La cuisine de france

La Cuisine

de France

by Mapie, the Countess de Toulouse-Lautrec

EDITED AND TRANSLATED BY

CHARLOTTE TURGEON

BONANZA BOOKS · NEW YORK

© MCMLXIV by The Orion Press, Inc.
Library of Congress Catalog Card Number: 64-24237
Designed by Wladislaw Finne
Illustrated by Jean Biagini
Manufactured in the United States of America
This edition published by Bonanza Books
a division of Crown Publishers, Inc.,
by arrangement with Grossman Publishers
a   b   c   d   e   f   g   h.

Contents

Introduction

All my life I have looked upon meal-time as the most agreeable moment of the day. My family, like almost all French families, considered that the cooking should be not merely good, but choice; and since I was brought up with these traditions, I have always wanted to see them applied. I began at the age of eight, in the immense vaulted kitchen in my grandmother's château, to learn the first rudiments of pastry cooking by making little cakes to serve with tea. Her cook made me understand that if in other kinds of cooking one can give free rein to one's imagination, in pastry cooking weights and measures must be rigorously observed under threat of ruining the cakes.

My mother had a remarkable chef, and while my brothers and sister were forbidden to come near the stoves, he was willing to let me watch him work because of the deep interest that, even at that early age, I was displaying in everything having to do with cooking. The making of my first omelet and my first crepes dates from that time, and it was by watching the cook make a ragoût or a sauce that I learned that you have to do a lot of tasting before you can decide that what you are making is right and ready for the table.

Some years later I was lucky enough to become the pupil of Dr. de Pomiane, the most genuine and best of our gastronomes. He used to talk about cooking as a scholar and an artist, and, in addition, he was a wonderful cook himself. His goal was not to teach his pupils how to prepare those elaborate dishes which are the prerogative of professional chefs, but rather how to make those dishes of high quality which are still simple enough to be within the capabilities of young women of limited means. It is to him, then, that I am indebted for the firm, and, I hope, gastronomical foundations of the kind of cooking that I present in this book. My dear old teacher has just died at the age of eighty-nine . . . the result of an auto accident. He had kept to the end his love of good food and great wines and had illustrated by example his lifelong opinion that "Gourmets are right, for they have the secret of mental poise and of good health."

In all cooking except pastry (which I exclude here for the reasons given above) one's individual personality can and must express itself. For years I have taught French cooking to a large number of girls and women, both French and foreign, at the *Académie Maxim's.* They all start with the same recipes and the same ingredients; yet when the dishes they have prepared reach the table, no two are exactly alike! Unconsciously each pupil has made some slight change in the recipe and has in this way expressed her own personality and taste.

I should like now to explain just what led me to be concerned professionally with cooking. During the war, in order to feed my children properly, I had been obliged to make all kinds of efforts to prepare decently the scarce and rather unappetizing foodstuffs that were available. After the war, since the whole mode of life had changed, I felt that it would be logical and right for me to go to work. I had the good fortune to be able to find a position with *Elle,* a large weekly magazine devoted to things that concern women, and much read in France. I became its food editor. Every week for fifteen years I have presented my readers with recipes. Shortly after joining *Elle,* I became the food editor also of the great monthly magazine, *Réalités.*

There could no longer be any question of the *haute cuisine* which had been practiced in the old days in my parents' home: that required too much expense, too many difficulties, and too much time spent over hot stoves.

Now what was necessary was to adapt that wonderful cooking to our times when all women work either in their own homes or outside, and when domestic service is rare and expensive. Encouraged by my readers, my friends and my family, I have done my best to succeed in this adaptation. Originality has helped me overcome the difficulties of certain recipes, but you will find in this book a great many classic recipes for main dishes, sauces and desserts.

I have often heard foreign friends of mine wonder how my compatriots happen to have such an unquestionable taste for good food and such refinement in their taste buds.

France is a country with resources that are as rich as they are varied; anyone who has traveled even a little bit in France has noticed how quickly the landscape changes with the great diversity of cultivation, cattle raising and wild life. In this country there are separate, distinctive and varied regions. Each one is peopled by men who from time immemorial have known how to get the very best out of what the seas, forests, fields, rivers and ponds offer them, so that regional types of cooking have been developed which have lovingly brought to perfection the most diversified local specialties. And since easier means of communication have allowed the man from Anjou to enjoy the truffles of Périgord, and the man from Périgord to savor lobster *à l'Armoricaine,* each one, far from proclaiming that his own little locality is the best of all and its cooking unrivaled, has profited with joy from his neighbor's masterpieces. And so it is that Paris has become not only the political but also the gastronomic capital of France, a capital where everyone rejoices in the immense variety that is brought to it from the diversified regional cuisines.

This eclecticism is applied also to a world-wide field: the natural products and the dishes which our explorers, or merely travelers, brought back from Africa, America or Asia have been seized upon, adapted and improved by our chefs who have finally assimilated them and enriched the French cuisine with them, for we have always been interested in and on the lookout for innovations.

Fundamentally this vitality of the French cuisine, this aptitude for seizing and appropriating all culinary ideas and all sorts of combinations which it transforms and by which it enriches itself, it shares with all the arts, at least all the arts that are vigorously alive and vital and constantly evolving.

For we consider cooking one of the fine arts, a minor one perhaps, but unquestionably one of them. Like painting or music, like poetry or choreography, isn't the purpose of cooking to beautify human life? Like them, does it not succeed in refining manners? And, like them, does it not have its creators, its performers, its critics who savor it and write its history? And the great painter, Henri de Toulouse-Lautrec, who was the cousin of my father-in-law, would not disagree with me, I am sure, except for having used the word "minor" in referring to cooking, for he was as much a gourmet himself as he was a fine cook.

Like the other arts, the art of cooking evolves and develops. Of course, we preserve our old recipes, using them when the circumstances are right for them, but we add others to them, either because they are better adapted to modern life, or simply because they enrich the gamut of our gustatory pleasures.

The composition of our menus has likewise changed very much, aiming constantly toward greater simplicity. In the archives of the cities of France we can find menus for meals served in the fifteenth and sixteenth centuries on great festive occasions by the various municipalities, menus which leave us aghast at their superabundance and studied elegance.

Later, customs became more simplified: when a great noble entertained King Louis XIV, the Sun-King, in 1656, the menu still had 168 separate dishes, although, of course, each guest touched only a few of them.

But I am talking, not of these great gala occasions, court and embassy receptions, but rather simply of those dinners to which our grandparents invited their friends in relatively recent times. A glance will show us the rapid changes that have taken place in the composition of a dinner.

Here, for instance, is a menu that I found in an old desk. It was for a dinner for twenty people given by my grandmother in 1882:

Menu I

POTAGES
(SOUPS)

Consommé Printanier
(Springtime Soup)

Bisque d'écrevisses
(Crawfish Bisque)

RELEVÉS
(REMOVES)

Turbot sauce aux huîtres
(Turbot with Oyster Sauce)

Filet de Boeuf à la Richelieu
(Beef Tenderloin, Richelieu Sauce)

———————

ENTRÉES

Timbales au Salpicon
(Individual Meat Timbales)

Foies de canard à la Toulousaine
(Duck's Livers à la Toulousaine)

Chaud-froid de gibier à l'écarlate
(Aspic of Game Birds à l'ecarlate)

———————

Sorbet au Thé
(Tea Sherbet)

———————

RÔTIS
(ROASTS)

Dinde truffé franquée d'ortolans
(Truffled turkey flanked with ortolans)

Faisans rôtis
(Roast Pheasants)

Entremets*
(side dish)

Petits pois à la Française
(Green Peas à la Française)

Cardons à la moëlle
(Cardoons with Marrow)

DESSERTS
(DESSERTS)

Nougat d'abricots
(Apricot Nougat)

*The word "entremets" has obviously changed its meaning. It now is used for the word "dessert."

Petits soufflés glacés à l'ananas
(Individual Cold Pineapple Soufflés)

Gâteau moka à la Parisienne
(Moka Cake à la Parisienne)

———————

In the time of the following generation, my parents', things were already much simpler. As an example, here is a menu dating from 1912 for an informal dinner for from ten to twelve people:

Menu II

Potage Mimosa
(Mimosa Soup)

Langouste gratinée
(Crayfish au gratin)

Quartier de pré-salé
(Roast Hind Quarter of Lamb)

Pommes de terre Anna
(Potatoes Anna)

Pintades rôties au cresson
(Roast Guinea Hen with Watercress)

Mousse de foie gras en aspic
(Foie Gras Mousse Aspic)

Salade de coeurs de laitues à la créme
(Hearts of Lettuce, Cream Dressing)

Haricots verts sautés
(Buttered String Beans)

Fromages
(Assorted Cheeses)

Fruits
(Assorted Fruits)

Bombe glacée
(Frozen Bombe)

Gâteau de Compiègne à la fraise
(Strawberry Cake à la Compiègne)

———————

Nowadays, for a similar occasion, my dinner would include simply one fish dish, or entrée; one meat dish, one vegetable in season, cheese and dessert. For instance:

Menu III

Coquilles Saint-Jacques au vermouth
(Scallops with Vermouth Sauce)

Aiguillette de boeuf en croûte
(Beef in Pastry)

Vermicelle grillé
(Grilled Vermicelli)

Asperges, Sauce Hollandaise
(Asparagus with Hollandaise Sauce)

Fromages
(Assorted Cheeses)

Nègre en Chemise
(Black and White Dessert)

———————

Just consider how the number of dishes has diminished in the space of two generations. But I do not think that the quality of the cooking has gone down. We have preserved our keen taste, and if we cannot allow ourselves the same ostentation, we are still, no doubt, as demanding when it comes to quality as our parents were.

Our customs concerning the order and importance of the different meals are essentially different from American habits. Our breakfast is light, including merely *café au lait* (very strong coffee served with a good deal of very hot milk), accompanied by croissants or toast, butter, marmalade, jam or honey.

As a general rule, lunch is the principal meal of the day. The menu is composed of eggs, for which we have multiple recipes, or an entrée; next comes a meat dish accompanied with vegetables, always served in a separate dish; then a salad, cheese and finally fruit. When we are at home, we eat a great deal of raw fruit.

On the other hand, a family dinner is very simple (soup, vegetables and dessert) except when we entertain guests. Obviously it is hard to entertain at lunch because the work schedule of many does not allow enough time, so that on such occasions, dinner becomes very important.

Except on rare occasions, such as balls or weddings, we never serve a cold buffet dinner. At home, for dinners that are limited to from twelve to twenty guests, everyone sits down at the table and is served normally by a butler or maid. Sometimes, of course, the mistress of the house cannot have service; then, she will not invite more than eight so that she herself can see to the needs of her guests.

In such a case she will also prepare her dishes, hot or cold, ahead of time, because many French dishes, such as *braisés,* ragoûts, *civets,* actually are better when reheated.

I think it very important to call your attention to this possibility of preparing things in advance, since it saves a great deal of time. If you are having guests on Tuesday, cook your *braisé* Monday evening at the same time you are preparing the family dinner for that evening. It will cook while you are straightening up the house or looking at television, and it will be ready when you want to go to bed. The next day it will take only a little time to reheat it, taste it for seasoning, and do the final cooking of the sauce.

I hope this book will be useful to you and that it will help you appreciate the cuisine of France. To conclude, let me add just one point, but an essential one: good cooking is accomplished only by love; love of one's husband, of one's children, and of one's friends.

Mapie, Countess de Toulouse-Lautrec
Paris, 1964

Editor's note

Mapie is a name well known to the housewives of France and to many cooking enthusiasts of other countries. It is the pen name of the Countess de Toulouse-Lautrec whose widely read recipes and culinary advices guide many people in planning and cooking food for their daily meals and for parties. The Countess is an exponent of modern French cooking. Despite the fact that she was brought up in a home where food was cooked in the splendid and sometimes complicated manner of the traditional great French cuisine, she has recognized the limitations of time and service that modern life imposes on housewives and has adapted her recipes and her methods of preparation to give French cooking a new look and an easier approach. Her recipes include the classic dishes for which France is famous as well as many of her own invention.

The author, who is a connoisseur of good food and a professional food editor, is also a teacher. When she explains certain procedures, she explains to the reader, as though he or she were one of her pupils at Maxim's cooking school, the reasons for doing it and what she expects as a result. Mapie is very explicit about the ingredients and the kind of seasoning that go into a dish but she feels that seasoning is a highly personal matter and does not care to dictate the exact amount. She urges her readers to taste constantly and relies on each cook to season according to one's own taste.

Countries vary in their culinary heritages, their kitchen practices and equipment and their sources of food supplies. In translating from one language to another and in transplanting kitchen preparations from one country to another there are many differences for which adjustments have to be made or substitutions be given. My task in preparing this book for the American readers has been to make these adjustments and to suggest the substitutions without detracting from the author's exceptionally delicious and uncomplicated recipes.

A few basic kitchen ingredients and condiments that vary slightly or may seem unusual to some readers are listed below. Others less generally used will be described in individual recipes.

Bouquet garni: This is an ingredient that appears very frequently in the recipes. It consists of a combination of fresh or dried herbs, often but not always 2 to 3 sprigs of parsley, ½ bay leaf and a sprig of thyme. If the fresh herbs are used, they are tied together with a piece of kitchen twine. If the dried herbs are used, it is a good practice to envelope and tie them in a small piece of cheesecloth. The *bouquet* is removed before the dish is served. *Bouquets* can vary in size and content. Each recipe will indicate the composition of the *bouquet*.

Butter: The butter generally used in France is what we call "sweet" or unsalted butter. Mapie believes that good cooking requires the best ingredients and uses only first-quality butter.

Calf's foot: Some recipes call for calf's foot, which adds gelatine and richness to many dishes. This is hard to find in most American markets, but pig's feet are widely marketed and can be used as second best.

Caramel: Caramel is used to line the molds for certain desserts and to color sauces. For the latter, Mapie scorns commercial substitutes and keeps a special little saucepan for making caramel. A lump or two of sugar is placed in the pan with a few drops of water. The sugar syrup boils until it turns dark brown and is added directly to the sauce.

Chervil: Chervil is sometimes called Italian parsley. It is not widely marketed but is easily grown. It resembles parsley but has a more delicate flavor.

Heavy Cream: French *crème fraîche* and American heavy cream can be used in the same way, though the former — because it is allowed to coagulate for a longer period of time — has a thicker consistency. The two creams do have approximately the same butterfat content. On the other hand, the American commercially soured cream, though similar in consistency to the *crème fraîche,* cannot be used as a substitute in cooking.

Flour: Unless otherwise specified, the flour referred to is the all-purpose variety. For certain recipes, especially in pastries and desserts, soft cake (or pastry) flour is used.

Oil: There is a large variety of oil in France as there is in the United States, but peanut oil is perhaps the favorite, with olive oil being used for certain dishes, especially those from the southern part of France.

Pepper: Black pepper is most commonly used in France. Freshly ground black pepper is the best and should be used unless otherwise indicated.

Saffron: Saffron can be bought in powdered or leaf form. It is a member of the crocus family and lends a subtle flavor and pretty yellow color to certain dishes. Since it is very expensive, in France turmeric is often used as a substitute. Both are used in this book.

Salt: Both fine salt and coarse sea salt are used in French cooking. The latter can be bought in some groceries and its use, when advisable, is indicated in the recipes. When a recipe calls for boiling salted water, the general rule is: 1½ teaspoons of salt per quart of water.

Tarragon: Tarragon is used a great deal more in French cooking than in American. It is a plant with small pungent leaves that have a faint anise flavor. It is easily grown in the garden. Dried tarragon is sold by many spice manufacturers.

Tomato Paste: French tomato paste is not seasoned with basil, so buy the American and not the Italian variety.

Vinegar: Both wine and cider vinegar are used in French cooking but unless otherwise specified, the vinegar called for is the red wine vinegar.

Cooking Utensils: Owning a French *batterie de cuisine* adds interest and enjoyment to French cooking but there are very few dishes that cannot be made with American cooking ware. French cooking utensils, however, are available in many hardware stores as well as in specialty shops dealing in foreign cooking supplies.

Sharp knives, wooden spoons and wire whips are the most essential hand tools.

A *moulinette* which is frequently prescribed in the recipes is a little hand grinder, sometimes called a *mouli* in American stores.

Heatproof serving platters and baking dishes are essential in any kitchen.

Special skillets for making crepes and an omelet pan are refinements that justify the expense.

A *bain-marie* is the term used for placing one pan in another containing hot water either on top of the stove or in the oven. We use a double boiler when cooking on top of the stove and usually place a baking dish in a roasting pan when cooking in the oven.

A charlotte mold is a moderate-sized round and straight-sided baking dish usually made of metal. Mapie uses such a pan in many recipes.

Electric gadgets such as electric beaters have the approval of the author when they save time and labor but she does not approve of the machines that turn into purées those foods that ought to retain texture.

Charlotte Turgeon

Sauces

Sauces

Sauces are the glory of the French cuisine. Each one demands care and attention. The refinement of flavor depends on the seasoning, which in turn depends entirely on the functioning of the taste buds of the cook. It is a recognized culinary truth that a good dish is achieved only if it is frequently and appreciatively tasted during the cooking process, and this is especially true of sauces.

Under the general title of sauces come any and all liquids that accompany foods. For example, the unthickened gravy (*jus*) that accompanies a roast is a sauce that requires great care. In the same way, the liquid in which ragout and braised dishes are cooked must be watched and tasted repeatedly. A good cook will keep a constant and careful check on the flavor of a sauce as the cooking progresses, adjusting the seasoning and adding little by little whatever is necessary. I say "little by little" because if one adds too much of anything, the excess cannot be removed, and the dish may be ruined. It is very important not to overseason. A sauce is an accompaniment that must never overshadow the food it accompanies. It is intended to point up and enhance the flavor. Remember too that all seasonings do not improve all foods.

What I have said about sauces for ragouts and braised dishes applies equally well to sauces that are made quite independently of the food it is to serve. These are emulsified sauces made with an egg base, white or brown sauces, and sauces made with meat, poultry, fish, or vegetable broth. All these sauces can be perfect if the cook gives them the attention they deserve, tasting, I repeat, frequently and carefully. If sauces are slimy because of too much flour or insipid because of indifferent seasoning, they will spoil any dish.

God be praised for the variety of our pleasure, and this includes the variety of sauces. Let us look at them. There are four main types:

1 EMULSIFIED SAUCES. Emulsified sauces made with eggs combined with butter or oil have a tendency to curdle if they are not carefully made. Fortunately, if this does occur, the sauce can be saved by adding a little cold water and beating vigorously. The cooked variety of these sauces are prepared in a *bain-marie* (or double boiler). Typical of this category are the sauces known as Béarnaise, Hollandaise, Mayonnaise, Vinot, Gribiche, Boyard, Rémoulade, Verte (Green Sauce), Aïoli (Garlic Sauce), Choron, and so on.

2 FLOUR-BASED SAUCES. The difference between white and brown sauces lies in the color of the butter, which changes according to the length of time it is cooked before adding the flour, and the kind of liquid that is used in the sauce.

White Sauces: White sauces are made by adding the flour as soon as the butter is hot. The liquid is light-colored, such as milk, white wine, chicken or fish broth. One must be careful that the sauce does not become lumpy when the liquid is added to the flour mixture. Some of the best-known white sauces are Béchamel, Normandy, Mornay, Ivory, Poulette, Horseradish, and Robert.

Brown Sauces: The butter for brown sauces is allowed to heat longer before adding the flour. The butter should become brown but never black. These sauces are made with beef broth, red wine, game broth, and tomato concentrate. Typical of these sauces are Madeira, Piquante, Tarragon, Miroton, Financière, and Quick Sauce (Vite Faite).

3 WINE AND TOMATO SAUCES. Certain sauces made with white or red wine or with tomato concentrate are made without a flour base. White wine sauces are made with beaten egg yolks and concentrated fish broth; red wine sauces are thickened, just before serving, with *beurre manié,* a cold mixture of flour and butter. Among these sauces let us mention Matelote, Mousse au Vin (Frothy Wine Sauce), Tomato Sauce, Hare Sauce.

4 MOTHER SAUCES. Mother sauces are also called culinary bases (*fonds de cuisine*). The cooking is long and slow, which makes it expensive for modern kitchens. However, I would nevertheless like to give the recipe for the benefit of those fortunate people who are still well equipped, that is, who have an old-fashioned stove, where such cooking is feasible. They will give themselves and others much pleasure in being able to provide these sauces.

White Base (Fonds Blancs):

3 pounds veal knuckle	3 well-trimmed leeks
2 pounds shoulder of veal	1 stalk celery
3 pounds chicken bones and giblets	*bouquet garni* (parsley, thyme, bay leaf)
2 medium-sized carrots	salt
5 medium-sized onions	

The meat should be boned and the bones broken or sawed into pieces. Place the bones in a deep kettle and cover with 6½ quarts of cold water. As the water begins to boil, add the vegetables cut in pieces, herbs, and salt. Let the combination simmer slowly and steadily for at least 4 hours. Cool in order to remove the fat more easily. Strain through a fine sieve.

The following base is used to enrich the sauces that accompany poultry or *blanquettes.*

Brown Base (Fonds Bruns):

3 medium-sized onions	4 tablespoons butter
3 medium-sized carrots	7½ quarts water
4 pounds soup bones	½ pound fresh pork skin

4 pounds shin beef

4 pounds veal knuckle

bouquet garni (parsley, thyme, bay leaf)

2 tablespoons salt

Prepare the vegetables and chop them fine. Saw or break the bones. Cut the meat into large pieces. Heat the butter in a large kettle and brown the vegetables, meat, and bones. Add 3 cups of water and the pork skin and cook slowly until the water has almost completely disappeared. Add 3 more cups of water and let that boil away. Repeat the process once more. Then add the rest of the water, the *bouquet garni,* and salt and cook very slowly for 8 hours. Cool in order to remove the fat. Strain through a fine sieve. This base will add immeasurably to braised beef and lamb dishes.

Aïoli sauce * Sauce aïoli

4 cloves garlic

2 egg yolks

salt and black pepper

1 cup (approximately) olive oil

2 teaspoons lemon juice

Aïoli, an emusified sauce, strongly flavored with garlic (hence the name) is a classic in Provence, particularly in Marseilles. A popular regional dish made of boiled salt cod, boiled vegetables (potatoes, carrots, turnips, and so on) molluscs, crustaceans is also called *aïoli,* but the sauce with its pungent odor is used with leftover beef, particularly boiled beef.

In a mortar or wooden bowl, pound the garlic with the salt and pepper to an oily consistency. Mix the egg yolks in well and start adding the oil very slowly as if making mayonnaise, beating constantly. Add a little lemon juice from time to time. If the sauce starts to curdle, add a few drops of lukewarm water to it and whisk vigorously. Do not store in the refrigerator. Too cold temperatures separate emulsified sauces.

Anchovy butter sauce * Sauce au beurre d'anchois
For grilled and broiled meat and fish

10 anchovy fillets

¼ pound unsalted butter

3 hard-cooked egg yolks

Vinaigrette Sauce (page 29)

Wash and wipe the anchovy fillets and mix them well with softened butter. Press the mixture through a sieve and pound in a mortar or wooden bowl with the egg yolks. Add the vinaigrette sauce.

Béarnaise sauce * *Sauce béarnaise*

For broiled meats, eggs, or fish

¼ cup wine or tarragon vinegar
4 teaspoons chopped parsley
4 teaspoons chopped tarragon
2 egg yolks

¼ pound soft unsalted butter
lemon juice
salt

Boil the finely chopped herbs in the vinegar in the top part of a double boiler over direct heat until the vinegar is reduced to about 3 teaspoonfuls. Remove from the fire and whisk in the egg yolks and a tablespoon of hot water. Place the pan over simmering water. Add the butter, bit by bit, stirring constantly. The sauce must never boil. (If the sauce should separate, move from the fire, add a teaspoon of lukewarm water and whisk very hard.) Season with salt and lemon juice.

Béchamel sauce * *Sauce béchamel*

3 tablespoons butter
5 tablespoons all-purpose flour

2 cups milk (variable)
salt and pepper

We owe a great debt to Louis de Béchamel, maître d'hôtel of King Louis XIV, for having invented béchamel sauce. It has become a culinary base in our kitchen, and is the starting point of many main dishes and desserts as well as the finishing touch for numerous gratin dishes. It is so essential that everyone who cooks at all must know how to make this sauce. There is only one difficulty, and that is to avoid a lumpy sauce. Contrary to general opinion, it is easier to avoid this if the milk is added all at once rather than little by little.

The quantity of liquid varies according to the desired thickness of the sauce.

Use a heavy metal saucepan. Cut the butter into pieces for uniform melting and heat over a moderate flame. Add all the flour at once and mix well with a wooden spoon, cooking for a few minutes until the mixture is pale gold. Too high a heat will brown the mixture. Remove the pan from the fire and pour in the cold milk. Stir well and put back on the fire, stirring until the mixture thickens. Season well. Pepper is indispensable to a good béchamel.

Bercy sauce * *Sauce bercy*

2 tablespoons butter
2 tablespoons chopped shallots
¾ cup bouillon
¾ cup dry white wine

1½ cups White Sauce (page 24)
1 tablespoon chopped parsley
salt and pepper

Melt 1½ tablespoons of butter and add the shallots, cooking until they are tender but not browned. Add the bouillon and white wine and cook until the liquid is reduced by half.

Meanwhile, make the white sauce. Combine the two mixtures and boil for 1 minute. Remove from the fire and add the remaining butter, the parsley, and the seasoning.

Bigarade sauce * Sauce bigarade

1 cup Brown Sauce (page 7)   4 tablespoons wine vinegar
2 oranges   ⅓ cup white wine
1 sugar lump

Prepare the brown sauce and let it simmer. With a sharp knife, remove the orange part of the orange skins in thin strips until you have 2½ tablespoonfuls. Throw into boiling water for 10 minutes and drain well. Squeeze the juice from the oranges.

Heat the sugar and vinegar in a saucepan over a low flame until lightly caramelized. Add the wine, and when that has almost boiled away, add the brown sauce and simmer 5 minutes.

Remove the saucepan from the fire and add the juice. Strain and add the orange peel. Season with salt and pepper, if necessary.

Boyard sauce (cold) * Sauce boyard

To accompany cold meats

1½ cups Mayonnaise (page 14)   1 tablespoon chopped chives
2 shallots   cayenne
⅓ cup white wine   salt and pepper

Make a very stiff mayonnaise. Chop the shallots fine and simmer them in the wine until the wine has almost disappeared. Cool before combining with the mayonnaise and chives. Season with salt, pepper, and cayenne.

Brown sauce * Sauce brune

Brown sauce is the modern simplification of Sauce Espagnole, in which the bouillon is the real *fond de cuisine,* brown base. Sauce Espagnole was brought to France by the Spanish chefs of Queen Anne of Austria, wife of Louis XIII and mother of Louis XIV. French chefs quickly adopted the sauce and improved it. Soon it became a pillar of French *haute cuisine*.

Because making the sauce is too time- and fuel-consuming for most modern cooks, the brown sauce has been devised, which uses homemade or store-bought stock or bouillon or even bouillon cubes.

6 tablespoons butter	1½ cups hot bouillon
5 tablespoons flour	salt and pepper

Heat the butter in a small saucepan over a moderate flame until the butter is brown. Add the flour and stir until smooth. Add the 1½ cups of bouillon and stir until completely blended. Season with salt and pepper and simmer 15 to 20 minutes. Add more bouillon if sauce is too thick. Taste again for seasoning.

Choron sauce * Sauce choron

Choron sauce is a béarnaise sauce to which is added tomato purée, in the proportion of 3 tablespoons of purée to every cup of sauce.

Cream sauce * Sauce à la crème

To accompany grilled lobster

3 tablespoons unsalted butter	mixed chopped herbs (optional)
½ cup very heavy cream	salt and pepper
juice of 1 lemon	

Heat the butter in the top part of a double boiler. Add the cream and the lemon juice. Heat over simmering water. Season with salt and pepper, and add a tablespoon of chopped herbs, if desired.

Cumberland sauce * Sauce cumberland

2 shallots	⅓ cup port
1 lemon	1 teaspoon French mustard
1 orange	cayenne
5 tablespoons currant jelly	powdered ginger

Peel and chop the shallots quite fine. Put in a small saucepan with 4 teaspoons of water and simmer 3 minutes. Using sharp knife, cut off the outer peel of the lemon and orange into tiny strips. Boil the strips in water for 10 minutes; drain well. Extract the juice from the orange and from half the lemon.

In still another saucepan, heat the jelly, and when it is melted, add the shallots, the fruit rinds, the fruit juices, port, mustard, and a pinch each of cayenne and ginger. Mix everything well.

Fines herbes sauce * Sauce aux fines herbes

3 teaspoons chopped parsley
3 teaspoons chopped chervil
1 shallot, chopped fine
⅓ cup dry white wine

⅔ cup Béchamel Sauce (page 6)
3 tablespoons heavy cream
3 teaspoons chopped tarragon

Simmer the parsley, chervil, and shallot in the wine until the wine has two thirds evaporated. Combine with the béchamel sauce. Cook 5 minutes and strain. Just before serving, add the cream and chopped tarragon.

Game essence sauce * Sauce au fumet de gibier

3-4 ounces raw game meat
   (hare, rabbit, partridge)
3 onions, chopped fine
1 bay leaf

2 sprigs thyme
¾ cup white wine
¾ cup bouillon
salt and pepper

Put the meat, onions, bay leaf, thyme, salt, pepper, and white wine in a saucepan. Bring to boil and simmer 15 minutes. Add the bouillon. Cover and simmer 1 hour. Strain the sauce and keep it hot in a double boiler until served.

Germaine sauce * Sauce germaine

For seafood cocktails

1½ cups Mayonnaise (page 14)
juice of ½ lemon
3 tablespoons catsup

3 tablespoons heavy cream
1 tablespoon cognac
salt and pepper

The mayonnaise should be fairly light in consistency. Season with the juice of half a lemon and salt and pepper. Add the catsup and then the cream, stirring constantly. Finally, add the cognac and taste for seasoning. (This can be made in an electric mixer or with a wire whisk.—*Ed.*) Chill before serving.

Green sauce * Sauce verte

1¼ cups Mayonnaise (page 14)   2 tablespoons chopped capers
1 large handful spinach leaves   2 tablespoons chopped pickles

Make the mayonnaise and color it green with 4 teaspoons of spinach juice. This is made by boiling the spinach leaves a few minutes, draining them, and then squeezing out the colored juice with your hands. Add the chopped capers and pickles and cool in the refrigerator before serving.

Gribiche sauce * Sauce gribiche

3 hard-cooked eggs   1 cup salad oil
4 teaspoons chopped mixed herbs 1 teaspoon wine vinegar
1 tablespoon French mustard   salt and pepper

Separate the yolks from the whites. Using a mortar or a wooden bowl, pound or rub the eggs with the chopped herbs and mustard. Gradually, drop by drop, add the oil, whisking constantly. Add the vinegar, salt, and pepper, and when well mixed, add the egg whites cut in small dice.

Hare liver sauce * Sauce au foie de lièvre

1 onion   ¾ cup good red wine
hare liver   2 sugar lumps
3 tablespoons butter   4 teaspoons flour
blood of the hare   salt and pepper
6 tablespoons red wine vinegar

Chop the onion and cut the liver into small pieces. Melt half the butter and cook the onion and liver in the butter for several minutes. Add the blood and the vinegar. Season with salt and pepper and simmer very gently for 1 hour. Strain the sauce and put it back into the saucepan. Add the wine and sugar.

Mix the rest of the butter with the flour, using a small wooden spoon. Add the mixture to the sauce bit by bit, stirring constantly. Do not let it thicken too much. At the last minute, pour the pan gravy into the sauce and serve in a preheated gravy dish.

Hollandaise sauce * Sauce hollandaise

4 eggs yolks   lemon juice
½ pound unsalted butter   salt and pepper

In the top part of a double boiler, whisk the egg yolks with 4 teaspoons of warm water. Place over simmering water and add little by little the softened butter, whisking constantly. The sauce must never boil. Season with salt, pepper, and lemon juice.

Horseradish sauces * Les sauces au raifort

For hare, rabbit, and pork

I

4 teaspoons Dijon mustard
4 teaspoons wine vinegar
2 tablespoons grated fresh horseradish
1 tablespoon sugar

pinch of salt
6 tablespoons heavy cream
⅓ cup soft breadcrumbs

Mix the mustard and vinegar in a small bowl. When well blended, add the remaining ingredients and mix well.

II

1½ cups Béchamel Sauce (page 6)
6 tablespoons dry white wine
4 teaspoons grated horseradish

2 tablespoons ground almonds
grated rind of ½ lemon

Combine the béchamel sauce, white wine, and horseradish in a saucepan and heat over a very low flame for 5 minutes. Just before serving, add the ground almonds and the grated lemon rind.

Ivory sauce * Sauce ivoire

For chicken

⅔ cup Béchamel Sauce (page 6)   1⅓ cups rich chicken stock

Make the sauce and beat it well with a wire whisk, adding the chicken stock. Always have twice the amount of stock as sauce. The stock must be completely free of fat. Let the sauce boil until it is medium thick.

This sauce is a classic for stewed chicken (*poule-au-pot*) and is naturally made with the broth.

Madeira sauce * Sauce madère

5 tablespoons butter
5 tablespoons flour
1½ cups bouillon

½ cup Madeira wine
salt and pepper
1 small can truffle peelings (optional)

Heat the butter slowly in a saucepan, and when it is light brown, add the flour. Mix well and cook a moment without letting the flour darken much. Gradually add the bouillon, whisking constantly. Add the wine, still stirring. Taste for seasoning and cook a moment longer. The sauce should not be too thick. Add the contents of the can of truffles if desired. Add bouillon, if necessary. All the cooking must be over a very low heat.

Maître d'hôtel butter * Beurre maître d'hôtel

⅔ cup unsalted butter	2 teaspoons lemon juice
3 teaspoons chopped tarragon	salt and pepper
3 teaspoons French mustard	

Cream the butter with the back of a wooden spoon until smooth. Work in the finely chopped tarragon and the mustard. Salt and pepper lightly and finally work in the lemon juice.

This can be served as decoration around a platter or served in a separate butter dish.

Mapie sauce * Sauce mapie

16-18 onions	1 teaspoon paprika
10 large tomatoes	¼ teaspoon cayenne
5 cups wine vinegar	2 tablespoons ground ginger
2 pounds light brown sugar	1½ teaspoons allspice
2 tablespoons salt	½ teaspoon mace
4 tablespoons dry mustard	2 teaspoons nutmeg
2 teaspoons white pepper	

Peel the onions and cut them into thin slices. Wash the tomatoes and cut them equally fine. Cook slowly for ½ hour and force through a strainer.

Combine with the vinegar and brown sugar and cook down over a moderate fire until sauce has the consistency of a medium béchamel sauce. Do not let the sauce burn. Add the remaining ingredients and cook a few minutes. This sauce is served both hot and cold, and can be stored in canning jars for future use.

Matelote sauce * Sauce matelote

2 shallots	2½ cups red wine, heated
5 tablespoons butter	1 large lump of sugar
4½ tablespoons flour	salt and pepper

Peel and chop the shallots very fine. Heat the butter very slowly and cook the shallots just until they are golden. Sprinkle with the flour and stir until the flour disappears. Add the hot red wine, stirring constantly, and cook just until the sauce begins to thicken slightly. Season with salt and pepper and color with sugar cooked until dark brown.

Note: If you are obliged to keep the sauce warm for a while before serving, use the lowest heat possible so that the sauce will not thicken.

Mayonnaise

Homemade mayonnaise is incomparably better than the commercial variety. It consists of nothing but egg, oil, a pinch of salt, and a little lemon juice or vinegar. It is essential that both the egg and the oil be at room temperature. Don't take an egg out of the refrigerator and expect to make a successful mayonnaise.

Place an egg in a very clean bowl. Be sure there is no egg white attached to the yolk. Mix *well* with a teaspoon of vinegar or lemon juice and a small pinch of salt, using a wooden spoon or wire whisk. Holding a cup of oil in one hand and stirring with the other, start adding oil *drop by drop* until the sauce becomes very thick. Then, and only then, thin the sauce with a little more vinegar or lemon juice, and add the oil in a fine thin stream, always stirring vigorously and in one direction. Once the emulsion has taken place, you can add as much oil as you like, although the usual proportion is 1 cup of oil to 1 egg yolk. Correct the seasoning with lemon juice or vinegar and salt.

If, on the other hand, the sauce turns, start with a fresh egg yolk in a clean bowl. Beat it well and start adding the turned sauce drop by drop. Once this has thickened, proceed as above, adding the oil. When the sauce is made, season it according to taste with vinegar or lemon juice and salt.

Variations: Besides varying the mayonnaise by making it with either lemon juice or vinegar, you can add a teaspoon of French mustard to the beaten egg before adding the oil. Herb mayonnaise is made by adding 2 teaspoons of chopped *fines herbes* (chives, parsley, chervil, tarragon, and so on) to the beaten egg before adding the oil. Tomato mayonnaise is made by adding a tablespoon of tomato paste or purée, which gives a different taste as well as a pretty color.

Melted butter sauce * *Sauce au beurre fondu*

For grilled fish, especially sole

7 tablespoons unsalted butter
2 tablespoons flour
½ teaspoon salt

2 egg yolks
1 teaspoon heavy cream
lemon juice

Melt 1 tablespoon of butter in a heavy saucepan. Stir in the flour over low heat. Add ¾ cup salted boiling water all at once and whisk vigorously until the sauce is smooth and reaching the boiling point.

In a small bowl, combine the egg yolks, cream, and a little lemon juice and pour the mixture into the saucepan. Mix well, but do not allow the sauce to boil.

Strain the sauce and beat in bit by bit the remaining butter without putting the sauce back on the heat.

Miroton sauce * Sauce miroton

3 medium-sized onions
3 tablespoons butter
4 teaspoons flour
1½ cups bouillon

1 lump sugar
4 teaspoons tomato purée
lemon juice or vinegar
salt and pepper

Peel and chop the onions very fine. Sauté them in butter until dark yellow, but not brown. Sprinkle with flour and stir in well. Meanwhile, heat the bouillon and sugar together and add to the flour mixture, stirring constantly. Add the tomato purée, mix well, and taste for seasoning. The sauce should not be thick; add more bouillon, if necessary. Finish the sauce with a little lemon juice or vinegar. The sauce should all be made over a moderate heat.

Monteynard sauce * Sauce monteynard

For hare or venison

3 tablespoons butter
3½ tablespoons dry breadcrumbs
1 onion
2 shallots

1 tablespoon chopped parsley
1 cup bouillon
1 tablespoon wine vinegar
½ pint heavy cream

Heat the butter over low heat until brown. Add the breadcrumbs and brown them.

Peel and chop the onion and shallots and add them and the chopped parsley to the buttered breadcrumbs. Stir in the bouillon and vinegar. Lower the heat as far as possible, cover the pan, and cook 2 hours.

Just before serving, pour in the pan gravy from the cooked game, add the cream and taste for seasoning.

Mornay sauce * Sauce mornay

For gratin dishes

Béchamel Sauce (page 6)   grated Gruyère cheese

Mornay sauce is béchamel sauce to which grated Gruyère cheese is added. For every 2½ cups of milk, allow 3 ounces, or approximately 1 cup, of grated cheese.

Mousseline sauce * Sauce mousseline

A classic sauce for grilled fish and for asparagus

Mousseline sauce is made by combining two parts hollandaise sauce and one part whipped cream.

Mustard sauces * Sauces moutarde

I

1½ teaspoons light Dijon mustard
6 tablespoons butter
1 teaspoon potato flour

white pepper
salt

Put the mustard in the top part of a double boiler and place over simmering water. Add the butter little by little, stirring constantly. Then add the flour in the same way. Thin the sauce by adding 6 tablespoons hot water and season with salt and pepper.

II

1 egg yolk
½ teaspoon vinegar
2 teaspoons French mustard

6 tablespoons soft butter
pinch of cayenne
salt

Beat the egg yolk slightly with the vinegar in the top of a small double boiler. Place over simmering water and add the mustard. Add the soft butter, bit by bit, stirring constantly. The sauce must never boil. If the sauce should separate, remove from the heat and beat in vigorously a tablespoon of ice water. When the sauce is blended, remove from the heat and season with salt and cayenne.

III

½ teaspoon dried capers
2 teaspoons chopped chervil
1 egg yolk
4 teaspoons light Dijon mustard

5 drops vinegar
1 tablespoon soft butter
white pepper
salt

Chop the capers very fine and combine with the chopped chervil in the top of a small double boiler. Mix with the egg yolk, the mustard, and the vinegar and place the pan over simmering water. Add the butter, bit by bit, stirring constantly as if you were making béarnaise sauce. Remove from the heat before adding salt and pepper.

Normandy sauce * Sauce normande

For fish and shellfish

3 tablespoons butter
4½ tablespoons flour
1¼ cups fish stock
½ pint heavy cream

2 egg yolks
1 or 2 tablespoons lemon juice
salt and pepper

Heat the butter and stir in the flour. Cook for a few moments and stir in the fish stock. Stir until it begins to thicken, remove from heat. Season with salt and pepper. Add the cream previously combined with the egg yolks and stir until well mixed. Add the lemon juice according to taste and taste again for seasoning. Keep warm over hot water without any more cooking.

Onion curry sauce * Sauce cari aux oignons

3 tablespoons butter
2 onions
4 tablespoons curry

1 cup bouillon
salt and pepper

In the heated butter, sauté the onions, sliced as thin as possible. When the onion is yellow and soft, add the curry. Cook a minute or two and add the bouillon. Taste for seasoning. When the sauce reaches the boiling point, reduce the heat and simmer 15 minutes. Strain before using.

Pepper sauce * Sauce poivrade

For marinated meats

2 medium-sized carrots
1 onion
3 tablespoons oil
1 sprig parsley
1 small sprig thyme
1 small bay leaf
¼ cup red wine vinegar

1⅓ cups marinade
6 tablespoons butter
3 tablespoons flour
2½ cups hot bouillon
8 large peppercorns
salt

Peel the vegetables and chop them coarsely. Place them in a saucepan with the oil, parsley, thyme, and bay leaf. Place over a moderate heat and cook until the vegetables begin to brown. Add the vinegar and half the marinade. Let the mixture cook uncovered until the liquid has been reduced to a third of its original volume.

In another saucepan, brown 3 tablespoons of butter and stir in the flour. Still stirring, add the hot bouillon and, when blended, add the vegetables. Simmer uncovered 45 minutes. Then, 10 minutes before the end of cooking, add the peppercorns slightly crushed and season with salt. Strain the sauce and add the rest of the marinade. Simmer a good half hour longer. Just before serving, add the rest of the butter.

Pheasant sauce * Sauce pour le faisan rôti

the pheasant livers
1 tablespoon butter
2 tablespoons French mustard

finely grated rind of 1 lemon
salt and pepper

Cut the pheasant livers into quarters and sauté them quickly in hot butter. Crush the livers with a fork and place them in a preheated gravy dish. Add the mustard, mix well, and season with salt and pepper, giving two grinds of the pepper mill. Add the lemon peel. Stir well and, still stirring, add the hot pheasant dish gravy.

Piquante sauce * Sauce piquante

1 shallot
⅓ cup red wine vinegar
1 sugar lump
3 tablespoons butter

5 tablespoons flour
1½ cups bouillon
2 tablespoons chopped pickles
salt and pepper

Chop the shallot fine and put it in a small saucepan with the vinegar and sugar. Heat until the vinegar is reduced by half. Take care because vinegar evaporates quickly.

Heat the butter in another saucepan until it turns brown. Add the flour and stir until brown. Stir in the bouillon, and when it begins to thicken, season with salt and pepper. Add the vinegar mixture and stir until it reaches the desired thickness. It should not be too thick. Before serving, strain the sauce and add the pickles.

Poulette sauce * Sauce poulette

4 tiny onions
4 mushrooms

pinch of thyme
small bay leaf

4 tablespoons butter
3 ½ tablespoons flour
¾ cup dry white wine or dry vermouth

2 egg yolks
1 teaspoon lemon juice
salt and pepper

Peel the onions and cook them in boiling salted water for 5 minutes. Clean the mushrooms and chop them very fine. Melt 1 tablespoon of butter in a small saucepan and sauté the mushrooms for a few moments.

In another saucepan, heat the remaining butter and add the flour. Stir just until blended and add the wine or vermouth. Add the salt, pepper, thyme, and bay leaf and the mushrooms and onions. Simmer 30 minutes. Remove the bay leaf. Just before serving, stir in the egg yolks previously mixed with the lemon juice. Taste for seasoning.

Pretty girl sauce * Sauce jolie fille

For boiled fish and boiled meats of every variety

4 teaspoons butter
1 ½ tablespoons flour
⅓ cup soft breadcrumbs
⅓ cup consommé
⅓ cup heavy cream

4 teaspoons chopped parsley
½ teaspoon onion juice
2 hard-cooked egg yolks
4 teaspoons lemon juice
salt and pepper

Heat the butter in a small saucepan and add the flour, mixing well. As soon as it is pale golden in color, add the breadcrumbs and stir for a minute before adding the consommé. Stir well, add the cream, and season with salt and pepper. Add the chopped parsley and the onion juice. Mix well, and as soon as it reaches the boiling point, remove from the fire and add the egg yolks and the lemon juice.

Provençale sauce * Sauce provençale

6 large tomatoes
¾ cup oil
a pinch of sugar

½ clove garlic
1 tablespoon chopped parsley
salt and pepper

Peel the tomatoes and cut them horizontally. Press out the seeds and chop the flesh rather coarsely. Heat the oil in a shallow saucepan, and when very hot, add the tomatoes. Sprinkle with salt, pepper, and sugar and add the well-crushed garlic and the chopped parsley. Cover and let cook over a very low flame for a half hour.

Raisin sauce * Sauce aux raisins secs

3 tablespoons seeded raisins
1 tablespoon finely grated lemon peel
⅔ cup brown sugar
2 tablespoons cornstarch

1 tablespoon French mustard
4 teaspoons wine vinegar
juice of 1 lemon

Soak the raisins 1 hour in warm water. Grate the lemon rind.

In a small saucepan place the brown sugar, the cornstarch, and the mustard. Stirring constantly, add the vinegar, the lemon juice, the grated lemon rind, and the drained raisins. Stir over low heat just to the boiling point. Simmer until the sauce thickens slightly. Serve hot or cold.

Red pepper and garlic sauce
Sauce au piment et à l'ail

For cold cooked fish and meat

4 hard-cooked egg yolks
4 tablespoons olive oil
3 cloves garlic
2 small red peppers

pinch of saffron *or*
1 teaspoon turmeric
4 teaspoons wine vinegar
salt and pepper

Crush the eggs with a pestle or the back of a wooden spoon in mortar or wooden bowl, incorporating the olive oil. Crush or press the garlic and mix them and the peppers, finely chopped, into the egg yolks. Stir in the saffron or turmeric. Season with salt and pepper and add the wine vinegar, stirring well. Strain before serving.

Rémoulade sauce * Sauce rémoulade

3 teaspoons French mustard
2 gherkin pickles, chopped
2 hard-cooked egg yolks

1 cup oil
salt and pepper

Put the mustard in a small bowl. Mix in well the pickles, egg yolks, salt, and pepper. Add the oil drop by drop, as you would in making mayonnaise .

Robert sauce * Sauce robert

For leftover beef and lamb

2½ tablespoons butter
4 tablespoons flour

1 teaspoon wine vinegar
1 teaspoon French mustard

3 or 4 onions, chopped fine   salt and pepper
1½ cups bouillon

Brown 2 tablespoons of the butter over a moderate heat and stir in the flour. When the flour is brown, add the finely chopped onions, the rest of the butter, and the bouillon. Stir until well blended. Cover and simmer 30 minutes. Just before serving, add the vinegar and mustard, adding more if you wish. Season with salt and pepper.

Soubise or onion sauce * Sauce soubise

4-5 onions   ⅓ cup bouillon
Béchamel Sauce (page 6)   ⅓ cup meat drippings
2 tablespoons butter   ⅓ cup heavy cream
⅓ cup dry white wine   salt and pepper

Peel the onions. Slice them thickly and cook in boiling water for 10 minutes. Meanwhile, prepare the béchamel sauce.

Drain the onions and put them in a saucepan with the butter, wine, bouillon, and meat drippings. Simmer 10 minutes, force through a strainer, add the béchamel sauce, and stir in the cream. Season and remove from the heat just before the sauce reaches the boiling point.

Supreme sauce * Sauce suprême

3 tablespoons butter   ¾ cup heavy cream
4 teaspoons flour   salt and pepper
1½ cups chicken broth

Heat the butter over a low flame. Add the flour and stir with a wooden spoon. Add the chicken broth and stir until the sauce begins to thicken. Add the heavy cream, salt, and pepper. Heat to the boiling point, but do not let it boil more than a few seconds.

Tarragon sauce * Sauce à l'estragon

1¼ cups dry white wine   4 teaspoons flour
3 sprigs of tarragon   1¼ cups bouillon
2 tablespoons butter   salt and pepper

Boil the wine down in a saucepan to half its original quantity. Add the leaves of two of the sprigs of tarragon and let it stand over very low heat without boiling until the odor of tarragon is quite pronounced. Meanwhile, chop the leaves of the remaining tarragon sprig.

Heat the butter until brown and stir in the flour. Stir in the bouillon and season with salt and pepper. When smooth, add the wine and tarragon mixture and cook very gently without letting it thicken. Just before serving, strain the sauce and then add the chopped tarragon leaves.

Tartar sauce * Sauce tartare

1 cup Mayonnaise (page 14)
1 large handful raw spinach
2 or 3 pickles

2 tablespoons capers
1 tablespoon French mustard

Make the mayonnaise. Wash the spinach, removing the stems. Throw the leaves into boiling water and cook 2 to 3 minutes. Drain. Squeeze the spinach with your hands over a small bowl. Save the juice.

Chop the spinach, the pickles, and the capers very fine. Combine with the mayonnaise and add the mustard. Mix well and color with the spinach juice. Keep in the refrigerator.

Tomato sauce * Sauce tomate

3 pounds tomatoes
6 ounces fat salt pork
6 medium-sized onions
1/3 cup chopped parsley

3 tablespoons oil
2 teaspoons sugar
salt and pepper

Dip the tomatoes in boiling water for a few seconds in order to remove the skins easily. Cut the tomatoes in quarters and press out the seeds. Cook in a large shallow pan over a low flame until they turn into a fairly thick juice.

Wash the salt pork in warm water to remove the excess salt. Cut in small pieces. Chop very fine along with the onions and the parsley or pass through a *moulinette* (a small food chopper). Cook this mixture in the oil over low heat for 20 minutes. Add the tomato and the sugar and taste for salt and pepper. Cover and simmer 45 minutes. If the sauce is too thick, add a little boiling water.

Venison sauce I * Sauce venaison

6 shallots
6 medium-sized onions

pinch of cayenne
2 tablespoons butter

2 medium-sized carrots
1½ cups wine vinegar
2 sprigs thyme
1 small bay leaf
2 teaspoons salt

4 teaspoons flour
marinade
1 teaspoon sugar
4 teaspoons chartreuse liqueur

Chop the shallots, onions, and carrots and boil with the vinegar, thyme, bay leaf, salt, and cayenne over a very low flame for 1 hour.

Brown the butter and blend in the flour. Stir in about a cup of the marinade in which the venison has been marinating. Add the vegetable purée and the sugar. Simmer 30 minutes. Then, 10 minutes before serving, add the chartreuse. Strain the sauce into a sauce bowl.

Venison sauce II (classic)
Sauce à l'ancienne pour venaison

When game is marinated before cooking, some of the marinade is used in the sauce.

20 cloves garlic
1 cup red wine vinegar
3 tablespoons butter

1 tablespoon flour
2½ tablespoons marinade
salt and pepper

Cook the peeled garlic cloves and the vinegar very slowly in an uncovered saucepan for 30 minutes. When the vinegar is greatly reduced and the garlic thoroughly cooked, mash the mixture into a purée.

In another saucepan, melt the butter and blend in the flour. Stir in the garlic purée. Add the marinade and the juice from the roast game, whisking very hard. Taste and season. If the sauce is too thick, add a little bouillon.

Vinot sauce * Sauce vinot

1 egg
salt and pepper
1 teaspoon wine vinegar

¾ cup olive oil
lemon juice

Separate the yolk from the white of the egg, leaving a little of the white with the egg yolk. Stirring constantly with a wire whisk (or an electric mixer—*Ed.*), add the salt, pepper, and the vinegar in a thin stream. Add 4 teaspoons of oil, drop by drop, and then the rest of the oil in a very small stream. The sauce will become firm. Beat the egg white stiff and add it by tablespoons, folding in thoroughly. Season with a little lemon juice.

White butter sauce * Beurre blanc

For salmon, pike, and other fresh-water fish

2 shallots	¾ cup unsalted butter
2½ tablespoons white wine vinegar	salt and pepper

This sauce was invented at the turn of the century by Mme. Clémence, who was proprietor chef of a little restaurant on the left bank of the Loire in Chebutte, about 15 miles from Nantes. Salmon was in great abundance, and the sauce she invented to serve with it has now become a classic accompaniment to salmon and other fresh-water fish. The sauce demands great care because the heat must be just right, but the perfect *beurre blanc* is worth the effort of making it.

Chop the shallots very fine and cook them very gently in half the vinegar until golden. Add 4 teaspoons of water, the vinegar, and some salt and pepper. Cook it down slowly to ⅓ its original volume. Still maintaining the low heat, whisk in the butter vigorously, adding the butter by small bits. The sauce will become frothy and very white.

White sauce * Sauce blanche

Follow the recipe for Béchamel Sauce, substituting water for the milk.

Marinades and marinating

What exactly is a marinade, which to the French sounds like a nautical term but is in fact a culinary process? Actually, the nautical sound to the word is very logical, because a marinade is a kind of brine made to conserve meats, a process perfected by sailors who had to go on long voyages.

All marinades have a basis of vinegar, wine, salt, and herbs. Part of the purpose of the marinade is to preserve the meat, or rather to stop the normal change meat undergoes. When you marinate meat, you not only slow down this process of change but you spice and tenderize the meat at the same time. This is why marinating has been used with venison for such a long time. In modern times, the process has been intelligently extended to flavor meat of domestic animals, especially when one wants a kind of wild flavor; domestic rabbits take on the flavor of hare, and a leg of lamb can taste rather like venison. The process is also used with fish, especially river fish with very little flavor.

Marinades can be made with both red and white wine, and they can also be used raw or cooked. Cooking a marinade reinforces the action of the salt and the herbs and makes the marinating process that much quicker. That is why cooked marinades are always used with large pieces of game, such as wild boar, elk, and so on. If a piece of meat needs to be marinated for a long time, the marinade can turn, but the cooked marinade can be recooked every four or five days and therefore does not turn.

Raw marinades can be used very successfully with young boar or venison, especially those caught in a short chase. In general, raw marinades are used with meat that you want to spice rather than tenderize and with the flesh of fish that you want to season but not change. The marinating process in these instances is short, a few hours at most.

In marinating, there has to be an exchange of flavors, because if a piece of meat takes on the flavor of wines, vegetables, and spices, it gives up some of its own flavor to the marinade. That is why some of the marinade is always used to make the sauce that will accompany the meat.

Marinating Rules:
1 In marinating meat or fish, use earthenware or enamel dishes, and never metal.
2 The length of time for the marinating process is determined by the outdoor temperature. In summer, game should marinate for much less time than in the winter.
3 Hare and rabbits are usually cut into pieces before being marinated. The pieces should be entirely covered with the liquid.
4 Ordinarily, a rabbit or hare will marinate 24 hours. Venison will marinate 2 to

5 days, depending on the age of the animal, the size of the meat, and the weather. For a haunch of wild boar 15 days is the average.

5 During the marinating process, the meat must be turned and basted frequently. Use wooden or bone utensils for both processes.

6 Cooked marinade must be absolutely cold before use, except in the case of wild boar, where it is poured over the meat while still boiling.

7 Cooked marinade should be recooked every 4 or 5 days. The meat is removed, the container is thoroughly washed, and the marinade is cooked and cooled before pouring it over the meat. ⅓ cup of each kind of liquid should be added to the marinade before boiling, to replace what has been lost by evaporation.

8 All marinated food can be cooked in every way—roasted, braised, fried, or broiled.

9 When you use a raw marinade, put half the vegetables in the bottom of the dish. Place the meat on the vegetables and cover it with the rest of the vegetables. Pour the liquid over it all.

Cooked wine marinade for small game, venison, or wild boar
Marinade cuite au vin pour gibier à poil, chevreuil, ou sanglier

1 onion	1 quart white or red wine
2 medium carrots	1 cup good wine vinegar
2 shallots	2 sprigs thyme
1 clove garlic	1 bay leaf
½ stalk celery	1 teaspoon salt
4 sprigs parsley	1 teaspoon peppercorns
4 tablespoons oil	

Cut the vegetables and the parsley in small pieces. Heat the oil in a saucepan, and when very hot, brown the vegetables and parsley. Add the wine, vinegar, thyme, bay leaf, salt, and pepper and bring to a boil. Reduce the heat and simmer ¾ hour.

For Other Game: Cool the marinade completely before pouring over the meat.
For a Boar: Pour boiling hot over the meat.

Cooked red wine marinade
Marinade cuite au vin rouge

For small meats, such as wild rabbit or hare, cut in pieces, venison chops, and so on

2½ cups red wine
1 carrot
1 onion
1 sprig thyme

1 bay leaf
pinch of rosemary
2 teaspoons juniper berries
salt and pepper

Combine the ingredients in a saucepan and simmer 30 minutes. Cool.

Cooked vinegar marinade for small game, venison, or wild boar
Marinade cuite au vinaigre pour gibier à poil, chevreuil ou sanglier

10 carrots
12 onions
2 pimientos
3 cloves
10 bay leaves
3 sprigs thyme

1 teaspoon peppercorns
1 tablespoon juniper berries
2 teaspoons salt
3 tablespoons butter
2½ cups wine vinegar
2½ cups bouillon

Slice the carrots and onions very thin. Combine with the pimientos, cloves, bay leaves, thyme, pepper, juniper berries, and salt. Heat the butter in a large saucepan and add the vegetable combination, stirring until the vegetables are lightly browned. Add the vinegar and bouillon. Bring to a boil and cook 2 minutes. Strain and pour over the meat hot, if marinating a boar; otherwise let cool before using with other game.

Raw red wine marinade for wild boar
Marinade crue au vin rouge pour sanglier

1 tablespoon juniper berries
3 onions, cut in slices
1 carrot, cut in rounds

½ teaspoon nutmeg
2 teaspoons salt
1 teaspoon peppercorns

1 stalk celery, sliced

2 sprigs thyme

2 bay leaves

¾ cup oil

5 cups red wine

Prepare the marinade. Place half the combined dry ingredients on the bottom of the container. Place the meat on them and cover with the remaining half. Combine the liquid and pour over the meat. The meat should be turned and basted morning and night for two weeks.

Raw red wine marinade for venison
Marinade crue au vin rouge pour chevreuil

For young venison

1 clove garlic, crushed

1 large carrot, cut in rounds

5 cups red wine

4 teaspoons kirsch

1 teaspoon salt

1 tablespoon juniper berries

1 tablespoon peppercorns

½ teaspoon rosemary

1 teaspoon chopped tarragon

4 tablespoons oil

Combine the ingredients and pour over the venison. Turn twice a day.

Raw red wine marinade for wild rabbit or hare
Marinade crue au vin rouge pour lapin de garenne

1 large carrot, cut in rounds

1 shallot

1 onion, stuck with

3 cloves

1 teaspoon peppercorns

1 teaspoon salt

2 sprigs thyme

1 bay leaf

4 sprigs parsley

4 tablespoons oil

2½ cups red wine

Combine the dry ingredients and place half of them in the dish. Add the hare, cut in pieces. Cover with the remaining half and pour the liquids over the hare.

Raw white wine marinade for wild rabbit or hare
Marinade crue au vin blanc pour lièvre

½ bottle dry white wine

dried rind of ½ orange, cut fine

1 bay leaf

sprig wild thyme

1 sprig thyme
1 teaspoon dried ginger
¼ teaspoon dried anise

1 teaspoon salt
½ teaspoon peppercorns
4 tablespoons oil

Combine the ingredients and pour over the rabbit, cut in pieces.

Raw white wine marinade for leg of lamb
Marinade crue au vin blanc pour gigot

1 bottle dry white wine
2½ tablespoons Ceylon tea
3 or 4 fresh mint leaves *or*
½ teaspoon powdered mint

2 sprigs thyme
1 teaspoon salt
1 teaspoon peppercorns

Combine and let the meat marinate for 3 days, turning 2 or 3 times a day.

Vinaigrette sauce (french dressing)
Sauce vinaigrette

4 tablespoons oil
4 teaspoons vinegar

salt
fresh ground black pepper

Whatever oil you use and whatever vinegar you prefer, the proportions are always the same: 4 tablespoons of oil to 4 teaspoons of vinegar. The vinegar and salt are placed in a salad bowl and stirred hard to dissolve the salt. The oil and pepper are then added. The best salad oil is a mild olive oil, and the best vinegar is wine vinegar.

Mustard french dressing
Vinaigrette à la moutarde

Add ½ teaspoon of French mustard to the salt and vinegar and stir well before adding the oil and pepper.

Egg french dressing * Vinaigrette à l'oeuf

Mix a raw egg yolk, ½ teaspoon French mustard, and the salt in the salad bowl and gradually add the vinegar, stirring constantly. Add the oil and pepper.

Cream french dressing * Vinaigrette à la crème

Substitute ⅓ cup of heavy cream for the oil in the basic recipe.

Lemon egg french dressing
Vinaigrette au citron et oeuf dur

Crush a hard-cooked egg yolk with a fork in the salad bowl. Add oil and lemon juice (instead of the vinegar), salt, and pepper. Mix to a creamy consistency.

Roquefort french dressing
Vinaigrette au roquefort

Crush 2 to 3 tablespoons of Roquefort cheese in the salad bowl and combine it with the basic French dressing.

Hard-cooked egg french dressing
Vinaigrette aux oeufs durs

Chop a whole hard-cooked egg in the salad bowl. Combine with French dressing and add 2 teaspoons each of chopped parsley and tarragon.

Herb french dressing * Vinaigrette aux fines herbes

Chop fresh young anise leaves, tarragon, parsley, basil, marjoram, chives, thyme, and mint, or as many of these as you can obtain, so that you will have about 2½ tablespoons of chopped mixed herbs. Double the basic recipe for French dressing (using lemon juice instead of vinegar, if you prefer) and add the herbs.

Soups

Soups

Soup is traditional in France. It used to constitute an entire meal—especially in the country. Before the war, when ladies used to think less of their waist measurements, one always served soup. In my childhood, we always had soup for breakfast. They used to say, "Soup is to make you grow tall," and the fact is that my five brothers, my sister and I all grew to be very tall.

In certain French provinces, those of the southwest, for example, both the noonday meal and the evening meal always begin with soup. These soups are particularly good, starting with a good piece of pork belly, which comes from the lard barrel, where it has been stored since the last time a pig was killed.

The difference between *la soupe* and *le potage* is great. The former is never strained, except bread soup, whereas the latter always is.

We often like bread with our soup; hence the French expression *"tremper la soupe,"* which means that one puts bread slices in the bottom of a tureen, and the contents of the soup kettle, in which meat, pork belly, and vegetables have been cooked, are poured over them. Making a good soup is not as simple as you think. Like all other dishes, its preparation demands care and testing.

Here are some traditional soups eaten all over France, from the beer soup of the north to the soups of Provence.

Artichoke soup (cold)
Consommé aux artichauts (froid)

FOR FOUR PEOPLE

4 artichokes	1½ cups bouillon
1½ cups Béchamel Sauce (page 6)	salt and pepper

Boil the artichokes in salted water for 45 minutes or until an outer leaf is easily detached. Drain. Remove the leaves and chokes, leaving only the bases, which should be large.

Make the béchamel. Mix with the bouillon.

Cut two of the artichoke bottoms in small dice. Force the others through a sieve. Combine the puréed artichoke with the bouillon mixture and season with salt and pepper. Chill in the refrigerator.

Serve the soup in individual soup plates and garnish with the diced artichoke.

Cream of artichoke soup
Potage crème d' artichauts

FOR EIGHT PEOPLE

7 artichokes
6½ cups thin Béchamel Sauce
  (page 6)
1 cup scalded milk

½ cup heavy cream
salt and pepper
croutons, fried in butter (optional)

Boil the artichokes in salted water for 45 minutes or until an outer leaf is easily detached. Drain. Remove the leaves and chokes and cut the bottoms into thin slices.

Meanwhile, make the thin béchamel sauce.

Add the artichoke slices to the sauce and continue cooking over a very low heat for 30 minutes. Pour the soup into another saucepan through a strainer. Force the artichoke pieces through the strainer. Add the hot milk and stir well. Season to taste and reheat, adding the cream. Serve hot and, if you like, serve a little bowl of croutons, fried in butter.

Asparagus soup * Soupe aux asperges

FOR SIX PEOPLE

2 pounds thin asparagus, white or green
3 tablespoons butter
4 teaspoons flour
1 egg yolk

¾ cup hot heavy cream
1 tablespoon chopped chervil
salt and pepper

Trim the asparagus and cut off the hard parts. Wash well and cut into 1-inch pieces. Cook in 6 cups of boiling salted water until very tender. Drain, but reserve the broth.

Heat the butter in a saucepan and stir in the flour. Add 5 cups of the asparagus broth. Season with salt and pepper and cook for several minutes.

Remove from the fire and beat in the egg yolk. Add the pieces of asparagus, the chervil, and the cream. Serve immediately.

Barley soup * Soupe à l'orge

FOR FOUR PEOPLE

2 carrots
1 onion
2 leeks

½ pound lean lamb shoulder
½ cup crushed barley
chopped parsley

4 tablespoons butter
9 cups hot chicken broth

celery salt
salt and pepper

Peel the carrots and cut them into thin strips. Peel the onion and trim the leeks, removing all the green. Chop them rather coarsely. Heat the butter in a deep kettle and sauté the vegetables gently for a few minutes before stirring in the chicken broth. If you do not have chicken broth on hand, use bouillon cubes and water.

Add the lamb cut in large pieces (as though for stew) and the barley. Season with celery salt, salt, and pepper. Simmer 1½ hours.

Remove the meat from the soup and cut it into small dice. Put the meat and the entire contents of the kettle into a soup tureen. Sprinkle with chopped parsley.

Horticultural bean soup
Potage purée de haricots rouges

FOR SIX PEOPLE

½ pound horticultural beans
1 large onion, cut in pieces
1 carrot, cut in pieces
bouquet garni (thyme, bay leaf, parsley)

¾ cup red wine
3 tablespoons butter
small croutons
salt and pepper

Unless the beans are fresh, soak them for several hours in water. Put them in a large saucepan and cover with cold water. Bring slowly to a boil and skim off any matter that floats to the top. When the liquid boils, add the onion, carrot, *bouquet garni,* wine, and salt. Reduce the heat, cover, and simmer very gently until the beans are soft. Remove the *bouquet garni* and vegetables. Reserve the broth and force the beans through a strainer or food mill.

Thin the resulting purée with the broth and taste for seasoning. Reheat to the boiling point, add the butter. As soon as it melts, serve the soup garnished with little croutons.

Beer soup I * Soupe à la bière I

FOR SIX PEOPLE

1 quart dark beer
½ lemon
½ teaspoon cinnamon
1 tablespoon cornstarch

2 egg yolks
2 cups scalded milk
toast
salt and pepper

Combine the beer, the peel of ½ lemon, and the cinnamon in a saucepan and bring to a boil. Boil 3 minutes.

Blend the cornstarch with a little cold water and add it to the hot beer.

Beat the eggs slightly and add the scalded milk, stirring constantly. Season with salt and pepper and stir this into the hot beer without letting the mixture boil. Pour over slices of dry toast. Serve very hot.

Beer soup II * Soupe à la bière II

FOR FOUR PEOPLE

1 quart beer	½ cup heavy cream
6 tablespoons sugar	3 egg yolks
8 small thin slices bread	salt and pepper
6 tablespoons butter	

Boil the beer and sugar for 10 minutes.

Fry the bread in butter until golden on both sides. Put the bread in a soup tureen.

Beat together the heavy cream and the egg yolks. When blended, season with salt and pepper. Remove the beer from the heat and beat into the egg mixture. Pour over the bread and serve immediately.

Beet soup * Potage de betteraves

FOR SIX PEOPLE

1 medium-sized cooked beet	1½ quarts hot bouillon
1 medium-sized onion	2 tablespoons chopped *fines herbes*
1 cup cut celery	(parsley, chervil, tarragon)
5 tablespoons butter	buttered croutons
1 tablespoon sugar	salt and pepper

Peel and cut the beet into thin strips.

Peel the onion and cut into thin strips.

Cut the celery into strips, lengthwise, the same size as the beet and onion.

Heat the butter in a saucepan and add the vegetables with the sugar and a little salt. Put on the cover and cook the vegetables very gently until tender.

Add the hot bouillon and simmer ½ hour. Add the chopped herbs. Season to taste, and when you serve the soup, pour it over little cubes of bread sautéed in butter.

Bourbon soup * Soupe bourbonnaise

FOR SIX PEOPLE

1 pound top round of beef	1 sprig chervil (or parsley)
½ boned chicken (raw)	9 cups boiling water

1 carrot
1 leek
1 stalk celery

12 small thin slices bread
6 tablespoons butter
salt and pepper

Chop the beef and chicken very fine and put them in a soup kettle. Peel and wash the vegetables and chop them very fine. Add the vegetables to the meats. Add the chervil and the boiling water. Season with salt and pepper and bring to a boil, stirring frequently. Lower the heat and cook 25 minutes. Taste again for seasoning.

Fry the bread in butter until golden brown on both sides. Put the bread in a soup tureen and pour the contents of the soup kettle over the bread.

Bread soup * Panade

FOR SIX PEOPLE

1½ pounds stale bread
10 tablespoons butter
3 egg yolks

1 cup heavy cream
salt and pepper

Break the bread into pieces and put it in a deep saucepan. Add water just to cover. Put over a slow heat and break the butter in pieces into the pan. Season with salt and pepper and cover. Simmer 2 hours, stirring frequently with a wooden spoon.

Force the mixture through a fine strainer and reheat over a very low heat.

Beat the egg yolks and cream together and season with salt and pepper. Remove the soup from the heat and stir in the mixture. Serve in heated soup plates.

Cauliflower and ham soup
Soupe au chou-fleur et jambon

FOR SIX PEOPLE

5 potatoes
1 large carrot
1 onion
1 stalk celery
5 tablespoons butter
4 tomatoes
several sprigs of parsley

1 small cauliflower
5 tablespoons ground ham
1 small sprig basil
9 cups boiling water
grated Parmesan cheese
croutons
salt

Peel the potatoes and the carrot. Cut the potatoes in thin slices and the carrot in rounds. Peel and chop the onion. Chop the celery.

Heat the butter in a deep pan and sauté the vegetables gently without letting them brown at all.

Add the tomatoes, cut in pieces, the parsley, the cauliflower, cut into flowerets, the ham, and the basil, finely chopped.

Add the water and cook a good half hour. Season with salt and pass everything through a food mill.

Serve very hot with grated cheese and with little croutons which have either been sautéed in oil or dried in the oven.

Cheese and shallot soup
Soupe au fromage et aux échalotes

FOR SIX PEOPLE

12 small thin slices bread
6 tablespoons butter
6 shallots
2½ tablespoons oil
1 tablespoon flour

9 cups boiling water
2 cups grated Gruyère cheese
½ cup heavy cream
salt and pepper

Cut the bread in very thin slices, halving the slices if the loaf is large. Brown them lightly on both sides in hot butter.

Peel the shallots and cut them in thin slices. Sauté them gently in hot oil until lightly colored. Sprinkle with the flour and add the boiling water. Stir and cook without a cover for 30 minutes. Season with salt and pepper.

In a soup tureen, put a layer of bread slices and sprinkle generously with cheese. Repeat the process until the bread and cheese is all used. Pour the shallots and the broth over the bread and add the heavy cream. Serve immediately.

Chicken soup * Soupe de poule

FOR SIX PEOPLE

4-pound chicken
2 carrots
2 leeks
⅛ teaspoon cayenne
bouquet garni (thyme, bay leaf)

2 teaspoons butter
3 eggs
¼ pound vermicelli
2 tablespoons chopped parsley
salt and pepper

Clean, truss, and tie the chicken. In a soup kettle with 2¾ quarts of water put the carrots, peeled and cut in large pieces, the leeks, trimmed and well washed, salt, pepper, cayenne, and the bouquet garni. Bring the water to a boil, skimming off any matter that floats to the top. Lower the flame and cook with the pan only half covered for 1½ hours.

Remove the chicken and let it cool. Skin and cut the meat from the bones. Cut it into thin strips, removing all the nerves and tendons.

Melt butter in a large skillet and pour in the eggs to make a very thin omelet, like a crepe. Cool and cut into shreds.

Strain the bouillon and reheat to the boiling point. Add the vermicelli. When cooked, add the chicken and the shredded omelet and chopped parsley.

Cucumber soup (cold) * Potage aux concombres

FOR FOUR PEOPLE

3 pounds cucumbers   paprika
4 teaspoons chopped tarragon   salt and pepper
1 cup heavy cream

Peel the cucumbers and with a little potato-ball cutter cut out 20 small balls. Boil them in salted water for 10 minutes. Drain.

Boil the rest of the cucumbers, cut in pieces, for 10 minutes. Drain and force the cucumbers through a strainer. You should have a thick liquid. Add the chopped tarragon and season with salt and pepper. Mix with the heavy cream and chill in the refrigerator.

Serve in individual soup plates garnished with cucumber balls and sprinkle with a little paprika.

Endive milk soup * Soupe au lait aux endives

FOR SIX PEOPLE

1 pound endive   2 quarts scalded milk
2 leeks   toast
3 potatoes   salt
6 tablespoons butter

Trim the endives. Wash them well and chop fine.

Trim the leeks, using only the white part. Chop fine.

Peel the potatoes and slice thin.

Heat the butter in a deep pan and sauté the endives, leeks, and potatoes gently without letting them brown.

Add the hot milk. Season with salt and cook 45 minutes. Do not strain this soup but serve very hot with small pieces of unbuttered toast.

Esau's soup * Potage esau

FOR FOUR PEOPLE

½ pound lentils   croutons

2 cups scalded milk   salt and pepper
3 tablespoons butter

Soak the lentils in water for several hours. Change the water and cook until tender.

Force the lentils through a food mill. Thin the purée with hot milk and some of the lentil broth. Cook the soup, stirring frequently, but do not let it get too thick. Season with salt and pepper, and just before serving, add butter and garnish with croutons.

Julienne soup * Potage julienne

FOR SIX PEOPLE

7 cups bouillon   2 cabbage leaves
2 carrots   chervil (or parsley)
2 white turnips   salt and pepper

This is made with bouillon from a *pot-au-feu* from which the fat has not been removed.

Skim the fat from the bouillon and put it in a deep pan.

Cut the vegetables into thin slices lengthwise and cut into small thin sticks about 1½ inches long. Cook the vegetables in the fat, covering the pan with a tight fitting cover. When the vegetables are soft, add the bouillon and simmer 20 minutes. Taste for seasoning and sprinkle with chopped chervil or, lacking that, chopped parsley.

Lamb curry soup * Soupe de mouton au cari

FOR SIX PEOPLE

3 pounds lean lamb shoulder   4½ quarts boiling bouillon or water
1 large onion   several sprigs parsley
5 tablespoons butter   ¼ pound uncooked ham
2½ tablespoons flour   ½ cup rice
8 tablespoons curry powder   salt

Ask the butcher to cut the meat in 12 pieces.

Peel the onion and chop it coarsely.

Heat the butter in a deep kettle, and when it is hot, put in the meat and the onion. Stir with a wooden spoon so that the meat will be lightly browned on all sides. Sprinkle with the flour and the curry powder and stir a few moments. Add the boiling bouillon or water, little by little, stirring constantly. Add the parsley and the raw ham, cut in dice. Bring to a boil. Cover and lower the heat. Cook gently for 2 hours.

Parboil the rice in salted water for 5 minutes.

Transfer the lamb and the ham to a hot tureen and keep warm.

Drain the rice and add it to the broth. Boil hard for 10 minutes and pour the broth over the meat. Serve very hot.

Leek and potato soup
Soupe aux poireaux-pommes de terre

FOR SIX PEOPLE

1½ pounds (6-8) potatoes
1 pound leeks
6 tablespoons butter

1 cup milk, scalded
dry bread
salt and pepper

Peel the potatoes. Wash them and cut them into large cubes.

Trim and wash the leeks, removing almost all of the green. Cut the white part into 1-inch pieces.

Heat the butter in a large saucepan and sauté the leeks over a low heat without letting them brown. Add 9 cups of water and the potatoes. Season with salt and pepper and cook over moderately high heat for 30 minutes. Add the milk and serve very hot, poured over small pieces of dry bread.

Lentil and tomato soup
Soupe aux lentilles et tomates

FOR SIX PEOPLE

¾ pound lentils
10 tomatoes
3 ounces pork belly
1 small bunch celery
½ onion

1 clove garlic (optional)
several sprigs parsley
4 teaspoons oil
8 tablespoons rice
salt

Put 2¼ quarts of cold water in a kettle and add the lentils. Bring to a boil and cook for 1 hour. Add the tomatoes, cut in pieces, and the fat, cut in dice. (If pork belly is not available, use lean salt pork and do not add salt to the soup.—*Ed.*) Add the celery, cut in pieces, the half onion, the garlic, if desired, the parsley, salt, and finally the oil. Cook a good half hour. Pass everything through a food mill.

Reheat the soup, and when it boils, add the rice, which will have been well washed under running water. When the rice is cooked, the soup is ready. Serve very hot.

Onion soup * Gratinée à l'oignon

FOR FOUR PEOPLE

3-4 onions
3 tablespoons butter
4 teaspoons flour
1½ cups heated dry white wine

8 thin slices French bread
5 ounces Gruyère cheese
salt and pepper

Peel the onions and slice them very thin. Melt the butter in a heavy pan. Add the onions and cook until they are golden. Sprinkle with flour and stir it in. Add the wine and 3 cups of boiling water and boil 1 minute.

Meanwhile, dry the bread in a hot oven and slice the cheese very thin. Alternate layers of bread and cheese in a heatproof soup tureen or a deep casserole. Pour the hot soup over the bread and cheese and brown in the oven (350° F.) for 30 minutes.

Onion soup with roquefort cheese
Gratinée au roquefort

FOR SIX PEOPLE

4 tablespoons butter
1½ pounds (5-6) onions
nutmeg
12 thin slices of French bread

3 ounces Roquefort cheese
2½ tablespoons cognac
4 tablespoons grated Gruyère cheese
salt and pepper

Heat the butter in a heavy pan and sauté the onions, peeled and finely chopped, until they are golden. Pour in 6 cups of boiling water and season with salt, pepper, and a little freshly grated nutmeg. Boil 5 minutes.

Meanwhile, dry the bread in a hot oven and put it in the bottom of a heatproof soup tureen or a deep casserole. Crumble Roquefort cheese over the bread and fill the tureen three fourths full with the soup. Add the cognac and sprinkle with the grated cheese. Bake at 350° F. for 25 minutes.

Tiny onion soup * Soupe aux petits oignons

FOR SIX PEOPLE

1¼ pounds (14-16) small onions
6 tablespoons butter
4-5 slices lean bacon, chopped fine
3 tablespoons tomato paste

¼ pound spaghetti
2 tablespoons chopped parsley
½ cup grated Gruyère cheese
salt

Peel the onions and sauté them in butter in a deep pan over a low heat along with the bacon until the onions are golden all over.

Stir the tomato paste into 9 cups of boiling water and add to the onions. Season with salt and cook 20 minutes.

Add the spaghetti, and when they are cooked, the soup is ready. Serve hot, sprinkled with chopped parsley. Serve a side dish of grated cheese.

Pea and pork soup * Soupe aux pois et au lard

FOR SIX PEOPLE

½ pound dried peas   1 pound potatoes
½ pound fresh pork belly   1 lettuce heart
½ pound leeks   1 loaf stale French bread
bouquet garni (thyme, bay leaf, parsley) salt and pepper
½ pound carrots

Soak the peas overnight in cold water.

Put 3½ quarts of water in a soup kettle and add the drained peas, the leeks, trimmed and carefully washed, the *bouquet garni,* and the fresh pork belly. (If you cannot find fresh pork belly, parboil salt pork 5 minutes, rinse, and use like the fresh pork.—*Ed.*) Season with salt and pepper and simmer covered for 2 hours.

At this point, add the carrots, peeled and cut in rounds, the potatoes and the lettuce heart. Cook gently for 2 hours longer.

Taste the soup for seasoning and pour over the bread. Serve very hot.

Chick pea soup * Soupe aux pois chiches

FOR SIX PEOPLE

1 pound chick peas   French bread
1 teaspoon baking soda   oil
bouquet garni (thyme, bay leaf,   salt and pepper
    orégano, green mint)

Soak the dried chick peas at least overnight in cold water to which baking soda has been added.

Cook the peas, preferably in very soft water, with the *bouquet garni,* salt, and pepper, until tender.

Meanwhile, fry small, thin slices of French bread in oil.

Put the croutons in a soup tureen and pour the broth over the toast. Add a large tablespoonful of chick peas per person to the tureen. Serve the rest of the peas in a vinaigrette sauce as an hors d'oeuvre the next day.

Red and green pepper consommé (cold)
Consommé aux poivrons verts et rouges

FOR FOUR PEOPLE

1 quart bouillon	1 red pepper
1 green pepper	salt and pepper

Prepare or buy an excellent bouillon.

Remove the seeds from the peppers and cut the peppers in thin matchlike sticks. Simmer 3 minutes in boiling salted water.

Cool and add to the cold bouillon. Taste for seasoning.

Provençale soup * Soupe provençale

FOR FOUR PEOPLE

1 large onion	5 tablespoons rice
3 tomatoes	2 tablespoons chopped *fines herbes*
½ celeriac	(parsley, chervil, tarragon)
4 tablespoons olive oil	salt and pepper

Peel the onion and slice it fine.

Wash the tomatoes and cut them in large dice.

Peel the celeriac and cut in small dice. (If you do not have celeriac, substitute a celery heart and chop it in large dice.—*Ed.*)

Heat the oil in a large saucepan and sauté the onions, celeriac, and tomatoes gently for about 6 minutes. Season with salt and pepper. Add 1 quart of boiling water. Cover and simmer for 1 hour; 15 minutes before the end of cooking, wash the rice and add to the soup.

Serve sprinkled with chopped *fines herbes*.

Pumpkin soup * Soupe au potiron

FOR FOUR PEOPLE

1 pound (2 cups) peeled pumpkin	6 slices French bread
3 cups scalded milk	salt and pepper
4 teaspoons sugar	

Peel the pumpkin and cut it into small pieces. Boil until tender in salted water and force through a sieve. Put the purée into a saucepan and mix it with hot milk until it has the consistency of cream. Season with sugar, salt, and pepper.

Place the bread in a soup tureen and pour the soup over the bread. Let it stand 3 minutes before serving.

Soup au pistou * Soupe au pistou

½ pound large wax beans
½ pound large green beans
½ pound carrots
½ pound leeks
½ pound turnips
1 pound zucchini
1 pound winter squash
2 pounds potatoes
2½ tablespoons soup pasta
salt

Pommade:
6 cloves garlic
1 large sprig basil
2 tomatoes
4 teaspoons tomato paste
1½ cups grated Gruyère cheese
¾ cup olive oil

Trim or peel all the vegetables. Wash them well and cut the beans, the carrots, the leeks, and the turnips into thin strips. Cut the zucchini, squash, and potatoes into large pieces. Add 9 cups of boiling water and salt. Bring to a boil and stir often. As the large pieces of vegetables become tender, mash them with a fork in the kettle. Cook 1½ hours.

Add small soup pasta in the form of tiny shells, if possible. Boil them, and halfway through their cooking, stir in the following pommade.

Pommade: In a mortar or wooden bowl, pound the garlic with all the basil leaves. Add the tomatoes, which have been peeled, halved, and seeded. Mix well and add the tomato paste, the grated cheese, and the olive oil. Mix thoroughly.

Stir this into the soup and keep stirring until the pasta is cooked.

Raisin soup * Potage aux raisins secs

¼ cup seedless raisins
½ cup shelled peas
½ cup small green beans
3 tablespoons butter

½ cup cooked rice
1½ quarts boiling water
salt

Soak the raisins in lukewarm water for 1 hour.
Shell the peas.
Cut the green beans in small pieces.

Heat the butter in a large saucepan. Heat the peas and beans in the butter. Add the water and season with salt. Cover and simmer very gently for 3 hours.

Then, 20 minutes before serving, add the rice and raisins. Serve without straining.

Saint germain soup * Potage saint-germain

FOR FOUR PEOPLE

½ pound dried peas
3 cups scalded milk
2 lumps sugar
½ cup heavy cream

3 tablespoons butter
buttered croutons
salt and pepper

Soak the peas overnight in cold water.

Put the peas in a saucepan with just enough cold salted water to cover. Bring to a boil and skim off any matter that floats to the surface. Cover and reduce the heat and cook over a moderate heat until the peas are tender.

Put the cooked peas in a blender or electric mixer and purée them. Thin the purée to the desired consistency with hot milk and blend it again until you have a smooth, creamy soup. Salt, if necessary, and season with pepper. Add the sugar, and as soon as it is dissolved, add the cream and butter.

Serve in hot soup plates, garnished with small triangular croutons sautéed in butter.

Cold sorrel soup * Soupe froide à l'oseille

FOR FOUR PEOPLE

3 eggs
1 pint sorrel
1 clove garlic, pressed
juice of 1 lemon

½ cup heavy cream
3 baby cucumbers
4 slices stale black bread
salt

Hard-cook 2 eggs in boiling salted water for 15 minutes. Plunge into cold water, peel, and cut into small pieces.

Trim and wash the sorrel using only a little of the stems.

Chop the sorrel coarsely. Boil them in 4 cups of salted water for 10 minutes and cool a little.

Beat the remaining egg and mix with the pressed garlic, the hard-cooked eggs, and a little lemon juice. Stir this into the soup and taste for seasoning. Chill in the refrigerator.

Just before serving, add the cream and the cucumbers cut in thin rounds. Cut the bread in small dice and pour the soup over them.

Sorrel bisque * Chiffonade d'oseille

FOR FOUR PEOPLE

1 quart sorrel	¼ cup heavy cream
3 tablespoons butter	2 egg yolks
1 tablespoon flour	1 lemon
1 tablespoon potato flour	salt and pepper

Wash the sorrel very carefully and chop it coarsely.

Heat the butter in a deep saucepan and sauté the sorrel until it wilts. Season with salt and pepper and sprinkle with flour.

Stir in the flour and add 6 cups of hot water gradually, stirring with a wooden spoon. Boil gently for 10 minutes.

Mix the potato flour with ¼ cup cold water. Stir it into the soup and boil 10 minutes longer.

Beat together the cream, egg yolks, and lemon juice. Remove the soup from the heat and stir in the mixture. Taste for seasoning and serve.

Tapioca bouillon * Potage velours au tapioca

FOR FOUR PEOPLE

4 cups beef or chicken bouillon	butter
3 large ripe tomatoes	chopped parsley
5 tablespoons tapioca	salt and pepper

If you do not have bouillon from a *pot-au-feu* on hand, use bouillon cubes dissolved in hot water.

Dip the tomatoes in boiling water for a moment and slip off the skins. Cut them and remove the seeds. Cook the tomatoes in the hot bouillon over a high heat for 10 minutes. Force them through a sieve and put the soup back on the heat. Season to taste with salt and pepper.

Bring the soup to a boil and add the tapioca, letting it fall gradually from your hand into the soup. Simmer a few minutes and serve.

Put about ¾ teaspoon of butter in each plate. Pour the soup over it and sprinkle with parsley.

Tomato consommé * Consommé à la tomate

FOR SIX PEOPLE

1 pound firm ripe tomatoes	salt and pepper
6 cups consommé	

Dip the tomatoes in boiling water for 1 minute and slip off the skins. Halve them and press out the seeds. Cut the flesh in small cubes. Cook the cubes in boiling salted water for 8 to 10 minutes.

Drain the tomatoes, and just before serving, add them to the consommé, which may be either hot or cold. Season with salt and pepper.

Royal tomato soup (cold) * Potage royal de tomates

FOR FOUR PEOPLE

1 quart bouillon	1 teaspoon sugar
4 tablespoons tomato paste	salt and pepper
4 egg yolks	

Mix the bouillon and tomato paste and stir thoroughly. Boil 3 to 4 minutes. Remove from the heat and add the egg yolks one by one, stirring constantly. Add the sugar and season with salt and pepper, if necessary. Chill in the refrigerator.

Classic vegetable soup of lorraine
Soupe aux légumes à l'ancienne
à la mode de lorraine

½ cup dried beans	1 sprig thyme
6 medium-sized carrots	1 bay leaf
4 leeks	6 tablespoons butter
6 potatoes	French bread, sliced thin
1 small trim cabbage	1 cup heavy cream
3 turnips	2 tablespoons chopped chervil
1 large onion	(or parsley)
1 clove garlic	sweet butter
1 stalk celery	

Soak the beans overnight.

Peel or trim and wash the vegetables very carefully. Leave the small cabbage whole and cut the other vegetables in two. Fill a deep soup kettle three quarters full with water. Bring to a boil and add all the vegetables. Add the thyme, bay leaf, and the butter. Season with salt and pepper and simmer for 3 hours.

Heat the soup tureen and cover the bottom with the bread. Cover with heavy cream and sprinkle with the chervil (using parsley if the chervil is not available— Ed.). Place a collander over the tureen and strain the broth gently through the collander.

Arrange the vegetables in a shallow heated dish. Put the cabbage in the center and surround it with the vegetables. Split the cabbage in two and put a large piece of sweet butter into the hollow. Serve at the same time with the soup.

Vichyssoise * Crème vichyssoise

FOR EIGHT PEOPLE

10 potatoes	1 cup heavy cream
6 leeks	4 teaspoons chopped chives
2 onions	nutmeg
¼ pound butter	salt and pepper
3¼ quarts chicken broth	

Peel the potatoes, leeks (using only the white part), and the onions. Wash them well and cut them in very thin slices.

Heat the butter in a deep kettle and sauté the leeks and onions gently until golden, stirring with a wooden spoon. Add the chicken broth and the potatoes and boil gently, uncovered, for 40 minutes. Force everything through a food mill and let it cool.

When the soup is cold, add the cream, the chopped chives, a dash of nutmeg, salt, and pepper. Mix thoroughly.

If the soup seems too thick, add cream or chicken broth. Serve cold, preferably.

Watercress soup * Soupe au cresson

FOR FOUR PEOPLE

1 pound (3-4) potatoes	4 tablespoons butter
2 cups scalded milk	4 teaspoons chopped chervil
1 bunch watercress	

Peel the potatoes and cut them in small pieces. Boil them in a quart of water. Do not strain but mash them in the saucepan. Add the milk and season with salt.

Trim the stems from the watercress and wash well. Add the leaves and cook the soup for 10 minutes. Just before serving, add the butter and chopped chervil. (Use parsley, if chervil is not available.—*Ed.*)

Fish soup * Soupe de poissons

FOR SIX PEOPLE

Although Bouillabaisse is a famous soup popular with French and American alike, it cannot be properly made except with fish only available in the Mediter-

ranean. Therefore, I will not include recipes for it in this book. However, there are many wonderful fish soups that can be made with fish found on both sides of the Atlantic.

2 pounds various fish (see below)
4 tablespoons olive oil
2 large tomatoes
2 onions
½ fennel root
3 cloves garlic, crushed

thyme, bay leaf
pinch of saffron *or*
1 tablespoon turmeric
¼ pound spaghetti
¾ cup grated Gruyère cheese
salt and pepper

Choose a variety of small fish (whiting, smelts, sole, sea bass, etc.) and have them cleaned and cut into pieces.

Heat the oil in a kettle and add the fish, the tomatoes, the onions, peeled and sliced, the fennel root, cut in pieces, the garlic, thyme, bay leaf, saffron or turmeric, salt, and pepper. Cook over a moderate heat for 3 to 4 minutes, stirring with a wooden spoon.

Add 9 cups of boiling water and skim off any matter that floats to the top. Cook gently for 20 minutes.

Strain the bouillon through a fine sieve and bring it to a boil. Add the spaghetti, broken into pieces, and cook 20 minutes longer. Serve very hot accompanied by the grated cheese.

Bilibi soup * Potage bilibi

FOR EIGHT PEOPLE

1 pound fish heads
1 *bouquet garni* (thyme, bay leaf,
   parsley)
3 quarts mussels
1 onion

1 stalk celery
2 cups white wine
½ cup heavy cream
salt and pepper

Put the fish heads in a kettle containing 6 cups of cold water, salt, and the *bouquet garni.* (If fish heads are not available, buy a pound of unboned fish.—*Ed.*) Bring to a boil and simmer 30 minutes. Drain the broth through a fine strainer and reserve.

Meanwhile, scrub and scrape the mussels.

Peel the onion and wash the celery and cut them into small pieces. Put the mussels in a pan with the vegetables and cook them over a high heat until the mussels open. Pour the mussel broth through a fine strainer and remove the shells from the mussels. Combine the fish broth, the mussel broth, and the white wine. Boil down to half its original quantity. Strain again.

Remove from the heat and add the cream and the mussels. Season to taste and serve very hot or cold.

Provençale housewives' soup
Soupe des ménagères provençales

FOR FOUR PEOPLE

½ pound potatoes
½ pound leeks
½ pound carrots
3-4 onions
2-3 cloves garlic
4 tablespoons olive oil
1½ pounds cleaned salt-water fish

fennel seeds, rosemary, thyme, bay leaf,
  basil
3 large tomatoes *or*
2 tablespoons tomato paste
¼ pound macaroni or spaghetti
saffron *or* turmeric
grated cheese
salt and pepper

Trim, peel, and wash thoroughly the vegetables as you would for an ordinary vegetable soup. Cut them in large pieces.

Pour the olive oil in a soup kettle and when it begins to heat, add the vegetables and cook until they are lightly colored. Add 1 quart of boiling water. Season with salt and cook until the vegetables are soft. Because soups of this kind tend to absorb water, have a kettle of boiling water at hand to add when necessary.

Add the fish. (In Provence they use *congre, rascasse, Saint-Pierre, mulet,* and so on. In America, where variety in marketed fish is limited, buy the freshest kinds of ocean fish available.—*Ed.*) Add the fennel, which is essential, rosemary, thyme, bay leaf, and fresh basil, if possible. Add the tomatoes or the tomato paste.

After 20 minutes, remove the fish, which can be eaten separately with Aïoli (page 5). Sometimes, the fish is forced through a food mill and added to the soup. Either way is good.

Strain the soup and put it back on the heat. When it boils, add the pasta and cook until tender. Season with saffron or turmeric, salt, and pepper. Serve very hot and pass a bowl of grated cheese.

The boss's fish soup
La soupe de poissons du patron

FOR EIGHT PEOPLE

This can be made only where a variety of fresh fish is available.—Ed.

1 cod's head
2 red perch
1 eel
1 mackerel
3 small skate

1 teaspoon fennel seeds
3 cloves garlic
½ teaspoon chopped parsley
3 tomatoes
2 tablespoons tomato paste

1 small flounder

2 large onions

¼ cup olive oil

1 teaspoon sea salt

pinch of saffron

dash of cayenne

2-3 potatoes (optional)

Sauce:

2 cloves garlic, crushed

Mayonnaise (page 14)

4 teaspoons tomato purée

All the fish should be scaled and cleaned. Use whatever heads are edible. Put all the fish in a kettle of cold water. Cover and bring to a boil. Skim off the matter that floats to the top.

Meanwhile, sauté in hot oil the onions, peeled and chopped fine.

Prepare the seasoning by mixing in a small bowl the sea salt, saffron, cayenne, fennel seeds, crushed garlic, and chopped parsley. Add this mixture and the sautéed onions to the fish kettle, the tomatoes cut in quarters, and the tomato paste.

As soon as the soup reaches the boiling point, cover, reduce the heat, and simmer 1½ hours. Add the potatoes, peeled and quartered, and cook 30 minutes longer.

Meanwhile, make the sauce. Crush the garlic in a bowl or force through a garlic press into a bowl. Mix with 2 cups of mayonnaise made with peanut or olive oil and the tomato purée.

Force the soup through a food mill, using a fine strainer. Serve very hot with little slices of French bread rubbed with garlic and fried in peanut oil and with the sauce (*la rouille*) served in a heated gravy bowl.

One can serve with this soup a whole lobster, cooked *au court-bouillon.* In this case, the lobster roe is added to the sauce.

Breton fish soup I * Cotriade bretonne I

FOR SIX PEOPLE

2 whiting

2 mackerel

1 small mullet

4 flounder fillets

3 onions

2 pounds (6-8) potatoes

2½ tablespoons oil

savory, tarragon, marjoram, anise seeds

thin slices of French bread, toasted

salt and pepper

Wash the whiting, mackerel, and mullet. (Other small fish can be substituted. —*Ed.*) Cut them in even, rather small slices. The flounder fillets should weigh about 2½ ounces each.

Chop the onions. Peel and quarter the potatoes.

Heat the oil in a soup kettle and brown the onions very lightly over a slow heat. Stir them with a wooden spoon so that they will be evenly browned. Add 9 cups of boiling water, the quartered potatoes, a pinch each of savory, tarragon, marjoram and anise. Cook covered over high heat for 15 minutes. Add the fish and cook uncovered for 10 minutes.

Transfer the fish to a hot platter and pour the soup over the toast.

*Breton fish soup II * Cotriade bretonne II*

FOR SIX PEOPLE

2 pounds fish heads (eel, red snapper, cod, whiting, haddock, flounder)
4 pounds varied fish (eel, red snapper, sole, cod, whiting)
2 small crabs
1 small lobster or 6 *langoustines*
1 quart mussels
3 tablespoons butter
4 large onions

1 quart Muscadet (dry white wine)
bouquet garni (mint, savory, burnet, chervil, marjoram, tarragon)
1 small sweet red pepper
1 pound carrots
1 pound turnips
2 pounds potatoes
salt and pepper

Ask the fish dealer to give you the fish heads in one package and a variety of cleaned fish in another. (If fish heads are not available, buy a 2-pound fish to take their place.—*Ed.*)

Wash the fish and cut into slices.

Wash the crab; cut the lobster in pieces; scrape and wash the mussels.

Heat the butter in a kettle and sauté lightly the onions, peeled and sliced thin. When the onions are golden, add the white wine, the *bouquet garni,* and the fish heads. Cover with water. Add the red pepper, salt, and pepper and bring to a boil. Add the carrots and the turnips, washed, peeled, and cut in pieces. When the vegetables are almost cooked, add the potatoes, peeled and cut in quarters. Cook until the potatoes are tender.

Remove the vegetables from the broth with a slotted spoon. Add a little of the fish stock and keep the vegetables warm. Pour the rest of the stock through a fine sieve into a large saucepan. Add the fish slices, the crab, and the lobster and boil just long enough to cook the fish. Do not overcook.

Taste for seasoning. Serve everything, the fish, the vegetables, and the broth in the same tureen.

*Fish and crab soup * Soupe aux poissons et crabes*

FOR SIX PEOPLE

4 pounds fish (see below)
2-3 soft-shelled crabs
1 pound tomatoes

½ cup oil
1 quart dry white wine
¼ pound thin spaghetti

3 onions   cayenne
2-3 leeks   salt and pepper
3 cloves garlic

This soup constitutes a whole meal. It is a good idea to buy good fish with as few bones as possible because the soup is not strained and the fish is served as a separate dish. Buy a combination of such fish as haddock, red snapper, whiting, smelt, and bass, properly cleaned and cut into pieces if too large. Buy cleaned, soft-shelled crabs. If not available, break hard-shelled crabs into pieces.

Dip the tomatoes in boiling water and peel off the skins.

Peel and chop the onions; trim the leeks, wash them well, and chop the white part only; crush the garlic.

Heat the oil in a deep kettle. Sauté the onion just until golden, add the leeks, garlic, and tomatoes. Heat the wine and add that along with 2 cups of boiling water. Season with salt and just a small dash of cayenne.

Add the crabs as soon as the liquid boils. Cover and boil gently for 15 minutes. Add the fish and boil 15 minutes longer.

Remove the crab and fish carefully from the broth and put them in a heated covered dish. Add the spaghetti to the broth and boil until tender. Serve the soup and fish as one or two courses according to your taste.

The real fisherman's soup
La vraie soupe des pêcheurs

FOR SIX TO EIGHT PEOPLE

The proportions for such a recipe cannot be exact, because it is made in indefinite amounts and with whatever fish is available.—Ed.

4-6 soft-shelled crabs   large *bouquet garni* (thyme, bay leaf)
2-3 pounds small rock fish   pinch of saffron *or*
4 tablespoons olive oil   2 tablespoons turmeric
3-4 onions   ¼ pound wide noodles
3-4 fennel leaves   grated Gruyère cheese
1 or 2 cloves garlic   salt and pepper
5-6 tomatoes *or*
3-4 tablespoons tomato purée

In the olive oil, along with chopped onion, fennel, and garlic, sauté the crabs and whatever small rock fish you can get. Add the fresh tomatoes, cut in pieces, or the tomato purée. Add the *bouquet garni* and cover with boiling water. Season with salt and pepper. Cook 1 hour.

Force everything through a food mill and reheat the soup, letting it cook

15 minutes. Strain the soup through a fine sieve. You will now have a thin soup, which should be reheated again.

Add some saffron or turmeric, and when the liquid boils, add the noodles. Simmer 20 minutes. Sprinkle with grated Gruyère and serve as hot as possible.

Marmite dieppoise ∗ *Marmite dieppoise*

FOR SIX PEOPLE

5 pounds varied fish (halibut, flounder, red snapper, or red perch)
1 pint mussels
1 pound leeks
1½ pounds (5-6) onions
1 celery heart
1 bottle dry white wine
1 *bouquet garni* (thyme, bay leaf, parsley)
6 tablespoons butter
1 pint heavy cream
buttered croutons
salt and pepper

Ask the fish dealer to cut the heads from the fish and to cut them in small pieces. (If fish heads are not available, buy an extra fish as a substitute.—*Ed.*) Cut the fish heads in pieces.

Scrape and wash the mussels. Put them in a saucepan and cook over a high heat until the mussels open. Strain the broth through a cheesecloth.

Trim the leeks, and using the white parts only, cut in pieces. Peel and chop the onions. Wash and chop the celery.

Combine the vegetables, the fish heads, the shucked mussels, and the mussel broth in a pan. Add the white wine and the *bouquet garni.* Simmer 30 minutes. Strain the broth through a fine sieve. This is called a *fumet de poisson.*

Cut the fish in large pieces and arrange them in a large pan. Season with salt and pepper. Add the fish *fumet,* the butter, and the cream. Simmer very slowly for 15 minutes. Taste for seasoning.

Arrange the fish in a shallow dish and serve the broth in a separate bowl. Accompany with a dish of croutons fried in butter.

Mussel soup ∗ *Soupe aux moules*

FOR FOUR PEOPLE

2 quarts mussels
½ cup dry white wine
2 teaspoons chopped parsley
small *bouquet garni* (thyme, bay leaf)
6 tablespoons butter
2 onions, finely chopped
1 clove garlic, chopped
½ cup hot milk
2 egg yolks
½ cup cream
juice of 1 lemon
8 small pieces fried French bread
salt and pepper

Put thoroughly washed and scraped mussels into a pan with the white wine, parsley, salt, and a very small *bouquet garni.* Cook for about 5 minutes or until the mussels are opened. Keep warm but do not cook any longer or the mussels will toughen. Strain the broth through cheesecloth.

Heat the butter in a deep soup kettle and sauté finely chopped onions and garlic until golden. Add the strained mussel broth, 3 cups of boiling water, and the milk. Simmer for 15 minutes. Remove the mussels from their shells and add to the soup.

Beat the egg yolks in the soup tureen with the cream and the juice of 1 lemon. Pour the soup over the mixture, stirring as you do it. Serve with the French bread slices fried in butter.

Mussel and rice soup * Soupe aux moules et au riz

FOR SIX PEOPLE

1½ quarts mussels	small *bouquet garni* (parsley, bay leaf)
1 onion	6 tablespoons rice
2 leeks	pinch of saffron *or*
2½ tablespoons olive oil	1 tablespoon turmeric
3 tomatoes	salt and pepper

Place the mussels in a pan over high heat and cook until the mussels open. Shell the mussels and strain the broth through a cheesecloth.

Slice the onion and leeks very thin and sauté in olive oil until golden. Add the tomatoes, peeled and cut into small pieces. Add 9 cups of boiling water, the *bouquet garni,* salt, and pepper. Cook 10 minutes.

Sprinkle the soup with the rice and add the saffron or turmeric. Boil vigorously for 10 to 12 minutes. Taste the rice. It should be slightly undercooked, because the soup must cook 2 minutes longer. Boil a little longer, if necessary. Add the mussels and the mussel broth. Cook 2 minutes. Remove the *bouquet garni* and serve very hot.

Oyster soup * Soupe aux huîtres

FOR FOUR PEOPLE

5 dozen oysters	1 *bouquet garni* (thyme, bay leaf,
¼ pound pork belly	parsley)
2 large potatoes	3 tablespoons butter
1 quart milk, scalded	salt and pepper

Open the oysters and put them and the liquor in a bowl.

Dice the pork belly quite fine and try it out in a skillet over a moderate heat.

(If fresh pork belly is not available, parboil salt pork 5 minutes, rinse, and use like the fresh variety.—*Ed.*)

Peel and boil the potatoes in water. Drain and mash them in the bottom of a soup kettle, adding the hot milk gradually. Add the *bouquet garni* and bring the mixture to a boil. When it boils, add the oysters and their liquor and simmer very gently for 3 minutes. Season with salt and pepper.

Put the butter in the bottom of the soup tureen and pour in the soup. You can also add to this soup some thin slices of toasted French bread.

Entrées

Entrées

The French horror of monotony in eating, which is clearly shown by our constant search for variety in menus from one meal to the next, from one week to the next, and from one season to the next, is also reflected in the fact that we refuse to serve only a single dish at a meal, even if it is accompanied by many vegetables.

What in other countries would be the only course of a meal, serves us as the main course, the *plat de résistance*. It generally consists of a meat, accompanied by vegetables and followed by a green salad, assorted cheeses, and dessert. But besides this, before attacking the main course, we like to amuse ourselves with something different, something lighter in character. This is a course that lends itself to all kinds of dishes, with a variety of taste as well as of presentation. These dishes are called entrées. It is because of its charming variations that the entrée is the course we *enter* a meal with.

Actually, in the classic French order of menus of bygone years, the *entrée* was the third course. First there were soups or hors d'oeuvres, then came what was then known as a "remove." It was only after that that there appeared the entrée, prelude to the main dishes, which—like today—consisted of meat, poultry, game, or large fish accompanied by sauces and vegetables.

Nowadays, except for formal banquets, the main course is very simply preceded at the noon meal by hors d'oeuvres or an entrée and in the evening by a soup or an entrée.

The hors d'oeuvres are either raw vegetables, fish, or *charcuterie* (sausage, ham, cold cuts, and so on). Usually, these hors d'oeuvres are cold. I have already described the soups to you.

The entrées are more impressive than soup or hors d'oeuvres, but still, they ought to remain just simple ambassadors of the main course that is to follow. Recipes for entrées are to be found not only in this chapter but in others also. An entrée can, after all, be simply a dish of eggs (only at lunch time, however), a delicate fish dish, an unusual dish of vegetables, such as a soufflé or a vegetable loaf, a dish of pasta (but a light and interesting one), or even, in summer, a salad, not a green salad but one made up of a variety of ingredients.

But there are also entrées that require more cooking. Formerly, for the third course that I referred to before, there used to be what one called a mixed entrée, that is to say, a dish that was almost important enough to constitute a main dish: quiches, pies, *vols-au-vent,* tarts, and so on. In other words, it was an entrée with a pastry base. We continue to serve these as simple entrées today, and you will find these in the following chapter. But you will also find recipes for fried entrées, for soufflés, for crepes, and for other dishes.

Personally, when I make my menus, whether it be for the family meal or for a party with many guests, I pay particular attention to the entrée. If the entrée pleases people, then the whole meal has every chance for success.

Entrées with pastry bases

Many of our best entrées are served with pastry bases—flaky pastry (*pâte feuilletée*), tart pastry (*pâte brisée*), and cream puff pastry (*pâte à chou*). If you turn to page 643, you will find directions for making these bases. Flaky pastry and tart pastry must be made in advance so that they will have time to rest. This is essential. In some cases, you will find definite proportions given for a particular recipe, but the method of making it is the same. If you have pastry left over, wrap it well and use it for making a dessert the next day.

Provençale barquettes * Barquettes provençale

TWENTY-FOUR BARQUETTES

Barquettes are individual oval tartlets. The tins for these can be bought at stores specializing in French cooking ware. If they are not available, round individual tartlet tins can be substituted.

Tart Pastry II (page 646)
Court Bouillon I (Page 163)
1 pound haddock
6 hard-cooked eggs

1 tablespoon tomato paste
1 cup Mayonnaise (page 14)
salt and pepper

Make a double recipe of the pastry. When it has rested, roll out and line individual tartlet tins as directed on page 645. Bake 15 minutes at 400° F. Cool and remove the tarts from the tins.

Cook the haddock in court bouillon. Withdraw the fish from the liquid when cooked and remove the skin and bones. Flake the flesh.

Chop the eggs rather coarsely and mix with the fish. Stir the tomato paste into the mayonnaise and mix with the fish and eggs. Stir well, seasoning with salt and pepper.

Fill the baked tartlets with the mixture and chill in the refrigerator.

Tuna barquettes * Barquettes au thon

TWENTY-FOUR BARQUETTES

Tart Pastry II (page 646)
1 small can green beans
1 small can red peppers

1 large can (16 ounces)
  oil-packed tuna fish
1 cup Mayonnaise (page 14)
salt and pepper

Make a double recipe of the pastry.

Drain the beans and red peppers.

Line the tartlet tins as directed on page 645. Bake about 15 minutes at 400° F. Cool and remove the tarts from the tins.

Chop the beans and peppers coarsely. Flake the tuna fish and mix with the vegetables, binding them with a mayonnaise highly seasoned with lemon juice, salt, and pepper. Mix well and chill in the refrigerator. Fill the tartlets with the mixture.

Cheese tartlets * Tartelettes au fromage

FOR FOUR PEOPLE

Tart Pastry II (page 646)
½ package cream cheese
2 tablespoons milk
2 eggs

¾ cup grated Gruyère cheese
1½ cups Béchamel Sauce (page 6)
4 teaspoons tomato paste
salt and pepper

Make the pastry in advance and let it rest. Roll it out very thin and line small tartlet tins. See page 645.

Soften the cream cheese with the milk in a small bowl and beat in the eggs. Add the grated cheese and mix well.

Make the béchamel and combine the mixtures, seasoning with salt and pepper to taste. Remember that grated cheese has a salty flavor. Finally stir in the tomato paste.

Fill the tartlets with the mixture. Bake about 15 minutes at 400° F. Serve as soon as they come out of the oven.

Mushroom tartlets * Tartelettes aux champignons

FOR TWENTY-FOUR TARTLETS

Tart Pastry II (page 646)
½ pound mushrooms
½ cup Béchamel Sauce (page 6)
1½ cups ground cooked veal

½ cup heavy cream
10 tarragon leaves
salt and pepper

Make the pastry, allowing it time to rest. Line individual tartlet tins and bake about 15 minutes in 400° F. oven. (See page 645 for instructions.) Cool and remove the tarts from the tins.

Trim the mushrooms. Wash them well and chop rather coarsely.

Make the béchamel and cook the mushrooms in the sauce for 1 or 2 minutes. Remove from the heat and stir in the ground veal, salt, pepper, and chopped tarragon.

Fill the tartlets with the mixture and chill in the refrigerator.

Mussel tartlets * Tartelettes de moules

FOR FIVE PEOPLE

Tart Pastry II (page 646)
1½ quarts mussels
½ cup Mayonnaise (page 14)

1 hard-cooked egg
2 tablespoons chopped chives

Make the pastry in advance and let it rest. Roll out very thin and cut into ovals or rounds. Line the tartlet tins as directed on page 645. Prick the pastry with a fork and bake about 12 minutes at 400° F. Cool and remove the tarts from the tins.

Scrape and wash the mussels and place them in a kettle. Put them over a high heat until the mussels open. Remove them from the shells and cool thoroughly.

Combine the mayonnaise with the egg, which has been cooked in salted, boiling water for 15 minutes, plunged into cold water, peeled, and crushed. Stir the mussels into the mixture.

Fill the baked shells with the mixture and decorate with chopped chives. Serve very cold.

Spinach tartlets * Tartelettes aux épinards

FOR SIX PEOPLE

Tart Pastry II (page 646)
2 pounds spinach
5 tablespoons butter

¾ cup heavy cream
2 hard-cooked eggs
salt and pepper

Make the pastry and let it rest. Line buttered oval or round tartlet tins with the pastry. Prick the pastry with a fork so that it will not swell during the baking. See page 645. Bake 12 to 15 minutes at 400° F. Remove the tarts from the tins.

Meanwhile, trim and wash spinach. Boil uncovered 5 minutes in a large amount of salted water. Drain thoroughly and force the spinach through a food mill. Put it in a saucepan with the butter and cook over a high heat for a few minutes in order to evaporate the remaining water from the spinach. Remove from the heat and add the cream. Season to taste with salt and pepper.

Fill the tartlets with the spinach and decorate each one with a slice of egg. Serve very hot.

Sweetbread tartlets I * Tartelettes de ris de veau I

FOR EIGHT PEOPLE

Tart Pastry II or III (page 646)
2 pairs sweetbreads
flour

1 pound mushrooms
6 tablespoons heavy cream
juice of ½ lemon

8 tablespoons butter

½ cup thick Béchamel Sauce
    (page 6)

salt and pepper

Make the pastry in advance.

Soak the sweetbreads in a bowl under a running faucet. Put them in a large saucepan of cold water. Bring to a boil and remove the sweetbreads from the pan and rinse them in cold water, removing the tissues and cartilages. Press the sweetbreads between 2 dish towels to remove the water. Cut each sweetbread into 2 pieces and dip them in flour.

Heat 4 tablespoons of butter in a skillet and cook the sweetbread pieces over a moderate heat, turning each one gently. Season with salt and pepper.

Make the béchamel sauce.

Line the individual tartlet tins with the pastry (see page 645). Bake them 10 minutes at 400° F. Remove the tarts from the tins.

Trim the mushrooms. Wash, dry, and chop them and sauté 4 to 5 minutes in the remaining butter. Put them in a shallow bowl and add enough of the béchamel gradually, stirring constantly, so that the mixture is not too thick. Add the cream, salt, and pepper.

Fill the tartlets with the mixture and top each one with a piece of sweetbread. Pour a little of the sweetbread butter, to which a little lemon juice has been added, over each one. Reheat in the oven for a moment before serving.

Sweetbread tartlets II * Tartelettes de ris de veau II

FOR TEN PEOPLE

Tart Pastry II (page 646)

6 artichoke bottoms

1 cup Béchamel Sauce (page 6)

¾ cup heavy cream

2 pairs sweetbreads

flour

6 tablespoons butter

1 lemon

salt and pepper

Make the pastry.

Boil the artichokes in boiling salted water for 45 minutes or until an outer leaf comes off easily. Discard the leaves and the choke, leaving just the bottoms. Or use canned artichoke bottoms. Grind them through a *moulinette* or force through a sieve.

Make the béchamel and mix it with the artichoke purée, cream, salt, and pepper.

Prepare the sweetbreads as in the preceding recipe but cut them in small slices before dipping them in flour and cooking them in butter. Season with salt and pepper.

Line the small tartlet tins with pastry as directed on page 645. Bake 10 to 12 minutes at 400° F. Remove the tarts from the tins. Fill each one with artichoke purée and top with a piece of sweetbread. Decorate with a small piece of lemon.

Sweetbread tartlets III
Tartelettes de ris de veau III

FOR EIGHT PEOPLE

Tart Pastry II (page 646)
2 pairs sweetbreads
6 tablespoons butter
1 small can peas
½ cup thin Béchamel Sauce
    (page 6)

8 tablespoons heavy cream
juice of 1 lemon
salt and pepper

Make the pastry in advance so that it can rest.

Prepare and cook the sweetbreads as in the first recipe for sweetbread tartlets, cutting each sweetbread in half so that you will have 8 pieces. Roll out the pastry. Cut and line round or oval tartlet tins. See page 645. Bake 12 to 15 minutes at 400° F. Remove the tarts from the tins.

Heat the peas.

Make the béchamel. Remove from the fire and stir in the cream.

Add the peas, well drained.

Put some of the mixture in each tartlet. Cover with a piece of sweetbread and pour a little melted butter, seasoned with lemon juice, over it.

Serve very hot.

Tomato tartlets * Tartelettes aux tomates

FOR SIX PEOPLE

Pastry:
3 cups flour
¼ pound butter
6 tablespoons water
½ teaspoon salt

Filling:
2 pounds (6-8 medium-sized) tomatoes
5 tablespoons olive oil
1 tablespoon chopped parsley
2 cans anchovy fillets
24 black pitted olives
salt and pepper

Make a tart pastry as directed on page 646, using 1 cup sifted all-purpose flour and 2 cups of sifted pastry flour. Let rest. When the dough is well rested, roll it out very thin on a floured marble or working surface. Cut into rounds and line 12 buttered tartlet tins. See page 645. Bake 12 to 15 minutes at 400° F. Remove the tarts from the tins.

Meanwhile, dip the tomatoes in boiling water for a few minutes and slip off the skins. Cut the tomatoes in pieces, removing the seeds. Heat the oil and sauté the tomatoes with the parsley, cooking until the tomatoes form a thick sauce. Season with salt and pepper.

Fill the tartlets with the tomato sauce. Cross 2 anchovy fillets on top of each one and garnish with 2 black olives, preferably the imported variety.

Fish rissoles * Rissoles de poissons

FOR SIX PEOPLE

Flaky Pastry (page 643)
1½ cups cooked fish
½ cup thick Béchamel Sauce
  (page 6)

1 tablespoon curry powder
2 lemons
salt and pepper

Make the pastry in advance, saving the final 2 "turns" for just before baking.

Make sure that the leftover cooked fish is free from skin and bones. Mix it with the thick béchamel and season with curry, salt, and pepper.

Roll the pastry out into a large, very thin square. Divide it into 2 equal rectangles.

Drop tablespoonfuls of the fish mixture onto one rectangle in mounds, spaced about 1¼ inches apart. With a pastry brush dipped in water, paint the lines between the mounds and around the edge. Cover with the other rectangle and press with your fingertips around each little mound.

Preheat the deep fat to 385° F.

Run a pastry wheel along the lines between the mounds and cut them into squares.

Fry in deep fat until golden brown. Drain on paper toweling and serve very hot, garnished with lemon slices.

Tuna rissoles I * Rissoles de thon à l'huile I

FOR FOUR PEOPLE

Flaky Pastry (page 643)
1 can oil-packed tuna fish
1½ cups Béchamel Sauce (page 6)

several sprigs parsley
Tomato Sauce (page 22) (optional)

This recipe is good for using up pastry trimmings. You need only about half the original recipe.

Cut the tuna into small pieces.

Make the béchamel and mix the two together.

Roll out the pastry very thin into a square, and on the nearer half place little mounds of the tuna mixture, spacing them ¾ of an inch apart. Run a pastry brush, dipped in water, over the lines that separate each one and around the edge. Fold the other half of the square over the mounds, pressing them together well. Using a cookie cutter, cut them into crescents.

Preheat deep fat to 385° F. Fry the crescents until golden brown. Drain on paper toweling.

Serve very hot on a napkin-lined platter garnished with fried parsley sprigs. Serve with tomato sauce, if desired.

Tuna rissoles II * Rissoles de thon à l'huile II

FOR FOUR PEOPLE

Flaky Pastry (page 643)
Tomato Sauce (page 22)
1 can (6 ounces) oil-packed flaked
    tuna
4 teaspoons tomato paste
1 tablespoon capers, chopped
2 lemons
salt and pepper

Make the pastry in advance and make the final 2 "turns" just before using. This will take about half the original recipe.

Make the tomato sauce, so that it will be ready when you need it.

Pound and rub the tuna in a mortar or wooden bowl with its oil to form a smooth paste. Add the tomato paste and the chopped capers and season to taste with salt and pepper.

Roll out the pastry very thin and cut it into 2½-inch rounds. Put a little of the stuffing on half of each round. Moisten the edges with a pastry brush dipped in water and fold the pastry over to form small turnovers. Press the edges together firmly.

Preheat the fat to 385° F. Fry in deep fat until golden brown. Drain on paper toweling and serve very hot, garnished with lemon slices and accompanied by tomato sauce.

Veal rissoles * Rissoles de veau

FOR FIVE PEOPLE

Flaky Pastry (page 643)
½ cup ground cooked veal
1 medium-sized onion
3 tablespoons butter
4 teaspoons flour
¾ cup hot bouillon
4 tablespoons chopped mushrooms
2 teaspoons chopped fines herbes
    (parsley, tarragon, chervil)
2 lemons
cayenne
salt and pepper

Make the pastry in advance and give the final 2 "turns" just before using.

Be sure that the veal is free from skin and gristle before grinding.

Chop the onion very fine.

Heat the butter in a small skillet and sauté the onion and the veal for a few minutes. Stir with a wooden spoon. Sprinkle with flour and stir that in. Add the bouillon and mix well.

Add the mushrooms, which have been trimmed, washed, and finely chopped. Add the chopped herbs and season with salt, pepper, and a dash of cayenne. Cool thoroughly.

Roll out the pastry very thin on a floured surface. Cut into 2½-inch rounds and on half of each round put a spoonful of stuffing. Moisten the edges with a pastry brush dipped in water and turn over the pastry to make little turnovers. Seal the edges well.

Preheat the deep fat to 385° F. Fry until golden brown. Drain and serve on a heated platter surrounded with lemon wedges.

You can use this same recipe with leftover chicken, meat, fish, or vegetables. You can also fill these *rissoles* with jam.

Ham and cheese turnovers
Chaussons au gruyère et jambon

FOR FOUR PEOPLE

Tart Pastry II (page 646)
1½ cups thick Béchamel Sauce
 (page 6)
1 cup grated Gruyère cheese

1 thick slice cooked ham
1 egg yolk
salt and pepper

Make the pastry in advance in order to let it rest.

Make the béchamel and remove it from the heat to stir in the cheese and the finely diced ham. Season highly.

Cut out 12 little rounds of pastry, about 2½ inches in diameter. Moisten the edges. Put a tablespoon of the ham-cheese mixture on half of each round. Fold over and press the edges together firmly.

Mix the egg yolk with a teaspoon of water and paint each little turnover. Bake 12 minutes at 400° F. Serve very hot.

Mushroom turnovers
Chaussons aux champignons

FOR FOUR PEOPLE

½ recipe Semiflaky Pastry (page 644)
¾ pound mushrooms
2 tablespoons butter
1½ cups Béchamel Sauce (page 6)

1 teaspoon chopped tarragon *or*
2 teaspoons chopped parsley
paprika
1 egg yolk
salt and pepper

Make the pastry, allowing time for resting.

Trim, wash, and slice the mushrooms. Sauté them 2 minutes in heated butter.

Make the béchamel and add the mushrooms. Season with the chopped herbs, salt, pepper, and paprika.

Roll out the pastry for the last 2 times, and after the sixth "turn," roll out the pastry to thickness of ⅛ inch. With a pastry wheel make 4 circles each 6 inches in diameter. Moisten the edges with water. Put a fourth of the mushroom mixture on one half of each circle. Fold over the other halves and seal the edges well.

Mix the egg yolk with a teaspoon of water and paint each turnover with the mixture. Bake 15 to 20 minutes at 400° F.

Frankfurters in flaky pastry
Saucisses en feuilletée

FOR FOUR PEOPLE

Flaky Pastry (page 643)   tarragon mustard
4 frankfurters

This will take about half the original recipe for flaky pastry. Prepare it in advance and give the final 2 "turns" just before using. Roll out the pastry very thin and cut into rectangles large enough to envelop the frankfurters. Spread the pastry with the mustard. Moisten the edges with a pastry brush dipped in water.

Place a frankfurter in each one and roll them up, sealing them like a package. Bake 10 minutes at 400° F.

Little quiches lorraines * Petites quiches lorraines

FOR TWELVE PEOPLE

Tart Pastry (page 646)   10 eggs
  (double recipe)   1 quart heavy cream
1¼ pounds thinly sliced   10 tablespoons butter
  Canadian bacon   salt and pepper

Make the pastry and let it rest several hours. Roll out on a floured surface to a thickness of ⅛ inch. Cut in rounds and line 24 round tartlet tins. Prick the pastry with a fork. See page 645.

Cut the bacon slices into small pieces and boil 5 minutes. Drain thoroughly.

Beat the eggs until thoroughly blended and add the cream. Season with salt and pepper.

Dot the uncooked tartlets with small pieces of butter and divide the bacon among the tarts. Pour the egg and cream mixture into the tartlets and bake 20 to 30 minutes in a 400° F. oven.

Crab quiche * Quiche aux crabes

FOR FIVE PEOPLE

Pastry:
3 cups flour
5 tablespoons soft butter
2½ tablespoons oil
1 egg
½ teaspoon salt

Filling:
3 eggs
2 cups heavy cream
1 large can crabmeat
salt and pepper

Make the tart pastry a day in advance, using ¾ cup sifted all-purpose flour and 2¼ cups sifted pastry flour. Combine with the other ingredients. See page 646. This pastry must rest a long time.

Roll out the pastry and line a tart or pie tin. Prick the pastry well. Bake 10 minutes at 350° F.

Beat the eggs in a bowl until blended. Add the cream and season with salt and pepper. Stir in the crabmeat, which has been coarsely flaked and freed from all cartilage.

Pour the mixture into the half-baked shell and continue baking for 20 to 25 minutes.

Quiche lorraine * Quiche lorraine

FOR SIX PEOPLE

7 tablespoons soft butter
2¼ cups flour
½ pound lean pork belly

4 eggs
1½ cups heavy cream
salt and pepper

Make a tart pastry as directed on page 646 by mixing the butter and ½ teaspoon of salt into the flour (½ cup all-purpose flour and 1¾ cups pastry flour), adding enough water to make a stiff dough that does not stick to your fingers. If it is too soft, add more flour. Let the dough rest for several hours. Roll it out into a circle and line a tart pan. Prick the pastry well with a fork.

Cut the pork fat into small dice. Parboil 5 minutes. (If necessary, substitute lean salt pork or bacon. —*Ed.*)

Beat the eggs until well blended. Stir in the cream and season with salt and pepper.

Sprinkle the diced pork fat into the tart. Pour over the egg mixture and bake 20 to 30 minutes at 400° F. Serve immediately.

Quiche with truffles * Quiche aux truffes

FOR TWELVE PEOPLE

Pastry:
5¾ cups flour
2½ tablespoons oil
10 tablespoons butter
2 egg yolks
1 teaspoon salt

Filling:
¾ pound mushrooms
5 tablespoons butter
5 eggs
2 cups heavy cream
1 large can truffle peelings
salt and pepper

Make the tart pastry a day in advance, using 2 cups sifted all-purpose flour and 3¾ cups pastry flour. Mix the ingredients just until blended. The pastry must rest a long time. Roll it out on a floured surface to a thickness of ⅛ inch. Line a large tart or pie tin. Prick the pastry well with a fork. Bake 10 minutes at 350° F.

Trim, wash, dry, and slice the mushrooms. Sauté them in butter for 5 minutes. Season with salt.

Beat the eggs until blended. Add the cream, the truffle peelings, the mushrooms, salt, and pepper. Stir well.

Pour the mixture into the half-baked shell. Bake about 20 minutes at 350° F.

Cheese and onion tart
Tarte aux oignons et fromage

FOR SIX PEOPLE

Tart Pastry (page 646)
1 pound (4-5) medium onions
3 tablespoons butter
3 eggs

4 teaspoons flour
1¼ cup heavy cream
1 cup grated Gruyère cheese
salt and pepper

Make Tart Pastry I or II. At the proper time, roll out and line a tart or pie tin. See page 645.

Peel and chop the onions very fine. Cook in boiling salted water for 15 minutes. Strain completely and sauté in the butter until golden.

Beat the eggs in a bowl with a fork and add the flour and the cream, beating continuously. Beat in the grated cheese and season with pepper. Do not add salt before tasting, because the cheese may be salty enough. Finally, stir in the onions.

Fill the tart with the mixture and bake 30 minutes at 400° F.

Onion tart colette * Tarte aux oignons colette

Tart Pastry II (page 646)
2 pounds onions
5 tablespoons butter
1 egg

1 tablespoon flour
¾ cup milk
1 pound tiny onions
salt and pepper

Make the pastry. Roll out and line a tart or pie tin with the pastry. See page 645.

Prick the bottom well with a fork so that it will not swell during the baking. Bake 15 minutes at 400° F.

Peel the onions and slice them thin. Sauté in 4 tablespoons of butter. When golden, remove from the heat and stir in a mixture of the egg, flour, and milk. Season with salt and pepper. Fill the tart with the mixture and bake 15 minutes at 400° F.

Meanwhile, parboil the little onions for 15 minutes in salted water. Drain and sauté in the remaining tablespoon of butter. Line these up on the cooked tart for decoration.

Onions tart brestoise * Tarte aux oignons brestoise

Tart Pastry (page 646) *or*
Flaky Pastry (page 643)
2 pounds onions

4 tablespoons oil
3½ ounces anchovy fillets
salt and pepper

Make the pastry of your choice, and when it is rested, roll it out to a thickness of ⅛ inch. Line a tart or pie tin but do not bake.

Peel the onions and chop them very fine. Cook them gently in a covered skillet in 3 tablespoons of hot oil until tender. Do not let the onions brown.

Pour the onions into the unbaked tart shell.

Rinse the anchovy fillets to remove excess salt and with them make a lattice pattern over the surface of the onion-filled tart shell. Bake 15 to 20 minutes in a 425° F. oven.

Poached egg and tomato tart
Tarte aux oeufs pochés et tomates

Tart Pastry (page 646)
1 pound onions

½ teaspoon anise seeds
6 eggs

2 cloves garlic

1 tablespoon white vinegar

5 tablespoons oil

tarragon leaves

2 pounds (7-8 medium-sized) tomatoes

paprika

1 sprig thyme

salt and pepper

2 bay leaves

Make the pastry in advance. When it has rested, roll it out on a floured surface with a floured rolling pin to a thickness of ⅛ inch. Line a buttered tart or pie tin. Prick well with a fork. Bake 15 minutes at 400° F.

Meanwhile, peel the onions and the garlic. Chop them well and put them in a skillet with 2½ tablespoons oil. Cover and simmer 30 minutes. Force the mixture through a strainer.

Wash and quarter the tomatoes and put them in another skillet with the rest of the oil, the thyme, bay leaves, and anise. Cook without a cover until it becomes a thick purée. Force through a strainer and combine with the onion purée. Season with salt and pepper.

Poach the eggs 3 minutes in simmering water to which the vinegar and a teaspoon of salt have been added. Transfer carefully with a slotted spoon to a towel to drain.

Spread the onion-tomato mixture in the baked tart. Arrange the eggs on top. Sprinkle with paprika and decorate with tarragon leaves. Serve hot.

Endive tart * Tarte aux endives

FOR SIX PEOPLE

Tart Pastry (page 646)

½ cup heavy cream

3 pounds Belgian endives

1 tablespoon tomato paste

1½ cups Béchamel Sauce (page 6)

salt and pepper

6 ounces Gruyère cheese

Prepare the pastry and roll it out with a floured rolling pin onto a lightly floured working surface to a thickness of ⅛ inch. Line a tart or pie tin with the pastry. Prick well with a fork so that the pastry will not swell during the baking. Preheat the oven to 400° F. and bake about 15 minutes. Let the tart cool in the tin.

Trim and wash the endive, removing any wilted leaves. Cook in boiling salted water for 45 minutes. Drain thoroughly, first in a strainer and then in toweling.

Meanwhile, make the béchamel. Remove from the heat and stir in 4 ounces (1 cup) freshly grated cheese.

Mix the cream with the tomato paste. Season with salt and pepper.

Arrange the endives in the tart. Cover with the sauce. Dice the rest of the cheese very fine and sprinkle over the top. Cover with the cream mixture. Reheat for 5 minutes in a 400° F. oven.

Leek tart * Tarte aux poireaux

FOR SIX PEOPLE

Flaky Pastry (page 643) *or*
Tart Pastry II (page 646)
3 pounds leeks
1½ cups Béchamel Sauce (page 6)

1 cup grated Gruyère cheese
2 tablespoons butter
salt and pepper

Make the pastry of your choice in advance in order to let it rest. You will need enough to line a large tart or pie pan.

Trim the leeks, discarding most of the green part. Wash well and boil 25 minutes in salted water. Drain completely. Chop the leeks fine.

While the leeks are cooking, make the béchamel. Season well with salt and pepper and mix in the chopped leeks.

Fill the tart crust. Sprinkle generously with grated cheese and dot with butter. Bake at 400° F. for 20 minutes.

Tart mapie * Tarte spéciale

FOR SIX PEOPLE

Pastry:
3 cups flour
¼ pound soft butter
6 tablespoons water
½ teaspoon salt

Filling:
5 ounces Gruyère cheese
spiced French mustard
1 can anchovy fillets
powdered thyme
1 pound tomatoes
2 onions
⅓ cup olive oil
salt and pepper

Make a tart pastry using ¾ cup of sifted all-purpose flour and 2¼ cups of pastry flour. Mix with the soft butter, the water, and salt. See page 646. Make a ball of the pastry and let it rest for at least 1 hour. Roll out on a floured surface to a thickness of ⅛ inch and line a large, buttered tart or pie tin. Prick the pastry with a fork and bake 10 minutes at 400° F.

Remove the tart from the oven and line the bottom with slices of cheese spread with mustard. Cover the cheese with a layer of anchovy fillets, crushed with a fork. Sprinkle with powdered thyme and cover with a layer of sliced tomatoes and a layer of thinly sliced onion rings. Season with a very little salt. Grind fresh pepper over the onions and sprinkle with the olive oil. Bake 15 minutes at 400° F. Serve very hot.

Mushroom tart * Tarte aux champignons

FOR SIX PEOPLE

Tart Pastry II (page 646)
1 pound mushrooms
juice of 1 lemon
5 tablespoons butter
5 tablespoons flour
¾ cup chicken or veal stock

pinch of thyme
pinch of powdered bay leaf
½ cup heavy cream
2 egg yolks
salt and pepper

Make the pastry in advance and let it rest. When it has rested, roll out to ⅛ inch thickness. Cut a large round of pastry and line a tart or pie tin. See page 645. Prick the bottom of the tart with a fork so that it will not swell during the baking. Bake 15 minutes at 400° F. Do not remove the baked tart from the tin but cool to luke-warm.

Meanwhile, trim, wash, and dry the mushrooms. Cut them in thin slices and put them in a saucepan with the lemon juice. Shake the pan so that the lemon juice will penetrate all the mushrooms. Add 3 tablespoons of butter. Sauté 4 to 5 minutes. Remove from the heat.

Heat 2 tablespoons of butter in a small saucepan and stir in the flour with a wooden spoon. Add the chicken or veal stock and whisk until blended. Season with salt, pepper, and the herbs. Lower the heat and beat in a combination of cream and egg yolks, seasoned with salt and pepper.

Put the well-drained mushrooms in a saucepan. Add the sauce and reheat gently. Do not boil. Pour the mixture into the hot tart and serve immediately.

Sole tart * Tarte aux soles

FOR FOUR PEOPLE

Tart Pastry II or III (page 646)
Court Bouillon I (page 163)
8 sole fillets
¾ pound mushrooms

1½ cups Béchamel Sauce (page 6)
juice of 1 lemon
¾ cup heavy cream
salt and pepper

Make the pastry and let it rest as long as necessary.
Prepare the court bouillon and let it cool.
Line a tart or pie plate with the pastry. Prick the bottom well so that the pastry will not swell. Bake 15 minutes at 400° F.
Flatten the fillets with the broad side of a large knife or a small cleaver so that they will not roll up during cooking. Put them in the cold court bouillon. Bring them to a boil slowly over a moderate heat, and as soon as the boiling point is reached, remove them to a towel to drain.
Trim the mushrooms, wash them well, and force them through a *moulinette* or spin them in a blender.

Make a béchamel and cook the mushrooms in it for 1 to 2 minutes. Season with salt, pepper, and lemon juice.

Spread the bottom of the baked tart with the mushroom mixture. Place the sole on top of the mixture and cover with cream. Season with salt and pepper and brown in the oven for 8 minutes. Serve very hot.

Spinach tart au gratin
Tarte gratinée aux épinards

FOR SIX PEOPLE

Tart Pastry II (page 646)
4 pounds spinach
6 tablespoons soft butter

½ cup heavy cream
3 ounces Gruyère cheese
salt and pepper

Make the pastry in advance. When it has rested, roll out on a floured surface and cut a large round. Line a tart or pie tin. Prick the pastry well with a fork and bake 15 minutes at 400° F.

Meanwhile, trim and wash the spinach thoroughly. Boil in a large amount of salted water for 5 to 6 minutes. Drain well, pressing out all the water possible with your hands. Do not chop the spinach but mix it with the butter and then with the cream. Season well with salt and pepper.

Put this combination in the baked crust and sprinkle with cheese, cut in small dice. Place in a 400° F. oven until the top is golden brown. Serve very hot.

Tomato tart * Tarte aux tomates

FOR SIX PEOPLE

Pastry:
3 cups flour
10 tablespoons butter
6 tablespoons water
½ teaspoon salt

Filling:
2 pounds onions
olive oil
2 cups soft breadcrumbs

½ cup milk
2 tablespoons chopped parsley
2 cloves garlic
pinch of thyme
pinch of powdered bay leaf
bouillon or hot water
2 egg yolks
9 small tomatoes
salt and pepper

Follow the instructions on page 646 for making the pastry, using 1 cup of sifted all-purpose flour and 2 cups of sifted pastry flour. After it has rested for several hours, roll it out and prick with a fork. Bake 20 minutes at 400° F.

Meanwhile, peel and slice the onions very thin. Heat 4 tablespoons of a rather light olive oil in a skillet and sauté the onions without letting them brown. The heat should be very low. Season with salt and pepper.

Soak the breadcrumbs in milk. Squeeze almost dry. Chop fine the parsley, the garlic, and a fourth of the cooked onions. Mix with the breadcrumbs. Heat 2 tablespoons of oil in another skillet and sauté the mixture for 3 minutes, seasoning with salt, pepper, and herbs. Moisten with 1 or 2 tablespoons of hot bouillon or water. Taste for seasoning. Remove from the heat and stir in the egg yolks. Cook over a very low heat while preparing the tomatoes.

Cut off the top third of each tomato and scoop out the seeds. Fill them with the breadcrumb mixture and put back the top of each tomato. Place them in a baking dish and sprinkle with 4 to 5 tablespoons of oil. Bake 15 minutes at 350° F.

Spread the rest of the cooked onions in the bottom of the tart. Place the tomatoes on the bed of onions and reheat 5 minutes in the oven. This tart is equally good hot or cold.

Fouée champenoise * Fouée champenoise

FOR SIX PEOPLE

Tart Pastry II (page 646)
1½ cups chopped walnuts
walnut oil

1½ cups heavy cream
2 tablespoons butter
salt and pepper

Make the pastry in advance and let it rest. Roll it out on a floured surface with a floured rolling pin to a thickness of ⅛ inch. Place a pastry circle or a bottomless layer-cake tin on a cold baking sheet and line either one to make a crust as you would a pastry or tart tin. Or you can line an ordinary tart or pastry tin. Prick well with the tines of a fork so that the crust will not swell.

Chop the walnuts fine. Put them in a bowl and work in enough walnut oil to make a thin paste. Spread this mixture in the tart. Season the heavy cream and spread it over the nuts. Dot with bits of butter and bake 20 to 30 minutes at 400° F.

Ham in flaky pastry * Gâteau plat au jambon

FOR TWELVE PEOPLE

Flaky Pastry (page 643)
1½ cups Béchamel Sauce (page 6)
1 pound lean ham, ground
½ cup heavy cream

2½ tablespoons tomato paste
3 eggs
1 egg yolk
salt and pepper

Make the pastry as directed on page 643. Make the last 2 "turns" just before using.

Make the béchamel and let it get cold. It should be rather thick. Put the ground ham in a bowl. Add the sauce, cream, tomato paste, eggs, salt, and pepper. Mix very thoroughly, beating with a wooden spoon.

Roll out the pastry on a lightly floured surface into a large square. Trim evenly and divide into 2 large rectangles of equal size.

Put the ham mixture on one rectangle, spreading it out evenly and leaving a ¾-inch margin on all sides of the rectangle. Moisten the margin with a pastry brush dipped in water. Cover with the other pastry rectangle and press the edges together firmly. Place on a baking sheet. Paint the surface with an egg yolk mixed with a teaspoon of water or with milk. Bake about 20 minutes at 400° F.

Salmon in flaky pastry * Feuilletée de saumon

FOR SIX PEOPLE

Flaky Pastry (page 643)
½ cup rice
4 hard-cooked eggs
3 tablespoons chopped herbs
   (parsley, chervil, tarragon)
1 pound chunk salmon

½ pound butter, melted
1 egg yolk
salt and pepper
1 cup heavy cream
½ lemon

This is an exquisite dish for a buffet, because it is as pretty to see as it is good to eat.

Prepare the pastry in advance. Do not give the final 2 "turns" until just before cooking.

Boil the rice and cool. Cook the eggs in boiling salted water for 15 minutes. Plunge into cold water, shell, and cut with an egg slicer.

Chop the herbs.

Cook the salmon in a court bouillon for 15 minutes. See page 163. Remove from the water. When cooled, flake the salmon, removing the bones. Cool.

Roll the pastry out quite thin into a large square and cut into 2 equal rectangles. Moisten the edges. Place one of the rectangles on a baking sheet and spread with a layer of rice leaving a ¾-inch border. Season with salt and pepper. Sprinkle with melted butter and then with chopped herbs and cover with egg slices. Then put on all the flaked salmon. Cover with more egg slices, with more chopped herbs, and finally with a layer of rice. Sprinkle very generously with melted butter. Cover with the other pastry rectangle, pressing the moistened edges together. Paint the entire surface with an egg yolk mixed with a teaspoon of water. Bake 20 minutes at 400° F.

This may be eaten hot or cold. Accompany with a bowl of heavy cream seasoned with lemon juice.

Pissaladière * Pissaladière

FOR SIX PEOPLE

2½ cups sifted all-purpose flour
1 package dry yeast
7 ounces salted anchovies
1 pound onions

8 tablespoons oil
3 tomatoes
¼ pound black olives (imported)
salt

The night before you serve this dish, make a dough by mixing the flour with the yeast, dissolved in ¼ cup lukewarm water, and a pinch of salt. Work together, adding just enough water to make the dough stick together. Knead until smooth. Put in a warm place, cover with a dish towel, and let stand.

Remove the bones from the anchovies and soak the fillets in water, changing the water several times.

Peel and slice the onions fine. Sauté in 6 tablespoons of oil until golden. Season with salt.

Dip the tomatoes in boiling water and peel off the skins.

Roll out the dough into a large circle. Place on a buttered baking sheet and roll the edges to form a rim. Prick the bottom well with a fork. Spread the bottom with the onions. Cut the tomatoes in large pieces and arrange on the onions, along with the freshened anchovy fillets and the olives. Sprinkle with 2 tablespoons of oil and bake 20 to 25 minutes at 400° F.

Chicken vol-au-vent * Vol-au-vent de volaille

FOR EIGHT PEOPLE

Vol-au-Vent (page 644)
3 tablespoons butter
4 teaspoons flour
⅔ cup hot bouillon
1 large can truffle peelings

⅓ cup Madeira
1 small can chicken quenelles*
2 cups diced cooked chicken
salt and pepper

Buy or bake the pastry shell (vol-au-vent).

Heat the butter in a saucepan and stir in the flour. Add the hot bouillon, the liquid from the truffle can, and the Madeira. Season with salt and pepper. Stir until blended and simmer gently without letting the sauce thicken. Poach the quenelles until thoroughly heated and cut in pieces.

Combine the quenelles, truffle peelings, chicken, and sauce and bring to a boil. Pour into the hot pastry shell and serve immediately.

*Quenelles are a kind of dumpling. They can be bought in cans in specialty shops.—Ed.

Macaroni vol-au-vent * Vol-au-vent de macaronis

FOR SIX PEOPLE

Vol-au-Vent (page 644)
¼ pound macaroni pieces
3 tablespoons butter
4 teaspoons flour
1 bouillon cube
2½ tablespoons Madeira

2 large slices cooked ham
12 small pitted green olives
12 pitted black olives
3 hard-cooked eggs
salt and pepper

Buy or bake the pastry shell (vol-au-vent).

Cook the macaroni in boiling salted water just until tender. Rinse in cold water and drain well.

Heat the butter in a saucepan and stir in the flour with a wooden spoon. Dissolve the bouillon cube in ½ cup of hot water, add to the butter-flour mixture, and stir until the sauce has thickened slightly. Add the Madeira and season to taste. Add the ham cut in dice, the olives, the eggs peeled and sliced, and the cooked macaroni. When very hot, pour into the hot pastry shell. Serve immediately.

If you have leftover meat or chicken, you can use that instead of the ham.

Cheese puffs * Ramequins au fromage

FOR FOUR PEOPLE

5½ tablespoons butter
⅛ teaspoon salt
1¼ cups sifted all-purpose flour

3 eggs
2½ ounces Gruyère cheese
milk

Bring 1 cup and 2 tablespoons of water, butter, and salt to a boil. Remove from the heat and add the flour all at once. Stir well. Put it back on the heat, stirring constantly, and cook until the mixture forms a ball, leaving a dry coating on the bottom of the pan. Remove from the heat again and beat in the eggs one by one, beating hard and long after each one.

Grate half the cheese and dice the rest quite fine. Add all the cheese to the dough.

With a pastry tube fitted with a medium-small tip, or with a teaspoon, drop little mounds of the mixture onto a buttered baking sheet, leaving space between each one. Paint each one with a little milk.

Bake 10 to 12 minutes at 400° F.

Pine cones * Pignatelles

FOR FOUR PEOPLE

½ recipe Cream Puff Pastry
   (page 649)

1 slice lean ham
½ cup grated Gruyère cheese

Make the pastry, leaving out the sugar. Mix in the ham, finely diced, and the freshly grated cheese.

Preheat the fat to 390° F. Drop the pastry in amounts as large as walnuts from the end of a tablespoon into the hot fat and fry until golden brown. Drain and serve very hot.

La gougère * La gougère

FOR SIX PEOPLE

10 tablespoons butter	4 egg yolks
2½ cups sifted all-purpose flour	4 egg whites, beaten stiff
½ pound Gruyère cheese	salt and pepper

Bring 1¼ cups of water, 8 tablespoons of the butter, a pinch of salt, and a little pepper to a boil in a saucepan. As soon as the mixture boils, remove from the heat and add the flour all at once. Stir well and replace the saucepan over heat. Continue stirring until the dough forms a ball, leaving a dry coating on the bottom.

Remove from the heat and cool 5 minutes.

Grate all but about 2 ounces of the cheese.

Add the egg yolks one by one to the dough, stirring constantly. Fold in the beaten egg whites and the grated cheese.

Preheat the oven to 400° F.

Butter a baking sheet with the remaining butter and make a circle of the dough on the sheet. Cut the rest of the cheese in very thin slices and place it on the circle. Bake 25 to 30 minutes.

Stuffed cream puffs for entrées
Petits choux fourrés et salés

FOR FOUR PEOPLE

Make the unsweetened cream puff pastry as directed on page 649.

Using a pastry bag fitted with a medium-sized tip, or using a teaspoon, drop little mounds of the pastry on a buttered baking sheet. Paint each one with a mixture of egg yolk beaten with a little milk. Bake 15 minutes at 400° F.

To fill the cream puffs, you either cut open the top third without cutting it off entirely, fill with a small spoon, and replace the cover, or you can make a little hole in the bottom and fill with a pastry tube.

Following are several suggestions for fillings:

Chicken filling ✳ Farce de hachis de volaille

1 cup finely ground chicken
½ cup heavy cream
juice of ½ lemon

paprika
cayenne
salt

Mix the finely ground cooked chicken with the heavy cream. Season with lemon juice, salt, paprika, and a dash of cayenne. The filling should be like a thin purée.

Sardine filling ✳ Farce de hachis de sardines

1 can smoked sardines
½ cup heavy cream

1 teaspoon tarragon

Pound the sardines, adding the cream and the chopped tarragon until you have a smooth purée. (This can be done with an electric mixer.—*Ed.*)

Mushroom filling ✳ Farce de champignons hachés

½ pound mushrooms
2 tablespoons butter

½ cup heavy cream
¼ cup grated Gruyère cheese

Trim, wash, and slice the mushrooms. Dry them in a towel and sauté 2 to 3 minutes in butter. Chop very fine and mix with the heavy cream and cheese.

Shrimp filling ✳ Farce aux crevettes

½ pound shelled shrimp
1½ cups Béchamel Sauce (page 6)

1 teaspoon curry powder
pepper

If the shrimp are salty, freshen them in running cold water. Boil 3 minutes, using salted water only if shrimp are fresh. Chop them fine and mix with the sauce. Season with curry powder and pepper.

Ham filling ✳ Farce au jambon

1 cup ground ham
1½ cups thick Béchamel Sauce
  (page 6)

2 tablespoons chopped *fines herbes*
  (parsley, chervil, tarragon)
salt and pepper

Combine the ground ham, sauce, and *fines herbes*. Season well.

Mussel saffron filling * Farce aux moules et safran

1 quart mussels	1 teaspoon turmeric *or*
pinch of thyme	pinch of saffron
pinch of powdered bay leaf	salt and pepper
1½ cups Béchamel Sauce (page 6)	

Scrape and wash the mussels thoroughly. Place in a saucepan with the powdered herbs. Put over high heat and cook until the mussels open. Remove from the heat and remove the mussels from the shells. Chop coarsely.

Make the béchamel and season with the turmeric or saffron, salt, and pepper. Add the chopped mussels to the sauce. Mix well.

Veal and raisin filling * Farce au veau et raisins secs

1 cup ground veal	1½ cups Béchamel Sauce (page 6)
¼ cup seedless raisins	salt and pepper

Grind veal that is completely free of skin or gristle.

Soak the raisins for 2 hours in water. Drain well.

Make the sauce. Combine with the veal and cook for a few minutes. Add the raisins and season with salt and pepper.

Poached eggs in cream puffs
Choux aux oeufs pochés

FOR FOUR PEOPLE

Cream Puff Pastry (page 649)	1½ cups Béchamel Sauce (page 6)
8 eggs	½ cup grated Gruyère cheese

Make the unsweetened cream puff pastry. Using a pastry bag fitted with a rather large tip, or using a tablespoon, make 8 mounds with the equivalent of 4 teaspoons of the pastry on a buttered baking sheet. Place them far apart, because they will swell during the baking.

Bake 20 minutes in a 400° F. oven. They should be dry, with no beads of moisture on the outside.

Meanwhile, poach and drain the eggs.

Make the béchamel. Remove from the heat and stir in the cheese.

Cut off the top third of each cream puff. Put a poached egg in each one. Cover with the sauce. Reheat in a 450° F. oven for a few moments to brown a little. Serve immediately.

Cheese éclairs * Eclairs au fromage

FOR SIX PEOPLE

5 tablespoons butter
1¼ cups sifted all-purpose flour
3 eggs
1 egg yolk

1½ cups Béchamel Sauce (page 6)
½ cup grated cheese
salt and pepper

Bring to a boil 1 cup plus 2 tablespoons of water, ½ teaspoon of salt, and the butter. Remove from the heat and stir in the flour all at once. Stir well and put back over the heat and continue stirring until the dough no longer sticks to the sides but leaves a dry coating on the bottom of the pan. Remove from the heat and cool a few minutes. Add the eggs one by one, beating hard after each addition.

Using a pastry bag fitted with a medium-small tip, force the dough in 3-inch strips onto a buttered baking sheet. Paint each one with the egg yolk mixed with a teaspoon of water. Bake 15 minutes at 400° F.

Meanwhile, make the béchamel. Remove from the heat and stir in the grated cheese. Season with salt and pepper.

Make a slit in the sides of the éclairs and fill with the cheese sauce. Reheat in the oven for a few moments before serving.

Foie gras brioches
Petites brioches à la mousse de foie gras

TWENTY BRIOCHES

20 small brioches

1 large can *foie gras mousse*

If you live near a French pastry shop, order the brioches. Otherwise, follow directions on page 668 for making small brioches. Whip the contents of the *foie gras* can with a fork.

Remove the tops of the brioches and scoop out the center part. Fill the center with the *foie gras mousse* and replace the tops before serving.

Ham and mushroom stuffed brioches
Brioches farcies au jambon et champignons

FOR SIX PEOPLE

12 brioches
¼ pound mushrooms
1½ cups Béchamel Sauce (page 6)

2 slices cooked ham
pinch of rosemary
salt and pepper

Buy or bake the brioches. See page 668. Cut off the tops and dig out the interior without piercing the outside.

Trim, wash, and slice the mushrooms and cook 5 minutes in 1 cup of slightly salted water. Strain but reserve the broth.

Make the sauce, using half-milk and half-mushroom broth as the liquid. When the sauce is thick, add the ham ground through a *moulinette* or chopped very fine and the mushrooms treated in the same way. Season with rosemary, salt, and pepper.

Fill the brioches, put back the tops, and reheat in the oven before serving.

Brioches stuffed with mushrooms
Brioches farcies aux champignons

FOR SIX PEOPLE

12 brioches
½ pound mushrooms
1½ cups Béchamel Sauce (page 6)

¾ cup grated Gruyère cheese
salt and pepper

If you cannot buy brioches, follow directions on page 668 for making them. Take off the tops and scoop out the interior without piercing the outside. Heat in a low oven.

Trim and wash the mushrooms. Grind them raw through a *moulinette* or grinder.

Make the béchamel and stir in the mushrooms and cheese. Season to taste with salt and pepper. Cook until the mixture is very hot. Fill the brioches with the mixture, replace the tops, and serve immediately.

Brioches with scrambled eggs
Brioches aux oeufs brouillés

FOR FOUR PEOPLE

4 brioches
6 eggs

2 tablespoons butter
salt and pepper

If you cannot buy brioches, follow directions on page 668 for making them. Remove the tops and scoop out the interior without piercing the outside. Heat in a low oven.

Make the scrambled eggs as on page 143. Fill the warm brioches with the scrambled eggs. Put back the tops and serve immediately.

Tarragon stuffed brioches
Brioches farcies à l'estragon

8 brioches	1 egg yolk
1½ cups Béchamel Sauce (page 6)	2 tablespoons chopped tarragon
1 cup grated Gruyère cheese	salt and pepper

Buy or make the brioches. See page 668. Cut off the tops and remove the centers without piercing the outside. Reheat in a moderate oven.

Make a thick sauce and stir in the grated cheese. Remove from the heat and beat in the egg yolk and the chopped tarragon. Season to taste.

Fill the brioches, replace the tops, and serve very hot.

Parisian poached egg soufflé
Soufflé (de paris) aux oeufs pochés

FOR EIGHT PEOPLE

5 tablespoons butter	2 cups grated Gruyère cheese
9½ tablespoons flour	1 tablespoon white vinegar
3 cups milk	salt and pepper
14 eggs	

Heat the butter and stir in the flour with a wooden spoon. Add the milk gradually and stir until the sauce thickens. Add the grated cheese, stir well, and remove from the heat. Cool to lukewarm.

Add 6 egg yolks, one by one, beating hard after each addition. Season with salt and pepper. Fold in 6 egg whites, beaten stiff.

Poach the remaining eggs in salted water to which a tablespoon of white vinegar has been added. Remove with a slotted spoon to a dish towel to drain.

Butter a large straight-sided serving dish that is heatproof. Put half the sauce in the dish. Arrange the poached eggs on the sauce and cover with the rest of the sauce.

Bake 10 minutes at 350° F. Increase the heat to 400° F. and bake 20 minutes longer. Serve immediately.

Cheese soufflé * Soufflé au fromage

FOR FOUR PEOPLE

3 tablespoons butter	1½ cups grated Gruyère cheese
8 tablespoons flour	4 egg whites, beaten stiff

2 cups milk	salt and pepper
4 egg yolks	

Heat the butter in a saucepan and stir in the flour with a wooden spoon. Add the milk gradually and stir until smooth and thick. Season with salt and pepper. Cool to lukewarm and add the egg yolks, one by one, beating hard after each addition. Stir in the cheese.

Fold in the stiffly beaten egg whites and pour into a buttered soufflé dish or other straight-sided baking dish. Fill the mold only ¾ full so that the soufflé will have a chance to rise.

Bake at 350° F. for 15 minutes. Increase the heat to 450° F. and bake 10 minutes longer. Serve immediately.

Endive soufflé * Soufflé d'endives

FOR FIVE PEOPLE

2 pounds Belgian endives	4 egg yolks
juice of 1 lemon	4 egg whites, beaten stiff
bread	salt and pepper
1½ cups thick Béchamel Sauce (page 6)	

Trim the endives and put them in a pan of boiling salted water containing the juice of a lemon and a piece of French bread or the heel of a loaf of white bread. These 2 elements are added to keep the endives white. Cook 30 minutes.

Remove the endives from the water and let them drain. When cooled to lukewarm, press them between the palms of your hands to extract all the water. Chop the endives very fine.

Meanwhile, make the béchamel. Remove from the heat and beat in the egg yolk. Mix in the endives. Season with salt and pepper.

Fold in the beaten egg whites, lifting the mass high as you fold so that the egg whites will not fall in baking.

Pour the mixture into a buttered soufflé dish or other straight-sided baking dish and bake 15 minutes at 350° F. Increase the heat to 450° F. and bake 10 minutes longer. Serve immediately. Soufflés cannot wait.

Fish soufflé * Soufflé de poisson

FOR SIX PEOPLE

1 cup milk	½ cup heavy cream
2⅔ cups dry breadcrumbs	4 egg whites, beaten stiff

1 pound raw haddock or pike   salt and pepper
4 egg yolks

You begin this recipe by making what is called a *panade,* which is a kind of bread base. Heat the milk to the boiling point. Remove from the heat and pour in the breadcrumbs. Add ½ teaspoon salt and wait until the bread has soaked up the milk. Put the pan back over high heat and stir vigorously until the mixture no longer sticks to the spoon. Remove from the heat and spread the mixture on a buttered baking sheet to cool.

With a rubbing motion, pound the raw fish in a mortar or wooden bowl to make a paste. Force it through a sieve and combine in a bowl with the *panade.* Add the egg yolks, one by one, beating hard after each addition. Stir in the cream and finally fold in the egg whites. Season highly with salt and plenty of pepper.

Pour into a buttered charlotte mold or other straight-sided baking dish and place in a pan of hot water. Bake 40 minutes at 400° F. Test by inserting a knife or needle. It should come out dry.

Unmold and serve with any sauce you wish. I suggest a tomato sauce or a béchamel with cheese.

Ham soufflé * Soufflé au jambon

FOR FIVE PEOPLE

5 tablespoons butter   ¼ pound ham
3 tablespoons flour   5 egg whites, beaten stiff
2 cups milk   salt and pepper
5 egg yolks

Heat the butter and stir in the flour with a wooden spoon. When the mixture is frothy, add the milk, stirring constantly to avoid lumps. Some people heat the milk before adding it. Cook the sauce until it thickens. Season but do not add too much salt, because the ham is salty. When the sauce is very thick, remove from the heat and cool to lukewarm. Add the egg yolks, one by one, beating hard after each addition. Stir in the ham, chopped very fine.

Fold in the beaten egg whites and pour the mixture into a buttered soufflé dish or other straight-sided baking dish. Bake 10 minutes at 350° F. and increase the heat to 450° F. Bake 20 minutes longer. Serve immediately.

Onion soufflé * Soufflé aux oignons

FOR FOUR PEOPLE

2 pounds onions   5 egg whites, beaten stiff
6 tablespoons butter   nutmeg

1½ cups Béchamel Sauce (page 6)   paprika
1 cup heavy cream   salt and pepper
5 egg yolks, slightly beaten

Peel and slice the onions very fine. Parboil in salted water for 15 minutes. Drain well and put in a saucepan with 3 tablespoons of butter. Cook gently until thoroughly cooked. Do not let them brown.

Make a thick béchamel and combine with the cooked onions. Season with salt, pepper, a dash of both nutmeg and paprika. Cook gently for 10 minutes, stirring constantly. Force the mixture through a strainer.

Melt the rest of the butter and add to the purée, along with the heavy cream, the egg yolks, and finally the beaten egg whites.

Pour the mixture into a buttered soufflé dish or straight-sided mold, filling the dish ¾ full. Bake 25 to 30 minutes at 400° F.

Spinach soufflé * Soufflé aux épinards

FOR FIVE PEOPLE

1½ pounds spinach   4 egg yolks, slightly beaten
2 tablespoons butter   ½ cup grated Gruyère cheese
¾ cup thick Béchamel Sauce   4 egg whites, beaten stiff
  (page 6)   salt and pepper

Trim and wash the spinach very carefully. Boil in salted water for 8 minutes. Drain and cool to lukewarm. Press the spinach between the palms of your hands to extract all the water. Force the spinach through a food mill and put it in a saucepan with the butter. Stir over high heat until any water evaporates and the spinach is quite dry. Make the béchamel and remove from the heat. Stir in the egg yolks, the spinach, and the grated cheese. Season with salt and pepper.

Finally, fold in the egg whites. Pour the mixture into a soufflé dish or other straight-sided baking dish. Cook 15 minutes at 350° F. Increase the heat to 450° F. and cook 10 minutes longer. Serve immediately.

Sweetbread soufflé * Soufflé de ris de veau

FOR SIX PEOPLE

1 pair sweetbreads   ¼ pound mushrooms
5 tablespoons butter   1 small can truffles
3 tablespoons flour   5 egg whites, beaten stiff
2 cups hot bouillon   Madeira Sauce with Truffles (page 11)
5 egg yolks   salt and pepper

Prepare and cook the sweetbreads. See page 428. Force them through a strainer.

Heat the butter in a saucepan and stir in the flour with a wooden spoon. When blended, add the hot bouillon and stir until smooth and rather thick. Season to taste with salt and pepper. Add the sweetbread purée and cool. Add the egg yolks, one by one, beating hard after each addition.

Trim, wash, and chop the mushrooms very fine. Add them and the can of truffles with their liquid.

Finally, fold in the beaten egg whites and pour the mixture into a buttered soufflé dish or other straight-sided baking dish. Place the dish in a pan of hot water and bake at 350° F. for 1 hour.

Meanwhile, make the sauce.

Unmold the soufflé and serve with the sauce.

*Truffle soufflé * Soufflé aux truffes*

FOR EIGHT PEOPLE

5 tablespoons butter
6 tablespoons flour
3 cups milk
12 egg yolks

4 tablespoons heavy cream
12 egg whites, beaten stiff
5 truffles
salt and pepper

Heat the butter in a saucepan. Stir in the flour with a wooden spoon and add the hot milk gradually, stirring constantly. When the sauce is thick, remove from the heat and cool to lukewarm. Add the egg yolks one by one, beating hard after each addition. Stir in the cream, season with salt and pepper, and finally, fold in gently the stiffly beaten egg whites.

Add the truffles, sliced in thin rounds, and stir in gently.

Pour the mixture in a large well-buttered soufflé dish or other straight-sided baking dish. Bake 15 minutes at 350° F. Increase the heat to 450° F. and bake 10 minutes longer. Serve immediately.

Crepes

Crepes form the basis for many delicious entrées. They must be carefully made. Keep a 5- to 6-inch skillet just for crepes, one that will never be washed or used for cooking any other food. The skillet, ideally made of heavy cast iron, can be kept clean by wiping it with paper toweling. If you wash the pan, the crepes will stick. Never grease the pan, because there is plenty of fat in the batter. The batter should be very thin, almost like water. If it seems too thick, do not hesitate to add cold water. Crepes must be *very* thin. You can keep cooked crepes warm while making others, either by placing in a warm oven, where they will become rather crisp, or by putting them between two soup plates posed on top of a panful of simmering water, where they will remain soft and pliable.

Once the batter is made, it should stand several hours. Stir well just before using. Pour about 1½ tablespoonfuls into the hot ungreased skillet and tilt it in a circular motion so that the batter covers the bottom. Turn up the heat for a few seconds and then lower it. Cook for 1 minute, turn with a wide spatula, and cook 1 minute on the other side. Continue the process until all the batter is used.

Once the crepes are made, they can be filled in a variety of ways. They serve as an entrée, an accompaniment to a main dish, or a dessert.

Crepe batter I * Pâte à crêpes I

ABOUT TWENTY CREPES

2 cups sifted cake flour	2 cups milk
½ teaspoon salt	7 tablespoons oil
3 eggs	

Make this batter several hours before using. Put the flour into a bowl. Fashion a small well in the center and into it put the salt and the eggs. Beat very hard with a wooden spoon and add the milk very gradually, beating constantly so as not to have a lumpy batter. If despite all this the batter does lump, strain it through a sieve. Finish by adding the oil. Follow the above directions for cooking.

Crepe batter II * Pâte à crêpes II

ABOUT TWENTY CREPES

2 cups sifted cake flour	10 tablespoons butter
2 cups milk	salt or sugar
4 eggs	

Put the flour in a bowl. Add the milk gradually, stirring constantly with a wooden spoon so that the batter will be very thin and without lumps. Break the 4 eggs into the batter and beat until well blended. Add salt or sugar, according to what you propose to fill the crepes with.

Melt the butter cut into small pieces in a double boiler. Pour the butter into the batter, stir well, and let the batter rest several hours, if possible.

Crepe cake mapie I * Gâteau de crêpes mapie I

FOR SIX PEOPLE

18 crepes
2 cups Béchamel Sauce (page 6)
2 heads Boston lettuce
1½ cups chopped cooked meat

1 cup grated Gruyère cheese
1 can tomato purée
paprika
salt and pepper

Make the crepe batter in advance. Let it rest. Cook the crepes and keep warm, following directions at beginning of section on crepes.

Make the béchamel.

Wash the lettuce and cook it in boiling salted water for 5 minutes. Drain thoroughly, squeezing out the water between the palms of your hands. Chop the cooked lettuce and mix with a little of the béchamel.

Chop the meat and mix it with some of the béchamel, enough to give it a spreading consistency. Season with salt, pepper, and paprika.

Put a hot crepe on a heatproof serving platter. Cover with cooked lettuce and sprinkle with grated cheese. Cover with a crepe and spread with the meat mixture. Cover with a crepe and spread with thick tomato purée. Repeat this alternation until all the crepes have been used.

Add the rest of the cheese to the rest of the béchamel. Pour it over the cake and brown 10 minutes in a 400° F. oven. Serve the cake in wedges, as you would a layer cake.

Crepe cake mapie II * Gâteau de crêpes mapie II

FOR SIX PEOPLE

18 crepes
1 cup Béchamel Sauce (page 6)
2 heads Boston lettuce
10 mushrooms

1 tablespoon butter
2 cans sardines
1 cup grated Gruyère cheese

Make the crepe batter in advance. Cook the crepes according to directions at beginning of section on crepes, and keep them warm between 2 soup plates over simmering water.

Make the béchamel.

Trim, wash, and cook the lettuce in boiling water for 5 minutes. Drain and press all the water out between the palms of your hands. Chop very fine. Bind with a little of the béchamel.

Trim, wash, and slice the mushrooms very fine. Sauté for a very few moments in the butter.

Pound the sardines to a smooth paste.

Place a crepe in a heatproof serving dish. Cover with some of the cooked lettuce. Sprinkle with grated cheese. Cover with a crepe and spread with the sardine paste; sprinkle with cheese. Cover with a crepe and spread with the sautéed mushrooms; sprinkle with cheese. Cover with a crepe and spread with tomato purée; sprinkle with cheese. Continue to alternate until you have a tall cake, using all 18 crepes.

Add the rest of the cheese to the sauce, which should be quite thick and strongly flavored with cheese. Add more cheese, if necessary. Brown 10 minutes in a hot oven (400° F.).

Crepes with bacon * Crêpes au lard fumé

FOR FOUR PEOPLE

1 can thick tomato purée	paprika
12 crepes	4 tablespoons oil
1 pound (4-5) onions	salt and pepper
6 slices Canadian bacon	

Make the crepe batter in advance.

Peel the onions and chop them fine.

Cut the bacon in small dice.

Sauté the onions and bacon in the oil until the onions are tender. Season with salt, pepper, and paprika.

Cook the crepes and keep them warm, as in the directions at beginning of section on crepes. Spread the crepes with the onion-bacon mixture. Roll up and serve on a heated platter immediately.

Banana crepes * Crêpes aux bananes

FOR FOUR PEOPLE

8 thin crepes	5 tablespoons butter
4 bananas	salt and pepper

Cook the crepes according to directions at beginning of section on crepes, and keep them hot between two soup plates posed on top of a pan of simmering water.

Buy ripe bananas. Peel them and split them in two, lengthwise. Heat the butter in a skillet and sauté the bananas until lightly browned and cooked. Place each banana half in a crepe. Roll and serve as an accompaniment to veal or roast chicken or turkey.

Minced chicken crepes
Crêpes aux hachis de volaille

FOR FOUR PEOPLE

12 crepes	1 cup Béchamel Sauce (page 6)
1½ cups minced cooked chicken	salt and pepper

Prepare the crepe batter in advance.

Chop the cooked chicken very fine or pass it through a grinder.

Make a highly seasoned béchamel sauce, seasoning it with plenty of pepper. Mix with the chicken.

Cook the crepes and keep them warm, as in the directions at beginning of section on crepes. Put a large tablespoon of the chicken mixture on each crepe and fold them in quarters, making a rounded triangle. Place on a heated serving platter. This makes a very pretty entrée.

Crepes with crabmeat * Crêpes au crabe

FOR FOUR PEOPLE

12 medium-sized crepes	pinch of thyme
2 ounces fat pork belly	pinch of powdered bay leaf
1 small onion	1 can crabmeat
1 pound (3-4 medium) tomatoes	salt and pepper
2 teaspoons chopped parsley	

Make the batter in advance so that it can rest.

Cook the crepes, keeping them hot. (See directions at beginning of section on crepes.)

Heat finely chopped pork fat in a small pan for 3 minutes to render some of its fat. (If pork belly is not available, parboil fat salt pork for 5 minutes. Rinse before chopping.—*Ed.*) Add the onion, chopped fine, and sauté until tender.

Dip the tomatoes in boiling water and slip off the skins. Cut the tomatoes in pieces and put them in the skillet with the parsley, salt, pepper, and powdered herbs. Cook over a slow heat, stirring frequently with a wooden spoon until the mixture has become fairly thick. Strain and combine with the crabmeat, which has been carefully picked over to remove all hard filaments. Reheat the mixture.

Fill the crepes with the crab mixture. Roll and serve very hot.

Crepes with hard-cooked eggs
Crêpes aux oeufs durs

FOR FOUR PEOPLE

12 crepes
6 hard-cooked eggs
1½ cups thick Béchamel Sauce
 (page 6)

½ cup grated Parmesan cheese
fresh tarragon leaves
salt and pepper

Make the crepe batter in advance. Cook the crepes and keep them warm. Follow directions at beginning of section on crepes.

Boil the eggs 15 minutes in salted water. Plunge in cold water. Shell and chop coarsely.

Make the béchamel. Add the eggs and cheese to the sauce and season highly with salt and pepper. If fresh tarragon is in season, add a few leaves to the sauce.

Fill the crepes with the egg mixture. Roll them up and serve on a heated platter.

Other fillings for crepes

Nuts, Roquefort cheese, and butter, pounded until smooth.

1 can salmon, 1½ cups Béchamel Sauce (page 6), 1 tablespoon tomato paste, paprika, salt, and a high seasoning of pepper.

Lean bacon, sautéed *cèpes* or mushrooms, garlic, oil, and Parmesan cheese.

Crepes with frankfurters * Crêpes frankfort

FOR FOUR PEOPLE

8 crepes
8 frankfurter sausages

herbed French mustard

Make the crepe batter in advance so that it can rest. Cook the crepes according to directions at beginning of section on crepes.

Simmer the frankfurters in water 10 minutes without letting them boil. Remove from the water and spread each one with mustard.

Roll each frankfurter in a crepe and serve on a heated platter.

Crepes with mushrooms * Crêpes aux champignons

FOR SIX PEOPLE

12 crepes
12 mushrooms
4 tablespoons butter
4 teaspoons flour

½ cup milk, scalded
1 cup grated Gruyère cheese
salt and pepper

Prepare the batter in advance so that it will have time to rest.

Trim and wash the mushrooms. Chop the stems and slice the heads. Heat 2 tablespoons of the butter in a small skillet and for 10 minutes cook the chopped stems over a slow heat with the cover on. Add the mushroom slices and continue to cook 5 minutes. Sprinkle with flour and season with salt and pepper, stirring gently. Add the milk and half the grated cheese.

Cook the crepes as described in beginning of section on crepes. When the 12 are made, put a little of the mushroom stuffing in each one. Roll them up and place in a shallow heatproof serving dish that has been lightly buttered.

Sprinkle with grated cheese and the rest of the butter, melted, and brown 5 minutes in a hot (400° F.) oven.

Mushroom crepe cake
Gâteau de crêpes aux champignons

FOR SIX PEOPLE

12 crepes
1 quart Béchamel Sauce (page 6)
¾ pound mushrooms
3 tablespoons butter

2 cups grated Gruyère cheese
½ cup heavy cream
salt and pepper

Make the crepe batter. Let it rest and cook the crepes, keeping them warm. See directions at beginning of section on crepes.

Make the béchamel.

Wash the mushrooms, having trimmed them carefully. Dry them well and chop them coarsely.

Heat the butter in a skillet and sauté the mushrooms over a slow heat, stirring them with a fork so that they will brown evenly and lightly. Mix with 1½ cups of béchamel sauce. Season with salt and pepper.

Mix another 1½ cups of béchamel with half the grated cheese. Season with pepper and stir until the sauce is smooth.

On a preheated serving platter place a crepe. Cover generously with a layer of the mushroom mixture. Cover with a crepe and spread with the cheese sauce.

Continue this alternation until all 12 crepes have been used.

Cover with the rest of the béchamel, to which the cream and the rest of the cheese have been added. This should be well seasoned with salt and pepper. Serve very hot. Cut in wedges. See also recipe for Crepes with Mushrooms.

Crepes with mussels * Crêpes aux moules

FOR FOUR PEOPLE

12 crepes	2½ tablespoons flour
2 quarts mussels	¾ cup white wine
1 onion	1 teaspoon chopped parsley
1 shallot	salt and pepper
6 tablespoons butter	

Make the crepe batter in advance.

Wash the mussels very thoroughly, scraping off the beards. Place them in a pan and heat until they open. Withdraw from the heat as soon as the shells are opened.

Chop the onion and shallot and sauté them in 3 tablespoons of butter until tender. Sprinkle with flour. Stir until the flour disappears and add the white wine and the mussel broth strained through a cheesecloth. Season with pepper and a little salt, if necessary. Shuck the mussels and add to the mixture. Add the rest of the butter and chopped parsley.

Cook the crepes following directions at beginning of section on crepes, and spread each one with the hot mixture. Roll and place on a heated platter. Serve very hot.

Crepes with sausages * Crêpes aux chipolatas

FOR FOUR PEOPLE

12 small crepes	2 tablespoons butter
12 long link sausages	

Make the crepe batter in advance. Cook 12 small crepes following directions at beginning of section on crepes. At the same time, brown the sausages in butter.

Wrap each sausage in a very hot crêpe and serve with applesauce.

Crepes soubise * Crêpes soubise

FOR FOUR PEOPLE

12 medium-sized crepes	1½ tablespoons heavy cream
1 pound (4-5) onions	salt and pepper

3 tablespoons butter
1 cup thick Béchamel Sauce
  (page 6)

paprika
nutmeg

Make the batter in advance so that it can rest. Cook the crepes and keep them warm, following directions at beginning of section on crepes.

Peel the onions and chop them fine. Cook in boiling salted water for 15 minutes. Drain them thoroughly and put in a saucepan with half the butter. Cook with a cover on until very tender. They must not brown at all.

Add the béchamel. Season with salt, pepper, paprika, and nutmeg and simmer 10 minutes over a low heat, stirring with a wooden spoon.

Press the mixture through a strainer and add the rest of the butter and the heavy cream. Reheat and fill the crepes with the mixture. Place on a heated platter and serve immediately.

Souffléed crepes * Crêpes soufflées

FOR FOUR PEOPLE

8 crepes
3 tablespoons butter
6 tablespoons flour
2 cups milk, scalded

¾ cup grated Gruyère cheese
4 eggs
salt and pepper

Make the crepe batter in advance. Cook the crepes and keep them warm between 2 soup plates, as directed at beginning of section on crepes.

Heat the butter in a medium-sized saucepan and stir in the flour. When the mixture is frothy, add the milk gradually, stirring constantly. Season with salt and pepper and freshly grated Gruyère cheese. Cook for about 5 minutes, still stirring. When the sauce is fairly thick, remove it from the heat. Cool to lukewarm and stir in the egg yolks.

Beat the egg whites stiff and fold them into the mixture.

In a rather deep heatproof serving dish, put a good layer of the soufflé mixture. Put a large tablespoonful of the mixture on each crepe and fold them in half. Arrange the crepes, one beside the other, in the dish on the layer of soufflé mixture; the crepes will open during the cooking.

Bake 15 minutes at 400° F. Serve from the baking dish.

Crepes with spinach * Crêpes aux épinards

FOR EIGHT PEOPLE

16 crepes
4 pounds spinach
6 tablespoons butter

1 cup grated Gruyère cheese
¾ cup milk
Tomato Sauce (page 22) (optional)

2½ tablespoons flour   salt and pepper

Make the crepe batter in advance so that it can rest. Cook the crepes and keep warm between two plates, according to directions at beginning of section on crepes.

Trim the spinach, removing all the large stems. Wash thoroughly and cook in boiling salted water for 10 minutes without a cover. Drain the spinach and run cold water through it immediately. Press the spinach between the palms of your hands to express all the water. Do this immediately or the spinach will darken. When the spinach leaves are almost dry, pass them through a very fine grinder, or, what is preferable, rub them through a sieve with a wooden mallet.

Heat the butter over a moderate heat until frothy. Add the spinach, mix with the butter, sprinkle with flour, and stir again. Add the cheese last and season to taste with salt and pepper.

Put a large tablespoonful of spinach in each hot crepe. Fold in quarters. Place the filled crepes in a ring around a heated platter, one overlapping the other. Serve very hot with or without a tomato sauce.

Crepes with scrambled eggs
Crêpes aux oeufs brouillés

FOR FOUR PEOPLE

12 crepes   3 tablespoons butter
10 eggs   salt and pepper

Make the crepe batter in advance. Cook the crepes and keep them warm, as in directions at beginning of section on crepes.

Break the eggs into the top of a double boiler. Beat them with a fork until blended. Season with salt and pepper. Put them over boiling water and stir continuously, especially on the bottom and the sides, where the eggs will cook more quickly. At the end of 5 minutes, add the butter cut into small pieces. When the eggs are smooth and creamy, remove from the heat.

Quickly put 2 large tablespoonfuls of scrambled eggs on each crepe. Fold them in quarters to form rounded triangles and serve immediately on a hot platter.

Fondue * La fondue

FOR SIX PEOPLE

1¾ pounds Emmenthal cheese   6 tablespoons kirsch
¾ pound Comté or Beaufort cheese   nutmeg
1 clove garlic   pepper
4½ cups dry white wine

(All the cheeses prescribed are of the Gruyère type but vary in flavor. If you do not live in one of the large cities where these cheeses are sold substitute Gruyère cheeses for them.—*Ed.*)

Grate the cheese and chop the garlic very fine. Mix with the white wine, without heating, until well blended.

Put in a heavy earthenware dish and stir over moderate heat with a wooden spoon, stirring the cheese as though you were making a cross. When the mixture begins to thicken, let it cook without stirring for 3 to 4 minutes and then put on a small food warmer after adding the kirsch. Season with pepper and a little freshly grated nutmeg. Let it stand over a very small flame while it is eaten.

To eat a fondue, put the dish on the warmer in the center of the table. At the right of each guest, place a dish containing small pieces of bread. With the help of a long fork, each guest dips his bread into the cheese fondue. Never drink water while you are eating a fondue. A little kirsch maybe, but never water.

NOTE: Do not be discouraged when you start cooking the fondue. It looks very unattractive to begin with, but stir with patience, and it will become smooth and appetizing.

Entrée à la chambord ∗ *Entrée à la chambord*

FOR EIGHT PEOPLE

5 cups heavy cream
8 eggs
2 cups sifted all-purpose flour
5 tablespoons butter

1½ cups grated Gruyère cheese
2 cups Béchamel Sauce (page 6)
salt and pepper

Put the cream in a heavy bowl.

Separate the whites from the yolks of the eggs, putting the whites in a deep bowl.

Add the egg yolks to the cream and mix them well with a whip. Add the flour and beat long and hard. Season highly with salt and pepper.

Beat the egg whites stiff and fold in the cream mixture gently with a wooden spoon or rubber spatula, lifting the mixture high as you fold. They must be completely blended with the cream mixture.

Heat a small heavy skillet with a little piece of butter. When the butter has melted, put in a ladle full of the batter. It should form a thick layer. The heat should be moderately low. After a few moments, lift a corner gently to see if the bottom is lightly colored. As soon as it is, put the skillet in a 350° F. preheated oven so that the pancake will cook without browning. It is cooked when it feels resistant to your finger. Protecting your hand with a glove or hot-pan holder, slide the pancake from the skillet onto a shallow heatproof serving dish and sprinkle with grated cheese. Keep warm.

Continue to make the pancakes, sliding one on top of the other (without touching it with your hand) and sprinkle each one with grated cheese. You will have a kind of layer cake.

Meanwhile, make the béchamel. Add the remaining cheese to the sauce. Pour the sauce over the cake and brown 5 minutes in a 450° F. oven.

Victoria cheese custards * Pains victoria

FOR FIVE PEOPLE

4 eggs	1 cup grated Gruyère cheese
2 cups milk	sauce (see below)

Beat the eggs slightly, adding the almost boiling milk. Stir continuously while adding both the milk and the cheese. Pour into well-buttered, deep individual molds or custard cups, filling them half full. Place the molds in a pan of hot water and bake 1 hour at 350° F. Remove from the molds.

Accompany with either a cream sauce or a tomato sauce.

Gnocchi parmentier * Gnocchi parmentier

FOR SIX PEOPLE

1½ pounds (4-5 medium) Idaho potatoes	2¾ cups flour nutmeg
5 tablespoons butter	¾ cup grated Gruyère cheese
2 eggs	salt and pepper

Peel and boil the potatoes in salted water. Drain well and mash thoroughly. Add 2 tablespoons of butter, the eggs, flour, salt, pepper, and freshly grated nutmeg. Mix very well.

Make little balls the size of walnuts with the mixture. Put them in a large pan of barely simmering salted water. Cook 10 minutes and remove with a slotted spoon to a well-buttered baking dish, which has been coated with the grated cheese. Alternate layers of gnocchi with layers of grated cheese, finishing with a layer of grated cheese. Sprinkle with melted butter and brown in a hot oven (400 °F.). When browned, serve immediately.

Fish quenelles à la lyonnaise
Quenelles de brochet à la lyonnaise

FOR EIGHT PEOPLE

Quenelles:	*Sauce:*
1 pike or, lacking that, ½ pound fresh salmon	¾ cup white wine 2 onions

1 quart milk

butter

5 cups all-purpose flour

11 eggs

nutmeg

bouquet garni (thyme, bay leaf)

2 tablespoons butter

2½ tablespoons flour

4 tablespoons heavy cream

salt and pepper

Clean and trim the fish and remove the flesh from the bones. You should have 1 cup of raw fish. Save the fish trimmings.

Bring the milk to a boil with 1½ teaspoons salt and 3 tablespoons of butter. When it boils, add the flour all at once and stir vigorously over heat until the mixture no longer sticks to the side but leaves a slight coating on the bottom. Remove and let the mixture cool a little. Add 3 eggs, one by one, beating hard after each addition.

In a mortar or wooden bowl, pound the fish well. Add 8 egg whites, one by one, pounding until blended. Season with salt and a little nutmeg. Combine this with the mixture in the saucepan and stir in the 8 egg yolks and ½ pound of butter cut into small pieces. Mix everything thoroughly. Let stand several hours before using.

Meanwhile, make the sauce. Put the fish trimmings in a saucepan with the wine, ¾ cup of water, the onions cut in slices, salt, pepper, and *bouquet garni*. Cover and simmer 1 hour.

Heat the butter and stir in the flour. Strain the fish broth into the pan and stir until well blended. Simmer 25 minutes. Season with salt and pepper, and just before serving, add the heavy cream.

Make little 2-inch sausagelike ovals with the fish mixture and poach them in barely simmering water for 10 minutes. Remove with a slotted spoon or skimmer and place on a heated platter. Cover with the sauce.

Renaissance entrée ∗ *Entrée renaissance*

FOR FOUR PEOPLE

2 pounds (4 large) mealy potatoes

½ pound cooked ham

4 eggs, slightly beaten

6 tablespoons butter

½ cup heavy cream

salt and pepper

Wash the potatoes, dry them, and bake in a 400° F. oven until cooked. Remove the pulp and force through a fine sieve or ricer. The French method is to weigh the cooked potatoes and mix them with half their weight of finely chopped ham along with the beaten eggs, butter, cream, salt, and pepper. (If you do not own scales, use the measurements given above.—*Ed.*) Beat everything together very well. If you have an electric mixer, use that. Put the mixture in a buttered fireproof serving dish and bake 15 minutes at 350° F. Serve from the baking dish.

Custard supremes, shrimp sauce
Suprêmes aux crevettes

FOR FOUR PEOPLE

½ pound small cleaned, cooked
  shrimps
1 quart milk
nutmeg
3 eggs
1 cup grated Gruyère cheese

1½ cups Béchamel Sauce (page 6)
4 teaspoons tomato paste
1 small can truffle peelings
4 large cooked shrimps
salt and pepper

Place small salty shrimp, which in many markets can be bought cooked and shelled, in a bowl of cool water. Place it under the water tap and let a thin stream of cold water run into it for ½ hour to remove the salt.

Meanwhile, boil the milk with salt, pepper, and a little nutmeg.

Beat the eggs slightly in a bowl and add the hot milk gradually, stirring constantly. Remove from the heat and stir in half the cheese.

Butter individual ramekins and pour the mixture into them. Place in a pan of hot water so that the water comes halfway up the sides of the ramekins. Bake these "supremes" 12 minutes at 450° F.

Make the béchamel and stir in the tomato paste, the rest of the cheese, and the well-drained shrimps. Mix well.

When the supremes are firm to the touch, unmold them onto a serving platter. Pour the sauce over them. Decorate with chopped truffles and with large shrimps.

Various toast canapés

Cheese canapés * Croûtes au fromage

FOR FOUR PEOPLE

Tomato Sauce (page 22)　　　　pepper
6 slices firm white bread　　　　paprika
1½ cups Béchamel Sauce (page 6)　　flour
2 eggs　　　　butter
1 cup grated Gruyère cheese

If you do not have tomato sauce on hand, begin the recipe by making it.

Without removing the crusts, slice the bread ⅜ inch thick.

Make a very thick béchamel, and when it is ready, remove from the heat and stir in the eggs and the grated cheese. Season highly with pepper and cool thoroughly.

Sprinkle a baking sheet with flour. Spread both sides of each slice of bread with the mixture and coat both sides with flour.

Fry in very hot butter in a heavy skillet, turning each piece so that they will be golden brown on both sides. Serve with the tomato sauce.

Crab toast canapés * Croûtes au crabe

FOR FOUR PEOPLE

2 hard-cooked eggs　　　　1 head lettuce
Vinaigrette Sauce (page 29)　　1 can crabmeat
2 teaspoons chopped parsley　　salt and pepper
4 slices firm white bread

Crush the eggs with ½ cup vinaigrette sauce that has been highly seasoned. Add the chopped parsley.

Toast the bread and cover each slice with a bed of lettuce. Cover generously with the crabmeat, free of all hard filaments. Sprinkle with the vinaigrette mixture.

Ham canapés * Croûtes au jambon béchamel

FOR SIX PEOPLE

6 slices firm white bread　　　　1½ cups Béchamel Sauce (page 6)

2 eggs   ⅓ cup grated Gruyère cheese
3 slices cooked ham   salt and pepper

Toast the bread in the oven.

Boil the eggs 15 minutes in salted water. Plunge into cold water. Shell and chop fine.

Chop the ham fine.

Make a béchamel, and while still hot, add the chopped eggs and ham. Season well with salt and pepper.

Put a thick layer of the mixture on each slice and place the canapés on a buttered baking sheet. Sprinkle with grated cheese and brown in a hot (400° F.) oven.

Hot canapés à la lorraine * Croûtes à la lorraine

FOR FOUR PEOPLE

firm white bread   2 ounces Canadian bacon
6 tablespoons butter   ¾ cup grated Gruyère cheese
4 eggs

These canapés must be served as soon as they are made.

Cut 8 slices of bread ⅓ inch thick. Remove the crusts and fry the bread very lightly on both sides. They should not brown.

Beat the eggs vigorously. Add the bacon, chopped fine, and the grated cheese. Do not salt, because the cheese and bacon are salty enough.

Put a good layer of the mixture on each slice of bread and bake 10 minutes at 400° F.

This is an entrée and not a cocktail canapé.

Roquefort canapés * Croûtes au roquefort

FOR FIVE PEOPLE

butter   3 ounces Roquefort cheese
10 slices dry white bread   1 egg
1½ cups thick Béchamel Sauce   nutmeg
   (page 6)   salt and pepper

Butter the bread and place the slices in a heatproof serving platter.

Make the béchamel, and while it is still on the heat, crumble the Roquefort into the sauce. Stir until well blended and remove from the heat. Add the egg and mix well. Season with pepper and nutmeg. Add salt, if necessary, although the Roquefort may make the sauce salty enough.

Generously cover each piece of toast with the mixture and brown in a hot oven (400° F.) for 5 minutes.

Sardine toast canapés * Croûtes aux sardines

FOR FOUR PEOPLE

16 small oil-packed sardines
white bread
10 tablespoons butter
1½ cups Béchamel Sauce (page 6)

1 cup grated Gruyère cheese
½ cup grated Parmesan cheese
cayenne
salt

Open the sardines to remove the backbone.

Cut the bread in 8 strips, 2¾ inches by 1¼ inches. Sauté them in butter. Spread the sautéed bread with butter and place on a heatproof serving platter. Put 2 sardines on each piece of toast.

Make the béchamel and add the grated Gruyère, salt, and a dash of cayenne. Pour the sauce over the canapés. Sprinkle with grated Parmesan and brown 10 minutes at 400° F. Serve very hot.

Scrambled egg and anchovy canapés
Croûtes aux oeufs brouillés et anchois

FOR AN INDEFINITE NUMBER OF PEOPLE

Sauté thin slices of firm white bread in butter so that they are lightly browned on both sides but not hard. Cover with scrambled eggs and garnish with split strips of anchovies. Serve immediately. Cut in small squares, these make wonderful cocktail canapés.

Tomato and black olive canapés
Croûtes aux tomates et olives noires

FOR AN INDEFINITE NUMBER OF PEOPLE

Sauté thin slices of firm white bread in oil until lightly browned but not hard. At the same time, sauté tomato slices in oil. Place the tomatoes on the sautéed bread. Garnish with pitted black olives (preferably imported). Heat the canapés in the oven before serving.

Cheese and bacon * Croûtes au gruyère et bacon

FOR AN INDEFINITE NUMBER OF PEOPLE

Sauté finely chopped onion in butter. When they are lightly browned, stir in the cheese. At the same time, sauté thin pieces of firm white bread in butter until lightly browned on both sides. Fry the bacon, allowing 1 slice for each canapé.

Spread each piece of sautéed bread with the cheese mixture. Cut each piece of bacon in half and put 2 strips on each canapé. Put in the oven until very hot. Serve immediately.

Deep-fat frying

Frying is the immersion of food into heated fat.

This immersion in hot fat "seizes" the food immediately and protects it so that it cooks the interior without letting it lose its juice or its soft inner texture.

In France, deep-fat frying is usually done in a kettle made especially for the purpose. It is rare that one tries to deep-fat fry in a skillet. The best medium for deep-fat frying is oil, preferably peanut oil.

The quantity of fat that is put in the kettle depends on the quantity of food to be fried. In every case, it is necessary that the fat completely cover the food.

The heat of the fat will vary with the kind of food to be fried. Foods containing a high percentage of water, such as fish, vegetables, or fruits, are cooked at a lower heat (370-380° F.), so that they can be cooked before browning. Partly cooked foods, such as fritters and croquettes, are cooked at a higher heat (385° F.). Very hot fat (390° F.) is required for small foods, such as tiny fish or cheese fritters, and other foods that have to be quickly browned.

Frying batter

ADVICE FOR MAKING FRYING BATTER

Like all batters, frying batter must be allowed to stand at least 2 hours before using. It can be made the day before. Rested batter will coat the foods to be fried much better than fresh batter, and because it ferments a little, it is lighter in texture. This is especially important for frying batter made with beer.

Obviously, if the batter recipe calls for a stiffly beaten egg white, that is added at the last moment.

The proportion of liquid (water, beer, or wine) to the flour is variable, because of the different types of flour. Some absorb more liquid than others. The batter should be slightly thicker than crepe batter, about the consistency of thin cream. It must be smooth and completely free of lumps.

The liquid for a batter should never be too cold. It is best to have it lukewarm, because the fermentation will be better.

Naturally, the flour must be sifted.

Make the batter in a bowl in the usual manner. After the flour is sifted into the bowl, with a wooden spoon fashion a well in the center to the bottom of the bowl. In this well, put the ingredients called for in the recipe, and work the flour into them gradually with the spoon, gradually adding the liquid, stirring continuously but gently. When the batter is made, let it stand in the kitchen but not in the refrigerator.

When frying fritters, the fat must be hot, but it must not be so hot that it burns them. Unless you have an automatic frying kettle, reduce the heat for 5 minutes between each batch of fritters, because as the fat heats during the cooking, it is apt to get too hot for the succeeding batch.

Drain the fritters on paper toweling, and keep them warm in a moderate oven (350° F.) with the door left open. Fritters must be fried just once before serving.

Frying batters * Les pâtes à frire

I

The frying batter of my former professor, docteur de pomiane:
La pâte à frire de docteur de pomiane, mon ancien professeur:

This batter is good for all frying, but especially for apple or strawberry fritters.

2 cups sifted all-purpose flour
2 teaspoons baking powder

½ teaspoon salt
1 egg

Mix the batter in the usual manner, adding enough water to give a creamy consistency that will coat the fritters well. Let rest.

II

Frying batter of alex humbert, chef at maxim's restaurant:
La pâte à frire d'alex humbert, chef des cuisines du restaurant maxim's:

2½ cups sifted all-purpose flour
1 teaspoon salt
4 teaspoons oil

⅔ cup beer
⅔ cup lukewarm water
3 egg whites, beaten stiff

Combine the flour, salt, oil, and liquids in the usual manner without beating too hard. Let the batter rest and fold in the beaten egg whites just before using.

III

Frying batter of my daughter adelaïde
La pâte à frire de ma fille, adelaïde

2 cups sifted all-purpose flour	½ teaspoon baking powder
1 egg	beer
½ teaspoon salt	

Combine the ingredients in the usual manner, adding enough beer to give the batter the consistency of a light custard. Let rest.

IV

Classic frying batter * *La pâte à frire à l'ancienne*

2 cups sifted all-purpose flour	1 tablespoon cognac
2 egg yolks	½ teaspoon salt
5 tablespoons olive oil	2 egg whites, beaten stiff
6 tablespoons milk	

Combine the ingredients in the usual manner, but do not add the beaten egg whites until the batter has rested and is ready to be used.

V

Frying batter of the baron brisse
La pâte à frire du baron brisse

This is the frying batter used by the famous gastronome of the 1890's.

2 cups sifted all-purpose flour	1½ tablespoons olive oil
4 egg yolks	2½ tablespoons cognac
2 egg whites	½ teaspoon salt

Mix the flour with the egg yolks, egg whites, olive oil, cognac, and salt. Add gradually enough lukewarm water, stirring constantly, until the batter is light and has the consistency of cream. Let it stand at room temperature for several hours.

VI

Frying batter monteynard
La pâte à frire monteynard

1¼ cups sifted all-purpose flour	2 eggs
1 scant cup water	2½ tablespoons oil
pinch of salt	

Combine the ingredients and mix them well, beating them vigorously. The batter should have a thickness that will make a ⅛-inch-thick coating on the back of a spoon.

VII

Batter especially for meat and brain fritters
La pâte à frire recommandée pour les beignets de viande et cervelle

2½ cups sifted all-purpose flour   1 tablespoon cognac
1 egg   milk
¾ teaspoon salt

Make the batter in the usual manner, adding gradually enough milk so that the batter will have the consistency of thin cream and will leave a 1/16-inch coating on the food that is to be fried.

VIII

Extra light frying batter
La pâte à frire ultra légère

1 cup sifted all-purpose flour   2 egg whites, beaten stiff
¼ teaspoon salt

Mix the flour and salt with enough water to give the batter the consistency of thick cream. Let rest. Just before using, fold in the egg whites. This is particularly recommended for apple fritters. The apple pieces are dipped in batter, plunged into deep fat (380° F.), and drained on paper toweling. Just before serving, they are thrown into the hot fat for a second frying.

Fritters

All fritters can be accompanied by a tomato sauce or by tartar sauce. Before making the fritters, read the preceding remarks about frying and frying batters. Allow time for the batter to rest before using.

Sorrel fritters * Beignets d'oseille

Wipe large sorrel leaves very well and dip them in the frying batter of your choice. Fry, drain, sprinkle with salt, and pile them high on a heated serving platter.

Cheese fritters * Beignets de fromage

FOR FOUR PEOPLE

¼ pound Gruyère cheese   frying batter

Cut the cheese into thin slices. Dip them in frying batter and fry them in very hot (390° F.) fat until golden brown. Serve very hot with a tomato sauce.

Cheese balls * Boulettes de fromage

FOR SIX PEOPLE

6 egg whites   fine breadcrumbs
¾ pound freshly grated Gruyère cheese

When you have egg whites left over, which is not infrequent in the kitchen, make this delicious and easy entrée.

Beat the egg whites until very stiff. Fold in the cheese. Make tiny balls of the mixture. Roll them in fine breadcrumbs and plunge into hot (390° F.) fat. These must be served immediately. The secret of this dish is that the balls must be made and fried at the last moment.

Cheese custard fritters * Crème frite au fromage

FOR SIX PEOPLE

1½ cups sifted all-purpose flour	2 cups finely grated Gruyère cheese
3 egg yolks	3 egg whites
3 eggs	fine breadcrumbs
2 cups scalded milk	salt and pepper

Mix the flour in a bowl with the egg yolks, eggs, salt, and pepper until you have a smooth batter. Put the mixture into a saucepan and gradually add the scalded milk, stirring constantly over moderate heat. Cook 6 minutes. Remove from the heat and stir in the grated cheese.

Pour the mixture onto a buttered baking sheet, smoothing it evenly to a thickness of about a ½ inch. Cool thoroughly.

A few minutes before serving, cut the mixture into small rectangles. Dip in egg white, beaten with a fork until frothy. Dip into breadcrumbs and deep-fry until golden brown at 390° F. Drain on paper toweling and serve immediately.

Variation: Along with the cheese you can add 2 slices of finely chopped ham.

Cheese delights * Délicieuses au fromage

FOR SIX PEOPLE

2 cups Béchamel Sauce (page 6)	3 egg whites
¾ cup grated Gruyère cheese	salt and pepper

Make the béchamel, and while it is still hot, stir in the cheese. Season with salt and pepper and cool thoroughly.

Beat the egg whites very stiff and fold them in gently, lifting the mixture high with a rubber spatula as you do it.

Drop tablespoonfuls of the mixture into very hot (390° F.) fat. Brown on all sides. Drain and cool.

Corn croquettes * Croquettes de maïs

FOR FOUR PEOPLE

2 cups corn kernels	2 eggs
1½ cups thick Béchamel Sauce (page 6)	fine breadcrumbs
	1 lemon
3 egg yolks	salt and pepper

Shuck corn cooked in boiling salted water until tender or use canned corn.

Make the béchamel and stir in the corn. Remove from the heat and stir in the egg yolks. Mix thoroughly and season with salt and pepper. Pour this mixture on a buttered baking sheet and cool thoroughly.

When the mixture is very cold, make little croquettes, about ¾ inch in diameter and 2 inches long.

Beat the eggs until blended. Dip the croquettes in the egg; then roll them in breadcrumbs. Fry them in deep fat at 385° F. until well browned. Serve on a heated platter garnished with lemon wedges.

You can also serve these with a tomato or curry béchamel sauce.

Egg and bacon croquettes
Croquettes aux oeufs durs

FOR FIVE PEOPLE

4 hard-cooked eggs
2 cups thick Béchamel Sauce
  (page 6)
1 large onion
2 tablespoons butter
4 slices Canadian bacon

1 large sprig parsley
1 egg
fine breadcrumbs
juice of 2 lemons
salt and pepper

Boil the eggs 15 minutes in salted water. Plunge in cold water. Peel and chop them coarsely.

Make the sauce and let it cool.

Peel and chop the onion coarsely. Sauté in the butter with the finely diced bacon.

Combine the 4 chopped eggs with the cold béchamel and stir in the onion-bacon mixture. Add the parsley, chopped fine or ground through a *moulinette.* Season with salt and pepper.

Form oval croquettes that are not very thick.

Beat the egg until blended. Dip the croquettes in egg and roll them in breadcrumbs. Fry in deep fat at 385° F. Serve very hot, sprinkled with lemon juice.

You can accompany this dish with a highly seasoned tomato sauce.

Lamb and artichoke croquettes
Croquettes de mouton aux artichauts

FOR FIVE PEOPLE

1 cup diced cooked lamb
4 artichoke bottoms

2 egg whites
dry breadcrumbs

1 cup Béchamel Sauce (page 6)   1 cup heavy cream
2 egg yolks   juice of 1 lemon
nutmeg   salt and pepper

Dice or chop coarsely lamb that is free of all skin and gristle.

Boil artichokes for 45 minutes in salted water and discard the leaves and choke. Or use canned artichoke bottoms. Cut the artichoke bottoms in very small dice.

Make the béchamel. Stir in the meat, artichokes, and egg yolks. Season with a pinch of nutmeg, salt, and pepper. Mix well and spread out on a baking sheet or marble to cool. When thoroughly cooled, form into little balls.

Beat the egg whites with a fork until frothy. Dip the balls in egg white and then in breadcrumbs. Deep-fat fry at 385° F. until golden brown. Drain well and keep hot in the open door of an oven, while completing the frying.

At the same time, scald the cream.

Serve the croquettes on a heated platter accompanied by the cream, seasoned with lemon juice, salt, and pepper.

Milanaise croquettes * Croquettes milanaises

FOR FOUR PEOPLE

2 medium-sized potatoes   2 egg yolks
1 cup thick Béchamel Sauce   2 egg whites
  (page 6)   fine breadcrumbs
¾ cup grated Gruyère cheese   several sprigs parsley
⅔ cup chopped ham   salt and pepper

Peel and boil the potatoes in salted water just until tender. Drain completely and force through a sieve.

Make the béchamel and, while still on the heat, mix in the cheese, potatoes, and ham. Season but do not add too much salt, because of the ham. Remove from the heat and cool a little before beating in the egg yolks.

Make croquettes the size of an egg and flatten them a little.

Beat the egg whites until frothy. Dip the croquettes first in the egg whites and then in the breadcrumbs. Fry in deep fat at 385° F. Fry the parsley at the same time.

Serve the croquettes piled high on a napkin-lined serving platter.

Mussel croquettes * Croquettes de moules

FOR FIVE PEOPLE

2 quarts mussels   ½ cup heavy cream
¾ cup dry white wine   2 egg yolks

pinch of thyme
pinch of powdered bay leaf
3 tablespoons butter
3 tablespoons flour
1 teaspoon turmeric *or*
small pinch of saffron

2 eggs
fine breadcrumbs
juice of 1 lemon
salt and pepper

Scrape and wash the mussels. Put them in a kettle with the wine and herbs. Cook uncovered over high heat until the mussels open. Remove the mussels from their shells and strain the broth through a very fine sieve. Chop the mussels coarsely.

Heat the butter in a saucepan until frothy. Stir in the flour with a wooden spoon. Stir in the mussel broth and cook until the sauce is very thick. Season with salt and pepper and add the saffron, cream, and mussels. Mix well. Cool slightly and stir in the egg yolks. Pour the mixture onto a working surface, preferably a marble, and cool thoroughly. Make small oval croquettes.

Beat the eggs until blended. Dip the croquettes in egg and then in fine breadcrumbs. Brown in deep, hot (385° F.) fat and drain on paper toweling. Serve very hot, sprinkled with lemon juice.

Veal croquettes ✻ *Croquettes de veau*

FOR SIX PEOPLE

1½ cups ground cooked veal
¼ pound mushrooms
3 cups thick Béchamel Sauce
    (page 6)
6 tarragon leaves

2 egg yolks
2 eggs
fine breadcrumbs
juice of 1 lemon
salt and pepper

Make sure that the veal is free of skin or gristle before grinding it.

Trim the mushrooms. Wash them well and chop coarsely.

Make the béchamel and cook the chopped mushrooms in it for 2 minutes. Season with salt and pepper and add the tarragon leaves, chopped fine, and the veal. Remove from the heat and beat in the egg yolks. Spread the mixture on a baking sheet or marble to cool.

Form oval croquettes of the mixture.

Beat the eggs slightly and dip the croquettes into egg and then into breadcrumbs. Fry them in deep fat at 385° F. Drain on paper toweling and serve very hot, sprinkled with lemon juice. Serve with a green salad.

Fish timbale de l'hôtel des colonies à vannes
Timbale de poisson de l'hôtel des colonies à vannes

FOR SIX TO EIGHT PEOPLE

4 pounds white fish (cod,
  haddock, whiting)
2 cups white wine
2 onions
2 cloves
2 shallots
1 teaspoon white peppercorns
2 cups soft breadcrumbs

¾ cup milk
1 tablespoon chopped parsley
1 egg
Court Bouillon I (page 163)
1 cup heavy cream
1 egg yolk
juice of 1 lemon
salt and pepper

Place the fish in a kettle with the white wine and an equal amount of water, the onions (each stuck with a clove), the shallots, and the peppercorns. Bring to a boil gently, and when the water starts to simmer, withdraw the kettle from the heat and let it stand covered for 15 minutes.

Take the fish from the liquid and remove all the skin and bones. Reserve the broth. Put the flesh in a mortar or wooden bowl. Add the breadcrumbs, soaked in milk and squeezed dry, salt, pepper, chopped parsley, and an egg. Pound everything together until you have a smooth paste. If it is too thick, add another whole egg.

Butter a timbale or a deep baking dish. After making sure that the mixture is well seasoned, put it in the timbale and place it in a pan of hot water. Bake at 350° F. for 1 hour.

Strain 1 cup of lukewarm court bouillon into a saucepan. Beat the cream, egg yolk, and lemon juice together and add to the court bouillon. Reheat but do not boil. Taste for seasoning, adding more salt, pepper, and lemon juice if necessary.

Unmold the timbale on a heated platter and surround with the sauce.

Eggs

Eggs

The age of eggs is very important. In ancient times, eggs eaten the day they were laid were called Golden Eggs by the Romans. Those laid the day before were called Silver Eggs, and those that were several days old were called Iron Eggs.

For certain preparations, such as boiled eggs, poached eggs, fried eggs, or eggs *mollet,* and also for shirred eggs, absolute freshness is essential.

When the egg is fresh, the shell is a little granular to the touch, as if covered with lime. If the egg is old, the shell is transparent. Another way to test the freshness of an egg is to put it in a glass of salt water. If it is fresh, it will drop to the bottom of the glass and will be an egg worthy of your best egg dishes. If it floats, it is not good. If it stays in suspension, it is not fresh enough to be served fried, poached or boiled but is perfectly good for omelets, scrambled eggs, cakes, sauces, etc.

An egg is a complete food in itself and is quickly digested if it is cooked without heavy or complicated sauces. Egg yolk is more easily digestible than the white and is much more caloric. An egg beaten into meat broth is very nourishing and is often prescribed for convalescents.

The exterior color of an egg is caused more by the breed of the hen than by what she has eaten.

Here are a few bits of information that are helpful when using eggs:

1 The least drop of egg yolk in egg whites will make it impossible to beat the egg whites absolutely stiff.
2 Add a pinch of salt to egg whites before beating them. This will make them easier to beat successfully.
3 Always beat egg whites just before using them; they will fall if they have to wait. It is easier to beat them in a bowl with a small bottom.
4 If you are making a sauce or a custard with egg yolks, do not let them boil, or the mixture will be full of little yellow threads.
5 Egg whites are not good if they are not used quickly. Use them the day you separate them from the yolks, or the next day, if you refrigerate them.
6 If you want an omelet soft and creamy, add a few bits of butter or a tablespoon of oil before putting them in the skillet.
7 It is absolutely necessary to plunge hard-cooked eggs in cold water as soon as they are cooked in order to peel them properly.
8 Only poach 1 or 2 eggs in a saucepan at a time. Drain poached eggs on a towel, and cut the whites with scissors to give them a trim appearance.

Boiled eggs in shells

Use strictly fresh, medium-sized eggs. Do not take the eggs directly from the refrigerator and put them into boiling water. Let them warm to room temperature.

There are various ways to boil eggs, but I prefer to lower the eggs with a spoon into boiling salted water and to cook them gently, allowing 3 minutes for those who like their eggs only slightly cooked, $3\frac{1}{2}$ minutes for soft-cooked, 4 minutes for medium-cooked, and $4\frac{1}{2}$ minutes for well-cooked eggs. Unless they are served immediately, keep them warm in a folded napkin.

Boiled eggs, served in their shells in egg cups, are accompanied by salt and pepper and small strips of buttered bread, toasted or plain which can be dipped in the egg.

An egg served this way is opened with a little spoon, never with a knife, preferably at the larger end. Once the egg is eaten, custom demands that the shell be crushed. Children may be told that this is done to keep the devil out of the egg shell, but the practical reason behind this custom is that empty egg shells are apt to roll off the plates onto the floor.

The best way to have really tender, hard-cooked eggs is to coddle them for 30 minutes. This means cooking the eggs in hot water just below the boiling point.

The more usual and quicker method is to boil the eggs for 15 minutes in salted water and to plunge them immediately into cold water. This makes it easier to shell the eggs.

Anchovy-stuffed eggs * Oeufs farcis aux anchois

FOR FOUR PEOPLE

6 eggs
¾ cup soft breadcrumbs
⅓ cup milk

1 can anchovy fillets
2 tomatoes

Boil the eggs 15 minutes in salted water. Plunge into cold water, shell, and cool. Cut the eggs lengthwise and remove the yolks.

Soak the breadcrumbs in milk and squeeze out the milk. Chop the anchovy fillets very fine. Crush the egg yolks and mix well with the breadcrumbs and anchovies. Stuff the egg whites with the mixture and put on a salad plate. Decorate with tomato slices. Serve very cold.

Stuffed eggs aurore * Oeufs farcis aurore

FOR SIX PEOPLE

6 eggs
2½ tablespoons chopped parsley
4 tablespoons grated Gruyère cheese
1½ cups Béchamel Sauce (page 6)

4 tablespoons tomato purée
2 tablespoons butter
salt and pepper

Boil the eggs in salted water for 15 minutes. Plunge in cold water and shell. Cool. Cut the eggs in half and remove the yolks. Mix 3 of the yolks with half the parsley and half the Gruyère.

Make the béchamel and add the purée. Season with pepper. Mix half of it with the egg yolk mixture and stuff the egg whites.

Place in a buttered baking dish and cover with the rest of the béchamel. Sprinkle with grated cheese and dot with butter. Bake 10 minutes in a hot (425° F.) oven.

Crush the rest of the egg yolks with the rest of the parsley. Just before serving, sprinkle this mixture over the eggs.

Little egg barrels * Petits oeufs en tonneaux

FOR FIVE PEOPLE

10 small eggs
anchovy paste

1 can anchovy fillets
corn salad or lettuce

Boil the eggs in salted water for 15 minutes. Plunge into cold water and shell. Cool.

Take off the top third of each egg and save it. Carefully remove the yolks with a small spoon. Crush the yolks in a small bowl and mix with anchovy paste. When well blended, put the mixture into the egg whites and re-form the eggs.

Cut the anchovy fillets into very thin strips and wrap them around the eggs so that they look like small wine barrels. Serve the eggs on a bed of corn salad or, lacking that, on shredded lettuce.

Brandied stuffed eggs * Oeufs farcis cognac

FOR SIX PEOPLE

6 eggs
6 black olives
2½ tablespoons capers
4 teaspoons minced tuna fish
½ teaspoon French mustard
pinch of allspice

2 tablespoons cognac
oil
3 tomatoes
2 cups cold cooked green beans
Vinaigrette Sauce (page 29)
pepper

Boil the eggs in salted water for 15 minutes. Plunge into cold water and shell. Cool and cut them in half, lengthwise. Remove the yolks. Crush them and mix well with the olives, which have been pitted and finely chopped, the capers, tuna, mustard, allspice, plenty of pepper, and cognac. Season with pepper and bind with a little oil so that you will have a smooth, rich mixture.

Fill the eggs, shaping the mixture into a dome. Put 3 capers on each one. Serve very cold on a salad platter garnished with tomato slices and green beans, which have been seasoned with vinaigrette sauce.

Crab-stuffed eggs (cold)
Oeufs farcis au crabe (froids)

FOR FOUR PEOPLE

8 eggs	1 tablespoon chopped parsley
1 small can crabmeat	lettuce
1 cup Mayonnaise (page 14)	salt and pepper
1 lemon	

Boil the eggs in salted water for 15 minutes. Plunge in cold water and shell. Cut the eggs lengthwise when they have cooled. Remove the egg yolks.

Flake the crabmeat, removing any hard filaments. Mix it with mayonnaise. Season to taste with salt and pepper and lemon juice and add the chopped parsley.

Fill the egg whites with the crabmeat mixture. Place each one on a small lettuce leaf and sprinkle with the egg yolks, which have been passed through a *moulinette* or forced through a strainer.

Egg Croquettes * Croquettes aux oeufs durs

FOR FIVE PEOPLE

5 eggs	1 tablespoon chopped parsley
1½ cups Béchamel Sauce (page 6)	fine breadcrumbs
1 large onion	lemon
4 slices Canadian bacon	salt and pepper
2 tablespoons butter	

Boil 4 eggs 15 minutes in salted water. Plunge them in cold water. Shell, cool, and chop them coarsely.

Make a thick béchamel and let it cool completely.

Peel and chop the onion. Dice the bacon. Sauté both in butter until the onions are golden.

Combine the eggs, onion, bacon, chopped parsley, and the cold béchamel. Mix well and form into small oval croquettes.

Beat the remaining egg and dip the croquettes first in egg and then in bread-crumbs. Fry the croquettes until golden brown in deep fat (385° F.). Sprinkle with lemon juice and serve very hot. You can also serve this with a tomato sauce.

Hot curried eggs * Oeufs farcis au cari (chauds)

FOR FOUR PEOPLE

6 eggs
3 cups Béchamel Sauce (page 6)
4 tablespoons curry powder

½ cup heavy cream
salt and pepper

Boil the eggs in salted water for 15 minutes. Plunge into cold water and shell. Cool and cut the eggs in half lengthwise.

Make the béchamel, and just before removing from the heat, add the curry. Mix well.

Remove the yolks from the egg whites and combine with enough of the sauce to make a smooth thick mixture. Fill the egg whites and put in a baking dish. Cover with the rest of the béchamel, to which the cream has been added.

Bake 10 minutes in a hot (425° F.) oven.

Cold curried eggs * Oeufs farcis au cari (froids)

FOR FOUR PEOPLE

8 eggs
⅓ cup heavy cream
1 tablespoon curry powder

3 large tomatoes
lettuce
salt and pepper

Boil the eggs in salted water for 15 minutes. Plunge them in cold water and shell. When they are cold, cut them in half lengthwise.

Remove the yolks and crush them with a fork. Combine with the cream and curry powder. Fill the egg whites with the stuffing.

Dip the tomatoes in boiling water and slip off the skins. Cut the tomatoes in 16 fairly thick slices.

Line a serving platter with lettuce leaves. Put the tomato slices on the lettuce and top each one with a stuffed egg. Serve very cold.

Frédéric eggs * Oeufs frédéric

FOR FOUR PEOPLE

8 eggs
1½ cups Béchamel Sauce (page 6)
½ cup Mayonnaise (page 14)

2 egg whites, slightly beaten
fine breadcrumbs
salt and pepper

Boil the eggs 15 minutes in salted water. Plunge into cold water and shell, cool, and cut them in half crosswise. These are going to be re-formed after they have been stuffed, so keep the halves together. Remove the yolks and crush them well with a fork.

Make the béchamel and mix with the crushed egg yolks and the mayonnaise. Heat very gently so as not to turn the mayonnaise. Season well.

Fill the eggs with some of the mixture. Put the halves together so that they look whole. Dip them in egg white and then in breadcrumbs. Fry them in deep fat for 1 minute at 385° F. Remove from the fat with a slotted spoon.

Put the rest of the mixture on a hot platter and surround with the fried eggs.

Egg delight * Oeufs ravissants

FOR FOUR PEOPLE

8 eggs	½ teaspoon celery salt
2 cups Béchamel Sauce (page 6)	pepper
½ teaspoon ginger	1 tablespoon spinach green or
½ teaspoon rosemary	3 drops green vegetable coloring
½ teaspoon powdered thyme	

Boil the eggs 15 minutes in salted water. Plunge into cold water, shell and cool them. Cut them with an egg slicer.

Make the béchamel and stir in all the spices. Obtain spinach green by parboiling 8 to 10 leaves in boiling water for 2 minutes and forcing them through a strainer. Add that or coloring to the sauce. Taste for seasoning. Mix in the eggs gently.

Chill in the refrigerator before serving.

Hard-cooked eggs aux fines herbes (cold)
Oeufs durs fines herbes

FOR FOUR PEOPLE

8 eggs	3 tablespoons chopped *fines herbes*
1½ cups Béchamel Sauce (page 6)	(parsley, chervil, tarragon)
¾ cup heavy cream	salt and pepper

Boil the eggs 15 minutes in salted water. Plunge into cold water and shell them. When they are cold, cut them into rounds, using an egg slicer.

Make the sauce and let it cool. It should be highly seasoned. Add the heavy cream and the herbs and mix with the eggs carefully. Chill in the refrigerator before serving.

Ham-stuffed eggs ✻ Oeufs farcis au jambon

3 ounces pork fat*
3 onions
2 tablespoons chopped parsley
1 tablespoon oil
1 can tomato paste
1 teaspoon sugar

9 eggs
1 small can truffle peelings
¼ pound mushrooms
8 thin slices cooked ham
½ cup grated Gruyère cheese
salt and pepper

Chop the pork fat, onions, and parsley very fine or pass them through a *moulinette.* Put these ingredients in a saucepan with the oil and simmer 20 minutes. Add the tomato paste, the same amount of water, and the sugar. Stir well and add more water if too dry. Season with salt and pepper and cook 30 minutes longer.

Boil the eggs 15 minutes in salted water. Plunge them in cold water. Shell and cool them. Cut 8 of the eggs in half. Remove the egg yolks. Mix them with the truffle peelings and with the mushrooms, which have been trimmed, washed, and chopped. Season with salt and pepper.

Stuff the egg whites with the mixture and roll each egg half in a half piece of ham. Place them in a baking dish.

Crush the remaining hard-cooked egg or pass it through a *moulinette* and add it to the tomato sauce. Pour this over the stuffed eggs and sprinkle with the grated cheese. Brown in a 400° F. oven for 10 minutes.

Shrimp-stuffed eggs ✻ Oeufs farcis aux crevettes

6 eggs
Court Bouillon (page 163)
¼ pound tiny shrimp
12 large shrimp

1½ cups Béchamel Sauce (page 6)
1 tablespoon tomato paste
cayenne
salt

Boil the eggs in salted water for 15 minutes. Plunge into cold water and shell. Cool. Cut the eggs in half lengthwise and remove the yolks.

Prepare a simple court bouillon. Simmer the shrimp 10 minutes. Shell the small ones, but not the large ones.

Make the béchamel. Crush the egg yolks and combine them with the shelled shrimp. Bind with a little béchamel. Season the mixture with salt and a little cayenne and fill the egg halves with it. Place the filled eggs in a buttered baking dish.

*If you cannot get pork fat, parboil salt pork 5 minutes. Rinse and use like fresh pork fat.—*Ed.*

Add the tomato paste to the rest of the sauce. Season with salt and pepper and pour it over the eggs. Bake 10 minutes in a hot oven (425° F.). Just before serving, place a large shrimp on each egg half.

Eggs mimosa * Oeufs mimosa

FOR FOUR PEOPLE

8 eggs
1 teaspoon French mustard
½ cup Mayonnaise (page 14)

2 tablespoons chopped *fines herbes* (chervil, tarragon, parsley)
lettuce
salt and pepper

Boil the eggs 15 minutes in salted water. Plunge them into cold water and shell, cool, and cut them in half crosswise. Remove the yolks and crush three fourths of them with a fork.

Mix the mustard with the mayonnaise and combine with the crushed yolks and chopped herbs. Season well with salt and pepper and stir until you have a smooth mixture.

Fll the egg whites with the mixture and place on a bed of lettuce leaves. Sprinkle with the rest of the egg yolks, forced through a strainer or a *moulinette*. Serve very cold.

Eggs à la tripe * Oeufs à la tripe

FOR FOUR PEOPLE

8 eggs
1 pound (4-5 medium) onions
3 tablespoons butter

2 cups Béchamel Sauce (page 6)
¼ cup heavy cream (optional)
salt and pepper

Boil the eggs 15 minutes in salted water. Plunge them in cold water. Shell, cool, and cut them into rounds with an egg slicer.

Peel the onions and cut them in thin slices. Heat the butter and sauté the onions until golden. Watch to see that they do not brown.

Meanwhile, make the béchamel, and add the cream, if desired. Mix in the eggs and the onions. Taste for seasoning and serve very hot.

Stuffed eggs on toast * Oeufs farcis sur toasts

FOR FOUR PEOPLE

8 eggs
¾ cups Béchamel Sauce (page 6)
¾ cup minced cooked meat
½ cup raw minced mushrooms

8 slices white bread
3 tablespoons butter
salt and pepper

Boil the eggs in salted water for 15 minutes. Plunge them into cold water. Shell them, cool, and cut them lengthwise, removing the yolks.

Make the sauce and combine with the minced meat and mushrooms. Season well and cook over a low flame just until well heated. The mixture should be thick. Stuff the egg whites.

Fry the bread lightly in butter on both sides. Put the toast on a baking dish. Put 2 egg halves on each piece of toast. Sprinkle with the egg yolks, which have been forced through a strainer or through a *moulinette*. Dot with butter and bake in a hot (425° F.) oven for 10 minutes.

Omelets

1 When making an omelet, use a spotlessly clean heavy iron or cast-iron skillet.
2 Never make an omelet with more than 12 eggs. Make two omelets if you have many guests. Serve them on one large platter.
3 Put just enough butter in the pan to keep the omelet from sticking, but not too much or the omelet will be greasy and indigestible.
4 Do not beat the eggs too much if you want a soft omelet. The more you beat the eggs, the more they will seem like a crepe.
5 Beat and season the eggs just before cooking.
6 The raw eggs are poured into hot butter, but the omelet is cooked over a moderate heat.

To make the omelet, break the eggs into a bowl, and beat them vigorously with a fork just until the yolks and whites are well blended. Season with salt and pepper.

Heat a little butter in the skillet, tilting the skillet so that it is evenly buttered all over, and when very hot, pour in the eggs. Reduce the heat. The eggs will coagulate immediately on the bottom. Lift up the corner of the omelet to let the liquid egg seep under. Stir gently until cooked so that the omelet will not stick. As soon as the omelet is cooked, slide a few bits of butter under the omelet to help loosen it from the pan and to give it a shiny appearance. When the omelet has browned slightly on the bottom, fold in two with a spatula, and slide it onto a warm platter. Serve immediately.

Asparagus omelet (cold) * Omelette boildieu

FOR FOUR PEOPLE

10 eggs
1 cup Vinaigrette Sauce (page 29)
2½ tablespoons chopped *fines herbes* (chervil, tarragon, parsley)

4 bunches asparagus
3 tablespoons butter
salt and pepper

Boil 2 of the eggs in salted water for 15 minutes. Plunge into cold water, peel, and cool. Crush the eggs with a fork. Make the vinaigrette sauce and stir in the crushed eggs and the *fines herbes.*

Cook the asparagus in salted water, having cut off the hard ends.

Beat the remaining eggs and add 1 tablespoon of butter, divided in small pieces. Season with salt and pepper. Heat the rest of the butter in a skillet and make the omelet as usual. Put the unfolded omelet on a heated serving platter. Put half of the asparagus on the omelet, sprinkle generously with the vinaigrette, and fold in two. Garnish the platter with the rest of the asparagus. Sprinkle the omelet with the sauce and serve after chilling.

Eskualduna omelet * Omelette eskualduna

FOR FOUR PEOPLE

1 onion
5 tablespoons butter
½ pound chicken livers

½ cup heated dry white wine
8 eggs
salt and pepper

Peel the onion and cut into very thin slices. Sauté the onion slices in 2 tablespoons of butter, and when they start to turn golden, add the chicken livers cut in small pieces. Add the hot wine, salt, and pepper and cook for just 3 minutes, no longer.

Beat the eggs and season with salt and pepper. Heat the rest of the butter in a skillet and cook the omelet as usual. Fold and slide it onto a heated serving platter. Cut the omelet down the center without going all the way through. Fill the slit with the chicken livers and their juice.

Omelet feydeau * Omelette feydeau

FOR FOUR PEOPLE

½ pound mushrooms
6 tablespoons butter
¾ cup Béchamel Sauce (page 6)

8 eggs
salt and pepper

Trim and wash the mushrooms. Chop them rather coarsely and sauté them in half of the butter. When the moisture has disappeared, add the béchamel and season well with salt and pepper.

Beat the eggs until blended. Add salt and pepper and make the omelet as usual. When the omelet is placed unfolded on a warm serving platter, cover the center of it with the mushroom mixture. Fold and serve immediately.

Omelet aux fines herbes * Omelette aux fines herbes

FOR FOUR PEOPLE

8 eggs
4 tablespoons chopped *fines herbes*
   (parsley, chervil, tarragon)

3 tablespoons butter
salt and pepper

Beat the eggs with their traditional omelet herbs, which should be very finely chopped. Add 1 tablespoon of butter divided into small pieces. Season with salt and pepper.

Heat the rest of the butter in a skillet. As soon as it is no longer frothy, add the eggs. At the end of 30 seconds, start lifting the corner of the omelet so that the liquid eggs will seep under.

As soon as the underneath is lightly browned, fold the omelet in two and slide onto a warm platter. Serve immediately.

Green omelet (cold) * Omelette verte (froide)

FOR FOUR PEOPLE

8 eggs	1 ½ cups cooked green peas
3 tablespoons chopped *fines herbes*	6 tablespoons butter
(parsley, chervil, tarragon)	salt and pepper

Break the eggs into a bowl and beat well. Add the chopped herbs and peas. Season with salt and pepper. Heat some of the butter well in a skillet. Pour in the eggs and cook 30 seconds before lowering the heat. When the omelet is completely cooked, add more butter under the omelet and turn it like a crepe. Brown the other side equally well, letting it cook 5 minutes.

Slip the omelet onto a serving platter and let it cool completely. Serve cold.

Ham omelet * Omelette au jambon

FOR FOUR PEOPLE

8 eggs	3 tablespoons butter
¾ cup diced cooked ham	salt and pepper

Beat the eggs and add the diced ham, 1 tablespoon of butter, divided into small bits, salt, and pepper.

Heat the rest of the butter in a skillet and proceed as usual.

Kidney omelet * Omelette aux rognons

FOR FOUR PEOPLE

1 veal kidney	1 teaspoon chopped parsley
6 tablespoons butter	salt and pepper
8 eggs	

Trim the kidney well, removing the fatty core and the filaments. Cut into rather small dice and sauté 3 to 4 minutes in 3 tablespoons of butter. Season with salt and pepper and keep warm.

Beat the eggs until blended. Season with salt and pepper. Heat the remaining butter in a skillet and make the omelet as usual. Slip the omelet onto a heated platter. Put the kidneys on the omelet. Fold the omelet, sprinkle with chopped parsley, and serve immediately.

Lorraine omelet * Omelette lorraine

FOR FOUR PEOPLE

6 very thin slices Canadian bacon
8 eggs
4 teaspoons very heavy cream

2 ounces Gruyère cheese, sliced thin
2 tablespoons butter
salt and pepper

Pan-broil the bacon for a few moments. Divide into small pieces. Break the eggs into a bowl and beat until well blended. Add the cream, bacon, cheese, salt, and pepper. Mix well.

Heat the butter in a skillet and make the omelet as usual.

Omelet massena * Omelette massena

FOR FOUR PEOPLE

1 marrow bone
2 artichokes
5 tablespoons butter

4 teaspoons tomato paste
8 eggs
salt and pepper

Preferably this omelet is made the day a *pot-au-feu* is cooking on the stove so that you will have the marrow bone. If not, poach the bone ½ hour in boiling salted water.

Cook the artichokes for 45 to 60 minutes in boiling salted water. Drain well and remove the leaves and choke, leaving just the bottoms. Cut the bottoms into slices and sauté them in 2 tablespoons of butter. Stir in the tomato paste.

Beat the eggs with salt and pepper and add the artichoke slices. Heat the rest of the butter in a skillet and make the omelet as usual. Fold it and slip onto a warm platter. Garnish with slices of hot marrow.

Mussel omelet * Omelette aux moules

FOR FOUR PEOPLE

1 quart mussels
6-8 eggs
1 large sprig chervil

3 tablespoons butter
salt and pepper

Put the thoroughly cleaned mussels in a pan and place over high heat. As soon as the shells are open, the mussels are cooked. Remove the shells.

Beat the eggs with finely chopped chervil (using parsley if chervil is not available—*Ed.*). Season with salt and pepper and add the mussels.

Heat the butter in a skillet, and when very hot, pour in the egg mixture and make the omelet as usual.

Curry mushroom omelet
Omelette aux champignons

FOR SIX PEOPLE

¼ pound mushrooms
5 tablespoons butter
pinch of curry

12 eggs
salt and pepper

Trim the mushrooms. Remove the caps, wash them well, and slice very thin. Save the stems for making soup.

Break the eggs into a bowl and beat until well blended. Add 1½ tablespoons of butter in small pieces to make the omelet very soft. Season with salt, curry, and pepper and stir in the mushrooms.

Heat the rest of the butter in a skillet. Pour in the egg mixture and make the omelet as usual.

Onion omelet * Omelette aux oignons

FOR FOUR PEOPLE

2-3 onions
5 tablespoons butter

8 eggs
salt and pepper

Peel and slice the onions very thin. Sauté in 2½ tablespoons of butter just until golden.

Beat the eggs until blended. Add the onions, salt, and pepper. Heat the rest of the butter in a skillet and make the omelet as usual.

Parmesan omelet * Omelette parmesan

FOR FOUR PEOPLE

8 eggs
1 cup grated Parmesan cheese

6 tablespoons butter
salt and pepper

Break the eggs into a bowl and add half the Parmesan cheese. Beat until the yolks and whites are blended, but no longer, or the omelet will be dry. Season with pepper and a very little salt.

Using a small skillet, heat a tablespoon of butter. When very hot, pour in one fourth of the liquid eggs. Make a small omelet but undercook it a little. In the same way, make 3 more small omelets. Roll the omelets up and place them side by side on a buttered baking sheet. Sprinkle with the rest of the Parmesan and dot with butter. Put in a hot oven (425° F.) just long enough to lightly brown the cheese.

Red pepper omelet (for cocktails)
Omelette aux piments

FOR TWELVE PEOPLE

6 canned red peppers
12 eggs

3 tablespoons butter
salt and pepper

Cut the peppers into small strips. Beat the eggs until the yolks and whites are blended. Add the peppers, salt, and pepper.

Heat the butter in a very large skillet, and when hot, pour in the eggs. Reduce the heat and cook the omelet as usual. When cooked, turn it over and continue to cook until the underside is browned.

Remove the omelet and let it cool. Cut in ¾-inch cubes and serve on cocktail sticks.

Potato omelet * Omelettes aux pommes de terre

FOR FOUR PEOPLE

2 medium-sized potatoes
6 tablespoons butter
8 eggs

1 teaspoon chopped parsley
salt and pepper

Peel the potatoes and cut them into small cubes. Heat 3 tablespoons of the butter in a skillet and cook the potatoes in the butter until tender. Season with salt, pepper, and chopped parsley.

Beat the eggs until blended. Season with salt and pepper. Add 1 tablespoon of the butter in small pieces. Heat the rest of the butter in a skillet and make the omelet.

Just before folding the omelet, put the potatoes on top. Fold and slip onto a heated platter.

Poulard omelet * Omelette poulard

FOR FOUR PEOPLE

8 eggs	5 tablespoons butter
¼ cup heavy cream	salt and pepper

Separate the yolks from the whites of 4 eggs. Put 4 egg yolks and 4 whole eggs in one bowl and 4 egg whites in another. Beat the 4 egg whites stiff and beat the contents of the other bowl until blended. Add the cream and season highly with salt and pepper. Fold in the egg whites rather than stirring them in. Lift the mixture gently. This is to keep the egg whites from falling.

Heat the butter in a large skillet and make the omelet as usual. Fold the omelet and put it on a very hot platter. Serve immediately.

Roquefort omelet * Omelette au roquefort

FOR SIX PEOPLE

12 eggs	4 teaspoons heavy cream
3 tablespoons butter	salt and pepper
2 ounces Roquefort cheese	

Beat the eggs until blended and season with salt and pepper. (Go lightly on the salt, because imported Roquefort is apt to be salty.—*Ed.*) Add 1 tablespoon of the butter in small pieces.

Crumble the Roquefort into a double boiler and heat. When it has melted a little, add the cream.

Heat the rest of the butter in a skillet and pour in the eggs, making the omelet as usual. Do not overcook, because the omelet should be quite soft. Spread the Roquefort mixture over the top while the eggs are cooking so that the cheese will penetrate the eggs.

Fold and slip onto a heated serving platter.

Savoy omelet * Omelette savoyarde

FOR FOUR PEOPLE

3 medium-sized potatoes	2½ ounces diced Gruyère cheese
6 tablespoons butter	salt and pepper
8 eggs	

Boil the potatoes in their jackets until tender. Peel them and cut into small dice. Sauté the diced potatoes in 3 tablespoons of butter until golden. Cool to lukewarm.

Beat the eggs well until blended. Season with salt and pepper and add the cheese. Stir in the potatoes.

Heat the rest of the butter in a skillet and pour in the mixture. Cook like an ordinary omelet.

Scallop omelet
Omelette aux coquilles saint-jacques

FOR FOUR PEOPLE

8 scallops in their shells*
pinch of thyme
pinch of powdered bay leaf
juice of ½ lemon
5 tablespoons butter

1 tablespoon cognac
1 tablespoon flour
¾ cup heavy cream
8 eggs
salt and pepper

Place the scallops in their shells, if available, in a kettle. Cook without water over high heat until the shells open. Remove from the heat and take out the white meat and the coral. Cook this in 1½ cups of simmering water with the herbs, salt, pepper, and the juice of ½ lemon.

Heat 2 tablespoons of butter in a small skillet and sauté the scallop meat for a few moments. Add the cognac and touch it with a lighted match. Remove from the heat.

Heat 3 tablespoons of butter in a saucepan. Stir in the flour with a wooden spoon, and when blended, add the strained scallop broth. Simmer for a few moments, stirring constantly. Remove from the heat. Stir in the cream and taste for seasoning. Keep hot.

Beat the eggs. Season with salt and pepper and make an omelet. Slide the omelet onto a heated serving platter. Pour the scallops and sauce over the omelet and serve very hot.

Sorrel omelet * *Omelette à l'oseille*

FOR SIX PEOPLE

½ pound sorrel
¼ pound butter

12 eggs
salt and pepper

Trim and wash the sorrel. Heat 5 tablespoons of butter in a skillet and add the sorrel. Cook over a very low flame for 8 minutes, stirring frequently. Remove and cool.

*Scallops are rarely sold in their shells in the United States. Only the white meat, sold by the pint or pound, is available. The pink "coral," which has a distinctive flavor, is not sold, but a little lemon juice approximates its flavor. Thus, with a few adjustments, this delicious dish can be served.—*Ed.*

Beat the eggs with salt and pepper until blended. Mix with the sorrel. Heat the rest of the butter in a skillet, and when very hot, pour in the eggs and make the omelet as usual. Serve very hot.

Tomato omelet * Omelette aux tomates

FOR FOUR PEOPLE

1 pound (3-4) tomatoes	3 tablespoons butter
2½ tablespoons oil	salt and pepper
8 eggs	

Dip the tomatoes into boiling water and slip off the skins. Heat the oil in a skillet and cook the tomatoes for 15 minutes, seasoning them with salt and pepper.

Beat the eggs until the yolks and whites are blended. Season with salt and pepper and pour into a skillet containing the very hot butter. Make the omelet as usual.

Put the omelet unfolded on a heated serving platter. Fill it with the cooked tomatoes and fold in two. Garnish with little mounds of cooked tomatoes at either end of the omelet.

Truffle omelet * Omelette aux truffes

FOR EIGHT PEOPLE

16 eggs	6 tablespoons butter
2 large truffles	salt and pepper
2½ tablespoons Madeira	

Beat the eggs until the yolks and whites are well blended. Add the truffles, sliced thin, the Madeira, salt, and pepper.

Heat some of the butter in a large skillet and make 2 omelets, using half of the mixture at a time. Serve both omelets on the same heated platter. Serve immediately.

Tuna omelet * Omelette au thon

FOR FOUR PEOPLE

1 small can oil-packed tuna fish	3 tablespoons butter
2½ tablespoons heavy cream	juice of 1 lemon
8 eggs	salt and pepper

Crush the tuna flakes with a fork, combining with the cream.

Beat the eggs until blended and stir in the tuna. Mix thoroughly.

Heat the butter in a skillet and make the omelet in the usual manner. Fold the omelet and slip it onto a heated platter. Sprinkle with lemon juice.

Eggs mollet

Eggs *mollet* are medium-hard-cooked eggs—cooked 6 minutes in boiling salted water, plunged into cold water, shelled, and served in many preparations, both hot and cold.

Shelling the eggs demands patience, because the egg is very fragile and must be peeled without breaking it. Give yourself time.

Like poached eggs, eggs *mollet* are kept warm in warm water until ready to be served.

Eggs mollet with espérance sauce (cold)
Oeufs mollets, sauce espérance

FOR FOUR PEOPLE

8 eggs	4 teaspoons flour
1 bunch watercress *or*	¾ cup milk
several spinach leaves	1 cup cream
3 tablespoons butter	salt and pepper

Boil the eggs 6 minutes in salted water. Plunge them immediately into cold water and shell very carefully so that they will not break.

Trim the stems from the watercress or spinach leaves and reserve a few of the leaves for decoration. Dip the leaves in boiling water for 2 minutes. Drain and chop the leaves and force them through a sieve. You will need 2½ tablespoons of the green purée.

Make a thin sauce by heating the butter and stirring in the flour. When blended, stir in the milk, cooking and stirring over a moderate heat, because the sauce must not thicken very much. Add the cream gradually, heating the sauce, but not allowing it to boil. Stir in the green purée. Season well.

Put the eggs carefully into a serving dish and cover with the sauce. Chill in the refrigerator and serve garnished with the remaining leaves.

Eggs mollet with fines herbes
Oeufs mollets aux fines herbes

FOR FOUR PEOPLE

8 eggs	2 tablespoons chopped *fines herbes*
10 tablespoons butter	(parsley, chervil, tarragon)

4 teaspoons flour
1½ cups bouillon

juice of ½ lemon
8 slices bread
salt and pepper

Boil the eggs in salted water for 6 minutes. Plunge immediately into cold water and shell very carefully. Put them in warm water while making the sauce.

Heat 5 tablespoons of butter in a saucepan and stir in the flour. Stirring with a wooden spoon, add the bouillon. When well mixed, add salt, pepper, and the chopped herbs, which have been finely minced or ground through a *moulinette.* Add 2 tablespoons more of the butter and cook very gently for 30 minutes. The sauce should not separate.

Remove from the heat and whisk in the rest of the butter. Add the juice of ½ lemon and taste for seasoning.

Meanwhile, prepare the croutons, which may be toasted and buttered or dried in the oven. Place the croutons on a heated serving platter. Put an egg on each one and cover with the sauce. Serve very hot.

Eggs mollet à la provençale or eggs mollet saint tropez
Oeufs mollets à la provençale ou oeufs saint tropez

FOR FOUR PEOPLE

Sauce:
2 ounces pork fat
4 teaspoons olive oil
1 onion
1½ pounds (5-6) tomatoes

Eggs Mollet:
1 loaf unsliced bread
7 tablespoons butter
9 eggs
2 teaspoons chopped parsley
salt and pepper

Sauce: Grind the pork fat through a meat grinder or a *moulinette* and heat it with the oil in a small skillet. (If necessary, use salt pork in the same way, but be careful not to add salt to the sauce.—*Ed.*) Grind the onion or chop it very fine and cook in the hot fat until golden.

Dip the tomatoes in boiling water and slip off their skins. Cut the tomatoes into large wedges and add them to the onion. Cook uncovered over a moderate heat for 30 minutes.

Eggs mollet: Meanwhile, cut the bread into ¾ inch slices and trim the crusts. Take out a little of the center from one side to make nests for the eggs. Fry the bread in butter until golden brown on both sides. Place them on a platter and keep warm.

At the same time, boil the eggs in salted water for 6 minutes. Remove 8 of them and plunge them into cold water. Peel very carefully. Continue cooking the remaining egg for 7 minutes longer. Chop the egg very fine or grind through a *moulinette* and mix with the chopped parsley.

Season the sauce to taste and force it through a sieve.

Put an egg on each crouton, cover with the sauce, and garnish with the egg and parsley mixture.

Eggs mollet à la russe (cold)
Oeufs mollets à la russe (froids)

FOR SIX PEOPLE

12 eggs	3 tomatoes
1½ pounds small green beans	1 sprig tarragon
½ cup Vinaigrette Sauce (page 29)	salt

Boil the eggs 6 minutes in salted water. Plunge them immediately into cold water and peel very carefully.

Trim the beans. Wash them and cook in boiling salted water for 20 minutes in an uncovered pan. Rinse quickly in cold water. Drain well and chop in small pieces. Season with half the vinaigrette.

Dip the tomatoes in boiling water and slip off the skins. Slice them and put them in a dish. Spoon the rest of the vinaigrette over them.

Spread the beans in a serving platter. Arrange the eggs on the beans and cover each one with a slice of tomato. Garnish the tomatoes with 2 crossed tarragon leaves. Serve very cold.

Scrambled eggs

Scrambled eggs * Oeufs brouillés

FOR FOUR PEOPLE

12 eggs   salt and pepper
3 tablespoons butter

My method of scrambling eggs is to cook them in a *bain-marie,* which is similar to the American double boiler. I do not add the butter until the end of the cooking. This gives the eggs their full flavor.

In my opinion, one must allow 3 eggs per person for ungarnished scrambled eggs. Break them into a heavy saucepan or top of a double boiler and beat them with a wire whisk until the yolks and whites are thoroughly blended and season with salt and pepper. Put the saucepan in a pan of hot water (the *bain-marie*) and beat the mixture with the whisk, paying especial attention to the bottom and sides where, obviously, the cooking is faster.

As soon as the eggs begin to coagulate, add the butter—little by little—without stopping the beating. When the eggs have a creamy consistency, pour them quickly into a heated serving platter so that the heat from the saucepan itself does not continue to cook the eggs.

If you have let your eggs cook too much, remove the pan from the heat and beat in a raw egg quickly.

If you want to mix in grated Gruyère cheese or heavy cream, do it while the eggs are still in the *bain-marie* (this despite certain theories about cooking cream).

If you make a scrambled egg tart, be sure that the crust is very hot when you pour in the scrambled eggs and quickly sprinkle the top with 1 or 2 slices of ham, chopped fine or passed through a *moulinette.* This makes a very pretty entrée.

Scrambled eggs in individual tartlets make an equally pretty entrée with the addition of cooked mushrooms, chopped truffles, puréed tomatoes or little green peas.

I often stuff crepes with scrambled eggs. They are delicious.

Croutons fried in butter are only served with scrambled eggs when they are served without a pastry crust on a platter.

Scrambled eggs à la blanchet
Oeufs brouillés à la blanchet

FOR FOUR PEOPLE

Tart Pastry I or II (page 646)
2½ tablespoons caviar
2½ tablespoons milk

8 eggs
juice of 1 lemon
pepper

Line 8 little tart tins with the pastry. Prick well with a fork so that the pastry will not rise. Bake 12 minutes at 450° F. Remove from the tins and keep warm.

Stir the caviar and milk together. Beat the eggs in a bowl until blended. Season with pepper and add the caviar mixture and a little lemon juice. Scramble the eggs in a double boiler. Stir with a wooden spoon until the eggs are cooked but still creamy. Pour the mixture into the warm tarts and serve immediately.

Scrambled eggs cinzano
Oeufs brouillés au cinzano

FOR FOUR PEOPLE

10 eggs
4 tablespoons butter
¼ pound cooked, shelled shrimp

½ cup dry Cinzano
salt and pepper

Break the eggs into a bowl and beat them with a whisk or fork until the yolks and whites are blended. Cook the eggs in a double boiler, stirring constantly, especially around the edges, so that the eggs will cook evenly. When the eggs begin to have a creamy consistency, add the butter and the shrimp, which, if they have been salted, should be freshened in cold water.

Remove the pan from the heat and pour in the Cinzano. Stir, taste for seasoning, adding salt and pepper as desired.

Scrambled eggs in cream
Oeufs brouillés à la crème

FOR SIX PEOPLE

14 eggs
3 tablespoons butter

⅔ cup heavy cream
salt and pepper

Beat the eggs with salt and pepper until the yolks and whites are blended. Cook in a double boiler, stirring constantly and especially around the edges to ensure even cooking. When the eggs begin to have a creamy consistency, add the butter in small bits, still stirring constantly.

Put the cooked eggs on a warm platter and pour the heavy cream in the center of them.

Scrambled eggs with croutons
Oeufs brouillés aux croûtons

FOR FOUR PEOPLE

4 thick slices white bread
6 tablespoons butter

12 eggs
salt and pepper

Trim the crusts from the bread and cut them into cubes. Heat 3 tablespoons of butter in a skillet and cook them gently, stirring so that they will brown lightly on all sides.

Make the scrambled eggs according to the recipe given above. Serve the croutons on a separate, small plate so that they won't be softened by the eggs.

Scrambled egg tarts
Croustades aux oeufs brouillés

FOR FOUR PEOPLE

Flaky Pastry (page 643)
8 eggs

3 tablespoons butter
salt and pepper

Line 8 individual tartlet pans or 1 large pie tin with pastry and prick the pastry well with a fork so that it will not rise. Bake 15 minutes at 425° F. Remove the tarts from the pans and keep warm.

Make the scrambled eggs as in the preceding recipes. Pour them into the tartlets and serve immediately.

N.B. For a delicious entrée, scatter finely shredded ham over the scrambled eggs or add cooked mushrooms, chopped truffles, cooked peas, or tomato sauce.

Scrambled eggs with tomato
Oeufs brouillés aux tomates

FOR FOUR PEOPLE

12 eggs
2 tablespoons tomato paste

3 tablespoons butter
salt and pepper

Break the eggs into a bowl and mix well with the tomato paste, salt, and pepper. Scramble the eggs as usual.

Poached eggs

Poached eggs are cooked in simmering water to which white vinegar and salt are added.

Never poach more than two eggs at a time in a saucepan.

When the eggs are cooked, transfer them with a slotted spatula to a clean towel and trim the whites with scissors to give them an even edge.

If not served immediately, keep the eggs in a pan of warm water.

Poached eggs with anchovy
Oeufs pochés au beurre d'anchois

FOR FOUR PEOPLE

8 slices white bread
5 tablespoons butter
8 eggs
4 tablespoons white vinegar

anchovy paste
1 lemon
salt

Fry the bread in butter on both sides.

Poach the eggs for 3 minutes in simmering water to which both salt and the vinegar have been added. Drain the eggs on a clean towel.

Spread each hot slice of bread with anchovy paste. Place the bread on a heated platter. Put a poached egg on each one, garnished with a thin slice of peeled lemon on top of the egg.

Poached eggs in aspic * Oeufs en gelée

FOR FOUR PEOPLE

1 meaty veal knuckle
1 calf's foot*
9 cups cold water
3 carrots
1 stalk celery
2 leeks

2 teaspoons cognac
8 eggs
4 tablespoons white vinegar
lettuce leaves
tarragon leaves
salt and pepper

*If a calf's foot is not available, use a pig's foot.—*Ed.*

In a deep pan, put the veal knuckle, sawed in several pieces, the calf's foot, the cold water, and 1 teaspoon of salt. Bring to a boil very slowly, skimming off the matter that floats to the top.

Wash the vegetables and cut them into pieces. When the liquid boils, add the vegetables and simmer gently for 4 hours.

Remove the meat bones from the bouillon and pour it through a strainer lined with a damp dish towel. Let the bouillon cool completely in the refrigerator. When it has jelled, skim off the fat that will have come to the surface.

Warm the jelly over a low heat; add the cognac and season to taste. Boil gently for 5 minutes. Let the bouillon cool to lukewarm.

Poach the eggs for 2½ minutes in simmering water to which a little salt and vinegar have been added. Transfer them to a clean dish towel with a skimmer and drain well. Put the eggs into individual molds or pyrex cups. Fill the molds with the lukewarm bouillon. Chill in the refrigerator for several hours.

Just before serving, unmold the eggs onto lettuce leaves and decorate with tarragon leaves.

Poached eggs à la crème aurore
Oeufs pochés à la crème aurore

FOR TWO PEOPLE

4 eggs	1 cup milk
4 tablespoons white vinegar	¾ cup heavy cream
2 tablespoons butter	4 teaspoons tomato purée
1 tablespoon flour	salt and pepper

Poach the eggs one by one in a small saucepan of water to which a little salt and vinegar have been added. Transfer them to a towel to dry.

Heat the butter and stir in the flour. When blended, add the milk and cook, stirring constantly, until the sauce begins to thicken. Season with salt and pepper and cool. Add the cream. Stir in 3 tablespoons of the tomato purée.

Put the eggs on a serving platter. Cover with the sauce and decorate the top of each one with a little tomato purée. Serve very cold.

Eggs bernis, béarnaise sauce
Oeufs bernis, sauce béarnaise

FOR FOUR PEOPLE

4 large artichokes	Béarnaise Sauce (page 6)
½ pound mushrooms	8 eggs

1 can truffle peelings
5 tablespoons butter

4 tablespoons white vinegar
salt and pepper

Cook the artichokes in boiling salted water. They are done when an outside leaf will tear off easily.

Drain the artichokes and remove the leaves and the choke. Save the leaves to eat as an hors d'oeuvre at another meal.

Cut the artichoke bottoms in small dice.

Trim and wash the mushrooms. Chop them coarsely.

Mix the mushrooms, the artichokes, and the truffles. Heat the butter in a skillet and sauté the mixture over a moderate heat. Season with salt and pepper.

Make a double recipe of the béarnaise sauce.

Poach the eggs in water to which a little salt and the vinegar have been added.

Spread the mushroom mixture on a heated platter. Arrange the eggs on top and cover with béarnaise. Serve immediately.

Curried poached eggs * Oeufs pochés au cari

FOR SIX PEOPLE

4 tablespoons seedless raisins
4 tablespoons butter
2½ tablespoons flour
3 tablespoons curry powder

2 cups milk
12 eggs
4 tablespoons white vinegar
salt and pepper

Soak the raisins in cold water for several hours.

Heat the butter and stir in the flour and curry powder. When well blended, stir in the milk and keep stirring until the sauce begins to thicken. Season with salt and pepper.

Poach the eggs in water to which the vinegar and salt have been added. Remove them from the water with a skimmer and drain them on a clean towel.

Put the eggs on a warm serving platter. Cover with the sauce and sprinkle with the raisins.

Poached eggs forestière * Oeufs pochés forestière

FOR FIVE PEOPLE

10 eggs
4 tablespoons white vinegar
10 large mushrooms
juice of 1 lemon
3 cups Béchamel Sauce (page 6)

¾ cup heavy cream
10 tarragon leaves, chopped
paprika
salt and pepper

Poach the eggs in simmering water to which the white vinegar and a little salt have been added. Transfer the eggs with a skimmer to a dry towel to drain.

Trim, cap, and wash the mushrooms. Poach the caps only for 3 minutes in boiling water to which the juice of a lemon has been added.

Make the béchamel. Add the cream and chopped tarragon leaves.

Place the caps on a warm platter. Put an egg in each one. Cover with the sauce and sprinkle with paprika.

Poached eggs à la grecque (cold)
Oeufs pochés à la grecque

FOR FOUR PEOPLE

2 pounds leeks	1 tablespoon tomato paste
12 small onions	½ teaspoon peppercorns
½ cup dry white wine	½ teaspoon paprika
½ cup olive oil	8 eggs
2 bay leaves	4 tablespoons white vinegar
½ cup water or bouillon	salt

Remove all the green part of the leeks. Cut the white part in ¾-inch pieces and boil them in salted water for 5 minutes. Drain well.

Peel the onions and put them, the leeks, the wine, oil, bay leaves, water or bouillon, tomato paste, peppercorns, and salt in a saucepan. Cook uncovered over a moderate heat for 1 hour. Cool completely.

Poach the eggs 3 minutes in simmering water to which the vinegar and salt have been added. Transfer to a clean towel with a skimmer. Trim the egg whites even with kitchen scissors.

Put the leeks in their sauce on a serving platter and cover with the cold eggs. Put the dish in the refrigerator and serve very cold.

Poached eggs with green sauce
Oeufs pochés sauce verte

FOR FOUR PEOPLE

10 eggs	1 cup oil
4 tablespoons white vinegar	onion, shallots, sorrel, tarragon,
2 teaspoons wine vinegar	watercress, parsley, chervil
1 teaspoon French mustard	salt and pepper

Poach 8 of the eggs 3 minutes in simmering water to which the white vinegar and some salt have been added. Transfer to a towel to drain and cool. Trim the whites evenly with scissors.

Hard-cook one of the remaining eggs in boiling salted water for 15 minutes. Plunge into cold water. Remove the yolk and put it, together with the raw yolk of the last remaining egg, into a small bowl. Pound the egg yolks with a teaspoon of wine vinegar and a teaspoon of mustard. Add the oil drop by drop as if you were making mayonnaise, whisking it with a small whip. When it thickens, add the oil in a thin stream. Season well with salt and pepper.

Chop the vegetables and herbs very fine. You should have about a cupful in all. Save out a little of the chopped herbs and force the rest through a food mill. Combine this with the sauce and add another teaspoon of wine vinegar.

Spread the sauce in a serving dish and put the poached eggs on top. Sprinkle with chopped herbs.

*Poached eggs maintenon * Oeufs pochés maintenon*

FOR EIGHT PEOPLE

Flaky Pastry (page 643)
16 eggs
4 tablespoons white vinegar
1 pound mushrooms
4 tablespoons butter

1½ cups Hollandaise Sauce (page 10)
juice of ½ lemon
1 cup Béchamel Sauce (page 6)
salt and pepper

Allow time for making the pastry and letting it rest. Roll it out on a floured surface and cut into large circles with a large cookie cutter or with the rim of a drinking glass. Line 16 small individual tartlet pans (or shallow muffin tins— *Ed.*) with the pastry. Prick them well with a fork to keep them from rising. Bake 10 minutes in a 400° F. oven. Remove from the pans and keep warm.

Before you make the rest of the recipe, poach the eggs, two at a time, in simmering water to which the vinegar and salt have been added. Poach the eggs 3 minutes and transfer them to a clean towel with a skimmer to drain. Trim the whites evenly with scissors.

Trim, wash, and chop the mushrooms. Sauté them in butter until the moisture disappears.

Make the béchamel and stir in the mushrooms. Season with salt and pepper. Let the mixture boil for just a moment.

Make the hollandaise and season with the juice of ½ lemon.

Spoon the mushroom sauce into each tartlet. Cover with a poached egg and spoon hollandaise over each egg. Serve immediately.

*Poached eggs montargis * Oeufs pochés montargis*

FOR FOUR PEOPLE

3 thin slices cooked ham

¾ cup grated Gruyère cheese

1½ cups cold cooked chicken or veal
¼ pound mushrooms
1½ cups thick Béchamel Sauce
   (page 6)

8 eggs
4 tablespoons white vinegar
salt and pepper

Slice the meats into thin strips, saving out a little of the ham for decoration.

Trim and wash the mushrooms. Boil them in a little salt water for 3 minutes. Drain. Cut in slices.

Make the béchamel. Mix in ¼ cup grated cheese, the meats, and the mushrooms. Pile this in a dome shape in the center of a heatproof serving dish. Sprinkle with the rest of the cheese and brown in the oven.

Poach the eggs, two at a time, in simmering water to which the vinegar and some salt have been added. Transfer them to a clean towel to drain and trim the whites evenly with scissors. Place the eggs around the dome and decorate each one with a strip of ham.

Poached eggs à la niçoise (cold)
Oeufs pochés niçoise

FOR FOUR PEOPLE

8 eggs
4 tablespoons white vinegar
1½ cups Mayonnaise (page 14)
1 lemon

4 teaspoons chopped chives
4 large tomatoes
4 teaspoons chopped chervil or parsley
salt and pepper

Poach the eggs 3 minutes in simmering water to which the vinegar and some salt have been added. Transfer them to a clean towel to drain and trim the whites with scissors when the eggs are cold.

Make the mayonnaise and season highly with lemon juice, salt, and pepper. Mix in the chopped chives.

Dip the tomatoes in boiling water for a moment and slip off the skins. Cut off the ends and then cut each tomato in two crosswise.

On a large serving platter place the 8 thick slices of tomato. Top each one with a poached egg. Cover with mayonnaise and sprinkle with chopped chervil or parsley. Serve very cold.

Saffron poached eggs with almonds
Oeufs pochés au safran aux amandes

FOR FOUR PEOPLE

Rice:
6 tablespoons oil

3 tablespoons flour
1½ cups milk

¾ cup rice
1 tablespoon turmeric *or*
pinch of saffron
½ cup ground almonds

Sauce:
3 tablespoons butter

4 teaspoons turmeric *or*
large pinch of saffron

Eggs:
8 eggs
4 tablespoons white vinegar
salt and pepper

Warm the oil in a deep skillet and stir in the rice. Cook 3 minutes, stirring constantly. Combine 1½ cups boiling water and turmeric or saffron and pour into the skillet. Season with salt and pepper. Reduce the heat, cover, and cook very slowly for 20 minutes or until the rice is just tender. Toast the ground almonds by putting them in a hot skillet and stirring until lightly browned. Add these to the cooked rice.

Meanwhile, make the sauce: Heat the butter and stir in the flour until blended; add the milk and turmeric or saffron. Stir until the mixture thickens. Season with salt and pepper.

Poach the eggs 3 minutes in simmering water to which the vinegar and some salt have been added. Transfer with a skimmer to a towel to drain.

Heap the rice on a serving platter. Surround with the eggs and pour the sauce over the eggs. Serve immediately.

Wilfrid poached eggs * Oeufs pochés wilfrid

FOR FOUR PEOPLE

Flaky Pastry (page 643)
Béarnaise Sauce (page 6)
8 eggs

4 tablespoons white vinegar
salt

Allow time for making and resting the pastry. Using about ⅔ of the recipe, roll out the pastry very thin into a long rectangle. Cut the pastry into 8 5-inch squares. Brush the edges with water.

Meanwhile, make the béarnaise and poach the eggs in simmering water to which the vinegar and some salt have been added. Transfer the eggs with a skimmer to a towel to drain. Trim the whites evenly.

Place an egg in the center of each square. Pinch 2 opposite corners and pull them up around the eggs. Do the same with the other corners so that the egg will be completely sealed in.

Fry in deep fat (385° F.) until golden brown and pile on a platter. Serve the sauce in a separate bowl.

Poached eggs in red wine
Oeufs pochés en matelote

FOR FOUR PEOPLE

8 eggs
12 tiny onions
3 cups red Burgundy
1 lump sugar
½ bay leaf
1 sprig thyme

⅛ teaspoon allspice
¼ pound butter
4 teaspoons flour
8 slices French bread
salt and pepper

Poach the eggs in simmering wine for 3 minutes. Transfer the eggs to paper toweling to drain and put them in warm water to keep warm. Peel the onions and add them to the wine seasoned with sugar, bay leaf, thyme, allspice, salt, and pepper. Boil until the wine is reduced to half its original quantity.

Meanwhile, work 3 tablespoons of butter and the flour together with your finger tips or with the back of a spoon until well blended. Remove the bay leaf and thyme from the wine and add the butter-flour mixture in small bits to the sauce, stirring with a wooden spoon over a low heat.

Fry the bread in 5 tablespoons of the butter and place on a warm serving platter. Cover with the poached eggs and pour over the sauce. Serve on heated plates.

Shirred eggs

Shirred eggs are usually cooked in butter in individual pyrex or earthenware dishes, on top of the stove rather than in the oven. The eggs are broken into the pans as soon as the butter is melted and are cooked over a low heat. You can pour a little butter on the egg yolk at the beginning of the cooking before seasoning with salt and pepper.

It is important that the heat be watched, because too high heat will burn the whites while the yolk is still uncooked. It is good to use an asbestos pad or wire trivet to protect the dish from the flame. For eggs shirred with bacon, no butter is used. The bacon is cooked first, and the eggs are cooked in the fat rendered by the bacon. If you use a skillet instead of the individual dishes, be sure that it is very clean.

Shirred eggs and sausages * Oeufs chipolata

FOR FOUR PEOPLE

4 small link sausages
3 tablespoons butter
4 eggs

Worcestershire sauce (optional)
salt and pepper

Cook the sausages in a small skillet.

Melt the butter in a large skillet. Add the eggs, leaving space between each one and cook gently so that the under part will not cook too quickly.

Place the eggs on a warm platter. Season with salt and pepper. Put the sausages between the eggs. Add a few drops of Worcestershire, if you like.

Eggs in cream * Oeufs cocotte à la crème

FOR FOUR PEOPLE

butter
4 or 8 eggs
heavy cream

chopped tarragon
salt and pepper

Butter individual ramekins, allowing 2 teaspoons of butter for each egg. Break very fresh eggs into each ramekin, season with salt and pepper. Cover the ramekins with heavy wax paper or aluminum foil and bake 5 to 6 minutes at 350° F. If the whites have completely set, the eggs are cooked.

Meanwhile, heat the cream. Allow 1 tablespoon of cream for each egg. Spoon the cream into the ramekins, sprinkle with pepper, and garnish with chopped tarragon.

Mustard eggs in ramekins
Oeufs cocotte à la moutarde

FOR FOUR PEOPLE

2 tablespoons butter	8 tablespoons heavy cream
8 very fresh eggs	salt and pepper
8 teaspoons French mustard	

Butter individual ramekins generously and break an egg into each one. Put a teaspoon of mustard on each egg and cover with a tablespoon of cream. Season with salt and pepper.

Put the ramekins in a pan of hot water and bake 6 to 8 minutes at 350° F. Serve immediately.

Assassin's eggs * Oeufs à l'assassin

FOR TWO PEOPLE

3 tablespoons butter	2 teaspoons wine vinegar
4 very fresh eggs	salt and pepper

Heat the butter in a skillet until light brown. Break the eggs into the skillet and season with salt and pepper. When partially cooked, turn the eggs over and complete the cooking. Transfer them to a warm, nonmetal platter and pour the vinegar into the skillet. Boil for a few seconds and pour the sauce over the eggs.

Country eggs * Oeufs campagnards

FOR FOUR PEOPLE

1 pound (4-5) potatoes	8 eggs
6 tablespoons butter	⅔ cup heavy cream
¾ cup grated Gruyère cheese	salt and pepper

Peel the potatoes. Wash them well and wipe them dry. Cut into fairly thin rounds.

Heat the butter in a deep skillet and add the potatoes. Cook over a moderate heat, stirring from time to time so that the potatoes will not stick. Season with salt and pepper.

When the potatoes are cooked, transfer them to a large shallow baking dish. Sprinkle with the grated cheese and break the eggs over the potatoes, leaving a little space between each one. Cover with the cream. Sprinkle with salt and pepper and brown in a hot (425° F.) oven until the whites have set. The yolks should not be hard.

Victoria eggs * Oeufs victoria

FOR FOUR PEOPLE

¼ pound butter	3 chicken livers
4 teaspoons flour	1 small can truffle peelings
1½ cups bouillon, heated	4 thin slices cooked ham
1 tablespoon cognac	8 very fresh eggs
¼ pound mushrooms	salt and pepper

Make a sauce: Heat 3 tablespoons of butter in a saucepan and stir in the flour. When well blended, add the hot bouillon, stirring constantly. Season with the cognac, salt, and pepper. Simmer a few minutes.

Trim, wash, dry, and cut the mushrooms into small pieces. Cut the chicken livers into small pieces also. Melt 3 tablespoons of butter in a skillet and sauté the livers and mushrooms for 3 minutes. Add them to the sauce, along with the entire contents of the can of truffles. Stir well but do not continue to cook or the sauce will become too thick.

Put the rest of the butter in the bottom of a large skillet. Halve the ham slices and place them in the skillet (use two skillets, if necessary). Break an egg on each slice of ham. Cook over moderate heat until the whites have set.

Transfer the eggs on the ham with a wide spatula to a warm serving platter. Spoon the sauce, dividing it equally, over each egg. Serve hot.

Fried eggs in cream * Oeufs frits à la crème

FOR FOUR PEOPLE

8 thin slices white bread	8 eggs
3 tablespoons butter	salt and pepper
1½ cups heavy cream	

Sauté the bread in butter until lightly browned on both sides.

Heat the cream and season with salt and pepper.

Fry the eggs in deep fat (385° F.), breaking the eggs just above the fat. Break the bubbles that will form in the whites with a fork. Fry 2½ minutes, turning the eggs over with a skimmer.

Place the fried bread on a warm platter. Put an egg on each one and cover with the hot cream.

Fried eggs in pastry * Oeufs frits en pâte

FOR FOUR PEOPLE

Flaky Pastry (page 643)
8 eggs

Tomato Sauce (page 22) *or*
Mornay Sauce (page 15)

Allow time to make and rest the pastry. Prepare the sauce of your choice.

Roll out a rectangle ⅛ inch thick, 16 inches long, and 8 inches wide. Divide this into 16 square pieces. Paint the edges with water, using a pastry brush.

On half of these squares, break 8 very fresh small eggs. Cover carefully with the remaining squares, being sure not to break the yolks. Press the edges together firmly.

Fry these in deep fat (385° F.) until golden brown. Serve with tomato or mornay sauce.

Piperade * Piperade

FOR FOUR PEOPLE

4 thin slices prosciutto
  or Bayonne ham
4 tablespoons diced ham fat
1 pound (3-4) tomatoes
2 green peppers

½ cup soft breadcrumbs
milk
6 eggs
salt and pepper

Heat the ham in a skillet and put aside in a warm place.

Try out the fat in the skillet. Peel the tomatoes and cut them in pieces. Add them and the green peppers, seeded and cut into small strips, to the fat. Season with salt and pepper and simmer 20 minutes.

Soak the breadcrumbs in a little milk and squeeze them almost dry.

Beat the eggs until the yolks and whites are blended. Add the breadcrumbs and the eggs to the mixture in the skillet. Stir carefully, and when cooked remove from the heat. Stir gently even after the skillet has been removed from the heat. Place on a heated platter. Cover with the ham slices and serve immediately.

Fish

Fish

Some of the same species of fish that are found in the coastal waters of France are found in the American coastal waters of the Pacific or the Atlantic oceans, but many are not. In some cases, there are species similar enough to be cooked in the same way. We will try to be as specific as possible about the various fish, giving suggestions for substitutions for fish not readily found in American markets. More fish recipes, such as fish loaf, fish soufflé, mussel tarts, tuna omelet, and so on, will be found in the entrée and egg chapters.—*Ed.*

How to Recognize Quality and Freshness in Fish

Fresh fish has no odor other than a slight sea smell.

Fresh fish should be rigid. Never buy a soft fish or one that has lost its elasticity.

Fresh fish have shiny scales and skin.

Fresh fish sold with their heads on will have bright shiny eyes. If the eye is damaged or grayish, the fish is no longer fresh.

Other signs of fresh fish: The inside of the gills should be red and shiny. Be careful of fish dealers, who will paint with beef blood the gills of not too fresh fish. Put your finger inside the gill, and you will know immediately if this is the case.

With herring and mackerel, the gills are black.

Notice that skate has a slight odor of ammonia. This disappears during cooking.

How to Prepare Fish

Count on 6 to 7 ounces of fish per person.

To scale fish easily, dip them in boiling water for 1 or 2 seconds.

To skin fish, put a dish towel around your fingers or dip them in coarse salt so that they will not slip. Make a little incision at the neck or tail, and pull off the skin with one single motion. An eel is skinned from head to tail; any member of the flounder or sole family is skinned from tail to head.

Small fish are cleaned through the gills. Large fish are usually split up the belly, and blood and intestines are removed.

Wash sea fish in salted water. Trim them and dry well. If they are not to be cooked immediately, sprinkle lightly with salt, and wrap them in a cloth.

A court bouillon should be prepared 30 to 60 minutes in advance before cooking the fish.

To keep a fish for several hours without a refrigerator, keep it covered in the court bouillon. Drain well before using.

Wrap a large fish in a towel or piece of cheesecloth in order to be able to lift it from the kettle without hurting it.

Never cook fish in boiling liquid. It should just be allowed to simmer lightly.

When frying fish fillets, dip them in milk before rolling them in flour. They will brown better.

When opening scallop shells, place them round side down in a dry pan, and place over high heat.

General Instructions for Cooking Fish

Very Small Fish: Little fish, such as whitebait, smelts, butterfish, and so on, are best fried in deep fat. They can be lightly dredged with flour or dipped in a thin frying batter, fried in hot fat, and piled high on a platter and garnished with lemon and fried parsley.

Individual Fish: Trout, perch, mackerel, small whiting, little mullets, and so on, are served broiled, fried, cooked in a court bouillon, or roasted.

Large Fish: Large fish that will serve many people are cooked in a court bouillon, baked, or braised in bouillon or red or white wine, but they are not broiled unless they are cut in slices. They can be served with a variety of sauces.

Fish in Aspic: The fish is cooked in a court bouillon made with wine and no vinegar and slightly colored with caramel (page 579). Put the fish in a fish boiler or other kettle. Add enough court bouillon just to cover the fish and let it barely simmer, allowing 20 minutes per pound. Transfer the fish to a platter. Boil down the court bouillon until it is very concentrated. Strain it, and spoon it over the fish. Chill in the refrigerator.

How to Broil Fish:

First and always, brush the fish with oil before broiling.

The grill or broiling rack should be very hot before you put the fish on it.

If the fish were not oiled or the grill heated, the fish would stick to the grill, which is a real catastrophe.

All sliced fish or fish steaks should be marinated in oil for a moment, seasoned with lemon juice, salt, and pepper.

When the first side of the fish has been browned on the very hot grill or broiling rack, it should be turned and the heat lowered.

All the rules for broiling fish apply to every cooking device that exists: a grill over a wood fire, a gas or electric oven broiler, a charcoal broiler like the barbecue. The best broiling is done over wine twigs, the smoke of which gives a definite and delicious flavor.

You can serve broiled fish with the following sauces:

Aïoli Sauce (page 5)   Gribiche Sauce (page 10)
Anchovy Butter Sauce (page 5)   Mustard Sauce (page 16)
Melted Butter Sauce (page 14)   Red Pepper and Garlic Sauce (page 20)
Maître d'Hôtel Butter (page 12)   Rémoulade Sauce (page 20)

Deep-Fat Fried Fish: Roll tiny fish or slices in flour or dip them in frying batter. Deep-fat fry in hot oil, drain, sprinkle with salt, and serve with fried parsley and lemon slices.

Court bouillon

Court bouillon is a prepared liquid usually composed of water, wine, or vinegar, butter, shallot, onions, sometimes carrots, thyme, bay leaf, parsley, salt, pepper, and garlic, if desired. The court bouillon is boiled for at least ½ hour before the fish is added and cooked over a low heat. Fish cooked in this manner is usually served with a tomato, mustard, or maître d'hôtel sauce. If the fish is rather tasteless, add celery and pepper to the court bouillon.

Court bouillon I (with vinegar)
Court bouillon au vinaigre

2 quarts water   2 shallots
⅔ cup vinegar   *bouquet garni* (thyme, bay leaf, parsley)
1 onion, sliced thin   salt

Combine the ingredients and simmer 30 minutes. Strain before adding the fish.

Court bouillon II (with white wine)
Court bouillon au vin blanc

For poaching fish

2-3 onions   *bouquet garni* (thyme, bay leaf, parsley)
1 quart white wine   2 teaspoons salt
1 quart water   ½ teaspoon peppercorns

Peel the onions and slice them thin. Put everything in a large pan and cook for 35 minutes. Strain before using.

Court bouillon III (with red wine)
Court bouillon au vin rouge

For fish stew

1 quart red wine	1 bay leaf
1 quart water	few sprigs parsley
1 large carrot	1 small stalk celery
1 large onion	2 teaspoons salt (preferably coarse)
1 sprig thyme	1 teaspoon peppercorns

Put everything except the peppercorns in a large pan and boil 40 minutes. Then 5 minutes before the end of cooking, add the peppercorns. Strain before using.

In this court bouillon you can cook large trouts, carps, and so on, besides using it for fish in wine sauce.

Court bouillon IV (à la nantaise)
Court bouillon à la nantaise

For finnan haddie (smoked haddock)

1 quart water	*bouquet garni* (thyme, bay leaf, parsley)
1 quart milk	½ teaspoon peppercorns

Put everything in a fish boiler or other kettle with the finnan haddie. Bring the liquid to a boil over a moderate heat. When it boils, remove from the heat, because the haddock will be cooked. Serve the haddock with melted butter and garnish with lemon slices.

Court bouillon V (au bleu)
Court bouillon au bleu

For trout

For 2 quarts:	*bouquet garni* (thyme, bay leaf)
2-3 carrots	1 large sprig parsley
3 large onions	2½ teaspoons salt, preferably coarse
2 quarts water	½ teaspoon peppercorns
1 cup vinegar	

Peel the carrots and onions and slice them. Place all the ingredients in a large pan except for the peppercorns. Boil 45 minutes, adding the peppercorns 10 minutes before the end of cooking. Strain the court bouillon. Trout cooked this way are thrown into the simmering court bouillon immediately after being killed and cleaned. They are cooked 5 minutes without actually boiling, which would break the fish into pieces. Serve immediately with melted butter and lemon slices.

Court bouillon VI * Court bouillon pour crustacés

For shellfish

For 2¾ quarts water:
3-4 carrots
2-3 onions
bouquet garni (thyme, bay leaf)

large sprig parsley
3 teaspoons salt, preferably coarse
½ teaspoon peppercorns

Peel the carrots and onions and cut them in thin slices. Put everything except the peppercorns in a large pan and cook covered for 1 hour over a moderate heat. Add the pepper 10 minutes before the end of cooking. Strain before using.

Salt-water fish

Florentine brill * Barbue florentine

FOR EIGHT PEOPLE

4-pound brill (or substitute) *
1 quart milk, scalded
bouquet garni (thyme, bay leaf, parsley)
3 pounds spinach
10 tablespoons butter

2 cups Béchamel Sauce (page 6)
¾ cup heavy cream
1¼ cups grated Gruyère cheese
salt and pepper

Clean and wash the fish and put it in a cold court bouillon made of scalded and cooled milk and an equal amount of water, *bouquet garni,* salt, and pepper. Bring to a boil over a moderate heat, and when the liquid boils, remove the skin and bones and detach the fillets.

Trim and wash the spinach and boil in salted water just until tender. Drain thoroughly, pressing out the excess water between the palms of your hands. Heat in a saucepan with the butter, and when well mixed, spread in the bottom of a heatproof serving dish.

Arrange the fish on the spinach and cover with a sauce composed of the béchamel, the cream, and the grated cheese. Season with salt and pepper and brown 10 minutes at 400° F.

*Brill does not exist in American coastal waters, but halibut and turbot make excellent substitutes. —Ed.

Breaded cod * Cabillaud pané

FOR FOUR PEOPLE

4 thin cod steaks	4 hard-cooked eggs
2½ tablespoons flour	4 lemon slices
1 egg, beaten slightly	4 rolled anchovies
½ cup fine breadcrumbs	2 tablespoons capers
¾ cup oil	salt and pepper

Ask your fish dealer to cut the steaks.

Put the flour, beaten egg, and breadcrumbs in different plates and dip the steaks first in flour, then in egg, and finally in breadcrumbs. Heat the oil in a skillet and cook the fish in the oil, turning the steaks twice and moving them a little so that they will not stick. Season with salt and pepper.

When the fish is cooked and well browned on both sides, put them on a heated platter. Decorate the platter with quarters of hard-cooked eggs and lemon slices topped with anchovy rolls and capers. Serve immediately.

Cod fillets with grapefruit
Filets de cabillaud aux pamplemousses

FOR SIX PEOPLE

6 large cod fillets	1 grapefruit
flour	2 hard-cooked eggs
7 tablespoons butter	1½ tablespoons chopped parsley
¼ cup heavy cream	salt and pepper
4 tablespoons oil	

Wipe the cod fillets well and dredge them lightly with flour. Heat half the butter and the oil in a skillet and sauté the fillets over a moderately low heat 12 to 15 minutes or until they are nicely browned on both sides.

At the same time, heat the rest of the butter in a saucepan. Add the cream, the juice of ½ grapefruit, and the eggs crushed fine with a fork. Season with salt and pepper and keep warm, but do not allow the sauce to boil.

Put the fish on a heated platter and pour over the sauce. Sprinkle with chopped parsley.

Garnish with half slices of grapefruit.

Cod loaf * Pain de cabillaud

FOR SIX PEOPLE

3 cups dry white wine	3 tablespoons soft breadcrumbs

1 onion

¾ cup milk

2 carrots

3 eggs

bouquet garni (thyme, bay leaf, parsley) 4 teaspoons flour

½ teaspoon peppercorns

1 egg yolk

1½ pounds cod fillets

½ cup heavy cream

7 tablespoons butter

juice of ½ lemon

nutmeg

salt and pepper

In a deep pan put the wine and an equal amount of water. Add the onion and the carrots, cut in slices, the *bouquet garni,* salt, and peppercorns. Cook over a moderate heat for 30 minutes and cool.

Put the fillets in the cold court bouillon. Bring to a boil and remove the fillets. Once the boiling point is reached, the fish is cooked. Drain and cool.

Pound and rub the fish in a mortar or wooden bowl. Add 5 tablespoons of soft butter, nutmeg, and breadcrumbs that have been soaked in milk and squeezed dry. Pound until well blended and force through a sieve. Add the eggs and pound again in the bowl or mortar until the paste is smooth. Butter a charlotte mold or other straight-sided baking dish. Fill with the fish mixture and place in a pan of hot water. Bake at 350° F. Cover with the sauce, made while the loaf is baking.

Heat 2 tablespoons of butter in a saucepan and stir in the flour with a wooden spoon. Add about a cupful of the court bouillon, stirring until you have a sauce the consistency of light cream. Simmer a few minutes and season with salt and pepper. Remove from the heat and stir in a well-blended mixture of egg yolk, cream, and lemon juice. This can be made with haddock, hake, or any other white fish.

Cod in flaky pastry ∗ *Cabillaud en pâte*

FOR SIX PEOPLE

Flaky Pastry (page 643)

2½ tablespoons curry powder

1½ pounds cod fillets

1 egg yolk

2 cups white wine

juice of ½ lemon

¼ cup milk

salt and pepper

1 cup heavy cream

Time the making of the pastry so that it will be ready when you want it. You will use about ⅓ of the pastry.

Poach the fish in white wine for 10 minutes. Drain and force it through a grinder or a *moulinette.* Put the fish in a saucepan with the milk and 2½ tablespoons of heavy cream and add the curry powder, salt, and pepper. Mix well and cool. The mixture should have the consistency of a thick purée.

Roll out the pastry very thin and divide into 2 rectangles of equal size and shape. Put the mixture on one of the rectangles, leaving a ½-inch border all around. Moisten the border with water. Cover with the other rectangle and press the edges together firmly. Paint with egg yolk, mixed with a teaspoon of water, and make little decorative lines on the surface with a sharp-pointed knife. Bake 20 minutes at 400° F. Serve with the rest of the cream, warmed and seasoned with lemon juice.

Sautéed cod with tomatoes
Cabillaud sauté aux tomates

FOR FOUR PEOPLE

1 pound cod	½ pound thin noodles
4 tablespoons curry powder	2 pounds tomatoes
flour	salt and pepper
7 ounces (14 tablespoons) butter	

Cut the cod in pieces approximately 1¼ inches square. Sprinkle with some of the curry powder and dip in flour. Sauté gently in half the butter until golden brown on all sides. Season with salt.

Cook the noodles for 2 minutes in a large pan of boiling salted water to which the rest of the curry powder has been added. Drain them quickly and lift up the noodles with a fork so that they will not stick.

At the same time, cook the tomatoes, peeled, seeded, and cut in pieces, in the rest of the butter until they have the consistency of a purée. Season with salt and pepper.

Make a ring of the noodles and put the fish in the center. Pour the cooking butter over the fish and season with salt. Edge the platter with the tomatoes. Serve very hot.

Broiled finnan haddie * Haddock grillé

FOR TWO PEOPLE

½ pound finnan haddie	1 teaspoon chopped tarragon
7 tablespoons butter	juice of ½ lemon
1 tablespoon chopped parsley	salt and pepper

Preheat the broiling pan and rack.

Melt the butter but do not let it brown.

Place the fish on the dry, heated broiling rack and broil under a medium heat, allowing 5 minutes to each side. Transfer the fish to a heated platter.

Reheat the butter still without letting it brown. Add the chopped parsley, juice of ½ lemon, tarragon, salt, and pepper and pour it over the fish. Serve with steamed or boiled potatoes.

Cold finnan haddie in cream
Haddock froid à la crème

FOR FOUR PEOPLE

1½ pounds finnan haddie
1 cup heavy cream
lemon juice

1 sprig tarragon, chopped
salt and pepper

Poach the finnan haddie either in water or milk for 15 to 18 minutes. It is best to place the fish flat in a pan. When it is cooked, drain it and cool, covered with a moist towel so that the fish will not dry out.

Put it on a serving platter. Cover with a sauce made by gradually adding lemon juice to the cream. Be guided by your taste. Season with salt and pepper. Chill thoroughly in the refrigerator. Serve with a cold rice or potato salad.

Finnan haddie in white wine
Haddock au vin blanc

FOR FOUR PEOPLE

10 small onions
¼ pound mushrooms
1¾ pounds finnan haddie
1 small sprig thyme
2 bay leaves
1 cup dry white wine

4 teaspoons fine breadcrumbs
3 tablespoons butter
1 cup heavy cream
juice of ½ lemon
pepper

Peel the onions and parboil them for 15 minutes in salted water.

Trim, wash, and slice the mushrooms quite thin.

Butter a shallow baking dish. Put in the finnan haddie, the onions and mushrooms, the thyme and bay leaves. Add the white wine and a pinch of pepper. Sprinkle with breadcrumbs and dot with butter.

Bake 15 minutes in a 350° F. oven, basting from time to time.

Heat the cream and season with the juice of ½ lemon.

Serve the fish on a heated platter and the cream in a separate bowl.

Finnan haddie with egg sauce
Haddock, sauce aux oeufs

FOR FOUR PEOPLE

1 pound finnan haddie

juice of 1 lemon

2 hard-cooked eggs

7 tablespoons butter

1 teaspoon chopped parsley

salt

Take out the large bone from the finnan haddie. Put the fish in a shallow heatproof dish with just enough water to cover. Bring to a boil and cook 3 minutes after it reaches the boiling point.

Crush the eggs with a fork.

Melt the butter and add the eggs along with the juice of 1 lemon, a little salt, and the parsley.

Place the fish on a heated serving platter.

Serve the sauce in a separate bowl.

Raw smoked finnan haddie * Haddock fumé cru

FOR FIVE PEOPLE

1 thick piece finnan haddie
 (approximately 1 pound)
2 lemons

toast

sweet butter

Using a very sharp knife, cut the fish as thin as possible, as you would for smoked salmon. Sprinkle with lemon juice.

Serve on a platter, accompanied by toast and fresh butter.

Hake à l'indienne * Colin à l'indienne

FOR FIVE PEOPLE

5 hake steaks*

5 tablespoons oil

2 onions, chopped fine

1 clove garlic, minced

1 tablespoon chopped parsley

1 cup dry white wine

2½ tablespoons curry powder

thyme

saffron

3 tablespoons butter

¾ cup heavy cream

juice of 1 lemon

salt and pepper

Order the steaks cut ¾ inch thick.

Heat the oil in a skillet and sauté the onions and garlic until transparent. Spread them in a heatproof serving dish. Sprinkle with the chopped parsley and place the fish steaks on the vegetables.

Mix the wine with the curry powder and a pinch each of thyme and saffron. Pour the combination over the fish and dot each fish steak with a piece of

*Where hake is not available, this recipe can be made with haddock or young cod (scrod).—*Ed.*

butter. Bake 10 minutes at 400° F. Add the cream, sprinkle with salt and pepper, and continue cooking 10 minutes longer. Serve sprinkled with lemon juice and accompany with boiled rice.

Hake à la niçoise * Colin à la niçoise

FOR SIX PEOPLE

6 hake steaks
flour
¾ cup olive oil
1 pound (3-4 medium) tomatoes
12 black olives (Greek or Italian)
2 tablespoons anchovy paste

1 clove garlic, minced
2 tablespoons capers
1 tablespoon chopped tarragon
3 lemons
1 can rolled anchovy fillets
salt and pepper

Order the steaks cut approximately ¾ inch thick. Coat the steaks lightly with flour.

Heat half the oil in a skillet, and when it bubbles, put in the fish. Do not keep the heat too high, because it will harden the fish. Allow 6 to 8 minutes for cooking, turning the steaks once or twice.

Dip the tomatoes in boiling water and slip off their skins. Cut them in pieces, removing the seeds. Cook them in the rest of the oil in another skillet. When they are soft, add the pitted black olives, anchovy paste, garlic, capers, and tarragon. Season with salt and pepper and mix well. Simmer a few moments.

Place the very hot fish steaks on a heated serving platter. Surround with the tomato mixture and decorate the platter by alternating slices of peeled lemon with rolled anchovy fillets.

Fresh broiled herring with mustard
Harengs grillés à la moutarde

FOR FOUR PEOPLE

8 herring
French mustard
dry breadcrumbs

oil
salt and pepper

Clean and wash the herring and wipe them very dry. Spread them with a light coating of mustard and powder them with dry breadcrumbs. Brush them with oil.

Preheat the broiling rack. Place the fish on the hot unoiled rack and broil 6 minutes on each side.

Serve very hot, accompanied with mustard and steamed or boiled potatoes.

Herring in white wine * Harengs au vin blanc

FOR FOUR PEOPLE

4 large or 8 small herring
flour
7 tablespoons butter

¾ cup dry white wine, heated
1 tablespoon chopped parsley
salt and pepper

Clean, wash, and dry the fish. Cut them into pieces and dredge them lightly in flour.

Heat half the butter in a pan and sauté the fish lightly on all sides. Add the hot wine, the balance of the butter, the salt, and the pepper. Cook for 10 minutes over a low heat.

Put the fish in a serving dish and sprinkle liberally with chopped parsley. Serve with steamed or boiled potatoes or boiled rice.

Broiled mackerel * Maquereaux grillés

FOR FOUR PEOPLE

4 1-pound mackerel
1½ tablespoons oil
7 tablespoons butter

2 lemons
1 tablespoon chopped parsley
salt and pepper

Clean the mackerel, cutting off their heads. Wash them and slit them down the front so that they will open flat. Remove the backbone and as many of the little bones as possible. Using a pastry brush, paint each fish with oil.

Place on a well-heated broiling rack and broil 5 minutes on each side. Season with salt and pepper.

Place the fish on a heated serving platter. Serve with a separate bowl of hot melted butter seasoned with the juice of a lemon and chopped parsley. Decorate the platter with lemon slices.

Mackerel à la boulonnaise
Maquereaux à la boulonnaise

FOR FOUR PEOPLE

Court Bouillon I (page 163)
2 good-sized mackerel
2 quarts mussels
Mayonnaise (page 14)

lemon
parsley
catsup

Prepare the court bouillon.

Clean and wash the mackerel. Cut off the heads and tails and cut the fish in pieces. Cook in the court bouillon over a low heat. When the flesh is cooked, re-move it from the liquid.* Drain and cool.

Scrape and wash the mussels and place them in a pan over high heat. When they open, they are cooked. Remove most of the mussels from their shells, saving a few in their shells for decoration. Cool.

Mix with a little mayonnaise.

Arrange the mackerel slices on a serving platter, separating them with little piles of mussels. Decorate the platter with the mussels in the shells, lemon slices, and sprigs of parsley. Serve the rest of the mayonnaise mixed with a little catsup in a separate bowl.

Mackerel fillets with onions
Filets de maquereaux sur lit d'oignons

FOR FOUR PEOPLE

Court Bouillon II (page 163)
4 1¼-pound mackerel
1½ pound (6-8) onions
3 tablespoons butter

¾ cup dry white wine
7 tablespoons heavy cream
juice of 1 lemon
salt and pepper

Prepare the court bouillon.

Clean and wash the mackerel and poach them in the court bouillon. Drain and remove the fillets.

At the same time, peel the onions and cut them into quite large pieces. Sauté them in butter until golden. Add the white wine, season with salt and pepper, and simmer 20 minutes. Remove from the heat and stir in 5 tablespoons of cream.

Put the onions in a shallow heatproof serving dish. Place the fillets on the onions. Sprinkle with lemon juice and spoon over the mackerel the rest of the cream, highly seasoned with pepper. Put in a 300° F. oven for 10 minutes. The sauce should not boil.

Mackerel maître d'hôtel
Maquereaux maître d'hôtel

FOR THREE PEOPLE

3 1-pound mackerel
7 tablespoons butter

juice of ½ lemon
salt and pepper

Buy mackerel that are absolutely fresh. Clean them, wash them, and cut the skin in several places without touching the flesh. Sauté in butter 10 to 20 minutes,

*Test the fish by inserting a fork. If the flesh flakes, the fish is cooked.—Ed.

turning the fish once. Season with salt and pepper. Transfer to a heated platter.
Squeeze the ½ lemon into the cooking butter and pour it over the fish. Serve
with boiled rice.

Sweet and sour mackerel * Maquereaux aigre-doux

FOR FOUR PEOPLE

2 large mackerel	2 bay leaves
1 carrot	1 teaspoon vinegar
1 onion	salt and peppercorns
2 sugar lumps	

Clean the mackerel and cut off their heads and tails. Cut each fish into 4 pieces.
Put in a saucepan and cover with water. Add the carrot and onion, cut in slices,
sugar, 2 bay leaves, a little salt, a pinch of peppercorns, and the vinegar. Simmer
about 30 minutes. You can eat this hot or cold equally well.

Mullet

Mullet is fished in southern Atlantic coastal waters, off Florida and the Carolinas. Sea Bass recipes can be used for mullet.

Cold stuffed mullet * Mulets froids farcis

FOR TEN PEOPLE

Fish:	Stuffing:
2 3-pound mullets (or sea bass)	2 cans truffle peelings
¾ cup vinegar	5 tablespoons cooked rice
3 carrots, sliced	5 tablespoons heavy cream
2 onions, quartered	5 tablespoons chopped shrimp
bouquet garni (thyme, bay leaf, parsley)	6 large mushroom caps
salt and peppercorns	2 lemons
	paprika
	Mayonnaise (page 14)
	salt and pepper

Clean the fish and wash it well. Do not cut off the heads or tails.
Prepare a court bouillon by boiling 3 quarts of water, the vinegar, carrots,
onions, bouquet garni, and 2 teaspoons of salt for 30 minutes. Add ½ teaspoon
of peppercorns 5 minutes before the end of cooking. Strain and cool.
Put the fish in the cold court bouillon and bring it very slowly to a boil over

low heat. When the water begins to boil, remove the fish from the liquid. Drain and cool completely.

Make the stuffing by chopping the truffle peelings and combining them in a bowl with the liquid from the truffle cans, the rice, cream, shrimp, and the mushroom caps sliced thin. Add the juice of 1 lemon and season with salt, pepper, and paprika. Mix well.

Before stuffing, remove the backbones from the fish. It will be much easier to cut. Stuff the fish and place them on a serving platter. Serve very cold with a dish of mayonnaise highly seasoned with the juice of the other lemon.

The duke's mullet * Mulet du duc

FOR FOUR PEOPLE

Court Bouillon II (page 163)
1 mullet or sea bass
   (approximately 2 pounds)
Green Sauce (page 10)

½ pound small mushrooms
juice of 1 lemon
6 large mushroom caps
4 hard-cooked eggs

Prepare the court bouillon. Strain and cool.

The fish should be scaled and washed. Clean the fish through the gills and cut off the fins.

Put the fish in the cold court bouillon. Bring it slowly to a boil, and as soon as it reaches the boiling point, remove from the heat and cool in the liquid.

Make the green sauce.

Remove the fish from the liquid. Drain completely.

Trim, wash, and boil the mushrooms 5 minutes in salted water. Drain and force through a sieve (or purée in a blender—Ed.). Add the juice of 1 lemon and 4 teaspoons of the green sauce to bind them.

Cook the mushroom caps separately in boiling salted water for 5 minutes. Drain and cool. Fill with the green sauce.

Halve the hard-cooked eggs. Crush the yolks and mix with a little of the sauce. Fill the whites.

Spread the mushroom purée on a serving platter. Place the fish on the mushrooms and surround with the stuffed eggs and the mushroom caps. Decorate the fish with the green sauce.

Mullet with grapes * Mulet aux raisins

FOR FOUR PEOPLE

2-3-pound mullet or sea bass
1 cup white wine
½ cup oil
1 large onion, sliced thin

bouquet garni (thyme, bay leaf, parsley)
1 bunch white grapes
salt and pepper

Put the fish, which has been scaled, cleaned, and washed, in an oval heatproof serving dish. Pour in the wine and oil and put the onion, divided into rings, all over. Add the *bouquet garni* and the grapes. Season with salt and freshly ground black pepper.

Bake 15 to 20 minutes at 400° F. Baste at least twice during the baking. Serve immediately with boiled rice or potatoes.

Mullet au gratin à la florentine
Gratin de mulet florentine

FOR FOUR PEOPLE

2 pounds spinach	1½ cups flaked, cooked mullet or
3 tablespoons butter	other white fish
4 teaspoons flour	1 cup grated Gruyère cheese
1½ cups scalded milk	salt and pepper

Trim and wash the spinach and cook, uncovered, in boiling salted water for 5 minutes. Rinse it quickly in cold water and drain well, pressing out the excess water between the palms of your hands. Spread the spinach unchopped in a shallow heatproof serving dish.

Heat the butter and stir in the flour. Add the hot milk and stir over heat until the sauce begins to thicken. Season with salt and pepper and add the cooked fish. Pour this over the spinach and sprinkle very generously with grated cheese. Brown well in a hot oven.

Mullet with lemon * Mulet au citron

FOR FOUR PEOPLE

1 large mullet	3 lemons
1½ tablespoons oil	4 teaspoons chopped parsley
1 clove garlic, crushed	salt and pepper

Scale the fish, clean, wash, and cut off the head and tail.

Cut in 2-inch steaks.

Heat the oil in a large pan. Add the garlic, the fish, 1 cup of water, and the juice of 3 lemons. Season with salt and pepper, and sprinkle with parsley. Simmer 20 minutes.

Arrange the fish carefully on a serving platter and sprinkle with the cooking juices, which will become jelly when you cool the fish.

Mullet loaf * Pain de mulet

3 tablespoons butter
2½ tablespoons flour
1½ cups scalded milk
4 tablespoons curry powder
1½ cups cooked mullet
   (or other white fish)

½ cup heavy cream
3 eggs
salt and pepper

Heat the butter and stir in the flour. Add the milk and stir until blended. Add the curry and continue cooking until the sauce is thick. Set aside to cool.

Pound the cooked fish to a smooth paste. Add to the sauce the fish, the cream, 1 whole egg and 2 egg yolks. Beat the egg whites and fold them into the mixture. Force the whole mixture through a sieve.

Place in a buttered mold and place in a pan of hot water. Bake at 400° F. for 30 minutes. Unmold and serve with curry sauce, which is a béchamel highly seasoned with curry powder.

Red mullet

These fish are small and delicately flavored. They are found on the Atlantic coast from Cape Cod to Pensacola and are also found off the west coast of Florida.

Red mullet en chaud-froid
Rougets en chaud-froid

FOR EIGHT PEOPLE

8 red mullet (5-7 ounces)
1 cup white wine
bouquet garni (thyme, bay leaf, parsley)
3 tablespoons butter
1 shallot

3 egg yolks
10 tablespoons heavy cream
cayenne
salt and pepper

Clean the fish and wash them. Place them in a baking dish with the white wine and an equal amount of water. Add the *bouquet garni,* salt, and pepper and place it uncovered over a low heat. Bring slowly to the boiling point, and just before it begins to boil, reduce the heat as low as possible and poach 10 minutes without actually letting the liquid boil. Carefully transfer the fish to a dish towel to drain, and then line them up on a serving platter. Save the cooking broth.

Heat half the butter in a saucepan and sauté the shallot, peeled and finely chopped. When it becomes pale yellow, add the cooking broth, strained through a fine sieve. Boil down to half its original quantity. Remove from the heat and stir in the egg yolks, beaten slightly with the cream. Cook over very low heat, stirring constantly until the mixture thickens. Do not let the sauce boil. Add the balance of the butter in small bits, stirring with a little whisk. Add a small pinch of cayenne and add salt and pepper, if necessary. Cover the fish with the sauce and chill in the refrigerator.

Cold red mullet à l'orientale
Rougets froids à l'orientale

FOR SIX PEOPLE

6 red mullet	1 clove garlic
flour	powdered thyme
oil	1 lemon
¾ cup white wine	salt and pepper
2 pounds (6-8) medium tomatoes	

Clean, wash, dry, and coat the fish with flour. Heat 4 tablespoons of oil in a skillet and sauté the fish 5 minutes on each side. Put them in a lightly buttered baking dish and pour in the white wine.

In a saucepan, cook for 30 minutes the peeled tomatoes and garlic with ⅓ cup of oil, a good pinch of thyme, salt, and pepper. Spoon the sauce over the fish and bake 3 minutes at 400° F.

Remove the fish from the baking dish to a serving platter. Boil the sauce down until thick and pour it over the fish. Serve cold, garnished with slices of lemon.

Quickly cooked red mullet * Rougets "vite faits"

FOR SIX PEOPLE

6 red mullet	juice of 1 lemon
¾ cup white wine	1 tablespoon chopped parsley
5 tablespoons butter	salt and pepper

Scale, wash, and dry the red mullet but do not clean. Cut off the fins and barbels. Place them in a well-buttered shallow baking dish. Season with salt and pepper and pour in the white wine. Cover with buttered wax paper. Bake 10 minutes in a 400° F. oven, basting frequently. The liquid should not boil but just slowly simmer. Transfer the fish to a heated serving platter. Add a large piece of butter to the liquid in the baking dish. Add the juice of 1 lemon and the chopped parsley. Heat, stir well, and pour over the fish.

Red mullet with fennel * Rougets au fenouil

FOR FIVE PEOPLE

5 red mullet
   (approximately 7 ounces each)
2 onions
¾ cup oil
1 stalk fennel

dry breadcrumbs
juice of 1 lemon
1 tablespoon chopped parsley
salt and pepper

Clean and wash the fish. Cut them slightly along the back with a sharp-pointed knife.

Peel and chop the onions fine. Sauté them in 2 tablespoons of oil, stirring so that they will be lightly browned all over. Chop the fennel fine and add to the onions. Season with salt and pepper.

Spread the vegetable mixture in the bottom of a baking dish. Place the fish on the mixture and season with salt and pepper. Cover generously with breadcrumbs and moisten them with the rest of the oil. Bake 15 to 18 minutes at 400° F.

Before serving, sprinkle with lemon juice and chopped parsley. Serve very hot with boiled rice.

Salt cod aïoli * L'aïoli de morue

FOR SIX PEOPLE

Fish:
2 pounds salt cod
½ bay leaf
½ pound dried white beans
4 artichoke bottoms
4 tomatoes
½ pound carrots
½ pound green beans
1 beet
2 pounds small potatoes
1 quart mussels
1 cup white wine
thyme, bay leaf
1 dozen snails (optional)
chervil (or parsley)

Sauce:
3 hard-cooked eggs
10 cloves garlic
1 egg yolk
1½ cups oil
½ lemon
salt and pepper

Soak the salt cod 8 to 12 hours, changing the water 3 times during the process. Remove the skin and bones. Cut in 6-inch pieces. Simmer the cod for 15 minutes with the bay leaf. Drain and keep warm.

Soak the beans overnight. Boil in salted water until tender.

Prepare and cook each vegetable separately in boiling salted water.

Clean the mussels and place them in a pan with the white wine and a pinch each of powdered bay leaf and thyme. Cook over high heat until the mussels open.

Boil the snails in salted water.

Put the cod in the center of a large platter. Surround with the boiled potatoes, hard-cooked eggs, the beet cut in thin slices, artichoke bottoms cut in quarters, beans, tomatoes, and carrots. Add the mussels and, if you like, the boiled snails. Sprinkle with chopped chervil and serve with aïoli sauce, made with 10 cloves of garlic (see page 5) and seasoned with the juice of ½ lemon.

Salt cod brandade * Brandade de morue

FOR FIVE PEOPLE

1¾ pounds salt cod	French bread
1 large potato	butter
2 cloves garlic	pepper
1 cup olive oil	

Soak the cod 8 to 12 hours, changing the water 2 or 3 times. Poach it in fresh water for 10 minutes. Remove any skin and bones and flake the fish.

Boil the potato in its jacket and peel off the skin.

In a mortar or wooden bowl, pound and then rub the garlic with the fish and the boiled potato. When you have a smooth paste, put it in a small saucepan, and over a very low heat, add the oil in a very thin stream, stirring constantly with a wooden spoon as though you were making mayonnaise. Season with freshly ground black pepper.

Serve with thin slices of French bread fried in butter.

Salt cod with potatoes and mushrooms
Morue aux pommes de terre et aux champignons

FOR FOUR PEOPLE

1½ pounds salt cod	1½ cups Béchamel Sauce (page 6)
4 large Idaho potatoes	½ cup grated Gruyère cheese
½ pound mushrooms	pepper
7 tablespoons butter	

Soak the salt cod 8 to 12 hours, changing the water 2 or 3 times. Poach 20 minutes. Drain the fish and flake it, removing any skin and bones.

Wash the potatoes and bake them for 1 hour at 375° F.

Make a thick béchamel sauce.

Cut off the top third of the potatoes, cutting them lengthwise. Scoop out the interiors and put the potato pulp in a bowl. Mash the potatoes and stir in the cod, the cooked mushrooms, and 3 tablespoons of the butter. Mix well and season with pepper. Fill the potatoes. Place them in a baking dish. Cover with the béchamel and sprinkle with grated cheese. Dot each potato with a little piece of butter. Bake 15 minutes at 400° F.

Provençale salt cod * Morue provençale

FOR EIGHT PEOPLE

3½ pounds salt cod fillets
bouquet garni (bay leaf, thyme, parsley)
4 cloves garlic
2 onions
several sprigs parsley
5 shallots

4 tomatoes
5 ounces (10 tablespoons)
  butter, melted
1½ cups olive oil
½ pound imported black olives
salt and pepper

Soak the cod 8 to 12 hours, changing the water 2 or 3 times. Put in a pan of cold water with the *bouquet garni* and bring to a boil. Remove from the heat and let the cod stand in the water for 15 minutes. Take the fish out of the liquid and drain.

Chop the garlic, onions, parsley, and shallots rather coarsely.

Dip the tomatoes in boiling water and slip off the skins. Halve and press out the seeds. Chop coarsely and combine with the other vegetables. Season with salt and pepper.

Spread half the vegetables in a large heatproof serving dish. Sprinkle with half the melted butter and oil. Place the cod on the vegetables and cover with the rest of the chopped vegetables. Surround with olives and sprinkle with the balance of the butter and oil. Bake 30 minutes at 400° F. Serve immediately.

Fish balls * Croquettes de morue

FOR SIX PEOPLE

1 pound salt cod
3 large potatoes
¾ cup milk, scalded
2 eggs, well beaten

2½ tablespoons heavy cream
Tomato Sauce (page 22)
flour
salt and pepper

Soak the cod overnight, changing the water 2 or 3 times. Drain. Poach 15 minutes in fresh water. Remove any skin and bones and drain well. Force the fish through a grinder or a *moulinette.*

Boil the potatoes in their jackets. Peel off the skins and force the potatoes through a sieve. Put the potatoes in a saucepan with enough milk to give a smooth but thick mixture. Add the cod and season to taste with pepper and add salt, if necessary. Remove from the heat and stir in the beaten eggs and cream. Let the mixture cool and stand for several hours.

Make the sauce.

Make little balls the size of pullet's eggs. Roll in flour and fry in deep fat (385° F.). Serve very hot with the sauce in a separate bowl.

Sardine dartois * Dartois de sardines

FOR SIX TO EIGHT PEOPLE

Flaky Pastry (page 643)
2 cans oil-packed sardines
3 tablespoons soft butter
1 egg yolk

3 tablespoons butter
½ cup heavy cream
juice of 1 lemon

This is a particularly good dish, and it is quickly achieved once the pastry is made. You will need about ¼ of the pastry recipe.

Roll out the pastry on a floured surface, using a well-floured rolling pin. Divide into 2 equal rectangles.

Preheat the oven to 400° F.

Crush the sardines with a fork, removing the tails and bones, if the sardines are large. Add the sardine oil and the soft butter. Mix well and spread over one of the rectangles, leaving a small border all around. Moisten the border with water. Cover with the other pastry rectangle and press the edges together firmly. Paint the surface with egg yolk mixed with a teaspoon of water. Bake 20 minutes.

Serve very hot accompanied with the following sauce, made while the *dartois* is baking: Melt the butter over a low heat. Add the cream and heat without letting it boil. Pour the sauce into a heated sauce bowl and at the last minute add the lemon juice.

Fresh sardines stuffed with almonds
Sardines farcies aux amandes

FOR FOUR PEOPLE

2 tablespoons seedless raisins
12 sardines*
½ cup dry breadcrumbs
¾ cup oil

allspice
bay leaves
salt and pepper

Soak the raisins in lukewarm water until soft.

Trim, clean, and wash the sardines, cutting off their heads and tails. Slit the

*Alewives or western pilchard are our nearest approximation to sardines.—*Ed*.

entire length of the bellies and remove the backbones.

Moisten the breadcrumbs with a little oil and mix with the raisins and almonds. Mix well, seasoning with salt, pepper, and allspice. The mixture should not be too thick.

Put a spoonful of the stuffing in each sardine and line them up, one pressed against the other, in a shallow oven dish. Put a piece of bay leaf between each sardine. Sprinkle with the rest of the oil and bake 30 minutes at 400° F. Cool thoroughly before serving.

Raw sardines with shallots
Sardines crues aux échalotes

This recipe is made with tiny fish, such as the New England herring or young alewife or the western pilchard. The fish must be extremely fresh. Cut off the heads and tails and slit open the bellies with scissors. Remove the backbone and cut the fish into strips.

Place the fillets on a platter and sprinkle generously with finely chopped shallots and lemon juice. Let stand overnight in a very cool place before serving.

Skate in dark butter * Raie au beurre noir

FOR SIX PEOPLE

3¾ pounds skate
½ cup white vinegar
2 teaspoons chopped parsley
¼ pound sweet butter

Dark butter:
¼ pound sweet butter
1 teaspoon white vinegar
4 teaspoons capers
salt

Fish: Cut the fish in pieces. Place them in a pan with enough cold water to cover, the vinegar and salt. Bring to a boil and simmer 10 minutes. Remove from the liquid. Drain and remove the skin. Place on a heated platter, sprinkle with parsley, and serve with the following sauce, made while the fish is cooking:

Dark Butter: Heat the butter over a low flame until it becomes dark brown (but not scorched). Pour the butter into a heated sauce bowl. Add the vinegar to the saucepan, heat, and add to the butter along with the capers.

Sole

The sole found in European waters differs in texture from that of our sole and is more highly prized. However, the name *sole* is used in America for various species of flounder—the lemon sole, the winter flounder, dab, gray sole, and yellow tail—and can be cooked like the so-called Dover sole. Sold in fillets or whole, they can be delicious, if properly prepared.

In many recipes, the trimmings (head, tails, bones, and skin) are called for. If you are dependent on a fish dealer who deals only in filleted and packaged fish, buy 1 or 2 pounds of some bony fish, cut in small pieces, to replace the sole trimmings.

Dover sole is imported by certain city fish markets and can be bought at a price.

Fillets of sole with bananas
Filets de soles aux bananes

FOR FOUR PEOPLE

⅔ cup rice	flour
2½ tablespoons curry powder	7 tablespoons butter
2 soles *or*	2 bananas
8 sole fillets	¾ cup fresh grapefruit juice

Cook the rice in salted water to which the curry powder has been added. See page 457.

Ask the fish dealer to remove the fillets from fresh sole or buy the fillets. Coat the fillets lightly with flour and sauté them in half the butter over a low heat.

Cut the bananas in 3 pieces and sauté them in butter in another skillet.

Heat the unsweetened grapefruit juice.

Put the rice on a serving platter. Arrange the fillets on the rice and place a piece of banana on each one.

Accompany with the grapefruit juice served in a separate bowl.

Broiled sole with tarragon
Soles grillées à l'estragon

FOR FOUR PEOPLE

4 1-pound sole or flounder	8 tarragon leaves, chopped
oil	juice of 1 lemon
7 tablespoons butter	salt and pepper

Buy the sole or flounder trimmed and cleaned. Wash and dry them carefully. Brush them with oil and season with salt and pepper.

Preheat the broiler and broiling rack. Place them on the hot ungreased rack and broil 5 minutes on each side.

Heat the butter and add the chopped tarragon and the lemon juice.

Serve the fish on a heated platter with the butter in a separate sauce bowl.

Sole en chaud-froid * Chaud-froid de soles

FOR EIGHT PEOPLE

8 1-pound sole *or*
32 small sole fillets
7 tablespoons butter
1½ cups dry white wine or hard cider

½ cup heavy cream
1 sprig tarragon
parsley
salt and pepper

Ask the fish dealer to fillet the fish but to give you the trimmings (heads, tails, bones, and skin). In a long shallow dish, place little bits of butter.

Roll the fillets up and line them up side by side on the butter. Season with salt and pepper and cover with the fish trimmings and the rest of the butter. Pour in the wine or cider and bake 10 to 20 minutes at 350° F.

Remove the rolled fillets and place them on a serving platter. Continue cooking the broth for 20 to 25 minutes. Add the cream. Bring it just to a boil. Remove the trimmings and strain the sauce through a fine sieve. Season to taste and pour over the fillets. Place in the refrigerator. When cold, the sauce will jell. Decorate with tarragon leaves and parsley.

Sole en chaud-froid with cucumbers
Chaud-froid de soles aux concombres

FOR FOUR PEOPLE

2 pounds cucumbers
3 8-10-ounce sole *or*
12 sole fillets
2 cups dry white wine
½ teaspoon anise seeds
1 teaspoon chopped tarragon

1 cup heavy cream
3 tablespoons butter
4 teaspoons flour
4 teaspoons tomato paste
salt and pepper

Ask the fish dealer to fillet the fish but to give you the trimmings (heads, tails, bones, and skin).

Place the fillets in a pan with 1 cup of white wine, 1 cup of cold water, salt, and pepper. Bring slowly to a boil, and when the liquid begins to boil, the fish is cooked. Drain and cool.

At the same time, cook the fish trimmings with 1 cup of wine, 1 cup of water, anise seeds, tarragon, salt, and pepper. Cook gently for 30 minutes.

Cut ¾ cup of cucumber balls with a small potato cutter. Dice the rest of the cucumbers. Boil the balls and the dice separately for 10 minutes in salted water. Mix the dice with half the cream. Spread them on a serving platter. Cover with the cold fillets.

Heat the butter and stir in the flour. Strain the fish broth into the mixture. Stir until smooth. Add the remaining cream and continue stirring and cooking until the sauce thickens. Color with the tomato paste. Cool the sauce to lukewarm and spoon over the fillets. Decorate with the cucumber balls and place in the refrigerator or some cool place.

Sole en chaud-froid with tomatoes
Chaud-froid de soles aux tomates

FOR FOUR PEOPLE

3 sole (approximately 8-10 ounces each)
or 12 sole fillets
1 cup dry white wine
tarragon

¾ cup heavy cream
4 teaspoons tomato paste
1 pound (3-4) tomatoes
salt and pepper

Put the cleaned and washed fish in a large pan with the wine, ½ cup of water, several tarragon leaves, salt, and pepper. Bring slowly to a boil. When the water boils, the fish are cooked.

Carefully remove the fillets, saving the skin and bones. Place the fillets between 2 plates to keep them flat. If whole fish are not available, provide yourself with a pound of bony white fish. Put the skin and bones of the sole or the bony fish in the cooking broth and boil gently with a cover on the pan for 20 minutes. Strain the broth into a saucepan. Add the cream and tomato paste. Season to taste and stir over a low heat for 10 minutes.

Boil the whole tomatoes 5 minutes. Skin them and remove the seeds. Crush the tomatoes in the bottom of a shallow serving dish, saving a little for decoration. Season with salt and pepper. Place the fillets on the bed of tomato. Cover with the sauce and decorate with little mounds of tomato placed here and there. This dish is eaten hot or cold.

Sole in cider * Sole au cidre

FOR FOUR PEOPLE

7 tablespoons butter
2 tablespoons chopped parsley
2-pound sole or
flounder

⅓ cup dry breadcrumbs
1 cup hard cider
4 tablespoons heavy cream
salt and pepper

Dot a large shallow heatproof serving dish with half the butter and sprinkle with half the parsley. Place a well-trimmed sole in the dish. Sprinkle with the rest of the parsley and the breadcrumbs and dot with the rest of the butter. Pour in the cider and season with salt and pepper.

Place the fish in a 350° F. oven and let the fish simmer (the liquid must not actually boil) for about 15 minutes or until the fish is cooked.

Just before serving, add the heavy cream. Serve the fish from the dish in which it has been cooked.

Fillets of sole in flaky pastry
Filets de soles en feuilleté

FOR EIGHT PEOPLE

Flaky Pastry (page 643)
3 tablespoons butter
1 shallot, finely chopped
1 tablespoon chopped parsley
¼ pound mushrooms

8 large sole fillets
¾ cup dry white wine or champagne
1 egg yolk
salt and pepper

Make the pastry and time it so that it will be ready when you want it. You will use about ¼ of the recipe.

Spread the butter in a shallow baking dish. Cover it with the finely chopped shallot, the parsley, and the mushrooms trimmed, washed, and thinly sliced. Put in the fish fillets and season with salt and pepper. Add the wine or champagne and cover with a piece of buttered wax paper. Place in a 350° F. oven and heat just until the liquid is at the boiling point. Remove the dish from the oven. Cool slightly.

Roll out the pastry and cut into 16 rectangles 5 × 3 inches.

Preheat the oven to 400° F.

Place a spoonful of the mushroom-shallot mixture and a fillet on 8 rectangles. With a pastry brush, moisten the edges with water. Cover each one with a pastry rectangle and press the edges together firmly. Paint with egg yolk mixed with a teaspoon of water. Place on a baking sheet and bake 15 to 20 minutes. Serve with hollandaise, if you like, but this is excellent without any sauce.

Sole meunière * Soles meunière

FOR FOUR PEOPLE

4 medium sole or flounder
flour
7 tablespoons butter

juice of 1 lemon
1 tablespoon chopped parsley
salt and pepper

Buy the sole trimmed and cleaned. Wash and dry thoroughly. Coat them lightly in flour.

Heat the butter in a skillet and sauté the fish 5 to 6 minutes on each side, according to their thickness. Season with salt and pepper.

Place on a heated serving platter and pour over the hot cooking butter. Season with lemon juice and sprinkle with chopped parsley. Serve immediately.

Sole ring * Couronne de soles

FOR SIX PEOPLE

Court Bouillon II (page 163)
3 sole *or*
12 sole fillets
2 lemons
1 whiting
1 cod steak (½-¾ pound)
½ pound mushrooms

½ cup soft breadcrumbs
¾ cup milk
3 eggs, slightly beaten
7 tablespoons butter
1 tablespoon flour
¾ cup heavy cream
salt and pepper

Prepare one half the recipe for the court bouillon.

Ask the fish dealer to remove fillets from fresh sole or buy the fillets. Wipe them well and sprinkle them with lemon juice. Butter a ring mold well and line the mold with the fillets in such a way that they will extend over both sides a little.

Cook the whiting and cod (or other white fish) in the court bouillon. Take the fish out of the liquid and remove the skin and bones. Force the fish through a grinder or *moulinette*. You will need about 2½ cups of fish. Boil down the broth to about 1½ cupfuls. Strain.

Trim and wash the mushrooms. Force them through a grinder and mix with the fish. Soak the breadcrumbs in milk. Squeeze dry and mix with the fish, 3 beaten eggs, half the butter, salt, pepper, and a little lemon juice. Mix thoroughly. Place the mixture in the ring mold and fold over the end of the fillets.

Cover with a piece of buttered wax paper and place in a pan of hot water. Bake 1 hour at 350° F.

Heat the rest of the butter in a saucepan and stir in the flour. Add the strained broth and stir until smooth and slightly thickened. Add the cream and the juice of ½ lemon. Taste for seasoning. Unmold the ring on a heated serving platter. Cover with the sauce. Serve with boiled rice.

Steamed sole * Sole à la vapeur

FOR ONE PERSON

1½-pound sole
3 tablespoons butter

1 lemon

Buy the sole cleaned and trimmed, with the skin removed from both sides. Place it in a plate.

Fill a pan full of boiling water and place the dish on top. Turn another plate upside down over the fish. The fish will cook by steam and will require no seasoning. Serve with melted butter and a cut lemon.

Steamship normandie's fillets of sole
Filets de sole, paquebot normandie

FOR SIX PEOPLE

3 sole *or*
12 sole fillets
1 pound mushrooms
3 cups Béchamel Sauce (page 6)

2 cups dry white wine
3 tablespoons butter
½ cup heavy cream
croutons fried in butter

Ask the fish dealer to clean, trim, and fillet the sole. You will need the trimmings, (head, tails, skin, and bones). If this is not possible, buy a pound of bony white fish cut in pieces.

Trim, wash, and wipe the mushrooms and chop them very fine.

Make the béchamel sauce. Add the chopped mushrooms to half the sauce. Keep hot.

In a shallow baking dish, put the fish trimmings or substitute. Add the cold white wine, and on top of this, place the fillets. Place in a 350° F. oven. When the liquid begins to boil, the fish is cooked.

Spread the mushroom mixture in a shallow serving dish. Arrange the fillets on the mushrooms. Cover with the rest of the béchamel, to which the butter and cream have been added. Season with salt and pepper and garnish with fried croutons.

Stuffed sole maichu * Sole farcie maichu

FOR SIX PEOPLE

1 large sole or flounder
 (approximately 4 pounds)
4 tablespoons oil
2 pounds (6-8) tomatoes

5 red or green peppers
fines herbes (parsley, chervil, tarragon)
¾ cup dry white wine
salt and pepper

Ask the fish dealer to clean the fish and to remove the backbone.

Heat the oil in a deep skillet. Add the tomatoes peeled and cut in pieces and the peppers seeded and cut in slices. Season with salt and pepper and cook until the vegetables become a thick purée. Fill the sole with the mixture. Place in a well-buttered shallow baking dish. Sprinkle with the chopped *fines herbes* and pour in the white wine. Season with salt and pepper.

Cover the dish with wax paper and bake 15 minutes at 350° F. Remove the paper and continue cooking 15 minutes longer. Lift up a little of the flesh with a fork. If it is perfectly white, the fish is cooked. Serve from the baking dish.

Tuna

When fresh tuna fish is in season, it is very good. The flesh is solid and compact, so that it is important to buy it by its weight and not by its size.

(The tuna referred to in these recipes is the white-fleshed variety such as the albacore or bonito, found in Pacific waters.—*Ed.*)

Tuna with bananas ∗ *Thon aux bananes*

FOR FOUR PEOPLE

4 thin slices of tuna
juice of 1 large or 2 small lemons
2 large onions
1 clove garlic
4 tomatoes
4 bananas
1 green pepper
3 tablespoons butter

2 cloves
bay leaf
thyme
flour
5 tablespoons oil
chopped parsley
salt and pepper

Put the tuna slices on a platter and sprinkle them generously with lemon juice. Marinate 30 minutes.

Peel the onions and garlic and chop them coarsely.

Dip the tomatoes in boiling water and slip off the skins. Cut them in pieces. Peel the bananas and slice them.

Slice the pepper thin, removing the seeds and filaments.

Heat the butter in a skillet. When it is hot, sauté the onions and garlic until pale yellow. Stir so that they will be sautéed evenly. Add the tomatoes, pepper, the bananas, the cloves, a pinch each of powdered bay leaf and thyme. Season with salt and pepper and simmer gently for 20 minutes.

Drain the tuna slices and coat them lightly with flour.

Heat the oil in a skillet and brown the tuna on both sides. Keep the heat moderate so that the fish will not stick to the skillet. Add the vegeables to the fish and simmer 30 minutes.

Serve sprinkled with chopped parsley.

Tuna with curry * Thon au cari

FOR FOUR PEOPLE

4 thin tuna steaks
⅓ cup oil
3 onions, chopped fine

2 tomatoes
2½ tablespoons curry powder
¾ cup dry white wine

Order the steaks cut very thin from the tail.

Heat the oil in a skillet and brown the steaks well on both sides. Season with salt and pepper and transfer them to a warm place.

Sauté the onions over high heat in the oil in which the steaks have browned. Peel, cut, and seed the tomatoes and cut them in large dice. Add to the onions. Add the curry. Stir well and add the white wine. Boil down for a few minutes and add the tuna. Lower the heat and simmer 30 minutes.

Serve with boiled rice.

Braised tuna with apples, cherries, and lemon
Thon braisé aux pommes, cerises et citron

FOR FIVE PEOPLE

2 pounds apples
10 tablespoons butter
2 pounds fresh tuna
2 lemons

1 pound cherries
cinnamon
salt and pepper

Peel the apples and cut them in wedges. Save out 2 to 3 apples. Melt 7 table-spoons of butter in a heavy pan, but do not let it brown. Sauté the tuna lightly on both sides. Season with salt and plenty of pepper. Add the apple slices and the juice of 1 lemon. Cover and cook gently for 45 minutes. Add the pitted cherries and a pinch of cinnamon. Continue to cook for 30 minutes.

Peel and slice the reserved apples into wedges. You should have about 20 pieces.

Heat the rest of the butter in a skillet and sauté the apples, letting them brown lightly on both sides but not allowing them to become too soft.

Place the tuna on a heated platter. Taste the sauce for seasoning, adding salt and pepper, if necessary. Pour this around the tuna and garnish with alternating wedges of apple and lemon.

Braised tuna with carrots
Thon braisé aux carottes

FOR SIX PEOPLE

2 pounds fresh tuna

1 pound carrots

4 tablespoons oil

¾ cup dry white wine

marjoram

juice of ½ lemon

orégano

salt and pepper

3 onions

Buy a thick tuna steak. Sauté in hot oil, turning it so that both sides will be nicely browned. Add a pinch of marjoram and *orégano*. Season with salt and plenty of pepper.

Cut the onions and carrots in rounds and brown them along with the fish. Pour in the white wine and sprinkle with lemon juice. Lower the heat, cover the skillet, and cook slowly for at least 1 hour.

This dish is never overcooked and is delicious warmed up. Before serving, taste for seasoning, adding more salt, pepper, and lemon juice, if necessary.

Broiled fresh tuna * Thon frais grillé

FOR FOUR PEOPLE

4 thin slices fresh tuna

1 teaspoon chopped tarragon

⅓ cup oil

salt and pepper

¼ teaspoon ginger

Marinate the fish for 2 to 3 hours in oil, seasoned with ginger, tarragon, salt, and pepper.

Preheat the broiler and broiling rack. Place the fish on the ungreased rack and broil 10 minutes on each side. Season with salt and pepper after cooking.

Serve very hot, sprinkled with the oil of the marinade.

You can also serve the tuna very hot on a bed of straw potatoes. Garnish the platter with strips of red pepper or other seasonable vegetable and accompany with a melted butter sauce.

Chartreuse of tuna * Chartreuse de thon

FOR SIX PEOPLE

1 pound carrots

¾ cup dry white wine

1 head lettuce

juice of 1 lemon

¼ pound sorrel

¾ cup oil

4 tomatoes

1 sprig thyme

4 onions

1 bay leaf

1 clove garlic

salt and pepper

1¾ pounds tuna

Wash, peel or trim, and chop all the vegetables very fine. Mix them well. Put half of them in the bottom of a deep heavy pan. Place the tuna on the vegetables. (If you can lard the fish by inserting small strips of fat salt pork, the dish will be that much more unctuous.) Cover with the rest of the vegetables and season with salt, lemon juice, and pepper. Pour in the white wine, lemon juice, and oil and add the thyme and bay leaf. Cover tightly and simmer very slowly for 3 to 4 hours.

Place the fish and the sauce on a serving platter and cool completely. You can place anchovy fillets on the tuna if you like the flavor.

Flambéed fresh tuna * *Thon frais flambé*

FOR FIVE PEOPLE

2 pounds tuna fish
5 tablespoons butter
5 tablespoons oil
1½ tablespoons cognac
cayenne
allspice
curry
nutmeg

1 onion, chopped fine
1 shallot, chopped fine
1 clove garlic, crushed
2 cups Muscadet or other dry white wine
4 tablespoons tomato paste
½ cup heavy cream
fried croutons or boiled rice
salt and pepper

Cut the tuna into thick pieces (you can use canned tuna). Heat the butter and oil in a deep heavy pan. Sauté the tuna, stirring so that it will be lightly browned on all sides. Add the cognac and touch with a lighted match. When the flames subside, add a pinch each of cayenne and allspice, a dash of curry and nutmeg, the onion, shallot, garlic, salt, and freshly ground pepper. Mix the wine and tomato paste and pour into the pan. Cook, allowing 30 minutes for 2 pounds.

Transfer the tuna with a slotted spoon to a heated platter. Keep warm. Strain the sauce into a saucepan and let it simmer for a few moments. Add the cream and reheat, but do not let the sauce boil. Pour over the tuna ringed with fried croutons or boiled rice.

Roast tuna fish * *Thon rôti*

FOR EIGHT PEOPLE

3 pounds tuna fish
¾ cup oil
juice of 1 lemon
4 teaspoons chopped chives
1 shallot, chopped fine
1 tablespoon chopped parsley

1 sprig thyme
1 bay leaf
4 tablespoons butter
4 teaspoons flour
salt and pepper

Remove the skin from the tuna fish and put in a marinade consisting of the oil, lemon juice, chives, shallot, chopped parsley, thyme, bay leaf, salt, and pepper. Let stand 2 hours.

Place the tuna on a rack in a roasting pan. Sprinkle with the marinade and dot with 2 tablespoons of butter. Roast at 300° F., allowing 15 minutes per pound.

Heat 2 tablespoons of butter in a saucepan. Stir in the flour, and when blended, add the liquid from the pan from which as much of the fat as possible has been removed. Place the tuna on a heated serving platter and serve the sauce in a separate bowl.

Vahine fish (uncooked) * Poisson des vahinés

FOR FOUR PEOPLE

1 pound (2 cups) raw white fish	2 hard-cooked eggs
juice of 6 lemons	salt and pepper
½ cup heavy cream	

The white fish (cod, scrod, halibut, and so on) should be completely free of skin and bones and cut in small pieces. Put them in an earthenware dish and cover them completely with lemon juice. Let stand overnight.

The next morning pour off half the lemon juice, season highly with salt and pepper, and mix with the cream. Place the fish on a serving platter and garnish with slices of hard-cooked eggs. Serve very cold.

Turbot

Turbot is a delicious, firm-fleshed fish abundant in French waters but occurring only along the northern Pacific coast in America. It belongs to the flounder family. For Easterners halibut (in steaks or fillets) or a species of flounder, popularly known as the window pane, weighing from 1 to 2 pounds and fished from Maine to the Carolinas, are satisfactory substitutes.

Turbot fillets au gratin * Filets de turbot au gratin

FOR FOUR PEOPLE

4 turbot fillets or substitute	2 egg yolks
(6-7 ounces each)	½ cup grated Gruyère cheese
¾ cup dry white wine	4 teaspoons fine breadcrumbs
10 tablespoons butter	salt and pepper
4 teaspoons flour	

Ask the fish dealer to take off the fillets for you but to give you the fish trimmings (bones, head, tail, and skin). Put the latter in a pan with white wine and an equal amount of water. Boil gently for 15 minutes.

Place the fillets in a shallow baking dish. Strain the court bouillon over the fish. Cover with a piece of buttered wax paper and bake 20 minutes at 350° F. Remove the fillets and continue cooking the broth for 30 minutes. Place the fillets on a heatproof serving platter.

Heat the butter over low heat and stir in the flour. Moisten with the hot fish broth. Stir until smooth and slightly thickened. Remove from the heat and add the rest of the butter, cut in small pieces. Then stir in the egg yolks. Taste for seasoning. Pour the sauce over the fish. Sprinkle with grated cheese and bread-crumbs. Brown in a 400° F. oven for 5 minutes.

Turbot à la granvillaise * Turbot à la granvillaise

FOR FOUR PEOPLE

4 turbot fillets or substitute
  (7 ounces each)
2 cups dry white wine
juice of 1 lemon

7 tablespoons butter
½ cup heavy cream
salt and pepper

Cut each of the fillets in 2 pieces. Place them in a large shallow pan. Add the wine and the juice of 1 lemon. Season with salt and pepper and bring to a boil. Simmer very gently for 20 minutes.

Transfer the fish to a heated platter and keep warm. Boil down the liquid in the pan to half its original quantity. Add the butter and cream. Do not boil but reheat, beating with a whisk until thick. Taste for seasoning.

Pour the sauce over the fish and serve with a side dish of rice with almonds and hazel nuts. See page 459.

Island turbot * Turbot des îles

FOR SIX PEOPLE

3-3½-pound turbot or substitute
3-4 potatoes
2 tomatoes
1 onion
2 cloves garlic
3 cups dry white wine

¾ cup oil
2 bay leaves
1 sprig thyme
2 lemons
salt and pepper

Clean, wash, and wipe the fish dry. Put it in a large shallow baking dish, large enough to let the fish lie flat.

Peel the potatoes and slice them thin, as you would for making potato chips.

Dip the tomatoes in boiling water and slip off the skins.

Peel the onion and garlic and chop them coarsely.

Surround the fish with the vegetables. Pour in the wine and oil and sprinkle with salt and freshly ground black pepper. Put in the bay leaves and thyme and add the lemons sliced fairly thick. Cover with buttered or oiled wax paper and bake 1 good hour at 350° F. Serve directly from the oven dish as soon as the fish comes out of the oven.

Poached turbot with hollandaise
Turbot poché, sauce hollandaise

FOR TEN PEOPLE

2 turbots (about 2 pounds each)	lemons
or substitute	chervil
¾ cup milk	salt
Hollandaise Sauce (page 10)	

Put the fish in a court bouillon made of cold milk, salt, and enough water just to cover the fish. Bring slowly to a boil and let the fish barely simmer for 10 minutes.

Make the sauce.

Remove the fish to drain. Place in a serving platter lined with a folded napkin. Garnish with lemon slices and little sprigs of chervil.

Serve the hollandaise in a separate sauce bowl.

Whiting

Whiting (*merlan*) is fished on the Atlantic coast and is sold both whole and filleted, fresh and frozen.

Creole whiting fillets * Filets de merlan créole

FOR SIX PEOPLE

1 egg, slightly beaten	10 tablespoons butter
flour	6 bananas
dry breadcrumbs	2 lemons
12 average-sized whiting fillets	salt and pepper

Put the beaten egg, flour, and breadcrumbs in 3 different plates and dip the fish fillets first in egg, then in flour, and then in breadcrumbs.

Heat 7 tablespoons of butter in a skillet, and when it is sizzling, sauté the fish 5 minutes on each side over a moderate heat. The fish should be well browned. Season with salt and pepper.

Heat the rest of the butter in another skillet. Peel and halve the bananas lengthwise. Sauté them on both sides, turning them carefully, and remove the skillet from the heat.

Alternate fish fillets and bananas on a heated platter. Sprinkle with lemon juice and garnish with lemon slices. Serve very hot with boiled rice or steamed potatoes.

Whiting fillets à la viennoise
Filets de merlan à la viennoise

FOR FOUR PEOPLE

2 eggs, slightly beaten	Mayonnaise (page 14)
2½ tablespoons flour	juice of 1 lemon
¼ cup fine breadcrumbs	several sprigs parsley
8 whiting fillets	salt

Put the eggs in one plate, the flour in another, and the breadcrumbs in another. Dip the fish fillets, first in egg, then in flour, and finally in breadcrumbs.

Fry in deep fat for 3 minutes at 380° F. Drain and sprinkle with salt. Serve on a heated platter with a mayonnaise highly seasoned with lemon juice and garnish with fried parsley.

Whiting à l'hôtelière * Merlans à l'hôtelière

FOR FOUR PEOPLE

4 ½-pound whiting	½ pound mushrooms
¾ cup milk	nutmeg
4 tablespoons flour	juice of 1 lemon
7 ounces (14 tablespoons) butter	1 tablespoon chopped parsley
1 onion	salt and pepper

Clean and wash the fish. Pour the milk in a soup plate and spread the flour on a plate. Dip the fish first in milk and then in flour.

Heat 7 tablespoons of butter in a large skillet and sauté the fish over moderate heat, turning each fish so that it will be well browned on both sides.

Peel and chop the onion very fine. Trim, wash, and chop the mushrooms. Heat 3 tablespoons of butter in a small skillet. Sauté the mushrooms and onion until the mushrooms are almost dry. Season with salt, pepper, and nutmeg.

Place the fish in a heatproof serving dish. Spread with the mushrooms. Place in a 400° F. oven for 1 minute.

Heat the rest of the butter until brown. Add the juice of 1 lemon and pour on the fish. Sprinkle with chopped parsley.

*Whiting red wine stew * Merlans en matelote*

FOR FOUR PEOPLE

4 ½-pound whiting
flour
6 tablespoons oil
1 onion
2 cups good red wine, heated

bouquet garni (thyme, bay leaf, parsley)
1 ½ tablespoons tomato paste
2 sugar lumps
salt and pepper

Clean and wash the fish. Cut off the heads and tails and cut them in 1½-inch pieces. Roll the fish pieces in flour.

Heat 4 tablespoons of oil in a skillet and sauté the fish over high heat, browning them on all sides.

Chop the onion fine and sauté in 2 tablespoons of oil in a large pan. When the onion is a pale yellow, sprinkle with 4 teaspoons of flour and stir with a wooden spoon for 1 minute. Add the hot wine and ¾ cup of boiling water. Add the *bouquet garni,* the tomato paste, sugar, salt, and pepper and simmer 15 minutes. Add the fish and simmer 15 minutes longer. Remove the *bouquet garni* and serve in a shallow dish.

Sauté thin slices of French bread in butter and serve with the sauce.

Fresh-water fish

*Carp, jewish fashion * Carpe à la juive*

FOR FOUR PEOPLE

2-pound carp
2 tablespoons chopped parsley
2 onions
2 cloves garlic
⅓ cup oil

2 tablespoons flour
½ teaspoon ginger
¼ pound mushrooms
salt and pepper

Buy the carp well scaled and cleaned. Be sure to buy a carp with roe. Cut the carp in slices and sprinkle it with salt and pepper. Keep in a cool place for 24 hours.

Chop the parsley, onions, and garlic very fine.

Heat the oil in a pan and stir in the flour. Add the chopped herbs and vegetables and add a cup of water, the ginger, salt, and pepper. Stir until blended. Add the fish slices and cook for 10 minutes without a cover. After 10 minutes, add the roe and the mushrooms, trimmed, washed, and chopped. Cook 10 minutes longer.

Re-form the fish on a heated serving platter. Boil down the sauce quickly until fairly thick and cover the fish with it.

Serve hot with noodles or cold with a salad.

Sweet and sour carp * Carpe aigre-douce

FOR FOUR PEOPLE

2-pound carp
3 tablespoons butter
4 teaspoons flour
1 onion, chopped fine
4 tablespoons seedless raisins

4 tablespoons yellow seedless raisins
3 tablespoons toasted slivered almonds
juice of ½ lemon
salt and pepper

Soak the raisins in water for 1 hour.

Buy the carp scaled and cleaned. Wash it well. Cut in pieces.

Heat the butter in a saucepan and add the flour. When blended, add 1 cup of water. Season with salt and pepper and add the onion, the raisins, and the fish pieces. Cook uncovered gently for 30 minutes.

Just before serving, add the almonds and the juice of ½ lemon.

Eels

Eels are more commonly eaten in France than in America. They can be found in great abundance all over the country but are usually sold only in certain large markets where the eels are kept alive in tanks. The one exception to this is at Christmas, where, thanks to the Mediterranean custom of eating eels at holiday time, they can be found in many markets.

The eels have to be skinned. The skin is slit around the neck and peeled off like a glove. A pair of pincers is a handy tool for this operation.

Boiled eels à l'angevine
Bouilleture d'anguilles à l'angevine

FOR SIX PEOPLE

3 eels (14-18 ounces each)
7 ounces (14 tablespoons) butter
½ pound mushrooms
2 cups dry white wine
   (preferably Anjou)

⅘ tablespoon heavy cream
salt and pepper

Skin and clean the eels and cut them into 1½-inch pieces. Throw away the heads. Put the butter in a large pan and add the eels and the raw mushrooms, trimmed and washed, left whole or cut in pieces, depending on size. Cover the pan and heat slowly for 5 to 6 minutes. Add enough wine to cover the eel pieces and put the pan on high heat until the liquid boils. Reduce the heat and simmer 10 minutes.

Remove the eel pieces to a heated serving dish with a slotted spoon. Cover to keep warm. Boil down the liquid rapidly to half its original quantity. Add the cream and beat the sauce with a fork for a few moments without letting the mixture boil. Season to taste with salt and pepper. Pour the sauce over the eels and serve immediately.

Eel on a spit * Anguille à la broche

FOR FOUR PEOPLE

1 live eel	Gribiche Sauce (page 10)
thin loaf French bread	salt
6 ounces (12 tablespoons) butter	

Cut off the head of a live eel and skin it. Cut into pieces approximately 2 inches long.

Cut small pieces of bread.

Alternate pieces of bread and eel on a long spit and brush them with melted butter and sprinkle with salt. Roast over a high heat, basting with the melted butter.

Serve the hot pieces of eel on the toasted bread and accompany with the sauce.

Eel stew * Matelote d'anguilles

FOR SIX PEOPLE

1 large onion	2 pounds eels
1 shallot	1½ tablespoons cognac
2 carrots	1 pound small onions
10 tablespoons butter	2½ tablespoons flour
2 cups good red wine	salt and pepper
bouquet garni (thyme, bay leaf, parsley)	

Peel the onion, shallot, and carrots and cut them into small pieces. In a pan, melt 3 tablespoons of the butter and sauté the vegetables until golden. Add the wine and *bouquet garni*. Simmer uncovered for 1¼ hours. Remove from the heat and cool.

Skin and clean the eel and cut in 2-inch pieces. Place the pieces in a saucepan and strain the wine sauce over the eel. Season with salt and pepper, add the cognac, and bring to a boil. The moment it boils, reduce the heat and barely simmer for 40 minutes.

Peel the small onions and boil them in salted water just until tender.

Work the balance of the butter and flour together until completely blended.

Transfer the eel to a heated serving dish with a slotted spoon. Add the onions to the eel pieces.

Drop the butter mixture by small bits into a simmering sauce, stirring constantly with a whip. Strain the sauce over eel and onions.

River perch

After trout, perch is considered the queen of the streams. Perch should be scaled as soon as it is caught. In America it is known as pike perch (although not related to a pike). The blue pike perch, which most closely resembles the French *perche* is fished mainly in the Great Lakes. Most of the fish weigh between 1 and 1½ pounds. In American markets, although occasionally sold whole, the perch is usually sold filleted. The following recipes can be made with the fillets.

Pike perch fillet fritters
Filets de perche en beignets

FOR FOUR PEOPLE

4 perch *or*	lemon wedges
8 perch fillets	parsley
flour	Mayonnaise (page 14)
Frying Batter III or IV (page 111)	

Cook the well-scaled and cleaned perch in boiling water for 10 minutes. Remove them from the water and take the two back fillets. The stomach fillets are full of bones. Don't bother with them.

Or poach perch fillets in water for 8 to 10 minutes. Cool the fillets.

Make the frying batter, allowing it time to rest.

Just before serving, dip the fillets first in the flour and then in frying batter and fry them at 380° F. just until they are golden. Serve immediately. Garnish with lemon wedges and fried parsley. Accompany with a bowl of mayonnaise.

*Pike perch meunière * Perches meunière*

FOR FOUR PEOPLE

4 1-pound pike perch	juice of 1 lemon
flour	salt and pepper
7 tablespoons butter	

Clean and wash well the scaled fish. Dip them in flour. If only fillets are available, dip them in flour and cook the same way.

Heat the butter in a skillet and sauté the fish 4 minutes on each side. Turn the fish carefully. Season with salt and pepper and sprinkle with lemon juice just before serving.

Pike à la georgienne * Brochet à la georgienne

FOR SIX PEOPLE

2-3-pound pike	red pepper, green pepper,
3 tablespoons butter	or hard-cooked eggs
½ cup heavy cream	salt
1¾ cups chopped walnuts	

Scale and clean the pike and bake in a 350° F. oven with the butter for 45 to 60 minutes. Season with salt and baste frequently during the baking. 10 minutes before the end of cooking, pour the cream, mixed with the chopped nuts, over the fish.

Serve on a heated platter. Decorate, as you wish, with red and green peppers or with quarters of hard-cooked eggs.

Pike with white butter sauce
Brochet au beurre blanc

FOR EIGHT PEOPLE

Court Bouillon II (page 163)	White Butter Sauce (page 24)
3-pound pike	

Cook the court bouillon. Cool to lukewarm.

Put the whole pike, cleaned and scaled (preferably with the head left on), in the lukewarm liquid and bring to a boil. As soon as it reaches the boiling point, reduce the heat and poach very gently for 25 minutes.

Make the sauce.

Transfer the fish to a well-heated platter. Remove the skin and spoon the sauce over the fish.

Roast pike with white wine
Brochet rôti au vin blanc

FOR SIX PEOPLE

7 ounces fat pork belly	2 cups good white wine
10 tablespoons butter	4 tablespoons flour
4-pound pike	salt and pepper

Have the fat cut in thin long strips as you would for larding a piece of beef. (If fresh pork fat is not available, parboil fat salt pork for 5 minutes and rinse.—*Ed.*) Lay the strips on both sides of the fish.

Dot the roasting pan with 3 tablespoons of butter and lay the fish on the butter. Season the fish with salt and pepper and roast at 400° F. for 20 to 25 minutes. Remove from the roasting pan to a heated serving platter. Keep warm.

Pour the wine into the roasting pan, scraping up all the juices adhering to the pan.

Heat the balance of the butter and stir in the flour. Add the wine and stir until blended. Simmer 5 minutes. Taste for seasoning and pour the sauce over the fish.

Sauger (yellow pike perch) * *Sandre*

FOR SEVEN PEOPLE

Sauger, also called wall-eyed or sand pike, are the most plentiful of the species of pike perch. It has delicious firm white meat.—Ed.

3-pound sauger
1 cup white wine vinegar
1 onion, sliced thin
1 shallot

bouquet garni (thyme, bay leaf, parsley)
Boyard Sauce (page 7)
salt and peppercorns

Scale the fish and clean it out through the gills and not by the stomach. Cut off the fins and wash well.

Place it in a fish boiler or other kettle. Cover with cold water and add the vinegar, onion, shallot, *bouquet garni,* salt (coarse salt, if possible), and a few peppercorns. Bring to a boil. Lower the heat and simmer about 35 minutes. Remove from the liquid to drain and cool. Serve the fish on a napkin-lined serving platter with a side dish of sauce.

Broiled salmon with white butter sauce
Saumon grillé au beurre blanc

FOR FOUR PEOPLE

4 5-ounce fresh salmon steaks
1½ tablespoons oil
White Butter Sauce (page 24)
1 tablespoon butter, melted

parsley
lemons
salt and pepper

Put the salmon on a plate and sprinkle with the oil. Let stand 30 minutes, turning occasionally.

Make the sauce.

Preheat the broiler. Brush the salmon with melted butter and place on the hot dry broiling rack. Broil 15 minutes, turning the steaks so that they will be browned on both sides. Season with salt and pepper.

Place the fish on a preheated serving platter. Decorate with parsley and lemon wedges and accompany with a side bowl of sauce.

Broiled salmon, maître d'hôtel butter
Saumon grillé, beurre maître d'hôtel

FOR EIGHT PEOPLE

8 5-6 ounce slices fresh salmon steaks   parsley
3 tablespoons oil   lemons
2 tablespoons butter   salt and pepper
Maître d'Hôtel Butter (page 12)

Follow the preceding recipe, substituting the maître d'hôtel butter for the white butter sauce.

Baked shad * Alose au four

FOR EIGHT PEOPLE

1 large shad (approximately   5 shallots, finely chopped
   4 pounds)   1 tablespoon chopped parsley
1½ pounds sorrel   2 cups dry white wine
7 ounces (14 tablespoons) butter   salt and pepper
3 egg yolks

Have the fish cleaned and scaled. Buy the shad with the roe.

Trim and wash the sorrel and put it in a saucepan with 2 tablespoons of butter and cook over a moderate heat until the sorrel wilts completely. Mix it with the shad roe and add 7 tablespoons of butter and the 3 egg yolks. Mix thoroughly. Season with salt and pepper. Stuff the shad with the mixture.

Butter the baking pan generously and sprinkle the butter with the chopped shallots and parsley. Pour in the wine and put in the fish. Put a piece of butter on the fish, season with salt and pepper, and bake 40 minutes at 400° F., basting frequently.

Trout with almonds * Truites aux amandes

FOR FOUR PEOPLE

4 average-sized trout   4 tablespoons heavy cream

flour

7 tablespoons butter

¼ cup toasted slivered almonds

salt and pepper

Clean and wash the trout, leaving their heads on. Coat them lightly with flour.

Heat the butter in a skillet and sauté the fish 6 minutes on each side. Season with salt and pepper. Place on a heated platter.

Add the cream and the almonds to the butter in the pan. Heat and pour over the fish.

Trout in cases * Truites en papillotes

FOR FOUR PEOPLE

4 trout

wax paper or aluminum foil

3 tablespoons salted butter

Clean, wash, and dry the trout, leaving the heads on.

Cut 4 long rectangles of wax paper or aluminum foil. Spread them with slightly salted butter and wrap a trout in each one, sealing in the fish completely. Place on a baking sheet and bake 20 minutes at 400° F. Serve very hot in the cases. Each diner will unwrap his own.

Trout in cream * Truites à la crème

FOR FOUR PEOPLE

4 average-sized trout

flour

7 tablespoons butter

½ cup sweet white wine or sweet cider

½ cup heavy cream

salt and pepper

Clean and wash the trout, leaving the heads on. Gash the trout slightly on both sides. Season with salt and pepper and coat lightly with flour.

Heat the butter in a skillet. When it is very hot, put in the trout and sauté 4 to 5 minutes on each side.

Pour in the white wine or cider and cook a few minutes over a low heat. Add the cream, season to taste with salt and pepper, and cook just until the sauce is blended and slightly thickened.

Cold trout with green sauce
Truite saumonée, sauce verte

FOR EIGHT PEOPLE

Court bouillon:

2 cups white wine vinegar

peppercorns

salt (preferably coarse)

1 pound carrots
2-3 onions
bouquet garni (thyme, bay leaf, parsley)

1 large (4-5 pound) trout
Green Sauce (page 10)
4 hard-cooked eggs
4 small tomatoes

Put 3¾ quarts of water in a large kettle and add the vinegar, carrots, onions peeled and sliced, *bouquet garni,* peppercorns, and 2 teaspoons of salt. Boil 1 hour. Strain and cool.

Put the fish wrapped in a towel or heavy cheesecloth on a rack in a fish boiler or large kettle. Pour in enough of the strained court bouillon to just cover the fish. Bring to a boil, and as soon as the boiling point is reached, reduce the heat and simmer, counting 20 minutes per pound. Remove from the heat and cool to luke-warm in the broth. Remove from the liquid to cool completely and drain.

Make the sauce.

Place on a serving platter. Surround with halves of hard-cooked eggs and small tomato halves hollowed and filled with green sauce. The rest of the sauce will be served in a separate bowl.

Trout à la lorraine * Truite à la lorraine

FOR FOUR PEOPLE

4 trout (approximately 7 ounces each)
3 tablespoons flour
7 tablespoons butter

1 cup heavy cream
salt

Clean and wash the trout, leaving the heads on. Dry them carefully in a towel and roll them lightly in the flour.

Heat half the butter in a skillet and sauté the trout a few moments on each side. Sprinkle with salt. Cover the skillet and simmer 7 to 8 minutes.

Arrange the fish on a heated platter. Add the balance of the butter and the cream to the butter in the skillet. Heat well but do not let the mixture boil. Pour very hot over the fish and be sure that your plates are heated also.

Whitebait omelet * Omelette aux petits poissons

FOR FOUR PEOPLE

Whitebait are tiny fish that look like minnows. They are eaten whole and uncleaned and are very delicious.—Ed.

8 eggs
½ pound whitebait
flour

3 tablespoons butter
salt

Beat the eggs as you would for any omelet. Season with salt.

Dredge the tiny fish well in flour and throw them into deep fat (385° F.). Fry until they are golden brown—this is a matter of a very few moments.

Drain well.

Heat the butter in a skillet and make the omelet in the usual manner. See page 130. Just before folding, put in the fried whitebait. Serve immediately.

Shellfish

For some unknown reason, the pretty term *fruits of the sea* or *seafood* does not apply to ordinary fish but only to shellfish: lobsters, crawfish, crabs, oysters, and so on, and does not apply to all crustaceans, molluscs, and even echinoderms (sea urchins, for example).

From time immemorial, France, loving good food and having a long sea coast, has always been particularly fond of shellfish, and despite all the wealth of food that the land has to offer, has always given an important place on the menu to *les fruits de mer.*

And what about today? New restaurants keep opening that specialize in nothing but shellfish. And although we prefer to eat shellfish caught off our own coasts, that does not seem to be enough, and our Breton fishermen, thanks to modern techniques, travel far to capture crawfish and *langoustes* in the waters off Ireland, Scotland, Africa, and Brazil and in the Caribbean and even in the Indian Ocean. Some time ago, there was a cod war between England and Iceland, and more recently there has been a lobster war between the French and the Brazilians, the latter worrying that our fishermen were trapping too many crawfish off their coast. Every year they hunt for new territories for fishing.

As for molluscs, the most popular are the oysters. They have been eaten in France from ancient times. The Romans coming to France left records about the great amount of oysters eaten by the Gauls. It is even said that the Romans, who were the ingenious inventors of oyster culture, took back to Italy the "Celtic oysters." All through our history, there are signs of this taste for oysters. In the eighteenth century, there was a relay service, of donkeys burdened with hampers filled with oysters, between the coasts and Paris, which was labeled "sea hunt."

Of course, until recently one could eat fresh oysters only by the sea, which is why our traditional cuisine offers so many recipes for cooked oysters: oyster soup, oyster pâtés, fried oysters, oysters soufflés, oysters *au gratin,* marinated oysters, and so on.

Now our rapid communications and the huge development of oyster culture let us have completely fresh and healthy raw oysters with their delicate flavor, and recipes for cooking oysters are all but forgotten. However, I am going to give you some that—paradoxically—are what the oyster growers have invented. They, who can have all the fresh oysters they want, have produced these recipes to vary the monotony of their menus. In my opinion, however, there is nothing better than the fresh, raw oyster.

Advice on crustaceans and molluscs

Crabs: Always buy heavy crabs. If a crab lacks a claw, stuff the opening with bread before cooking the crab, or the crabmeat will become water-soaked during the cooking. Plunge the live crab in a court bouillon or boiling salted water and cook, allowing 8 minutes per pound. Cool to lukewarm before removing the claws and breaking open the shell. Take out the meat with a pointed knife and serve with a Vinaigrette Sauce (page 29) to which a hard-cooked egg has been added.

Crabmeat: Crabmeat does not travel far except in cans or frozen. In America, the people on the west coast enjoy the famous Dungeness crab, which weighs from 1½ to 3½ pounds. Further north, there is the excellent King Crab of Alaska, which weighs from 5 to 12 pounds and which is sold very successfully in a frozen state all over the country. The Atlantic coast is rich in crab, but the best comes from the Maryland coast. The shell of all crabs is very hard and has to be broken with a hammer, but the meat that comes after the tedious work of picking it out is well worth the effort.

Shrimps: The *crevettes grises* are small shrimp, which are less decorative but more flavorful than the large and pink variety. In America, the small variety is found only in the San Francisco Bay area and occasionally off the New England coast. They are so tender that you can boil them and eat them shell and all. Served with salt and buttered bread, they make a marvelous dish. The large shrimps should be cooked with a highly seasoned court bouillon to give them more flavor.

Lobster: Lobster, which must be very much alive until it is cooked, is plunged into boiling water or court bouillon. When the lobster is cooked, always remove the "stomach," which is found in the head and the bitter intestinal strip down the center of the tail.

Spiny Lobster (Langoustes): These are lobsters without claws and are also called crayfish or just lobster. The best French variety are the brownish colored, which are far superior to the green *langouste* fished off the African coasts. In America, the best crawfish or spiny lobsters are found around San Francisco, but they are available all along the Pacific and southern Atlantic coasts. Recipes for spiny lobster can be made with lobsters. Never overcook either lobster or spiny lobster, because the overcooked flesh becomes soft and stringy.

Cockles: Cockles are found in the French market all year round. They are eaten like oysters, raw, seasoned with lemon juice, or cooked in a court bouillon. Opened over a high heat like mussels, they are delicious in rice pilaffs. Cockles are not marketed in America except in jars.

Scallops: Scallops are sold in their shells in France. Only the scallop meat and the coral are kept. In America, the scallop meat is sold without the shells and without the coral.

Mussels: Choose mussels that are not too large. Scrape them carefully and wash them well before putting them in a pan without water and heating them until the mussels open. If you have gathered them yourself and only in that case, you can eat them raw like oysters. Mussels should not be gathered in harbors or anywhere where sewage might poison them. Away from the coast it is best to eat them in the R months.

Crawfish (écrevisses): These fresh-water crustaceans are called crawfish, crayfish, or crawdabs and are available in the northwest and some states of the midwest. They look like tiny lobsters. They are rarely sold in the Eastern markets.

Crab in shells * Coquilles de tourteau

FOR FOUR PEOPLE

1 pound crabmeat
⅔ cup sliced mushrooms
3 tablespoons butter
1½ cups Béchamel Sauce (page 6)
3 egg yolks

juice of 1 lemon
fine breadcrumbs
melted butter
salt and pepper

Buy the fresh crabmeat or boil crab (enough to give you a pound—2 cups—of crabmeat) in salted water for 15 minutes and pick out the pieces, leaving some of the claw meat to use as a garnish.

Trim, wash, and slice the mushrooms and sauté them 2 minutes in butter.

Make the béchamel sauce. Add the crabmeat, except for the garnish, the mushrooms, salt, and pepper. When well heated, remove from the heat and stir in the egg yolks slightly beaten with the lemon juice.

Fill scallop shells or shallow ramekins with the mixture. Cover with fine breadcrumbs and sprinkle with a little melted butter. Brown slowly in a 350° F. oven. Garnish with pieces of claw meat.

Toulon crabs * Crabes toulonnais

FOR FOUR PEOPLE

2 large crabs
Court Bouillon (page 163)
1 hard-cooked egg
½ clove garlic
small stalk fennel
lemon juice

2 pounds mussels
1 tablespoon flour
¾ cup scalded milk
fine breadcrumbs
salt and pepper

Cook the crabs in a court bouillon, which should be highly seasoned. Remove from the court bouillon. Cool to lukewarm and remove the crabmeat. Keep the claw meat in a warm place. Wash some pieces of the body shell and save them.

With a mortar and pestle or a wooden bowl and pounder, pound and rub the egg, the yellowish tamale and the roe, found in the bodies, the garlic, fennel, and a few drops of lemon juice until well blended.

Scrape and wash the mussels and put them in a pan over high heat. When they open, sprinkle with salt and pepper and remove from the heat. Remove the mussels from the shells and chop them coarsely.

Heat 3 tablespoons of oil and brown the flour very lightly in a deep skillet. Add the hot milk and ¾ cup of the strained mussel liquor and stir until the sauce has the consistency of light cream. Stir in the pounded mixture, then the mussel and claw meat. Taste for seasoning and cook uncovered for a few minutes. Fill the crab shells with the mixture and cover with fine breadcrumbs. Sprinkle with oil and brown in a 450° F. oven for a few minutes.

Crawfish bouquet
Buisson d'écrevisses cardinalisées

FOR SEVEN TO EIGHT PEOPLE

4 pounds very lively crawfish (see page 209)
Court bouillon:
2 small onions
6 shallots
4 cloves garlic
several sprigs parsley

2 quarts white wine
2 cloves
½ bay leaf
1 sprig thyme
cayenne, paprika
salt and white pepper

Wash the crawfish. Pull out the center back flipper, which will bring with it the intestinal strip.

Chop the onions, shallots, garlic, and parsley quite fine. Put them in a large pan with the white wine and add the cloves, bay leaf, and thyme made into a *bouquet garni.* Bring to a boil and boil down one third. Add the seasoning, using a pinch of cayenne and paprika, sea salt, and white pepper.

Bring back to a full rolling boil and throw in the live crawfish. Cook 3 to 5 minutes or until they are bright red. Remove from the court bouillon, and when cooled, arrange them on a serving platter in a kind of pyramid. Just before serving, sprinkle with some of the court bouillon. Garnish with a small bouquet of parsley placed in the top of the pyramid.

Crawfish au gratin * Gratin de queues d'écrevisses

FOR SIX PEOPLE

Court Bouillon VI (page 165)
45 crawfish (see page 209)
1 cup Béchamel Sauce (page 6)
7 tablespoons butter
1 tablespoon *fine champagne*

1 truffle, diced fine
¼ pound mushrooms
1½ cups heavy cream
½ cup grated Gruyère cheese
salt and pepper

Prepare the court bouillon.

Wash the crawfish and pull out the center flipper on the tail. This will remove the intestinal strip.

Simmer the crawfish in the court bouillon for 20 minutes. Drain and remove the meat from the tails.

Make the béchamel.

Pound or pulverize enough crawfish shells to give you 3 tablespoons. Mix with an equal amount of butter, and when well blended, force the mixture through a fine strainer.

Melt the rest of the butter in a heavy pan and sauté the crawfish tails. When they have been lightly sautéed on all sides, add the cognac and touch with a lighted match. Add the diced truffle and the mushrooms, washed, trimmed, and thinly sliced. Season with salt and pepper.

Add the cream to the béchamel and heat slowly, adding bit by bit the crawfish butter and a little of the truffle juice from the can and season with salt and pepper.

Preheat the oven to 400° F. Put the crawfish and the rest of the contents of the pan in a shallow heatproof serving dish. Cover with the sauce and sprinkle with grated cheese. Brown 10 minutes in the oven. (This is excellent made with African lobster tails.—*Ed.*)

Broiled spiny lobster, sauce gérard
Langouste grillée, "sauce gérard"

FOR FOUR PEOPLE

1 large spiny lobster (2¾ pounds, approximately)
oil
½ cup wine vinegar
4 shallots, chopped
1 teaspoon crushed peppercorns
1 sprig each tarragon, parsley, chervil

4 egg yolks
½ pound butter
fine champagne
½ teaspoon chopped tarragon
cayenne
salt and pepper

Preheat the oven to 450° F.

Split the lobster in half and remove the intestinal strip.

Remove the roe. Season the meat, brush it with oil, and broil 15 to 20 minutes.

In the top part of a double boiler, boil down the vinegar with the shallots, peppercorns, and herb sprigs to a third its original quantity. With it make a béarnaise, using the egg yolks and butter. See page 6.

Cook the roe with 2 tablespoons of *fine champagne* or very good cognac for 2 to 3 minutes and force it through a sieve. Add this to the béarnaise and taste for seasoning. Add the chopped tarragon. Keep the sauce just warm, not hot, in a double boiler.

Serve the lobster very hot, accompanied by the warm sauce, and serve with boiled rice.

Fisherman's spiny lobster * Langouste du pêcheur

FOR FOUR PEOPLE

2 haddock heads	2 ¾-pound spiny lobster
⅓ cup oil	4 teaspoons turmeric *or*
2 cups dry white wine	1 large pinch saffron
bouquet garni (thyme, bay leaf)	1 quart mussels
1 clove garlic, chopped	boiled potatoes

Ask your dealer to give you the haddock heads, or lacking these, buy 2 pounds of unboned finnan haddie. Put it in a kettle with the oil and heat without browning for several minutes. Add the wine and an equal amount of water, the *bouquet garni,* salt, pepper, and garlic. Simmer, covered, for 30 minutes. Add the live lobster and the turmeric or saffron and cook 30 minutes longer.

Wash, scrape, and cook the mussels in their own juice.

Remove the lobster and strain the broth. Cut the lobster in pieces.

Put the lobster on a heated, deep serving platter. Surround with the cooked mussels and the boiled potatoes. Pour the broth over everything.

Spiny lobster with port or sherry
Langouste au porto ou xérès

FOR FOUR PEOPLE

2 ½-pound spiny lobster	2 teaspoons flour
2 onions	⅓ cup port (or sherry)
7 tablespoons butter	salt and pepper
2 cups heavy cream	

Cut the lobster into pieces.

Peel and chop the onions and sauté them in 5 tablespoons of butter with the lobster pieces, shell side down, over high heat. When the lobster pieces are light red, add the salt, pepper, and cream. Turn the lobster pieces over, cover, and cook gently for 30 minutes.

Remove to a heated platter with a slotted spoon.

Mix the remaining butter with the flour. Add this in small pieces to the sauce and add the wine. Stir well and pour over the lobster. Serve with boiled rice.

Potted spiny lobster * Civet de langouste

FOR SIX PEOPLE

4 onions	4 teaspoons chopped parsley
3 cloves garlic	2 tablespoons tomato paste

5 ½ pounds live spiny lobster
½ cup oil
5 tablespoons butter
6 tablespoons cognac

3 cups dry white wine, heated
cayenne
3 egg yolks
salt and pepper

Chop the onions and garlic quite fine and put in a saucepan with enough cold water just to cover. Cover and simmer 30 minutes. Drain well.

Cut the lobsters into pieces. Heat the oil and butter in a skillet large enough for the pieces to lie flat, shell side down, one against the other. Do not let the lobster meat touch the fat or it will take on an unpleasant flavor.

Once the lobsters are very red, transfer them to a preheated kettle with a slotted spoon, with the kettle placed over a low heat. Sprinkle with 2 tablespoons of cognac and touch with a lighted match. Remove from the heat when the flame subsides.

Add the onion and garlic to the fat in the skillet along with the chopped parsley and tomato paste. Stir over low heat until hot and well blended and add to the lobster. Add the hot wine and season highly with salt, pepper, and cayenne. Cover and cook gently for 15 minutes. Add the rest of the cognac and simmer 10 minutes longer.

Beat the egg yolks and stir them into the lobster thoroughly. Taste for seasoning. This dish should be highly seasoned. Pour into a heated serving dish and serve hot.

Spiny lobsters éloi ✳ *Langouste éloi*

FOR SIX PEOPLE

Court Bouillon VI (page 165)
9 small live spiny lobsters
4 truffles
4 tablespoons cognac
1 onion
2 cloves garlic

¼ pound mushrooms
4 egg yolks
2 cups grated Gruyère cheese
10 tablespoons butter
salt and pepper

Prepare the boiling court bouillon and plunge the live lobsters into it. Cook 20 minutes. Remove from the court bouillon. Cool and split them in half. Carefully remove the meat and clean out the shells. Let the shells dry.

Meanwhile, marinate the truffles in brandy for 1 hour.

Trim, wash, dry, and chop the mushrooms.

Chop the onion and garlic. Dice the truffles and mix them all together with the lobster meat, coarsely chopped, and the cognac. Season with salt and pepper. Bind all this together with slightly beaten egg yolks. Fill the shells with the mixture.

Sprinkle the filled shells with cheese and dot each one with several pieces of butter. Bake in 400° F. oven until golden brown, basting frequently with the butter that runs into the pan. Serve immediately.

Lobster à l'armoricaine * Homard à l'armoricaine

FOR SIX PEOPLE

4 onions
1 clove garlic
5 pounds live lobsters
5 tablespoons butter
7 tablespoons oil
¼ cup cognac

2 tablespoons chopped parsley
1 ½ tablespoons tomato paste
2 cups dry white wine, heated
cayenne
salt and pepper

Chop the onions and garlic quite fine and boil them 10 minutes in a little water. Drain them well and force them through a fine sieve.

Cut the live lobsters into large pieces, using a heavy cleaver or large heavy knife.

Heat the butter and oil in a large skillet and put in the lobster shell side down so that the lobster meat will not brown. When the shells are red, transfer them to a kettle standing over a low heat, and sprinkle with 1 ½ tablespoons of the cognac. Touch with a lighted match.

In the skillet in which you have sautéed the lobsters, add the onion purée, the parsley, and the tomato paste. Stir until blended and pour over the lobster. Add the hot white wine. Season with salt, pepper, and cayenne. Cover and cook over a low flame for 15 minutes. Add the rest of the cognac and simmer 10 minutes longer. Taste the sauce for seasoning.

Serve with boiled rice.

Cardinal lobster * Homard cardinal

FOR SIX PEOPLE

3-pound lobster
¼ pound mushrooms
2 tablespoons butter
1 ½ cups Béchamel Sauce (page 6)
red vegetable coloring

cayenne
1 large truffle
¼ cup grated Gruyère cheese
salt and pepper

Fill a large kettle of water and bring to a full rolling boil with a tablespoon of salt. Put in the live lobster. Boil 30 minutes. Remove from the kettle and cool.

Put the lobster on a cutting board. Pull off the claws close to the body with your hands. Remove the head. Break the claws, remove the meat, and cut into very small pieces. Remove also the tamale (greenish liver).

Trim and wash the mushrooms. Slice the caps and cut the stems into small pieces. Sauté briefly in butter.

Make the béchamel and color it pink with a drop or two of vegetable coloring.

Combine the lobster meat, tamale, and mushrooms in a bowl and add a little of the sauce. This should be a rather thick mixture. Season to taste with salt, pepper, and a little cayenne, if you like lobster highly seasoned.

Lay the lobster flat on the board, and using a pair of scissors, cut away everything in the body shell, leaving it empty, and remove the meat from the tail. Fill the body and tail shell with the mixture. Cut the tail meat in slices and cut the truffle in thin slices. Alternate slices of lobster meat and truffle over the filling so that the entire shell is filled. Spoon over the rest of the sauce, which should not be very thick. Place on a heatproof serving platter. Sprinkle lightly with grated cheese and put the lobster in a hot oven just to let it reheat. It must not dry out. Serve with boiled rice.

Lobster in champagne * Homard au champagne

FOR TWO PEOPLE

1¼-1½-pound lobster
3 tablespoons butter
4 tablespoons Madeira
fish stock
1 truffle

1 cup heavy cream
¾ cup champagne
2 egg yolks
salt and pepper

Cut a live lobster in approximately 1¼-inch slices. Sauté them in butter until red. Season with salt and pepper, Madeira, and enough fish stock to come halfway up the lobsters. If possible, add a truffle. Cover and cook gently for 20 minutes.

Remove the lobster from the pan with a slotted spoon and remove the meat from the shells. Slice the lobster meat and the truffle and place in a serving dish. Keep covered and warm while preparing the sauce.

Strain the cooking broth and boil it down to 1 cup. Add the heavy cream and heat without boiling. Add the champagne, and taking the pan from the heat, stir in the egg yolks. Pour the sauce over the lobster and serve immediately. This dish cannot wait.

Curry of lobster mapie * Homard au cari mapie

FOR SIX PEOPLE

3 2-pound lobsters
3 medium-sized onions
7 tablespoons olive oil
8 teaspoons curry powder
2 cups white wine

3 egg yolks
¾ cup heavy cream
juice of 2 lemons
salt and pepper

Plunge the live lobsters into a large kettle of boiling salted water and cook 3 minutes. Remove them from the water. Cut the tails and claws into pieces.

Chop the onions and sauté them in olive oil just until pale yellow. Add the lobster pieces and continue cooking for five minutes. Sprinkle with curry and add about 2 cups of wine or enough to come halfway up the lobster pieces. Season with salt and cook with the cover on the pan until the liquid has been reduced by half.

Transfer the lobster pieces with a slotted spoon to a deep serving platter.

In a small bowl beat the egg yolks with the cream and some lemon juice. Remove the lobster sauce from the heat and add the egg mixture to the sauce. Stir and taste, adding more salt, pepper, and lemon juice, if necessary. Pour the sauce over the lobster pieces and serve with boiled rice.

Lobster daniel lacombe * Homard daniel lacombe

FOR EIGHT PEOPLE

4 1½-pound lobsters
7 ounces butter
5 tablespoons chopped herbs (parsley, chervil, chives)
2 onions
2 shallots
⅓ cup armagnac

1 tablespoon flour
cayenne
1⅓ cups bouillon
2 cups heavy cream
½ cup grated Gruyère cheese
salt and pepper

Cut the live lobsters into pieces with a cleaver or 2 sharp, heavy knives.

Heat 10 tablespoons of butter in a large skillet and sauté the lobster pieces until bright red. Remove the pieces from the skillet with a slotted spoon and put them aside for the moment.

Make a mixture of finely chopped herbs and vegetables and sauté it in the same butter until the onions are soft. Put back the lobster pieces and add the armagnac. Touch with a lighted match.

When the flames subside, sprinkle with flour and season with salt, pepper, and a dash of cayenne. Add the rest of the butter. Reduce the heat, cover, and simmer 20 minutes. Add the cream and the cheese. Heat but do not boil for 10 minutes. Taste for seasoning. Serve very hot.

Sherry lobster * Homard au xérès

FOR FOUR PEOPLE

2½ pounds live lobster
7 tablespoons butter
cayenne
5 tablespoons sherry

4 egg yolks
10 tablespoons heavy cream
salt

Buy 1 large or 2 1¼-pound lobsters. Boil them in salted water for 20 to 30 minutes, depending on size. Remove from the water and cool. Remove the meat from the shells and cut into average-sized pieces. Take out the tamale (greenish liver) and put it in a bowl.

Melt the butter in the top of a double boiler. Add the lobster and a pinch of cayenne. Cook 5 minutes. Add the sherry and a pinch of cayenne.

Add the egg yolks and the cream to the tamale and beat well. Pour this mixture onto the lobster and stir constantly until the mixture thickens. Do not let it boil. Taste before adding salt.

Serve in a *vol-au-vent* for a formal dinner.

Bathing lobsters * Homards à la nage

FOR FOUR PEOPLE

2¾ cups white wine	2 *bouquets garnis* (thyme, bay leaf)
1 cup veal or chicken stock	4 1-pound live lobsters
1 onion	1 tablespoon white vinegar
2 carrots	½ pound soft butter
2-3 sprigs parsley	lemon juice (optional)
6 shallots	salt and pepper

The bath: Combine in a saucepan the white wine, stock, onion, carrots cut in slices, parsley and shallots chopped fine, and a *bouquet garni.* Add 2 teaspoons of salt and cook until the vegetables are soft.

The lobsters: Plunge the live lobsters in a large kettle of boiling water to which salt, a tablespoon of white vinegar, and a small *bouquet garni* have been added. Boil 20 minutes. Remove from the heat, but let the lobsters stay in the water for another 5 minutes. Drain them and split them lengthwise, removing and saving the tamale (greenish liver). Shell the lobster claws and tails.

While the lobsters are cooking, put the soft butter in a bowl and place it in a bowl of ice. Beat vigorously with a whip. Add the hot bath mixture to the butter gradually, stirring constantly. Add enough to give you a slightly thickened sauce. Add the tamale. Taste the sauce, adding lemon juice, if you like.

Arrange the lobster meat on a platter and spoon the sauce over it all.

Mussels poulette * Moules poulette

FOR FOUR PEOPLE

3 quarts mussels	1 tablespoon flour
¾ cup white wine	¼ pound (scant) mushrooms
3 onions, chopped	1 egg yolk, beaten slightly
7 tablespoons butter	2 teaspoons chopped parsley

bouquet garni (thyme, bay leaf,
   parsley)

juice of ½ lemon
salt and pepper

Scrape and wash the mussels well under running water. Put them in a kettle with the wine, the chopped onions, and the *bouquet garni.* Heat without a cover until the mussels open.

Place the mussels in a shallow platter, removing the top shell from each one.

Heat the butter in a saucepan and blend in the flour. Add the mussel broth strained through a fine sieve and stir until blended. Add the mushrooms, trimmed, washed, and cut into pieces. Simmer over a low heat for 30 minutes.

Just before serving, remove the sauce from the heat and add the egg yolk, chopped parsley, salt, pepper, and the juice of half a lemon. Pour this sauce, which should be very hot, over the mussels.

Mussels saint jean * Mouclade saint jean

FOR EIGHT PEOPLE

7 quarts mussels
2¼ cups white wine (preferably
   Muscadet)
7 tablespoons butter
6 tablespoons flour
1 quart milk, scalded

2 tablespoons heavy cream
1 egg yolk
curry powder
sea salt
pepper

Scrape and wash the mussels. Put them in a pan and add enough wine to come halfway up the mussels. Heat until the mussels open. Remove the top shells of the mussels. Keep warm.

In a large saucepan, heat the butter and stir in the flour. When well blended, add the milk and stir until the mixture boils. Season with sea salt and black pepper.

In a bowl mix the cream, egg yolk, and a good pinch of curry. Pour this into the boiling milk sauce and stir vigorously until well blended. Taste for seasoning, adding more curry if the sauce is not sufficiently colored or flavored.

Add about ¼ cup of the wine in which the mussels cooked. Place the mussels in a heated serving dish and pour the sauce over them. Keep on a table warmer, because the mussels must be served very hot.

Surprise mussels on skewers
Brochettes de moules surprise

FOR SIX PEOPLE

1 quart mussels

fine breadcrumbs

6 slices bacon

2 thick slices cooked ham

1 egg, slightly beaten

10 tablespoons butter

juice of 1 lemon

salt and pepper

Put the mussels, which have been thoroughly scraped and washed, in a kettle and place over high heat until they open. Remove from the heat, cool to luke-warm, and remove the mussels from their shells.

Cut the bacon and the ham into 1-inch squares.

Alternate a mussel, a square of ham, and a square of bacon on 6 small skewers until everything has been used. Dip them in beaten egg and then in breadcrumbs, seasoned with salt and pepper.

Heat the butter in a large skillet and brown the filled skewers on all sides. Serve on a heated platter and sprinkle with lemon juice.

Mussels with spinach
Moules farcies aux épinards

FOR SIX PEOPLE

Stuffing:

¾ pound spinach

5 ounces cooked ham

2 tablespoons butter

2½ tablespoons olive oil

1 tablespoon chopped parsley

2 cloves garlic, chopped fine

⅓ cup soft breadcrumbs

milk

½ cup grated Gruyère cheese

1 egg

salt and pepper

Sauce:

2 medium-sized onions

2 shallots

2 cloves garlic

2½ tablespoons olive oil

2 tablespoons butter

3-4 tomatoes

4 teaspoons tomato paste

2 cups white wine

bouquet garni (thyme, bay leaf,
    parsley)

salt and pepper

Scrape and wash the mussels.

Set aside the 24 large mussels. Open the rest by putting them in a large kettle and cooking them over high heat until they open. Remove the mussels from the heat, and when lukewarm, remove the mussels from the shells. Save the broth and strain it through a very fine sieve.

In salted water boil thoroughly the washed spinach just until tender. Drain well.

Chop the cooked mussels, the ham, and the spinach, and when well mixed, sauté them lightly in a mixture of butter and oil for 10 minutes. Add the garlic, parsley and the breadcrumbs, soaked in a little milk and squeezed dry, and cook 10 minutes longer. Remove from the heat and add the cheese and raw egg. Mix thoroughly.

Open the large mussels with a knife. Stuff them well between the two parts of the mussels, which line the shells. Close and bind the mussels with 2 pieces of kitchen twine. These will simmer 1 hour in the following sauce.

To make the sauce: Sauté the chopped onions, shallots, and garlic in a mixture of the oil and butter. When golden, add the tomatoes, peeled, seeded, and chopped and simmer 15 minutes. Add the tomato paste and cook for another 15 minutes. Add the white wine, *bouquet garni,* and ¾ cup of strained mussel broth. Season with salt and pepper. Boil for about 5 minutes.

Add the stuffed mussels and simmer covered 1 hour. Remove the cover from time to time so that the sauce will become quite thick.

Remove the twine before serving.

Oysters

One of the compensations that the summer is over and that September, the first of the months with the letter R, has arrived is that it is again the time for oysters.

The oyster's most important quality is freshness. If uncooked, it must be eaten alive. If there is any suspicion, throw it away. Do not eat it. Once the top shell is removed, touch the oyster. If it retracts, it is alive.

Oysters are served on the half shell, on a bed of ice, accompanied by lemon wedges and buttered rye bread. A perfect sauce for oysters is made by adding salt and finely chopped shallots to vinegar. Very cold dry white wine is the best drink to go with oysters served this way.

Remember: Oysters should not be opened until just before serving.

Raw oysters are much better when eaten very cold. Serve them, if possible, on cracked ice.

When you open oysters, wrap your left hand in a towel for safety's sake.

When you cook oysters, take care never to let them boil.

Broiled oysters * *Huîtres sur le gril*

FOR FOUR PEOPLE

4 dozen oysters	juice of 1 lemon
7 tablespoons butter	fine breadcrumbs
1 large sprig parsley	salt and pepper
2 shallots	

Remove the oysters from the shells and put them and their juice into a small saucepan. Heat, but do not boil, until they stiffen slightly. Remove from the juice with a slotted spoon and put them in a skillet with the butter and chopped parsley and shallots. Sauté over a low heat, without letting them boil, until the edges curl. Season with pepper and add salt, if necessary.

Wash out the shells and put 1 (or 2) oysters with their sauce in each one. Sprinkle with a little lemon juice and cover with breadcrumbs. Place under a very hot broiler until they plump up. Serve immediately.

Fried oysters * Huîtres frites

FOR FOUR PEOPLE

2 dozen oysters

Frying Batter:
1¼ cups sifted all-purpose flour
1 egg yolk
¾ cup beer
1 teaspoon cognac
salt

Marinade:
2½ tablespoons wine vinegar
1 bay leaf
1 lemon
1 tablespoon chopped parsley
1 small onion, chopped
½ teaspoon powdered basil
1 clove

Begin by making the frying batter, because it should rest several hours before using. Sift the flour into a bowl. Fashion a well in the center, and into it put the egg yolk, beer, cognac, and a pinch of salt. Beat well with a wooden spoon.

Remove the oysters from the shells and let them drain in a sieve. Make a marinade by combining the ingredients and let the oysters soak in it for 1 hour. Remove them from the marinade and dry them on toweling.

Dip each one in the frying batter and fry in deep fat at 385° F.

Hot oysters in the shell * Huîtres en coquille

FOR FOUR PEOPLE

2 dozen oysters
2 shallots, finely chopped
3 tablespoons chopped raw mushrooms
1 tablespoon chopped parsley

fine breadcrumbs
butter
salt and pepper

Open the oyster shells and scrape out the oysters with their juice into a saucepan. Heat so that they will stiffen but do not boil.

Wash out the bottom shell of each oyster. Dry well.

Chop and combine the shallots, mushrooms, and parsley. Season with salt and pepper.

Put the oysters back in the shell. Sprinkle with the mushroom mixture. Cover with fine breadcrumbs and dot each one with a small piece of butter.

Bake 10 minutes at 400° F.

Parmesan oysters * Huîtres au parmesan

FOR FOUR PEOPLE

2 dozen oysters
butter
1 tablespoon chopped parsley

6 tablespoons champagne
½ cup grated Parmesan cheese
pepper

Remove the oysters from the shells and drain them well.

Butter a shallow baking dish and arrange the oysters in the dish. Sprinkle with chopped parsley and freshly ground pepper.

Sprinkle with champagne and finally with grated cheese.

Cook in a 400° F. oven for 10 minutes or until well browned. Do not let boil.

Flambéed scallops
Coquilles saint-jacques flambées

FOR SIX PEOPLE

2 pints scallops
1 cup white wine
½ pound mushrooms
7 tablespoons butter

1½ tablespoons cognac
½ cup heavy cream
salt and pepper

Cook the scallops in white wine over a moderate heat for 15 minutes.

Trim and wash the mushrooms and cut them into small pieces.

Then 10 minutes before serving, heat the butter in a skillet and sauté the mushrooms. Stir with a wooden spoon, and when the mushrooms begin to get firm, add the well-drained scallops. Cook 5 to 6 minutes. Add the cognac and touch with a lighted match. Add the heavy cream and season with salt and pepper. Bring to a boil and serve immediately.

Scallops with vermouth
Coquilles saint-jacques au vermouth

FOR FIVE PEOPLE

1½ pints scallops
1 cup vermouth
¾ pound mushrooms
7 tablespoons butter
¾ cup white wine

1 onion, chopped fine
1 tablespoon flour
3 egg yolks
¾ cup heavy cream
salt and pepper

Cook the scallops with the vermouth in a small saucepan for 10 minutes.

Wash, trim, and slice the mushrooms and sauté them in half the butter for 5 minutes.

In another saucepan cook the wine and onion together for 15 minutes.

Heat the rest of the butter in a larger saucepan and stir in the flour. Add the wine with the onions and stir until smooth. Strain the broth from the scallops into the pan and continue stirring. Season with salt and pepper.

Beat the egg yolks and cream until blended and add that to the sauce. Reheat but do not let the sauce boil.

Put the scallops in the center of a heated serving dish. Surround with the mushrooms and pour the sauce over everything. Serve very hot.

Snails

Snails, a great favorite with some, are detested by others. The better varieties are those harvested in dry places, far from swamps and marshes. Those growing in the vineyards are the best. They are good for the health, but because they are hard to digest, they are always seasoned with garlic.

If you gather snails yourself or buy them alive, you must always let them fast for a week in a large earthenware pot. The day before you cook them, wash them well and put them back in the pot with a handful of coarse salt, which will make them froth. Then cook them in a court bouillon (page 163) for 15 to 20 minutes. When they are easily removed from their shells, they are cooked and ready for final preparation.

Burgundy snails * Escargots à la bourguignonne

FOR FOUR PEOPLE

4 dozen snails	2 onions
¾ cup red wine vinegar	3 shallots
1 tablespoon coarse salt	3 cloves garlic
2½ tablespoons flour	1¾ cups butter
1 quart white Burgundy wine	½ cup finely chopped parsley
bouquet garni (bay leaf, thyme)	fine breadcrumbs
2 carrots	salt and pepper

Wash the snails in several changes of water. Remove the veils that close the openings with a sharp-pointed knife. Put the snails in a pan with the vinegar, salt, and flour. Let stand for 2 hours, stirring occasionally.

Wash the snails again and put them in a kettle of cold water. Bring to a boil, skimming off any matter that comes to the surface. Simmer 8 minutes. Remove and drain well.

Bring 3 cups of the wine and an equal quantity of water to a boil. Add the *bouquet garni,* the carrots and onions cut in rounds, 1 shallot, 1 clove of garlic chopped fine, and ½ teaspoon of peppercorns. Add the snails and cook, covered, over a very low heat for 3½ hours.

Make a mixture of the butter, 2 shallots and 2 cloves of garlic, chopped very fine, the parsley, salt, and pepper, blending it all very thoroughly.

Drain the snails. Take each one out of the shell and cut off the little black filament at the end of the snail. Wash and dry the shells. Put a little of the butter mixture in each shell. Insert the snails and fill the shells with more of the butter mixture, pressing it down with your thumb. Sprinkle with a little fine breadcrumbs. Put the prepared snails in a shallow baking dish. Sprinkle with the remaining Burgundy. Bake 8 minutes at 450° F. and serve immediately.

Snails à la curnonsky * Escargots à la curnonsky

FOR FOUR PEOPLE

4 dozen prepared snails (page 223)	2 onions
4 cups red wine	2 cloves
3 cloves garlic	bay leaf
½ red pepper	pinch of wild thyme or marjoram

Prepare the snails.

Bring the wine and the garlic and onions, chopped fine, to a boil. As soon as the mixture boils, add the red pepper, chopped fine, the rest of the seasonings, and the snails. Cook over a moderate heat for 25 to 30 minutes. Serve in a soup tureen with the broth.

N.B. Because this is hard to eat delicately, have plenty of paper napkins on hand.

Snails in herb butter * Escargots au beurre

FOR FOUR PEOPLE

½ teaspoon peppercorns	3 tablespoons finely chopped parsley
4 dozen snails	2 tablespoons soft breadcrumbs
7 tablespoons butter	pepper
4 cloves garlic	

Wash the snails and boil them in water for 20 minutes.

Remove the snails from the shells. Rinse out the shells carefully and put back the snails.

Pound together the butter, the garlic peeled and finely chopped or pressed, the parsley, and the breadcrumbs. Pound to a smooth paste and season with freshly ground black pepper. Put a little of this mixture in each shell.

Place a dozen snails in 4 individual heatproof plates and put them in a 450° F. oven. Heat until the butter is sizzling. Serve in their shells.

Squid in their ink ∗ Encornets dans leur encre

FOR FOUR PEOPLE

1 pound squid
½ pound (2 medium-sized) onions
1 clove garlic
½ cup oil

¼ small red pepper
1½ tablespoons armagnac
fried croutons
salt

Remove the heads of the squid and slit open the bellies, removing all the intestines but carefully saving the black liquid, the "ink" in the stomach. Chop the squid in pieces.

Chop the onions and garlic very fine and sauté them in the skillet with the oil and the squid pieces. Season with salt. When the onions are soft, add the ink, diluted in ½ cup of boiling water. Add the red pepper, finely chopped, and the armagnac. Cover and simmer 2 hours. Serve with croutons fried in butter.

Stuffed squid ∗ Encornets farcis

FOR FOUR PEOPLE

10 squid
1 large onion
2 large sprigs parsley
3 ounces pork fat
½ cup cooked rice

7 tablespoons butter
2 carrots
1½ tablespoons cognac
6 tablespoons white wine
salt and pepper

Buy the squid all cleaned and prepared for stuffing.

Wash thoroughly. Chop 2 squid quite fine. Chop the onion and the parsley, keeping them separate. Dice the pork fat and try it out in a skillet. (If fresh pork fat is not available, boil salt pork 5 minutes, rinse, and use like fresh pork fat.— Ed.) Add the onion and sauté with the chopped squid until golden-colored. Season with salt and pepper. Add the chopped parsley and the rice. Taste again for seasoning.

Stuff the squid with the mixture and sew up the openings. Heat the butter in a deep dish and sauté the carrots cut in thin rounds with the squids. When lightly browned on all sides, pour in the cognac and touch with a lighted match. Add the white wine, salt, and pepper and simmer covered for 1½ hours.

Large seafood turnover
Chausson aux fruits de mer

FOR SIX PEOPLE

Flaky Pastry (page 643)
1 quart mussels
4 frozen lobster tails
½ pint scallops
white vinegar
½ pound butter

3 shallots
4 teaspoons *fine champagne* or cognac
4 teaspoons chopped parsley
1 egg yolk
juice of 1 lemon
salt and pepper

Make the pastry, timing it so that it will be ready when you want it.

Wash and scrape the mussels. Place them in a pan over high heat until they open. Remove them from their shells.

Cook the lobster tails in boiling salted water for 10 minutes. Drain and remove them from their shells. Cut in slices.

Cook the scallops 10 minutes in boiling water to which a little white vinegar and salt have been added. Remove from the liquid and cut them across in 2 slices, if they are large.

Heat 3 tablespoons of butter in a saucepan and sauté the shallots, chopped fine, until tender. Add the scallops and lobster. Sprinkle with salt and pepper and sauté for 2 minutes. Add the liqueur and touch with a lighted match. Add the chopped parsley. Remove from the heat and stir in the mussels.

Preheat the oven to 400° F.

Roll out the pastry into a large round. Moisten the edges and put the seafood mixture on half the round. Fold over the other half and press the edges together.

Place on a buttered baking sheet.

Paint the surface with egg yolk mixed with a teaspoon of water. Bake 20 minutes.

Melt the rest of the butter and season with lemon juice and salt. Serve in a separate sauce dish.

Poultry
and game

Poultry

In the old days, poultry was more expensive than meat. Nowadays, it is rather the other way around, at least for industrially bred chicken. However, we much prefer what we call farm chicken, by which we mean chicken that are naturally bred, allowed to run freely in the farmyards, and fed with good grain. With the standardization of merchandising, the consumer need no longer scrutinize every bird that is bought, but can depend on the label it bears, which tells the source, the weight, and the quality.

Game is more commonly marketed in France than in most parts of the United States. State laws differ. Some states allow game to be sold, and others do not. In both countries, game is more expensive than domestic poultry, but its wild taste makes it prized among gourmets. Again, unless your game comes directly from the hunter's bag, the consumer must depend on the market for reliable merchandise.

Because both game and poultry are increasingly popular, it has been necessary to leave the beaten path of the classic recipes and to try some new ones.

In the following chapter, I will give you some of the classic recipes and some of more recent invention. But before you cook a chicken, you must know how to choose one.

For roasting: Choose a young, tender broiler (2-2½ pounds), a so-called fryer (2½-3½ pounds), or a roasting chicken (3½-6 pounds). The flesh should be moist and white. Or choose a capon (4-8 pounds), which has the same qualities as a chicken.

For fricassees: Choose a young, tender pullet (2½-5½ pounds) or a lean cockerel—or even a rooster or a hen, which are less succulent but lend themselves very well to preparations with sauces. It is a rooster or hen that you will use for boiled chicken.

In the city, chickens are usually sold all cleaned and ready for cooking. A young chicken should be chosen for its supple flesh, which is smooth and bluish white. The flesh is tender and the wish bone soft. A large chicken has large rounded thighs, a strong neck. Both breast and back should be covered with tender flesh and a thin layer of pale yellow fat.

If the chicken is sold with feet on, cut them off below the ankle; otherwise, in cooking, the skin will retract and the bone will appear. In general, the best way to cook poultry is on the spit, but whether they are cooked in the oven or on a spit, they take the same length of time. Never salt roasted poultry or game until the end of cooking, except when specifically indicated. To tell when a chicken is done, prick it with a fork. If the liquid that comes out is perfectly clear-colored, the chicken is ready to eat. Always save the bones and the carcass to make soup with.

Chicken

Roast chicken * *Poulet rôti*

FOR FOUR TO FIVE PEOPLE

1 large roasting chicken   salt and pepper
3 tablespoons butter

Buy the chicken dressed and ready for roasting. Leave the liver in the inside.
Preheat the oven to 400° F.

Spread the outside of the chicken with butter. Place the bird in a roasting pan
and roast in the oven, allowing 20 minutes per pound.

From time to time, put a few tablespoons of boiling water in the pan. Salt the
juices (not the bird) and baste frequently. To see if it is cooked, test the chicken
by inserting a fork in the thigh. If the juice that comes out is clear-colored and
not rosy, it is done.

Transfer the chicken to a heated platter. Add a little boiling water to the pan
and scrape off the juice adhering to the pan. Season with salt and pepper. Pour
the sauce into a heated gravy bowl and serve with the chicken.

Alsatian chicken * *Poulet à l'alsacienne*

FOR FOUR PEOPLE

2½-3-pound chicken   4 tablespoons turmeric
2 pounds fresh peas   ¾ cup grated Parmesan cheese
¼ pound noodles   ¼ pound butter
large pinch of saffron *or*   salt and pepper

Roast the chicken, basting often. (See preceding recipe.) Do not salt until the
last moment.

Shell the peas and boil in salted water until tender.

Cook the noodles in a large pan of salted water to which the saffron or turmeric
has been added. Drain, and if the peas are not ready, cover the collander so that
they will not cool.

Mix the noodles, peas, cheese, and butter and place on a heated serving platter.
Put the chicken, whole or cut up as you wish, on the mixture.

Put 2 tablespoons of boiling water in the roasting pan, scraping the juices from
the pan with a fork and blending them with the water. Serve in a separate bowl.

Chicken à l'armagnac * Poulet à l'armagnac

FOR FOUR PEOPLE

2½-3-pound chicken
4 tablespoons butter
paprika
1½ tablespoons armagnac

½ pound mushrooms
4 tablespoons heavy cream
salt and pepper

Have the chicken cut in 8 pieces. Heat the butter in a heavy pan with a tight-fitting flat cover. Brown the chicken pieces in the butter, adding salt, pepper, and a dash of paprika. Add the armagnac and cook uncovered for 2 minutes. Cover the pan and put a little water on the cover. Simmer very gently for 30 minutes.

Trim and wash the mushrooms. Boil 5 minutes in salted water. Drain. Then, 10 minutes before the chicken is cooked, add the mushrooms. Just before serving, add the heavy cream and serve very hot on a heated serving platter.

Chicken in aspic * Poulet en gelée

FOR FIVE PEOPLE

1 calf's foot
1 veal bone
4 carrots
3 tomatoes
fines herbes (parsley, tarragon,
    chervil)

3-3½ pound chicken
tarragon leaves
salt and pepper

Put 3 quarts of water in a soup kettle with a calf's foot (substituting a pig's foot, if necessary—Ed.). Add a veal bone sawed in several pieces, the carrots peeled and cut in large pieces, and the tomatoes cut in quarters. Add a sprig each of parsley, tarragon, and chervil and season with salt and pepper. Bring to a boil and cook 1 hour, skimming off the matter that floats to the surface.

Add the chicken, cleaned and trussed, to the bouillon. It should be completely covered. Add water, if necessary. Simmer 1½ hours. Remove the chicken from the bouillon and let it cool. Remove the skin and carve the chicken into serving pieces.

Strain the bouillon through a sieve lined with a cold wet dish towel. Let the bouillon cool, and when it has cooled to a syrupy consistency, but before it has jelled, it is ready for the next step.

Place the chicken pieces on a trivet over a shallow platter. Spoon the aspic over each piece several times. You can use again the liquid that falls into the platter. Arrange the chicken in a serving dish. Decorate each one with tarragon leaves and pour the liquid aspic around the chicken. Chill in the refrigerator.

Chicken with bananas * Poulet aux bananes

FOR FIVE PEOPLE

3-pound chicken	½ cup white wine
2 tablespoons butter	pinch of ginger
4 tablespoons oil	5 bananas
1½ tablespoons rum	salt and pepper

Have the chicken cut in pieces. Heat the butter and oil in a deep skillet or *sauteuse,* and when hot, brown the chicken over a moderate heat. Stir the chicken with a wooden spoon so that it will be well browned on all sides. Season with salt and pepper and add the rum. Touch with a lighted match and stir until the flame subsides.

Add the white wine and a pinch of ginger and cook covered over a low heat for 1 hour.

Peel the bananas and poach them in simmering water for about 2 minutes. Drain, cut in rounds, and keep warm.

Put the chicken with its sauce on a heated platter and surround with the banana slices.

Basque chicken * Poulet basquaise

FOR FIVE PEOPLE

3-pound chicken	3 green peppers
1 large slice raw ham (½ inch thick)	3 tomatoes
1 bunch small green onions	cayenne
5 tablespoons butter	salt and pepper
1½ tablespoons armagnac	

Clean and truss the chicken.

Dice the ham and trim the onions.

Heat the butter in a heavy pan and brown the chicken, ham, and onions together, stirring with a wooden spoon so that the chicken will brown on all sides. Season lightly with salt and pepper.

Add the armagnac and touch with a lighted match. Stir gently until the flames subside.

Add the peppers seeded and cut into rather small pieces and the tomatoes, which have been peeled and seeded. Add a dash of cayenne.

Cover and cook 1¼ hours over a moderate heat. Transfer the chicken to a heated serving platter and keep warm. Boil down the sauce in the pan to about two thirds its quantity and place it around the chicken.

Chicken belle armurière ∗ Poulet belle armurière

FOR FIVE PEOPLE

3 pairs lamb's brains
4 tablespoons armagnac
1 can truffle peelings
1 roasting chicken

1 canned truffle
6 tablespoons butter
salt and pepper

Soak the brains 2 hours in cold water. Remove the filament that covers them. Wash them, dry them, and put them in a bowl with the armagnac. Let them stand 1 hour, spooning the armagnac over the brains from time to time. Chop them coarsely and mix with the truffle peelings, which have been drained. Season with salt and pepper.

Clean and truss the chicken as though for roasting. Slice the truffle very thin, and lifting the skin from the flesh on both sides of the bird, slide the truffle in with your fingertips. Season the interior with salt and pepper and fill with the truffled brains. Sew up the opening.

Spread the chicken generously with butter and put in a roasting pan. Place in a preheated 400° F. oven and roast 20 minutes per pound. Salt the drippings from the chicken and baste often with the drippings.

Accompany with straw potatoes or chestnuts.

Chicken au blanc ∗ Poularde au blanc

FOR SIX PEOPLE

3-4-pound chicken
2 cups boiling bouillon
1 onion
4 cloves
bouquet garni (thyme, bay leaf, parsley)

3 tablespoons butter
1 tablespoon flour
2 egg yolks
½ cup heavy cream
juice of ½ lemon
salt and pepper

Clean and truss a chicken as though for roasting and put it in a pan just large enough to hold it. (Oval pans especially made for cooking chicken are found in most hardware stores.—*Ed.*)

Pour over the hot bouillon and add the onion, peeled and stuck with the cloves, and the *bouquet garni*. Season with salt and pepper. Cover with a piece of buttered paper so that the chicken will not brown. Cover and bring to a boil over high heat. Reduce the heat and cook gently for 20 minutes. Remove the paper, turn over the chicken, replace the paper and the cover, and cook 20 to 25 minutes longer. Prick the chicken. If the juice that comes out is at all rosy, the chicken is not sufficiently cooked and should be cooked until the juice is colorless.

Prepare the sauce: Pour off almost all of the chicken broth, leaving only enough to let you keep the chicken in a warm place without drying out.

Melt the butter in a saucepan over a low heat and stir in the flour with a wooden spoon. Add the chicken broth and stir while the sauce cooks for a few minutes. Beat the egg yolks slightly with the cream and the juice of ½ lemon. Remove the sauce from the heat and stir in the egg mixture. Season to taste with salt and pepper. Place the chicken on a hot serving platter and cover with the sauce. Serve with boiled rice.

Chicken blanquette * Blanquette de poulet

FOR FIVE PEOPLE

3½-4-pound chicken	4 teaspoons flour
3 carrots	¾ cup heavy cream
3 onions	1 teaspoon chopped tarragon
5 tablespoons butter	salt and pepper

Have the chicken cut in small pieces. Place in a pan with 2½ quarts of cold salted water. Bring to the boiling point and remove any matter that floats to the surface.

Add the carrots peeled and sliced very thin and the onions cut in quarters. Cover and cook over a moderate heat for 30 minutes. At this point, the chicken is cooked.

Heat the butter in a saucepan and stir in the flour with a wooden spoon. Add about 3 cups of strained chicken broth, stirring until the sauce has the consistency of thin cream. Season with salt and pepper.

Beat the egg yolk slightly with the cream. Remove the sauce from the heat and stir in the egg mixture. Add the chopped tarragon to the sauce. Place the chicken on a heated serving platter and cover with the sauce. Serve with rice.

Bohemian chicken * Poulet à la bohémienne

FOR SIX PEOPLE

3½-4-pound chicken	1½ cups croutons
10 tablespoons butter	2½ tablespoons oil
6 artichokes	1 teaspoon chopped tarragon
½ pound mushrooms	2 teaspoons chopped parsley
4 teaspoons tomato paste	salt and pepper

Clean and truss the chicken for roasting. Save the chicken liver carefully. Spread the chicken with butter and roast in a preheated 450° F. oven for 50 to 60 minutes. Add a little water gradually to the drippings that will fall in the pan. Season with salt and baste frequently with the mixture, adding water when necessary.

Boil the artichokes in salted water until the outer leaves are easily detached. Remove the leaves and the chokes and dice the bottoms in large pieces. (Use canned artichoke bottoms, if necessary.—*Ed.*) Sauté these in 2 tablespoons of butter. Combine with the mushrooms, which have been previously trimmed, washed, dried, and gently sautéed in 2 tablespoons of butter over a low heat.

Sauté the chicken liver in a little butter. Chop it coarsely and combine with the artichoke-mushroom mixture, tomato paste, and the chicken pan juices. Season with salt and pepper.

Fry the croutons in the oil and remaining butter until brown on all sides.

Place the chicken on a heated platter. Pour the mushroom mixture over the chicken and surround with croutons. Sprinkle with chopped tarragon and parsley.

Boiled chicken béarnaise * Poule au pot béarnaise

FOR SIX PEOPLE

3-pound chicken
2 carrots
3 onions
1 shallot
5 ounces Canadian bacon
1 pound tomatoes
bouquet garni (thyme, parsley, bay leaf)

4 tablespoons oil
1½ tablespoons cognac
2 cloves garlic
1½ cups good red wine
salt and pepper

Have the chicken cut in pieces.

Peel the carrots and cut them in rounds. Peel the onions and cut them in large pieces. Peel and chop the shallot. Dice the bacon. Dip the tomatoes in boiling water and slip off the skins. Prepare the *bouquet garni.*

Heat the oil in a heatproof earthenware casserole. When hot, put in the chicken, the shallot, and the bacon and sauté until the chicken is golden brown on all sides. Add the cognac and touch with a lighted match.

When the flames subside, add the tomatoes, the carrots, the garlic, the *bouquet garni,* the red wine, salt, and pepper. Cover and simmer 2 hours. Serve this dish in the casserole.

Broiled chicken * Poulet grillé

FOR FOUR PEOPLE

2½-3-pound broiler
10 tablespoons butter

½ cup fine breadcrumbs
salt and pepper

Have the chicken cut in 4 pieces and flatten each one. Melt the butter and brush each piece of chicken with the butter. Sprinkle with salt and pepper. Bake 15 minutes at 450° F.

Take out the chicken and roll each piece in breadcrumbs. Brush again with butter and broil 15 minutes. Season with salt and pepper and serve with a separate dish of tartar sauce.

Young broiled chicken mapie * Jeunes poulets grillés

FOR FOUR PEOPLE

2 small broilers	1 large ripe tomato
12 tablespoons butter	1 tablespoon cognac
fine breadcrumbs	½ teaspoon French mustard
2 shallots	2 tablespoons chopped *fines herbes*
4 teaspoons flour	(parsley, chervil, tarragon)
1½ cups dry white wine	salt and pepper

Split the broilers and flatten them. Melt half the butter and brush the broilers with butter. Broil 10 minutes on each side, brushing the other side with butter when you turn them. Remove from the heat and roll each piece in breadcrumbs and sprinkle with butter. Put back under the broiler, allowing 5 minutes more for each side.

Serve with the following sauce: Heat the rest of the butter in a saucepan and sauté the shallots chopped fine. When golden, stir in the flour. At the same time, boil the wine down quickly to half its quantity. Add the wine to the flour mixture and stir until smooth. Cut the tomato and force it through a fine strainer. Add 2½ tablespoons of the tomato juice, the cognac, the mustard, and the drippings from the broiled chicken to the sauce. Season with salt, pepper, and the chopped herbs. Simmer 10 minutes. Taste the sauce for seasoning.

Chicken burdin * Poulet gratiné burdin

FOR FOUR PEOPLE

2-3-pound chicken	4 teaspoons flour
2 carrots	3 egg yolks
2 onions	1 cup heavy cream
2 bay leaves	½ cup grated Gruyère cheese
6 tablespoons butter	salt and pepper
½ pound mushrooms	

Make a chicken stock by cooking the chicken trimmings (wing tips, feet, neck, gizzard) in 4 cups of water with carrots, onions, bay leaves, salt, and pepper for 1 hour in a covered pan over low heat. Poach the chicken in the stock for 30 minutes. Test by inserting the tip of a knife. If the liquid that seeps out is clear, the chicken is cooked. If not, poach a few minutes longer.

Trim, wash, and chop the mushrooms and sauté them in 3 tablespoons of butter for 5 minutes.

Heat the rest of the butter in a saucepan and stir in the flour with a wooden spoon. Add the broth from the chicken into the saucepan and stir until blended. Add the mushrooms and their liquid. Simmer 10 minutes.

Remove the pan from the heat and stir in the egg yolks beaten with the cream.

Cut the chicken in 4 pieces and place it on a heatproof serving platter. Spoon the sauce over the chicken. Sprinkle with grated cheese and brown in a hot (450° F.) oven.

*Burgundy chicken * Poulet de bourgogne*

FOR FIVE PEOPLE

3½-4-pound chicken
2 tablespoons butter
2½ tablespoons oil
1 tablespoon flour

1¼ cups white Burgundy
4 shallots, finely chopped
1 lemon rind, finely grated
salt and pepper

Have the chicken divided into pieces. Heat the butter and oil in a heavy pan and brown the chicken on all sides. Sprinkle with flour and stir with a wooden spoon until the flour disappears.

Heat the wine and add to the chicken. Add the shallots and season with salt and pepper. Cover and cook gently for 45 minutes.

Just before serving, taste the sauce for seasoning and add the rind of a lemon, finely grated.

*Carmen chicken * Poulet carmen*

FOR SIX PEOPLE

4-pound chicken
3 tablespoons butter
4 red peppers
2 pounds fresh green peas
½ cup rice

1 teaspoon chopped tarragon
1½ cups Mayonnaise (page 14)
1 teaspoon French mustard
salt and pepper

Spread the chicken with butter and roast according to directions on page 230. Cool. Cut off all the flesh from the bones, removing the skin. Cut the flesh in small dice.

Cut the peppers in half and remove the seeds. Broil them in an oiled broiling pan for 5 minutes. Cut them in small pieces.

Shell and cook the peas in boiling salted water until tender. Drain and cool.

Boil the rice in salted water just until tender (12 to 15 minutes). Rinse in cold water. Drain and cool.

Combine the chicken, peppers, peas, rice, and chopped tarragon and bind with the mayonnaise mixed with the mustard.

Chicken and celery * Poulet aux céleris

FOR SIX PEOPLE

4-pound chicken	1 bunch celery
⅓ cup olive oil	1 pound (3-4) tomatoes
1 pound (4-5) onions	salt and pepper

Clean and truss the chicken.

Heat the oil in a heavy pan and brown the chicken on both sides. Add the onions peeled and sliced fine. Sauté them lightly without letting them brown.

Trim the celery and cut the stalks into pieces. Boil them 15 minutes in salted water. Drain and add them to the chicken and season with salt and pepper.

Dip the tomatoes in boiling water. Slip off the skins. Halve them and press out the seeds; cut them in pieces and add to the chicken. Cover and cook over moderate heat. The total time for cooking the chicken is 1¼ hours.

Chicken charentaise * Poularde charentaise

FOR SIX PEOPLE

4-5-pound chicken	10 tablespoons butter
2 carrots	2½ tablespoons flour
2 leeks	4 egg yolks
2 onions	¾ cup Pineau de Charente*
1 stalk celery	juice of ½ lemon
½ pound mushrooms	salt and pepper

Cook the chicken, properly cleaned and trussed, for 1 hour in salted water to cover with the carrots, leeks, onions, and celery, washed, trimmed, and cut in pieces. Remove the chicken and keep it warm.

Trim, wash, and chop the mushrooms very fine.

Melt 6 tablespoons of the butter in a large saucepan and stir in the flour with a wooden spoon. Add some of the chicken broth and stir until it has the consistency of light cream. Season with salt and pepper.

Remove from the fire and stir in the egg yolks and the wine. Add the chopped

*Pineau de Charente is a fortified white wine. If you cannot buy it, substitute a good dry white wine, and add a teaspoon of cognac.—*Ed.*

mushrooms seasoned with the juice of ½ lemon. Season with more salt and pepper, if necessary.

Carve the chicken and place the pieces on a heated serving platter.

Stir the rest of the butter into the sauce and spoon the sauce over the chicken. Serve very hot with boiled rice.

Chicken chasseur * Poulet chasseur

FOR FIVE PEOPLE

3½-4-pound chicken
2 tablespoons butter
2 tablespoons oil
1½ tablespoons cognac
½ cup dry white wine

1 cup bouillon
2 tablespoons chopped *fines herbes*
　(parsley, chervil, tarragon)
2 tablespoons tomato paste
salt and pepper

Have the chicken cut into pieces. Heat the butter and oil in a heavy pan and brown the chicken lightly on all sides. Add the cognac and touch with a lighted match. When the flames have subsided, add the wine and bouillon, season with salt and pepper, and sprinkle with the *fines herbes.* Cook over a moderate high heat for 20 minutes.

Stir in the tomato paste and reduce the heat. Cook 15 minutes longer. Serve with sautéed potatoes.

Chicken chaud-froid * Chaud-froid de poulet

FOR FIVE PEOPLE

3½-4-pound chicken
1 calf's foot*
2 carrots
bouquet garni (thyme, bay leaf)
5 tablespoons butter

2½ tablespoons flour
1¼ cups heavy cream
2 egg yolks
1 truffle
salt and pepper

Clean and truss the chicken. Put it in a pan with 2 quarts of cold water and add the carrots, cut in rounds, *bouquet garni,* the calf's foot, salt, and pepper. Boil 1½ hours. Cool the chicken and carve into pieces. Strain the broth.

Heat the butter in a small saucepan and stir in the flour. Add 1½ cups of hot chicken broth and simmer 10 minutes to let it thicken. Season with salt and pepper and remove from the heat. Add the cream and stir in the slightly beaten egg yolks. Cool to lukewarm.

Dip each piece of chicken twice in the sauce to coat well and put it on a rack

*If a calf's foot is not available, substitute a pig's foot or a knuckle bone sawed in pieces.—*Ed*.

to cool. Arrange the cold chicken on a serving platter and decorate each piece with a slice of truffle. If you prefer, you can reconstruct the chicken around the chicken carcass.

Chicken chops pojarsky
Côtelettes de poulet pojarsky

FOR FOUR PEOPLE

1 pound boned chicken breasts	flour
2 cups soft breadcrumbs	1 egg, slightly beaten
½ cup milk	fine breadcrumbs
½ pound butter	juice of 1 lemon
½ cup heavy cream	salt and pepper
nutmeg	

Be sure that the chicken is free of skin and tendons. Chop fine in a wooden bowl.

Soak the soft breadcrumbs in milk and squeeze them dry. Add them and 10 tablespoons of butter to the chicken and continue chopping and mixing, adding the cream little by little. Season with salt, pepper, and a little nutmeg. Divide the mixture into 10 balls. Roll them in flour. Flatten and shape them to look like lamb chops. Dip each "chop" in beaten egg and then in fine breadcrumbs.

Just before serving, heat 6 tablespoons of butter in a skillet, and when hot, sauté the "chops" for 20 minutes, turning them halfway through the cooking. Serve on a hot platter and sprinkle with the cooking butter and the juice of a lemon. Any vegetables can accompany this dish.

Coq au vin * Coq au vin

FOR SIX PEOPLE

3-pound cockerel	bouquet garni (thyme, bay leaf,
2½ tablespoons oil	parsley)
5 ounces pork belly	croutons
20 tiny onions	2 cloves garlic
½ pound mushrooms	2 tablespoons butter
1½ tablespoons cognac	1 tablespoon cornstarch
1 bottle red burgundy	salt and pepper

Have the chicken cut in 7 pieces. Heat the oil in a deep skillet and brown the chicken on all sides.

Dice the pork belly and try it out until it renders some of its fat. (If pork belly is not available, substitute fat salt pork boiled 5 minutes and rinsed.—*Ed.*) Add the onions, which have been peeled, and the mushrooms, which have been trimmed, washed, and cut in pieces. When the onions are lightly colored on all sides, add the chicken pieces and pour in the cognac. Touch with a lighted match.

When the flames subside, add the red wine and season strongly with salt and pepper. Add the *bouquet garni* and the garlic. Bring to a boil. Turn down the heat and cook at least 45 minutes.

Make the croutons by frying bread cubes in butter or drying them in the oven.

Work the butter and cornstarch together with the tips of your fingers and add the mixture to the sauce in small bits, whisking vigorously as you do it. Let the sauce thicken a little and taste for seasoning. Serve in a deep serving dish garnished with croutons.

Stuffed baby chicks ∗ *Poussins farcis aux riz*

FOR FOUR PEOPLE

4 baby chicks or small Rock Cornish hens
¼ cup rice
4 teaspoons turmeric *or*

a pinch of powdered saffron
5 tablespoons oil
6 tablespoons butter
salt and pepper

Prepare the small birds for stuffing.

Cook the rice in a pan of salted boiling water to which the turmeric or saffron has been added. When the rice is just tender, rinse and drain it thoroughly. Mix with the oil, salt, and pepper. Stuff the birds with the stuffing and close the openings with small skewers.

Heat the butter in a deep skillet. Brown the birds well on both sides. Sprinkle with salt and cover. Cook over a low heat for 15 to 20 minutes.

Serve with green salad and hard-cooked eggs. These little birds are good eaten either hot or cold.

Creole chicken ∗ *Poulet créole*

FOR FIVE PEOPLE

3-3½-pound chicken
6 tablespoons butter
1 large onion
1 small red pepper
2½ tablespoons curry powder

a pinch of powdered saffron
4 teaspoons sugar
1 coconut
salt

Have the chicken cut into pieces. Heat the butter and sauté briefly the onion, cut in thin slices. Add the chicken and continue to sauté until slightly colored on all sides.

Chop the pepper very fine and add it, the curry, the saffron, the sugar, and salt to the chicken. After a few moments, remove the chicken from the pan and cover the pan. Simmer very slowly for 20 minutes.

Bore a hole in the coconut and drain off the milk. Open the coconut and remove the white flesh. Grate it and crush it, stirring it with the coconut milk, mixed with ¾ cup boiling water.

Put the chicken back into the pan and cook 35 minutes. Then 10 minutes before the end of cooking, pour the coconut mixture over the chicken.

Chicken croquettes * Croquettes de poulet

FOR FOUR PEOPLE

⅔ cup diced cooked chicken
2 large slices lean cooked ham
½ pound mushrooms
2 tablespoons butter
1½ cups thick Béchamel Sauce
  (page 6)

3 egg yolks
2 egg whites
¾ cup fine breadcrumbs
parsley sprigs
salt and pepper

Make sure that there are no tendons or skin left on the chicken. Dice the chicken and the ham quite fine.

Trim, wash, and chop the mushrooms. Sauté them 5 minutes in butter.

Make the béchamel. Add the meat and mushrooms and cook gently 5 minutes. Season with salt and pepper. Remove from the heat and stir in the egg yolks. Mix well and cool thoroughly. Let the mixture stand in the refrigerator for several hours before proceeding.

Form the mixture into thin, long oval croquettes.

Beat the egg whites until frothy. Dip the croquettes first in egg white and then in fine breadcrumbs.

Fry the croquettes in deep fat (385° F.). Drain thoroughly on paper toweling. Pile them high on a napkin-lined serving platter and garnish with fried parsley sprigs.

Chicken and cucumber aspic
Pavé de poulet aux concombres

FOR SIX PEOPLE

5-pound roasting chicken
1 calf's foot
3 carrots
2 leeks

2-pound cucumber
3 sugar lumps
1 bunch watercress
2 hard-cooked eggs

2 white turnips

bouquet garni (thyme, bay leaf, parsley)

salt and pepper

Clean and truss the chicken and put in a kettle containing 3 quarts of salted cold water. Bring to a boil, skimming off any matter that floats to the surface. Add the calf's foot (substituting a pig's foot if necessary—*Ed.*). Add the vegetables peeled and cut in pieces and the *bouquet garni.* Cook for 2 hours.

Peel the cucumber and remove the seeds and filaments. Cut the cucumber in large dice and boil in salted water for 15 minutes. Drain thoroughly and cool.

Remove the cooked chicken from the kettle and set aside to cool. Strain the broth through a sieve lined with a cold damp dish towel. Season the broth to taste.

Make a caramel (page 579) with the sugar and water and color the broth with it. Cool and then chill until the aspic is the consistency of heavy syrup without being jelled. Pour a thin layer in a wide, rectangular dish. Let it set in the refrigerator.

Remove the skin from the chicken and slice the meat, both breast and leg meat. Put a rectangular layer of chicken on the aspic and cover with a layer of cucumber. Repeat the process. Pour over the syrupy aspic and chill in the refrigerator.

Unmold on a bed of watercress and decorate with hard-cooked egg slices. Serve with a watercress and potato salad.

Chicken fricassée à l'angevine
Fricassée de poulet à l'angevine

FOR SIX PEOPLE

3½-4-pound roasting chicken
6 tablespoons butter
12 small onions
3 cups dry white wine

½ pound mushrooms
1 pint extra heavy cream
salt and pepper

Have the chicken cut in 8 pieces. Season with salt and pepper. Melt the butter in a saucepan and add the chicken. Cover and simmer 7 to 8 minutes. Peel and add the onions. Put back the cover and cook gently for 20 minutes. Add the white wine and continue cooking gently with the pan covered for 50 minutes. Add the mushrooms, which have been trimmed, washed, and dried, and cook for 15 minutes. At this point, the chicken should be well cooked.

Remove the chicken with a slotted spoon and place on a serving platter. Keep hot.

Add the cream and let it simmer for a few minutes. Taste the sauce for seasoning.

Flambéed chicken * Poulet flambé

FOR FOUR PEOPLE

2-2½-pound chicken	½ cup heavy cream
6 tablespoons butter	2 egg yolks
1½ tablespoons Calvados	salt and pepper

Have the tender young chicken cut in 4 pieces. Put 4 tablespoons of butter in the skillet and brown the chicken well on all sides.

Season with salt and pepper. Lower the heat, cover, and cook gently for 30 minutes. At this point, the chicken should be cooked, but make sure by pricking it with the tip of a knife. If the fluid that comes out is clear-colored, the chicken is cooked.

Pour over the Calvados and touch with a lighted match. When the flames subside, add the cream beaten slightly with the egg yolks. Do not let the sauce boil after this. Stir to release the juices sticking to the pan. Add the rest of the butter bit by bit. Keep the sauce just below the boiling point. Season with salt and pepper and serve hot.

Gascony chicken livers
Foies de volaille de gascogne

FOR TWO PEOPLE

4 chicken livers	¾ cup very good red wine
3 ounces fat pork belly	½ cup bouillon
2½ tablespoons goose fat	*bouquet garni* (thyme, bay leaf)
10 very small onions	French bread
1 teaspoon sugar	garlic
1 tablespoon flour	salt and pepper

Cut the chicken livers in half and season with salt and pepper.

Dice the pork fat. (Substitute, if necessary, fat salt pork that has been boiled 5 minutes and rinsed.—*Ed.*) Try the fat out in a skillet until it has rendered some fat. Add the chicken livers and cook gently for 5 minutes, turning the livers occasionally. Remove from the pan.

Heat the goose fat in a saucepan. Add the peeled onions and let them brown lightly. Sprinkle with sugar and flour and stir well. Heat and add the wine and bouillon. Season with salt and pepper and add the *bouquet garni.* Cover, reduce the heat, and simmer 1 hour.

Slice the bread thin and toast on both sides. Rub the toast with the cut side of a garlic clove.

Remove the *bouquet garni* and taste the sauce for seasoning. Reheat the livers in the sauce.

Serve the livers in a heated dish garnished with the croutons.

Chicken with grapefruit * Poulet au pamplemousse

FOR FOUR PEOPLE

2½-3-pound chicken	¾ cup chicken broth
flour	⅓ cup sherry
6 tablespoons butter	1 grapefruit
4 teaspoons cognac	salt and pepper

Quarter the chicken and dip it lightly in flour.

Heat the butter in a deep skillet or *sauteuse* and cook the chicken over fairly high heat, turning the pieces so that they will brown on all sides. Add the cognac and touch with a lighted match. Season with salt and pepper.

When the chicken is cooked, transfer it to a serving platter and keep hot. Add the chicken broth, the sherry, and the juice of ½ grapefruit to the chicken butter and stir well, loosening all the juices adhering to the pan. Let it boil down to half its original quantity. Add the sections of the other half of the grapefruit, from which all the white filaments have been removed. Season with salt and pepper.

Pour the sauce over the chicken and serve with green beans.

Chicken au gratin with foie gras
Poulardes gratinées

FOR EIGHT PEOPLE

2 chickens (3½ pounds each)	⅓ cup grated Gruyère cheese
10 tablespoons butter	⅓ cup grated Parmesan cheese
8 tablespoons flour	8 2-ounce slices *foie gras*
1 quart milk, scalded	1 truffle
4 egg yolks	salt and pepper

Spread the chickens, properly cleaned and trussed for roasting, with 4 tablespoons of butter. Roast 45 minutes at 450° F., basting often with the juices that form in the pan.

Heat 6 tablespoons of butter in a large saucepan and stir in the flour. When thoroughly blended, remove from the heat and cool. Pour the scalded milk into the mixture and beat hard with a whisk. Season with salt and pepper and add the egg yolks, beating very hard again with the whisk. The sauce should have the consistency of light cream. Add the cheese, saving out just a little for the final step. Mix carefully.

When the chickens are cooked, remove them from the oven. Arrange in a large ovenproof serving platter the slices of *foie gras* and place a slice of truffle on each one. Divide each chicken into 4 pieces (breasts and legs) and place one piece on each slice of *foie gras*. Pour the sauce over the chicken and sprinkle with a little cheese. Brown 10 minutes in a hot (450° F.) oven.

Chicken au gratin henri iv ∗ Gratin henri iv

FOR FOUR PEOPLE

½ cup rice
3 cups diced cooked chicken
1 cup Béchamel Sauce (page 6)
¾ cup grated Gruyère cheese

¼ pound mushrooms
2 tablespoons butter
salt and pepper

Make a rice pilaff according to directions on page 455.

Remove the skin and tendons from the chicken and dice quite small.

Make the sauce and stir in the cheese.

Trim, wash, and slice the mushrooms quite fine. Sauté them in butter over a slow fire for 5 to 6 minutes.

Combine the chicken, mushrooms, and sauce and season well with salt and pepper. Heat together.

In an ovenproof serving dish, put a layer of rice. Cover with a layer of the chicken mixture. Repeat the process. There should be several layers. Bake at 400° F. for 15 minutes.

Chicken liver loaf ∗ Pain de foies de volaille

FOR FOUR PEOPLE

4 chicken livers
½ cup soft breadcrumbs
½ cup milk
1 onion, finely chopped

5 tablespoons soft butter
2 tablespoons chopped parsley
3 eggs
salt and pepper

Force the raw chicken livers through a sieve. Put in a mortar bowl or in a wooden bowl with the breadcrumbs, which have been soaked in milk and squeezed dry. Add the onion, butter, and parsley and pound together with the egg yolks. Season with salt and pepper. When very thoroughly blended, add the egg whites, beaten stiff. Put the mixture in a buttered charlotte mold or other straight-sided mold and place in a pan of hot water. Bake at 350° F. for 45 minutes.

Unmold and serve hot with a piquante sauce.

Chicken marengo ∗ Poulet marengo

FOR FIVE PEOPLE

3½-4-pound chicken
4 tablespoons olive oil
1 shallot

¾ cup dry white wine
4 teaspoons tomato paste
5 eggs

2½ tablespoons water or bouillon   salt and pepper
½ pound mushrooms

Cut the chicken into 8 pieces. Heat the oil in a deep skillet or *sauteuse* and chop the shallot. Brown the chicken and shallot lightly in the oil. Add the water or bouillon and cook over a moderate heat for 15 minutes.

Trim, wash, and cut the mushrooms into large pieces. Add them, salt, and pepper to the chicken. Cover and cook until the chicken is tender.

Remove the chicken from the pan and keep hot. Add the wine, scraping the juices adhering to the pan with a fork. Stir in the tomato paste. Season and simmer 10 minutes.

Meanwhile, heat deep fat to 385° F. Just before serving the chicken, deep fry the eggs. Serve the chicken on a heated platter. Pour the sauce over the chicken and garnish with the fried eggs.

Paella basque ∗ *Paella basque*

FOR EIGHT PEOPLE

8 tomatoes
3 green peppers
2 red peppers
1-3 cloves garlic
¾ cup olive oil
2 cups chick peas or green peas
1 quart mussels and clams
½ pound crabmeat (fresh or canned)
12 large shrimp

3½-4-pound chicken
3 slices Canadian bacon
2 large veal cutlets
8 link sausages
½ pound long rice
large pinch of saffron *or*
1 tablespoon turmeric
salt and pepper

Make a *ratatouille:* Cut in small dice the vegetables and as much garlic as you like to use. Cook them over high heat with 4 tablespoons of olive oil until all the vegetables are tender. Season with salt and pepper. Remove from the heat.

Cook the chick peas or green peas in boiling salted water until tender. Add to the *ratatouille.*

Place the thoroughly cleaned mussels and clams in a pan and cook over high heat without water until the shells open. Let cool and shuck them. Add the mussels and clams to the vegetable mixture along with the crabmeat cut into small dice.

Cook the shrimp in salted water for not more than 5 minutes. Do not shell.

Have the chicken cut in 8 pieces. Heat the rest of the oil in a deep skillet and fry the chicken for 20 minutes, turning each piece. Drain the chicken and keep hot. Sauté the bacon, the cutlets, and the sausage in the same skillet. Cut the meat into pieces.

Meanwhile, make a rice pilaff with the saffron or turmeric. Just before serving, mix all the meats, vegetables, shellfish—except the chicken and shrimp—and the rice together carefully so as not to crush the ingredients. Put in a deep earthenware dish and arrange the pieces of chicken and the shrimp on top.

Paprika chicken * Poulet au paprika

FOR SIX PEOPLE

4-pound chicken	1½ tablespoons paprika
2 large onions	1 cup dry white wine
1 clove garlic (optional)	¾ cup heavy cream
5-ounce piece of bacon	cayenne
3 tablespoons lard	salt and pepper

Have the chicken cut in pieces. Chop the onions, garlic, and bacon coarsely.

Heat the lard in a heavy pan, and when melted and very hot, sauté the chicken, onions, garlic (if desired), and the bacon until well browned on all sides. Sprinkle with paprika and stir in well. Add the white wine and enough boiling water to cover. Season with salt, pepper, and a small pinch of cayenne. Cover the pan and cook about 35 minutes.

Remove the chicken pieces with a slotted spoon and boil down the sauce quickly. The sauce should be slightly thick. Put the chicken back in the sauce. Add the cream and taste for seasoning. Reheat the sauce and serve with boiled rice.

Chicken in pastry * Poulet en feuilleté

FOR SIX PEOPLE

Flaky Pastry (page 643)	2 onions
3½-pound chicken	2 thin slices cooked ham
1 can truffle peelings	powdered thyme
1 can *foie gras mousse*	powdered bay leaf
4 teaspoons cognac	1 egg yolk
6 tablespoons butter	salt and pepper
2 carrots	

You will require a large square of pastry, large enough to envelop the chicken completely.

Prepare the chicken for stuffing. Make a mixture of drained truffle peelings, the *foie gras,* cognac, salt, and pepper. Mix well and put into the chicken. Sew up the opening and truss the chicken.

Heat the butter and sauté the onions and carrots, grated or ground through a *moulinette,* and the ham cut into thin strips. Season with salt, pepper, thyme, and bay leaf. Cook gently until the vegetables are tender and remove them with a slotted spoon. Using the same butter, brown the chicken lightly on both sides. Season with salt and pepper.

Roll out the pastry very thin. Spread the vegetables in the center. Place the chicken on the vegetables and wrap the pastry around it like a package, pressing the edges in place to make a tight seal. Make an opening on top of the pastry and insert a small roll of paper to serve as chimney. Paint the pastry well with an egg yolk mixed with a teaspoon of water.

Bake 1 hour at 400° F.

Chicken with peanuts * Poulet aux arachides

FOR FIVE PEOPLE

3-pound chicken	2 small red peppers
½ lemon	1⅓ cups roasted peanuts
2 onions	4 tablespoons peanut oil
2 large tomatoes	salt and pepper

Have the chicken cut in small pieces. Put them in a saucepan with 1½ quarts of salted water, ½ lemon, pepper, and 1 onion peeled and cut into large pieces. Bring to a boil and cook 15 minutes.

Pound together with mortar and pestle (or with a wooden pounder and bowl) the tomatoes, the peppers, and ¼ of the remaining onion.

Crush the peanuts, blending them with a little salt and ½ cup water.

Drain the chicken thoroughly. Heat the oil in a heavy pan and brown the chicken pieces. Add the tomato mixture and the peanuts. Cook 20 minutes, and 5 minutes before the end of cooking, add the rest of the onion sliced thin.

Chicken pie mapie * Poulet en croûte

FOR SIX PEOPLE

Flaky Pastry (page 643)	5 shallots
3½-4-pound chicken	4 slices Canadian bacon
6 tablespoons butter	4 hard-cooked eggs
½ bottle excellent dry white wine	1 egg yolk
4 teaspoons sherry	salt and pepper
½ pound mushrooms	

You will require enough pastry for a top crust.

Have the chicken cut in pieces. Heat half the butter in a shallow pan or *sauteuse* and sauté the chicken, turning it so that it will be lightly colored on all sides. Season with salt and pepper, reduce the heat, and cook gently for 20 minutes. Transfer the chicken pieces to a deep earthenware baking dish.

Add the wine to the pan in which the chicken was sautéed and scrape the juices from the pan with a fork. Stir well and let the wine boil down for a few minutes. Add the sherry.

In the remaining butter, sauté the mushrooms, which have been washed, trimmed, and cut in pieces and the shallots chopped quite fine. Season with salt and pepper.

Add the wine sauce and the mushroom mixture to the chicken. Cover with the slices of bacon and the hard-cooked eggs cut in quarters. Moisten the rim of the dish.

Roll out the pastry to fit the dish. Put in place, pressing the edges to the rim. Make a little hole in the pastry and put in a tiny paper roll to act as a chimney for the steam to escape. Paint the pastry with an egg yolk mixed with a teaspoon of water. Bake 15 to 20 minutes at 400° F.

Chicken with white port * Poulet au porto

FOR SIX PEOPLE

2½-3-pound chicken	2 cups heavy cream
6 tablespoons butter	1 egg yolk
1 pound mushrooms	salt and pepper
1 cup white port	

Clean and truss the chicken. Heat the butter in a deep pan and brown the chicken on both sides.

Trim the mushrooms, wash them well, and remove the caps. Put the caps with half the port and half the cream in the pan with the chicken. Season highly with salt and pepper. Cover and cook over a moderate heat for 30 minutes. Add the rest of the port and cream, season with salt and pepper, and continue to cook for 20 minutes.

Just before serving, remove the pan from the fire and take out the chicken. Stir the egg yolk into the sauce. Carve the chicken into serving pieces and put them back to re-form the chicken. Surround with the mushroom caps and pour the sauce over everything. Serve with boiled rice or with green beans.

Provençale chicken * Poulet provençal

FOR FOUR PEOPLE

2½-3-pound chicken	¼ cup pitted black olives (preferably
2½ tablespoons olive oil	Italian or Greek)
¾ cup dry white wine	½ teaspoon powdered basil
1 clove garlic	salt and pepper
4 tomatoes	

Have the chicken quartered. Heat the oil and brown the chicken well on all sides in a deep skillet or *sauteuse*. Add the white wine, the garlic, the tomatoes, which have been peeled, seeded, and cut in pieces, and the black olives. Season with basil, salt, and pepper. Cook uncovered for 15 minutes or until tender.

Chicken with rice * Poule au riz

FOR SIX PEOPLE

1 stewing chicken	chicken broth
1 pound carrots	3 egg yolks
1 pound leeks	1 cup heavy cream
1 stalk celery	½ cup rice
3 tablespoons butter	juice of 1 lemon
4 teaspoons flour	salt and pepper

Clean and truss the chicken as though for roasting. Put in a large pan of cold water. Salt with sea salt, if available. If not, use ordinary salt. Bring to a boil, skimming off any matter that floats to the surface. When the liquid is boiling, add the vegetables, peeled, washed, and cut in large pieces. Cook 2 hours, skimming occasionally.

Melt the butter in a saucepan and stir in the flour. Add 2 cups of the strained chicken broth and cook until the sauce begins to thicken.

Boil the rice.

Beat the egg yolks with the cream. Remove the sauce from the heat and add the egg mixture. Thin with more broth, if necessary. The sauce should have the consistency of light cream. Season with lemon juice, salt, and pepper.

Carve the chicken into serving pieces. Spread the rice in a shallow serving dish. Cover with chicken pieces and pour over the sauce. Sprinkle with paprika.

Coq au riesling * Coq au riesling

FOR FIVE PEOPLE

3½-4-pound cockerel	1½ cups Riesling wine
5 tablespoons butter	1 small can *foie gras*
3 shallots	½ cup heavy cream
¼ pound mushrooms	salt and pepper

Have the chicken cut in pieces.

Heat the butter in a deep pan and brown the chicken pieces well on all sides. Season with salt and pepper.

Chop the shallots. Trim, wash, and chop the mushrooms.

Add the wine and stir until the wine boils.

Add the shallots and mushrooms and the *foie gras,* which will melt immediately. Taste for seasoning. Cover and simmer ½ hour. Add the cream and simmer ½ hour longer.

The sauce should be quite thick. Taste it again for seasoning. Serve on a heated platter with boiled rice.

Chicken rissoles * Rissoles de poulet

FOR FOUR PEOPLE

Flaky Pastry (page 643)
1 cup cooked chopped chicken
1 onion, finely chopped
3 tablespoons butter
1 tablespoon flour

¾ cup chicken broth
1 tablespoon Madeira
1 small can truffle peelings
1 lemon
salt and pepper

Prepare the flaky pastry in advance.

Make sure that the chicken is free from all skin and tendons. Chop quite fine.

Sauté the chopped onion and the chicken in heated butter until golden. Sprinkle with flour and stir well with a wooden spoon. Stir in the hot broth and add the Madeira and the truffle peelings. Simmer 3 minutes, season with salt and pepper, and remove from the fire. Cool thoroughly.

Roll out the pastry very thin on a floured working surface. Cut the pastry in 12 3-inch circles. Moisten the edges and put a little spoonful of stuffing on each half of each circle. Fold like turnovers, pressing the edges together.

Fry until golden brown in deep fat (385° F.). Drain on paper toweling and serve on a heated platter garnished with lemon slices.

Chicken with roquefort cheese * Poulet au roquefort

FOR FIVE PEOPLE

2½-3-pound chicken
4 tablespoons white raisins
2 ounces Roquefort cheese
½ cup soft breadcrumbs
½ cup milk
3 ounces liver paté

3 tablespoons butter
1½ tablespoons cognac
½ cup champagne or dry white wine
½ cup heavy cream
salt and pepper

Prepare the chicken for stuffing.

Soak the raisins 1 hour in warm water.

Make a stuffing by mixing the Roquefort, the breadcrumbs soaked in milk and squeezed almost dry, half the raisins, and the liver paté. Knead them together thoroughly and stuff the chicken with the mixture, sewing up the opening.

Heat the butter in a deep pan, and when it is hot, brown the chicken lightly on both sides. Add the cognac and touch with a lighted match. When the flames have subsided, add the champagne, salt, and pepper. Cover the pan completely and simmer very slowly for 1½ hours.

Then 10 minutes before the end of cooking, add the cream and the rest of the raisins. Taste for seasoning.

Serve very hot, accompanying the dish, if you like, with sautéed mushrooms.

Chicken à la romaine * Poulet à la romaine

FOR FIVE PEOPLE

3-3½-pound chicken	2 sweet red peppers
¼ pound Canadian bacon	6 tablespoons butter
1 shallot	¾ cup dry white wine
2 onions	¾ cup bouillon
2 carrots	salt and pepper

Clean the chicken and prepare for stuffing.

Put the bacon through a meat grinder or chop very fine. Stuff the chicken and sew up the opening.

Peel and chop all the vegetables.

Heat the butter in a heavy pan and sauté the chicken and all the vegetables, turning the chicken and stirring the vegetables so that they will be evenly sautéed. Season with salt and pepper and add the wine and bouillon. Cover and cook slowly for 1 hour and 15 minutes. Serve with rice.

Roast chicken sans surveillance
Poulet rôti sans surveillance

FOR FOUR PEOPLE

2½-3-pound chicken	2 tablespoons butter
oil	salt and pepper

To avoid watching and basting the chicken while it roasts, rub the bird all over for several minutes with oil. Do not use butter, because butter will burn too quickly.

Sprinkle inside and out with salt and pepper and put the butter inside the chicken. Sew up the opening so that the bird will not dry out and cover it with heavy wax paper, well oiled on both sides. Do not enclose the bird completely.

Put the chicken in a preheated 500° F. oven and roast 15 minutes. Reduce to 250° F. and cook about 45 minutes, depending on the oven and the size of the chicken. You will find that you don't have to be a poultry chef to serve a perfect chicken, which your guests will think has been turned on a spit.

Chicken sauté with mayonnaise
Sauté de poulet mayonnaise

FOR SIX PEOPLE

3-3½-pound chicken
2 tablespoons butter
4 tablespoons oil
1½ tablespoons cognac
¾ cup dry white wine

4 teaspoons chopped *fines herbes*
  (parsley, tarragon, chervil)
1½ cups Mayonnaise (page 14)
salt and pepper

Have the chicken cut in pieces. Heat the butter and oil in a heavy pan, and when very hot, brown the chicken pieces well on all sides. Add the cognac and touch with a lighted match. When the flames subside, add the wine and chopped herbs. Season with salt and pepper. Cook gently for 20 to 25 minutes or until the chicken is cooked.

Meanwhile, make the mayonnaise with lemon juice and spread it on the serving platter. Place the chicken pieces on the mayonnaise and serve with rice or potato straws.

Chicken on skewers (cold)
Brochettes de poulet (froid)

FOR TEN PEOPLE

1 large cold roasted chicken
10 tomatoes
¾ pound Gruyère cheese

2 hard-cooked eggs
1½ cups Vinaigrette Sauce (page 29)

Remove the skin from the chicken. Cut the flesh into ¾-inch cubes. Wash and wipe the tomatoes and cut them into large dice. Cut the cheese in smaller dice. Alternate the chicken, tomato, and cheese on small skewers. Chop the eggs coarsely and combine them with the vinaigrette.

Each guest will season his skewer with the vinaigrette just before eating.

Chicken sauté with sweet red peppers
Poulet sauté aux piments doux

FOR FOUR PEOPLE

2½-3-pound chicken
2 tablespoons butter

½ cup white wine
12 pitted black olives (preferably

2 ½ tablespoons oil
1 can red peppers
1 teaspoon anise seeds

Greek or Italian)
salt and pepper

Order the chicken cut in pieces.

Heat the butter and oil in a deep skillet or *sauteuse,* and when very hot, brown the chicken pieces on both sides. Lower the heat and add the red peppers cut in pieces. Season with salt and pepper and the anise seeds.

Pour in the white wine. Cover and cook gently for 30 minutes. Taste the sauce, adding, if too dry, some more white wine mixed with a little hot water. Season again with salt and pepper and add the black olives 5 minutes before serving.

Chicken in shells with spinach
Coquilles de poulet aux épinards

FOR FOUR PEOPLE

2 pounds fresh spinach
3 tablespoons butter
1 ½ cups diced cooked chicken

1 ½ cups Béchamel Sauce (page 6)
¾ cup grated Gruyère cheese
salt and pepper

Trim and wash the spinach and place it, uncovered, in boiling salted water. Cook for 4 minutes once the spinach has started boiling. Drain. Cool slightly and press the spinach between the palms of your hands to squeeze out all the water. Reheat with a little butter and season with salt and pepper.

Mix the diced chicken, free from all skin and tendons, with béchamel sauce. Heat well and add ½ cup of cheese. Season with salt and pepper to taste.

Put a layer of spinach in natural or porcelain shells, or lacking those, use shallow ramekins. Cover with the chicken mixture. Sprinkle each one with grated cheese and dot with a little piece of butter. Brown in a hot (450° F.) oven.

Chicken on skewers (hot)
Brochettes de poulet (chaud)

FOR SIX PEOPLE

3-4-pound chicken
4 tablespoons oil
juice of 1 lemon

½ pound mushrooms
salt and pepper

Cut the flesh from the raw chicken, removing the skin and tendons. Cut it in pieces of a size suitable for threading on skewers. Put the chicken in a bowl with oil, lemon juice, salt, and pepper and let stand for an hour.

Trim and wash the mushrooms. Using the caps, alternate them with pieces of chicken on metal skewers. If the mushrooms are large, cut them in halves or quarters.

Broil the chicken and mushrooms under a high flame, turning them to brown on all sides. Season with salt and pepper and serve them with boiled rice and a green salad.

Chicken soufflé * Soufflé de poulet

FOR FIVE PEOPLE

1½ cups ground cooked chicken
2 cups thick Béchamel Sauce
  (page 6)
5-6 tarragon leaves

2 egg yolks
5 egg whites
salt and pepper

Be sure that the chicken is free of skin and tendons before grinding it.

Make the béchamel very thick and add the chicken. Chop the tarragon leaves and add to the sauce. Season with salt and pepper. Remove from the flame and stir in the egg yolks, mixing everything thoroughly.

Beat the egg whites very stiff and fold them into the chicken sauce, lifting the mixture high in the process. Taste for seasoning and put into a buttered soufflé dish.

Bake in a preheated slow (300° F.) oven for 15 minutes. Raise the temperature to 450° F. and bake 10 minutes longer. Serve immediately, because soufflés cannot wait.

Stuffed boiled chicken * Poule au pot farcie

FOR FIVE PEOPLE

small (3-4-pound) roasting chicken
2 pork chops
2 slices cooked ham
2 shallots
⅔ cup soft breadcrumbs
½ cup milk
1 tablespoon chopped parsley

1 egg
1 pound carrots
1 pound small white turnips
1 pound leeks
2 large cabbage leaves
salt and pepper

Clean and truss the chicken. Cook the pork chops thoroughly and chop the meat, the ham, and the shallots quite fine. Soak the breadcrumbs in the milk and squeeze them almost dry. Mix this with the meat and add the parsley and egg. Stir until thoroughly blended. Season with salt and pepper.

Put half the stuffing in the chicken and sew up the opening. Place the chicken in enough boiling salted water to cover. Add the carrots, turnips, and leeks, properly peeled and washed.

Make a ball of the rest of the stuffing and cover it with the cabbage leaves. Put the ball in a piece of cheesecloth and tie with a knot. Place this in the kettle with the chicken. Simmer 1½ hours.

Serve the chicken very hot, surrounded with the vegetables. Remove the stuffing ball from the cheesecloth and cut it in slices. Arrange these on the same platter.

Tarragon chicken * Poulet à l'estragon

FOR SIX PEOPLE

3½-4-pound chicken
2 ounces fat pork belly
3 large sprigs tarragon
6 tablespoons butter
2 carrots

2 onions
3 cups hot bouillon or water
4 teaspoons Madeira
1 teaspoon potato starch
salt and pepper

Clean the chicken and prepare it for stuffing. Chop the pork fat very fine with the chicken liver and the leaves of 1 sprig of tarragon. (If fresh pork fat is not available, parboil salt pork and rinse before using.—Ed.) Season the mixture with salt and pepper (using less salt if salt pork has been substituted). Stuff the chicken with the mixture and sew up the opening. Truss the chicken.

Melt the butter in a covered baking dish and add the carrots and onions very thinly sliced. Put the chicken on the vegetables. Cover and cook over a very low heat for 20 minutes. Add the liquid, salt, and pepper and cover again. Bake in a 400° F. oven for 50 minutes.

Remove the chicken from the pan and keep warm. Strain the sauce through a fine sieve into a saucepan. Add 4 teaspoons of chopped tarragon leaves and the Madeira. Boil down the liquid to half its original quantity. Mix the potato starch with a little cold water and stir into the sauce.

Put the chicken on a serving platter. Pour over a little of the sauce and serve the rest in a separate bowl.

Chicken tart with poached eggs
Tarte de poulet aux oeufs pochés

FOR FIVE PEOPLE

Tart Pastry (page 646)
2 cups chopped cooked chicken
1 cup Béchamel Sauce (page 6)
5 eggs

4 teaspoons white vinegar
paprika
salt and pepper

Make the pastry in advance. Roll it out thin and line a pie plate. Prick the pastry well with a fork so that it will not bubble. Bake 15 minutes in a preheated hot (450° F.) oven.

Be sure that the chicken is free of skin and tendons. Chop quite fine.

Make the béchamel, add the chicken, and let the mixture heat, seasoning with salt and pepper.

Poach the eggs 2½ minutes in simmering water to which vinegar and salt have been added.

Spread the chicken mixture in the baked shell and put the poached eggs on them. Sprinkle with paprika and serve immediately.

Chicken with new vegetables
Poulet cocotte aux primeurs

FOR FIVE PEOPLE

3½-4-pound chicken	1 pound new carrots
5 ounces lean pork belly	1 pound small tomatoes
6 tablespoons butter	1 pound small green peas
½ pound small mushrooms	1 pound tiny new potatoes
1 bunch green onions	salt and pepper

Clean and truss the chicken. Dice the lean pork belly quite small. (If pork belly is not available, boil lean salt pork in fresh water for 5 minutes and rinse well before using.—*Ed.*) Sauté the chicken and pork in 1½ tablespoons of butter until the chicken is lightly browned on both sides. Sprinkle with pepper and salt. (Salt very sparingly, if salt pork has been used.—*Ed.*) Cover and cook 1 hour in a 350° F. oven.

Meanwhile, cook all the vegetables separately. Trim, wash, and sauté the mushrooms in 1 tablespoon of butter. Peel the onions and carrots and parboil them separately in boiling salted water for 15 minutes. Drain and sauté lightly in butter. Cut the tomatoes in half and sauté them on both sides in butter. Boil the peas and steam the potatoes in their jackets. Then 5 minutes before the chicken is cooked, add the potatoes to the chicken so that they will brown lightly.

Transfer the chicken to a heated serving platter. Place the vegetables in little piles around the chicken and pour over the chicken juices with the diced pork belly.

Chicken with wine vinegar * Poulet au vinaigre

FOR FOUR PEOPLE

2½-3-pound chicken	5 teaspoons white wine
6 tablespoons butter	4 tablespoons wine vinegar

2 cloves garlic

3 teaspoons French mustard

4 teaspoons tomato purée

4 teaspoons heavy cream

1 teaspoon Worcestershire sauce

salt and pepper

Choose a chicken that is not too fat. Have it cut in pieces and cook it in a covered heavy pan with the butter and unpeeled garlic, salt, and pepper for 25 to 30 minutes or until the chicken is cooked.

Meanwhile, mix in a bowl the mustard, tomato pureé, and white wine.

When the chicken is cooked, add the vinegar. Cover the dish and cook until the chicken is almost dry. Remove the chicken and keep hot in a serving platter. Put the mustard mixture into the pan and cook down a little without a cover. Add the cream and the Worcestershire. Stir well and pour over the chicken.

Walnut chicken * Poulet aux noix

FOR FIVE PEOPLE

3½-4-pound chicken

2 carrots

2 white turnips

1 leek

5 tablespoons butter

5 small onions

pinch of thyme

2½ tablespoons wine vinegar

2 cups walnut meats

salt and pepper

Cut the chicken in 8 pieces.

Make a stock by cooking the chicken trimmings (neck, feet, wingtips, gizzard) in a quart of water with the carrots, turnips, and leek peeled and cut in pieces. Cook covered for 2 hours. Strain.

Heat the butter in a heavy pan and brown the chicken lightly on all sides. Peel and add the onions, salt, and pepper and cover with the stock. Add the thyme and vinegar. Cover and cook over a medium heat for 30 minutes.

Meanwhile, grind the walnut meats through a food chopper or chop them very fine. Add them to the chicken and cook 15 minutes longer. The sauce should be rather thick. If it is too thin, boil it down rapidly without a cover.

Pour everything into a deep dish—chicken and sauce. This is also very good cold. Chill thoroughly in the refrigerator.

Chicken waterzoi * Waterzoi de poulet

FOR SIX PEOPLE

3-3½-pound chicken

1 carrot

7 leeks

1 small celery leaf

4 onions

several sprigs of parsley

6 tablespoons butter

6 egg yolks

1½ cups heavy cream

salt and pepper

Cut the chicken in pieces. Put the trimmings (neck, gizzard, feet, wingtips) in a pan with a pint of water, the carrot cut in small pieces, the white part of 1 leek, and the celery leaf. Season with salt and pepper, cover, and simmer 1 hour.

Trim and peel the remaining leeks and cut them in thin strips. Peel the onions and cut them in thin strips of the same size. Chop the parsley.

In a large pan, melt the butter and cook the leeks, onions, and parsley over low heat for 30 minutes. It is essential that the vegetables do not brown.

Put the chicken pieces on the vegetables. Strain the broth over the pieces and cook 1¼ hours. In a warm soup tureen put the egg yolks, beaten with the cream. Pour the chicken mixture into the tureen and serve very hot.

Turkey

The turkey is no longer reserved for holidays but is eaten all year round. Available in small broiler size as well as in the larger sizes, turkey can be served in a variety of ways, roasted, braised, or poached.

Turkeys are sold drawn, cleaned, and prepared for stuffing. Remove the innards, which will usually be found trimmed and cleaned in the body cavity. Turkeys can be stuffed in both the neck and body cavities. They are trussed for roasting like chicken (see page 230).

Turkey and artichokes au gratin
Gratin de dinde aux artichauts

FOR SIX PEOPLE

4 cups cooked turkey	6 tablespoons butter
1½ cups Béchamel Sauce (page 6)	½ cup grated Gruyère chese
6 artichoke bottoms	salt and pepper

Force the meat through a food chopper, using a fine blade.

Make the béchamel and mix it with the turkey. It should be a thick, smooth mixture. Season with salt and pepper to taste.

Make a purée of artichokes by forcing cooked or canned artichoke bottoms through a food mill. Heat it in 5 tablespoons of the butter and season to taste with salt and pepper.

Put the turkey mixture in a shallow baking dish. Cover with the artichoke purée and sprinkle with grated cheese. Dot with butter and brown in a hot (450° F.) oven for 10 minutes.

Braised turkey with mushrooms * Dinde aux cèpes

9-pound turkey
½ cup soft breadcrumbs
½ cup milk
5 ounces ground veal
½ pound very lean pork belly
4 pounds mushrooms*

6 tablespoons butter
1 egg
½ cup oil
nutmeg
salt and pepper

Prepare the turkey for stuffing.

Make a stuffing by combining the breadcrumbs soaked in milk and squeezed dry, the ground veal, and about a third of the pork belly chopped fine. (If pork belly is not available, use lean salt pork parboiled 5 minutes and rinsed.—*Ed.*) Trim, wash, and chop 1 pound of the mushrooms. Add them and the egg to the stuffing and season with salt, pepper, and nutmeg. Stuff the turkey. Sew up the openings and truss the bird as though for roasting.

Heat the butter in a pan large enough to hold the turkey. Brown very well on both sides. Cover and cook gently for 1½ hours over moderate heat or in a 350° F. oven.

Chop the rest of the mushrooms and sauté them in oil for 10 minutes. Chop and sauté the rest of the pork fat. Add the mushrooms and fat to the turkey. Season with salt and pepper and cook 30 minutes longer or until the turkey is cooked. Test by pricking with a fork; when done, the juice that seeps out is colorless.

Place the turkey on a platter. Remove the skewers and twine and surround with the pork and mushrooms.

Turkey canapés * Toasts de dinde

3 cups chopped turkey
10 tablespoons butter
1 tablespoon flour
½ cup Madeira
1 cup turkey bouillon

3 tablespoons chopped green olives
juice of ½ lemon
6 slices white bread
salt and pepper

The turkey should be free of skin and tendons and chopped rather coarsely.

Heat 3 tablespoons of butter in a saucepan and stir in the flour with a wooden spoon. Add the Madeira and the bouillon. Season with salt and pepper and cook until the sauce thickens. Add the turkey and the chopped olives. Add the lemon juice and taste for seasoning.

*The original recipe calls for *cèpes,* which have a distinctive flavor. Dried wild mushrooms, imported from France, can be used. They approximate the flavor.—*Ed.*

Fry the bread lightly in the rest of the butter. Cover each toast with a thick mound of the turkey mixture and serve very hot.

Turkey aux girolles * Dinde aux girolles

FOR EIGHT PEOPLE

Girolles *or* chanterelles *are wild mushrooms that are found only in some parts of the United States and are rarely marketed. Imported, dried* girolles *or Chinese mushrooms are found in most markets dealing with foreign foods and make an excellent substitute. Soak according to directions on the package.*—Ed.

5-pound turkey broiler
6 tablespoons butter
⅔ cup oil
2 shallots, finely chopped
3-ounce piece lean bacon

1½ cups dry white wine
2 pounds *girolles*
2 tablespoons chopped parsley
   and chervil
salt and pepper

Have the broiler cut into pieces.

Heat the butter in a large heavy pan. Melt the butter and half the oil. When the mixture is hot, brown the turkey, the shallots chopped fine, and the bacon diced small. When well browned, add the white wine. Season with salt and pepper. Cover and simmer 1½ hours. Turn occasionally.

If you use fresh *girolles,* trim and wash them carefully. Otherwise, drain and dry the soaked variety. Sauté in the rest of the oil for about 20 minutes or until almost dry. Season with salt and pepper.

Put the turkey on a heated platter and surround with the mushrooms. Serve very hot. Sprinkle with the chopped herbs.

Magic turkey * Dinde magique

FOR TWELVE PEOPLE

10-12-pound turkey
3 tablespoons Calvados
Tart Pastry (page 646)
4 pounds apples
1 3-ounce package cream cheese

2 tablespoons heavy cream
10 tablespoons butter
huckleberry jam
salt and pepper

The magic of this recipe is the injection of the liqueur into the raw turkey, an operation that requires a hypodermic needle.

Buy the turkey the day in advance, prepare it for roasting, and inject the Calvados once on each side. Let it stand 24 hours.

Make the pastry.

Peel and core one pound (4-6) of the apples and shred them fine.

Mix the cheese with the cream, and when well blended, mix with the shredded apples. Spread this in the bottom of the roasting pan. Season with salt and pepper.

Spread the turkey with butter. Roast at 400° F. for 1¾ hours. Baste frequently.

Peel and core the remaining apples and put a little butter in each one. Place around the edge of the roasting pan and continue cooking for 45 minutes. Test the turkey by piercing the flesh with a fork. The liquid that comes out should be colorless.

Line with pastry small oval tins or, lacking those, tiny muffin tins. Prick with a fork and bake at 400° F. for 10 minutes. Let cool, unmold, and fill with huckleberry jam.

Serve the turkey surrounded by the apples and jam tarts.

Turkey mapie * Dinde à la crème

FOR EIGHT PEOPLE

1 small turkey broiler (4-6 pounds)
18 tablespoons butter
2½ ounces lean pork belly
16 tiny onions
20 small new carrots

10 potatoes
½ cup heavy cream
1 tablespoon paprika
salt and pepper

Prepare the small turkey as though for roasting. Heat 6 tablespoons of butter in a heavy pan large enough to hold the turkey and some vegetables. Brown the bird well on both sides. Reduce the heat, cover, and cook gently for 45 minutes, basting frequently and turning occasionally. Season with salt and pepper.

Dice the pork belly (using lean salt pork, parboiled 5 minutes and rinsed, if necessary—*Ed.*). Add to the turkey.

Peel the vegetables, cutting the potatoes in quarters. Heat 12 tablespoons of butter in a skillet and sauté all the vegetables in the butter for about 10 minutes. Season with salt and pepper.

Add the vegetables and put the covered pan in a preheated 350° F. oven. Cook 45 minutes longer. Just before serving, add the heavy cream and 1 tablespoon of paprika. Season to taste with salt and pepper. Reheat but do not let the sauce boil.

Place the turkey on a heated platter. Remove the skewers and twine and surround with the vegetables in the sauce.

Turkey pot-au-feu * Dinde au pot

FOR TWELVE PEOPLE

10-12-pound turkey
4 onions

2½ tablespoons flour
3 egg yolks

1 pound white turnips
1 pound carrots
4 cloves
3 tablespoons butter

¾ cup heavy cream
juice of 1 lemon
salt and pepper
bouquet garni

Prepare the turkey as though for roasting. Place it in a large kettle of cold, salted water. Add the vegetables peeled and washed, the cloves, and the *bouquet garni* and simmer 5 hours, skimming off from time to time the matter that floats to the surface.

Heat the butter over a slow heat and stir in the flour with a wooden spoon. Add 3 cups of the turkey broth, stirring constantly. Stir until the sauce starts to thicken. Remove from the heat and stir in the egg yolks beaten with the cream and the juice of the lemon. Season with salt and pepper.

Serve the turkey on a heated platter surrounded with some of the sauce. Serve the rest of the sauce in a separate bowl and accompany the turkey with boiled rice.

Roast turkey * Dinde rôtie

FOR TEN PEOPLE

10-12-pound turkey
Chestnut Stuffing *or*
Rice Stuffing

6 tablespoons butter
salt pork
salt and pepper

Prepare the turkey for stuffing.

Make the stuffing of your choice and stuff both the body and neck cavities. Sew them up and bind the legs and wings to the body of the bird with skewers or kitchen twine. Skewer the neck skin over the opening.

Place small dots of butter all over the bottom of the roasting pan. Place the turkey in the pan and drape the bird with paper-thin slices of salt pork.

Roast 1½ hours at 450° F. Baste frequently with the drippings in the pan seasoned with salt and pepper. Remove the pork fat to let the turkey brown and continue cooking, still basting, for another hour.

Transfer the turkey to a heated platter and remove the skewers and twine. Add a little water to the roasting pan. Scrape the juices adhering to the pan and strain the sauce into a heated sauce boat.

Rice stuffing * Farce au riz

FOR TEN-POUND TURKEY

¾ cup rice
½ pound mushrooms
2 tablespoons butter
2 cups ground cooked meat

½ pound pork fat
2 eggs, slightly beaten
salt and pepper

Boil the rice in salted water just until tender, Rinse and drain.

Trim, wash, and chop the mushrooms. Sauté in butter for 5 minutes. Combine the ground meat and the fat. Mix everything together, seasoning with salt and pepper and mix in the beaten eggs.

Chestnut stuffing * *Farce aux marrons*

FOR TEN-POUND TURKEY

2½ pounds chestnuts
½ pound lean pork belly
turkey giblets, liver, heart, gizzards
2½ cups stale bread

1 cup milk
2 tablespoons chopped parsley
2 eggs, slightly beaten
salt and pepper

Using a sharp-pointed knife, slash the chestnuts, starting at the base on one side and continuing over the top of the chestnut and down on the other side. Put the chestnuts in a pan of cold water. Bring to a boil and boil 6 to 7 minutes. Drain and peel off both the outer and inner skins while the nuts are hot. Boil 30 minutes longer.

Chop the pork belly as fine as possible. (If pork belly is not available, use lean salt pork boiled 5 minutes and rinsed.—*Ed.*)

Chop the giblets, liver, heart, and gizzard—very fine.

Soak the bread in milk and squeeze dry.

Mix the fat, giblets, bread, and parsley together well and stir in the eggs. Season with salt and pepper. Stir in the chestnuts, taking care not to break them more than necessary.

Fill the neck and body cavities.

Turkey rissoles * *Emincés de dinde en fritot*

FOR SIX PEOPLE

Tart Pastry (page 646) *or*
Flaky Pastry (page 643)
12 slices cooked turkey

6 tomatoes
3 tablespoons butter
parsley

Make the pastry in advance. Roll it out on a floured working surface. Cut into 12 squares, using a pastry wheel. Moisten all the edges and lay a piece of turkey on each one. Fold over and press the edges together firmly.

Fry in deep fat (385° F.) until golden brown. Drain on paper toweling and serve on a heated platter garnished with tomatoes halved and sautéed lightly in butter and with parsley fried in the deep fat with the *rissoles.*

Turkey roi soleil * Dinde roi soleil

FOR TEN PEOPLE

8-pound turkey	6 tablespoons butter
10 ounces blood sausage	salt and pepper

Prepare the turkey for stuffing. Remove the skin from the sausage and place the sausage in the body cavity of the turkey. Sew up the opening. Truss the turkey and spread with butter.

Place in a roasting pan and roast at 450° F. until the turkey is well browned. Reduce the heat to 400° and cook 1¾ to 2 hours in all, basting often with the drippings in the pan. Season the juices in the pan with salt and pepper toward the end of the cooking. If the turkey browns too much, cover it with aluminum foil.

Remove the twine and skewers from the turkey and spoon the stuffing into a heated dish. Place the turkey on a platter and add a little water to the roasting pan, scraping the juices that adhere to the pan. Strain into a sauce boat and serve.

Victor emmanuel turkey * Dinde victor-emmanuel

FOR TEN PEOPLE

7-pound broiler turkey	juice of 1 orange
5 ounces raw chicken breast	juice of 1 grapefruit
½ pound raw veal	bouillon
½ pound pork belly	*bouquet garni* (thyme, bay leaf,
5-ounce can *foie gras mousse*	parsley)
2 egg whites	4 tablespoons seedless raisins
10 tablespoons butter	4 tomatoes
¾ cup sherry	2 tablespoons flour
2 cups dry white wine	salt and pepper

Prepare the turkey for stuffing.

Grind the chicken meat, the veal, and the pork belly as fine as possible. (If pork belly is not available, substitute fat salt pork boiled 5 minutes and rinsed.—*Ed.*) Mix with the *foie gras mousse.* Season with salt and pepper. Fold in the stiffly beaten egg whites. Stuff the turkey with the mixture. Sew up the openings and truss the turkey.

Heat 7 tablespoons of the butter in a large braising pan or, lacking that, use 2 medium-sized roasting pans, one of which will serve as a cover. Brown the turkey well on both sides. Add the sherry, the white wine, the juices of both the orange and the grapefruit, and enough bouillon to come halfway up the turkey. Add the *bouquet garni* and the raisins and sprinkle with salt and pepper. Cover and braise in the oven for 1½ hours at 350° F.

Peel the tomatoes and cut them in quarters.

Melt 3 tablespoons of butter and stir in the flour. Add 1 cup of the bouillon from the turkey, stirring until the mixture begins to thicken. Add the quartered tomatoes and pour the mixture into the braising pan. Continue cooking for 30 minutes.

Transfer the turkey to a heated platter. Remove the twine and skewers and carve the turkey. Rebuild the turkey around the carcass and cover with a little of the sauce, which has been poured through a fine strainer. Serve the rest of the sauce in a gravy boat. Accompany the dish with buttered spinach.

Duck

In France, there are three types of duck that can be found in the market: the *Nantais,* the *Rouennais,* and the *Barbarie.*

The *Barbarie* is large enough for a whole family. The best time to eat this type is in September.

The *Nantais* and the *Rouennais* are smaller birds, with more delicate flesh. They weigh between three to four pounds and cannot serve more than four people.

A duck for roasting must always be young and tender. Never buy a duckling weighing less than 3½ pounds.

The only duckling marketed nationwide in the United States is the Long Island Duckling, which weighs between 4 and 5½ pounds. It is excellent for roasting, and will lend itself admirably to other French ways of preparing duck.

To cook duck. We like to cook duck medium-rare, which means cooking them 15 minutes per pound at 450° F. Although the *Rouennais* duck is sometimes cooked much rarer, the flavor is best if the meat is rosy in color. Englishmen and Americans in general like duck well done (25 minutes per pound), but much of the flavor is lost in overcooking duck.

Ducks are sold cleaned and ready for cooking. To prepare for roasting or sautéing, simply remove the innards, found in the cavity, and any excess fat found at the neck or tail end or in the cavity. If the duck is stuffed, sew up the opening and bind the wings and legs and neck skin to the body with skewers or kitchen twine. Prick the skin in several places to let the extra fat seep out during the cooking.

Duck is very fat, so that it is only necessary to paint the skin lightly with butter before roasting or braising it. Do not salt the raw duck, but salt the cooking juices and baste often with them. It is important to remove with a spoon as much fat as possible from the sauce before serving.

Duck béarnaise * Canard à la façon du béarn

FOR FOUR PEOPLE

4-5-pound duck
10 tablespoons butter
bouquet garni (thyme, bay leaf,
    parsley, chives, basil, 2 cloves)
¾ cup white wine (preferably
    Jurançon*)

6 large onions
1 tablespoon flour
juice of ½ lemon
salt and pepper

Truss the duck as though for roasting. Heat 5 tablespoons of butter in a large pan and sauté the duck until browned on both sides. Season with salt and pepper. Tie all the herbs in a bouquet, covering them with a little square of cheesecloth.

Add the *bouquet garni* and the wine to the duck. Cover and cook gently until tender. Test with a fork.

Peel and chop the onions very fine. Sauté them in a skillet with the rest of the butter. Season with salt and pepper. When lightly colored, sprinkle with flour. Stir with a wooden spoon and add the cooking broth from the duck. Cook until the sauce has the consistency of a thin purée. Taste for seasoning. Add the juice of ½ lemon.

Carve the duck into serving pieces and serve on a heated platter with the sauce.

Duck with beer and grapes
Canard à la bière aux raisins

FOR FOUR PEOPLE

4-4½-pound duck
1 onion
6 tablespoons butter
10 ounces beer

bouquet garni (thyme, bay leaf,
    parsley)
1 large bunch seedless grapes
salt and pepper

Prepare the duck as though for roasting.

Chop the onion very fine. Heat the butter in a large pan, and when very hot, sauté the duck and onion together, turning the duck so that it will brown lightly on both sides. Add the beer and the *bouquet garni* and season with salt and pepper. Cover and cook until tender, basting often. When the duck is cooked, remove it from the pan and keep hot.

Remove the *bouquet garni* from the sauce and add the grapes. Simmer for a few moments.

Divide the duck into serving pieces. Cover with the sauce and serve with boiled rice.

*Jurançon wine comes from the Pyrenees and is pale yellow and rather fruity in flavor. Some of the Northern New York State wines are very similar to it.—*Ed.*

Braised nantua duck with apples
Canard nantais aux pommes

2 tablespoons seedless raisins	1½ tablespoons Calvados (optional)
1 duck	2 pounds apples
5 tablespoons butter	salt and pepper
1 cup Muscadet wine	

Soak the raisins in cold water for at least 30 minutes.

Prepare a duck as though for roasting. Heat half the butter in a deep oven dish and brown the duck gently for 15 minutes, turning it so that it will brown evenly. Add the Muscadet or other good dry white wine. Season with salt and pepper and add the raisins. Cover and braise in the oven at 400° F. for 45 minutes or until tender when pricked with a sharp knife.

Taste the sauce for seasoning, removing the excess fat. Add the Calvados, if desired.

Meanwhile, peel and core all the apples. Leave 2 of them whole and cut the rest into eighths. Sauté the sections gently in the rest of the butter. Wrap the other two apples in aluminum foil and bake in the oven with the duck.

Place the duck on a serving platter. Decorate with the apple slices and put a whole apple at each end. Strain the sauce over the duck and serve very hot.

Braised duck with peas
Canard braisé aux petits pois

1 duck	10 small onions
5 ounces lean pork belly	1 carrot
10 tablespoons butter	1 small can green peas
¾ cup dry white wine	salt and pepper
bouquet garni (thyme, bay leaf, parsley)	

Have the duck cut into serving pieces.

Dice the pork belly. (If pork belly is not available, parboil lean salt pork for 5 minutes and rinse before using.—*Ed.*)

Heat 6 tablespoons of butter in a large pan, and when hot, sauté the pork and the cut duck until browned on all sides. Season with salt and pepper and add the white wine. Add the *bouquet garni.* Cover and cook over a moderate flame for 45 minutes or until tender.

Meanwhile, peel the onions and slice the carrot very thin. Sauté in the rest of the butter, and when they are cooked and well browned, add the drained peas, cooking them just until they are heated. Add this to the duck shortly before serving.

Serve very hot on heated plates.

Duck with grapefruit * Canard au pamplemousse

FOR FOUR PEOPLE

1 duck	½ cup sherry, heated
6 tablespoons butter	1 grapefruit
4 teaspoons cognac	salt and pepper
1 cup bouillon	

Prepare the duck as though for roasting. Heat the butter in a large pan and brown the duck well on both sides. Add the cognac and touch with a lighted match. When the flames have subsided, add the bouillon, sherry, and the juice of ½ grapefruit. Season with salt and pepper. Simmer 45 to 60 minutes or until the duck is well cooked. When you prick it with a fork, the juice should be colorless and not rosy.

Meanwhile, peel the remaining half of the grapefruit, taking care to remove all the white filaments. A few minutes before the end of cooking, add the grapefruit sections to the sauce.

Duck with olives * Canard aux olives

FOR FOUR PEOPLE

1 duck	6 tablespoons butter
46 small green pitted olives	1½ tablespoons cognac
6 tablespoons soft breadcrumbs	¾ cup bouillon
¼ cup milk	salt and pepper
1 egg	

Prepare the duck for roasting, saving carefully the liver.

Chop about 20 of the olives. Chop the liver. Soak the breadcrumbs in milk and squeeze them as dry as possible. Mix everything together. Season with salt and pepper and bind with a slightly beaten egg.

Stuff the bird, sew the opening, and truss for roasting. Heat the butter in a large pan, and when very hot, brown the duck on both sides. Add the cognac, bouillon, salt, and pepper and cook 45 to 60 minutes or until the bird is tender when pricked with a pointed knife.

Then 15 minutes before the end of the cooking, add the rest of the olives to the sauce. Carve and serve very hot on preheated plates.

Chocolate duck * Canard au chocolat

FOR FOUR PEOPLE

1 duck
4 tablespoons oil
4 teaspoons wine vinegar
¼ cup sherry
juice of 1 lemon
1 bay leaf
2 sprigs parsley

2 carrots, sliced thin
2 squares bittersweet chocolate,
    shredded
⅔ cup bouillon
12 link sausages
salt and pepper

Prepare the duck as though for roasting. Heat the oil in a large deep dish and brown the duck well on both sides. Add all the other ingredients and cover the pan very tightly. Lower the heat and simmer 1½ hours. Serve with boiled rice.

Duck à l'orange * Canard à l'orange

FOR FOUR PEOPLE

1 duck
6 tablespoons butter
1½ cups bouillon
¾ cup dry white wine

1 veal knuckle, sawed in pieces
5 oranges
salt and pepper

Prepare and truss the duck as though for roasting. Heat the butter in a large pan and brown the duck well on all sides over a moderate heat. Season with salt and pepper and add the bouillon, wine, and veal bones. Cover and simmer for 2 hours.

Remove from the pan and strain the sauce. Put the sauce back in the pan and add the juice of 2 oranges and their rind cut in thin strips and boiled 2 minutes. Use only the colored part of the orange rind.

Put the duck on a serving platter. Garnish with orange slices cut in halves or in star shapes.

Reheat the sauce, letting it boil for a second or two, and pour over the duck. Serve with boiled rice.

Duck paillard * Canard paillard

FOR FOUR PEOPLE

1 duck
6 shallots
½ pound fat pork belly
7 tablespoons butter

¾ cup red wine
small *bouquet garni* (thyme, bay leaf)
1 teaspoon meat extract
salt and pepper

Prepare the duck for stuffing, carefully saving the liver.

Chop three of the shallots and half the liver together. Shred the pork fat. (If pork belly is not available, parboil fat salt pork 5 minutes, rinse and chill before shredding.—*Ed.*) Mix the fat with the shallots and liver, season with salt and pepper, and stuff the duck with the mixture. Sew up the opening and truss the duck.

Spread the duck with 3 tablespoons of butter and roast at 450° F., allowing 15 minutes per pound. Watch the cooking, because the duck must not be over-cooked. The flesh should be rosy when carved.

Meanwhile, chop the remaining shallots and the other half of the liver and put them in the saucepan with the wine, *bouquet garni,* salt, and pepper. Cook until the liquid has boiled down a little and add the meat extract. Stir well, and just before serving, add the rest of the butter in small bits, whisking vigorously. Taste for seasoning.

Carve the duck in serving pieces and place on a heated platter. Surround the duck with the sauce.

Duck pâté mapie * Pâté de canard mapie

FOR EIGHT PEOPLE

paper-thin salt pork (see below)	½ pound boned veal
10 ounces finely ground, mildly seasoned sausage meat	1 bay leaf
	1 sprig thyme
1 can truffle peelings	1½ tablespoons cognac
1 duck, boned	salt and pepper

(Except in special stores, it is hard to get the sheet of pork fat known as *barde.* Ask the butcher to give you a paper-thin wide slice or several narrow slices of salt pork. Rinse in cool water.—*Ed.*)

Line an earthenware dish with the pork fat, letting it hang over the edges so that eventually it will fold over and cover the pâté.

Put a layer of sausage meat on the fat. Sprinkle with salt and pepper and with some of the truffles coarsely chopped.

Ask the butcher to bone the duck for you. If that is not possible, cut the meat in small pieces from the raw duck. Cut the veal in thin slices also. Place the duck and the veal in the dish and sprinkle with salt and pepper. Cover with the rest of the sausage meat. Sprinkle with the rest of the chopped truffles.

Fold the pork fat ends over the pâté and place the bay leaf and thyme on top. Pour the cognac over it all and cover the dish. Cook 1 hour at 400° F. and 2 hours more at 300° F. Cool and then chill in the refrigerator. This can be kept for several days.

Serve as a first course or as an accompaniment to a green salad.

Duck with peaches * Canard aux pêches

FOR EIGHT PEOPLE

2 ducks
¼ pound butter
1 tablespoon sugar
½ cup hot bouillon

½ cup Madeira
1 can peaches
salt and pepper

Prepare the ducks as though for roasting. Heat the butter in a pan that can be covered and is large enough to hold both ducks. (Lacking something better, 2 medium-sized roasting pans, one to be used as a cover, can serve.—*Ed.*)

Sauté the ducks on both sides, sprinkling them with sugar. When well browned, add the hot bouillon, salt, and pepper. Cover and simmer very slowly about 1 hour and 15 minutes or until tender.

Remove the ducks from the pan to a large serving platter. Spoon off as much of the fat as possible from the sauce and add the Madeira and peaches. As soon as the sauce is very hot, pour it around the ducks. Serve immediately.

Roast duck with sage dressing
Canard farci à la sauge

FOR FOUR PEOPLE

1 duck
1½ cups soft breadcrumbs
½ cup milk
3 duck livers
2 ounces veal kidney fat

5 sage leaves
1 egg
3 tablespoons butter
salt and pepper

Prepare the duck for stuffing.

Soak the breadcrumbs in milk and squeeze as dry as possible. Chop very fine the duck livers, the fat, and the sage leaves. Mix thoroughly with the breadcrumbs, season with salt and pepper, and bind with the egg. Stuff the duck with the mixture and sew up the opening.

Truss for roasting and spread the duck with butter. Roast at 450° F., adding a little boiling water to the pan occasionally, and season with salt and pepper. Baste frequently. Allow 15 minutes per pound for medium-rare duck. Serve very hot.

Duck with turnips * Canard aux navets

FOR FOUR PEOPLE

1 duck

1 cup dry white wine

3 ounces lean pork belly	pinch of thyme
12 tablespoons butter	1 pound small white turnips
1 shallot, chopped	salt and pepper

Prepare the duck as though for roasting.

Dice the pork belly. (If pork belly is not available, use salt pork boiled 5 minutes and rinsed.—*Ed.*)

Heat half the butter in a large pan. Add the pork, shallot, and duck. Brown the duck well on both sides. Add the white wine. Season with salt, pepper, and thyme. Cover and cook gently for 45 to 60 minutes or until tender when pierced with a a sharp-pointed knife.

When the duck is cooking, peel the turnips and cut them in small dice. Brown them in the rest of the butter. Cook until tender over a moderate heat, stirring them frequently so that they do not stick to the pan. Shortly before the duck is cooked, add the turnips. Serve very hot on preheated plates.

Wild duck in wine * Canard sauvage au vin

FOR FOUR PEOPLE

1 young wild duck,* plucked, singed, and cleaned	*bouquet garni* (thyme, bay leaf)
flour	12 tiny onions
3 ounces lean pork belly	1 teaspoon sugar
6 tablespoons butter	½ pound mushrooms
2¼ cups red wine	1½ tablespoons cognac
	salt and pepper

Cut the duck in pieces and coat them with flour. Dice the pork belly and sauté in the butter until golden. (If pork belly is not available, parboil lean salt pork for 5 minutes and rinse before using.—*Ed.*) Add the duck and brown very well on all sides. Sprinkle with flour, and when that has disappeared, add the wine, *bouquet garni,* salt, and pepper. Cover and simmer 1 hour.

Heat the rest of the butter on a small skillet and sauté the onions sprinkled with sugar. When golden, add them to the duck.

Trim, wash, dry, and slice the mushrooms. Then 5 minutes before the duck is cooked, add the mushrooms and taste the sauce for seasoning. Pour in the cognac and touch with a lighted match. Serve with buttered noodles.

Braised wild duck in cider
Canard sauvage braisé au cidre

FOR FOUR PEOPLE

1 wild duck, plucked,	10 tablespoons butter

*If the duck is not young and its flesh is hard, hang it 3 to 4 days before plucking, and then marinate it 24 hours in the red wine, which will later be used to cook the duck.

cleaned, and singed
2 tablespoons cream cheese
2 teaspoons heavy cream
paper-thin slice(s) fat salt pork
2 pounds cooking apples

1½ tablespoons Calvados
2 cups hard cider
½ cup heavy cream
salt and pepper

Spread the interior of the duck with a mixture of the cream cheese and cream. Sprinkle with salt and pepper. Wrap the bird in salt pork, which has been rinsed to remove excess salt and patted dry. Bind with kitchen twine. Meanwhile, peel, quarter, and core the apples.

Heat the butter in a large pan and brown the duck well on both sides. Pour in the Calvados and touch with a lighted match. When the flames subside, add the apples and let them brown very lightly. Reduce the heat, sprinkle with salt and pepper, and add the cider. Cover and simmer for 1 hour. Test with the point of a knife to see if it enters easily.

Add the cream and taste for seasoning. Do not crush the apples. They should have retained their shape.

Put the duck on a serving platter. Remove the twine and fat. Surround with the apples.

Domestic rabbit

When you buy a rabbit, choose it carefully. It should have a short neck, and the front paws should be very flexible. (In the United States rabbit is growing increasingly popular, and although freshly killed rabbit is sold only in some areas, excellent frozen rabbit is now distributed nationwide.—*Ed.*)

To roast a rabbit: The classic way to prepare a rabbit for roasting is to truss it by drawing back the front legs and drawing forward the back legs, holding them in place with a skewer or kitchen twine. The head is placed upright and run through with a skewer to the back. If this is too gruesome for the tenderhearted, the rabbit can be cut off at the shoulder and only the meaty back and legs roasted. Baste a rabbit frequently and roast 45 to 60 minutes at 400° F., depending on size.

To cut up a rabbit: If a rabbit is to be made into a stew or sauté, it should first be cleaned and then laid on its side. Cut off the legs, both front and back, and the neck at the base. The back is cut across in 3 or 4 pieces.

If you want to give the rabbit a slightly gamy taste, marinate it in the following mixture:

Classic white wine rabbit marinade
Marinade classique au vin blanc pour un lapin

1 carrot	2 sprigs thyme
1 onion	1 clove
1 shallot	⅔ cup wine vinegar
½ cup oil	1 quart dry white wine
1 bay leaf	salt

Peel and chop the carrot, onion, and shallot. Heat the oil over very low heat. Add the vegetables, herbs, and spices. Stirring frequently with a wooden spoon, brown the vegetables lightly. Add the vinegar and wine. Simmer 45 minutes. Cool thoroughly before using.

Roast argentinian rabbit * Lapin à l'argentine

FOR FOUR TO FIVE PEOPLE

1 rabbit	4 tarragon leaves
6 cloves garlic	dash of cayenne
2 sprigs thyme	¾ cup oil
1 bay leaf	3 tablespoons wine vinegar
1 teaspoon paprika	salt and pepper

Prepare the rabbit for roasting.

Pound the garlic with the herbs and spices, including the salt and pepper, until you have a smooth paste. Add the oil and vinegar and mix well.

Put the rabbit in a shallow platter and smear the rabbit with the mixture, using your hands. Let stand 12 hours, basting with the mixture occasionally. Roast 1 hour at 400° F., basting with the marinade.

Dijon rabbit * Lapin dijonnaise

FOR SIX PEOPLE

1 large rabbit	¾ cup heavy cream
1 small jar Dijon mustard	salt

Prepare a rabbit for roasting and spread it generously with mustard. Roast at 400° F. for 45 to 60 minutes or until tender. Transfer the rabbit to a heated platter. Add the cream to the roasting pan and heat without boiling, scraping the juices that adhere to the pan. Season with salt and serve the sauce in a separate bowl.

Serve with steamed potatoes.

Jugged rabbit * Civet de lapin

FOR SIX PEOPLE

1 rabbit
3 tablespoons lard
1½ tablespoons flour
2 cloves garlic
1 medium-sized onion
2 cups red wine, heated

bouquet garni (thyme, bay leaf,
   parsley)
5 ounces lean pork belly or salt pork
2 tablespoons butter
20 small onions
salt and pepper

Cut the rabbit into pieces and save out the liver. Heat the lard in a heavy pan and brown the rabbit pieces well on all sides. Sprinkle with the flour and add the garlic crushed with the flat side of a knife and the onion chopped well. Season with salt and pepper. Stir a moment and then add the hot wine. Add the *bouquet garni* and simmer 30 minutes.

Meanwhile, parboil the pork fat 5 minutes and cut into small dice. Sauté them and sauté the onions separately in butter until golden. Add both to the rabbit and cook 30 minutes longer. Then 10 minutes before the end of cooking time, add the liver cut in 4 pieces. If the sauce is not dark enough, add a little caramel (page 579 .

If you start with a live rabbit, you will save the blood, which should be mixed with a tablespoon of vinegar. Add this to the sauce at the last minute.

Rabbit with olives * Lapin aux olives

FOR FOUR PEOPLE

4 pieces of rabbit
6 tablespoons oil
4 onions
4 teaspoons flour
¾ cup dry white wine

½ teaspoon rosemary
¼ cup pitted black olives
chopped parsley
salt and pepper

Choose meaty back or leg pieces.

Heat the oil in a deep skillet or in a *sauteuse,* and when very hot, brown the rabbit well on all sides. Add the onions, cut in pieces, and sprinkle with flour. Let the onions and flour brown lightly before adding the white wine. Season with salt, pepper, and rosemary. Cover and cook gently for 30 minutes or until tender. Halfway through the cooking, add the olives (preferably the imported variety).

Serve very hot, sprinkled with chopped parsley. Serve with steamed potatoes.

Rabbit with sausage * Lapin à la chipolata

FOR FIVE PEOPLE

1 large rabbit

bouquet garni (bay leaf, 2 sprigs

2 tablespoons butter
2 tablespoons lard
¼ pound lean pork belly
¾ cup white wine
¾ cup bouillon

thyme, 1 sprig parsley)
12 chestnuts
8 small spicy link sausages
salt and pepper

Cut the rabbit into pieces.

Heat the butter, lard, and diced pork belly in a heavy pan and heat slowly. (If pork belly is not available, parboil salt pork for 5 minutes and rinse before dicing.—*Ed.*) When the fat is hot, add the rabbit pieces and brown lightly, turning each piece. Add the wine and bouillon slowly. Add salt, pepper, and the *bouquet garni.* Cook gently for 1 hour.

Meanwhile, slit the chestnuts and brown them very slowly for 25 to 30 minutes so that they will cook without burning. Peel off both skins.

Prick the sausages and poach in ¼ inch of water until the water evaporates. Brown the sausages lightly.

Just before serving, add the cooked chestnuts and sausages.

Hare

Hare, called jack rabbit in the southern part of the United States, is delicious when properly cooked. It should be drawn and dressed as soon after being killed as possible. For most preparations, it is essential to save the blood and the liver.

Hare in champagne ∗ *Lièvre au champagne*

FOR EIGHT PEOPLE

1 large hare
2 wide paper-thin slices fat salt pork
2 onions
5 shallots
5 cloves garlic
bouquet garni (thyme, bay leaf,
    parsley)

¾ cup white wine
1 bottle champagne
1½ tablespoons armagnac
1 cup heavy cream
salt and pepper

Once the hare is prepared for cooking, wrap it in a slice of pork fat that has been rinsed and dried. Bind to the body at both ends with kitchen twine. Season with pepper.

Line a large deep dish with another slice of salt pork (or several narrow slices, if necessary) and place the hare on it. Add the onions, cut in two, the shallots, the garlic, and the *bouquet garni.* Add the white wine. Cover and simmer covered for 2 hours.

In another pan, boil the champagne down to half its original quantity. Add the armagnac and pour the mixture over the hare. Simmer 1½ hours longer.

At the last minute, add the cream and season with salt and pepper.

Place the hare on a heated platter. Remove the pork fat and strain the sauce over the hare.

Hare à la galopade * *Lièvre à la galopade*

FOR EIGHT PEOPLE

1 large hare
7 tablespoons butter
2 tablespoons flour
3 cups hot red wine
bouquet garni (thyme, bay leaf, parsley)

20 small onions
½ pound small mushrooms
salt and pepper

When the hare is dressed, reserve the blood.

Tenderize the hare by pounding it with the flat side of a cleaver. Cut in serving pieces.

Heat 5 tablespoons of butter in a large pan and brown the hare well on both sides. Sprinkle with flour, and when that disappears, add the hot red wine. Season with salt and pepper, the blood of the hare, and the *bouquet garni.* Cook over high heat for 30 minutes.

Meanwhile, sauté the onions in the rest of the butter. Trim, wash, and wipe the caps of the mushrooms. When the hare has cooked ½ hour, add the onions and mushrooms. Season the sauce to taste with salt and pepper and cook ½ hour longer.

Serve with fried croutons and boiled potatoes.

Jugged hare * *Civet de lièvre*

FOR TEN PEOPLE

1 large hare
4 teaspoons vinegar
1 bottle good red wine
2 carrots
1 large onion
bouquet garni (thyme, bay leaf, parsley)

4 tablespoons oil
½ pound lean pork belly or salt pork
25 small onions
3 tablespoons butter
2 ounces pork fat, chopped
4 teaspoons flour
salt and pepper

When the hare is drawn and dressed, save the blood and liver in a small bowl. Add the vinegar to prevent coagulation.

Cut the animal in pieces and place them in a deep bowl with the wine, the carrots and onion cut in thin slices, the *bouquet garni,* salt, and 2 teaspoons of peppercorns and 2½ tablespoons of oil. Marinate 24 hours, turning the pieces occasionally.

Cut the lean pork fat into small dice and parboil 5 minutes.

Peel the small onions.

Heat the butter and the rest of the oil in a heavy pan.

Sauté the parboiled pork dice and the onions until golden. Remove them from the pan and add the chopped pork fat and the pieces of hare that have been wiped dry. Brown them on all sides and sprinkle with flour. When the flour has disappeared, add the wine from the marinade, and the *bouquet garni,* and cook covered for 1 hour. Season to taste. Add the pork dice and the onions and the blood with the liver which has been crushed with a fork. Simmer very slowly for another hour.

Serve with steamed potatoes.

Saddle of hare in white wine
Râble de lièvre mariné au vin blanc

FOR FOUR PEOPLE

1 saddle of hare	3 tablespoons butter
1½ cups white wine	1 wide paper-thin slice salt pork
1½ tablespoons cognac	3 tablespoons heavy cream
1½ tablespoons Madeira	4 teaspoons currant jelly
1 onion	1 teaspoon peppercorns
1 carrot	salt and pepper
pinch of thyme	

Put the saddle (the back of the animal extending from the lower shoulders to the tail) in a bowl with the white wine, cognac, Madeira, the onion and carrot cut in thin slices, thyme, salt, and peppercorns. Marinate for 3 hours, basting frequently with the liquid.

Remove the saddle from the marinade and wipe it dry. Place in a roasting pan and spread it with butter. Cover with the slice of salt pork, which has been rinsed and dried to remove the excess salt. Roast at 400° F. for 25 to 30 minutes, depending on the age and tenderness of the hare. Baste frequently with a cup of hot marinade, spooning a tablespoon over the meat every few minutes.

Just before serving, add the cream and jelly to the sauce in the pan. Season the sauce to taste with salt and pepper.

Hare with prunes and chestnuts
Lièvre aux pruneaux et marrons

FOR SIX PEOPLE

1 hare, including blood and liver
1 bottle good white wine
1 carrot, sliced
1 onion, sliced thin
thyme
½ pound prunes
flour

tea
5 tablespoons oil
1½ tablespoons cognac
8 small onions
½ pound Canadian bacon, diced
rosemary
salt and pepper

Cut the hare in pieces. Combine the white wine, sliced carrot, sliced onion, salt, pepper, and a pinch of thyme in a bowl and soak the hare in this marinade for 24 hours.

Soak the prunes in strong tea for several hours. Take out the pits.

Remove the hare from the bowl and wipe each piece well. Dip it into flour.

Heat the oil in a deep pan and sauté the hare on all sides. Add the cognac and touch with a lighted match. Strain enough of the marinade over the hare so that the liquid comes just to the top of the meat.

Peel the onions and cut the bacon into small dice. Boil the bacon 5 minutes and sauté in a little oil.

Add the onions, bacon, a pinch of rosemary and thyme, salt and pepper. Cover and cook over moderate heat for 1 hour.

Slit the skin of each chestnut and roast them in a pan made especially for the purpose or in the oven. Remove after 10 minutes and peel off the outer and inner skins. At the end of the first hour of cooking, add the chestnuts. Continue the cooking for 2 hours.

10 minutes before serving, add the blood and the liver, forced through a strainer. Add the prunes. Taste the sauce. If it is too thin, continue cooking, but this time without a cover. Serve the hare on a platter and surround it with.small croutons of bread fried in oil.

Hare en saupiquet * *Lièvre en saupiquet*

FOR EIGHT PEOPLE

1 pound chestnuts
1 young hare, including the liver
4 teaspoons cognac
5 tablespoons goose fat
3 medium-sized onions
2½ ounces bacon

2½ tablespoons wine vinegar
3 cups good red wine
bouquet garni (thyme, bay leaf,
   parsley)
½ clove garlic
salt and pepper

When the hare is killed, the blood must be saved. Chop the liver and put it in a bowl with the blood and the cognac.

Spread the hare with 3 tablespoons of goose fat and roast it 1 hour at 400° F. During the cooking process, sprinkle the drippings with salt and baste occasionally. Add a little hot water to the pan, if necessary.

While the hare is roasting, sauté the onions, peeled and sliced thin, and the bacon, cut in small dice, in the rest of the goose fat. When the onions are golden, add the vinegar, the red wine, the *bouquet garni,* garlic, salt, and pepper. Simmer slowly until the sauce is a third of its original quantity. Strain the sauce. Reheat slowly. Add the liver mixture. Stir once and remove from the heat. Put in a a separate bowl and serve with the roast hare.

Wild rabbit

Wild rabbit is tenderer than hare. We are presuming that the purveyor of your rabbit, whether it be a storekeeper or a hunter, will give you the rabbit skinned, dressed, and ready for cooking.

Wild rabbit stew ✳ *Gibelotte de lapin de garenne*

FOR FOUR PEOPLE

1 teaspoon peppercorns	12 small onions
1 wild rabbit	1½ cups white wine
5 ounces lean pork belly	¾ cup bouillon
1½ tablespoons butter	1 teaspoon chopped rosemary
1½ tablespoons oil	salt and pepper

Cut the rabbit into serving pieces.

Dice the lean pork fat. (If pork belly is not available, parboil lean salt pork 5 minutes. Rinse before using.—*Ed.*)

Heat the butter and oil in a heavy pan. Sauté the pork dice, and when golden, add the rabbit. Brown well and add the onions.

Gradually add the wine and bouillon. Season with salt and pepper and the rosemary. Cover and cook gently for 1 hour.

Wild rabbit and cabbage
Lapin de garenne au chou

FOR SIX PEOPLE

1 wild rabbit, cleaned and
   cut into pieces
3 tablespoons butter
1 large cabbage
½ pound lean salt pork

pork skin (see below)
fat salt pork (see below)
½ cup bouillon
salt and pepper

Sauté the rabbit in butter until lightly browned on all sides.

Remove the stem and core from the cabbage and wash the leaves well. Parboil in salted water for 5 minutes. Drain well.

Rinse the salt pork in cold water. Dry and cut in thin slices.

Ask the butcher for pork skin, but if this is not possible, parboil bacon or salt pork rind for 5 minutes. Rinse and pat dry. Ask him also for 2 wide paper-thin slices of salt pork.

Line the bottom of a casserole with the pork skin or substitute. Cover with a layer of cabbage leaves and then a layer of lean salt pork slices and a layer of rabbit pieces. Cover this with another layer of cabbage leaves and grind some pepper over them. Cover with a slice of fat salt pork. Put in all the rabbit pieces. Cover with another slice of fat salt pork and another layer of cabbage leaves. Sprinkle with pepper. Put on one more layer of lean salt pork and top with a layer of cabbage leaves. Add the bouillon. Cover and simmer very gently for 3 hours.

Wild rabbit sauté with lemon
Lapin de garenne sauté au citron

FOR SIX PEOPLE

1 large wild rabbit
½ cup oil
2 cups white wine
1 shallot

6 tablespoons butter
juice of ½ lemon
chopped parsley
salt and pepper

Cut the rabbit into serving pieces.

Heat the oil in a heavy pan and brown the rabbit well on all sides.

Reduce the heat. Season with salt and pepper. Cover and simmer 20 to 25 minutes. Transfer the rabbit to a platter and keep hot.

Pour the wine into the pan in which the rabbit has been sautéed and add the shallot, peeled and finely chopped. Cook 15 minutes without a cover. Season the sauce to taste with salt and pepper. Then stir in the butter by bits and add the lemon juice. Pour this sauce over the rabbit and sprinkle with chopped parsley.

Wild rabbit à la saint aignan
Lapin de garenne à la saint aignan

FOR FOUR PEOPLE

1 wild rabbit
¼ pound butter
bouillon or water
1 pound (4-5) onions

pinch of cayenne
2½ tablespoons tomato paste
½ cup heavy cream
salt and pepper

Cut the rabbit in pieces. Heat the butter in a deep heavy pan and brown the rabbit on all sides.

At the same time, and in the same pan, sauté the onions which have been peeled and sliced very thin. Season with salt and pepper. When the rabbit is lightly browned, add enough bouillon or water to cover. Cover the pan and cook over moderate heat for 1 hour. During the cooking, add a pinch of cayenne. At the end of the cooking, stir in the tomato paste and the cream. Taste for seasoning.

Make a caramel (page 579) with 2 lumps of sugar and add it to the sauce. Serve the rabbit on a heated platter with the sauce poured over it.

Marinated wild rabbit * Lapin de garenne mariné

FOR FIVE PEOPLE

Marinade:
2 cups red wine
1 carrot, sliced
1 shallot, sliced
1 onion stuck with
3 cloves ·
1 teaspoon peppercorns

bouquet garni (thyme, bay leaf,
   parsley)
1 large wild rabbit
4 tablespoons oil
flour
½ cup seedless raisins
4 teaspoons cognac

Prepare the marinade. Cut the rabbit in pieces and put them in the marinade for 24 hours. Turn them occasionally.

Remove the rabbit pieces, dry them well. Sauté the pieces in oil and sprinkle with a good tablespoon of flour. Mix well and add 2 cups of the strained marinade. Cover and cook 40 minutes or until tender.

Meanwhile, soak the raisins in warm water to which the cognac has been added. Just before serving, add the raisins to the sauce.

Venison and wild boar

Roast venison grand veneur
Gigue de chevreuil grand veneur

FOR EIGHT PEOPLE

2 quarts good red wine
3 lumps sugar
1 tablespoon peppercorns
3 cloves
6 bay leaves
1 tablespoon curry powder

3 sage leaves
pinch of rosemary, nutmeg, and thyme
1 leg young venison
several strips (¼-inch thick) fat pork
6 tablespoons butter
salt and pepper

Boil together for 30 minutes the wine, sugar, and all the herbs and spices.

Put the venison in a large dish and strain the wine mixture over it. Let it stand 10 days, turning the leg twice each day.

At the end of this time, remove the venison and wipe it dry. Lard the meat by running strips of pork with a larding needle against the grain of the meat.

Place the venison in a roasting pan and smear it with the butter. Roast 60 to 70 minutes at 400° F., basting often with some of the marinade.

Serve very hot, accompanied by a pear compote flavored with cinnamon.

Larded venison * Fricandeau de chevreuil

FOR SIX PEOPLE

1 haunch of young venison
Red Wine Marinade (page 28)
15 strips fat salt pork
1 very wide paper-thin piece pork fat
2 carrots
2 onions

2 stalks celery
bouquet garni (bay leaf, thyme,
  parsley)
1 quart bouillon
½ cup heavy cream
salt and pepper

Marinate the haunch of venison in a red wine marinade.

Cut as large a piece of the meat from the haunch as possible. Lard it with small strips of salt pork that have been rinsed to remove excess salt and dried. Run the strips *with* the grain of the meat. Sprinkle the meat with salt and pepper and surround it with a very wide piece or several narrow pieces of salt pork that has been rinsed and dried. Bind with kitchen twine.

Place in a braising pan with all the vegetables peeled and finely chopped, *bouquet garni,* bouillon, salt, and pepper. Cover and cook gently for 4 hours.

Remove the pork fat from the venison and transfer the venison to another deep pan. Scrape all the juices on the bottom of the pan and strain the sauce through a fine sieve. Remove as much fat as possible and pour the sauce over the meat. Boil down over a high heat until the sauce is quite thick. Turn the meat so that it will be browned on all sides. Just before serving, add the cream and taste the sauce for seasoning. Serve with chicory in cream.

Juniper venison stew
Civet de chevreuil au genièvre

FOR FOUR PEOPLE

2 pounds venison	*bouquet garni* (thyme, bay leaf,
6 tablespoons butter	parsley)
2 cups good red wine	1 tablespoon juniper berries
2 onions	1 teaspoon potato flour
2 cloves garlic	salt and pepper

This dish can be made from the breast meat or any other cut. Cut venison meat in pieces.

Heat the butter in a heavy pan and sauté the meat until lightly browned on all sides. Add the wine and an equal amount of water. Add the onions and garlic cut thin, the *bouquet garni,* the juniper berries, salt, and pepper.

Cover and cook over a moderate heat for 1 hour. Test to see if the meat is cooked by inserting a fork. Season the sauce to taste, and continue cooking, if necessary. If the sauce is too thin, boil it down without the cover.

When the venison is tender, place it in a heated dish. Strain the sauce and remove as much of the fat as possible. If it is still not thick enough to suit you, sprinkle with a little (1 scant teaspoon) potato flour and beat hard with a whisk until the sauce thickens. Pour the sauce over the venison.

Venison chops * Côtelettes de chevreuil

FOR FOUR PEOPLE

8 venison chops	6 tablespoons butter
16 small strips fat salt pork	¾ cup beef bouillon
Cooked Red Wine Marinade	juice of ½ lemon
(page 27)	salt and pepper

Insert into the chops tiny strips of salt pork that have been rinsed to remove excess salt and patted dry. Let the chops marinate 12 hours in the marinade.

Heat butter in a heavy pan and brown the chops on both sides. Add the bouillon, juice of ½ lemon, salt, and pepper. Cook without a cover over moderate heat until the sauce becomes very concentrated. Taste the sauce for seasoning.

Serve the chops with a chestnut purée, an onion purée, or with pears baked without sugar.

Braised shoulder of venison with olives
Epaule de chevreuil braisée aux olives

FOR FIVE PEOPLE

1 shoulder of venison	2 ounces fat pork belly
Cooked Red Wine Marinade	¾ cup pitted green olives
(page 27)	1 scant teaspoon potato starch
10 small strips fat salt pork	salt and pepper

Remove the interior bone of the shoulder, leaving the exterior shank bone intact. Marinate for 3 days, turning the meat occasionally.

Using a larding needle, thread little strips of the salt pork, which have been seasoned with pepper, in the interior of the shoulder. Roll and tie with kitchen twine.

Dice the pork fat. (If pork belly is not available, parboil a piece of fat salt pork for 5 minutes. Rinse and dry before dicing.—*Ed.*) Put the venison in a deep pan with the pork fat and let it cook very gently in its own juice for 1 to 1½ hours, depending on the age of the animal.

Boil the olives in water for 15 minutes.

When the venison is tender, remove it from the pan. Spoon off as much fat as possible from the sauce and add the olives. Let it boil a moment. Sprinkle with the potato starch, beating hard with a whip to avoid lumps in the sauce. Taste for seasoning.

Carve the venison and arrange on a heated platter. Pour the sauce over the meat.

Roast wild boar * Sanglier mariné rôti

FOR EIGHT TO TEN PEOPLE

Marinade:	nutmeg
¾ cup oil	4 teaspoons juniper berries
1 carrot, cut in slices	*Wild boar:*
1 stalk celery, cut in pieces	1 wild boar leg
3 onions, sliced	6 tablespoons butter
1 quart red wine	1½ tablespoons cognac
bouquet garni (thyme, bay leaf)	salt and pepper

Heat the oil and sauté the vegetables in it. Add the wine, *bouquet garni,* juniper berries, salt, a teaspoon of peppercorns and a good pinch of nutmeg. Bring to a boil and pour boiling hot over the wild boar leg. Marinate 2 weeks, turning the leg twice a day.

Before cooking, remove the boar leg from the marinade and wipe it well. Spread with butter, salt, and pepper and place in a roasting pan. Put into a 350° F. oven. As soon as the butter has melted, pour over the cognac and touch it with a lighted match. Add 1½ cups of the marinade and roast for about 45 minutes.

Wild boar à la mode * Sanglier à la mode

FOR SIX PEOPLE

3-pound boned shoulder of wild boar
3 ounces fat salt pork
5 tablespoons butter
3 cups dry white wine
¾ cup bouillon or water

bouquet garni (thyme, bay leaf, parsley)
½ lemon
salt and pepper

Unless you have a willing game merchant to do it for you, lard the piece of meat with thin strips of salt pork, which have been rinsed to remove excess salt. Use a larding needle.

Heat the butter in a deep dish and brown the meat on both sides. Add the white wine, bouillon, the *bouquet garni,* salt, pepper, and ½ lemon, cut in thin slices. Cover and simmer 4 hours.

Serve with brussels sprouts sautéed in butter.

Goose

Goose is not as popular as turkey with some people because it has a stronger and sometimes oily flavor, but a young goose is very delicious. A good quality young goose will have very white fat and a fine-grained skin. Buy small geese. In France, geese weighing 6 to 8 pounds are the most desirable. In the United States, the smallest birds sold are 8 to 9 pounds.

When you roast a goose in the oven, always place it on a trivet in the roasting pan in order to let the fat drop into the pan. If the goose is cooked in its own fat, the meat becomes greasy and very indigestible.

Draw off the fat from the pan several times during the cooking. Save it, because it makes the best cooking fat imaginable. Never boil a goose; the broth is too strong, and the meat will become too dry. The skin of the goose should be well browned. Roast in a hot oven and count 18 minutes per pound.

No matter how much fat you remove from the pan, the juices will still be fatty at the end of cooking. Add a cup of well-seasoned bouillon (preferably veal) to the juices to make the dish gravy.

The famous *foie gras* (fattened goose liver) is not produced in America and must be imported from France. It can be bought in cans weighing from 1½ to 15 ounces. Fresh goose liver flown in from France can be obtained in certain specialty shops but at great expense. However, for the sake of real enthusiasts of the delicacy, we include two recipes.

Goose with cherries * Oie aux cerises

FOR EIGHT PEOPLE

1 small goose
4 tablespoons butter
1 large jar unsweetened cherries

¾ cup good red wine or port
salt and pepper

Place the goose on a trivet in a roasting pan and spread with butter. Place in a preheated 450° oven and roast. Allow 18 minutes per pound.

At the end of 15 minutes, baste the goose and siphon or spoon off the fat and put in a bowl for future use. Repeat this process every 15 minutes for the first hour of roasting. Season with salt and pepper. At the end of cooking there should be about 2 cups of drippings in the pan.

Drain the cherries and put them in a saucepan with the wine or port. Boil 2 minutes.

Remove the cooked goose from the oven. Pour the juices from the pan into the saucepan containing the cherries. Carve the goose and put the pieces on a heated platter. Pour the cherries over the goose.

Preserved goose * Confit d'oie

This is used in such hearty dishes as *Cassoulet*.

Cut a small goose in quarters, but do not remove the bones. Save the liver for other purposes. Put the pieces of goose in a deep bowl and sprinkle generously with salt. Cover with a towel and let stand for at least 24 hours. Remove the pieces from the bowl and wipe them well.

Heat the goose fat slowly in a kettle, and when the fat is liquid, put in the pieces of goose. Cook them in the fat for 1 hour over very low heat. Be sure the goose is cooked by testing it with a straw. The meat should be tender. Put the meat in an earthenware pot and strain the fat over the goose. Let cool thoroughly and cover with a ½-inch layer of lard to preserve the meat.

The goose should stand 3 months before being eaten. It will be good for many months provided it is stored in a cool, dry place.

Roast goose with orange * Oie à l'orange

FOR EIGHT PEOPLE

1 small goose	1 cup concentrated bouillon
3 tablespoons butter	½ teaspoon cornstarch
4 oranges	salt and pepper
½ cup dry white wine	

Spread the goose with a very thin layer of soft butter and place it on a trivet in a roasting pan. Roast at 450° F., allowing 18 minutes to the pound. Every 15 minutes for the first hour, baste the goose and then siphon or spoon off all the fat from the pan. Season with salt and pepper halfway through the cooking.

Squeeze the juice from 2 of the oranges. Peel off the orange part of the rind and cut it into thin strips. Cook 5 minutes in boiling water. Peel the other oranges carefully and divide into sections.

Transfer the goose to a heated platter. Spoon off all possible fat from the pan juices and pour the juices into a small saucepan. Add the white wine, the orange juice, and the bouillon. Sprinkle with the cornstarch, stirring until the sauce is slightly thickened. Add the orange peel to the sauce. Taste for seasoning.

Carve the goose and arrange the pieces on the serving platter. Surround with a little of the sauce. Serve the rest in a gravy bowl. Garnish the platter with the orange sections.

Fresh foie gras slices with grapes
Escalopes de foie d'oie aux raisins

FOR FOUR PEOPLE

flour	½ cup armagnac
4 slices fresh *foie gras*	1 teaspoon meat extract
6 tablespoons butter	1 bunch seedless grapes
4 slices white bread	salt and pepper

Flour the slices of *foie gras* lightly on both sides. Cook gently in 2 tablespoons of butter, allowing 1½ minutes on each side. Season with salt and pepper.

At the same time, in another skillet, fry the bread slices lightly on both sides in 2 tablespoons of butter. Place on a heated platter and put the liver slices on the bread. Keep hot.

Pour the armagnac into the pan in which the liver has cooked. Simmer 5 minutes. Add the extract, dissolved in a little water. Add the grapes and simmer for 10 minutes. Remove the pan from the heat and whisk in the remaining butter.

Pour the sauce over the liver slices and serve very hot.

Roast goose with plums * Oie rôtie aux prunes

FOR SIX PEOPLE

1 small goose	6 tablespoons sugar
3 tablespoons butter	salt and pepper
4 pounds plums	

Roast the goose as in the preceding recipes.

Stone the plums and cook them in a saucepan with a very little water and the sugar for 15 minutes.

Serve the goose on a heated platter and surround with the cooked plums.

In a separate bowl, serve the dish gravy, from which as much fat as possible has been removed. It should be very hot.

Poached fresh foie gras * Foie gras frais poché

FOR FIVE PEOPLE

large *foie gras* (1¾ pounds)	¼ teaspoon allspice
(see introductory remarks)	¾ cup bouillon
½ cup cognac	salt and pepper
½ cup Madeira	

Remove the filaments from the liver. Marinate it 1 hour in cognac, Madeira, allspice, salt, and pepper. Baste it frequently.

Wrap the liver in a cheesecloth and put in a saucepan with the bouillon. Bring just to the boiling point and reduce the heat. The liquid should never actually boil. Poach for 25 to 30 minutes.

Guinea hen

Guinea hen has a fine flavor, but the meat is apt to be dry, so that when roasting, it should be covered with a thin slice of pork fat, or if it is braised, the flesh should be studded with bits of pork fat. Guinea hen, which is found only in specialty shops, weighs from 2 to 3 pounds.

Guinea hen d'auvergne
Pintade à la façon d'auvergne

FOR FOUR PEOPLE

1 large guinea hen (3 pounds)	5-6 sprigs parsley
paper-thin slice fat salt pork	4 teaspoons juniper berries
4 teaspoons oil	7 tablespoons butter
3-4 chicken livers	2 cups mellow white wine
3-4 chicken gizzards	*bouquet garni* (bay leaf, thyme,
⅛ pound uncooked ham	tarragon)
1 clove garlic	4 large slices white bread
2 onions	salt and pepper

Prepare the guinea hen for roasting, reserving carefully the liver, gizzards, and, if possible, the lungs. Rinse the slice of salt pork, which should be large enough to envelop the hen. Substitute several narrow, paper-thin slices if a wide one is not obtainable. Bind the fat to the bird with kitchen twine. Put the oil in a roasting pan and roast the hen at 400° F. for about 45 minutes, basting frequently with the drippings seasoned with salt and pepper.

Chop the guinea hen innards very fine with the chicken livers, the gizzards, the raw ham, the garlic, the onions, and the parsley. Add the juniper berries. Season with salt and pepper.

Heat 5 tablespoons of butter in a pan and sauté the mixture for 8 minutes. Reserve about a quarter of the mixture for future use and put the rest in a saucepan with the white wine, ½ cup of water, the *bouquet garni,* and a little salt and pepper. Cook over a moderate heat for 30 minutes. Force the mixture through a strainer into another saucepan, pressing hard to extract all possible juices. Taste the sauce for seasoning.

Brown the bread lightly in the remaining butter on both sides and spread with the mixture you have saved out.

Quarter the cooked guinea hen and place a piece on each crouton. Pour the sauce over the meat and serve immediately.

Braised guinea hen with peaches
Pintades braisées aux pêches

FOR EIGHT PEOPLE

2 large guinea hens	powdered thyme and bay leaf
2 onions	5 tablespoons peach liqueur
½ pound carrots	1 teaspoon cornstarch
3-ounce piece of bacon	1 jar peaches
5 tablespoons butter	salt and pepper

Prepare the guinea hen for roasting.

Peel and slice the onions and carrots and dice the bacon.

Use a pan deep enough to hold the guinea hens and still be covered. Line the bottom of the pan with the onions, carrots, and diced bacon. Dot with butter. Sprinkle with salt and pepper and with a pinch each of powdered thyme and bay leaf. Place the guinea hens on this foundation and roast in a 450° F. oven until the birds are browned on both sides. Pour the liqueur over the birds and touch with a lighted match. If you have no peach liqueur, use a mixture of armagnac and curaçao. When the flames subside, add the bouillon. Cover the pan tightly and cook 45 minutes at 400° F. Remove the hens to a heated platter and keep hot. Strain the sauce through a fine sieve. If the sauce is too thin, whip in the corn-starch and boil 5 minutes.

Put the peach halves in a large pan so that each one lies flat on the pan. Pour in the sauce and simmer 5 minutes.

Surround the hens with the peaches and pour the sauce over the hens and the peaches.

Guinea hen with cider * Pintade au cidre

FOR FOUR PEOPLE

4 tablespoons seedless raisins
2-2½-pound guinea hen
wide paper-thin slice fat salt pork
3 tablespoons butter
¼ cup walnut pieces

¾ cup hard cider
1½ tablespoons Calvados
¼ cup heavy cream
salt and pepper

Soak the raisins in lukewarm water for 30 minutes.

Prepare the guinea hen as though for roasting. Rinse and dry the wide piece of salt pork and envelop the bird. (Use several narrow pieces of paper-thin salt pork, if necessary.)

Heat the butter in a deep heavy pan. Add the guinea hen and nuts and pour over the cider, the Calvados, and the heavy cream. Season with salt and pepper. Cover and simmer 30 minutes.

Add the soaked and drained raisins and cook 20 minutes longer.

Remove the pork fat from the hen and place the hen in a roasting pan. Brown in a 450° F. oven for 10 minutes.

Remove the nuts and raisins from the sauce with a slotted spoon and put them around the edge of a heated serving platter. Boil down the sauce a little. Place the guinea hen on the platter and pour the sauce over everything.

Stuffed guinea hen * Pintades farcies

FOR TWELVE PEOPLE

3 guinea hens

2 eggs, slightly beaten

1 pound chicken livers	2 pounds carrots
½ pound shallots	1 pound onions
½ pound butter	2 cups port
¾ pound sausage meat	2 cups bouillon
2 small can truffle peelings	salt and pepper

Prepare the hens for stuffing.

Chop the guinea hens and chicken livers and half the shallots. Melt 6 table-spoons of the butter and sauté the livers and the shallots over low heat. When lightly browned, season with salt and pepper and remove from the heat. Add the sausage meat, the truffle peelings, and the eggs. Mix thoroughly and stuff the birds with the mixture. Sew up the openings and truss the birds.

Melt ¼ pound of butter in a deep roasting pan.

Peel and slice the rest of the vegetables very thin and sprinkle them over the butter. Spread the birds with the rest of the butter and place them on the vegetable bed. Roast 30 minutes at 350° F. Add the port and the bouillon and sprinkle with salt and pepper. Cover and cook 30 minutes longer.

Place the guinea hens on a heated platter and strain the sauce through a fine sieve over the birds.

Serve with a purée of chestnuts.

Feathered game

Birds should be plucked just before cooking.

To pluck: Begin by removing the breast feathers. Force the wings under the bird to clear the breast. Hold the bird far from you when you pull out the feathers. After the breast, pull out the feathers from the back and neck. Cut off the wingtips with a small cleaver.

To singe: It will be easier if you singe the bird before you cut off the neck and the feet, and besides, that way you will not get burned. Hold the bird by the neck and feet as you pass it over a brightly burning flame.

To clean: Cut the neck at the base. Remove the crop where the stones are found. Remove the oil sac at the tail. Laying the bird on its back, cut an opening under the right thigh. Draw the bird, removing all of its innards. Save the gizzard, liver, and heart. Break open the gizzard to remove the stones. Remove the gall without breaking.

To truss: Pull the legs backward and pierce the thigh with a kitchen needle threaded with twine. Run it through the bird, bringing it out in the corresponding place on the other thigh. Fold over the neck skin. Pass the needle through one wing, through the neck skin, through the other wing, and tie firmly. The bird is ready to roast.

Squabs

Young squabs have either a pale rose or bluish white flesh, depending on the breed. Older birds have a darker complexion. The small squab, weighing ¾ pound, is served whole for 1 person. The larger squab, 1-1½ pounds, can be split, and will serve 2 people. Roast squabs weighing 1 pound are cooked for 30 minutes. They are prepared like roast chicken.

Squab stew * Pigeons en matelote

FOR FOUR PEOPLE

2 1½-pound squabs	1½ cups good red wine, heated
5 tablespoons butter	1 *bouquet garni* (thyme, bay leaf)
2 onions	2 lumps sugar
4 teaspoons flour	salt and pepper

Clean and truss the squabs. Melt the butter in a large pan and brown the squabs lightly on both sides. Remove from the pan and split the squabs in two.

Brown the onions very lightly, peeled and sliced thin, in the same butter. Add the squabs and sprinkle with flour. When the flour has mixed with the butter, add the wine. Add salt, pepper, the *bouquet garni,* and the sugar. Cover and cook over very low heat for 2 hours. Put an asbestos mat or wire trivet under the pot so that the cooking will be extremely slow. Serve with boiled rice or steamed potatoes.

Sautéed squabs * Pigeonneaux sautés

FOR FOUR PEOPLE

4 squabs (¾ pound each)	4 teaspoons cognac
6 tablespoons butter	½ cup bouillon
¼ pound mushrooms	1 teaspoon paprika
2 slices cooked ham	pinch of ginger
1 onion	salt and pepper

Cut each squab in quarters. Heat the butter in a large pan and sauté the squabs gently on all sides.

Trim, wash, dry, and chop the mushrooms fine. Cut the ham in thin strips. Slice the onion thin.

Add the cognac to the squab and touch with a lighted match. Add the mushrooms and ham and sauté for 5 minutes. Add the bouillon. Season with the paprika, ginger, salt, and pepper. Cover and cook over moderate heat for 20 minutes.

Serve with boiled rice and sautéed tomatoes.

Squabs with fresh peas * Pigeons aux petits pois

FOR FOUR PEOPLE

2 large squabs
¼ pound lean salt pork
2½ tablespoons butter
12 tiny onions
4 teaspoons flour

¾ cup bouillon
2 cups very fresh peas
bouquet garni (2 bay leaves,
    2 sprigs thyme)
salt and pepper

Prepare the squabs as though for roasting.

Dice the lean salt pork and cook for 5 minutes. Rinse and drain dry.

Heat the butter in a deep heavy pan and gently sauté the diced pork fat. When golden, but not brown, remove from the pan with a slotted spoon and set aside in a dish.

Sauté the peeled onions in the same butter. They should be golden also, but not brown. Remove them to the same dish.

Still using a moderate heat, sauté the squabs gently on both sides. Keep the pan uncovered and turn the squabs. When well browned, remove them to a small platter.

Stir the flour into the pan, and when well blended, add the bouillon and cook gently for 2 to 3 minutes. Sprinkle with pepper.

Put the squabs and any juice that may have seeped out, the pork, and the onions into the pan. Add the fresh peas and the *bouquet garni.* Cover and cook over a moderate heat for 30 minutes. Taste for seasoning.

If the peas are not tender at this point, cook a little longer.

Serve the squabs on a heated platter surrounded with the peas.

Partridge

A la Saint Rémi
Tous les perdreaux sont perdrix.

If you have the choice, choose a gray partridge instead of a red one, because the meat is tenderer and the flavor better. Partridge are eaten soon after they are shot. Hunters say they should be eaten *"au bout de fusil,"* which means as soon as they are shot. Obviously, this is not possible, but they should be eaten within two or three days.

Young partridge (*perdreaux*) are best eaten roasted, but when the birds grow bigger (*perdrix*) and their beaks become stiff, they are best eaten braised. Never pluck the bird until shortly before cooking. Cooking time for a young partridge is 25 to 30 minutes. The meat should remain faintly pink. Croutons on which roast partridge are served should be fried very lightly in not too hot butter so that they will be soft.

Roast partridge * Perdreaux rôtis

FOR FOUR PEOPLE

4 young partridge
10 tablespoons butter
4 grape leaves
4 paper-thin slices salt pork

4 thin slices white bread
1 lemon
salt and pepper

Pluck the partridge at the last moment. Draw, singe, and truss them as described in the introduction to this section. Smear the birds with butter. Cover each one with a clean grape leaf and then with a paper-thin slice of salt pork, which has been rinsed and dried. Wrap string around the birds twice to keep the fat in place.

Put in a roasting pan. Pour a little melted butter over each bird and put in a 450° F. oven. When the fat is browned on one side, turn the birds to brown on the other. At the end of 10 to 12 minutes, take off the string, fat, and leaves and continue to cook. About 18 minutes should be enough for the average partridge. Do not baste the birds during the cooking.

Meanwhile, sauté the thin slices of bread in 2 tablespoons of butter over a low flame. The bread must remain soft. Place the bread on a heated platter. It is essential that both the platter and the sauce bowl be preheated.

Place the birds on the pieces of sautéed bread. Remove the twine. Pour 1 or 2 spoonfuls of water into the roasting pan and scrape the bottom to release the juices. Blend and strain into a heated sauce boat.

Broiled partridge * Perdreaux grillés

FOR SIX PEOPLE

3 large young partridge
½ cup olive oil
3 tablespoons butter
4 teaspoons flour
½ cup red wine

½ cup bouillon
juice of ½ lemon
2 shallots
salt and pepper

Prepare the partridge as though for roasting. Heat the oil in a large skillet and brown the partridge well on both sides. Remove from the oil and cool.

When the partridge are cold, broil them for 30 minutes, turning them often.

Heat the butter in a saucepan and stir in the flour with a wooden spoon. Add the wine, the bouillon, and the juice of ½ lemon. Season with salt and pepper and add the shallots chopped fine.

Cut the partridge in half lengthwise and place on a heated platter. Cover with the sauce. Serve with straw potatoes.

Partridge with cabbage * Perdrix aux choux

FOR FOUR PEOPLE

2 large partridge	2 ounces pork skin or rind
1 large green cabbage	1 large onion
7 ounces fat salt pork	1 clove
¼ pound uncooked sausage	6 tablespoons dry white wine
½ pound carrots	salt and pepper

Prepare the partridge for roasting and brown quickly in a hot oven. Remove as soon as the breasts are lightly browned. This is just preliminary cooking.

Trim and cut the cabbage, removing the center core. Cook in boiling salted water for 15 minutes. Drain and soak in cold water for 10 minutes. Drain and press the water from the cabbage with the palms of your hand.

Put the cabbage in a heavy deep pan with the salt pork (which has been washed to remove the excess salt), the sausage, the carrots peeled and left whole, the pork skin, the onion stuck with the clove, pepper, and a very little salt. Add the white wine. Cover and cook gently for 1 hour.

Add the partridge and cook 1 hour longer.

Remove the partridge and cut into serving pieces. Remove the pork skin and cut into small rectangles. Remove the carrots and sausage and cut into rounds.

Place the cabbage in a deep serving dish and arrange the partridge on it. Garnish with the pork pieces and surround with the sausage and carrot rounds.

Partridge casserole * Perdreaux en cocotte

FOR TWO PEOPLE

2 young partridge	¼ pound mushrooms
10 tablespoons butter	4 teaspoons juniper berries
2 carrots	1½ tablespoons cognac
2 medium-sized onions	2½ tablespoons dry white wine
2 stalks celery	salt and pepper

Prepare the birds for roasting.

Heat 5 tablespoons of butter in a deep skillet. When the butter is very hot, sauté the birds over moderate heat for 10 minutes, turning them so that they will brown on both sides. Set the pan aside.

Peel the carrots and onions and cut them, the celery, and the cleaned mushrooms into small thin strips. Heat the rest of the butter in a heavy saucepan and cook the vegetables in the butter with the pan covered over very low heat for 1 hour.

Place half the vegetables in a casserole. Put the partridge on the vegetables and cover with the rest of the vegetables. Season with salt and pepper. Crush the berries slightly and add them, the cognac, and the white wine to the casserole. Cover tightly and cook 30 minutes at 400° F. Serve from the casserole.

Partridge essendiéras * Perdreaux essendiéras

FOR TWO PEOPLE

2 young partridge	1 bunch grapes
¼ pound butter	salt and pepper
2 medium-sized oranges	

Prepare the partridge as though for roasting. Heat the butter in a large skillet and sauté the birds gently for 15 minutes, turning them so that they will brown on both sides. Season with salt and pepper.

Peel the oranges, dividing them in sections and removing all the white fibers and filaments. There should be a dozen sections of orange and a cupful of stemmed grapes.

Put the partridge in a deep pan. Surround with the fruit and pour the butter from the skillet over the birds. Cover tightly and bake 25 to 30 minutes in a hot (400° F.) oven.

Partridge with cherries * Perdreaux aux cerises

FOR SIX PEOPLE

6 small partridge	1 large can small unsweetened
½ package cream cheese	pitted cherries
¾ cup heavy cream	7 tablespoons butter
1 small can (2¾-oz.) *foie gras mousse*	1½ tablespoons fine cognac
6 slices white bread	salt and pepper

Pluck and clean the partridge. Do not cut off their heads and carefully save the livers, hearts, and gizzards. Pound these with the cream cheese, 2 tablespoons of heavy cream, and the *foie gras mousse* to make a stuffing. Season with salt and pepper. Reserve enough to spread the croutons and stuff the birds with the rest. Put in 3 or 4 cherries for each bird. Sew the openings and truss the birds, making sure that the heads are in place and the feet crossed. These are essential points for making a proper presentation of the partridge.

Heat 5 tablespoons of the butter in a very large pan or *sauteuse,* preferably one made of copper. When very hot, brown the partridges on both sides. Season with salt and pepper and add the cognac. Touch with a lighted match. When the flames subside, add the rest of the cherries, saving out about 2 dozen for decoration. Add the rest of the cream. Reduce the heat and cook very, very gently for ½ hour. Watch carefully that they do not become too dry. Taste for seasoning.

Remove the crusts from the bread and brown the slices lightly in 2 tablespoons of butter on both sides. Spread with the reserved stuffing. Place on a heated platter.

To serve: Spear cherries on toothpicks and insert 3 or 4 on the back of each bird. Place the birds on the croutons and pour the sauce, which should be rather thick and very hot, over the birds. Serve immediately.

Partridge with hazel nuts * Perdreaux aux noisettes

FOR EIGHT PEOPLE

4 large young partridge	8 tablespoons butter
½ cup oil	6 ounces Canadian bacon
3 cups dry white wine	1 tablespoon cognac
3 lemons	white bread
2 carrots	½ cup shelled hazel nuts
6 small onions	white peppercorns
bouquet garni (thyme, bay leaf)	salt

Pluck, singe, and clean the partridge. Split them and marinate them 48 hours in a mixture of the oil, wine, lemon sliced thin, the carrots, and 1 onion peeled and sliced thin, *bouquet garni,* salt, and 2 teaspoons of white peppercorns. Turn the partridge several times during the marinating process.

Remove the partridge from the marinade and wipe them carefully. Heat 6 tablespoons of the butter in a large deep pan. Sauté the bacon cut in small dice and the remaining onions, which have been peeled. When golden-colored, add the partridge and brown them well. Add the cognac and touch with a lighted match. When the flames subside, remove the partridge from the pan and add the marinade. Boil the sauce until it begins to thicken. Put back the partridge. Cover and cook 20 minutes.

Meanwhile, cut the bread into 8 triangles and sauté them gently in 2 tablespoons of butter.

Then 10 minutes before the end of cooking, chop the hazel nuts fine and add half of them to the partridge. Place the partridge on a heated platter. Pour the sauce, seasoned to taste, over the birds and sprinkle with the remaining nuts. Alternate lemon wedges and croutons around the edge of the platter.

Normandy partridge ✳ *Perdreaux normande*

4 small partridge
4 paper-thin slices salt pork
10 tablespoons butter
pinch of powdered thyme

1 pound apples
⅔ cup heavy cream
1½ tablespoons Calvados
salt and pepper

Prepare the partridge as though for roasting. Place a piece of salt pork, washed to remove excess salt and patted dry, over each bird and tie in place.

Heat half the butter in a deep earthenware or iron pot, and when very hot, brown the birds on all sides. Season with salt and pepper and sprinkle with thyme.

At the same time, peel the apples and slice them thin. Let them cook in the rest of the butter in a separate pan for 5 minutes. Add the apples to the browned birds and cook over a moderate heat for 20 minutes. Add the cream and Calvados. Taste the sauce for seasoning and cook just until the sauce is thoroughly heated. Serve immediately on a heated platter.

Pheasant

Pheasants are particularly good in the late fall. The young pheasants (under 1 month) have short, rounded claws; the older birds have long, sharp ones.

The hen pheasant has a light skin, and the meat is more delicate than that of the male, which is often dry. When the pheasant has hung a little while, its perfume is remarkable. A pheasant can be stuffed, roasted, and braised.

Braised pheasant with apples *Faisan braisé aux pommes*

4 tablespoons seedless raisins
1 pheasant
7 tablespoons butter
1½ pounds apples
½ cup heavy cream

juice of ½ lemon
1½ tablespoons Calvados
½ teaspoon cinnamon
salt and pepper

Soak the raisins 2 hours in tepid water.

Prepare the pheasant as though for roasting. Heat 2 tablespoons of butter in a large pan and brown the pheasant well on both sides. Remove from the pan.

Peel, core, and cut the apples in thin slices. Heat the rest of the butter in a large skillet, and when very hot, sauté the apples quickly so that they will be lightly browned on the outside but not cooked.

Put a good layer of apples in the bottom of the pan in which the pheasant was browned. Place the bird on the apples and surround with the rest of the apples. Pour in the cream previously mixed with the juice of ½ lemon, the Calvados, and cinnamon. Season with salt and pepper and add the drained raisins. Cover and cook over a moderate heat for 2 hours.

Pheasant with apples and chestnuts
Faisan braisé aux pommes et marrons

FOR FOUR PEOPLE

1 large young pheasant	⅔ cup bouillon
½ apple	salt and pepper
½ package cream cheese	*Chestnuts in Bouillon:*
1 tablespoon heavy cream	2 pounds chestnuts
4 teaspoons cognac	2 cups bouillon
½ teaspoon rosemary	2 sugar lumps
¼ teaspoon sage	2 tablespoons butter
1 wide paper-thin slice lean salt pork	*Buttered Apples:*
3 tablespoons butter	8 apples
⅓ cup port	1 lemon

Prepare the pheasant for stuffing.

Chop the liver with ½ apple. Mix the cheese and cream and add to the liver mixture along with the cognac, salt, pepper, and herbs. Stir thoroughly and stuff the pheasant with the mixture. Sew the opening and cover the pheasant with the salt pork rinsed and dried. Bind with kitchen twine to the bird.

Prepare the chestnuts. See below.

Heat the butter in a deep pan and put in the pheasant. Add the port. Cover and cook over a moderate heat for 45 minutes. Baste several times. Prick with a sharp-pointed knife to see if the pheasant is tender.

Prepare the apples. See below.

Remove the pheasant from the dish and take off the salt pork. Place the bird on a heated serving platter and surround with the apples and chestnuts, which have been cooking at the same time. Heat the sauce in the pan with the bouillon and pour over the pheasant.

Chestnuts in Bouillon: Buy large chestnuts and remove the outer skin with a sharp knife. Dry the nuts in a roasting pan in a slow oven for a few minutes. The inner skin will lift off easily.

Put the chestnuts in a pan just big enough to hold them. Cover with bouillon and add the sugar and a pinch of salt. Heat. When the liquid boils, add the butter. Cover and simmer for 1 hour. Do not stir; the chestnuts will absorb the bouillon and will remain whole.

Buttered Apples: Choose sweet, medium-sized apples. Peel them without cutting and rub them with lemon so they will not darken. Cut off the top at the stem end to serve as cover. Remove the seeds with an apple corer. Fill the holes with butter and put back the covers. Put in a buttered baking dish, add ¾ cup water, and cook until tender but not mushy. It is impossible to give an exact time because of the variety in size and type of apples. Test with a knife.

Broiled deviled pheasant
Faisandeaux grillés à la diable

FOR FOUR PEOPLE

6 tablespoons butter	French mustard
2 young pheasants *or*	cayenne
1 tender large pheasant	½ cup fine breadcrumbs
6 tablespoons butter	salt

Split the prepared young pheasants in half, or quarter a large pheasant. Season the pieces with salt and brush them with butter. Roast 20 minutes at 400° F. Remove them and brush them while they are still warm, with mustard to which you have added a dash of cayenne. Coat them with fine breadcrumbs and sprinkle with melted butter. Finish cooking by broiling, turning each piece at least once.

Serve with commercially prepared devil sauce or hot raisin sauce.

Pheasant in cream * Faisan à la crème

FOR FOUR PEOPLE

5 tablespoons butter	juice of ½ lemon
1 large pheasant	1 tablespoon paprika
1 onion	salt and pepper
1 cup heavy cream	

Heat the butter in a casserole. When it is hot, put in the pheasant. Add the onion peeled and quartered. Cover and braise over moderate heat for 30 minutes.

Add the cream and the juice of ½ lemon and a tablespoon of paprika. Season with salt and pepper. Continue cooking over very low heat for 15 minutes.

If the pheasant is mature, prolong the first part of the cooking.

Pheasant with grapes * Faisan aux raisins

FOR FOUR PEOPLE

1 large pheasant
paper-thin slice(s) salt pork
2 pounds white grapes
24 walnuts
½ cup sour cream

2 tablespoons butter
1½ tablespoons cognac
3 lumps sugar
salt and pepper

Prepare the pheasant as though for roasting. Rinse a wide slice or several narrow slices of paper-thin salt pork to remove excess salt. Pat dry and envelop the bird in the fat, binding with kitchen twine.

Save out a few grapes for decoration and force the rest through a strainer to extract the juices.

Put the bird and the walnut halves in a deep pan. Add three fourths of the grape juice, cognac, all the cream and butter, and some salt and pepper. Cover the pan and cook gently for 30 minutes.

Make a very thin caramel (see page 579) with the sugar. Add the caramel and the rest of the grape juice. Continue cooking for 20 minutes.

Remove the pheasant and take off the twine and fat. Put the pheasant in a very hot (450° F.) oven to brown. When nicely colored, place the pheasant on a heated serving platter. At the same time, remove the nuts from the sauce with a slotted spoon and quickly boil down the sauce for a few moments. Season to taste with salt and pepper and strain the sauce over the bird. Surround with the nuts and grapes. Serve immediately.

Pheasant pot-au-feu * Faisan au pot

FOR FOUR PEOPLE

1 large pheasant
paper-thin slice(s) salt pork
1 quart bouillon
½ quart dry white wine
2 onions
2 carrots
2 stalks celery

bouquet garni (thyme, bay leaf,
    parsley)
6 tablespoons butter
4 teaspoons flour
1 egg yolk
juice of 1 lemon
½ cup heavy cream
salt and pepper

Prepare the pheasant for boiling. Wrap it in paper-thin salt pork rinsed and dried. Bind with kitchen twine.

In a deep kettle, put the bouillon, wine, and the vegetables, all sliced very thin, and the *bouquet garni.* Season with salt and pepper and boil gently for 30 minutes, occasionally skimming off the matter that floats to the surface. Add the pheasant and cook 30 to 40 minutes or until tender.

In a saucepan, melt the butter and stir in the flour. Simmer 5 minutes. Add 1½-2 cups of the pheasant broth and cook ½ hour, stirring frequently. Remove from the heat.

Beat together the egg yolk, lemon juice, and cream. Add the mixture to the sauce, season with salt and pepper, and strain the sauce.

Carve the pheasant and place the pieces on a heated platter. Cover with the sauce. Serve with celery purée.

Roast pheasant ∗ *Faisan rôti*

FOR FOUR PEOPLE

1 large young pheasant
2 ounces lean pork belly
1 tablespoon cream cheese
1 teaspoon heavy cream
6 walnuts (optional)

20 grapes (optional)
bacon
butter
salt and pepper

Prepare the pheasant for stuffing. Save out the liver.

Pound together the liver and the pork belly. (If pork belly is not available, parboil lean salt pork for 5 minutes and rinse before using.—*Ed.*) Blend the cheese and heavy cream and combine with the liver mixture. If you would like something a little special, add the coarsely chopped walnuts and grapes. Season with salt and pepper and stuff the bird. Sew up the opening.

Spread the surface with butter. Put strips of bacon over the bird and bind them with kitchen twine and roast at 400° F. for about ½ hour or until the bird is tender when you insert a knife. Season the drippings with salt and pepper and baste frequently.

Serve on a heated platter with straw potatoes.

Wild pigeon

Stuffed wild pigeon aux fines herbes *Palombes farcies aux herbes*

FOR FOUR PEOPLE

2 wild pigeons
½ cup soft breadcrumbs

3 tablespoons chopped *fines herbes*
   (parsley, chervil)

½ cup bouillon

2 eggs

2 ounces pork belly

3 tablespoons butter

salt and pepper

When wild pigeons are sold in the store, they should be prepared for cooking, but if brought home in a hunter's bag, they should be dry-plucked, cleaned, and hung for a day before cooking.

Soak the breadcrumbs in the bouillon and squeeze them dry. Put them in a bowl with the raw eggs and the pork belly, chopped fine. (If pork belly is not available, use fat salt pork, boiled 5 minutes and rinsed.—*Ed.*) Chop the herbs equally fine and mix everything well, seasoning with salt and pepper.

Stuff the birds and sew the opening. Place the pigeons in a roasting pan and brush them with melted butter. Roast 35 minutes at 400° F., basting frequently with melted butter. Do not salt until the end of cooking.

Serve with a green salad seasoned with lemon juice.

Quail

Roast quail ✳ *Cailles rôties*

FOR TWO PEOPLE

4 quail

5 tablespoons cognac

4 grape leaves

6 tablespoons butter

4 small paper-thin slices salt pork

4 slices white bread

1 lemon

salt and pepper

Quail should be cooked as soon after killing as possible. It is one kind of game that cannot wait. Pluck the birds at the last moment. Draw them and singe well. This is very important because otherwise the flesh would be oily. Pour over the cognac and touch with a lighted match.

Season each bird with salt and pepper and envelop in a washed and dried grape leaf; spread with butter and then cover with a piece of pork fat. Bind with twine. Roast 10 minutes, preferably on a spit, but if not, in a 400° F. oven. Cooking time is the same. Remove the birds. Take off the fat and leaves.

Meanwhile, fry the white bread lightly in the rest of the butter.

Serve the birds on the croutons on a heated platter. Garnish with lemon wedges.

Flambéed quail with grapes
Cailles flambées aux raisins

8 quail

8 grape leaves

8 small paper-thin slices fat salt pork

6 tablespoons butter

3 tablespoons cognac

¼ cup white wine

1 bunch grapes

¼ cup heavy cream

salt and pepper

Follow the preceding recipe for preparing and wrapping the birds.

Heat the butter in a large pan and sauté for 10 minutes, turning the birds once. Remove the birds to a roasting pan and remove the fat and grape leaves. Pour over hot cognac and touch with a lighted match.

Add the white wine to the butter in which the quail has cooked. Simmer 10 minutes and add the grapes and cream and season to taste with salt and pepper. Bring just to the boil and add the quail. Cook 5 minutes longer.

Serve with sautéed apples.

Teal

Teal with mushrooms * Sarcelles aux champignons

The European teal and the American teal are somewhat different but can be prepared in the same way.—Ed.

2 teal

2 shallots

½ pound mushrooms

3 tablespoons butter

nutmeg

1½ tablespoons cognac

1 lemon

salt and pepper

Pluck and clean the teal and remove the four breasts.

Chop the shallots.

Trim, wash, dry, and slice the mushrooms.

Heat the butter in a heavy pan and sauté the shallots and the breasts. Season with a dash of nutmeg, salt, and pepper. When lightly browned on both sides, add the cognac and touch with a lighted match. When the flames subside, add the mushrooms. Cook 15 minutes.

Serve with lemon quarters.

Woodcock

Woodcock in white wine * Bécasse au vin blanc

FOR TWO PEOPLE

1 woodcock
paper-thin slice fat salt pork
4 tablespoons butter

½ cup dry white wine
4 teaspoons *foie gras mousse*
salt and pepper

Woodcock should not be eaten until 5 or 6 days after it is bagged. The flesh should be slightly greenish before cooking.

Pluck the bird, but do not draw it. Envelop in a slice of salt pork that has been rinsed and dried. Bind with twine.

Spread the bird with 2 tablespoons of butter and sprinkle with pepper. Place in a small pan. Roast 25 to 30 minutes at 400° F., basting often. Sprinkle with ¼ cup of white wine, and when that boils, remove the bird from the oven.

Remove the innards without crushing the bird and crush them with a fork, working in the *foie gras mousse* and ¼ cup of white wine. Heat the sauce, but do not let it boil. Spread the sauce on a heated platter and place the woodcock on the sauce. Serve immediately with straw potatoes.

Meat

Meat

To roast beef

Because there is no international agreement about cutting beef, it is difficult to be too precise about universal directions for roasting beef. However, there are certainly some basic truths about roasting, no matter where it is done.

1 Never roast any but the best cuts of beef. In France this means you may roast *le filet, le contrefilet, le rumsteck, la tranche* or *le rond* (less savory), *les côtes,* or *l'entrecôte.* These correspond approximately to the roasts that in America are called tenderloin, sirloin, face of the rump, top of the round, roast ribs of beef, or thick rib steak. In most American retail markets tenderloin fillets seldom weigh more than 2 to 3 pounds, and a sirloin roast is used in its place in recipes calling for larger beef fillets.

2 Small roasts should be wrapped and tied in a paper-thin layer of beef fat, pork fat, or salt pork.

3 Roasts should be placed on a rack in an open roasting pan and put into a well-preheated oven. They should never be salted before roasting, but when drippings appear in the pan, they are salted and used to baste the meat. A little pan of hot water or bouillon should be at hand to use for basting also if the meat is dry. This process is started halfway through the cooking. Ideally, a roast is basted every five minutes but never with a cold liquid.

4 Roasts should be served on time. An uncut roast can wait several minutes, but once cut it should be served.

5 Preheat the oven to 400° F. Larger roasts can be cooked at 350° F. For very rare meat count on 12 minutes per pound. 15 minutes per pound will cook the meat medium rare, or *à point.* French people in general like meat cooked rarer than most Americans do. Increase the cooking time by 2 to 3 minutes per pound, if desired.

6 Be sure both platter and gravy bowl are heated before using.

To lard meat

Wash a long block of fat salt pork and parboil 5 minutes to remove the excess salt. Rinse and cut the fat into ¼-inch-thick long strips. Insert the strips in the end of a larding needle, and, unless a recipe gives special instructions, push the needle across the grain into one side of the piece of meat and out the other. Trim the ends even with the meat. If you do not have a larding needle, poke holes into the meat with a sharp thin knife, and insert the strips with your fingers.

Roast beef * Côte de boeuf rôtie

FOR EIGHT PEOPLE

6-pound rib roast   salt and pepper
10 tablespoons butter

A rib roast is one of the best cuts. The larger the cut, the better the flavor.
Preheat the oven to 400° F.

Rub the entire surface with butter. Place on a rack in a roasting pan. I like to
count on 12 to 15 minutes per pound, but many Americans like meat better done,
so cook longer if necessary. Overcooked meat loses much of its flavor.

When drippings fall in the pan, sprinkle with salt. Baste very frequently with
the drippings.

Let the roast stand on the platter for 10 minutes while making the sauce. Pour
a little boiling water in the roasting pan and stir with a fork to loosen the juices
adhering to the pan. Stir vigorously until it boils. Strain into a heated gravy bowl.

Yorkshire pudding has crossed the channel to some French homes and restaurants. Here is how it is made:

Yorkshire pudding * Yorkshire pudding

FOR EIGHT PEOPLE

beef drippings   nutmeg
4 eggs   1 teaspoon salt
2 cups milk   pepper
2 cups flour

Pour most of the beef drippings into a shallow roasting pan. Place in the same
oven with the beef. Beat up the eggs, milk, and flour. Season with salt, pepper,
and a pinch of nutmeg.

Approximately 15 minutes before serving the beef, pour the batter into the
preheated pan and bake. The pudding is cooked when an inserted knife comes
out dry.

Cut in large squares and surround the beef with them.

Beef fillet rossini * Filet de boeuf rossini

FOR TEN PEOPLE

7½-ounce can whole *foie gras*   ¾ cup Madeira
4 tablespoons butter   salt and pepper
3-pound beef tenderloin or sirloin

Chill the *foie gras* for an hour or two so that it will cut easily.

Preheat the oven to 400° F. Heat the butter in a heavy deep pan or iron casserole. Sauté the tenderloin in the butter, turning it so it is lightly browned on all sides. Add the Madeira, sprinkle with salt and pepper, and roast 30 minutes.

Slice the *foie gras* very thin. Remove the meat from the pan and let the juices boil down a little. Slice the meat and arrange on a platter, alternating slices of beef and *foie gras*. Pour the sauce over the meat. Serve at once.

Rump roast of beef with onion sauce
Pointe d'aiguillette soubise

FOR EIGHT PEOPLE

3-4-pound beef roast (face of the rump)
5 tablespoons butter
1 pound new onions
salt and pepper

Sauce:
2 pounds (10-12) onions
1½ cups Béchamel Sauce (page 6)
5 tablespoons butter
¾ cup heavy cream (optional)
salt and pepper

Roast: Have the roast tied firmly. Season with pepper and brown it in butter in the roasting pan, turning it to brown all sides. Remove the meat from the pan and add the onions, finely chopped, and sauté until golden. Spread smooth in the pan and place the meat on the onions. Roast at 400° F., allowing 15 minutes per pound. If the onions are old, boil them for a minute or two after chopping them and drain well before putting them in the roasting pan.

Sauce: Make the sauce while the meat is roasting. Cut the onions into thin slices and boil them in salted water for 10 minutes. Drain. Make the béchamel while the onions are boiling. Heat the butter in a skillet and cook the onions in it over a very low heat until tender without letting them brown. Combine with the béchamel and season with salt and pepper. Force this through a sieve or a food mill (or spin a moment in the blender—*Ed.*). Just before serving, add 2 teaspoons of butter and the heavy cream.

Place the meat on the platter, season with salt, slicing a good part of it. Pour the juice from the pan over the meat and serve the sauce in a separate heated bowl.

Roast beef jardinière * Rôti de boeuf jardinière

FOR EIGHT PEOPLE

The only difficulty with this dish is making everything come out at once. Read the whole recipe in order to understand it thoroughly before beginning.—Ed.

3-4-pound beef roast
½ pound butter
½ pound mushrooms
8 small tomatoes

8 artichoke bottoms
2 pounds young green beans
½ teaspoon baking soda
salt

Order a securely tied sirloin or face of the rump roast. Paint the surface with melted butter and roast at 400° F., allowing 15 minutes per pound. Season the drippings and baste frequently.

Melt the butter.

Wash, trim, and chop the mushrooms stems very fine. Sauté them quickly and briefly in 2 tablespoons of butter. Boil the caps for 1 minute. Drain.

Boil the tomatoes for 1 minute in salted water. Remove the skins and place them in an ovenproof dish. Sprinkle them with melted butter. Allow them to brown in the oven for 15 minutes before serving.

Boil fresh artichokes in salted water for 30 to 40 minutes. Discard all but the bottoms, which will be stuffed. Or, use canned artichoke bottoms and heat them with a little butter in the oven. Fill with the chopped mushrooms and cover with the mushroom caps. Keep warm.

Boil the green beans in a large pan of water to which the soda but not salt has been added. Do not cover. Boil just until tender (10 to 15 minutes). Drain.

Heat the rest of the butter.

Place the meat on a heated platter. Pour ¾ cup of hot water into the roasting pan, stirring until the juices are dissolved in the water.

Pour hot butter over the vegetables and alternate little bunches of beans with the tomatoes and artichokes around the edge of the platter. Pour the sauce over the meat.

Roast beef with mushrooms and chestnuts
Rôti de boeuf aux champignons et marrons

FOR SIX PEOPLE

2-pound beef rump, sirloin or
  eye of the round roast
3 tablespoons butter

12 large mushrooms
2 pounds chestnuts
salt and pepper

Preheat the oven to 450° F.

Rub the roast with butter and place in the oven. At the end of 10 minutes, add 4 teaspoons of boiling water, pouring it over the meat. Baste with a teaspoon of hot water every 5 to 10 minutes. Allow 12 minutes per pound for roasting unless you like it better done, in which case count 15 minutes per pound. 5 minutes before the end of cooking, sprinkle with salt and pepper.

Meanwhile, trim, wash, and wipe the mushrooms. Chop the stems fine and place them in the mushroom heads. Brush with oil and bake 15 minutes in the oven.

Prepare the chestnuts by slashing each one around the center and put them in a skillet lined with a trivet (a metal round pierced with holes). (A pressure cooker pan, without the cover, is good for this.—*Ed.*) Cook over moderate heat 25 to 30 minutes, shaking the pan frequently. When cooked, the outer and inner shell of the chestnuts will come off easily.

Remove the roast from the pan and let it stand while boiling down the gravy just a little. Alternate the mushrooms and chestnuts around the edge of the platter and pour the sauce over the meat.

Beef fillet mapie * Filet de boeuf aux pruneaux

FOR FOUR PEOPLE

16 small prunes
2 cups very strong tea
1 small can *foie gras* pâté
2 tablespoons butter

1 1/4-pound beef tenderloin
1/2 cup Madeira
salt and pepper

Soak the prunes in strong tea for several hours. Remove the stones and fill the cavity with the *foie gras*. Place on a baking sheet. These will be heated in the oven just before serving.

Preheat the oven to 450° F. Heat the butter in a heavy pan or iron casserole. Put in the fillet. Pour in two thirds of the wine and sprinkle with salt and pepper. Roast 15 minutes basting frequently, and for the last 3 minutes place the prunes in the oven.

Serve the meat on a platter surrounded with the prunes. Stir the rest of the wine into the pan, bring quickly to a boil, and pour over the meat.

Beef fillet in pastry * Filet de boeuf en croûte

FOR EIGHT PEOPLE

4 cups sifted all-purpose flour
10 tablespoons soft butter
3 eggs
1/4 cup oil
2 teaspoons salt

3/4 pound fine sausage meat
1 box truffle peelings
3-pound beef tenderloin or sirloin

Sift the flour into a mound on a pastry marble or board. Fashion a hole into the center and cut the butter into small pieces directly into the hole. Add two of the eggs, the oil, and the salt. Using the fingers of one hand, gradually work the flour into the center, adding only as much water as necessary to make the dough workable. Knead with the palm of the hand until you have a smooth shiny ball.

Let rest in the refrigerator at least an hour, but if possible, make the pastry a day ahead.

Flour a rolling pin and roll out the pastry to a thin rectangle on a lightly floured surface. Trim the edges evenly. Spread with the sausage meat and sprinkle with the truffles chopped very fine or passed through the hand mill (*moulinette*). Put the fillet in the center of the rectangle and wrap the pastry around it, moistening the parts that touch each other so that they will stick together well.

With a sharp, pointed knife, make a hole the size of a dime in the top and insert a chimney made of a roll of white paper. Cut some decorative lines on the pastry with the tip of the knife, and then paint the whole surface twice with the remaining egg yolk mixed with a teaspoon of cold water.

Bake 45 minutes at 400° F. If the pastry gets too brown, cover with a piece of paper. Serve this dish warm, not hot.

Beef fillet in aspic * Filet de boeuf en gelée

FOR TEN PEOPLE

1 pound short ribs of beef	⅓ cup port
1 pound bottom round of beef	2 eggs
4 pounds shin bone	4-pound center cut beef sirloin
1 calf's (or pig's) foot	3 tablespoons butter
3 carrots	salt and pepper
3 leeks	

This recipe must be made the day before serving.

In a large kettle of cold salted water, place the short ribs, the bottom round, the shin bone, and the calf's or pig's foot. Bring to a boil over a moderate heat, skimming off carefully the matter that floats to the surface. Wash and peel the vegetables and add them, skimming until the water returns to the boil. Simmer with the kettle three quarters covered for 4 hours over a moderate heat. Strain the broth and cool. Taste for seasoning. Chill in the refrigerator so that all the fat will rise to the surface. Remove the fat. Reheat the bouillon with the port, adding the whites of the eggs slightly beaten and the egg shells crushed. Let the bouillon simmer 20 minutes and then pass it through a fine strainer, lined with a spotless dish cloth.

Place the meat on a rack in an open roasting pan. Spread it with the butter and roast 45 to 50 minutes at 400° F., basting it frequently with the drippings in the pan. Season the drippings but not the meat with the salt.

Cool the meat completely. Slice very thin and arrange on a platter, letting each slice be partly covered by the one next to it.

Cool the aspic to lukewarm and spoon it carefully over the meat. Chill before serving.

Braising beef

Braising is a method of cooking that permits us to use cuts of beef that are not tender enough to broil or roast.

Braising is done in a closed pot or pan to avoid evaporation. Braised meats do not have to come from young animals as do roasts and broiled meats. Slow cooking in a closed pot tenderizes them.

For this reason, it is difficult to give exact cooking times, because this can vary an hour or more, according to the age of the animal. Beef is usually braised in bouillon or wine but rarely in just water, because the sauce would lack flavor.

Here is my method for braising beef: It is always preferable to marinate the meat for several hours in red or white wine. This will serve to moisten the meat.

The butter, oil, or lard is put in a heavy saucepan, Dutch oven, or iron pot and heated well so that the sides of the meat will be immediately *saisi,* thus keeping the juices inside the piece of meat. When the meat is well browned on all sides, it is usually taken out of the pot or pan, and if it is a dry piece of meat, such as the bottom round, it is best, when it is lukewarm, to surround it with a thin piece of pork fat and to tie it in place.

Wipe out the pan in which the meat has been browned so that it is perfectly clean, and add the vegetables of the marinade. If the meat has not been marinated, put in raw chopped onions and carrots. On these vegetables put several strips of fat pork and the *bouquet garni.* Place the meat on this foundation, and pour over some of the marinade or simply red or white wine. Cook this uncovered over high heat until the liquid is reduced by half. Add strong bouillon, season with salt and pepper, and cover the pan. Cook over very low heat until tender. Test this by inserting a skewer or knitting needle into the meat. If no blood escapes and it feels tender, the meat is cooked.

During braising, as soon as the meat is no longer covered with liquid, it is important to baste often with the cooking liquid and to turn the meat, or obviously the exposed part would dry out.

Once the cooking is completed, one must take the meat out and let it stand for a while. In cooling, the meat retracts, which makes it easier to carve thin, unbroken slices. While waiting, strain the sauce, pressing the vegetables gently through the strainer with the back of a wooden spoon. After it is strained, put the sauce in a saucepan, and skim off the fat with a metal spoon. As the sauce cools, the fat rises to the top, which makes this process easier.

Once the grease is removed, the sauce is reheated and poured over the meat, which has been sliced and arranged on a heated platter. To present the meat properly, it should be sliced like a roast, or, in other words, with three fourths of the roast sliced and arranged on the platter with overlapping slices extending from the "heel" of meat.

In the family the sauce is poured over the vegetables and meat all on the same platter and not in a separate bowl, as one would do otherwise. The accompaniments of braised beef are numerous. The ever-faithful potato can be replaced by vegetables, purées, braised salad greens, or by pastas.

Some practical rules for braising beef

1 Never buy a small piece of meat to braise. If you have only two or three at table, buy a piece that will be eaten in two meals. Braised meat reheats very well and also makes delicious cold dishes.

2 If you make a marinade, use chopped carrots and onions in the proportion of 4 tablespoons to a pound of meat, a *bouquet garni* (thyme, bay leaf, parsley), and peppercorns.

3 It is absolutely necessary to clean the pot or pan in which the meat is browned because all overheated fat is bad for the health and in any case gives a bad flavor to the sauce.

4 If you add several pieces of pork skin and half a calf's foot, you will achieve a sauce that will jell when it cools.

5 Bouillon cubes and hot water can substitute for bouillon.

6 Don't forget that the cooking for braising must be slow, but nevertheless there must be a constant slight bubbling of the liquid.

7 If you find there is too much sauce, boil it down rapidly in an uncovered saucepan.

8 Braised meat must be well cooked and tender, but do not overcook, for it will lose its flavor and savor.

Boeuf à la mode, or pot roast ∗ *Boeuf à la mode*

FOR FOUR PEOPLE

1½-pound rump roast	2 onions
salt pork	2 cloves
2 tablespoons butter	cayenne and paprika
½ calf's foot*	*bouquet garni* (thyme, bay leaf, parsley)
pork skin*	2½ cups white wine
3-4 carrots	salt and pepper

Lard the beef with thin strips of salt pork. Sauté the beef in heated butter, using a heavy pan or casserole. When colored (but not browned) on all sides, add the calf's foot and the pork skin or substitutes.

Peel the carrots and cut them into rounds; peel the onions and stick each one with a clove. Add them to the meat, along with a small pinch of each of the spices, herbs, salt, and pepper. Add the white wine and ½ cup of water. Bring to a boil and cover. Lower the flame and barely simmer for 5 hours, or cook in 275° F. oven. At the end of this time, taste the sauce for seasoning. If there is too little sauce, add wine and cook 30 minutes longer.

Place the meat on a heated platter. Surround with the carrots, onions, and calf's

---

*If necessary substitute ½ pig's foot for calf's foot and rind of salt pork or bacon, parboiled 5 minutes.—*Ed.*

foot. Discard the *bouquet garni* and the pork skin or rind. Pour the sauce through a sieve lined with a towel dampened in cold water. Pour over the meat and serve with steamed potatoes.

Braised beef rump with mushrooms in pastry
Aiguillette de boeuf en croûte

FOR TWELVE PEOPLE

Pastry:
5 ¼ cups flour
½ pound butter
1 egg
1 teaspoon salt

Beef:
3-pound rump or boneless loin roast

beef bone, sawed in pieces
¼ pound butter
1 ½ cups dry white wine
1 ½ cups bouillon
1 calf's foot
1 ½ pounds mushrooms
1 ½ cups Béchamel Sauce (page 6)
salt and pepper

Pastry: Make a mound of the flour on a pastry board or marble. Fashion a well in the center and place in it the soft (not melted) butter, egg, and salt. Pour approximately 1 ½ cups of cold water gradually into the well, working in the flour toward the center with your fingers. When the pastry forms a ball that no longer sticks to your fingers, flatten it slightly, cover, and let it rest at room temperature or in the refrigerator, if weather is hot.

Beef: Order the roast and ask for a beef bone sawed in pieces at the same time. Melt 5 tablespoons of butter in a large heavy pan and sauté the meat until brown on all sides. Remove the meat and pour off the butter, wiping the pan clean. Put the meat back in the pan. Add the wine, bouillon, the bone and calf's foot. (If necessary, substitute ½ pig's foot.—*Ed.*) The liquid should just barely cover the meat. Add salt and pepper. Cover and simmer for 4 hours. Remove the meat from the liquid and boil the liquid down with the bone and foot until the sauce is about one third its original quantity.

Trim, wash, and drain the mushrooms. Chop them very fine and sauté them over high heat in 3 tablespoons of butter for 2 minutes.

Mix the béchamel sauce and combine it with the mushrooms. The mixture should be thick.

Taste for seasoning.

Divide the pastry in two and roll each half out into rectangles of equal size. Moisten the edges with water.

Cut the beef into very thin slices and spread each slice with the mushroom mixture. Re-form the spread slices into a roast, pressing the pieces one against the other. Place the meat on one of the rectangles and cover with the other. Seal the edges well and make a little chimney by putting a small roll of white paper or a porcelain tube in a small hole. Cook 40 minutes at 400° F. Strain the sauce into a gravy bowl and serve separately.

Braised short ribs in aspic * Basse côte en gelée

FOR FOUR PEOPLE

2 pounds short ribs
2½ cups red wine
3-4 carrots, sliced
2-3 onions, sliced
bouquet garni (thyme, bay leaf, parsley)
⅛ teaspoon each nutmeg, ground
    cloves, ginger

2½ tablespoons butter
1½ cups bouillon
2-3 pieces pork skin*
2-3 soup bones, sawed in pieces
salt and pepper

Let the meat marinate overnight in the red wine, to which carrots, onions, bouquet garni, spices, salt, and pepper have been added.

Remove the meat and wipe it dry with paper toweling. Heat the butter in a heavy saucepan and brown the meat on all sides. Remove the meat from the pan, pour off the butter, and wipe out the pan completely. Replace the meat. Add salt, pepper, the bouillon, pork skin, the soup bones, the vegetables from the marinade, and the wine. Bring to a boil, reduce the heat, and simmer without a cover for 3 hours.

Remove the meat and slice it. Arrange on a platter and garnish with the vegetables. Line a fine sieve with a dish towel dampened in cold water and pour the sauce through that over the meat. Cool and then place in the refrigerator.

Braised ribs of beef in white wine
Côtes de boeuf au vin blanc

FOR SIX PEOPLE

3-pound rib roast (boned and rolled)
1 bottle dry white wine
1 pound small prunes
½ cup seeded raisins
6 tablespoons butter

4 teaspoons sugar
¾ cup bouillon
6 tablespoons sliced almonds
salt and pepper

Marinate the roast 4 days in winter and 2 days in summer in white wine. Turn the roast occasionally during each day. The night before cooking the meat, put the prunes and raisins to soak in water.

* If necessary, substitute salt pork or bacon rind washed and parboiled 5 minutes.—Ed.

Heat the butter in a heavy pan. Place the meat in the butter and sprinkle with sugar. Turn the meat until it is brown on all sides. Pour in the marinade and the bouillon. Cover and cook 3 hours. Add the prunes and the raisins. Taste the sauce for seasoning and cook 5 minutes longer. Sprinkle with the almonds just before serving.

Braised beef à la grecque (cold)
Aiguillette de boeuf à la grecque

FOR EIGHT PEOPLE

3 tablespoons butter
3-pound eye of the round or rump roast
4 carrots, sliced thin
2 medium-sized onions, chopped
1½ cups dry white wine
bouquet garni (thyme, bay leaf, parsley)
2 pounds leeks

24 small onions
¾ cup oil
1½ cups bouillon or water
2½ tablespoons tomato paste
1 bay leaf
paprika
salt and pepper

Heat the butter in a deep heavy saucepan. Sauté the meat, the carrots, and the larger onions, turning the meat until lightly browned on all sides. Add ¾ cup of wine, salt, and pepper and cover tightly. Braise 3 hours in a 300° F. oven or over a very low heat on top of the stove. Turn occasionally. When cooked, remove from the pan and cool.

While the meat is cooking, cook the rest of the vegetables. Take off most of the green from the leeks. Trim and wash carefully and cut the leeks into 2-inch pieces. Place them in a saucepan with the little onions, properly peeled, the oil, the bouillon or water, the tomato paste, bay leaf, ½ teaspoon of salt, *bouquet garni,* and 1 tablespoon of peppercorns. Cook over a good heat for 45 minutes. Remove from the stove to cool.

Serve the meat, sliced thin and well arranged on a platter, surrounded with the leeks and onions, and sprinkle with paprika.

Flemish carbonnades of beef
Carbonnades de boeuf flamande

FOR FOUR PEOPLE

1½ pounds boneless sirloin of beef
10 tablespoons butter
5 large onions

bouquet garni (thyme, bay leaf)
12 ounces beer
salt and pepper

Ask the butcher to slice the meat in ½-inch slices. There should be 8 slices. Heat half the butter in a skillet and sauté the little steaks 2 minutes on each side. Sprinkle with salt and pepper, transfer to a platter, and keep in a warm place. Pour off the butter from the skillet. Peel and chop the onions rather coarsely. Heat the rest of the butter and sauté the onions until pale yellow. Season with salt and pepper.

In an earthenware casserole, place 4 steaks and cover with a layer of onion. Put in 4 more steaks and cover with the rest of the onions. Add the *bouquet garni.* Pour the beer into the skillet and stir over high heat until it comes to a boil. Pour the liquid into the casserole and cover. Bake 3 hours at 300° F. Remove the *bouquet garni* before serving and serve with boiled potatoes.

Burgundy beef * Boeuf bourguignon

FOR SIX PEOPLE

2½-pound beef sirloin or rump roast
6 tablespoons butter
1 large tablespoon flour
1 bottle red Burgundy
6 onions
bouquet garni (thyme, bay leaf, sage)
salt and pepper

Cut the beef into 1½-inch cubes. Heat the butter in a heavy pan and sauté the beef so that it is lightly seared on all sides. Sprinkle with the flour and stir with a wooden spoon until the flour is pale yellow. Add the wine, stirring constantly. Add the onions and *bouquet garni,* salt, and pepper. Simmer covered for 4 hours, tasting occasionally for seasoning. Serve with a cabbage purée.

Braised beef rump mapie
Aiguillette de boeuf mapie

FOR SIX PEOPLE

5 tablespoons lard
2-pound beef rump roast
⅓ pound pork skin*
4 onions, sliced
4 carrots, sliced
24 ounces beer
nutmeg
ginger
½ calf's foot*
6 ginger snaps (crushed)
6 tablespoons seedless raisins
6 tablespoons ground almonds
salt and pepper
⅓ pound unsliced lean bacon with rind

Heat the lard and sauté the beef just long enough to sear it on all sides without

*If pork skin and calf's foot cannot be bought, substitute salt pork or bacon rind, parboiled 5 minutes and ½ pig's foot.—*Ed.*

browning. Cut off the rind and dice the bacon or cut it in small strips. Add to the meat along with the sliced onions and carrots. Continue to cook a few minutes. Add the beer, pork skin, salt, pepper, nutmeg, ginger, and calf's foot. Cover and simmer or cook in a 300° F. oven for 4 hours. Taste for seasoning.

Remove the meat from the pan. Strain the sauce into a saucepan. Add the crushed ginger snaps and boil 10 minutes. Add the raisins and almonds and taste for seasoning. Cut the meat in slices on a platter and pour the sauce over the meat.

Braised beef with cabbage
Boeuf braisé aux choux

FOR FOUR PEOPLE

1 cabbage
10 tablespoons (5 ounces) lard
1 pound stew beef
2 onions
1 cup bouillon or water

1 apple
3-4 tomatoes
1 teaspoon sugar
4-5 potatoes
salt and pepper

Trim the outer leaves, if damaged, from the cabbage. Cut into quarters and cook in rapidly boiling salted water for 5 minutes. Drain.

Heat the lard in a heavy saucepan and brown the beef on all sides, along with the onions, peeled and sliced fine.

Stir in the bouillon or water. Add the cabbage and the apple, peeled, cored, and sliced thin. Peel the tomatoes; cut in two, press out the seeds, and then cut in quarters. Add these, the sugar, salt, and pepper. Mix gently, cover, and simmer for 2 hours. Peel and quarter the potatoes. Add them to the pan and continue cooking for 1 hour. Taste for seasoning.

Braised beef with carrots
Boeuf braisé aux carottes

FOR SIX PEOPLE

1 pound (4-5 medium) carrots
3 tablespoons butter
3-pound eye of the round or
    top round roast
¾ cup dry white wine

¾ cup bouillon
2 tablespoons tomato paste
bouquet garni (bay leaf, thyme, parsley)
salt and pepper

Peel the carrots and cut into very thin rounds. Heat the butter in a heavy pan or casserole and brown the meat an all sides. Then add the wine and bouillon.

Add the carrots, the tomato paste, the *bouquet garni,* salt, and pepper.

Bring the liquid to a boil. Cover tightly and simmer very gently for 3½ to 4 hours. Watch the meat to see that too much liquid does not evaporate. Add a little bouillon or water, if need be.

Remove the meat from the liquid and cut in slices. Arrange on a heated platter. Garnish with the carrots. Pour the sauce through a sieve lined with a dish towel dampened in cold water and onto the meat.

Braised curry of beef
Culotte de boeuf braisée au cari

FOR SIX PEOPLE

3 tablespoons lard	2½ cups bouillon
5 ounces lean bacon (unsliced)	½ calf's foot
3-pound rump roast of beef	½ ginger root
2 onions	8 teaspoons curry powder
4 carrots	salt and pepper
2½ cups dry white wine	

Heat the lard in a heavy pan or casserole. Add the lean bacon, cut in small pieces, and when that is pale yellow, add the meat. Sear on all sides without letting the meat get too brown. Peel the onions and carrots and slice them very fine. Add these to the meat and pour in the wine and bouillon, using bouillon cubes if you do not have bouillon on hand. Add the half foot (using a pig's foot if calf's foot is not obtainable—*Ed.*), the ginger root, salt, and pepper. Bring to a boil, lower the heat as far as possible and barely simmer for 4 hours. Keep the pan covered.

Pierce the meat with a fork to be sure it is thoroughly cooked. Add the curry, taste for salt and pepper, and continue cooking for 10 minutes longer. Remove the meat to a heated platter. Strain the sauce through a fine sieve. Cut slices from the beef, but leave part of the meat unsliced. Pour some of the sauce over the meat and serve the rest in a gravy bowl. Accompany with rice.

Beef carbonnades monteynard
Boeuf en carbonnade monteynard

FOR SIX PEOPLE

2 pounds individual beef steaks	¾ cup bouillon
¾ cup lard	1 large slab French bread
4-5 onions	French mustard
1½ teaspoons mixed powdered herbs	salt and pepper
6 ounces beer	

Order individual steaks that are small but fairly thick ($\frac{1}{2}$ to $\frac{3}{4}$ inch), cut from the eye of the round, weighing about $\frac{1}{4}$ pound each. Heat 4 tablespoons of the lard in a skillet and sear the steaks on both sides without letting them cook. Set the steaks aside and pour off the lard, wiping the skillet clean.

Melt the rest of the lard in the skillet and sauté the onions, sliced thin, over a moderate heat, letting them turn yellow but not allowing them to brown.

In the bottom of a heavy deep pan or earthenware casserole, place half the onions and cover with the steaks. Spread the rest of the onions over the meat. Sprinkle with salt and pepper and a mixture of powdered herbs. This can be a commercially prepared mixture or one of your own making, using powdered thyme, bay leaf, tarragon, fennel, sage, and so on. No one herb should dominate. Pour the beer and bouillon over the onions. Cover everything with a large slab of bread spread generously on both sides with mustard. Cover the pan or casserole tightly and cook at 275° F. in the oven or simmer very slowly on top of the stove for 4 hours.

Arrange the meat and onions on a heated platter. Pour the sauce through a sieve lined with a dish towel dampened in cold water. Reheat and serve separately, along with rice or boiled potatoes. This dish is even better if made a day in advance and reheated. It makes a particularly fine dish if the cooked steaks are placed on an ovenproof platter, covered with flaky pastry, painted with egg yolk, covered with well-oiled brown paper, and baked 45 minutes at 300° F. Accompany with the vegetables.

Burgundy oxtail * Queue de boeuf bourguignonne

FOR FOUR PEOPLE

Although oxtails are not commonly marketed in America, there are specialty shops where they can be found and for those adventurous enough to seek them out, here are two recipes.—Ed.

1 oxtail, cut in 2-inch pieces	*bouquet garni* (small bay leaf,
3 tablespoons lard	parsley, thyme)
4 medium-sized onions, chopped fine	10 small onions
1 can tomato paste	3 tablespoons butter
$\frac{3}{4}$ cup bouillon	1 teaspoon sugar
$\frac{1}{2}$ bottle red Burgundy	salt and pepper

Brown the oxtail pieces in very hot lard in a heavy pan. When browned on all sides, pour off the fat, removing any particle of burnt fat.

Add the onions, tomato paste, bouillon, red wine, *bouquet garni,* salt, and pepper. Cover, bring to a boil, and simmer very gently for $3\frac{1}{2}$ hours.

Peel the little onions and boil them in salted water for 15 minutes. Drain. Melt the butter in a skillet. Stir in the sugar and add the onions. The onions will be nicely glazed when they are cooked. Stir gently with a wooden spoon from time to time.

Serve the oxtail with the sauce, removing the *bouquet garni,* and surround with the little onions. Be sure that the sauce is properly seasoned.

Oxtails with sausages
Queue de boeuf aux saucisses

FOR SIX PEOPLE

2 oxtails	*bouquet garni* (bay leaf, thyme, parsley)
5 tablespoons lard	1 pound small link sausages
2½ cups bouillon	salt and pepper
¾ cup dry white wine	

Have the tails cut into pieces. Heat the lard in a heavy pan and over a moderate heat, simmer the pieces with the cover on for 15 minutes. Add the bouillon, white wine, *bouquet garni,* salt, and pepper. Simmer very gently for 4 hours. Remove the cover. If the sauce is too thin, let it cook down. 15 minutes before serving, add the sausages. Taste the sauce for seasoning.

Braised beef provençale
Daube de boeuf provençale

FOR FOUR PEOPLE

2 pounds top round of beef	1 large clove garlic
4 teaspoons lard	2 tomatoes
4 teaspoons olive oil	2 shallots
2 tablespoons diced salt pork	1 celery root
2 tablespoons diced lean bacon	1 stalk celery
3 onions	1¼ cups red wine
2 cloves	small piece orange rind
2 carrots	cinnamon, ginger, peppercorns
½ calf's (or pig's) foot	salt
bouquet garni (bay leaf, thyme, sage)	

Have the beef cut in 2½-inch cubes.

Heat the lard, oil, and salt pork in a heavy pan. When well heated, add the bacon, and when that begins to turn yellow, add 2 onions, peeled and quartered, and a third onion, peeled but left whole with the cloves stuck in it. Add also the carrots, peeled and cut in slices, the half calf's foot, the beef squares, the *bou-*

quet garni, and the garlic. Sauté all together for several minutes. Then, add the tomatoes, peeled and quartered, the shallots, the celery root and stalk and pour in the wine. Add the orange rind, a pinch each of cinnamon and ginger, 6 peppercorns, and some salt. Bring to a boil. Cover and cook as slowly as possible for 6 hours. Serve with macaroni.

Smothered beef * Estouffade de boeuf

FOR SIX PEOPLE

3 pounds beef rump steak
10 ounces fat salt pork (with rind)
4 shallots
2 cloves garlic
2 tablespoons chopped parsley

2 cups good red wine
marjoram
sage
salt and pepper

Ask the butcher to cut the meat into small 4-inch-square steaks about ¼ inch thick. Remove the rind from the salt pork. Cut in pieces and place on the bottom of a heavy pan or casserole.

Wash the salt pork and parboil 5 minutes to remove the excess salt, and chop fine. Chop also the shallots, garlic, and parsley and mix well.

Put a layer of steaks in the pan, spread each piece with the salt pork mixture, sprinkle with pepper, and cover with a layer of steaks. Do this until all the meat has been used up. Pour in the red wine and add a pinch of marjoram and sage. The minute the mixture comes to a boil, cover the pan and lower the heat or place the casserole in a 275° F. oven for 6 hours.

Remove the steaks to a heated platter. Pour the sauce, seasoned to taste, onto the steaks through a sieve lined with a towel dampened in cold water.

Hungarian goulash * Goulache hongroise

FOR EIGHT PEOPLE

2 pounds boned pork shoulder
2 pounds bottom round of beef
5 tablespoons butter
¾ cup oil

7-8 medium onions
8 teaspoons Hungarian paprika
8 potatoes
salt and pepper

Cut the meat into 1½-inch cubes. Keep pork and beef separate. Heat the butter and oil in a heavy pan or enamel-lined casserole. Put in the onions, which have been peeled and chopped fine. Cook over a low heat until the onions become transparent but not brown. Stir frequently. Add 4 teaspoons of paprika, 5 cups of boiling water and the beef. Season with salt and pepper. Cook covered for 30 minutes. Remove the cover and continue cooking until the water has completely disappeared. Add 5 more cups boiling water, cover and cook 1 hour longer. Add the pork and cook for another hour. 20 minutes before the end of cooking, add the potatoes, peeled and quartered, and 4 more teaspoons of paprika. Serve very hot.

Russian goulash * Goulache à la russe

FOR SIX PEOPLE

3 pounds beef round
12 tablespoons lard
3-4 medium-sized onions

bouquet garni (thyme, small bay leaf, parsley)
4 tablespoons tomato paste
salt and pepper

Cut the beef into 1½-inch cubes. Melt the lard in a heavy pan and cook the onions, peeled and chopped fine, until they are golden. Add the meat, stir well, and cover. Cook over a moderate heat for 10 minutes. Add the *bouquet garni,* tomato paste, and 1½ cups of water. Season with salt and pepper and bring to a boil. Cover and cook over very low heat or in a 275° oven for 4 hours.

Remove the *bouquet garni,* pour into a deep serving dish, having tasted for seasoning, and serve with boiled potatoes.

Braised beef with horticultural beans, or hungarian braised beef
Boeuf braisé aux haricots rouges, ou boeuf à la hongroise

FOR SIX PEOPLE

horticultural shell beans
2 pounds beef round
4 medium-sized onions
2 carrots
2 cloves garlic

2 large tomatoes
5 tablespoons lard
4 tablespoons rice
salt and pepper

Allow ½ cup of beans per serving. This means shelling about 2 pounds of fresh beans or soaking 2 cups of dried beans overnight.

Order the meat tied as though for roasting. Peel and slice the onions and carrots. Peel and coarsely chop the garlic.

Put all the ingredients in a large covered casserole. Cover completely with water. Bring everything to a boil. Cover and cook as slowly as possible or place in a 200° F. oven for 12 hours.

The pot-au-feu

The *pot-au-feu* is one of the best dishes in the classic French tradition. It is a category unto itself and the source of many other dishes. The broth or bouillon makes an excellent soup and is the basis for many others. The meat, which should consist of two kinds, one fat and one lean, provides both hot and cold main dishes. When a *pot-au-feu* is first made, it is usually served with the vegetables used for seasoning and with boiled potatoes, cooked apart. Potatoes cooked in the *pot-au-feu* cloud the bouillon. Always serve mustard and mayonnaise (see page 14) or tomato sauce (see page 22) with *pot-au-feu*. Never be afraid to serve a cold sauce with a hot meal. It may surprise your guests, but it will delight them.

If you want to have a good aspic, add a calf's foot (or, if necessary, use a pig's foot—*Ed.*) to the *pot-au-feu*. Once the meat is cooked and removed from the kettle, continue to cook the bone and calf's or pig's foot for another 2 hours. The feet can be served cold, split and accompanied by a vinaigrette sauce (see page 29). This makes an excellent hors d'oeuvre. Always cook the *pot-au-feu* in a copper or stainless steel kettle. Ordinary metal gives the broth an inferior taste.

Never cook less than 4 pounds of beef.

When starting a *pot-au-feu*, always start in cold water, and as the water comes to a boil, skim off all the matter that floats to the surface. This is most important for both flavor and appearance. Never overseason with too many vegetables or spices.

Pot-au-feu with marrow bone
Le pot-au-feu avec l'os à moëlle

FOR SIX PEOPLE

2 pounds chuck beef
1 pound bottom round of beef
1 tablespoon salt
2 pounds carrots
2 pounds turnips
2 pounds leeks

1 onion
1 clove
3 cloves garlic, crushed
1 stalk celery
1 large marrow bone
Caramel (page 579)

Even if this recipe seems simple, it is important to take care if your *pot-au-feu* is to be successful.

Put 5 quarts of cold water in a deep pot. Add the meats and the salt (preferably sea salt). Bring to a slow boil, skimming off all the matter that comes to the top. When the liquid is boiling, put on a cover, leaving one edge uncovered so that the steam can escape.

Wash and prepare the vegetables. Stick the clove in a piece of onion. Cut the vegetables into large pieces. Add them to the meat and skim for the next few minutes. Simmer 2½ hours.

Wrap the marrow bone in cheesecloth so that the marrow will not escape. Place it in the kettle and simmer 1 hour longer. Color the broth with a little caramel.

Serve the meat on a heated platter surrounded by the vegetables and accompany with a bowl of boiled potatoes. Serve mayonnaise, tomato sauce, and mustard at the same time. The marrow is served on a small plate surrounded by fried croutons and lemon slices.

Short rib pot-au-feu nivernais with crapiaux
Plat de côtes nivernais avec ses crapiaux

FOR SIX PEOPLE

1 pound dry white beans	6-8 potatoes
4 pounds thick short ribs	2 onions
3-4 carrots	½ cup oil
4 leeks	¾ cup flour
3 white turnips	¾ cup milk
2 stalks celery	3 eggs, slightly beaten
1 small fresh ham (2-3 pounds)	6 tablespoons grated Gruyère cheese
1 pound fresh Toulouse or Polish sausage	4 tablespoons diced raw Morvan ham or Canadian bacon
1 cabbage	salt and pepper
1 pound lean bacon, unsliced	

Soak the white beans in water overnight.

Place the short ribs in a casserole or kettle containing 5 quarts of cold water. Bring to a boil slowly, skimming off the matter that floats to the surface. Wash, peel, and cut the vegetables in pieces. When the liquid reaches a full boil, add the vegetables and the fresh ham. Skim again while the liquid is returning to the boiling point. Season with salt and pepper and cover three quarters of the way. Cook 3½ hours.

One hour before serving, boil the white beans with the sausage in one pan and in another cook the cabbage, cut in wedges with the bacon. Peel the potatoes and time them to be boiled and drained at the time of serving.

At the same time, prepare the savory garnish by chopping the onions quite fine and sautéing them until golden in 4 tablespoons of oil. Blend the flour and milk in a bowl. Add the beaten eggs, the cheese, the ham, and the onions. Add 4 tablespoons of oil and season with salt and pepper. Heat 2 tablespoons of oil in an iron skillet. Pour in the batter, which should be quite thick. Bake 8 to 10 minutes on each side at 350° F. Cut into thin wedges.

To serve: Cut the short ribs, ham, and bacon in serving pieces and arrange in a deep, preheated platter. Surround with the vegetables and boiled potatoes and garnish with the omelet wedges. Serve the beans and sausage, cut in serving pieces, in a separate dish.

Rich (classic) pot-au-feu
Pot-au-feu riche, ou à l'ancienne

FOR EIGHT PEOPLE

3-pound round roast of beef	3 leeks
1 small knuckle of veal	1 large turnip
1 pound uncooked ham	½ celery root
4-5 pound hen, cleaned and trussed	1 parsnip
1 tablespoon salt	3 cloves
1 cabbage	½ bay leaf
1 large onion	toasted French bread
4 carrots	salt and pepper

Put the meats in a large casserole or kettle. Cover with cold water and add the salt. Bring to a slow boil, skimming carefully and frequently. Do not cover completely, so that the steam can escape. Simmer for 2 hours.

Prepare the vegetables by washing and peeling them, cutting only the large vegetables. Cook 1 hour longer and add the cloves and bay leaf. Continue cooking 2 hours longer.

Place slices of toasted bread in a soup tureen. Through a sieve lined with cheesecloth or dish toweling, strain broth over the toast. Put half of the vegetables in the tureen. Season with pepper and add more salt, if necessary.

In a deep platter place the meats and surround with the rest of the vegetables. Serve at the same time. Serve with mayonnaise, tomato sauce, and mustard.

Beef aspic ring * Couronne de boeuf en gelée

FOR EIGHT PEOPLE

2-pound chuck roast of beef	Caramel (page 579)
1 pound top round	2 slices ham
2 calf's (or pig's) feet	3 hard-cooked eggs
2-3 ounces bacon rind	3 gherkin pickles
6-8 carrots	2 tablespoons capers
6-8 leeks	6-8 tomatoes
1 onion	Vinaigrette Sauce (page 29)
1 clove	salt
bouquet garni (bay leaf, thyme, parsley)	

Place the meats in a casserole or kettle containing 5 quarts of water and a tablespoon of salt (preferably sea salt). Bring it slowly to a boil, skimming off all the matter that floats to the surface. When the water boils, add the feet, the bacon rind, the carrots, and leeks, properly washed and trimmed, the onion, peeled and stuck with the clove. Continue skimming while the water returns to the boil. Add the *bouquet garni,* cover the kettle three quarters of the way, and simmer 3½ hours.

Remove the meats from the kettle and allow them to cool completely. Line a sieve with a dish towel dampened in cold water and pour the broth through. This will take away the fat from the broth. Taste for seasoning. Color the bouillon with caramel, using 2 lumps of sugar and 4 teaspoons of water. Cool and then place in a bowl of ice, stirring frequently. When it reaches the syrupy stage, it is ready for use.

Cut the meat in strips and the ham in small dice. Cut the eggs and pickles in thin rounds. Combine these ingredients with the capers and mix carefully, trying not to break the egg rounds. Put the mixture in a large ring mold and fill with the cold syrupy aspic. Allow to set several hours in the refrigerator.

Unmold on a large round platter and garnish with tomato slices seasoned with a vinaigrette sauce.

Tied beef ✳ *Boeuf à la ficelle*

FOR TWO PEOPLE

1 small sirloin roast (¾-1 pound)   5 cups beef or chicken bouillon✳

Ask the butcher to tie the meat as though for roasting. Bring the bouillon to a full boil in a pan just large enough to hold the meat. Boil very hard for 6 to 8 minutes. Remove the meat to a heated platter and serve with boiled vegetables from a pot roast or au gratin potatoes. This meat must be very rare to be good.

Grilling or broiling meat

Grilling meat is the process of cooking meat by direct heat. The meat is placed on a grill or in a folding grill and cooked over or under hot coals. In most home kitchens, the meat is placed on a preheated grill in a broiling pan and cooked under an electric or gas broiler. Still another method is pan-broiling. The heavy frying pan or skillet is heated to a high temperature and either sprinkled with salt or brushed with a little oil or butter before cooking the meat. With any method, the meat is brushed with fat before being cooked.

If herbs are to be added to the meat, they should be pressed into the raw meat before brushing the meat with fat. Always turn the meat with a spatula rather than a fork so that juices will not escape. Turn the meat only once, and do not

---

✳If you do not have prepared bouillon, use meat extract or bouillon cubes mixed with the required amount of water.—*Ed.*

salt the meat before grilling. Sprinkle with salt once the meat is turned and again just before serving.

Thin steaks, such as beefsteaks (*biftecks*), which are sometimes solid meat and other times patties made of ground beef, are grilled with a very high heat. 1 minute on each side will give you a blue steak that is almost raw; 2 minutes on each side will give a very rare steak; and 3 minutes on each side will render the steak medium rare. Thicker steaks (porterhouse, sirloin, T-bone, rumpsteak, and so on) are seared with a high heat, and then the heat is reduced or the meat placed further away from the source of heat until the meat is sufficiently cooked.

To give the characteristic lattice grill marks on broiled meat, shift the meat 90 degrees halfway through the searing process.

Steaks are most often served with a maître d'hôtel sauce or a Béarnaise sauce, but let me introduce you to a few less usual recipes for serving steaks.

Rib steak forestière * Entrecôte forestière

FOR TWO PEOPLE

1 boneless rib or club steak
   (approximately ¾ pound)*
¼ pound lean bacon (in one piece)
¼ pound mushrooms

4 tablespoons butter
½ cup dry white wine
salt and pepper

Trim the steak well. Dice the bacon. Wash, wipe, and slice the mushrooms.

Boil the bacon in salted water for 5 minutes. Drain.

Divide the butter between 2 skillets. Pan-broil the steak when the first pan is very hot, turning when the meat is well seared on one side.

Sauté the mushrooms and bacon in the other skillet for a few minutes, keeping them separate. Season the mushrooms with salt and pepper.

Put the steak on a heated platter. Pour the wine into the steak skillet, stirring to release the juices adhering to the pan. Boil just long enough to give you time to put the bacon on one side of the meat and the mushrooms on the other. Pour the sauce over the meat.

Pepper steak * Entrecôte au poivre

FOR TWO PEOPLE

1 boneless rib or club steak
   (approximately ¾ pound)**

⅓ cup water or bouillon
4 teaspoons cognac or armagnac

*For serving larger numbers, use a porterhouse, rump, or T-bone steak.

**This recipe is good with porterhouse, rump, T-bone steak.

1 teaspoon peppercorns	½ teaspoon cornstarch
1½ tablespoons butter	salt
1½ tablespoons oil	

Trim the steak. Crush the peppercorns on a dish towel with a rolling pin. A peppermill makes the pepper too fine. In eating this dish, you actually crunch the pepper with your teeth. Press the pepper into both sides of the steak with your fingers, so that it sinks into the meat.

Heat the butter and oil in a large skillet, and when it is very hot, put in the meat. The high heat will help seal in the pepper. Turn, salt, and cook according to your taste. Remove to a heated platter and keep warm while you make the sauce.

Add the bouillon or water and stir well. Add the best cognac you have and mix over a moderate heat. Sprinkle with the cornstarch and keep stirring until the sauce boils. Taste and add salt, if necessary. Pour over the meat.

Beefsteaks

Biftecks is a word well known to everyone who has eaten in France, because beef is eaten so often this way. They are individual steaks, cut from the sirloin, the ribs, the eye of the round, or the rump. They may be of various thicknesses but are usually ⅓ to ½ inch thick.

Biftecks may also mean fine ground beef patties. They are also pan-broiled.

*Beefsteaks with roquefort * Biftecks au roquefort*

FOR FOUR PEOPLE

4 quarter-pound beefsteaks	3 tablespoons Roquefort cheese
2 tablespoons butter	salt and pepper

Pan-broil the beefsteaks with a very high heat, allowing 2 to 3 minutes on each side. Cream together the butter and Roquefort cheese with a fork.

Place the steaks on a hot platter. Sprinkle lightly with salt and pepper. Put a piece of the Roquefort mixture on each steak and serve immediately.

*Beefsteaks on horseback * Biftecks à cheval*

FOR FOUR PEOPLE

4 quarter-pound beefsteaks	8 eggs
6 tablespoons butter	salt and pepper

Take 2 large skillets and put half the butter in each one. Heat one very hot and the other moderately hot. Pan-broil the steaks in one and place on a hot platter. Cook the eggs in the other, putting a cover over the eggs while cooking. Place 2 eggs on each steak. Pour the cooking butter from both skillets over the eggs. Season lightly with salt and pepper.

Beefsteaks à la bordelaise
Biftecks à la bordelaise

FOR FOUR PEOPLE

2½ tablespoons oil
1 onion, chopped fine
1 shallot, chopped fine
4 quarter-pound beefsteaks

4 teaspoons flour
¾ cup red Bordeaux
salt and pepper

Heat the oil in a skillet. Sauté the onion and shallot over a moderately high heat until golden, but do not burn. Add the beefsteaks and sprinkle with salt and pepper. When browned on one side, turn and sprinkle with the flour. Pour in the wine and stir the sauce well. Lower the heat and cook until the sauce thickens.

Place the beefsteaks on a heated platter and strain the sauce over the steaks.

Anchovy beefsteak * Bifteck à l'anchois

FOR EACH SERVING

¼ pound ground beef chuck
½ teaspoon butter

½ teaspoon anchovy paste
salt and pepper

Divide the meat into 2 thin patties. Spread one with the mixture of butter and anchovy paste. Cover with the other and press together firmly. Cook 4 minutes on each side in a hot skillet. Sprinkle with salt very lightly because of the anchovy but more heavily with freshly ground pepper. Serve at once.

Beefsteaks with gruyère
Biftecks hachés au gruyère

FOR FOUR PEOPLE

1 pound ground beef chuck
4 thin slices Gruyère cheese

2 tablespoons butter
salt and pepper

Divide the ground beef into 4 patties. Split each one in half and insert a slice of cheese. Press the patty back into shape. Season with salt and pepper. Heat the butter in a skillet, and when very hot, grill the patties, allowing about 5 minutes to each side.

*Beefsteaks with ham * Biftecks au jambon*

FOR TWO TO FOUR PEOPLE

1 pound ground beef chuck	4 teaspoons butter
French mustard	1 teaspoon anchovy paste
2 thin slices cooked ham	salt and pepper

Make 8 thin patties from the ground beef. Sprinkle half of them with salt and pepper and spread with a thin layer of mustard. Put half a slice of ham on the same patties, trimming if necessary so that the ham will not go over the edges. Cover with the other patties and press together firmly.

Combine the butter and anchovy paste.

Heat a skillet until very hot. Cook 3 minutes on each side. Sprinkle with more salt and pepper. Garnish each one with a dab of anchovy butter. Serve with French fried potatoes.

*Beefsteaks with onion * Biftecks hachés à l'oignon*

FOR FOUR PEOPLE

1 pound ground beef chuck	3 tablespoons butter
4 medium-sized onions, chopped fine	salt and pepper

Make 8 very thin patties of equal dimensions. Cover half of them with a thick layer of chopped onion. Cover with the other patties and press together firmly. Heat the butter in a skillet, and when very hot, pan-broil 4 minutes on each side. Season with salt and pepper.

Various beef dishes

Besides roasting, braising, broiling, and grilling beef, there are other ways of preparing it that fall into no special category. Some are based on raw meat, but many more are intended to use up leftover cooked meat. Hundreds of recipes might be listed, but the following are typical and excellent.

Beef stroganoff * Boeuf stroganoff

FOR FOUR TO SIX PEOPLE

1½ pounds sirloin steak
5 tablespoons butter
paprika

2 shallots
⅓ cup extra heavy cream
cayenne, salt, and pepper

Cut the meat in ½-inch slices and cut the slices into pieces approximately 2 inches wide. Heat 4 tablespoons of butter in one skillet and the rest in a small saucepan. Sauté the steak in the skillet for 5 minutes. Season with salt, pepper, and paprika. Chop the shallots very fine and sauté just until tender.

Combine the meat and shallots and stir in the cream. Heat without boiling. Taste for seasoning, adding a little cayenne. Serve at once.

Beef fillet on skewers * Brochettes de filet de boeuf

FOR SIX PEOPLE

1 pound boneless sirloin tip
12 slices lean bacon
10 tablespoons butter, melted

soft breadcrumbs
salt and pepper

Cut the meat into small cubes and the bacon into squares. Alternate the meat and bacon on 6 small skewers. Paint carefully with melted butter and turn in a plate of breadcrumbs. Season with salt and pepper.

Heat the rest of the butter in a skillet and pan-broil over a moderate heat, turning when necessary. Serve with a green salad.

Beef fillet on skewers with green peppers
Brochettes de filet de boeuf aux poivrons verts

FOR SIX PEOPLE

Follow the preceding recipe, alternating slices of seeded green peppers with the meats.

Steak tartare * Steak tartare

FOR ONE PERSON

Steak Tartare is always prepared for an individual serving. Only the best and leanest steak should be used.

¼ pound fresh ground lean beef
1 egg yolk
1 teaspoon chopped parsley
3 teaspoons capers
1 medium onion, chopped fine

oil
Worcestershire sauce
French mustard
salt and pepper

Place the beef in a patty on a plate. Make a deep indentation in the center to hold the raw egg yolk. Sprinkle with chopped parsley and surround with little piles of capers and the chopped onion. Serve with the condiments so that the diner can season his own steak.

Burgundy beef fondue
La fondue bourguignonne

FOR SIX PEOPLE

This popular dish is cooked at the table by the diners themselves. It consists of beef cubes, cooked in a boiling combination of butter and oil and served with a variety of sauces. Each person is provided with a long wooden-handled fork or, lacking these, with two ordinary forks, so that one fork may cool while the other is being used. The meat is dipped into the boiling fat and then into the sauces. Two plates are placed before each guest, one containing the meat; the other is used for the sauces. Serve with plenty of French bread and good red wine.

Tomato Sauce (page 22)
Gribiche Sauce (page 10)
Mayonnaise (page 14)

1½ pounds sirloin or tenderloin
¾ cup butter
¾ cup oil

Prepare the sauces and have them in readiness. The tomato sauce is served hot and the others cold. Place them in attractive bowls.

Cut the meat into ¾-inch cubes and divide them among six plates.

Combine the butter and oil in a small saucepan or flameproof dish. Heat to the boiling point and place on an electric hot plate or candle burner.

Beef salad * Salade de boeuf

FOR SIX PEOPLE

12 thin slices boiled beef
6 hard-cooked eggs
3 large tomatoes
1 small can peas

1 bunch watercress
Mayonnaise (page 14)
Vinaigrette Sauce (page 29)

Place the meat in the center of a large platter. Surround the meat with a pretty arrangement of sliced, hard-cooked eggs, sliced tomatoes, well-drained peas, and watercress. Serve the mayonnaise and vinaigrette sauce in two bowls and accompany the platter with a large dish of French fried potatoes.

Beef slices with eggplant * Miroton aux aubergines

FOR SIX PEOPLE

3-4 onions, chopped fine
2 medium-sized eggplant
12 slices cooked beef (boiled or braised)
4-5 tomatoes
¾ cup oil
4 teaspoons flour

¾ cup bouillon or water
½ teaspoon French mustard
4 teaspoons Caramel (page 579)
soft breadcrumbs
salt and pepper

Peel the onions and chop quite fine. Slice the eggplant lengthwise, without peeling, and about ½ inch thick. Slice the meat about ⅛ inch thick and slice each tomato in half.

Heat 4 tablespoons of oil in a skillet and sauté three fourths of the onions just until tender. Spread them in the bottom of a large shallow baking dish. Cover the onions with the meat and cover the meat with the eggplant. Sprinkle with salt and pepper.

Heat 4 more tablespoons of oil and sauté the rest of the onions until tender. Stir in the flour and remove from the heat. Stir in the bouillon or water and return to the heat for 5 minutes. Add the mustard and the caramel. Stir well and pour over the contents of the baking dish. Cover with the tomato halves. Sprinkle with the rest of the oil and with breadcrumbs. Sprinkle once more with salt and pepper and bake 1 hour at 375° F.

Minced beef martinique * Hachis martiniquais

FOR SIX PEOPLE

1 cup rice
¼ teaspoon saffron or
2 tablespoons turmeric
oil
3 onions, chopped fine

3 cups minced cooked beef
6 tomatoes
6 bananas
6 eggs
salt and pepper

Boil the rice with the saffron or turmeric. Place in a well-oiled ring mold and keep hot in the oven.

Heat 2½ tablespoons of oil in a heavy skillet and sauté the chopped onions until golden. Add the minced beef. Season with salt and pepper and cook 3 minutes.

In another pan, heat a little oil and sauté the tomatoes, split in half. Remove them to a heated platter, spacing them around the edge. Sauté the bananas, cut lengthwise, and place them between the tomatoes.

At the same time, fry the eggs 3 minutes in a skillet containing boiling hot oil 1½ inches deep. Place the eggs strategically in the same border.

Turn the rice ring onto the platter and fill the center with the minced beef.

Hot parsley beef ∗ Persillade

FOR FOUR PEOPLE

8-12 thin slices boiled beef
1½ cups hot bouillon
⅓ cup chopped parsley

juice of 1 lemon
salt and pepper

Put the beef slices in a pan with the bouillon and parsley. Simmer 15 minutes. Add the juice of half a lemon. Simmer 15 minutes more. Taste and add more lemon juice, salt and pepper, if necessary. Serve with rice.

Minced beef with provençale tomatoes
Hachis de boeuf aux tomates provençales

FOR FOUR PEOPLE

8 medium-sized tomatoes
⅔ cup olive oil
1 large clove garlic
1 tablespoon chopped parsley
4 cups minced cooked beef (or lamb)

4 large onions
4 teaspoons flour
1½ cups hot bouillon
salt and pepper

Cut the tomatoes in half. Heat ⅓ cup of oil in a large skillet and place the tomatoes, cut side down, in the skillet. Pierce each tomato with a fork. Cook 5 minutes and turn. Chop the garlic and the parsley and sprinkle the tomatoes with a mixture of the two. Sprinkle also with salt and pepper. Reduce the heat and cook slowly until the tomatoes are very soft.

Grind the beef. Peel and chop the onions. Put the rest of the oil in another skillet and sauté the onions until golden. Add the meat, stir well, and sprinkle with the flour. Stir until the flour disappears and then stir in the bouillon. Season with salt and pepper and cook 5 minutes.

Put the beef in a shallow heatproof platter. Place the tomatoes on the beef. Pour the cooking juices from the tomato pan over everything and heat 5 minutes in a 400° F. oven.

Minced beef in ramekins * Boeuf en ramequins

FOR FOUR PEOPLE

1½ cups ground cooked beef
3 tablespoons butter
1 onion, chopped fine
4 teaspoons flour
¾ cup hot bouillon
1 tablespoon tomato paste

8 eggs
paprika
1 tablespoon mixed chopped herbs
   (parsley, chives, tarragon)
salt and pepper

Grind the meat.

Heat the butter in a skillet and sauté the chopped onion until golden. Add the beef, mix well, and sprinkle with the flour. Stir until the flour disappears and add the bouillon and then the tomato paste. Season with salt and pepper and simmer 5 minutes.

Poach the eggs in simmering salted water for 3 minutes.

Butter 8 individual ramekins. Line each one with a layer of the beef mixture. Cover with a poached egg and top each one with a layer of beef. Bake in a 400° F. oven for 2 minutes. Sprinkle with paprika and chopped herbs and serve immediately.

Minced beef parmentier * Hachis parmentier

FOR SIX PEOPLE

2 cups potato purée
3 tablespoons butter
2 large onions, chopped fine
2 tomatoes

3 cups leftover boiled or braised beef,
   minced
½ cup grated Gruyère cheese
salt and pepper

Prepare potato purée and spread half of it in a buttered shallow oven dish.

Sauté the chopped onion, and when pale yellow, add the tomatoes, which have been peeled, seeded, and diced. After 3 minutes, add the minced beef. Season with salt and pepper and mix well. Heat 3 minutes longer.

Spread the beef mixture over the potatoes and cover with the rest of the potatoes. Sprinkle with grated cheese and brown in a hot oven.

Beef loaf with tomato sauce
Pain de boeuf, sauce tomate

FOR FOUR PEOPLE

Tomato Sauce (page 22)
1¼ cups ground boiled beef

4 egg yolks
4 egg whites, beaten stiff

½ cup ground lean ham   salt and pepper
3 tablespoons soft butter

Unless you have tomato sauce on hand, start by making the sauce, which takes slightly longer to cook than the loaf.

Pound the ground meat, the butter and egg yolks, with mortar and pestle or with a potato masher and wooden bowl. When well blended, season with salt and pepper and fold in the egg whites.

Put the mixture in a well-buttered charlotte mold or loaf tin. Place in a pan of hot water and bake 45 minutes at 375° F. Unmold hot and serve with the sauce.

Beef-mushroom croquettes with madeira
Croquettes de hachis de boeuf au madère

FOR FOUR PEOPLE

1½ cups Béchamel Sauce (page 6)	Tomato Sauce (page 22)
¼ pound mushrooms	flour
3 cups minced cooked beef	dry breadcrumbs
3 tablespoons butter	several sprigs parsley
⅓ cup Madeira	salt and pepper

Make a thick béchamel sauce. Wash, trim, and chop the mushrooms. Grind or chop the leftover beef to make 3 cups of minced beef.

Heat the butter in a skillet. Sauté the mushrooms a minute. Add the beef and the Madeira and season with salt and pepper. Cover and cook over a low flame 5 to 10 minutes. Combine with the béchamel and cool. The mixture should be well seasoned and very thick.

Make the tomato sauce.

Chill and divide the mixture into croquettes the size of small potatoes. Dip in flour and then in breadcrumbs.

Fry in deep fat (385° F.) until golden brown. At the last minute, fry the parsley.

Serve the croquettes very hot and pass the sauce in a separate bowl.

Veal

Very good veal is veal with flesh that is white, tender, but firm and moist. This is not easy to find. In most countries, veal is not really veal but young beef. Even in some parts of France, where the art of raising and butchering veal is the fruit of centuries of experience, this meat is not always of the very best. It is only in Paris, where the most exacting culinary clientèle still exists, that one can always find perfect veal—at a price. The milk diet and the days of rest and tranquility before butchering are very important for good veal, but this fortunately is not our concern. We don't have to raise the veal; we only have to cook it.

In America the meat is cut differently, so that it is difficult to produce exactly the same results. However, if you have a French or Italian butcher in your vicinity, he will understand how to cut the meat, especially the *escalopes* (cutlets). If not, perhaps you can instruct him after reading the following paragraph:

To cut *escalopes* (French-cut cutlets): Cut the meat on the bias in thin slices (about ⅓ inch thick) from the top of the leg. Each piece should weigh 3 to 4 ounces apiece and should be free of fat or gristle. Unless the meat is very young and tender, it will have to be pounded a little or flattened with a rolling pin.

Generally speaking, veal requires long slow cooking and frequent basting. In most recipes, the veal is browned in fat before being braised or roasted and is usually cooked with added fat. It lends itself to other subtle flavors to make many delicious dishes. Chops and cutlets should not be cut too thick, and your butcher or you should always slash the edges so that they will lie flat in cooking.

Breaded veal cutlets * Escalopes de veau panées

FOR FOUR PEOPLE

4 French-cut veal cutlets
1 egg
3 tablespoons flour

1 cup fresh breadcrumbs
6 tablespoons butter
salt and pepper

Order cutlets weighing about ¼ pound each and all of equal thickness and shape.

Beat the egg slightly in a shallow dish. Put the flour in one plate and the breadcrumbs in another. Dip each cutlet first in the flour, then in the egg, and finally in the breadcrumbs. Let them stand a little while, preferably in the refrigerator.

Heat the butter in a skillet and fry the cutlets 8 to 10 minutes on each side. Season with salt and pepper. Serve on a hot platter and accompany with sautéed potatoes.

Veal cutlets with apple brandy cream
Escalopes de veau à la crème calvados

FOR FOUR PEOPLE

4 French-cut veal cutlets
3 tablespoons butter
3 tablespoons oil
¼ pound mushrooms

4 teaspoons Calvados, or apple brandy
4 tablespoons heavy cream
salt and pepper

Order cutlets weighing approximately ¼ pound each.

Heat the butter and 1½ tablespoons of oil in a skillet. Brown the cutlets well on both sides. Season with salt and pepper. Add 4 teaspoons of warm water and cook, covered, over a very low flame for 30 minutes, turning occasionally.

Meanwhile, trim, wash, and slice the mushrooms. Heat the rest of the oil and sauté the mushrooms over a high heat. Shortly before serving, spread the mushrooms over the cutlets. Add the apple brandy and touch with a lighted match. Add the cream and bring to a quick boil. Taste for seasoning.

Serve very hot with sautéed potatoes, green beans, or braised carrots.

Veal cutlets with stuffed mushrooms
Escalopes de veau farcis aux champignons

FOR FOUR PEOPLE

4 French-cut veal cutlets
½ pound mushrooms, including
   4 very large ones
2 tablespoons oil
1 stalk white celery

2 teaspoons chopped parsley
5 tablespoons butter
4 tablespoons heavy cream
salt and pepper

Order cutlets weighing approximately ¼ pound each.

Wipe clean 4 large mushroom heads. Paint the exterior with oil and bake 20 minutes in a 350° F. oven.

Wash the rest of the mushrooms; mince them fine or grind in a meat chopper. Chop the celery very fine and combine with the mushrooms and parsley. Season with salt and pepper and sauté in the rest of the oil for 2 minutes.

Brown the cutlets on each side in butter. Reduce the heat, cover, and continue cooking for 20 minutes, turning once or twice. Season with salt and pepper. Arrange the cutlets on a preheated platter. Surround with the mushroom heads stuffed with the celery-mushroom mixture. Put the rest of the mixture on the cutlets. Add the cream to the pan in which the veal has been cooked. Bring just to a boil, scraping the juices from the bottom of the pan. Pour this over the meat.

Breaded veal cutlets with roquefort
Escalopes de veau panées au roquefort

FOR FOUR PEOPLE

4 French-cut veal cutlets
6 tablespoons butter
1 ounce (2 tablespoons) Roquefort
   cheese
flour

1 egg, slightly beaten
1 cup soft breadcrumbs
5 teaspoons oil
lemon wedges
salt and pepper

Order cutlets weighing ¼ pound each and sliced very thin.

Cream together 2 tablespoons of butter with the cheese until you have a smooth paste. Spread this on one side of the cutlets. Dip the cutlets in flour, then in beaten egg, seasoned with salt and pepper, and finally in breadcrumbs, pressing the crumbs into both sides of the cutlets. Let stand a little while, if possible.

Heat the rest of the butter and the oil in a skillet. Fry the cutlets 8 to 10 minutes on each side, depending on the thickness of the cutlet. Serve with lemon wedges and sprinkle with salt and pepper.

Veal cutlets in cases
Escalopes de veau en papillotes

FOR FOUR PEOPLE

4 French-cut veal cutlets
6 tablespoons butter
5 ounces mushrooms
1 small can truffle pieces

4 teaspoons armagnac or cognac
4 thin slices cooked ham
salt and pepper

Order cutlets cut thin and weighing ¼ pound each. Heat the butter in a skillet. Brown the cutlets on each side. Reduce the heat and cook slowly with the cover on for 15 minutes. Remove from the skillet but keep warm.

Meanwhile, trim, wash, and dry the mushrooms. Chop them and the truffles very fine. Add this mixture and the armagnac or cognac to the butter in the skillet and cook 5 minutes. Season to taste.

Cut rectangles of heavy parchment paper (or aluminum foil—*Ed.*) large enough to contain a cutlet. Paint each rectangle with oil. Place a half slice of ham on half of each rectangle. Cover with a cutlet and top with another slice of ham. Spoon the mushroom sauce over the meat and fold the other part of the rectangle over the meat, rolling the edges so that nothing will escape. Place on an ovenproof serving platter and bake 10 minutes at 400° F. Serve individually without removing the paper.

Veal cutlets with tarragon
Escalopes de veau à l'estragon

FOR FOUR PEOPLE

4 French-cut veal cutlets	2 tablespoons tomato paste
flour	16 tarragon leaves
3 tablespoons oil	paprika
½ cup dry white wine	salt and pepper

Order cutlets weighing approximately ¼ pound each.

Dip both sides of each cutlet in flour. Heat the oil in a skillet and brown the cutlets well on each side. Reduce the heat to low and cover the skillet. Cook 20 minutes, turning occasionally. Add the white wine, taking care to scrape the juices from the bottom of the pan. Stir in the tomato paste and the 10 tarragon leaves, minced fine. Season with salt and pepper and continue cooking 10 minutes.

Arrange the cutlets on a heated platter. Pour the sauce over the meat and sprinkle with more chopped tarragon and paprika.

Veal cutlets romanichel
Escalopes de veau romanichel

FOR FOUR PEOPLE

4 French-cut veal cutlets	1 egg, slightly beaten
4 slices ham	½ cup soft breadcrumbs
4 slices Gruyère cheese	5 tablespoons butter
flour	salt and pepper

Order 3-ounce cutlets, trimmed as squarely as possible. Cut thin slices of ham and Gruyère cheese to exactly the same dimensions, pressing them very firmly together. Dip each set first in flour, then in beaten egg and then in breadcrumbs. Use plenty of coating so that veal, ham, and cheese will stick together.

Heat the butter in a skillet and sauté the cutlets 8 to 10 minutes on each side. Season with salt and pepper. Serve with buttered spaghetti.

Parslied veal cutlets with kirsch
Escalopes de veau persillées au kirsch

FOR FOUR PEOPLE

4 French-cut veal cutlets	5 tablespoons chopped parsley
3 tablespoons oil	¾ cup heavy cream
4 teaspoons kirsch	salt and pepper

Order cutlets weighing 3 to 4 ounces each.

Heat the oil in a skillet. Brown the cutlets well on both sides. Sprinkle with salt and pepper. Turn the heat very low and cook 30 minutes, turning occasionally. When the cutlets are thoroughly cooked, add the kirsch and touch with a lighted match. Spoon the liquid over the meat until the flames die down. Place the cutlets on a heated platter.

Stir the parsley into the pan juices. Add the cream and bring to a boil, stirring constantly. Season with salt and pepper. Boil 1 to 2 minutes and pour the sauce over the meat. Serve immediately. This is also an excellent way to prepare veal chops.

Flambéed veal cutlets with grapes
Escalopes de veau flambées aux raisins

FOR FOUR PEOPLE

4 French-cut veal cutlets
3 tablespoons butter
⅔ cup dry white wine

1 large bunch seedless grapes
4 teaspoons armagnac or cognac
salt and pepper

Order cutlets weighing about ¼ pound each.

Heat the butter in a skillet and brown the cutlets well on each side. Add the white wine, season with salt and pepper, and cover. Cook 30 minutes over very low heat.

10 minutes before the end of cooking, add the grapes, free from any stems. Just before serving or, if you prefer, at the table, add the armagnac and flame with lighted match. Veal chops may be prepared in the same way.

Viennese cutlets * Escalopes de veau à la viennoise

FOR FOUR PEOPLE

4 French-cut veal cutlets
flour
1 egg, slightly beaten
1 cup soft breadcrumbs
5 tablespoons butter
3 tablespoons oil

2 hard-cooked eggs
1 tablespoon chopped parsley
4 slices lemon
4 anchovy fillets
salt and pepper

Order cutlets weighing 3 to 3½ ounces each. Season with salt and pepper. Put flour in one plate, a beaten egg in another, and the breadcrumbs in still another. Coat each cutlet with flour and dip it in egg and then in the breadcrumbs. Let stand in the refrigerator for a while, if possible.

Heat the butter and oil in a large skillet, and when it smokes, sauté the cutlets 6 minutes on one side and 4 minutes on the other.

Meanwhile, prepare the garnish: Chop the egg whites and yolks separately and arrange them and the parsley around the edge of a preheated serving platter in little piles.

Place the cutlets in the center of the platter. Place a lemon slice on each one and put a rolled anchovy fillet on each lemon slice.

Sherried veal cutlets * Escalopes de veau au xérès

FOR FOUR PEOPLE

4 French-cut veal cutlets	½ cup heavy cream
5 tablespoons butter	¼ cup grated Gruyère cheese
6 tablespoons sherry	salt and pepper

Order cutlets weighing 3 to 4 ounces each. Heat the butter in a skillet. Brown the cutlets on both sides. Reduce the heat, cover, and cook 30 minutes, turning occasionally. Add the sherry and stir to scrape the juices from the pan. Add the cream, stir, season with salt and pepper, and let the sauce cook down for a few minutes.

Put the cutlets in a shallow heatproof platter. Pour the sauce over the meat, sprinkle with grated cheese, and brown under the broiler.

Veal birds with olives
Paupiettes de veau aux olives

FOR FOUR PEOPLE

4 French-cut veal cutlets	5 tablespoons butter
1¾ cup ground ham	1 carrot, grated
2 tablespoons diced black olives	4 teaspoons cognac
3 tablespoons soft breadcrumbs	pinch of ginger
1 egg, slightly beaten	salt and pepper

Order very thin cutlets weighing about 3 ounces each. Have the butcher pound them very flat.

Grind the ham and olives together and mix with the breadcrumbs and egg. Season with salt and pepper. The stuffing should have the consistency of a purée. Spread the stuffing on the cutlets and roll them up tightly, tying them both around and lengthwise so that none of the stuffing will escape.

Heat the butter in a skillet and brown on all sides. When well browned, stir in the grated carrot and half the cognac. Touch with a lighted match. Season with salt and pepper. Cover, reduce the heat, and cook slowly for 45 minutes, turning occasionally.

Put the "birds" on a preheated platter. Add a pinch of ginger to the cooking juices. Add the rest of the cognac, scraping the pan to release all the juices. Pour this sauce boiling hot over the meat and serve.

Martinique veal birds
Paupiettes de veau martiniquaises

FOR FOUR PEOPLE

4 French-cut veal cutlets
4 very ripe small bananas
3 tablespoons butter
1 carrot

4 tablespoons rum
½ cup heavy cream
salt and pepper

Order cutlets cut very thin, weighing 2 to 3 ounces, and have them pounded flat. On each cutlet, crush a banana with a fork and roll up the cutlets into tight rolls, tying them with kitchen twine.

Heat the butter in a deep skillet and brown the "birds" well on all sides. Add the peeled carrot, cut in thick slices. Add ¾ cup of water. Sprinkle with salt and pepper. Cover and cook 30 minutes over a low heat, turning occasionally.

Just before serving, add the rum and cream. Stir until it reaches the boiling point. Serve immediately with rice.

Veal birds with leeks
Paupiettes de veau aux poireaux

FOR SIX PEOPLE

6 French-cut veal cutlets
2 pounds leeks
1 3-ounce can liver paste
4 tablespoons canned tomato purée
2 hard-cooked eggs

¼ teaspoon dried anise seed
1 raw egg
5 tablespoons butter
¼ cup soft breadcrumbs
salt and pepper

Order cutlets weighing 3 to 3½ ounces each. Flatten them. Cut off most of the green tops of the leeks. Wash them well and boil 30 minutes in salted water. Drain well, squeezing out all the water with the palms of your hands.

Make a stuffing by mixing the liver paste, the tomato purée, finely chopped hard-cooked eggs, anise, salt, and pepper, using the raw egg as a binder. Mix until thoroughly blended. Spread the stuffing on the cutlets, roll them up tightly, and tie them around and lengthwise with kitchen twine. Chop the leeks.

Heat the butter in a skillet, and when very hot, brown the "birds" in the butter, turning them so that they will brown evenly. Reduce the heat, add the leeks. Sprinkle with breadcrumbs, salt, and pepper. Cover and cook very slowly for 45 minutes.

Braised veal chops ✳ Côtelettes de veau braisées

FOR FOUR PEOPLE

4 thick loin veal chops	3 carrots
4 tablespoons butter	salt and pepper
4 teaspoons cognac	

Order chops weighing slightly less than ½ pound each. Heat the butter in a skillet and brown the chops well on each side. Add the cognac and touch with a lighted match.

Peel the carrots and slice them very thinly into the skillet. Season everything with salt and pepper. Reduce the heat to very low, cover, and cook for 30 minutes or until the chops are thoroughly cooked. Put the chops on a heated platter and strain the sauce over the chops.

Veal chops with orange sauce
Côtelettes de veau à l'orange

FOR FOUR PEOPLE

4 loin veal chops	1 teaspoon flour
5 tablespoons butter	1 egg, well beaten
4 slices bacon	¼ cup heavy cream
1 large juice orange	salt and pepper

Cook the chops in 4 tablespoons of butter, browning them first over high heat and then reducing the heat to finish the cooking, allowing 7 to 10 minutes on each side, depending on the thickness of the chops. Sauté the bacon with a tablespoon of butter in another skillet. Keep warm.

At the same time, peel off the outer orange layer of the orange and cut it into thin strips. Throw the strips into boiling water for 5 minutes. Squeeze the juice from the orange. You should have ½ cup of juice.

When the chops are cooked, sprinkle them with salt and pepper and place them on a preheated platter. Keep warm. Stir the flour into the skillet with a wooden spoon over low heat, add the orange juice and 2 to 3 tablespoons of hot water. Add the parboiled orange strips and simmer the sauce 5 minutes, stirring constantly. Season with salt and pepper. Remove from the heat and whisk in cream previously mixed with the beaten egg. Reheat but do not boil.

Veal chops nanciennes
Côtelettes de veau nanciennes

FOR FOUR PEOPLE

4 loin veal chops
1 egg, beaten slightly
½ cup soft breadcrumbs
1 shallot, chopped fine
2 teaspoons chopped parsley

2 tablespoons butter
2 teaspoons flour
½ cup bouillon
1 tablespoon French mustard
salt and pepper

Dip the chops in the beaten egg and then in a mixture of breadcrumbs, chopped shallot, and parsley, seasoned with salt and pepper. Grill them in a moderately hot, lightly greased skillet, allowing 8 minutes to each side.

At the same time make a small quantity of thin sauce by heating the butter and stirring in the flour. Stir in the bouillon and season with the mustard, salt, and pepper. Stir until smooth.

Serve the chops on a preheated platter and spoon the sauce over the chops.

Veal chops with grapefruit and white wine
Côtelettes de veau aux pamplemousses

FOR SIX PEOPLE

6 loin veal chops
5 tablespoons butter
4 carrots
4 teaspoons cognac
1½ cups white wine

2 small grapefruit
1 sprig thyme
1 small bay leaf
salt and pepper

Brown the chops well on both sides in butter. Add the carrots, peeled and cut into thin rounds. Season with salt and pepper. Sprinkle with the cognac and touch with a lighted match, spooning the flaming liquid over the chops. Add the white wine, the juice of one of the grapefruit, the thyme, and the bay leaf. Cover and simmer 10 to 15 minutes. Peel, slice, and seed the other grapefruit.

Put the chops and the sauce on a preheated platter. Decorate with the grapefruit slices. Serve with buttered noodles.

Veal chops à la jeanne * Côtelettes de veau jeanne

FOR FOUR PEOPLE

4 loin veal chops
2 tablespoons butter

4 teaspoons chopped parsley
¾ cup milk

3 eggs	salt and pepper
2 tablespoons flour	

Sear the chops in a hot ungreased skillet for 2½ minutes on each side. Season well with salt and pepper.

Spread the butter in the bottom of a shallow ovenproof dish and arrange the chops in the dish.

Beat the eggs enough to mix the yolks and whites well. Add the flour and beat again very hard. Add the chopped parsley, and, beating constantly, add the milk gradually. Be sure there are no lumps in the mixture. Pour over the chops and bake 25 minutes in a 400° F. oven or until the top is golden brown.

Serve with rice or a green vegetable.

Grilled veal chops with basil
Côtelettes de veau au basilic

FOR FOUR PEOPLE

4 large loin veal chops	4 teaspoons finely chopped fresh basil
3 tablespoons butter	salt and pepper

Brown the chops in an ungreased skillet over a moderate heat, allowing 7 to 10 minutes on each side, depending on the thickness of the chops. When one side is done, turn and sprinkle with salt and pepper.

Meanwhile, cream the butter and fresh basil together into a smooth paste. Put the chops on a heated platter. Divide the butter among the four chops. Serve with straw potatoes and a tossed salad seasoned with basil.

Flambéed veal chops with asparagus
Côtelettes de veau aux asperges

FOR FOUR PEOPLE

2 pounds asparagus	2½ tablespoons cognac
6 tablespoons butter	½ cup heavy cream
4 large loin veal chops	salt and pepper

In France, where our asparagus is blanched in the growing process, we trim and pare it for this recipe so that only the tender inner part is used. Ten minutes are necessary for parboiling. For the green asparagus more common in American markets, you need simply wash and trim it and parboil in salted water 3 to 5 minutes, depending on the thickness of the stalks. Drain immediately.

Heat the butter in a deep skillet and brown the chops on both sides. Add the asparagus and sauté them on all sides too. Reduce the heat, cover and simmer until the veal chops are cooked, allowing 7 to 10 minutes for each side.

Remove the cover and add the cognac. Touch with a lighted match and spoon the flaming liquid over the chops. Add the cream and season well with salt and pepper. Bring the sauce to a boil for just a few moments and serve. If there seems to be too much liquid in the pan to make a rich sauce, boil the juices down before adding the cognac and cream.

Curried veal * Veau en cocotte au cari

FOR SIX PEOPLE

2½-pound boned loin roast of veal	3 medium-sized tomatoes
½ pound lean salt pork	2 tablespoons curry
5 onions, chopped fine	salt and pepper

Order the roast tied tightly. Parboil the salt pork 5 minutes; rinse and cut it into strips. Heat in a heavy pan over a moderate flame until the pork renders its fat. Brown the roast on all sides in the fat. Don't hurry this operation; it takes time.

When the meat is nicely browned, add the onions, and the tomatoes, which have been peeled and cut into pieces. Add the curry, salt, and pepper. Reduce the heat, cover and simmer 2½ hours. Watch to see that the sauce does not become too concentrated. If need be, add a little warm water.

Put the meat in a covered dish to cool slightly. Strain the sauce through a fine sieve lined with a cold damp dish towel. Reheat the sauce to the boiling point.

Cut several slices of the veal on the platter, leaving about a third of the meat uncut. Pour the sauce over the meat and serve with curried noodles.

Loin of veal with walnuts * Longe de veau aux noix

FOR SIX PEOPLE

2½-pound loin of veal, boned and rolled	*bouquet garni* (parsley, tarragon)
2 carrots, grated	1 cup walnuts, chopped fine
2 onions, chopped fine	2 tablespoons Roquefort cheese
3 tablespoons butter	¾ cup heavy cream
¾ cup bouillon	salt and pepper

Order the meat tied tightly.

Prepare the vegetables and sauté them in a deep casserole or heavy pan in butter until soft. Add the meat and continue cooking until the meat is browned lightly on all sides. Sprinkle with salt and pepper. Add the bouillon and the *bou-*

quet garni; cover and cook 2 hours over a low heat, turning the meat occasionally. Remove the meat from the pan and cool.

Slice the meat into 12 slices. Spread each one with a thin layer of the nuts well blended with the Roquefort cheese. Put the roast back into its original form and tie it up again. Place back into the pan and continue cooking for another hour.

Place the meat on a heated platter. Remove the strings. Strain the sauce over the meat. Pour the cream over the top and brown quickly under a hot broiler.

Veal orloff * Le veau orloff

FOR SIX PEOPLE

2-pound round of veal roast	1 cup milk
10 tablespoons butter	4 tablespoons heavy cream
2 carrots, grated	juice of 1 lemon
2 onions, chopped fine	2 egg yolks
¾ cup white wine	½ cup grated cheese
10 ounces mushrooms	paprika
3 tablespoons flour	salt and pepper

Order a roast cut from the top of the round and tied tightly. It should be about 4 inches in diameter.

Heat 5 tablespoons of butter in a deep casserole or heavy pan. Sauté the grated carrots and chopped onions until the onions are golden. Add the veal and continue cooking until the meat is lightly browned on all sides. Season with salt and pepper, add the wine, cover, and cook gently for 1½ hours.

Wash, dry, and chop the mushrooms rather coarsely. Sauté in 2 tablespoons of butter until the moisture disappears.

Heat 3 tablespoons of butter in a small saucepan. Blend in the flour and add the milk, stirring until the mixture thickens. Season with salt and pepper. Pour half of the sauce into a small bowl and add the mushrooms, the cream, and the juice of a lemon. Season to taste.

Cut the veal into slices and spread each slice with the mushroom mixture. Put the roast back in its original form on a heatproof serving platter.

Whisk the egg yolks into the rest of the sauce and strain the sauce from the casserole into the saucepan. Pour this over the meat. Sprinkle with the grated cheese and a little paprika and brown in a very hot oven.

Cold veal ragoût * Ragoût de veau froid

FOR FOUR PEOPLE

1½ pounds veal knuckle	*bouquet garni* (bay leaf, thyme)
5 tablespoons butter	¼ pound mushrooms

3 tablespoons oil
6 small onions
1 cup bouillon

1 tablespoon flour
2 egg yolks
salt and pepper

Order the knuckle sawed in rather small pieces.

Heat 3 tablespoons of the butter and oil in a deep pan. Peel the onions and add them and the meat to the fat. Season with salt and pepper and brown on all sides. Add the bouillon and the *bouquet garni.* Cover and simmer 1 hour. Then 10 minutes before the end of cooking, add the mushrooms, which have been washed and sliced thin.

Put the meat, onions, and mushrooms on a shallow serving platter. Discard the *bouquet.*

Heat 2 tablespoons of butter in a saucepan and stir in the flour. Add the broth from the veal and stir until smooth. The sauce should be thin, so add bouillon if necessary. Taste for seasoning. Cook a few moments, then cool for 3 minutes. Stir in the egg yolks, which have been slightly beaten. Pour the sauce over the meat and chill in the refrigerator.

Veal sauté poulette * Sauté de veau poulette

FOR FOUR PEOPLE

1¾ pounds boned veal shank
¾ cup oil
¼ teaspoon rosemary
¼ teaspoon thyme
1½ cups bouillon (veal or chicken)

2 egg yolks
1 lemon
1 tablespoon chopped parsley
salt and pepper

Have the meat cut for stew.

Heat the oil in a heavy pan. Brown the veal lightly in the oil. Add the rosemary and thyme and the bouillon. Season with salt and pepper. Cover and simmer 1½ hours.

If the meat is tender when you insert the tip of a knife, it is cooked. Beat the egg yolks with lemon juice and parsley. Add the mixture slowly to the meat but do not let the sauce boil. Put the meat in a heated platter. Pour the sauce over it. Serve with braised endive.

Veal sauté mapie * Sauté de veau mapie

FOR FOUR PEOPLE

1¾ pounds shoulder of veal
6 tablespoons butter
6 slices bacon
½ teaspoon ginger

¾ cup dry vermouth
¾ cup bouillon
4 artichoke bottoms
salt and pepper

Have the meat cut for stew meat. Brown it in 3 tablespoons of butter and at the same time fry the bacon in another pan until half cooked. Add the bacon to the veal. Add the ginger, a very little salt, some pepper, the vermouth and the bouillon. Cover and simmer 1½ hours.

Boil artichokes in salted water until the outer leaves can be pulled off easily. For this recipe you will use only the bottoms. Cut the bottoms in slices and brown them lightly in 3 tablespoons of butter.

Taste the veal for seasoning and add salt and pepper if necessary. Place in a warm dish and garnish with the artichokes.

Veal roger * Veau roger

FOR SIX PEOPLE

2¾ pounds of shoulder of veal
3 large onions
1 clove garlic (optional)
6 ounces fat bacon (in a piece)
4 tablespoons diced lard

4 tablespoons paprika
1 cup dry white wine
¾ cup heavy cream
cayenne
salt and pepper

Order the meat cut in large pieces as for stew.

Chop the onions, garlic, and bacon rather coarsely. Heat the lard in a heavy pan until it boils. Sauté the chopped ingredients in the hot lard until golden. Sprinkle with the paprika. Stir well and add the white wine and enough hot water to almost cover the meat. Season with salt and pepper and a dash of cayenne. Cover, lower the heat, and simmer 1½ hours.

Prick the meat with the point of a knife to be sure it is very tender. If the sauce is very thin, remove the cover and boil it down a little.

Then 3 minutes before serving, add the cream. Mix well, taste for seasoning. Heat but do not let the sauce boil.

Serve with boiled rice, potatoes, or green vegetables.

Veal sauté from the hill country
Sauté de veau de la colline

FOR FOUR PEOPLE

1¾ pounds breast of veal
¾ cup olive oil
3 ounces fat bacon (in a piece)
2 onions
1 clove garlic
1½ cups rosé wine

large pinch *orégano*
½ teaspoon powdered basil
6-8 tomatoes
½ cup pitted black olives
salt and pepper

Order the veal cut in squares.

Heat the olive oil in a deep frying pan.

Dice the bacon and chop the onions and garlic quite fine. Add these and the veal to the oil at the same time and sauté until golden. Add the wine, *orégano,* and basil. Sprinkle with salt and pepper. Cover and simmer 1 hour.

Add the tomatoes, which have been peeled, halved, seeded, and diced. Continue to cook without the cover for 30 minutes longer. About 5 minutes before serving, taste for seasoning and add the olives. (Use the imported variety if possible.—*Ed.*)

Serve with zucchini that have been diced, boiled 5 minutes, and then sautéed in oil.

Veal sauté with celery * Sauté de veau au céleri

FOR SIX PEOPLE

2 ½ pound breast of veal
1 large celery heart
6 tablespoons butter

1 ½ cups dry white wine
juice of ½ lemon
salt and pepper

Order the veal cut in large pieces.

Wash the celery and cut it into ¾-inch pieces. Boil in salted water for 10 minutes, drain.

Heat 5 tablespoons of the butter without browning in a heavy pan and sauté the veal until yellow on all sides. Add the celery and 1 cup of wine. Sprinkle with salt and pepper. Cover and simmer 1 ½ hours.

Put the veal and celery in a serving dish. Pour ½ cup of wine into the pan and stir with a fork to loosen the juices. Add a tablespoon of butter and the juice of ½ lemon and cook the sauce for 5 minutes. Pour this over the meat and serve with fried potatoes.

Bohemian veal sauté * Sauté de veau bohémienne

FOR FOUR PEOPLE

2 pounds veal riblets and
   breast of veal
2 ½ tablespoons oil
5 tablespoons butter
6 tablespoons dry white wine
1 pound (3-4) tomatoes

10 small onions
1 pound fresh or canned chestnuts
4 link sausages
juice of 1 lemon
salt and pepper

Have the meat cut for stew. Sauté in the oil and 3 tablespoons of the butter in a heavy pan until well browned on all sides. Pour off a little of the fat and add the wine. Season well with salt and pepper. Cover, reduce the heat, and simmer 1 ½ hours.

Meanwhile, cut the tomatoes in small pieces; peel and boil the onions in salted water just until tender; drain and sauté lightly in 1 tablespoon of butter; boil the chestnuts 25 minutes and peel them or use the canned variety (unsweetened); sauté the sausages in a tablespoon of butter.

Remove the meat. Boil down the liquid to about half its original quantity. Put back the meat and add the tomatoes, onions, chestnuts, and sausages. Cook for 5 minutes. Taste for seasoning, adding more salt and pepper, if necessary. Cook 15 minutes longer. Sprinkle with lemon juice. In France, this is served with wild mushrooms called *girolles*.

Veal chaud-froid * Chaud-froid de veau

FOR EIGHT PEOPLE

This excellent aspic dish is used as a first course or as a main dish for a summer meal. The use of a calf's foot makes a jellied broth that is very different from that made with artificial gelatine. The knowledge of this difference separates amateurs from connoisseurs.

2½-pound round of veal roast	4 teaspoons flour
10 tablespoons butter	2 egg yolks
1½ cups warm bouillon or water	⅔ cup heavy cream
1 calf's foot*	10 ounces mushrooms
2-3 ounces pork skin*	salt and pepper

Order the roast cut from the round about 3 to 4 inches in diameter and tied tightly. Heat 6 tablespoons of the butter in a heavy casserole. Brown the roast on all sides. Sprinkle with salt and pepper. Add the bouillon, calf's foot, and pork skin. Cover and cook 2 to 2½ hours, depending on the thickness of the roast. Remove the meat from the casserole and let it cool completely. Strain the sauce through a strainer lined with a cold damp dish towel.

Wash and trim the mushrooms and put them through a food grinder or chop quite fine. Cook them without water in a small skillet for 3 minutes so that they will render their water.

Heat 3 tablespoons of butter in a small saucepan and add the flour. Add 2 cups of the strained and fat-free veal broth. Stir until the sauce begins to thicken. Remove from the fire and whisk in the eggs and cream. Taste for seasoning. Stir frequently while the sauce cools. Placing the pan in a bowl of ice will speed up the process.

Cut the cold veal in thin slices and spread with the mushrooms mixed with half the sauce. Put the roast back in its original form and place on a small platter. Pour the rest of the sauce over the roast and chill before serving.

---

*When calf's foot is not available, use a pig's foot. Substitute bacon rind, parboiled 5 minutes, for pork skin, if necessary. —*Ed.*

Veal with bacon * Veau au bacon

FOR SIX PEOPLE

2¼-pound round of veal roast
2 carrots, grated
2 onions, chopped fine
3 tablespoons butter
¾ cup bouillon
2 sprigs parsley

10 tarragon leaves
12 slices Canadian bacon
¾ cup heavy cream
¼ cup grated Gruyère cheese
salt and pepper

Order the round tied.

Prepare the vegetables and sauté them in the butter in a casserole or heavy pan over a moderate heat. Add the meat and brown that lightly on all sides. Season with salt and pepper and add the bouillon, parsley, and tarragon. Cover and simmer 2 hours. Remove from casserole. Let the meat cool.

Cut the meat in 12 slices. Between the slices slide a thin slice of Canadian bacon. Retie the roast, put it back in the pan, and cook 1 hour longer. Place the meat on a heatproof serving platter. Remove the string. Strain the sauce over the meat. Pour the cream over the sauce. Sprinkle with the grated cheese and brown in a hot oven.

Loin of veal gendarme * Longe de veau gendarme

FOR TEN TO TWELVE PEOPLE

5-pound boned loin of veal
3 ounces bacon
3 ounces pickled beef tongue
3 carrots
2 large onions
6 tablespoons butter

1½ cups dry white wine
1½ cups bouillon
1 calf's foot
bouquet garni (thyme, bay leaf, parsley)
salt and pepper

Most American butchers will bone, roll, and tie the meat, but few will know how to lard with bacon and beef tongue. Cut the pieces of bacon and the tongue in long strips. Lard the veal with the strips (page 311).

Peel and cut the carrots in thin slices. Peel and chop the onions. Heat the butter in a deep casserole or pan. Brown the meat lightly, along with the carrots and onions. Do not let them burn. Turn the meat frequently.

Add the white wine, bouillon, salt, pepper, the calf's foot, and the *bouquet garni*. Cover and simmer 2 hours. (Substitute ½ pig's foot, if necessary.—*Ed.*)

Remove the meat from the sauce. Trim off the ends to give it a good shape and place in a deep serving platter. Pass the sauce through a strainer lined with a cold damp dish towel. Reheat quickly and pour it over the meat.

Baked shoulder of veal with bananas
Epaule de veau rôtie aux bananes

FOR FIVE PEOPLE

1¾-pound veal shoulder clot
3 tablespoons butter
¼ teaspoon anise seeds
¾ cup bouillon

¾ cup white wine
5 very ripe bananas
salt and pepper

Order the veal boned and tied for roasting.

Heat the butter in a deep fireproof casserole. Brown the roast on all sides. Sprinkle with the anise, salt, and pepper. Cover and braise 1 hour at 300° F., spooning 3 to 4 tablespoons of a combination of the bouillon and white wine over the roast from time to time.

Remove the roast to a heated platter. Cut the bananas in slices and heat them 2 minutes in the sauce, which should be fairly concentrated. Meanwhile, slice the roast, surround with the bananas, and pour the sauce over everything. Serve very hot with boiled rice.

Breast of veal stuffed with rice and pistachios
Poitrine de veau farcie au riz et pistaches

FOR SIX PEOPLE

½ cup rice
pinch of saffron *or*
1 tablespoon turmeric powder
1 cup (5 ounces) diced ham
3 tomatoes
½ cup pistachio nuts

2 tablespoons chopped parsley
1 egg
1 veal breast with pocket
6 tablespoons oil
salt and pepper

Boil the rice 12 minutes or until just tender in 4 cups of boiling salted water to which a pinch of saffron or the turmeric has been added. Drain.

Dice the ham. Peel the tomatoes, press out the seeds, and dice them. Add these, the nuts, and the parsley to the rice and mix well, binding with the raw egg. Season with salt and pepper.

Fill the pocket of the veal breast with the mixture and sew the opening up tightly.

Heat the oil in a deep casserole or heavy pan. Brown the meat on all sides. Season with salt and pepper and cover. Cook very slowly for 1 hour.

Serve hot with its own juices for gravy or serve cold with a mayonnaise seasoned with lemon juices and *fines herbes*.

Cold veal with tuna * Veau froid au thon

FOR SIX PEOPLE

2-pound round of veal roast
1 can oil-packed tuna fish
1 small can anchovy fillets
1 onion
2½ cups dry white wine

6 tablespoons oil
juice of 2 lemons
4 teaspoons chopped pickle
salt and pepper

Order the veal tied tightly.

Put the veal in a *small* casserole or pan. Flake the tuna directly into the casserole. Add the anchovy fillets, cut in small pieces, the onion, peeled and sliced thin, salt, and pepper. Cover with the white wine. Cover and cook over a low flame for 2 hours.

Remove the veal to small serving dish. Strain the rest through a food mill to give a purée. (The same may be accomplished in a blender.—*Ed.*) Mix with the oil and the juice of 2 lemons. Pour this over the meat and sprinkle with the pickles. Cover and keep in a cool place for 24 hours.

Roast shoulder of veal * Epaule de veau rôtie

FOR SIX PEOPLE

2½-pound veal shoulder clot
3 tablespoons oil
juice of ½ lemon

1 teaspoon anchovy paste
salt and pepper

Order the shoulder boned, rolled, and wrapped in a paper-thin covering of pork fat. The roast should be tightly tied. Roast in 400° F. oven, allowing 25 minutes per pound.

Combine the oil, lemon juice, and anchovy paste in a small bowl. Season very lightly with salt but generously with black pepper. Spoon this over the roast in small quantities during the cooking.

Alsatian breast of veal
Poitrine de veau à l'alsacienne

FOR SIX PEOPLE

1 veal breast
½ pound ground raw veal
½ pound sausage meat

8 tablespoons butter
1 egg
⅛ teaspoon powdered cloves

4 onions	¼ teaspoon nutmeg
6 carrots	⅛ teaspoon allspice
2 white turnips	salt and pepper

Order from your butcher the breast of veal with pocket, ground veal from the neck, and lean sausage meat.

Peel the vegetables and cut them into thin match sticks. Put all the vegetables in a heavy saucepan with 2 tablespoons of the butter for 1 hour over a very low heat. Combine with the ground veal, sausage meat, raw egg, spices, salt, and pepper and mix very well. Put the stuffing in the pocket of the breast and sew up the opening.

Heat 6 tablespoons of butter in a deep casserole or heavy pan. Brown the meat on both sides. Reduce the heat, cover, and cook 2 hours or place in a 300° F. oven.

When serving this as a leftover, place slices of the meat on very hot sauerkraut and serve with dry white wine.

Filet mignon of veal au gratin
Noisettes de veau gratinées

FOR EIGHT PEOPLE

8 *filets mignons* of veal	¾ cup soft breadcrumbs
8 onions	2 cups white wine
10 tablespoons butter	cayenne
1¼ cups grated Gruyère cheese	salt and pepper

The *filet mignons* are small steaks cut from the boned sirloin 1½ inches thick and weighing approximately ¼ pound each.

Peel and slice the onions very thin. Heat the butter in a deep casserole or heavy pot and sauté the onions over a moderate heat until they are golden and tender. Spread the onions smooth in the bottom of the casserole and place the *filets mignons* on the onions. On each one place two heaping tablespoons of grated cheese and a heaping tablespoon of soft breadcrumbs. Season each steak with salt, pepper, and a dash of cayenne. Sprinkle with the white wine. Cover the casserole tightly. Bake 4 hours at 275° F. Do not baste, but watch to be sure the meat does not become too dry. Add a little water or wine if necessary.

Mixed grill on skewers * Mixed grill de maïs

FOR FOUR PEOPLE

4 fresh ears of corn	2 slices calf's liver
2 French-cut veal cutlets	butter

4 large link sausages   salt and pepper
4 thick slices bacon

Husk the corn and slice into 1-inch rounds. Cut all the meats into pieces and thread everything on small skewers, alternating pieces of meat with pieces of corn.

Broil for 10 minutes, turning often. Season with salt and pepper and serve with melted butter.

Grenadins of veal nemours
Grenadins de veau nemours

FOR SIX PEOPLE

Grenadins *are small thick (¾ to 1 inch) slices cut on the bias like an* escalope *from the top of the round or cut straight from the boned loin of veal.—Ed.*

6 *grenadins*   2 cups bouillon
3 ounces bacon   10 ounces mushrooms
3 ounces fresh pork rind   3-4 potatoes
1 onion, chopped fine   butter
1 carrot, grated   salt and pepper
6 tablespoons dry white wine

Order *grenadins* weighing 4 to 5 ounces each.

Dice the bacon and pork skin. (If it is impossible to get fresh pork rind, buy 6 ounces fat bacon including the rind and parboil it 5 minutes.—*Ed.*) Heat the dice in shallow casserole to render some fat. Add the chopped onion and grated carrot. Sauté over a low heat for a few moments. Spread the vegetables smooth in the pan and place the meat on the vegetables. Cook slowly until lightly browned on both sides. Add the wine and cook until evaporated. Add 6 tablespoons of bouillon and let that evaporate also. Add the rest of the bouillon. Sprinkle with salt and pepper. Cover and cook in 350° F. oven for 1½ hours, basting often. Ten minutes before serving, remove the cover to brown the meat.

Wash, trim, and slice the mushrooms. Peel and slice the potatoes. Sauté the mushrooms and potatoes in butter, using separate skillets. Place the meat on a heated platter. Strain the sauce over the meat and garnish with the mushrooms and potatoes.

Blanquette of veal * Blanquette de veau

FOR FOUR PEOPLE

This is a classic recipe and is absolutely delicious because of its creamy and subtly flavored sauce.

1 pound shoulder of veal	*bouquet garni* (bay leaf, thyme, parsley)
1 pound breast of veal	4 teaspoons flour
1 carrot	2 egg yolks
1 onion	½ cup heavy cream
6 tablespoons butter	juice of 1 lemon
1 veal bone	salt and pepper

Have the meat cut in 8 pieces. I advise the two cuts of veal, because experience has taught me that some like the lean pieces, whereas others like the fatter morsels.

Cut the carrots in pieces and the onion in quarters. Over a low heat, melt 3 tablespoons of butter in a medium-sized casserole or pan. Without increasing the heat, add the veal. Cover and cook 10 minutes so that the meat will render some juice but will not color. Add enough boiling water to cover the meat—no more. Add the carrot, onion, veal bone, *bouquet garni* and a little salt. Cover and simmer 1½ hours.

Heat the rest of the butter in a small saucepan. Stir in the flour and add enough of the veal broth to make a thick sauce. Simmer 5 minutes.

Beat the egg yolks slightly, adding the cream and the juice of 1 lemon. Remove the sauce from the fire and whisk in the egg mixture. Season to taste. Replace on the heat to warm, but do not let the sauce boil.

Transfer the meat with a slotted spatula to a hot platter. Pour the sauce over the meat and serve with boiled rice.

Knuckle of veal à la provençale
Jarret de veau à la provençale

FOR SIX PEOPLE

1 large meaty veal knuckle or shank	1 large clove garlic
3 tablespoons flour	¾ cup bouillon
3 tablespoons lard	*bouquet garni* (thyme, bay leaf, sage)
4-5 medium-sized onions	juice of 1 lemon
¾ cup dry white wine	salt and pepper
6 medium-sized tomatoes	

Ask the butcher to saw the knuckle into 6 slices.

Sprinkle the knuckle with salt, with pepper, and then with flour. Heat the lard in a deep casserole or pan and brown the knuckle well, turning the pieces frequently. Reduce the heat and add the onions, chopped very fine. Cook until the onions are pale yellow and add the wine. Cook 5 minutes.

Peel the tomatoes, halve them, and press out the seeds. Add them, the garlic, peeled and crushed, the bouillon, and the *bouquet garni*. Cover and cook slowly on top of the stove or in the oven (300° F.) for 1½ hours. Just before serving, add the juice of 1 lemon. Taste for seasoning.

Veal on skewers with tagliatelli
Brochettes de veau aux tagliatelles

FOR SIX PEOPLE

1½ pounds round of veal
thyme
4-5 tomatoes

½ pound thin noodles
salt and pepper

Order the veal cut into 24 pieces.

Sprinkle the veal with powdered thyme. Cut the tomatoes into 24 pieces.

Alternate the veal and tomatoes on small skewers. Broil or fry them for 30 minutes, turning frequently. Season with salt and pepper.

Boil the *tagliatelli* (thin noodles) in a large kettle of boiling salted water for 3 to 5 minutes or just until tender, stirring occasionally with a fork so that they will not stick together. Drain the noodles thoroughly and place them on a heated platter. Place the skewers on the noodles and pour the juice from the pan over everything.

Veal riblets à la bourgeoise
Tendrons de veau à la bourgeoise

FOR SIX PEOPLE

Riblets (tendrons) *are crosscuts of the middle breast of veal, from which the flank and bone have been removed. They are cut in pieces for serving.—Ed.*

8 veal riblets
3 tablespoons butter
4 teaspoons oil
1 large onion
1 large carrot
3 ounces fat salt pork
2 cups dry white wine
⅔ cup bouillon or water
bouquet garni (thyme, bay leaf, parsley)

Garnish:
20 tiny onions
20 very small carrots
3 tablespoons butter
1 teaspoon sugar
salt and pepper

Riblets: Order the riblets cut 1½ inches thick. Heat 3 tablespoons of the butter and the oil in a shallow casserole or pan. Brown the riblets well on both sides.

At the same time, chop the onion and grate the carrot. Dice the salt pork and throw into boiling water for 3 minutes. Drain.

When the riblets are browned, season with salt and pepper. Add the white wine, stirring with a wooden spoon to mix in the juices adhering to the pan. Boil down the wine a few moments. Add the bouillon or hot water, the onion, the carrot, the parboiled fat, and the *bouquet garni.* Cover and simmer 1½ hours.

Garnish: Thirty minutes before serving, put the tiny onions and carrots in separate saucepans. Barely cover the vegetables with cold water and add 3 tablespoons of butter, a pinch of sugar, and a pinch of salt to each pan. Boil down slowly without covers until the water has evaporated and the vegetables are glazed.

Place the riblets on a heated platter. Surround with the vegetables. Spoon off as much fat as possible from the sauce. Season highly with salt and pepper and strain the sauce over the meat. Serve with boiled or steamed potatoes.

Veal riblets à l'orientale
Tendrons de veau à l'orientale

FOR FOUR PEOPLE

2 pounds veal riblets (see preceding recipe)	4 small eggplant
6 tablespoons butter	1½ cups boiled rice
3 teaspoons curry powder	soft breadcrumbs
¾ cup white wine or bouillon	salt and pepper

Dip the veal riblets, cut in serving pieces, in flour. Heat 3 tablespoons of the butter in a deep skillet. Brown the riblets on all sides. Add the curry and mix well with a wooden spoon. Season with salt and pepper. Add ¼ cup of wine or bouillon. Lower the heat to simmer. Cover and cook for 1 hour adding a little liquid when necessary. The secret is not to have an excess of liquid but also not to let the riblets get dry. Test the meat by piercing with a fork; it should be tender and the liquid that comes out should be colorless.

At the same time, boil the eggplant in salted water 10 to 15 minutes or just until tender. Remove from the water and split each one down the middle. Remove the center part of each half, leaving a ½ inch shell and dice the flesh. Mix with the rice and season well. Stuff the eggplant and sprinkle well with breadcrumbs and with melted butter. Bake 30 minutes at 350° F.

Place the riblets on a heated platter. Surround with the eggplant. Add a little water to the riblet pan, scraping the juices from the bottom of the pan with a fork. Pour the sauce over the meat.

Almond veal balls * Boulettes de veau aux amandes

FOR FOUR PEOPLE

½ pound (1¼ cups) ground cooked
   veal
1 egg
½ cup ground almonds
1½ cups water

1 teaspoon chopped parsley
3 tablespoons oil
juice of 1 lemon
salt and pepper

Grind veal that is completely free of skin or muscle.

Beat the egg until well blended and add the meat. Season with salt and pepper and form the mixture into small balls the size of pullet eggs.

Put the almonds, water, and parsley in a small saucepan and bring to boil. Add salt, pepper, oil, and the little balls. These should be covered with the liquid. Reduce the heat, cover, and simmer very gently for 2 hours. Serve very hot, sprinkled with the juice of the lemon.

Lamb

In France, lamb is sold as *agneau de lait* (suckling lamb), *agneau* (young lamb), or *mouton* (lamb). The suckling lamb, killed before it is weaned, is what Americans call Early Spring Lamb or Easter Lamb. Except at specialty shops and in Greek and Jewish markets near religious holidays, small lambs of this size are very hard to find in America. They are usually cooked whole on a spit, or the "baron"—the saddle and two legs—is roasted in one piece. *Agneau* corresponds to a young spring lamb weighing from twenty to thirty pounds. A large animal is called a *mouton,* but this would be called Spring Lamb in America and is the size most commonly found in the markets. Over 90 per cent of lamb sold in the United States is sold as spring lamb, and most of it, unfortunately, is larger than what is considered ideal in France, so that certain adaptations must be made in the cutting of the meat.

Chops *(côtelettes)* are cut in pretty much the same way both sides of the Atlantic.

If a recipe calls for a 4-to-5-pound leg of lamb, and the butcher only has legs weighing 6 to 7 pounds, ask him to cut off some steaks before preparing the leg for roasting. In France, a bit of the shank bone is left on to serve as a kind of handle. Frenchmen like lamb rare. Some Americans want to increase the cooking time.

A spring lamb shoulder usually weighs 5 to 6 pounds, which is more than these recipes require. A cooperative butcher will sell you the shank end of the shoulder of the proper weight, or if you are obliged to buy the entire piece, you can slice off some pieces for a *ragoût* and still have the required cut for stuffing or braising or boiling.

Shoulder of lamb cannot be roasted satisfactorily because of its dry, fibrous quality. If it is to be oven-cooked, it should be stuffed, because the stuffing yields juices that the meat absorbs. This cut is ideal for braising. The shoulder should always be boned regardles of the way it is to be cooked.

Young kid can be cooked in the same way lamb is.

Roast lamb with shell beans ∗ *Gigot rôti aux haricots*

FOR TEN PEOPLE

It is a long-standing tradition that says that lamb must be seasoned with garlic. If the flavor pleases you, honor the tradition by inserting small slivers of garlic, but do so with care because the fine flavor of lamb should not be hidden.

1 small leg of lamb

butter

10 pounds fresh shell beans

2 tablespoons chopped parsley

juice of 1 lemon

salt and pepper

Spread 6 tablespoons of butter over the lamb and sprinkle with black pepper. Roast in a 425° F. oven, allowing 9 to 10 minutes per pound. Put a little boiling water in the roasting pan. Salt the juice that comes from the roast and baste frequently with it.

Beans: Count on 1 pound of unshelled beans per person. Shell them and start cooking them in cold water with 1½ tablespoons of butter for each pound of beans. Skim the matter that floats to the surface. Simmer slowly, and halfway through the cooking, add a cup of cool water. When the beans are tender, drain them. Melt 6 tablespoons of butter in a deep pan. Add the parsley and the cooked beans. Season with salt and pepper and cook until the butter has permeated the beans. Just before serving, season with lemon juice.

Flageolets, or dried white beans, can be soaked, cooked, and served in the same way, or you may serve a mixture of fresh green beans and shell beans.

Summer lamb (cold) * Gigot d'été

FOR EIGHT PEOPLE

1 small leg of lamb (4-5 pounds)

4 paper-thin slices of salt pork

2 carrots

2 onions

2 shallots

1 clove garlic

½ calf's foot

butter

salt and pepper

Ask the butcher to bone the leg but to leave a little of the shank intact. The leg meat should be tied tightly. Ask him also to supply you with 4 wide strips of salt pork. If this is not possible, buy several thin strips—enough to line the pan and to cover the lamb. Wash the strips to remove excess salt. Dry well.

With the pork strips line a deep, heavy pan large enough to hold the lamb. Peel the carrots and cut them into thin rounds and place them on the fat. Pass the onions, shallots, and garlic through a *moulinette,* or chop them very fine. Put these on top of the carrots. Sprinkle with salt and pepper.

Place the lamb on the vegetables, add the calf's foot, and cover with strips of salt pork. (Substitute ½ pig's foot if calf's foot is not available.—*Ed.*) Spread a piece of heavy paper with butter and place it under the pan cover, which is then put in place. The dish must be hermetically sealed. Cook in a 250° F. oven for 6 hours.

Remove the lamb, cut it in slices, and pour over the pan juices and vegetables, which have been forced through a strainer. Cool and then refrigerate for several hours.

Montaigue roast lamb * Gigot montaigu

FOR EIGHT PEOPLE

1 pound dry white beans
2 pounds (8-10) onions
10 tablespoons butter
2 pounds (6-8) potatoes

1 small leg of lamb (3½-4 pounds)
¾ cup bouillon
salt and pepper

Soak the beans at least 3 hours. Bring to a boil in cold salt water and cook at least 1 hour. The length of cooking will vary with the age of the bean. Watch it carefully.

Peel the onions and cut them in thin slices. Sauté them gently in 3 tablespoons of butter.

Peel the potatoes and cut them in thin slices also.

In a large baking dish spread half of the sautéed onions. Cover with a good layer of cooked beans and a layer of raw potatoes. Dot liberally with butter and sprinkle with salt and pepper. Repeat the process.

Put the lamb well coated with butter on the vegetables. Roast 1 hour at 400° F. Baste several times during the cooking with hot bouillon. Season the meat with salt and pepper at the end of cooking.

Leg of baby lamb in pastry
Gigot d'agneau en croûte

FOR SIX PEOPLE

1 small boned baby leg of lamb*
3 or 4 lamb kidneys
3 tablespoons butter
1 teaspoon chopped herbs (rosemary, sage, thyme, basil, bay leaf)

Flaky Pastry (page 643)
1 egg yolk
salt and pepper

Remove all the fat from the kidneys and split them in half. Sauté the kidneys in hot butter for 3 minutes and sprinkle them with salt and pepper. Place the kidneys in the cavity and sprinkle with chopped herbs. Tie the roast firmly and sprinkle with salt and pepper. Roast in a very hot oven (450° F.), allowing 10 minutes to the pound. Turn the meat occasionally. Remove and let cool to lukewarm.

*This recipe calls for a leg of lamb weighing 2 pounds. Because this is difficult to find in American markets, ask the butcher either to split a small leg or better yet, to saw off the shank end of a 5- to 6-pound leg to give you a 3½-pound roast. In either case, the exterior bone should be properly trimmed but left intact; the interior bone and gland should be removed. Excellent steaks can be cut from the rest of the leg.—Ed.

At the same time—or before—make the pastry, and after the final turns, roll out the pastry ¼ inch thick and envelop the meat with an overlap of ½ inch. Moisten the edges with water to make a proper seal. Paint the pastry with an egg yolk mixed with a teaspoon of water. Bake 15 minutes at 450° F. Serve hot with au gratin potatoes or cold with a garnish of tomatoes, stuffed with a mixture of boiled rice, chopped meat, and herbs.

Breton leg of lamb * Gigot à la bretonne

FOR EIGHT PEOPLE

1 small leg of lamb (4-5 pounds)	6 ounces lean bacon (in one piece)
1 pound dried white beans	¾ cup heavy cream
1 carrot	10 tablespoons butter
1 onion	soft breadcrumbs
1 clove	salt and pepper
bouquet garni (thyme, parsley, bay leaf)	

Order the leg with a part of the shank left on.

Soak the beans overnight. Drain and place in a pan of cold salted water. Add the carrot, the onion stuck with the clove, and the bouquet garni. Cook until tender. Drain and remove the bouquet garni, carrot, and onion. Season with salt and pepper.

Cut the bacon into small dice and brown them in a hot skillet. Drain and add to the beans, along with the cream and 5 tablespoons of butter. Place in a shallow baking dish. Cover with soft breadcrumbs and dot with pieces of butter. Bake about 15 minutes.

Spread the gigot with butter and roast at 400° F., allowing 12 minutes per pound and timing it to be ready when the beans are cooked. Baste frequently with water or bouillon. Sprinkle with salt and pepper at the end of the roasting.

The roast may be served in the same dish with the beans, but the sauce, which is the juice coming from the roast, is served in a separate bowl.

Roast leg of baby lamb à la normande
Gigot d'agneau à la normande

FOR SIX PEOPLE

1 small leg of lamb	1½ cups heavy cream
8 tablespoons butter	2 teaspoons flour
¼ cup bouillon	salt and pepper
3 tablespoons Calvados, or apple brandy	

Unless a small leg of lamb weighing 2½ to 3½ pounds is available, order a small leg of lamb and have two or three steaks cut off, leaving a 3½ pound roast. See preceding recipe.

Sprinkle the lamb with pepper. Place it in a shallow roasting pan in which 5 tablespoons of butter have been melted. Roast at 15 minutes per pound at 300° F., turning the roast often, basting the meat each time with the drippings in the pan. Halfway through the cooking, sprinkle with salt. Place the roast in a shallow ovenproof platter. Keep warm.

Pour the bouillon and Calvados into the pan and bring to a boil on top of the stove, scraping the bottom of the pan with a fork. Simmer 3 minutes.

Cream the remaining 3 tablespoons of butter with the flour and add that in small pieces to the sauce, stirring constantly. Add the cream and simmer a few moments. Pour the sauce over the lamb and cook in the oven, basting constantly with the sauce. Serve with fresh peas.

Suckling lamb on a spit * Agneau grillé à la broche

FOR EIGHT TO TEN PEOPLE

A suckling lamb is not found in many American markets, but around Easter time it is worth hunting for. The lamb should be well trimmed and cleaned. Sprinkle the interior with a good handful of chopped herbs—thyme, bay leaf, chervil, and tarragon—and salt and pepper. If you like the flavor of garlic, insert little slivers of it all over the meat. Place the lamb on a spit over a dripping pan. Do not brush the animal with fat, but once the fat begins to drop into the dripping pan, baste frequently as the lamb turns. Do not salt until the lamb is half cooked.

The lamb should be cooked over hot coals. The traditional source of heat is the wood of fruit trees, which gives a strong steady heat. Cook 40 minutes. The French way to test the lamb is to insert a needle into the thickest part and then to touch it to your lips. If the needle feels warm, the meat is rare; if the needle feels hot, it is well cooked; if it is cold, the meat is not sufficiently cooked.

To carve the lamb: Begin by removing the two legs and the two shoulders. If the lamb is sufficiently cooked, this is an easy process. Separate the chops from the saddle (lower back) with a cleaver, and carve the saddle like a duck, with slices cut on the bias.

Serve the lamb with chestnuts that have been peeled, boiled until three quarters done, and roasted in the dripping pan for the final 20 minutes the lamb is cooked. Allow 4 to 5 chestnuts per person.

Seven-hour leg of lamb * Gigot de sept heures

FOR EIGHT PEOPLE

Here is a marvelous recipe given to me by the actress Charlotte Lyses, who was the wife of the great author-actor Sacha Guitry. It is long in cooking but easy to make because it needs little attention.

1 small leg of lamb (4-5 pounds)	10 large onions
½ veal knuckle	3 tablespoons butter
10 tablespoons oil	10 tomatoes
4½ cups hot beef bouillon	salt and pepper
cayenne	

Ask the butcher to remove the interior bone and gland of the leg but to leave a little of the shank bone intact. Have it tied. Buy a good meaty knuckle.

Heat the oil in a Dutch oven or heavy pan, and when it is very hot, brown the lamb on all sides. Pour the hot bouillon over the meat. Season with salt, pepper, and a dash of cayenne. As soon as the bouillon boils, reduce the heat, cover, and simmer 4 hours.

Place the knuckle in a deep dish with a little hot water. Simmer uncovered for 3 hours, adding hot water when necessary.

Peel the onions and cut them in large pieces. Sauté them in butter until golden. Peel and quarter the tomatoes.

When the lamb has cooked 4 hours, add the knuckle, the onions, and the raw tomatoes. Cover and simmer 3 hours. Taste occasionally for seasoning. If the sauce is too liquid, remove the cover and boil down the sauce over a high flame.

Remove the lamb carefully to a heated platter. The knuckle is not served, and can be used for another meal. Ladle the sauce, which should be quite thick and not strained, around the meat. Serve with rice, vermicelli, or a purée of white beans.

Leg of lamb, brown onion sauce
Gigot sauce soubise brune

FOR SIX PEOPLE

1 small leg of lamb (4-5 pounds)	1½ tablespoons flour
8-10 young carrots (1 pound)	Caramel (page 579)
2-3 white turnips (1 pound)	2 sugar lumps
8-10 onions (2 pounds)	salt and pepper
allspice	
1½ tablespoons butter	

Order the leg with the interior bone and gland removed but the shank bone left intact. Tie well.

Place the lamb in a deep, heavy kettle. Cover with boiling water. Add the carrots, the turnips, and 3 of the onions, all of which have been peeled and cut in pieces. Season with salt, pepper, and a little allspice.

Peel the rest of the onions and chop them very fine or grind them through the meat chopper. Place them in a pan without water. Cover and steam. Make a thin mixture by heating butter with the flour and adding ¾ cup of the lamb broth, bringing it to a boil but not letting it thicken. At the same time, make the caramel with the sugar. Combine the onions, *roux,* and caramel. Taste for seasoning with salt and pepper.

Carve the lamb and place it on a very hot platter. Pour the onion sauce over the meat.

Marinated leg of lamb with apples, wine sauce
Gigot mariné aux pommes, sauce au vin

FOR EIGHT PEOPLE

1 small leg of lamb (4 pounds)	*Sauce:*
1 quart red Burgundy	6 shallots
1 onion	6 onions
1 carrot	1 medium-sized carrot
2 cloves garlic, crushed	1 cup red wine vinegar
bouquet garni (thyme, bay leaf, parsley, rosemary)	thyme, bay leaf, cayenne
	2 tablespoon butter
1 teaspoon peppercorns	1½ tablespoons flour
5 tablespoons butter	1 sugar lump
8 cooking apples	4 teaspoons green chartreuse liqueur
juice of 1 lemon	salt

Lamb: Ask the butcher to bone the leg but to leave a small piece of the shank intact. The meat should be larded and rolled and tied. Probably 2 to 3 steaks will have to be cut off to give a leg of the proper size.

In order not to waste wine, place the lamb in a casserole that will just hold the meat. The meat must be barely covered by the marinade. Peel and slice thin the onion and carrot. Add them, the garlic, the *bouquet garni,* salt, and a teaspoon of peppercorns. Let this marinate 2 or 3 days, turning the meat morning and evening.

Remove the meat from the marinade and wipe it dry. Paint it well with butter and roast in a 400° F. oven, allowing 12 minutes to a pound.

Peel and core the apples. Cook 3 minutes in boiling water to which the juice of a lemon has been added. Drain and put the apples in a buttered baking dish. Sprinkle with a little water and cook in a slow oven just until tender.

Sauce: Peel and chop the shallots, onions, and carrot. Simmer them 1 hour in the vinegar, with a pinch of thyme, the bay leaf, and a little cayenne. Force the mixture through a strainer or food mill (or spin in the blender.—*Ed.*) Heat the butter and stir in the flour. Slowly add 1 cup of the marinade, stirring with a wooden spoon. Add the purée and the sugar. Simmer 30 minutes. Add the char-treuse 10 minutes before the end of cooking.

Place the lamb on a heated platter. Surround with the apples. Pour a little of the sauce over the meat; serve the rest in a separate bowl.

Hunter's leg of lamb * Gigot des chasseurs

FOR SIX PEOPLE

1 small leg of lamb
1 quart dry white wine
2½ tablespoons oil
1 tablespoon red wine vinegar
2 carrots
2 shallots

1 clove
1 teaspoon peppercorns
rosemary, thyme, 2 bay leaves
5 tablespoons butter
salt and pepper

Ask the butcher for a leg of lamb weighing 3 to 4 pounds. To do this, he will probably have to cut off 2 or 3 steaks. Ask him to remove the interior bone and gland but to leave the shank intact. Ask him to lard the meat. If this is not possible, buy a ¼-pound piece of salt pork. Rinse and cut it into small strips. Cut little incisions in the meat and insert the salt pork pieces.

Put the meat in a non-metal deep dish large enough to hold the lamb. Add the wine, oil, vinegar, the carrots cut in rounds, the shallots finely chopped, the clove, peppercorns, 2 teaspoons of salt, ½ teaspoon each of rosemary and thyme and 2 bay leaves. Let this stand 4 days, turning the meat twice a day.

Remove the lamb from the marinade and wipe it dry. Spread it with butter and roast it in a 400° F. oven, allowing 12 minutes per pound. Baste often with the marinade. Place on a hot platter and serve the pan juices in a sauce bowl.

Serve with a purée of chestnuts and currant jelly.

Lamb shoulder with foie gras
Epaule de mouton au foie gras

FOR SIX PEOPLE

2-3 pounds boned lamb shoulder
1 can *foie gras* mousse
1 small can truffle peelings
½ cup soft breadcrumbs
½ cup milk

1 raw egg
5 tablespoons butter
4 teaspoons cognac
salt and pepper

Order the shoulder boned and prepared for stuffing.
Spread out the meat, skin side down.

In a bowl, combine the *foie gras* mousse, the truffle peelings, the breadcrumbs, which have been soaked in milk and squeezed dry, the egg, salt and pepper. Mix these ingredients thoroughly and spread them on the meat. Roll and tie securely.

Heat the butter in a heavy pan and brown the meat. Sprinkle with salt and pepper. Pour in the cognac and touch with a lighted match. Cook very slowly for 1½ hours, adding occasionally 1 or 2 tablespoons of hot water in order to moisten the meat. Serve with fresh spinach.

Stuffed shoulder of lamb à l'orientale
Epaule de mouton farcie à l'orientale

FOR SIX PEOPLE

3 pounds shoulder of lamb	cayenne
2 cups Curried Rice (page 457)	1 cup dry white wine
½ cup seedless raisins	3 tablespoons curry
1½ cups ground ham	6 tablespoons butter
1 egg	salt and pepper
2½ tablespoon oil	

Order the shoulder of lamb boned and ready for stuffing.

Combine the rice with the raisins, which have been soaked in water for several hours. Add the ham, raw egg, and oil. Mix well, season with salt, pepper, and a pinch of cayenne. Spread this stuffing on the meat. Roll up and tie well.

Heat the wine in a saucepan with the curry. Add a little salt, pepper, and cayenne.

Heat the butter in a heavy deep pan and brown the meat on all sides. Add the white wine. Reduce the heat and simmer slowly for 3 hours, turning the meat often. Pierce the meat with a pointed knife to see if it is tender. If not, continue cooking.

This may be served with a curried rice pilaff, to which you may add raisins and diced ham.

Salmon stuffed shoulder of lamb
Epaule d'agneau farcie au saumon

FOR FOUR PEOPLE

2-3 pounds boned lamb shoulder	sage
¼ pound lean lamb	butter
3 eggs	salt and pepper
1 small can salmon	

Order the lamb shoulder unrolled and ask the butcher to grind the extra meat.
Boil 2 of the eggs 15 minutes in salted water. Peel and chop.

Combine the ground meat, chopped eggs, and the salmon. Bind with a raw egg and season with a pinch of sage, salt, and pepper.

Put the stuffing in the middle of the shoulder. Roll and tie firmly. Spread butter over the meat, place in a buttered roasting pan, and roast 45-60 minutes at 400° F. depending on the weight of the shoulder.

Braised shoulder of lamb
Epaule de mouton braisée

FOR FOUR PEOPLE

2 pounds boned shoulder of lamb	4 medium-sized onions
3 tablespoons lard	3 potatoes
4-5 medium-sized carrots	salt and pepper

Order the shoulder boned, rolled, and tied.

Heat the lard in a deep heavy pan and brown the meat on all sides. Add the carrots and onions, cut in pieces, and add 1½ cups of water, seasoned with salt and pepper. Bring to the boiling point, cover, and simmer very slowly for 2 hours.

Peel and dice the potatoes and brown them.

Place the shoulder on a hot platter and surround with the vegetables. Pour the juice from the pan over the meat.

Shoulder of lamb with mustard
Epaule de mouton à la moutarde

FOR SIX PEOPLE

2½ pounds boned shoulder of lamb*	1 egg, slightly beaten
6 tablespoons butter	½ cup soft breadcrumbs
French mustard	salt and pepper
flour	

Ask the butcher to cut the lamb into cubes.

Heat half the butter in a heavy pan and brown the lamb cubes on all sides. When well browned, sprinkle them with salt and pepper and remove them from the pan to cool.

Spread the cold lamb pieces lightly with mustard. Coat them with flour and

*This is also made with breast of lamb.

dip them in the beaten egg and then in the breadcrumbs seasoned with salt and pepper.

Reheat the butter in the pan and cook the pieces of lamb in it for 10 minutes, stirring gently with a wooden spoon. Heat the rest of the butter in a saucepan.

Put the lamb on a heated serving platter. Pour over the melted butter. Serve with puréed potatoes.

Home style stuffed shoulder of lamb
Epaule de mouton farcie "comme chez soï"

FOR SIX PEOPLE

3-4 pounds shoulder of lamb
2 cups dry bread
1½ cups dry white wine
2 cups leftover chopped cooked meat
1 hard-cooked egg, chopped
4 ounces raw calf's liver, chopped
4 ounces cooked ham
1 clove garlic, minced

1 onion, chopped fine
2 teaspoons chopped parsley
½ teaspoon chopped tarragon
6 tablespoons lard
1 lump sugar
2 tablespoons tomato paste
salt and pepper

Order the shoulder boned and ready for stuffing. Place it on a working surface, skin side down.

Chop the bread coarsely. Soak it in a little of the wine. Squeeze it fairly dry and combine it with the meat, egg, liver, ham, garlic, and onion. Sprinkle with salt, pepper, parsley, and tarragon and mix well.

Spread the stuffing on the lamb. Fold in two, so that the long edges meet. Sew together with kitchen string and then tie with string, like a package.

In a deep heavy pan, heat the lard and brown the meat on both sides. Add the sugar lump and ½ cup of white wine. Sprinkle with salt and pepper. Reduce the heat and cook gently for 3 hours, basting often. Taste for seasoning and add the tomato paste. Cook 1 hour longer. Turn the meat from time to time.

Place on a heated platter. Remove as much grease as possible from the sauce and pour it over the meat. Be sure that your plates are very hot so that the sauce will not cool. Serve this meat with rice, puréed potatoes, green vegetables, or turnip purée.

Breaded lamb chops * Côtelettes de mouton panées

FOR FIVE PEOPLE

5 large loin lamb chops (¾ inch thick)
juice of 1 lemon
2½ tablespoons oil

thyme, bay leaf, rosemary, oregano
1 cup soft breadcrumbs
salt and pepper

Place the lamb chops in a shallow dish. Sprinkle with the lemon juice, 1½ tablespoons of oil, and a pinch each of the powdered herbs. Marinate for 1 hour.

Remove the chops from the marinade, dry them with toweling, and paint them with the rest of the oil. Sprinkle them with salt and pepper and dip them in the breadcrumbs. Broil or grill them with very high heat, turning them. Serve with a purée of fresh boiled peas.

Shoulder of lamb with garlic
Epaule de mouton à l'ail

FOR SIX PEOPLE

3-4 pounds shoulder of lamb	3 cloves garlic
pork fat strips	½ teaspoon chopped tarragon
6 tablespoons butter	2 teaspoons chopped parsley
1 lump sugar	1 teaspoon potato flour
5 large onions	salt and pepper
2 carrots	

Order a small shoulder of lamb, asking the butcher to leave on a little of the shank. The shoulder should be boned, larded, rolled, and tied. In this case, the larding is done by inserting about ten strips of fat pork. (If you use salt pork, wash it and parboil 5 minutes to remove excess salt.)

Heat the butter in a deep heavy pan. Brown the shoulder on all sides and add the sugar and ¾ cup hot water. Season highly with salt and pepper. Add the onions, peeled but left whole, and the carrots cut in slices, the garlic, tarragon, and the parsley. Lower the heat and simmer very gently for 5 hours.

Remove the meat to a heated platter. Remove the garlic. Pour the potato starch very slowly into the cooking liquid in the pan, stirring hard with a wire whisk. Strain some of the sauce over the meat and serve the rest in a separate bowl.

Broiled lamb steaks with thyme
Agneau grillé au thym

FOR FOUR PEOPLE

2 lamb steaks	4 tablespoons olive oil
1 clove garlic	3 tablespoons butter
thyme	salt and pepper

Order the steaks cut from the leg where the leg meets the body. They should be about ¾ inch thick and weigh approximately 10 ounces each. Ask the butcher to bone and trim them.

Cut a garlic clove in two and rub the steaks with it so that there will be just a suggestion of the flavor. Sprinkle with the thyme and press the herbs into the flesh with your fingers. Paint both sides with olive oil. Grill or broil 5 minutes on each side with a moderately high heat.

Place the steaks on a hot platter. Add a good piece of butter to each steak and sprinkle with salt and black pepper. Serve immediately.

Grilled lamb chops, chervil butter
Côtelettes de mouton grillées

FOR FOUR PEOPLE

4 large lamb chops	1 tablespoon chopped chervil*
3 tablespoons butter	salt and pepper

Order English lamb chops, which are cut from the leg end of the loin. Preheat the grill or broiler until very hot. Broil or grill the chops, allowing 3 minutes on each side. Sprinkle with salt and pepper at the end of the cooking.

Work the butter and chopped chervil to a smooth paste. Place the chops on a preheated platter, dot with the butter, and serve with French fried potatoes.

Lamb chops champvallon
Côtelettes de mouton champvallon

FOR FOUR PEOPLE

4 large lamb chops (¾ inch thick)	*bouquet garni* (thyme, bay leaf, parsley)
6 tablespoons butter	4 medium-sized potatoes
3 onions	salt and pepper
1 cup hot bouillon	

Order thick chops from the leg end of the loin. Have them well trimmed.

Brown the chops in 3 tablespoons of butter, turning each chop once.

At the same time, chop the onions very fine and sauté them in the rest of the butter. Place the chops in a small, shallow, fireproof dish. Cover with the onions and add bouillon to fill the dish up to the top of the chops, enough to cover them and the potatoes. Add the *bouquet garni* and bring the liquid to a rapid boil. Sprinkle with salt and pepper and put in a 400° F. oven. At the end of 10 minutes, surround the meat with the potatoes sliced very thin. Continue to cook 20 to 30 minutes or until the potatoes are soft. Baste often with the bouillon in the dish. Do not worry if the potatoes break; this is probably an advantage.

*Substitute parsley if chervil is not available.—*Ed.*

Braised lamb chops
Côtelettes de mouton braisées aux tomates

FOR FOUR PEOPLE

4 large lamb or mutton chops
6 tablespoons lard or shortening
2 large onions

2 large tomatoes
¼ teaspoon anise seeds
salt and pepper

Order the chops well trimmed. Either loin or shoulder chops are suitable.

Heat 4 tablespoons of lard in a heavy pan. Cut the onions in thin slices and the tomatoes in pieces and sauté them in the fat. Season with anise, salt, and pepper.

At the same time, sauté the chops in the rest of the lard in a large skillet. When they are well browned, transfer them to the heavy pan. Lower the fire and cook very slowly for 1 hour. Serve with rice.

Cheese-coated lamb chops
Côtelettes de mouton panées au fromage

FOR FOUR PEOPLE

4 large lamb chops (½ inch thick)
flour
1 egg, slightly beaten
½ cup soft breadcrumbs

¼ cup grated Parmesan or Gruyère
  cheese
3 tablespoons butter
1 lemon
salt and pepper

Order well-trimmed lamb chops. Sprinkle each one with salt and pepper and dip first in flour, then in egg, and then in a mixture of breadcrumbs and cheese. Pat the breadcrumb mixture in to make a smooth coating.

Heat the butter in a skillet and brown the chops on each side over moderately high heat. Turn the chops with a spatula and shake the skillet frequently so that the chops will not stick. Reduce the heat and cook a few minutes longer or until the chops are cooked. Serve with peas. Garnish with lemon.

Lamb on skewers * Brochettes d'agneau

FOR FOUR PEOPLE

10 ounces lean lamb
5 ounces lean bacon
fresh mint leaves

3 tablespoons olive oil
salt and pepper

Have the lamb cut in 1¾-inch cubes, preferably from the top of the leg. Cut the sliced bacon in strips the same length.

Alternate pieces of lamb with the bacon and mint leaves on small skewers. Sprinkle with salt and pepper and brush with olive oil. Broil 10 minutes, turning frequently.

Lamb chops grandmont
Côtelettes de mouton grandmont

FOR FOUR PEOPLE

4 large lamb chops (¾ inch thick)
2 onions
2 cups Béchamel Sauce (page 6)
½ clove garlic
1 egg yolk

½ cup grated Parmesan cheese
3 teaspoons chopped parsley
½ cup soft breadcrumbs
cayenne
salt and pepper

Broil the lamb chops 2 minutes on each side.

Peel and chop the onions very fine. Boil them in salted water for 15 minutes and force them through a strainer (or spin in the blender.—*Ed.*).

Make the béchamel sauce and add the onion purée, the garlic, finely minced, and beat in the egg yolk. Add half the grated cheese and 2 teaspoons of the parsley. Reheat the sauce in a double boiler and season well with salt, pepper, and a little cayenne. Stir well.

Spread a little of the sauce in the bottom of a shallow heatproof platter. Place the chops on the sauce and cover with the rest of the sauce. Sprinkle with breadcrumbs previously mixed with a teaspoon of chopped parsley. Place the chop platter in a pan of hot water and brown 6 to 10 minutes in a 450° F. oven.

Lamb chops with onion purée
Côtelettes de mouton à l'oignon

FOR FOUR PEOPLE

4 loin lamb chops (¾ inch thick)
3 tablespoons butter
2 onions
2 medium-sized carrots
¾ cup bouillon
1 clove

Purée:
3 pounds (12-15) onions
5 tablespoons butter
¾ cup heavy cream
salt and pepper

Lamb Chops: Brown the lamb chops in butter lightly on both sides. Grate or finely chop the carrots and onions and add them to the chops. Add the bouillon, the clove, salt, and pepper and simmer 1 hour.

Purée: Thinly slice enough onions to measure 6 to 7 cups. Melt the butter in a deep skillet and cook the onions very slowly for 30 minutes, stirring frequently. They must not brown. Add the cream and let the mixture boil down to thicken. Season to taste with salt and pepper and put through a strainer. The mixture should be fairly thick.

Place the chops around the edge of a heated platter and fill the center with the purée.

Lamb chops with fruit
Côtelettes de mouton aux fruits

FOR FOUR PEOPLE

4 shoulder lamb chops	1 large orange
3 tablespoons butter	1 large grapefruit
2 tablespoons oil	salt and pepper

Order chops weighing ½ pound each.

Put half the butter and oil in one skillet and half in another. Heat them both. In one skillet, sauté the lamb chops, and when well browned on both sides, reduce the heat and cook for 5 minutes.

In the other skillet sauté the orange and grapefruit, which have been peeled, stripped of all fibers, and sliced. When the slices have all been sautéed, add them to the meat. Season with salt and pepper and serve very hot with rice.

Lamb and green peppers on skewers
Brochettes de mouton aux poivrons verts

FOR FOUR PEOPLE

10 ounces lamb fillet	1 tablespoon oil
5 ounces (6-7 slices) lean bacon	1 lemon
4 green peppers	salt and pepper

Ask the butcher to cut clear meat from the loin into pieces approximately 1 inch square. Cut the bacon strips into 1-inch pieces.

Cut the peppers in half and remove the seeds. Cut into strips ¾ inch wide. Thread small skewers with a piece of lamb, a piece of bacon, and a piece of pepper, continuing in that order until all the skewers have been filled with an equal number of pieces. Sprinkle with salt and pepper and brush with oil. Broil about 10 minutes. Serve with wedges of lemon.

Lamb on skewers à la persane
Brochettes de mouton persanes

FOR SIX PEOPLE

1¼ pounds shoulder of lamb	juice of 2 lemons
½ pound fat bacon	mint leaves
1 onion, chopped fine	salt and pepper

Cut the lamb and the bacon in square pieces. Put them in a bowl with the chopped onion, the juice of 2 lemons, salt, and pepper. Let stand 1 or 2 hours.

Thread the meat and bacon on the six small skewers, putting a half mint leaf between each piece. Broil 10 minutes, preferably over hot charcoal. Turn frequently.

Lamb mixed grill on skewers
Brochettes de côtelettes d'agneau

FOR FOUR PEOPLE

8 small rib chops	8 mushroom caps
8 slices bacon	oil
8 very small tomatoes	salt and pepper
8 small link sausages	

Order the chops with the rib bone trimmed down. Cut the bacon slices in half. Wash the tomatoes and the mushrooms.

Thread a tomato, a sausage, a chop, a piece of bacon, a mushroom, another tomato, a sausage, a chop, a piece of bacon, and finally another mushroom on each of 4 skewers. Sprinkle with salt and pepper. Brush well with oil and broil about 10 minutes, turning frequently.

Toulouse cassoulet ∗ Le cassoulet toulousain

FOR FIVE PEOPLE

2 pounds shoulder of lamb	1 can tomato paste

1 pound pork skin or rind
1 pound dried white beans
1 sprig thyme
2 bay leaves
6 tablespoons lard or goose fat

2½ tablespoons *fine* cognac
¾ pound Toulouse sausage
1 cup soft breadcrumbs
1 cup *confit d'oie* (if possible)

Ask the butcher to cut the lamb (bones included) into twelve pieces. Ask him also to sell you a pound of pork skin. (If none is available, use the rind of pork, bacon or salt pork.—*Ed.*) Boil the rind 5 minutes to remove the excess salt.

Cut the pork skin in pieces, and the day before cooking the *cassoulet,* put the rind in a deep pan. Add 2¾ quarts of water. Cover and simmer 3 hours. Remove and cool. The next morning you will have a firm jelly.

Soak the beans overnight in cool water.

The next day, heat the pork jelly, and when it is melted, add the beans, the thyme and bay leaves.

Heat the lard or goose fat and sauté the lamb pieces, browning them lightly on all sides. Reduce the heat, cover, and cook 30 minutes.

Add the meat to the beans and stir in the tomato paste and the cognac. Simmer 30 minutes.

(Toulouse sausage may be available only in large cities, but Polish or Italian dry sausage will do very well.—*Ed.*) Brown the sausage lightly in a skillet. Cut in 5 pieces and add to the beans. Pour the cassoulet into a casserole. Sprinkle with some of the breadcrumbs and bake 15 minutes in a hot oven (400° F.). Remove from the oven, stir with a fork, sprinkle again with breadcrumbs, and return to the oven 15 minutes again. Repeat this process 5 times in all. If you have some *confit d'oie* (cooked goose preserved in salted clarified goose fat), serve it cold on top of the cassoulet, which is served very hot.

Moussaka * Moussaka

FOR SIX PEOPLE

12 large eggplants
Tomato Sauce (page 22)
1⅔ cups oil
2 pounds shoulder of lamb,
   cut in pieces
¾ cup sliced mushrooms

3 large onions, sliced thin
4 tablespoons chopped herbs (parsley,
   rosemary, chervil, tarragon)
3 eggs
3-4 teaspoons paprika
salt and pepper

Wash the eggplant. Cut 6 of them in half lengthwise. Slit the flesh in several places and cover them with coarse salt. Turn them upside down on a platter and leave them for 25 minutes. This is to drain them.

If you do not have tomato sauce on hand, start it at this point.

To continue with the moussaka, heat ½ cup of oil in a large skillet and sauté the eggplant halves over low heat for 15 minutes, taking care to turn them carefully so that the skin does not break. Do not let them brown. As soon as the flesh is soft to the touch, place the eggplant, skin side up, on paper toweling. Remove the skins carefully, without tearing the skin. Save the skins and put the flesh in a bowl.

Do not peel but slice the remaining eggplant into thin rounds. Heat another ½ cup of oil in the skillet and sauté the rounds for 15 minutes, turning occasionally. Season with salt and pepper.

At the same time, heat ⅓ cup oil in another skillet and cook the meat 15 minutes, stirring frequently; put the cooked meat through a food chopper.

Cook the mushrooms and onions in a pan with ⅓ cup oil just until tender, stirring frequently.

Combine the ground meat with the eggplant flesh, onions, mushrooms, *fines herbes,* and raw eggs. Mix thoroughly and season with paprika, salt, and pepper.

Grease a straight sided round mold (a charlotte mold) and line the bottom and sides with eggplant skins, shiny side out. The interior must be completely covered. Put a good layer of the meat mixture in the bottom. Cover with a layer of eggplant rounds. Alternate these layers until the mold is filled. Cover with eggplant skins. Bake 45 minutes in 300° F. oven.

Unmold the moussaka on a hot serving platter and serve with tomato sauce.

Stuffed breast of lamb (cold)
Poitrine de mouton farcie

FOR SIX PEOPLE

1 breast of lamb	⅓ cup oil
10 ounces pork sausage meat	1 tablespoon vinegar
¼ pound mushrooms, chopped	2 teaspoons mixed chopped herbs,
2 onions, chopped	(parsley, tarragon)
3 teaspoons paprika	salt and pepper
½ cup soft breadcrumbs	Vinaigrette Sauce (page 29)
1 tablespoon chopped parsley	
bouillon	
3 hard-cooked eggs	

Ask the butcher to cut a pocket in the breast for stuffing. Sprinkle the interior with salt and pepper.

Make a stuffing with the sausage, the mushrooms, onions, paprika, breadcrumbs, and parsley. Mix well. Season with salt and pepper. Fill the pocket with the mixture. Sew the pocket closed and cook it in enough bouillon to half cover the meat for 2 hours. Cool completely.

Cut the meat in slices and arrange on a platter. Cover with well-seasoned vinaigrette sauce to which have been added the hard-cooked eggs, finely chopped, and the *fines herbes.*

Lamb sauté à la poulette
Sauté de mouton à la poulette

FOR FOUR PEOPLE

1½ pounds boned lamb shoulder	allspice
6 tablespoons oil	2 eggs
2 cups hot bouillon	juice of ½ lemon
1 tablespoon chopped parsley	salt and pepper

Have the meat cut in bite-size pieces. Brown it in hot oil in a deep pan. When thoroughly browned on all sides, add the bouillon, salt, pepper, chopped parsley, and spice according to taste. Simmer for 1 hour. When the tip of a knife enters the meat easily, the meat is cooked.

Prepare a binding by beating the egg yolks with the juice of ½ lemon and chopped parsley. Add the binding to the sauce gradually, stirring constantly. Don't let the sauce boil.

Put the lamb in a shallow platter and pour the sauce over it. Serve very hot with rice or shelled beans.

Lamb ragoût with red wine
Ragoût de mouton au vin rouge

FOR SIX PEOPLE

2 pounds stew lamb	1½ cups red wine
½ pound piece lean bacon	*bouquet garni* (parsley, thyme, bay leaf)
3 tablespoons butter	½ pound mushrooms
1 pound tiny onions (18-20)	croutons
3 tablespoons flour	salt and pepper

Ask the butcher for well-trimmed lean meat, cut in 1½-inch squares.

Cut the bacon into rather small dice and throw them in boiling water for 2 minutes. Drain, dry, and sauté them in butter in a deep heavy pan. Add the small peeled onions and sauté until they are golden. Add the meat and brown lightly on all sides, stirring with a wooden spoon.

Sprinkle with flour and stir until the flour has taken on a little color. Add the wine and 1½ cups of water and mix well. Add the *bouquet garni,* salt, and pepper. Cover and simmer 1 hour.

Remove the meat with a slotted spoon. Strain the sauce. Wipe out the pan. Put back the meat and the sauce and add the mushrooms. Taste for seasoning. Simmer 1 hour longer. Add the onions.

(At this point, a small glass of pig's blood should be added to the sauce, but this is unlikely to be available in most home kitchens.—*Ed.*)

Fry small squares of bread in butter. Serve the ragoût in a deep platter garnished with the croutons.

Lamb à la saintonge * Mouton à la saintonge

FOR FOUR PEOPLE

1½ pounds breast of lamb
¾ cup oil
½ cup rice
4 large tomatoes

4 bananas
4 eggs
salt and pepper

Cut the breast meat into small pieces. Brown them in ¼ cup hot oil. Season with salt and pepper. Cover and simmer 1 hour.

Boil the rice as you would for pilaff.

Divide the remaining oil between 2 skillets. Cut the tomatoes in half and sauté them in one skillet; in the other, sauté the bananas cut in two lengthwise.

3 minutes before serving, fry the eggs in deep fat (385° F.).

Make a ring of rice on a serving platter. Fill the center with the lamb. Alternate the eggs, tomatoes, and bananas around the rice.

Lamb blanquette * Blanquette d'agneau

FOR FOUR PEOPLE

1½ pounds breast of lamb
1 onion
1 clove
2 carrots
bouquet garni (thyme, bay leaf)
3 tablespoons butter

1 tablespoon flour
½ pound mushrooms
2 egg yolks
4 tablespoons heavy cream
juice of 1 lemon
salt and pepper

Have the meat cut in 2½-inch cubes. Place in a saucepan and cover with cold water. Add the onion stuck with a clove, the carrots, peeled and sliced, the *bouquet garni,* salt, and pepper. Bring to a boil, lower the heat, cover, and simmer about 35 minutes.

Heat the butter in another saucepan and stir in the flour. Stir in 2 cups of the meat broth and cook 5 minutes, stirring with a wooden spoon. Season to taste with salt and pepper.

Wash, trim, and slice the mushrooms and add them to the sauce. Cook 5 minutes. Remove the sauce from the heat and stir in the egg yolks slightly beaten with the cream and the juice of a lemon.

Drain the meat and place it on a warm serving platter. Cover with the sauce. Serve with rice.

Spring navarin of lamb
Navarin printanier d'agneau

FOR EIGHT PEOPLE

4 pounds boned shoulder of lamb
6 tablespoons lard or shortening
½ teaspoon sugar
6 tablespoons flour
bouillon or water
3 medium-sized tomatoes
1 clove garlic

bouquet garni (thyme, bay leaf, parsley)
20 tiny onions
20 small new potatoes
20 little carrots
20 small spring turnips
1 pound fresh peas
salt and pepper

Ask the butcher to cut the lamb into pieces approximately 2½ ounces each.

Melt the fat in a deep ovenproof pan and add the lamb. Season with salt and pepper and sprinkle with sugar. Brown the lamb well, stirring the meat frequently. Pour off three fourths of the fat. Sprinkle the meat with flour and stir until the flour disappears. Then add enough bouillon or water to cover the meat. Add the tomatoes, peeled and chopped, the garlic, and the *bouquet garni.* Cover and cook for 1 hour in a 300° F. oven.

During this time, prepare and cook the vegetables in separate pans. The vegetables should be cooked just until tender but not soft. Add all of them to the lamb and continue cooking for 20 minutes. Taste for seasoning. Remove as much as possible of the fat from the surface with a metal spoon and serve very hot.

Lamb sauté with lemon * Sauté d'agneau au citron

FOR EIGHT PEOPLE

2½ pounds boned shoulder of lamb
4 tablespoons oil
1 lemon
¾ teaspoon cinnamon

1 large pinch saffron *or*
3 teaspoons turmeric
salt and pepper

Order the lamb cut for stew. Heat the oil in a deep pan and brown the meat on all sides.

Slice the lemon very thin and spread all of it—except the ends—on the meat. Add a cup of hot water and season with cinnamon, saffron or turmeric, salt, and pepper. Cover tightly and simmer 1 hour.

Lamb ragoût à la grecque
Ragoût d'agneau à la grecque

FOR FOUR PEOPLE

2 pounds lean boned breast meat
  of lamb
10 small onions
3 tablespoons lard or shortening
1 cup bouillon
4-5 tomatoes

1 bay leaf
paprika
1 cup rice
juice of 1 lemon
salt and pepper

Cut the meat in 2-inch cubes. Peel the onions.

Heat the lard in a deep pan and add the meat and onions. Cook 15 minutes over a moderately high heat for 15 minutes, stirring constantly. Add the bouillon and continue cooking 5 minutes. Add the tomatoes, peeled and quartered, the bay leaf, and a good pinch of paprika and season with salt and pepper. Cook 10 minutes. Add enough boiling water to cover and remove the bay leaf and the onions. Keep the onions warm.

Add the rice, cover, and cook 20 minutes. Season with salt, pepper, and a little lemon juice. Serve on a heated platter with the onions.

Malayan curry * Cari malais

FOR EIGHT PEOPLE

2 pounds veal for stew
1¼ pounds lean pork
1 pound lamb for stew
7 tablespoons curry powder
4 teaspoons anise powder
3 teaspoons cinnamon
oil
5 onions, chopped fine

4 shallots, chopped fine
3 cloves garlic
4 small red peppers
cayenne
2 large potatoes
¾ cup coconut milk or milk
salt and pepper

Order the meat cut in pieces approximately 1½ inches square.

Mix the curry and anise powder with the cinnamon.

Sauté the onions and shallots in a little oil in a large, heavy pan that will be used to cook the meat. When they are golden brown, remove them to a side plate. Put in as much meat as will fit in the bottom of the pan. Cook until lightly browned. Turn the meat over and sprinkle with the curry mixture. Brown the other side, turn again, and sprinkle with the curry. Cook 2 to 3 minutes. Remove to another side plate, scraping the bottom of the pan to remove all the curry powder. Repeat the process with the rest of the meat, using a little more oil, if necessary. When all the meat has been browned and seasoned, put it back into the pan with the onions and add enough water to just cover. Add the garlic, the red peppers, plenty of salt, a good pinch of cayenne and black pepper and the potatoes, cut in dice. Cover and simmer at least 2 hours or until the meat is well cooked. Then, 15 minutes before serving, add the coconut milk. Serve very hot, preferably from a covered dish kept on a food warmer.

Broiled épigrammes of lamb
Epigrammes d'agneau grillées

FOR SIX PEOPLE

Epigrammes, *sometimes called riblets in America, are pieces taken from the breast, with bone and flank removed. Often used only for stews, they serve well for nobler dishes because of their delicious flavor.—Ed.*

2 pounds lean breast meat of lamb	2 teaspoons chopped parsley
6 tablespoons butter	1/8 teaspoon pepper
4 teaspoons flour	salt

Order the meat cut in 6 slices.

Boil the pieces of breast meat in salted water for 15 minutes. Drain and wipe dry. Broil 3 minutes on each side.

Work the butter, flour, and parsley together with a spatula until well blended. Season with a little pepper.

Put the broiled meat on a heated serving platter and dot liberally with the butter mixture.

Breaded épigrammes of lamb
Epigrammes d'agneau panées

FOR FOUR PEOPLE

1½ pounds lean breast meat of lamb	1 large clove garlic
1 onion	2 tablespoons chopped parsley
1 carrot	½ cup breadcrumbs
bouquet garni (thyme, parsley, bay leaf)	salt and pepper
6 tablespoons butter	

Order the meat cut in 8 slices.

Shred the onion and carrot and put in a large saucepan of water with the *bouquet garni,* a teaspoon of salt, and a few peppercorns. Boil 10 minutes before adding the meat. Boil 10 minutes longer. Drain and dry the meat in a clean towel.

Dot the bottom of a shallow casserole with the butter. Cover with the meat. Chop the garlic fine and combine with the chopped parsley. Spread the combination over the meat. Sprinkle with salt and pepper and finally with the bread-crumbs. Brown in a hot oven (400° F.) for 10 minutes.

Braised lamb's neck with chestnuts
Collier de mouton braisé aux marrons

FOR SIX PEOPLE

3 pounds lamb's neck (in one piece)	pinch of ginger
5 tablespoons butter	¾ cup dry white wine
2 carrots	2 pounds chestnuts
1 onion	salt and pepper

Brown the meat in butter in a deep heavy pan along with the carrots and onion, chopped fine. When well browned on all sides, sprinkle with salt and pepper and a little ginger and add the white wine. Cover and simmer 3 hours, turning the meat occasionally.

Cut the shell of each chestnut around the center with a sharp, pointed knife. Broil them in the oven or pan-broil them in a frying pan fitted with a trivet. Remove the shell and skin while the chestnuts are hot. Add the chestnuts ½ hour before serving. The meat must cook a long time or it will remain attached to the bone and won't be as delicious as it should be.

Lamb curry * Cari de mouton

FOR SIX PEOPLE

5 tablespoons butter	4 tablespoons slivered almonds
2½ pounds lamb or mutton neck meat, cut for stew	4 tablespoons seedless raisins
5 tablespoons curry powder	½ cup orange marmalade
½ teaspoon allspice	chutney sauce
2 bananas	salt
2 apples	

Heat the butter in a deep heavy pan until frothy. Add the meat and cook over a low fire until the meat is slightly cooked on all sides. The meat must not brown. Add 3 cups of water in which the curry powder, allspice, and salt have already been mixed. Add the bananas, cut in large pieces, and the apples, which have been peeled and cut into quarters or eighths, if the apples are large. Cover and simmer for at least 2 hours. If the sauce thickens too much, add water.

Serve very hot with boiled rice, and in little side dishes, serve the slivered almonds, raisins, orange marmalade, and chutney sauce.

Lamb and artichoke croquettes
Croquettes de mouton aux artichauts

FOR FIVE PEOPLE

4 artichoke bottoms
1½ cups leftover lamb
1½ cups thick Béchamel Sauce
  (page 6)
2 eggs

pinch of nutmeg
soft breadcrumbs
juice of 1 lemon
1 cup heavy cream
salt and pepper

If using fresh artichokes, boil them in salted water for 45 minutes. Drain and discard all but the bottoms. Lacking fresh artichokes, use the canned or frozen variety. Cut the artichoke bottoms into small dice.

Chop rather coarsely or dice the leftover lamb, which should be free from all gristle.

Make the béchamel sauce and add the artichokes, lamb, 2 egg yolks, nutmeg, salt, and pepper. Mix it well and spread it out on a marble or other working surface to cool.

When cold, make small balls of the mixture. Dip each one into egg white, which has been beaten to a froth, and then into the breadcrumbs. Fry the balls in deep fat (385° F.) until golden brown.

At the same time, heat the cream without boiling and season it lightly with the salt, pepper, and the lemon juice.

Drain the croquettes on paper toweling and serve hot accompanied by the hot cream.

Pork

The saying is that you can eat every bit of a pig from snout to tail, and this is true not only of the fresh meat but of preserved pork. Even before Mr. Appert at the beginning of the nineteenth century invented the famous "boîtes Appert," which was the beginning of the modern system of canning meat, fish, and vegetables, our ancestors had found ways to conserve pork.

Fresh pork must be sufficiently cooked, whether one is roasting a loin, broiling a chop, or braising a shoulder butt. Like all white meat, including chicken and veal, pork should *never* be served rare. This is a matter of hygiene as well as one of flavor.

The American butcher cuts pork somewhat differently from the French butcher, but there seems to be greater similarity in pork cuts than in other meats. Loin and tenderloin roasts are similar enough in flavor to duck, so that some classic treatments of duck are equally good with pork, in my opinion, particularly when combined with fruit. For example, Pork with Cherries is as delicious as the well-known *Canard Montmorency,* and Pork with Orange is a good competitor for *Canard à l'Orange.* Roast Pork with Pineapple is excellent, if unusual, and we all know how well apples and prunes complement pork.

The classic vegetable accompaniments to pork are potatoes, chestnuts, all kinds of cabbage—red and white—Brussels sprouts, cauliflower, and broccoli.

As for *charcuterie,* which means all kinds of pork products that are smoked, salted, or preserved in brine, there are too many to mention, and some of them are strictly local and not exported.

The preparation of these we will leave to the specialists, but the use of them will add greatly to our menu, and I will give recipes for those meats that are available both in France and in the United States.

Roast pork à la boulangère
Rôti de porc à la boulangère

FOR FOUR PEOPLE

2 pounds boneless pork roast	3 tablespoons butter
6-8 potatoes	rosemary
3-4 apples	salt and pepper

Order the roast well tied. If you prefer, buy a 3½-pound unboned loin roast. Peel the potatoes and apples and cut them in thick slices.

Dot a shallow oven dish with bits of butter. Put in the apples first and then the potatoes. Place the pork on the potatoes. Sprinkle with salt, pepper, and a teaspoon of rosemary. Bake for 1 hour at 400° F., basting often. When the meat is well browned, cover it with buttered paper or aluminum foil. Serve the dish from the oven dish in which it is cooked.

Pork for autumn * Porc d'automne

3 pounds loin of pork
8 tablespoons butter
1 medium-sized cabbage
¾ cup red wine

6-8 apples
2 pounds chestnuts
salt and pepper

Ask the butcher to tie the roast well. Spread 2 tablespoons of butter in a roasting pan and place the pork on the butter. Roast at 350° F., allowing 25 minutes per pound. The meat should be very white. Baste occasionally.

Meanwhile, remove the outer hard leaves of the cabbage and shred the cabbage fine. Put in a deep, enamel-lined dish with 3 tablespoons of butter and the red wine. Cook slowly.

Peel the apples and cut them in 8 or 10 slices and sauté them in 3 tablespoons of butter over a moderate heat. They should be lightly browned but not so soft that they will lose their shape.

At the same time, cut slashes around the chestnuts and put them in a hot frying pan fitted with a trivet or under the broiler. Grill 15 minutes. Remove the shells.

Place the cooked roast on a hot platter, carving about three fourths of it. Surround it with the vegetables and fruits. Remove the grease from the pan juices and pour a little over the meat and the rest in a small sauce bowl. If you serve a salad at the same time, choose watercress.

Pork loin roast with pine nut cakes
Carré de porc au bacon et galettes de pignes de pin

2½ pounds boned pork loin
4 slices bacon
3 tablespoons butter

Pine Nut Cakes:
1½ cups thick Béchamel Sauce
   (page 6)
1 egg
2 ounces pine nuts
oil
butter
salt and pepper

Roast: Ask the butcher to lard a lean, fat-trimmed piece of loin with the bacon or do it yourself with the help of a larding needle. The bacon should run through the middle of the roast. Spread the roast with butter and roast 1 hour at 425° F.

Pine Nut Cakes: Make the thick béchamel sauce, remove from the stove, and beat in a raw egg. Season with salt and pepper and spread it out on a baking sheet to a smooth sheet about ⅛ inch thick. Let it cool completely. Cut in rounds with a 2½-inch cookie cutter. Stick the pine nuts at random into the rounds. Sauté in a mixture of half oil, half butter until golden brown on both sides. Slice the pork and arrange the slices, slightly overlapping, on a hot serving platter. Garnish with the cakes.

Roast pork montmorency
Rôti de porc montmorency

FOR EIGHT PEOPLE

3-pound boneless pork roast	1 can red cherries
4 tablespoons butter	salt and pepper
1½ cups red wine	

Ask the butcher to bone either a loin or a shoulder but to give you a compact, well-tied roast. You will need the bones also.

Put the roast in a shallow oven dish, preferably earthenware. Spread the roast with butter and sprinkle with pepper. Place the bones on either side of the roast. Put the dish in a 400° F. oven and roast 1¼ hours. After 10 minutes of cooking, add a large spoonful of boiling water. Do this 3 more times every 5 minutes. Salt the gravy that results from this process and use it to baste the meat frequently. Prick the meat with a fork when the cooking is done. If the juices that run out are colorless, the meat is cooked; if pink, the meat should cook a little longer.

Meanwhile, pour the wine into a small saucepan. Add the cherries that have been thoroughly drained. Simmer 10 minutes.

Put the pork on a heated serving platter. Slice three fourths of it, overlapping the slices on the platter. Sprinkle the slices with part of the dish gravy. Remove the cherries from the wine with a slotted spoon and mix them with the rest of the dish gravy. Put the cherries and the gravy on two sides of the platter and serve very hot with strong mustard.

Pork in beer * Porc à la bière

FOR EIGHT PEOPLE

3-pound loin pork roast	4 tablespoons soft breadcrumbs

5 tablespoons lard

8 onions

bouquet garni (thyme, bay leaf, parsley)

2 cups (16 ounces) beer

salt and pepper

Order the roast well tied. Heat 2 tablespoons of the lard in a skillet and brown the roast on all sides. Remove the roast and add the rest of the lard.

Peel the onions and chop them coarsely. Sauté them in the hot fat until golden, stirring them frequently with a wooden spoon.

Line the bottom of the casserole with a layer of half the onions. Place the meat on the onions. Sprinkle with salt and pepper and cover with the rest of the onions. Add the *bouquet garni.* Sprinkle with more salt and with the breadcrumbs. Pour in the beer. Cover and bake at 350° F. for 2½ hours. Do not let the meat cook too fast. Reduce the heat if the liquid is bubbling hard.

Transfer the meat to a heated platter and cut several slices. Spoon off as much of the fat as possible from the sauce. Pour a little sauce over the meat. Serve the rest in a separate bowl.

Pork with pineapple * Porc à l'ananas

FOR EIGHT PEOPLE

3-pound boneless pork roast

5 ounces fat bacon

1 bay leaf

1 sprig thyme

1 clove

1 cup pineapple juice

salt and pepper

Have the pork tied well. Dice the bacon very fine and cook it in a deep, heavy dish until it begins to brown. Add the roast and brown it lightly on all sides. Sprinkle with salt and pepper. Add the bay leaf, thyme, and clove and pour in the pineapple juice. Bring to a boil, cover, and cook slowly for 2 hours.

Slice the meat and arrange on a hot platter. Remove the bay leaf, thyme, and clove and pour the sauce over the meat.

Serve with rice or with braised endive.

Pork with orange * Porc à l'orange

FOR FIVE PEOPLE

2 pounds pork tenderloin

1 pound veal bones

3 tablespoons butter

4 carrots

4 teaspoons cognac

1½ cups dry white wine

1 sprig thyme

1 bay leaf

3 oranges

salt and pepper

Ask the butcher for the thickest part of the tenderloin. Order the veal bones sawed.

Brown the pork in butter in a deep heavy pan. At the same time, brown the carrots cut in thin rounds and add the bones. When the pork is browned on all sides, add the cognac and touch it with a lighted match. Add the white wine, the thyme, and the bay leaf. Season with salt and pepper and let it simmer covered for 2 hours.

Remove the orange part of the rind of 2 oranges with a sharp knife and cut it into thin strips. Cook the rind in boiling water for 2 minutes. Squeeze the juice.

Transfer the pork to a long serving platter and keep it warm. Strain the sauce through a sieve lined with a cold damp dish towel. Add the orange juice and the orange rind. Bring the sauce to a boil again.

Slice the pork and arrange the slices on the platter. Decorate the edge of the platter with half slices of peeled orange from which all seeds and fibers have been removed. Pour the sauce over the pork.

Roast pork stuffed with prunes
Rôti de porc aux pruneaux d'agen

FOR SIX PEOPLE

1 pound small prunes	6 cooking apples
2½ pounds pork loin roast	salt and pepper
2½ tablespoons butter	

Soak the prunes long enough for them to be easily pitted. Make incisions in the pork and insert as many prunes as necessary to make a rich stuffing. Do this a little in advance, so that the flavor of the prunes will permeate the meat. Spread the meat with a little butter. Roast at 425° F. for 1 hour, basting frequently. Halfway through the cooking, sprinkle with salt and pepper.

Peel the apples carefully, leaving a band of skin intact around the middle. Core the apples and insert a piece of butter and a prune in each apple. Bake in a slow oven (300° F.) for 1 hour. (If you have only one oven, bake the apples first and keep them warm.—Ed.)

Carve the meat and arrange it on a hot platter. Place the apples around the edge and serve the sauce in a heated sauce bowl.

Pork in milk * Porc au lait

FOR SIX PEOPLE

2¼ pounds tenderloin of pork	1 clove garlic
2 tablespoons butter	*bouquet garni* (thyme, bay leaf,
4½ cups milk	parsley, chervil)

2 carrots   salt and pepper
1 onion

Brown the tenderloin in hot butter on all sides in a deep, heavy pan. Add enough milk to cover the pork completely. Add the carrots, peeled and sliced in rounds, the onion, peeled and quartered, the clove of garlic, and a small *bouquet garni*, salt, and pepper. Cook uncovered over a very low flame for about 3 hours.

After this amount of cooking you should have a smooth gravy. Strain it and pour over the meat, which is served on a heated platter. If the cooking has been too fast, you will have to add more milk. If it has been too slow, increase the heat at the last minute to boil down the milk.

Pork in pastry (cold) * *Porc en croûte*

FOR SIX PEOPLE

2-pound boneless pork roast   French mustard
Semiflaky Pastry (page 644)   1 sprig tarragon

Order a small, compact piece of boneless pork, preferably from the tenderloin.

Make the pastry. Roll out the pastry to a large round. Spread all the surface with mustard and place the roast in the center. Divide the tarragon sprig in two and place it on the pastry. Roll the pastry around the roast so that it looks like a large sausage.

Bake 1 hour a 400° F. When the pastry is browned, cover it with heavy paper so that it will not burn. The meat requires more time than the pastry to cook.

Cool and serve cold with a well-seasoned salad.

Braised pork shoulder butt with peas
Porc braisé aux pois cassés

FOR FOUR PEOPLE

1 pound dried peas   pinch rosemary
12 tablespoons butter   4 eggs
2 pounds boneless pork shoulder butt salt and pepper
¾ cup dry white wine

Soak the peas in cold water overnight or at least for several hours. Drain them and cook them in fresh salted water over a high heat approximately 1 hour or until tender. The time will vary depending on the size and age of the peas.

Heat 2 tablespoons of butter in a deep dish large enough to hold the shoulder butt. Brown the meat on all sides over a moderate heat. Sprinkle with salt and pepper and add the white wine and a pinch of rosemary. Cover the dish and simmer 1 hour.

Drain the peas when tender and force them through a strainer or food mill (or purée them in a blender—*Ed.*). Add 8 tablespoons of butter and enough of the water of the peas to give a smooth purée. Taste for seasoning.

Beat the egg yolks slightly and add them to the purée. Beat the egg whites until stiff and fold them into the purée. Put the mixture into a buttered baking dish or mold and place the dish in a pan of hot water. Bake 30 minutes at 350° F.

Slice the meat and arrange it on a hot serving platter with the slices slightly overlapping. Pour the sauce over the meat. Unmold the pea *gâteau* onto a hot plate to accompany the meat.

Breton pork shoulder * Palette de porc bretonne

FOR SIX PEOPLE

3 pounds lightly cured pork
   shoulder butt
3 small cabbages

6-8 potatoes
dry sausage (salami, *cervelas*, Polish)

Wash the shoulder butt in running water. Cut the cabbages in large pieces and boil them for 10 minutes in a deep kettle. Add the shoulder butt and cook with the cabbage for 1½ hours over a moderate heat.

Cook the potatoes and add them 5 minutes before serving along with six good-sized pieces of sausage.

Braised pork slice with eggplant
Daube de porc aux aubergines

FOR FOUR PEOPLE

2-pound-slice pork shoulder
6 tablespoons oil
10 small onions

1 pound small eggplants
1 small red pepper
salt and pepper

Brown the shoulder slice in the oil on both sides in a deep, heavy pan.

Peel the onions and add them to the meat and let them brown with the meat. Season with salt and pepper. Cover and cook over low heat for ¾ hour. Watch to see that the meat does not become so dry that it sticks to the pan. Add water if necessary, but theoretically the meat and onions should cook in their own juices.

Peel the eggplants and add them to the meat. (If only large eggplants are available, cut one in thick slices instead of using 4 small ones.—*Ed.*) Cool 30 minutes.

Just before serving, remove the meat and vegetables to a heated platter. Crush a little of the red pepper into the sauce, which should be dark brown. Taste for seasoning.

Roast suckling pig * Cochon de lait rôti

FOR EIGHT PEOPLE

1 small suckling pig
  (approximately 8 pounds)
7 ounces fat bacon
7 ounces lean pork belly
3 hard-cooked eggs
1½ cups soft breadcrumbs
milk
½ cup chopped parsley
1 sprig tarragon, chopped

1 large can truffle peelings
15 large prunes (scalded and pitted)
6 tablespoons kirsch
butter
16 small apples
currant jelly
salt and pepper

Order a suckling pig, preferably with the head on. It will save you trouble if the pig has been thoroughly cleaned and singed and prepared for roasting. Set aside the liver and sprinkle the interior with salt and pepper.

Prepare the stuffing by chopping the bacon and pork belly. (If you cannot get pork belly, buy a piece of lean salt pork and parboil it 5 minutes. Rinse well.— *Ed.*) Chop the hard-cooked eggs. Soak the breadcrumbs in a little milk and squeeze it dry. Mix all these together with the parsley, tarragon, truffle peelings, prunes, and coarsely chopped pig's liver. Season with kirsch, salt, and pepper and mix thoroughly. Put this stuffing in the pig and skewer or sew the opening.

Place the pig on a grill in a roasting pan. Spread the surface with a thick coating of butter and protect the ears with heavy paper or aluminum foil. Roast 1½ hours at 350° F. Peel and core the apples and put a little butter in the centers. Bake at 350° F. in a shallow dish for 30-40 minutes or until tender but not soft. Serve the pig on a large platter surrounded by the apples. Fill the apple centers with currant jelly.

Pork shoulder in beer * Echine de porc à la bière

FOR FOUR PEOPLE

2 pounds pork shoulder butt
3 tablespoons lard or shortening
8-10 medium-sized onions

4 tablespoons soft breadcrumbs
2 cups (16 ounces) beer
bouquet garni (bay leaf, thyme, parsley)
salt and pepper

Ask the butcher for a small roast cut from the shoulder. It should be well tied.

Heat 2 tablespoons of the lard or shortening in a skillet and sauté the onions, peeled and finely chopped, until golden, stirring them frequently with a wooden spoon. Remove from the skillet, and with the remaining fat, brown the pork on all sides.

Line a deep casserole with half the onions. Place the meat on the onions and cover with the rest. Season with salt and pepper. Sprinkle with breadcrumbs. Add the beer and the *bouquet garni.* Cover and cook 2½ hours in a slow (300° F.) oven. Watch to see that the liquid is not bubbling hard. The cooking must be slow.

Remove as much fat as possible from the sauce with a metal spoon. Serve with potato purée.

Braised pork shoulder with red cabbage
Echine de porc braisée aux choux rouges

FOR SEVEN PEOPLE

3 pounds pork shoulder butt	1½ cups red wine
1 large red cabbage	3 lumps sugar
5 tablespoons butter	salt and pepper

Buy the shoulder butt with the skin left on.

Remove the outer leaves from the cabbage. Wash the head and cut it into long thin strips. Parboil in boiling water for 5 minutes. Drain well.

Heat the butter in a heavy pan. Brown the shoulder butt on all sides. Add the cabbage, the red wine, sugar, salt, and pepper. Cover and simmer for 2 hours.

Shoulder blade of pork with lentils
Palette de porc aux lentilles

FOR FOUR PEOPLE

1 pound dried lentils	2 carrots
2 pounds shoulder blade of pork	*bouquet garni* (thyme, bay leaf)
½ pound fat bacon	chopped parsley
4 onions	salt and pepper

Soak the lentils overnight. Drain well before using.

Put the shoulder blade, the fat bacon, the lentils, whole peeled onions, carrots, *bouquet garni,* salt, and pepper in a kettle and cover with cold water. Bring slowly to a boil, skimming the matter that floats to the surface. When it boils, reduce the heat, cover, and simmer a full hour.

If the lentils are not cooked, remove the meat but continue to cook the lentils until tender. Otherwise, remove the onions, carrots, and *bouquet garni.* Drain the lentils and place them on a serving platter. Cover with slices of bacon and shoulder. Sprinkle with chopped parsley. Serve very hot.

Stuffed pork chops with apples
Côtelettes de porc farcies aux pommes

FOR SIX PEOPLE

6 thick (¾-inch) pork chops
flour
oil
3 cooking apples

Stuffing:
1½ cups soft breadcrumbs
¾ cup chopped celery
4 tablespoons milk
3 tablespoons soft butter
salt and pepper

Pork Chops: Split each chop through the center right to the bone. Dip each chop in flour and brown lightly in oil on both sides. Season with salt and pepper.
　　Peel, core, and halve the apples.

Stuffing: Mix the ingredients of the stuffing and season well. Spread the stuffing between the split halves of the chops and close them with wooden toothpicks.
　　Put the chops in a baking dish. Place half an apple on each one and cook 30-35 minutes at 350° F.

Braised pork chops with corn
Côtelettes de porc braisées au maïs

FOR FOUR PEOPLE

4 onions
1 green pepper
3 tablespoons butter
4 loin pork chops

1 small can corn
juice of ½ lemon
salt and pepper

Peel and chop the onions. Split the green pepper. Remove the seeds and chop quite fine. Sauté the onions and pepper in half the butter for a few moments. Add the chops and sauté them until lightly browned on both sides. Season with salt and pepper. Cover and simmer 1 hour, turning the meat occasionally.
　　Drain the corn and heat it in the rest of the butter. Season with salt and pepper.
　　Spread the corn in a hot serving platter. Arrange the chops on the corn. Add the juice of ½ lemon to the sauce in the pan and pour it over the chops.

Pork chops with bananas
Côtelettes de porc aux bananes

FOR FOUR PEOPLE

8 bananas	4 loin pork chops
nutmeg	½ cup chopped toasted almonds
3 tablespoons butter	salt and pepper

Peel and slice the bananas. Put the round slices into a bowl containing ½ cup water, a pinch of salt, and ½ teaspoon ground nutmeg. Soak for 15 minutes.

Heat the butter in a skillet and sauté the chops over a moderate heat until browned on both sides. Cover and cook 10 to 15 minutes or until the chops are thoroughly cooked. Season with salt and pepper.

Force the bananas through a sieve (or purée them in a blender—*Ed.*). Heat over a low flame and spread the purée in a heated platter. Place the chops on the purée and sprinkle with coarsely chopped toasted almonds.

Marinated pork chops, sauce robert
Côtelettes de porc marinées, sauce robert

FOR FOUR PEOPLE

4 loin pork chops	2 cloves
¾ cup oil	salt and pepper
2 bay leaves	Sauce Robert (page 20)

Put the chops in a shallow, nonmetal dish containing the oil, bay leaves, cloves, salt, and pepper. Marinate the chops 3 days, turning them morning and evening. When it is time to cook them, put them in a skillet containing 3 tablespoons of the marinade. Cook them over a moderate heat for 20 minutes or until well cooked. Serve on a platter with sauce robert.

Milanaise pork chops
Côtelettes de porc à la milanaise

FOR FOUR PEOPLE

4 pork shoulder chops	4 tablespoons oil
1 egg, slightly beaten	12 small pitted green olives
1 cup soft breadcrumbs	juice of ½ lemon
½ cup grated Parmesan cheese	salt and pepper

Ask the butcher to pound the chops well. Place the beaten egg in one shallow dish and combine the breadcrumbs and cheese in another. Dip each chop first in the egg and then coat well with the breadcrumb mixture, patting the latter into the meat with your hand.

Brown the chops in hot oil on both sides. Add the olives, lemon juice, salt, and pepper. Cover and cook 20 minutes over moderately low heat. Serve with spaghetti.

Pork chops with apricots, curry sauce
Côtelettes de porc aux abricots, sauce cari

FOR FOUR PEOPLE

Sauce:
2 onions, chopped fine
3 tablespoons butter
1 tablespoon flour
1 tablespoon curry powder
¾ cup bouillon
salt and pepper

Chops:
¼ pound mushrooms
4 loin pork chops
6 tablespoons butter
2 apricots
salt and pepper

Sauce: Begin this recipe by making the sauce. Sauté the onions in butter until tender. They should be brown but not charred. Sprinkle with flour and add the curry. Cook 1 or 2 minutes and then add the bouillon. Season with salt and pepper. Bring the sauce to a boil, lower the heat, and simmer 30 minutes. Force through a strainer or food mill.

Pork Chops: Wash briefly, chop, and sauté the mushrooms over high heat for a few minutes. Sauté the chops in 3 tablespoons of butter until browned on both sides. Place half an apricot on each chop and cover with the curry onion sauce. Spread the mushrooms over the sauce, sprinkle with salt and pepper, cover, and cook gently for 30 minutes.

Hungarian goulash * Goulache hongroise

FOR EIGHT PEOPLE

2 pounds pork shoulder butt
2 pounds beef rump
6-8 onions
5 tablespoons butter

¾ cup oil
8 teaspoons Hungarian paprika
6-8 potatoes
salt and pepper

Order the meat cut in 1¾-inch squares.

Peel the onions and chop them fine. Heat the butter and oil in a heavy, deep pan. Add the onions and cook them over a very low heat until transparent. Add 4 teaspoons of the paprika, 4½ cups of boiling water, and the beef. Season with salt and pepper. Cover and cook for 30 minutes. Remove the cover and boil down the liquid until it practically disappears.

Add another 4½ cups of boiling water and the pork. Cover and cook 1 hour longer. Then, 20 minutes before the end of cooking, add the potatoes, peeled and cut in large pieces, and 4 teaspoons of paprika. Serve very hot.

Baked pork chops with apples
Côtelettes de porc aux pommes en l'air

FOR FOUR PEOPLE

4 loin pork chops	4 medium-sized cooking apples
3 tablespoons butter	salt and pepper

Sear the chops on both sides in very hot butter, allowing 1 minute to each side. Reduce the heat and continue cooking for 10 minutes.

Peel the apples and cut them first in quarters and then in thin slices.

Arrange the almost-cooked chops in an oven dish and pour the pan juices over it. Arrange the apple slices around the chops. Season with salt and pepper and bake in a 300° F. oven just until the apples are tender—approximately 10 minutes.

Pork goulash with cider * Goulache de porc au cidre

FOR FOUR PEOPLE

1½ pounds pork shoulder butt	¾ cup hard cider
4 onions	¾ cup bouillon
3 tablespoons butter	*bouquet garni* (thyme, bay leaf)
3 teaspoons Hungarian paprika	1½ pounds chestnuts
4 teaspoons flour	salt and pepper

Have the meat cut in 1¾-inch squares. Peel the onions and cut them in thin slices.

Heat the butter in a deep heavy pan. Sauté the onions until golden. Add the meat and sauté, stirring occasionally so that the meat will brown lightly on all sides. Add the paprika and flour, stir well. When the flour has disappeared, add the cider, bouillon, *bouquet garni,* salt, and pepper. Cover and simmer 45 minutes.

Meanwhile, make a circular cut around each chestnut. Broil them or grill them on a trivet in a heavy frying pan. Peel them and add them to the meat, adding more bouillon if necessary to cover the chestnuts. Cook 45 minutes longer.

Before serving, taste the sauce for seasoning.

Veal and pork pie * Pie de porc et veau

FOR SIX PEOPLE

⅓ recipe Flaky Pastry (page 643)
1½ pounds shoulder slice of pork
1½ pounds veal round
½ pound lean bacon (in one piece)
6 tablespoons butter
4 carrots
4 white turnips

1½ cups bouillon
juice of ½ grapefruit
2 bay leaves
savory
1 egg
salt and pepper

Prepare the flaky pastry.

Cut the meat into 1½-inch cubes. Dice the bacon quite small. Sauté the meat in 4 tablespoons of butter over a very low heat. Do not let it brown. At the same time, sauté in 2 tablespoons of butter the carrots and turnips peeled and cut in thin rounds.

Add the vegetables to the meat. Mix gently and pour in the bouillon and grapefruit juice. Season with salt, pepper, the bay leaves, and a good pinch of savory. Cover and simmer 1½ hours. Taste for seasoning. Set aside for the moment.

Roll out the pastry after the fourth "tour" into a round that will cover a deep pie dish containing the meat mixture. Put a little porcelain chimney into the dish, or lacking that, fashion one out of aluminum foil or heavy paper. Make a hole in the pastry and slip it over the chimney onto the pie dish pressing the pastry edge onto the rim. Paint the pastry with slightly beaten egg and bake 25-30 minutes at 400° F.

Easter pork pâté (cold) * Pâté de pâques au porc

FOR FIVE PEOPLE

½ recipe Flaky Pastry (page 643)
6 eggs

2 cups ground pork
salt and pepper

After its final "tour" roll out the pastry into a long rectangle.

Trim the edges even. Moisten the edges with cold water.

Hard-cook 5 eggs in salted water for 20 minutes. Shell them and cut each one in half lengthwise.

Spread half the rectangle with the ground pork, leaving a margin on all sides. Dispose the egg halves on the meat. Sprinkle with salt and pepper. Fold the other half of the rectangle over the meat and eggs and press the edges together. Place on a baking sheet, paint the entire surface with slightly beaten egg, and bake 1 hour at 400° F. Cool and then put in the refrigerator.

The pâté is eaten cold.

Pork on skewers * Brochettes de porc poêlées

FOR FOUR PEOPLE

1 pound lean pork	3 tablespoons lard
8 slices bacon	lemon
bay leaves	salt and pepper

Cut the meat into small pieces, approximately ¾ inch square. Cut the bacon in small pieces. Alternate meat, bacon, and half bay leaves on small skewers, filling each skewer.

Heat the fat in a skillet and fry the skewered meat for 15 minutes, turning often. Salt very lightly, but be generous with freshly ground black pepper. Sprinkle with lemon juice.

Serve with potato purée.

Potée bretonne * Potée bretonne

FOR FOUR PEOPLE

1 pound lightly cured pork shoulder	8 carrots
1 pound lean pork belly or salt pork	½ pound Polish sausage
1 large cabbage	salt and pepper

Wash the pork meats to remove excess salt.

Trim the cabbage, removing the hard outside leaves, and parboil the cabbage in salted water for 10 minutes. Drain.

Put the pork meats, the cabbage cut in pieces, the carrots cut in rounds, and a little pepper in a casserole. Cook covered for 2 hours.

Then 10 minutes before the end of cooking, put in the sausage cut in two pieces. Serve with boiled potatoes.

Potée auvergnate * Potée auvergnate

FOR FOUR PEOPLE

½ pound dry white beans	4 turnips
½ small cured pig's head	4 carrots
1 *cervelas* or ½ pound other	1 clove garlic, crushed
dry sausage	*bouquet garni* (bay leaf, thyme, parsley)
1 cabbage	1 stalk celery
1 large onion	4 large potatoes
4 leeks	4 slices French bread

½ pound lean pork belly or salt pork   salt and pepper

Soak the beans for at least 3 hours.

Wipe the pig's head well. Place it and the pork belly (or salt pork parboiled 5 minutes) in a deep kettle. Cover with 3¼ quarts of water. Bring to a boil slowly, skimming off the matter that floats to the surface. When the liquid boils add the onion, leeks, turnips, and carrots, all peeled and cut in large pieces. Add also the garlic, the *bouquet garni,* and the celery cut in large pieces. Cover and cook gently, for 1 hour.

Cut the cabbage in quarters and parboil 10 minutes. Parboil the beans 10 minutes. Add both vegetables. Season with pepper and add salt, if necessary. Continue to cook 1½ hours. Add the potatoes, cut in two, and the *cervelas.* Cook 35 minutes more.

Place the meats on a serving platter and surround with the vegetables. Serve the broth from a soup tureen in which you have placed the French bread slices dried in the oven. Serve very hot.

Ham

In France, cooked hams are called *jambon de Paris* if they are boneless and *jambon d'York* if the bone has been left in, no matter what part of France they come from. Uncooked hams, on the contrary, are named specifically for the locality they come from: *jambon de Bayonne, de Lozère, de Mayence,* and so on. The quality and type of pig differs from place to place, but what is most characteristic is the difference in curing and smoking.

In America, most of the hams sold in the market have been partly or wholly precooked and require neither prolonged soaking nor cooking. This is a mixed blessing. Uncooked hams can be bought, and for the most part, I would recommend the uncooked as the kind to get.

A whole ham weighs from 10 to 12 pounds and will feed 20 to 24 people. It is possible to buy a half ham (preferably the butt end), or a shoulder ham called picnic, or cottage, ham, which is more suitable for most families' requirements.

Imported canned hams are very satisfactory for recipes calling for cooked ham.

Burgundy ham * Jambon à la bourguignonne

FOR EIGHT PEOPLE

1 small uncooked or partially cooked ham	1 sprig thyme
4 sprigs parsley	1 teaspoon peppercorns
2 onions	2 cups red Burgundy wine
3 cloves	2 cups bouillon
	1½ teaspoons arrowroot or cornstarch

Soak the ham in water for 24 hours unless otherwise indicated by the directions on the ham wrapping. Rinse it well.

Put the ham in a deep kettle with parsley, onions in which the cloves are stuck, thyme, and peppercorns. Cover with boiling water and boil gently for 1½ hours.

Remove the ham and take off the skin and extra fat, leaving a coating about ½ inch thick.

Put the ham in a casserole. Add the wine and bouillon. Cover and bake 1 hour at 300° F.

Mix the arrowroot in a small bowl with ½ cup of the liquid in which the ham is cooking. Pour it into the casserole and continue cooking for 15 minutes. Taste for seasoning. Slice the ham and serve with potato purée.

Ham in aspic * Jambon en gelée

FOR TWELVE PEOPLE

1 large ham
1 calf's (or pig's) foot
4 carrots
4 leeks
1 stalk celery

1 large *bouquet garni* (thyme, bay leaf, parsley)
2 tablespoons cognac
2 lumps sugar
1 truffle
salt and pepper

Place the ham and calf's foot in a large kettle. Cover it with cold water, 2 teaspoons of salt, and a teaspoon of peppercorns. Bring slowly to a boil, skimming off all the matter that floats to the top. When the liquid boils, add the vegetables, washed, trimmed, and cut in pieces, and the *bouquet garni.* Cover and simmer gently for 3 hours.

Remove the ham and let it cool. Cut off the skin and fat. When thoroughly cold, cut the ham in thin slices and arrange them on a serving platter.

Meanwhile, pour the broth through a strainer lined with a cold damp dish towel to remove the fat. Boil down the broth to about 3 cups. Add the cognac and color it with caramel made with 2 lumps of sugar (page 579). Let cool until syrupy but not set. Decorate the ham with thin slices of truffle and spoon the sauce over the ham. Refrigerate until the aspic is firm.

Roast ham * Jambon rôti

FOR EIGHT PEOPLE

1 small boned fresh ham
1 bottle white wine
¾ cup oil

1 tablespoon salt
1 teaspoon peppercorns
bouquet garni (thyme, bay leaf, sage)

Ask the butcher to bone the ham. Remove the skin and most of the fat, leaving a covering of about ½ inch. Place the ham in a nonmetal container with the wine, oil, salt, peppercorns, and *bouquet garni.* Marinate for 2 days.

Remove the ham from the marinade, tie the ham, and roast it at 300° F., allowing 35-40 minutes per pound. Baste often with the marinade.

Serve with chestnut purée.

Ham with prunes * Jambon aux pruneaux

FOR TWELVE PEOPLE

1 large uncooked ham
2 pounds prunes

2 cups port
salt and pepper

Put the ham in a large kettle of cold water without any seasoning. Bring to a boil, lower the heat, and continue to simmer, allowing 20 minutes to the pound.

Take the ham from the water and remove the skin and most of the fat. Place in a casserole or Dutch oven just large enough to contain the ham. Add the wine and the prunes, which have been soaked in advance. Season with salt and pepper. Cover and braise ½ hour.

Place the ham on a serving platter. Cut some off in thin slices and surround with prunes. Pour the sauce over the ham.

Ham with mushrooms * Jambon aux champignons

FOR FOUR PEOPLE

8 slices cooked ham (¼ inch thick)
¾ pound mushrooms
6 tablespoons butter
4 teaspoons flour
½ cup milk
¾ cup heavy cream
salt and pepper

If the ham slices are unusually large, buy 4 and cut them in half. They should be of equal size and shape.

Wash the mushrooms. Take about a quarter of them and slice thin. Throw them into boiling water for 2 minutes. Drain. Chop the remaining mushrooms and boil them in salted water for 2 minutes also. Drain.

Make a béchamel sauce, using 2 tablespoons of the butter, the flour, and milk. Season well and mix in the chopped mushrooms.

Heat the cream with the remaining butter, but do not let it boil. Place 4 slices of ham in a lightly buttered shallow oven dish. Spread the mushroom sauce over the ham and cover with the remaining 4 slices. Cover with the hot cream. Sprinkle with salt and pepper. Decorate with the sliced mushrooms and brown in a hot oven for 4 to 5 minutes.

Ham birds * Jambon en paupiettes

FOR FOUR PEOPLE

1 celery root (celeriac)
2 apples
½ cup chopped walnuts
¾ cup thick Mayonnaise (page 14)
juice of ½ lemon
1 can *foie gras* mousse
8 slices cooked ham (⅛ inch thick)

Peel the celery, boil it 5 minutes in salted water, drain, and cool. Cut in small dice. (If celery root is not available, substitute 2 celery hearts and do not blanch.—*Ed.*)

Peel, core, and dice the apples and mix the celery, apples, and chopped nuts. Bind with mayonnaise well seasoned with lemon juice.

Spread each slice of ham with *foie gras* mousse. Cover with a good layer of the apple mixture. Roll up each piece. Serve with a green or tomato salad.

Ham with grapes * Jambon aux raisins

FOR FOUR PEOPLE

8 slices cooked ham	bouillon
Brown Sauce (page 7)	1 bunch large white seedless grapes
2 tablespoons Madeira	salt and pepper

Trim the edges of the ham if the skin has been left on and roll each one up. Place them in a shallow oven dish.

Make the sauce and season it with Madeira, salt, and pepper. Add enough bouillon to make a thin sauce. Add the grapes, free from stems, and pour the sauce over the ham. Put in a 350° F. oven until the ham is thoroughly heated.

Ham with tarragon sauce
Jambon sauce brune à l'estragon

FOR FOUR PEOPLE

Tarragon Sauce (page 21)	2 tablespoons butter
8 slices boned cooked ham (¼ inch)	

Make the sauce. It should be rather thin.

Warm the ham in a large skillet containing the butter. Do not fry the ham; it should be simply heated.

Heat a serving platter. Arrange the ham on the serving platter, each slice overlapping the other slightly.

Pour the sauce over the meat and serve very hot. Serve with braised endive, Brussels sprouts, or simply with steamed potatoes.

Croque-monsieur * Croque-monsieur

FOR FOUR PEOPLE

16 very thin slices white bread	6 tablespoons butter
4 large slices cooked ham	2 tablespoons oil
16 thin slices Gruyère cheese	

Assemble the bread, ham, and cheese. The ham should be cut in two and be the same size and shape as the bread and cheese.

Butter the bread. Cover half the slices with a slice of cheese, a slice of ham, another slice of cheese, and finally a piece of bread.

Heat butter and oil in a skillet and fry the sandwiches 2 minutes on each side. Serve hot.

Ham and cheese croquettes * Croquettes de jambon

FOR SIX PEOPLE

1¼ cups flour	2 cups grated Gruyère cheese
5 eggs	2 large thin slices cooked ham, minced
2 cups boiling milk	fine breadcrumbs
	salt and pepper

Mix the flour, 2 egg yolks, and 3 whole eggs in a bowl, stirring until you have a smooth paste. Put in a small saucepan and add the boiling milk, stirring constantly. When the mixture boils, reduce the heat and cook 6 minutes. Remove from the heat and stir in the cheese and ham. Season with salt and pepper. Take care, the cheese is salty.

Pour this mixture onto a small baking sheet, smoothing it into a sheet ¾ inch thick. Chill completely.

Shortly before serving, beat the 2 egg whites until frothy. Cut the croquette mixture into rectangles. Dip each rectangle first in egg white and then into breadcrumbs. Fry in deep fat (385° F.). Drain and serve very hot with a green salad or with tomato sauce.

Ham soufflé * Soufflé de jambon

FOR EIGHT PEOPLE

3¼ cups ground cooked ham	6 egg yolks, beaten slightly
2 cups thick Béchamel Sauce (page 6)	8 egg whites, beaten stiff
cayenne	salt and pepper
¾ cup heavy cream	

Use ham that is very lean.

Make the sauce, and when it is cooled to lukewarm, season with salt, pepper, and cayenne. Stir in the cream and the ground ham. Mix well and add the egg yolks. Finally, fold in the beaten egg whites. Pour into a buttered mold or baking dish. It should fill the dish about two thirds of the way so that the soufflé can rise.

Bake in a 350° F. oven for 25 minutes.

Ham mousse with spinach
Mousse de jambon aux épinards

FOR SIX PEOPLE

3 cups thick Béchamel Sauce (page 6)
1 cup ground lean cooked ham
4 eggs yolks
½ cup heavy cream
few drops red coloring

4 eggs whites, beaten stiff
4 pounds spinach
½ cup grated Gruyère cheese
salt and pepper

Make the béchamel sauce and remove from the heat. Put aside ¾ cup. Into the rest, stir the ham, the egg yolks, and the cream. Season and add a few drops of red coloring. Fold in the stiffly beaten egg whites and mix well. Put in a buttered mold and bake in a pan of hot water for 45 minutes at 350° F.

Boil the fresh spinach just until tender (or substitute 2 boxes of frozen leaf spinach—Ed.). Drain the spinach well and place it in a shallow oven dish. Unmold the mousse on the spinach. Add the cheese to the reserved sauce and spread it over the mousse. Put back in the oven for 15 minutes.

Ham cornucopias (cold) * Jambon en cornets

FOR SIX PEOPLE

2 cups cooked, mixed vegetables
   (macédoine)
1 cup Mayonnaise (page 14)
6 large, very thin slices cooked ham

6 small tomatoes
1 head garden lettuce
salt and pepper

Prepare the vegetable macédoine and mix in the mayonnaise, saving out a little for decorating. Season well.

Roll the ham into cornucopias and fill each one with the mixture.

Cut the tomatoes in half and place them cut side down on a serving platter. Spread them with mayonnaise so that they resemble mushrooms. Surround the edge with 6 large lettuce leaves and place a cornucopia on each leaf.

Salt pork and cabbage * Petit salé aux choux

FOR SIX PEOPLE

3 pounds very lean salt pork (in one piece)
2 small cabbages

6 carrots
bouquet garni (bay leaf, thyme)
½ teaspoon peppercorns

Wash the salt pork in running water for 30 minutes to remove the excess salt.

Remove the hard outer leaves of the cabbage, quarter them, and boil them in a kettle of boiling water for 5 minutes. Drain well.

Peel the carrots and leave whole.

Put the salt pork in a kettle containing 3½ quarts cold water. Add the *bouquet garni* and the peppercorns. Bring to a boil, skimming off the matter that floats to the surface. Reduce the heat, cover about three fourths of the way, and cook 30 minutes.

Add the cabbage and the carrots and cook 1½ hours.

Remove the cabbage from the kettle with a slotted spoon and let it drain well before putting it on a heated serving platter. Remove the carrots and place them around the edge, and finally put the salt pork on the cabbage. Serve immediately with steamed potatoes and mustard.

Sausages on skewers * Brochettes de chipolatas

FOR FOUR PEOPLE

20 small link sausages
16 small mushroom caps

1 tablespoon olive oil
4 tomatoes

Alternate small sausages with mushroom caps, brushed with oil, and pieces of tomatoes on small skewers. Broil or grill over charcoal for 10 minutes, turning often. Serve with mustard.

Sausages in pastry * Chipolatas en robe

FOR TWELVE PEOPLE

1 recipe Flaky Pastry (page 643)
½ cup oil
2½ pounds link sausages

tarragon mustard
small cup milk
Tomato Sauce (page 22)

Make a flaky pastry in advance.

Heat the oil in a skillet and brown the sausages on all sides. Remove from the skillet and drain.

After the final "tour," roll out the pastry as thin as possible. Cut into rectangles 2 by 3 inches. Spread each rectangle with a little tarragon mustard, which can be bought in fine grocery shops. Place a sausage on each rectangle and fold up like a package. Brush each one with milk.

Bake 10 minutes in a preheated 400° F. oven. Serve very hot with tomato sauce and an endive or green salad.

Sauerkraut

It is customary in most places to buy the sauerkraut all prepared so that all we need do is add wine, herbs, and pork products.

This excellent dish was introduced into France in the eighteenth century by the Princess Palatine, mother of the Regent. This Bavarian princess scandalized and shocked the lords and ladies of the Court, who found the odor of cooking sauerkraut revolting. It is quite true that the odor is disagreeable; if you want to avoid it, every time you cook cabbage, put a large piece of bread in a clean towel or cheesecloth. Tie it well, and put it in the pot with the cooking cabbage.

Alsatian sauerkraut * La choucroute

FOR FOUR PEOPLE

3 tablespoons lard
2 onions
1 sprig thyme
1 bay leaf
1 teaspoon peppercorns
2 cloves
½ bottle dry white wine

2 pounds sauerkraut
½ pound pork belly
¼ pound fat bacon
1 pound cured boneless pork
    shoulder butt
4 large Frankfurt sausages
8 new potatoes

Heat the lard in a deep pan. Peel and slice the onions very thin. When they are transparent, add the thyme, bay leaf, peppercorns, and cloves. Add the white wine and simmer 5 minutes. Add the sauerkraut and stir well. Reduce the heat and add the pork belly and bacon. (If pork belly is not available, add pork jowl or fat salt pork, parboiled 5 minutes.—*Ed.*) Cover and cook 30 minutes. Add the pork shoulder and simmer 4 hours. Then, 10 minutes before serving, add the sausages.

Boil the potatoes in their jackets. Peel them and serve with the sauerkraut.

Sauerkraut with champagne
Choucroute au champagne

FOR EIGHT PEOPLE

Sauerkraut cooked in this way is perfectly delicious and very easy to digest. It is a meal in itself. If there are any leftovers, keep covered in a cool place and three or four days later it will be very good reheated.

6 tablespoons lard
3 onions
1 sprig thyme
1 bay leaf
1 teaspoon peppercorns
1 bottle dry champagne
4 pounds sauerkraut

½ pound fat bacon
½ pound fresh pork belly
2 pounds cured boneless pork
    shoulder butt
1 pound boned pork loin
8 large Frankfurt sausages
8-10 small potatoes

Heat the lard in a large deep kettle. Sauté the onions until transparent. Add the thyme, bay leaf, pepper, and dry champagne. Simmer 5 minutes and add the sauerkraut, fat bacon, and pork belly. (Substitute parboiled pork jowl or fat salt pork, if necessary.—*Ed.*)

Cook gently for 30 minutes. Add the pork meats and continue cooking for 4 hours. Then, 10 minutes before serving, add the sausages. Serve with steamed potatoes.

Variety meats

What are known as *abats* in France, offal in England, and variety meats in America are different names for the edible innards of animals. Some strange sensitivity has kept Americans not only from giving these delicacies a proper name but from even enjoying this section of gastronomy to the fullest. But times are changing in this respect, and people are becoming more adventurous. This is good, because properly prepared meats in this category are among the most nutritious and delicious offerings of the French cuisine.

In France, there are special shops called *triperies* where all manner of variety meats are prepared for final cooking or completely cooked for the customers. This does not exist in America. Below are a few directions for preparing and pre-cooking the variety meats for which recipes follow.

Brains:
To prepare: Soak the brains for 1 hour in cold water to which white vinegar has been added. Remove the membrane and bloody tissue and put them into fresh cold water.

To precook: Cook 30 minutes in simmering water (enough to cover) to which a tablespoon of white vinegar and a teaspoon of salt have been added. Drain and dry.

Calf's Head:
Buy the calf's head boned and cleaned. Soak at least 6 hours in water to which white vinegar has been added. Change the water occasionally. Before cooking, rub the head with the cut side of a lemon so that the flesh will not darken. Wrap the head in a cheesecloth and place in a kettle of cold water. The water should come 1 inch above the head. Cook over high heat to begin with, skimming off the matter that comes to the surface. Reduce the heat and simmer 4 hours (less if the head has been cut in pieces).

Cold *tête de veau* is served with a variety of sauces. It can be served hot au gratin as fritters, sautéed with black butter and parsley, or in a kind of stew called *matelote*.

Tongue:
Tongue must be soaked 5 to 6 hours in cold water and then plunged in boiling water to loosen the skin, which must be removed.

Sweetbreads:
See individual recipes.

Liver:
See individual recipes.

Tripe:

To prepare: Parboil fresh tripe for a few minutes. Drain and rinse in cool water. Remove the skin and scrape the exterior. Soak 12 hours in cold water, changing the water occasionally.

To precook: Boil 1½ to 3 hours or until tender in water strongly flavored with vinegar.

(Pickled tripe is much more available in the United States than fresh tripe. Before using, wash in several changes of cool water and soak several hours. Simmer 5 minutes in salted water. Drain and rinse. Simmer 2 hours).

Calf's brains fritters * Beignets de cervelle de veau

FOR FOUR PEOPLE

1 set calf's brains
wine vinegar
Frying Batter VII (page 112)

parsley
salt

Follow the introductory instructions for preparing and precooking the brains.

Prepare the frying batter; wash and dry the parsley. Preheat the deep fat to 385° F.

Cut the well-drained brains in large squares. Dip them in the batter and fry until golden brown. Fry the parsley a few seconds.

Serve the brains on a napkin-lined platter and sprinkle with salt. Garnish with the parsley. This should be eaten *very* hot.

Brain pâté * Pâté de cervelle de veau

FOR TWELVE PEOPLE

2 sets veal brains
2 onions
1½ cups oil
2 tablespoons chopped parsley
2 tablespoons chopped chervil

1 tablespoon chopped tarragon
12 eggs
3 tablespoons coarsely chopped
  pistachio nuts
salt and pepper

Follow the introductory instructions for preparing the brains. Rinse and precook 5 minutes in boiling salted water.

Peel the onions and chop them very fine. Place in a saucepan with the oil and chopped herbs and cook gently for 5 minutes. Drain the brains and add them to the mixture in the saucepan and add 1½ cups water. Season with salt and pepper and cook uncovered until all the water has disappeared.

Cut the brains in large pieces. Beat the eggs as you would for an omelet or just until the yolks and whites are well blended. Add the pistachio nuts and season again with salt and pepper. Oil a preheated mold, pour in the brain mixture, and bake 15 minutes at 350° F. Unmold when cold.

Fried beef brains * Cervelle de boeuf frite

FOR FOUR PEOPLE

1 set beef brains
Frying Batter VII (page 112)
Tomato Sauce (page 22)

8 sprigs parsley
4 lemon quarters
salt

Follow the introductory instructions for preparing and precooking the brains (see above). At the same time, make the batter and the tomato sauce. Wash the parsley and dry on toweling. Preheat the deep fat (preferably vegetable oil) to 385° F.

Cut the brains in pieces and dip the pieces one by one into the batter and then into the boiling fat. Fry to a golden brown. Do not fry more than 5 or 6 pieces at a time or the fat will become too cool. When the brains are cooked, place them on a heated platter. Fry the parsley for a few seconds. Garnish the platter with the parsley and lemon. Sprinkle the meat with salt and serve with the tomato sauce.

Brain loaf * Pain de cervelle de veau

FOR FOUR PEOPLE

1 set calf's brains
4 eggs
½ cup heavy cream

Madeira Sauce (page 11)
salt and pepper

Follow the introductory instructions for preparing the brains. Rinse and precook in boiling salted water for 15 minutes. Drain well and place in a mortar or in a wooden bowl.

Separate the yolks from the whites of the eggs.

Pound the brains with the cream, the egg yolks, salt, and pepper until it becomes a smooth paste. Beat the egg whites stiff and fold into the brain mixture.

Butter a mold—preferably a classic charlotte mold—and pour in the brain mixture. Place in a pan of hot water and bake 1 hour at 350° F. Unmold and serve with a Madeira sauce, prepared while the loaf is baking.

Lamb's brains in brown butter with apples
Cervelle de mouton au beurre noir et pommes

FOR FOUR PEOPLE

4 large lamb's brains
2 pounds apples
sugar
6 tablespoons butter

8 teaspoons wine vinegar
4 teaspoons capers
2 tablespoons chopped parsley
salt and pepper

Follow the introductory instructions for preparing the brains. Precook 25 minutes.

Peel and core the apples and cook them in a small amount of water just until tender. Force them through a strainer or food mill and sweeten them lightly.

Brown the butter in a small saucepan. Add the capers, 4 teaspoons of vinegar, and the chopped parsley, salt, and pepper.

Drain the brains thoroughly and cut them in two longitudinally. Place them on a hot platter. Pour the hot brown butter over the brains and serve with the applesauce.

Tripe victorine * Gras-double victorine

FOR FOUR PEOPLE

4 onions
¾ cup oil
4 shallots
2 cloves garlic
1½ pounds precooked or
  pickled tripe (page 421)
2 tablespoons cognac

2 tablespoons Italian tomato paste
¾ cup dry white wine
thyme
2 teaspoons chopped parsley
salt and pepper

Peel the onions and cut them in very thin slices. Heat half the oil in a skillet and cook the onions gently without letting them take on any color.

Peel the shallots and cook them for 5 minutes in boiling water. Mince the garlic.

Slice the tripe in strips and sauté them in the rest of the oil in a heavy, shallow saucepan until golden. Add the onions and the shallots. Add the cognac and touch with a lighted match. Stir while the flames subside. Add the garlic, the tomato paste, the white wine, ¾ cup water, and seasonings. Stir well and place in a casserole dish. Cook covered in a 350° F. oven for 1 hour.

Veal heart in white wine
Coeur de veau au vin blanc

FOR SIX PEOPLE

2 pounds veal heart	2 teaspoons chopped parsley
¼ pound butter	2 teaspoons chopped chives
¼ cup cognac	1 teaspoon chopped tarragon
¾ cup dry white wine	salt and pepper

Cut the heart lengthwise in very thin slices. Heat the butter in a large skillet and sauté the slices over a moderate flame for 2 minutes, turning each piece once. Keep warm while preparing the sauce.

Stir the cognac into the butter in the skillet and touch with a lighted match. When the flames subside, add the wine, salt, and pepper and let the sauce boil for a few minutes. Reheat the heart slices in the sauce, but do not let the sauce boil, or they will become tough.

Serve on a heated platter and sprinkle with the herbs. Rice is the best companion to this dish.

Calf's liver bercy * Foie de veau bercy

FOR FOUR PEOPLE

4 slices calf's liver (¼ pound each)	2 teaspoons chopped parsley
6 tablespoons butter	juice of 1 lemon
4 teaspoons flour	salt and pepper

Trim the filament from the liver. Heat half the butter and dip each slice in it and sprinkle lightly with flour. Grill or broil with moderate heat for 5 to 8 minutes.

Cream the balance of the butter with the chopped parsley. Place the liver on a hot platter. Sprinkle with salt and pepper. Place a piece of the parsley butter on each slice and sprinkle with lemon juice.

Broiled calf's liver with marrow
Foie de veau grillé à la moëlle

FOR FOUR PEOPLE

1 marrow bone	4 thick slices calf's liver
3 tablespoons butter	flour
1 lemon	salt and pepper

Ask the butcher to saw a good marrow bone for you and just give you the raw marrow. Poach this 5 minutes in simmering salted water.

Melt the butter and add the juice of ½ lemon to it.

Trim the filament from the liver. Season with salt and pepper. Dip the liver pieces in flour. Paint with the melted butter and broil or grill 5 minutes.

Preheat a serving platter and decorate it with lemon slices. Place the liver slices on the platter, and in the center of each one, place a round of marrow, taken directly from the hot water.

Calf's liver with apples * Foie de veau aux pommes

FOR FOUR PEOPLE

4 slices calf's liver (¼ pound each)	2 lemons
flour	4 teaspoons apple brandy
2 cooking apples	2 teaspoons chopped parsley
5 tablespoons butter	salt and pepper

Trim the filament from the liver. Sprinkle with salt and pepper and dip each side in flour.

Peel, core, and slice the apples very thin.

Using two frying pans, heat half the butter in each one. Cook the apples very gently in one, taking care that they do not turn into applesauce, but are just softened. In the other pan, fry the liver, allowing 3 to 5 minutes on each side, according to preference. Sprinkle with lemon juice.

Place the liver on a heated platter. Pour the apple brandy on the apples. Touch with a lighted flame and pour the apples over the liver. Decorate with lemon slices and chopped parsley.

Liver and bacon on skewers
Brochettes de foie de veau au bacon

FOR FOUR PEOPLE

10 ounces calf's liver	4 tablespoons olive oil
4 bacon slices (⅛ inch thick)	powdered thyme
4 small tomatoes	salt and pepper

Cut the liver in 2-inch cubes. Cut each slice of bacon into 4 pieces and the tomatoes into wedges.

Alternate the liver, bacon, and tomato pieces on 4 small skewers. Using a pastry brush, paint them with olive oil. Sprinkle them with powdered thyme and grill or broil for about 10 minutes, turning them occasionally. Sprinkle with salt and pepper before serving.

Calf's liver with white grapes
Foie de veau aux raisins

FOR EIGHT PEOPLE

1 whole calf's liver
2 slices paper-thin fat salt pork
6-ounce chunk salt pork
2 onions, chopped fine
3 carrots, grated
½ cup dry white wine

½ cup bouillon
bouquet garni (thyme, bay leaf, parsley)
1 large bunch white grapes
⅔ cup heavy cream
salt and pepper

Order a whole liver and ask the butcher to tie it like a roast, enveloping it with a paper-thin covering of fat salt pork. Sprinkle with black pepper.

Wash the chunk of salt pork and parboil 5 minutes to remove the excess salt. Cut in small dice and heat in a deep heavy saucepan to try out the fat. When the liquid fat is very hot, remove the pork pieces, put in the liver, and brown lightly on all sides. When this is accomplished, pour off half the fat.

Add the chopped onion and grated carrot and cook gently for 5 minutes. Add the wine and bouillon, the *bouquet garni,* and a little more pepper. Cover and barely simmer for 2¼ hours. The pan can be put in a 275° F. oven, if you wish. The liver should be turned and basted occasionally.

Remove the liver from the pan and keep warm. Strain the sauce through a fine sieve. With a spoon, skim off as much fat as possible from the sauce as you reheat it. Add the grapes, free from stems, and the cream. Taste for seasoning and heat without boiling for 5 minutes.

Remove the covering and strings from the liver. Slice on a preheated platter and cover with the sauce. Serve immediately.

Home style tripe * Gras-double de chez nous

FOR FOUR PEOPLE

2 pounds precooked or pickled tripe
   (page 421)
5 tablespoons butter
4 large onions

1 tablespoon chopped parsley
1 cup dry white wine
salt and pepper

Slice the tripe very thin.

Using 2 skillets, heat half the butter in each one. Peel the onions and slice them very thin. Sauté until golden.

At the same time, sauté the tripe slices over a very high flame until golden. Add the onions to the tripe. Season with salt, pepper, and parsley. Mix well. Place in an earthenware shallow dish that has been preheated. Pour the wine into the tripe pan and stir in order to scrape off the cooking juices in the bottom of the pan. Pour over the tripe. Eat very hot.

Pork liver loaf * Gâteau de foie de porc

FOR SIX PEOPLE

1 pound pork liver	4 eggs
1 pound pork fat	⅓ cup Madeira
1½ cups milk	1 tablespoon cognac
1½ cups flour	salt and pepper

Force the raw liver through a strainer into a bowl. Heat the pork fat over a low flame to render the liquid fat.

Mix the milk and flour to a smooth paste. Stir in the eggs and cook over a moderate flame until the mixture no longer sticks to the sides. Stir constantly. Add the melted fat, the raw liver, and the wine and cognac. Season highly with salt and pepper. Force again through a strainer and pour into a baking casserole or bread tin. Bake 1½ hours in 375° F. oven. Cool before placing in refrigerator. Serve cold.

Pork pâté * Pâté de grillotin

FOR SIX PEOPLE

1 pound fresh boned pork	1 small box truffle peelings
1 pound pork liver	⅓ pound pork skin *or*
1 pound pork fat	½ pound bacon strips
5 tablespoons cognac	

Chop separately the pork, the liver, and the pork fat. Mix them well and stir in the cognac, truffles, salt, and pepper.

Ask the butcher to cut off a large piece of pork skin when he is cutting up a pork. If this is impossible, use bacon strips. Line an earthenware terrine with the pork skin *(couenne)* or bacon strips in such a manner that ends hang over the edges long enough to cover the pâté when the terrine is filled.

Fill the terrine with the pâté and fold the ends over. Bake 1 hour at 375° F. Let the pâté cool in the terrine.

Pork liver with onions * Foie de porc aux oignons

FOR SIX PEOPLE

6 quarter-pound slices pork liver	2 tablespoons butter

salt and pepper

flour

2 large onions

2½ tablespoons wine vinegar

3 tablespoons oil

1 tablespoon chopped parsley

Trim the filament from the liver slices, sprinkle with salt and pepper, and dip each slice lightly in flour.

Chop the onions quite fine and sauté them in butter until golden. Add the vinegar. Season with salt and pepper and cook 2 minutes. Keep warm.

Fry the liver in oil over a moderate flame until cooked but not overcooked. Place the slices on a heated platter. Spoon the onions over the slices and sprinkle with chopped parsley. Serve with puréed or sautéed potatoes.

Breaded lamb liver * Foie d'agneau pané

FOR FOUR PEOPLE

4-8 slices lamb's liver

oil

½ teaspoon rosemary powder

1 cup dry breadcrumbs

juice of 1 lemon

½ cup heavy cream, warmed

salt

Soak the liver slices in oil for 30 minutes, turning them occasionally. Sprinkle each piece with rosemary and salt and coat with breadcrumbs. Place on a baking sheet and broil 4 minutes on each side.

Place on a heated serving platter. Sprinkle with lemon juice and serve with warm cream to which a little lemon juice has been added.

Sweetbreads in cream * Ris de veau à la crème

FOR FOUR PEOPLE

2 pairs sweetbreads

5 tablespoons butter

1 small can truffle pieces

½ pint heavy cream

salt and pepper

Put the sweetbreads in cold water for 2 hours, changing the water several times. Then put the sweetbreads in a pan of cold water and bring to a boil. Simmer 1 minute and plunge into cold water. Remove the membranes and bloody tissues, and when the sweetbreads are cold, press them in clean toweling to remove moisture. Cut the sweetbreads in ¼-inch slices.

Sauté the slices in butter over a moderate heat, allowing 5 minutes to each side. Season with salt and pepper and place on a heated platter.

Meanwhile, heat the truffles and the cream, but do not let the sauce boil. Season with salt and pepper and pour over the sweetbreads.

Sweetbreads clamart * Ris de veau clamart

FOR FOUR PEOPLE

1 large sweetbread	2-3 pounds fresh peas
flour	juice of ½ lemon
6 tablespoons butter	salt and pepper

Put the sweetbread to soak in cold water for several hours, changing the water 2 or 3 times. Bring to a boil from cold water, simmer 2 minutes, and put back into cold water. Remove the membranes and bloody tissues.

Cut the sweetbread into thin slices. Dip each piece in flour and sauté in the butter over moderate heat, allowing 5 minutes to each side.

Meanwhile, shell and cook the peas in boiling salted water until tender. Drain well and put in the center of a heated serving dish. Place the sweetbread slices on the peas in a ring. Sprinkle the lemon juice into the butter in the pan. Add salt and pepper and stir hard to remove the cooking juice from the bottom of the pan. Pour over the sweetbreads and peas. Serve very hot.

Braised sweetbreads * Ris de veau braisé

FOR FOUR PEOPLE

2 pairs sweetbreads	4 teaspoons cognac
6 tablespoons butter	salt and pepper
3 carrots	

Soak the sweetbreads in water for 2 to 3 hours. Put them in a pan of cold water and bring them to a boil. Simmer 2 minutes. Put them in a bowl of cool water and remove the membranes and bloody tissues.

Heat the butter in a heavy saucepan. Cut the carrots in thin slices into the butter and sauté lightly. Add the drained sweetbreads and cook over the same moderate heat until they are golden. Add the cognac and touch with a lighted match. Cover and simmer 20 minutes. Sprinkle with salt and pepper.

Place the sweetbreads on a preheated serving platter and strain the sauce from the pan over them.

Sweetbreads with truffles * Ris de veau aux truffes

FOR FOUR PEOPLE

1 pair sweetbreads	1 large truffle
1 tablespoon white vinegar	4 teaspoons flour
flour	¾ cup bouillon

7 tablespoons butter	⅓ cup Madeira
1 goose liver	salt and pepper

Soak the sweetbreads for 1 hour in warm water to which a tablespoon of vinegar has been added. Boil 3 minutes in salted water. Plunge into very cold water and remove the membranes and bloody tissues.

Cut the sweetbreads into 4 slices, dip in flour. Using one large skillet or two smaller ones, heat in 4 tablespoons of butter, allowing 5 minutes of gentle cooking to each side. At the same time, sauté the fresh goose liver, cut in 4 slices and dipped in flour. Allow 3 minutes to each side. Slice the truffle and heat the slices 1 minute on each side.

Heat 3 tablespoons of butter. Stir in the flour, and when well blended, stir in the bouillon and Madeira. Season with salt and pepper and simmer 10 to 15 minutes.

Alternate the slices of sweetbread, liver, and truffles on a heated serving platter and strain the sauce over them.

Sweetbreads on skewers * Brochettes de ris de veau

FOR SIX PEOPLE

2 pairs sweetbreads	6 tablespoons butter
½ pound mushrooms	soft breadcrumbs
6 slices bacon (⅛ inch thick)	salt and pepper

Soak the sweetbreads 5 to 6 hours in cold water, changing the water several times. Bring the sweetbreads to a boil, simmer 2 minutes, drain and put into cold water again. Remove the membranes and bloody tissues. Put them in clean toweling and press out the moisture.

Wash, wipe, and slice the mushroom heads. Cut the sweetbreads and the bacon into squares.

Alternate the sweetbreads, mushroom slices, and bacon on six small skewers. Sprinkle with salt and pepper. Melt the butter and spread the breadcrumbs out on a large plate. Brush each skewer generously with melted butter and roll in the breadcrumbs. Broil or grill under low heat for 15 minutes, turning the skewers frequently.

Normandy sweetbreads * Ris de veau à la normande

FOR FOUR PEOPLE

2 small pairs sweetbreads (1¼ pounds)	4 teaspoons apple brandy or Calvados
2 pounds apples	½ cup heavy cream

7 tablespoons melted butter   salt and pepper
fried croutons

Soak the sweetbreads in warm water for 1 hour. Remove the membranes and bloody tissues. Put in a pan of boiling salted water and simmer 3 minutes. Drain and cool.

Peel, core, and quarter the apples and cook in covered shallow pan with 2 tablespoons of butter.

Place the sweetbreads in a pan containing 5 tablespoons of melted butter. Sprinkle with salt and pepper and cover with a piece of buttered paper to keep the sweetbreads from darkening. Cover the pan and cook very gently for 30 minutes.

Cut into squares 3 to 4 thick slices of white bread from which the crusts have been removed and fry them in butter. Remove paper from sweetbreads, add the apple brandy, and touch with a lighted match.

When the flames have subsided, place the sweetbreads on a heated platter. Add the cream to the pan and stir hard while heating. Pour over the sweetbreads. Surround with the fried croutons. Serve the apples in a separate dish.

Sweetbread turnover Louis XIV
Chausson de ris de veau Louis XIV

FOR TWO PEOPLE

1 sweetbread   1 thin slice boiled ham
   (approximately ½ pound)   1 egg
1 small truffle   4 tablespoons Brown Sauce (page 7)
1 slice smoked tongue   1 tablespoon Madeira
2 tablespoons butter   salt and pepper
Flaky Pastry (page 643)

This recipe is usually made with the trimmings of flaky pastry, but can be made with other unsweetened pastry. Provide yourself with enough pastry to make a single crust pie.

Soak the sweetbread for about 3 hours in cold water, changing the water from time to time. Put in a pan of cold water and bring to a boil. Simmer 2 minutes and then plunge into cold water. Remove the membranes and bloody tissue and drain the sweetbreads thoroughly. Using a very sharp knife, make little incisions all over the sweetbread and stick in little pieces of truffle and tongue, pushing them in so that they will not fall out. Heat the butter in a skillet and sauté the sweetbread gently on both sides. Sprinkle with salt and pepper.

Roll out the pastry into a circle large enough to accommodate the sweetbread and leave a ¾-inch border. Moisten the edges. Place the boiled ham on one half of the circle, and on that, place the sweetbread. Fold over the other half and press the edges together. Make a hole in the top to let the steam escape. Insert a pastry tube tip. Paint the surface twice with the egg yolk, mixed with 1 teaspoon of water. Bake 30 to 40 minutes at 400° F. When cooked, pour a mixture of the brown sauce and the wine through the hole. Serve hot.

Breaded sweetbread scallops with mushrooms
Escalopes de ris de veau aux champignons

FOR FOUR PEOPLE

1 large pair sweetbreads	juice of ½ lemon
1 egg, slightly beaten	6 tablespoons butter
flour	¾ cup heavy cream
dry breadcrumbs	salt and pepper
1 pound mushrooms	

Soak the sweetbreads in cold water 2 to 3 hours, changing the water three times. Put in a pan of cold water and bring to a boil. Simmer 5 minutes and then plunge the brains into a bowl of very cold water. Remove the membranes and bloody tissues. Drain well and press in clean toweling to remove moisture.

Cut the sweetbreads in 4 slices. Dip each scallop in flour, then in the beaten egg, and finally in the breadcrumbs.

Trim, wash, and slice the mushrooms very thin. Sprinkle with lemon juice and sauté briefly in 1½ tablespoons of butter. Season with salt and pepper and add the cream. Heat well but do not allow the sauce to boil.

At the same time, sauté the scallops in the rest of the butter, allowing 5 minutes of gentle cooking to each side.

Spread the mushroom mixture on a preheated platter and place the scallops on top. The mushrooms can be replaced by tomato sauce.

Sweetbread filling for vol-au-vent
Garniture de vol-au-vent au ris de veau

FOR EIGHT PEOPLE

1 pair sweetbreads	5 tablespoons flour
6 tablespoons butter	½ cup heavy cream
1 cup chicken broth	juice of 1 lemon
1 cup mushrooms	1 can truffle pieces
2 thick slices ham	salt and pepper

Precook the sweetbreads as in the preceding recipe. Cut into squares. Melt 3 tablespoons of butter in a saucepan. Add the diced sweetbreads and the chicken broth. Place a piece of buttered heavy paper right on the scallops to keep them from darkening. Cover the pan and simmer 20 minutes.

Trim, wash, and slice the mushrooms and sauté them briefly in 1 tablespoon of butter. Dice the ham.

Make a sauce by heating the remaining butter and blending in the flour. Add the broth from the sweetbreads and the heavy cream. Stir until smooth. Season highly with lemon juice, salt, and pepper. Simmer very gently for 10 minutes. Add the sweetbreads, mushrooms, truffles, and ham. Mix well. The filling will be placed in a warm vol-au-vent.

Sweetbread croquettes * Croquettes de ris de veau

FOR FIVE PEOPLE

1 pair (½ pound) sweetbreads
1½ cups Béchamel Sauce (page 6)
¼ pound mushrooms
1 tablespoon butter
3 ounces smoked tongue
Madeira Sauce with Truffles (page 11)

flour
2 eggs
dry breadcrumbs
parsley sprigs
salt and pepper

Soak and precook the sweetbreads as in the above recipe.

Make a very thick, highly seasoned béchamel sauce. Clean and chop the mushrooms and sauté them very briefly in butter.

Chop the cold sweetbreads, the mushrooms, and the tongue quite fine and mix with the sauce. Spread the mixture out on a buttered platter and chill in the refrigerator.

Prepare the madeira sauce.

Divide the mixture into croquettes (round, oval, or flat) of about 1½ tablespoons each. Dip them first in flour, then in slightly beaten eggs, and finally in breadcrumbs.

Preheat the deep fat to 385° F. Fry the croquettes until golden brown, doing four or five at a time. Drain on paper and serve on napkin-lined platter, garnished with parsley, fried at the last minute. Season to taste.

Sweetbread tarts (3 methods)
Tartelettes de ris de veau (3 méthodes)

Sweetbread tarts are usually served at the beginning of a meal. Each of the following recipes are served in tarts made with Tart Pastry (page 646) and require

2 pairs of sweetbreads. *Precook the sweetbreads:* Soak them several hours in cool water, changing the water several times. Place the sweetbreads in a pan of cold water. Bring the water to a boil. Remove the pan from the heat. After a moment or two plunge the sweetbreads into very cold water. Remove the membranes and bloody tissues. Rinse again and press out the excess moisture in clean toweling.

I. With mushrooms * Aux champignons

FOR EIGHT PEOPLE

8 4-inch tarts	¾ pound mushrooms
sweetbreads	¾ cup heavy cream
flour	juice of 1 lemon
6 tablespoons butter	salt and pepper
¾ cup Béchamel Sauce (page 6)	

Make and bake the tarts. Precook the sweetbreads. Cut each sweetbread into 4 pieces, dip in flour, and cook gently for 10 minutes in 4 tablespoons of butter, turning them occasionally.

Make the béchamel sauce.

Trim, wash, and chop the mushrooms. Cook them 3 minutes in 2 tablespoons of butter. Remove to a shallow bowl and stir in the béchamel, which should not be too thick. Add the cream, salt, and pepper. Fill the tarts with the mixture. Place the sweetbreads on top. Squeeze a little lemon juice into the pan in which the sweetbreads were cooked. Stir hard for a moment and pour over the sweetbreads. Serve immediately.

II. With peas * Aux petits pois

FOR EIGHT PEOPLE

8 4-inch tarts	1 can tiny peas
sweetbreads	¼ cup heavy cream
flour	juice of 1 lemon
6 tablespoons butter	salt and pepper
¾ cup Béchamel Sauce (page 6)	

Make and bake the tarts. Precook and cook the sweetbreads as in the first method.

Make a medium thick béchamel sauce and heat the canned peas in the remaining butter. Combine with the béchamel and the cream. Season with salt and pepper.

Fill the tarts with the peas and place the sweetbreads on top. Sprinkle lemon juice into the butter in the pan in which the sweetbreads cooked and pour over the sweetbreads.

III. With artichokes * Aux artichauts

8 4-inch tarts
sweetbreads
flour
6 tablespoons butter
6 artichokes

1½ cups Béchamel Sauce (page 6)
¾ cup heavy cream
1 lemon, sliced thin
salt and pepper

Make and bake 8 tarts. Precook and cook the sweetbreads as in the first method.

Boil the artichokes in a large kettle of boiling salted water for 45 minutes. Drain and discard all but the bottoms. Pass this through a food mill (or spin in blender—*Ed.*).

Make the béchamel sauce and stir this and the cream into the artichoke purée. Season well and keep warm.

Fill the tarts with the artichoke mixture. Cover with the sweetbreads and place a slice of lemon on each one.

Lamb kidneys on skewers with artichokes
Brochettes de rognons de mouton
aux fonds d'artichauts

8 lamb kidneys
8 small tomatoes
8 artichoke bottoms
    (cooked or canned)

oil
salt and pepper

Remove the outside filament and the hard core from the kidneys. Cut each one in 4 pieces. Wash and cut the tomatoes in quarters and cut the artichokes in quarters also.

Alternate the kidney, tomato, and artichoke pieces on small skewers. Using a pastry brush, paint each skewer with oil and sprinkle with salt and pepper. Grill or broil 10 minutes, turning frequently.

Veal kidneys in champagne
Rognons de veau au champagne

This can also be made with Cinzano vermouth. The dish is prepared very quickly and just before serving.

FOR SIX PEOPLE

2 veal kidneys	3 tablespoons butter
½ pound mushrooms	¾ cup champagne or Cinzano
juice of ½ lemon	salt and pepper

Remove the filament and hard fat from the kidneys. Cut into thin slices. Trim and wash the mushrooms. Slice and sprinkle with lemon juice.

Heat half the butter in a skillet. Sauté the kidneys over a fairly high heat for 1 minute. Add the mushrooms and sauté 2 minutes longer. Add the champagne or Cinzano. Lower the heat and add the rest of the butter and season with salt and pepper. Stir well but do not let the sauce boil.

Veal kidneys à la berrichone
Rognons de veau à la berrichone

FOR SIX PEOPLE

The sauce for this dish is made in advance and can be kept overnight in the refrigerator. It is made with the delicate white wine of Sancerre, a famous district in the Loire valley. For those who cannot have a Sancerre wine, substitute a light dry white wine.

Sancerre Sauce:	Kidneys:
2½ tablespoons butter	1 large veal kidney
4 teaspoons chopped onion	¼ pound fat bacon
1¼ cups Sancerre wine	1½ tablespoons butter
1 sprig thyme	3 tablespoons sliced mushrooms
1 bay leaf	¾ cup Sancerre wine
pinch of salt	1 teaspoon chopped parsley
	salt and pepper

Sancerre Sauce: Melt 1 tablespoon of the butter in a saucepan and sauté the onion just until pale yellow. Add the wine, thyme, bay leaf, and salt and barely simmer uncovered for almost an hour or until the wine has been reduced to half its quantity. Strain the sauce and melt 2 tablespoons of butter in it without reheating.

Kidneys: Remove the filament and hard fat from the kidney. Split it in two lengthwise and cut into ½-inch slices.

Cut the bacon into small squares and boil them for 5 minutes. Drain. Heat the butter in a heavy pan and sauté the diced bacon and mushrooms until pale yellow. Remove from the pan with a slotted spoon, and using the same butter, sauté the kidney pieces over a high heat for 5 minutes, stirring frequently. Sprinkle with salt and pepper and add them to the mushrooms and bacon. Add the wine and boil down rapidly for a few moments. Add the Sancerre sauce, the chopped parsley, the mushrooms, and the bacon and cook 2 minutes before adding the kidneys. Reheat but do not let the kidneys boil. Serve immediately.

Sautéed veal kidneys with herbs
Rognons de veau sautés aux fines herbes

FOR FOUR PEOPLE

2 veal kidneys
10 tablespoons butter
2 tablespoons mixed chopped herbs
   (parsley, tarragon, chervil)

juice of 1 lemon
salt and pepper

Trim the kidneys, removing carefully all filaments and hard fat. Cut in thin slices.

Heat 3 tablespoons of the butter in a skillet, and when it is hot, sear the slices on both sides. This should take about 1½ minutes. Place the kidney slices on a preheated platter. Season with salt and pepper and keep warm.

Heat the rest of the butter in a small saucepan, and when it is bubbling, pour it into a heated gravy bowl. Stir in the chopped herbs and the juice of a small lemon. Serve the kidneys and let each person help himself to the sauce.

Veal kidneys flambéed with mustard
Rognons de veau flambés à la moutarde

FOR FOUR PEOPLE

1 large veal kidney
3 tablespoons butter
4 teaspoons cognac
1 tablespoon French mustard

1 teaspoon flour
¾ cup bouillon
3 tablespoons heavy cream
salt and pepper

Remove the filament and hard fat from the kidney. Cut in two through the thickness of the kidney and then cut into small dice.

Heat the butter in a skillet, and when it is very hot, add the kidney. Sauté over a moderate flame 4 to 5 minutes, stirring gently with a wooden spoon. Pour the cognac over the kidneys. Touch with a lighted flame, and as soon as the flames subside, remove the kidneys with a slotted spoon. Stir the mustard and flour into the butter, and still stirring, add the bouillon. Sprinkle with salt and pepper and cook a few minutes. Add the cream and the kidneys and cook just long enough to reheat the kidneys. Serve at once.

Flambéed veal kidneys * Rognons de veau flambés

FOR FOUR PEOPLE

2 veal kidneys
6 tablespoons butter
½ cup cognac

1 scant teaspoon juniper berries, pounded
salt and pepper

Trim the kidneys of filament and hard fat and leave whole.

Heat the butter in a heavy pan, and when it is frothy, sauté the kidneys until browned on all sides. Remove the kidneys from the butter and pour in the cognac. Touch immediately with a lighted match. Add the pounded berries and simmer 2 to 3 minutes. Add 6 tablespoons of hot water. Simmer a few minutes longer.

Cut the kidneys in large dice (the meat should be pink inside). Put the kidneys in the sauce just long enough to reheat. Do not let the sauce boil. Serve immediately. Season to taste.

Veal kidneys with vermouth
Rognons de veau au vermouth

FOR SIX PEOPLE

3 veal kidneys
6 tablespoons butter
1 teaspoon flour
½ cup dry vermouth

¾ cup dry white wine
1 cup bread cubes
salt and pepper

Remove the filaments and hard fat from the kidneys. Cut them in pieces. Heat 6 tablespoons of the butter in a skillet and sauté for about 3 minutes, stirring with a wooden spoon. Remove the kidneys with a slotted spoon. Stir in the flour, and when well blended, add the vermouth and wine. Sprinkle with salt and pepper and simmer 5 to 6 minutes.

Meanwhile, heat the remaining butter in a small skillet and sauté the bread cubes.

Put the kidneys back in the sauce just long enough to reheat. Serve on a hot platter and garnish with the fried croutons.

Cold beef tongue express * Langue froide expresse

FOR SIX PEOPLE

6-8 small potatoes
1 pound green string beans
Vinaigrette Sauce (page 29)

18 thin slices cooked tongue
3 hard-cooked eggs, sliced
3 pickles, sliced

Cook the potatoes in their jackets in boiling salted water. Cool, peel, and slice very thin.

Trim and wash the beans and boil in salted water for 20 minutes. Drain.

Mix the potatoes and beans carefully with the vinaigrette sauce, taking care not to crush the potatoes. Heap in the center of a serving platter and surround with slices of tongue. On each piece of tongue place a round of egg, and on the egg slices, place small rounds of pickles.

Braised beef tongue mapie
Langue de boeuf braisée mapie

FOR EIGHT PEOPLE

1 beef tongue (3-3½ pounds)
5 tablespoons lard
5 ounces lean salt pork
2 medium-sized onions
4 carrots
16 ounces beer

½ teaspoon nutmeg
½ teaspoon ginger
½ calf's (or pig's) foot
2 tablespoons seedless raisins
salt and pepper

Order the tongue well trimmed. Heat the lard in a heavy saucepan and sauté the tongue on all sides without browning. Wash the salt pork to remove the excess salt and cut it into small dice. Add that, the onions, peeled and sliced thin, and the carrots, sliced equally thin. Cook several minutes.

Add the beer, the seasonings, and the calf's foot. Cover and simmer 4 hours.

1 hour before the end of cooking, put the raisins in warm water. Just before the end of cooking, add the raisins. Remove the calf's foot and the tongue. Slice the tongue and place on a heated platter. Pour the unstrained sauce over the tongue. Serve with boiled rice.

Parmesan beef tongue
Langue de boeuf au parmesan

FOR SIX PEOPLE

1 beef tongue
    (approximately 2 pounds)
5 tablespoons lard
2 onions
3 carrots
1 cup white wine

2 tablespoons chives
1 tablespoon chopped parsley
½ pound piece Parmesan cheese
2 tablespoons butter
salt and pepper

Buy a well-trimmed beef tongue and ask the butcher to lard it lightly. Heat the lard in a heavy pan and sear the tongue gently on all sides. Peel and slice the onions and cut the carrots into thin rounds. Add the vegetables to the tongue and continue to cook several minutes. Season with salt and pepper and add the white wine, chives, and parsley. Cover and simmer for 3 hours. Cool the tongue in the sauce.

Remove the tongue from the pan and cut into very thin slices. Slice the Parmesan cheese as thin as possible and lightly grease an ovenware dish. Put a layer of Parmesan cheese slices on the bottom. Cover with a layer of tongue. Sprinkle with the sauce in which the tongue cooked. Repeat this process until the dish is full, ending with a layer of cheese. Sprinkle with melted butter and cook in a 375° F. oven for 15 minutes, turning the broiler on for the last few seconds.

Tongue pot-au-feu * Langue de boeuf au pot

FOR TEN PEOPLE

1 large beef tongue
1 pound soup bones
2 pounds carrots
1 pound leeks
3 white turnips
3 onions

1 stalk celery
salt and pepper
Tomato Sauce (page 22) *or*
Vinaigrette Sauce with Herbs (page 30)

Place a well-trimmed beef tongue and the bones in a large kettle of cold water. Bring slowly to a boil, skimming off the matter that floats to the top.

Meanwhile, prepare the vegetables: Wash the carrots and cut them into pieces; remove most of the green part of the leeks, wash very carefully, and tie in 2 bunches; peel the turnips and cut in thick slices; peel the onions and cut in wedges; cut the celery in large pieces.

When the water boils, add the vegetables, salt, and pepper. Cover and simmer 4 hours.

Serve the tongue and vegetables with the desired sauce.

The bouillon is very good and can be used like that of a beef *pot-au-feu.*

Beef tongue salad * Salade de langue de boeuf

FOR SIX PEOPLE

3 cups diced cold tongue
1 small bunch white celery
1 head garden lettuce
3 large, cold boiled potatoes

4 tomatoes
4 hard-cooked eggs
5 small dill pickles
1½ cups Mayonnaise (page 14)

Dice the tongue and the well-washed celery. Wash the lettuce and place it in the refrigerator, after having drained it thoroughly.

Cut the potatoes into thin slices. Peel and cut the tomatoes into small pieces. Peel the eggs and cut them into thin slices. Chop the pickles rather coarsely.

Combine the tongue, celery, potatoes, tomatoes, eggs, and pickles with well-seasoned mayonnaise and serve very cold on leaves of lettuce.

Calf's head vinaigrette * Tête de veau vinaigrette

FOR FOUR PEOPLE

1 calf's head, boned	*bouquet garni* (bay leaf, thyme, parsley)
2 carrots	Vinaigrette Sauce (page 29)
2 leeks	2 tablespoons chopped herbs (parsley,
1 onion	chives, chervil, tarragon)

Prepare the calf's head as suggested in the introduction to this section. When the water boils, add the prepared vegetables and *bouquet garni.* Cook slowly 1½ to 2 hours or until meat is tender. Drain and cut into thin slices. Serve hot or cold with vinaigrette sauce, to which the chopped herbs are added.

Pig's head pot-au-feu * Tête de porc au pot

FOR SIX PEOPLE

2 small pig's heads	1 stalk celery
1 onion	8-10 potatoes
1 clove	Tomato Sauce (page 22) *or*
1 clove garlic	Mayonnaise (page 14) *or*
2 pounds carrots	Vinaigrette Sauce (page 29)
2 pounds leeks	salt and pepper
2 pounds turnips	

Read the introduction to this section. Prepare pig's heads as you would calf's head.

Place the heads in a very large kettle and cover them completely with cold water. Bring to a rapid boil, skimming off all matter that comes to the surface. Meanwhile, prepare the vegetables: peel the onion and stick it with a clove; peel the garlic and bruise it slightly; scrub the carrots, peeling only if necessary. Wash the leeks and remove all but a third of the green part. Tie in bunches of two or three. Wash the turnips and cut into large pieces. Wash the celery.

Put the vegetables in the kettle. Season with 1 tablespoon of salt and ½ teaspoon of peppercorns. Skim again until the water boils. Then cover three quarters of the way and simmer 2 hours.

Withdraw the heads from the kettle and remove the bones. Cut the meat in slices and place on a large platter surrounded with the vegetables. This is usually served with boiled potatoes and either a tomato sauce or mayonnaise. It is also served cold with a vinaigrette sauce and accompanied by potato salad.

Jugged pig's feet à l'aveyronnaise
Civet de pieds de porc à l'aveyronnaise

FOR EIGHT PEOPLE

8 pig's feet	1 stalk celery
1 quart red wine	*bouquet garni* (bay leaf, thyme, parsley)
1 clove and 2 onions	¼ pound pork skin or bacon rind
1 carrot	salt and pepper

Ask the butcher to cut the feet into quarters. Put them in a deep kettle. Cover with 2½ cups of water and add the red wine, the peeled onions, one of which will be stuck with a clove, a carrot, cut into slices, the celery, broken into pieces, the *bouquet garni,* pork skin, salt, and pepper. Bring to a boil and simmer covered for 3 hours. If the sauce is too thin, remove the cover and cook down.

Arrange the feet on a heated platter and keep warm. Remove the *bouquet garni* and the pork skin and strain the sauce over the feet. Serve with boiled potatoes.

Grilled pig's feet * Pieds de porc grillés

FOR SIX PEOPLE

6 pig's feet	½ teaspoon peppercorns
3 carrots	1 teaspoon salt
3 leeks	6 ounces butter
2 white turnips	dry breadcrumbs
bouquet garni (bay leaf, thyme, parsley)	mustard

Start cooking the feet in a kettle containing 5 quarts of cold water. Prepare the vegetables and put them in the kettle. Add the *bouquet garni,* pepper, and salt. Bring gradually to a boil, skimming off all the matter that floats to the top before the water reaches the boiling point. Place the cover on three quarters of the way and cook slowly for 3 hours.

Remove the feet from the kettle. Cool, split, and remove the bones.

Melt half the butter. Using a pastry brush, paint each piece liberally on all sides with the butter. Dip into soft breadcrumbs and put on a baking sheet or in a grill. Broil or grill with a hot flame for 5 minutes on each side. Heat the rest of the butter.

Serve the feet on a preheated platter. Cover with hot butter and serve with mustard.

Potatoes, rice, and pasta

Potatoes

In France potatoes perhaps even more than bread are the basic food. They appear every day at table. Potatoes contain a lot of water, which means that they take up a lot of space in the stomach and satisfy hunger very quickly. They are also very digestible and the richness in potassium and other minerals make them an important part of the daily diet. To avoid losing these valuable qualities, the best way to cook them, both from the point of view of flavor as well as health, is to bake them in their jackets, but there are many other delicious ways of preparing potatoes. Here are a few general rules:

1 Start boiling potatoes in cold salted water.
2 The best puréed potatoes are made from baked potatoes.
3 If you want sautéed potatoes that will not crumble, start with raw potatoes.
4 Don't try to deep-fry potatoes with less than 7 cups of fat.

(There are more varieties of potatoes grown in Europe than in the United States. Some types are better than others for certain preparations. We will try to indicate which of the few American varieties are best in each recipe.—*Ed.*)

Potato purée * Pommes de terre en purée

FOR FOUR PEOPLE

4 pounds potatoes
5 tablespoons butter

1 cup boiling milk
salt and pepper

Peel the potatoes and cut them in quarters. Put the potatoes in a pan with enough cold water to just cover the potatoes. Season with salt, using the coarse sea salt, if possible. Bring to a boil and simmer uncovered for 20 minutes or just until tender. Test them by inserting a knife blade. The potatoes should not be overcooked.

From now on, you should act quickly. Put a strainer over a large saucepan or a casserole. Remove the potatoes from the water in small lots with a slotted spoon or skimmer so that they will drain. Force them through the strainer as quickly as possible. Potatoes should always be puréed while very hot. (We prefer this method, but if you prefer, you may use a food mill or potato ricer, but do not use a potato masher or a blender. The essential point is that as much water as possible must be drained from the potatoes before puréeing them).

Put the potatoes over medium heat and add the butter. Beat with a whip adding the hot milk gradually. Season with fine salt. Serve immediately. Potato purée is like soufflé and cannot wait.

Potatoes anna * Pommes de terre anna

FOR FOUR PEOPLE

2 pounds new or small potatoes   salt and pepper
6 tablespoons butter

Peel the potatoes and slice in 1/16-inch rounds. You should have 5 to 6 cups of potato slices.

Butter a charlotte mold or other straight-sided metal baking dish liberally and line the bottom and sides with rows of potato slices. Dot the bottom layer with bits of butter, sprinkle with salt and pepper, and cover with another layer of potatoes. Continue this process until the mold is three quarters filled. The potatoes should be tightly packed. Cover with a buttered round of heavy paper and bake 45 minutes at 450° F. The potatoes are cooked if they feel tender when a knife is inserted.

Unmold carefully on a heated platter. There should be a golden crust on the outside, and the inside should be soft.

Baba potato pie * Tourte baba

FOR SIX PEOPLE

Pastry:
2 cups all-purpose flour
8 tablespoons soft butter
1 teaspoon salt
6 tablespoons cold water

Filling:
5-6 potatoes
2 tablespoons *fines herbes*
   (chervil, parsley)
5 tablespoons butter
1 egg yolk
¾ cup heavy cream
salt and pepper

Put the flour in a bowl and fashion a well in the center. Add the butter and salt, and adding the water gradually, work the flour into the butter with the tips of your fingers until you have a smooth ball. Let the pastry rest for several hours. Divide in 2 parts and roll each one into a round or square shape, depending on the shape of your pie dish.

Butter the pie dish and line it with pastry.

Peel the potatoes and slice them very thin as you would for potato chips. Put a layer of potatoes in the pie dish. Sprinkle with chopped herbs, salt, and pepper and dot with butter. Repeat this process until the potatoes are all used. Moisten the edge of the pastry and put on the top crust.

Cut a 4-inch circle in the top pastry to make a cover that will be removed later. Trace a design on the top pastry with a sharp-pointed knife and brush with beaten egg yolk. Bake 35 minutes at 425° F. If the top crust browns too quickly, cover it with heavy wax paper. When the pie is cooked, take off the little cover and pour in the fresh cream, tilting the pie so that the cream will run all through. Serve very hot.

Potatoes à la basquaise
Pommes de terre à la basquaise

FOR FOUR PEOPLE

4 large Idaho potatoes
2 tablespoons butter
3 tomatoes
1 clove garlic, minced
1 green pepper

2 slices of Bayonne or Italian ham, chopped
1 tablespoon chopped parsley
½ cup olive oil
salt and pepper

Bake the potatoes in a hot (450° F.) oven for 50 minutes or until cooked. Cut off the top third lengthwise and scoop out the potatoes. Purée or mash the potatoes, working in the butter and seasoning with salt and pepper.

Peel the tomatoes. Cook them with the garlic, the green pepper seeded and cut into thin strips, the ham, and the parsley in the oil until the tomatoes and the peppers are tender and the mixture is not too liquid.

Place a layer of potato purée in each shell and fill with the ham and vegetable mixture. Cover with breadcrumbs and sprinkle with oil. Brown in a very hot oven.

Byron potatoes * Pommes de terre byron

FOR SIX PEOPLE

8 large baking potatoes
6 tablespoons butter
½ cup heavy cream

½ cup grated Parmesan cheese
salt and pepper

Wash the potatoes and bake them at 450° F. for 50 minutes or until cooked. Remove all the potato from the jackets.

Heat the butter in a pan and brown the potatoes in it. Season with salt and pepper. Put the potatoes in a buttered round baking dish so that it looks like a kind of cake. Pour on the heavy cream. Sprinkle with the grated cheese and brown in the oven.

Cheese potato cake * Gâteau de pommes de terre

FOR FOUR PEOPLE

4 medium-sized Idaho potatoes
1½ cups Béchamel Sauce (page 6)

½ pound Gruyère cheese, grated
2 tablespoons butter

4 egg yolks   salt and pepper
4 egg whites, beaten stiff

Peel the potatoes. Start them in cold salted water, bring to a boil, and cook until tender.

Make the béchamel sauce.

Drain the potatoes, mash them well, and stir them into the hot sauce. Mix well over moderate heat. Season, but remember that the cheese will add salt to the mixture.

Beat in the egg yolks one by one, beating hard after each addition. Fold in the egg whites and finally the grated cheese.

Butter generously either a charlotte mold or a straight-sided baking dish. Put the potato mixture in the dish and place the dish in a pan of hot water. Bake 1 hour at 375° F.

Serve with a sauce of your choice in a separate bowl.

Sautéed cheese potatoes
Pommes de terre sautées au fromage

FOR SIX PEOPLE

4 pounds small potatoes   ½ cup grated Gruyère cheese
½ cup oil   3 tablespoons heavy cream
3 tablespoons butter   salt and pepper

Peel the potatoes and cut them in quarters. Cover with cold salted water. Bring to a boil and cook until tender. Drain thoroughly and cut into small dice.

In a deep skillet, heat the oil and butter. Add the potatoes and crush them slightly, stirring in the cheese at the same time. Season with salt and pepper and sauté until the vegetables are golden brown without letting them burn. Turn onto a serving platter and cover with the cold heavy cream. Serve immediately.

Duchess potatoes * Pommes de terre duchesse

FOR FOUR PEOPLE

4-5 large baking potatoes   1 egg yolk slightly beaten
10 tablespoons butter   salt and pepper
4 egg yolks

The key to successful Duchess potatoes is to work with dry potato pulp. The easiest way to do this is to bake the potatoes, but if you prefer to boil them, special care must be taken to dry them. Start to cook the potatoes in cold salted water.

Bring to a boil and cook until tender. Drain and force them through a strainer or food mill or mash them thoroughly. Put the cooked potatoes in a saucepan and stir over moderate heat to let the extra moisture evaporate. If you use boiled potatoes, the process is slightly longer.

Remove from the heat and beat in the butter and 4 egg yolks. Season well with salt and pepper. Make balls of the mixture and put them on a floured working surface. Cut them into thick rectangles or squares. Cut decorative lines on the tops. Dip them in flour and paint them with a slightly beaten egg yolk. Brown in a hot (450° F.) oven or fry in butter until golden brown on both sides.

Potato chips * Pommes de terre chips

The infallible way to succeed with making potato chips is to soak the potatoes overnight.

Peel 2 pounds of potatoes and cut them into *very* thin slices. (There are many gadgets to help with this process.) Leave them overnight in a large bowl of water. The next day, lift them out of the water and dry them in toweling. All the starch will remain in the water.

Fry in deep fat (385° F.) until golden brown. Drain and sprinkle with salt.

Potato crepes vonassiennes
Crêpes de pommes de terre vonassiennes

FOR FOUR PEOPLE

3 large baking potatoes
¾ cup scalded milk
6 eggs, slightly beaten
4 tablespoons flour

4 tablespoons heavy cream
3 tablespoons butter
salt and pepper

Peel the potatoes and boil in salted water until tender. Drain well and force them through a strainer or food mill. Add the hot milk and beat over moderate heat until the mixture is hot. Beating constantly, add the eggs, the flour and the heavy cream. Stir well, until the mixture is the consistency of very thick cream. Season with salt and pepper.

Heat the butter in a large skillet and drop small portions of the mixture (about 2 teaspoonfuls at a time) from the end of a tablespoon into the butter, keeping them far enough apart to allow for spreading. When golden brown on one side, turn and brown the other side. Serve very hot.

Dauphine potatoes * Pommes de terre dauphine

FOR FOUR PEOPLE

These delicious creations are a combination of cream puff pastry and potato purée.

Cream Puff Pastry:
1 cup water
1 teaspoon salt
6 tablespoons butter
1 cup flour
3 eggs

Potato Purée:
3 baking potatoes
6 tablespoons butter
4 egg yolks
salt and pepper

Bring the water, salt, and butter to a boil in a saucepan. Remove from the heat and pour in the flour, all at once. Stir vigorously. Return to the heat and dry the mixture by stirring it until it no longer sticks to the pan but starts to leave a thin film on the bottom. Set aside to cool slightly. Add the eggs one by one, beating the mixture for 5 minutes after each addition.

At the same time, boil the potatoes, which have been peeled, quartered, and placed in cold salted water. When tender, drain them well and force them through a strainer or mash them well. Put in a heavy pan and place over a moderate heat, adding butter bit by bit until all the butter has been worked in. Remove the pan from the heat and add the egg yolks one by one, beating hard after each addition.

Beat in the pastry mixture and season well with salt and pepper.

Dip small spoonfuls of the mixture into flour and drop into hot deep fat (350° F.). Fry until golden brown.

Potatoes au gratin dauphinois I
Gratin dauphinois I

FOR FIVE PEOPLE

3 pounds small potatoes
1½ cups milk
1 clove garlic
5 tablespoons butter

½ cup heavy cream
4 tablespoons grated Gruyère cheese
salt and pepper

Peel and wash the potatoes. Cut them in thin slices.
Scald the milk with the garlic.
Butter a round baking dish. Melt the rest of the butter.
Spread a thick layer of potatoes in the pan. Sprinkle with half the melted butter and the cream. Season well with salt and pepper and sprinkle with cheese. Cover with the rest of the potatoes. Sprinkle with the rest of the butter, salt, and pepper.

Remove the garlic from the milk and pour the hot milk over the potatoes. Bake 30 minutes at 400° F. Insert a knife, and if the potatoes feel tender, they are ready to serve.

Potatoes au gratin dauphinois II
Gratin dauphinois II

FOR FOUR PEOPLE

6-8 small potatoes	1 egg
3 tablespoons butter	½ cup milk
1 clove garlic	⅔ cup grated cheese
nutmeg	salt and pepper

Peel the potatoes and slice quite thin. Spread butter in a shallow earthenware dish rubbed with garlic. Put in the potato slices. Sprinkle with salt, pepper, and a little nutmeg.

Beat the egg well with the milk and pour over the potatoes. Sprinkle all over with the grated cheese and dot with butter. Bake 40 minutes at 350° F.

Milanaise croquettes * Croquettes milanaises

FOR FOUR PEOPLE

2 large baking potatoes	2 egg yolks
1½ cups thick Béchamel Sauce (page 6)	2 egg whites
	½ cup fine breadcrumbs
¾ cup grated Gruyère cheese	several sprigs parsley
2 ⅛-inch slices cooked ham, chopped	salt and pepper

Peel the potatoes and cook them in salted water until tender. Drain them very dry and force them through a food mill or strainer.

Meanwhile, make the béchamel sauce. Mix the sauce, the potatoes, the cheese, and the ham, stirring over moderate heat. Season with pepper and just a little salt (not too much because of the ham). Remove from the fire and beat in the egg yolks.

Beat the egg whites until frothy. Make little croquettes of the potato mixture. Flatten them and dip them in egg white and then in fine breadcrumbs. Fry in deep fat (385° F.) and serve with parsley, which has been fried in deep fat also.

Darfin potato garnish * Pommes de terre darfin

FOR FOUR PEOPLE

2 pounds small potatoes
4 teaspoons oil

6 tablespoons butter
salt and pepper

Peel the potatoes and cut them into very thin, matchlike strips.

Heat the oil and butter in a skillet, and when it is very hot, put in a small hand-ful of potato sticks and spread them out like a thin pancake. When well browned on one side, turn it over to brown on the other side. When cooked and while still hot, remove from the pan, sprinkle with salt and pepper, and roll into a cornu-copia. Keep warm while making the rest in the same manner.

This is made to accompany all kinds of roasts.

Fondant potatoes * Pommes de terre fondantes

FOR FOUR PEOPLE

2 pounds boiling potatoes
6 tablespoons butter

5 tablespoons oil
salt and pepper

Peel the potatoes and cut them in quarters. With a sharp knife, round off the edges so that they are uniformly round ovals. Put in a pan of cold salted water; bring to a boil and cook 5 minutes. Drain thoroughly.

In a covered casserole or heavy saucepan, heat the butter and oil. Add the po-tatoes and sauté them well without letting them brown too much. Sprinkle with salt and pepper. Reduce the heat, cover, and cook very slowly for 1 hour, shaking the pan occasionally. Just before serving, add about 4 teaspoons of water. This will be immediately absorbed and will tenderize the potatoes.

Potato fritters * Pommes de terre en beignets

FOR FOUR PEOPLE

8 small Idaho potatoes
3 tablespoons heavy cream
2 egg yolks

2 egg whites, beaten stiff
salt and pepper

Peel the potatoes and steam them until tender or boil them and drain very dry. Pass them through a food mill or strainer. Beat in the cream and the egg yolks. Season with salt and plenty of pepper.

Fold in the beaten egg whites. Form the mixture into little balls, throw them in deep fat (385° F.), and fry until golden brown. Drain on paper toweling. Serve very hot.

Meat-stuffed potatoes * Pommes de terre farcies

FOR FOUR PEOPLE

8 medium-sized Idaho potatoes
½ pound pork belly*
1 onion
2 tablespoons chopped *fines herbes*
   (chives, parsley)

½ pound ground beef
1 egg
1 cup bouillon
salt and pepper

Peel the potatoes and hollow them out for stuffing.

Dice the fat very fine; peel and slice the onion; chop the herbs.

Put the fat in the skillet and heat until it has rendered some of the fat. Add the onion and the ground meat and sauté until lightly browned. Remove from the heat and stir in the chopped herbs and the raw egg. Season with salt and pepper.

Stuff the potatoes with the mixture. Put them in a shallow baking dish. Sprinkle with the bouillon and bake 1 hour at 400° F., basting occasionally.

Paprika potatoes * Pommes de terre au paprika

FOR FOUR PEOPLE

2 pounds small boiling potatoes
3 onions
2½ tablespoons oil

2 firm tomatoes
2 teaspoons paprika
salt and pepper

Peel the potatoes and put in a bowl of cold water.

Peel and chop the onions very fine.

Heat the oil in a frying pan and sauté the onions until transparent. Do not let them brown.

Dip the tomatoes in boiling water and slip off the skins. Halve them and press out the seeds. Cut the tomatoes in pieces and add them and the paprika to the onions. Slice the potatoes into the pan. Season with salt and add enough boiling water to come just to the top of the potatoes. Put in a 350° F. oven for 20 to 25 minutes or until the potatoes feel tender when you insert a fork.

Sage potato purée
Purée de pommes de terre à la sauge

FOR EIGHT PEOPLE

5 pounds Idaho potatoes
2 onions

½ teaspoon chopped sage
¼ pound butter

*If pork belly is not available, parboil fat salt pork for 5 minutes. Rinse and use like pork belly.—
Ed.

4 teaspoons oil   salt and pepper
4 cups bouillon

Peel the potatoes. Cover them with boiling salted water and boil until tender.

Meanwhile, peel and chop the onions quite fine. Sauté in the oil just until transparent. Add 2 cups of bouillon, the sage, salt, and pepper and boil the combination until it has boiled down about one third of its volume.

Force the potatoes through a food mill or mash thoroughly and mix with the sage bouillon. Add the butter and mix thoroughly over moderate heat. Add as much of the rest of the bouillon as necessary to give a smooth purée. Season with salt and pepper and serve very hot with roast or braised pork.

Potato soufflé * Pommes de terre en soufflé

FOR SIX PEOPLE

8 medium-sized potatoes   3 egg yolks
6 tablespoons butter   3 egg whites, beaten stiff
¾ cup scalded milk   salt and pepper

Cover the washed potatoes with cold salted water. Bring to a boil and cook until tender. Drain, peel the potatoes, and force them through a food mill or mash thoroughly. Beat in the butter and milk, using a wire whisk. Season with salt and pepper. Still whisking, add the egg yolks, one by one, beating hard after each addition. Fold in the egg whites carefully.

Butter a soufflé or other straight-sided baking dish. Put in the potato mixture and bake in a 425° F. oven 20 to 25 minutes or until golden brown.

Straw potatoes * Pommes de terre paille

FOR FOUR PEOPLE

2 pounds Idaho potatoes   salt

Peel the potatoes. Wash them and cut them into little sticks the size of a match. Wipe them well in a towel.

Fry the sticks in hot (380° F.) fat until very light brown. Do not fry too many sticks at once or the temperature of the fat will fall too much. Keep the potatoes warm and, just before serving, put them all back for a few moments into very hot (390° F.) fat. Drain and sprinkle with salt. Serve on a hot platter.

Rice

Rice is a delicious and quickly prepared accompaniment to meat, poultry, and fish and can be eaten as a salad or as a dessert. Unfortunately, few people cook it well, although it is very simple to prepare.

Boiled rice * Riz créole

rice
salted water

oil or butter

Allow 2 heaping tablespoons of rice to a serving. Bring a large amount of salted water to a full, rolling boil. Pour in the rice gradually so that the water continues to boil. Boil 12 minutes and start testing the rice. It should be just tender but not soft. Continue testing constantly. Different rices require different amounts of cooking time—though the variations are only a matter of moments. Rice must never be overcooked.

Rinse the rice thoroughly with cold water to remove the excess starch. Drain well and put in an ovenproof dish. Sprinkle with a little oil or dot with butter and let it dry and reheat in a moderate oven. Stir occasionally with a fork. The rice must be dry but not dried out to the point of being crisp.

Pilaff rice * Riz pilaf

FOR FOUR PEOPLE

2 tablespoons butter
½ cup rice

1 cup boiling bouillon or water
salt

Heat the butter or an equal amount of oil in a pan or heatproof casserole. Add the rice and stir until the rice is transparent. Add the hot bouillon or water, seasoned with salt. Bring the liquid to a boil again. Reduce the heat to very low, cover, and simmer 20 minutes. Do not stir. Once the cooking is complete, you may add meat, fish, or diced vegetables.

Basque pilaff * Pilaf à la basquaise

FOR EIGHT PEOPLE

1 large onion
3 red peppers

¼ teaspoon saffron leaves or
3 tablespoons turmeric

¾ cup olive oil

1¼ pounds lean pork

¾ cup dry white wine

3 quarts mussels

1 cup long grain rice

1½ cups water

12 *langoustines**

2 cups fresh or canned peas

3 thick slices bacon

12 slices Mexican sausage

salt and pepper

Chop the onion very fine and cut the peppers in thin strips. Sauté them in 6 tablespoons of oil. Reserve a few strips of red pepper for decoration. When tender, add the pork, cut in small pieces. Brown lightly and add the white wine. Season with salt and pepper. Cover and simmer 1½ hours. Test to be sure that the pork is tender by inserting the point of a knife.

Place thoroughly cleaned mussels in a pan. Heat over a moderately high flame until the shells open. Save about 10 of the best ones for decoration and shell the rest.

Measure the rice and for every cup of rice use 1½ cups of water. Bring the water to a boil with the saffron leaves (or turmeric). Season with salt and pepper.

Heat 6 tablespoons of olive oil in a heavy pan. When it begins to heat, add the rice and stir until the rice is transparent. Add the saffroned water and bring it again to a boil. Cover, lower the heat as much as possible, and let the rice cook without stirring for 20 minutes or just until tender. Turn off the heat and keep the rice covered.

Cook the *langoustines* (or shrimp) in salted water for 5 to 6 minutes. Freshen in cold water. Do not shell. Cook fresh peas or reheat well-drained canned peas in a double boiler. Dice the bacon and sauté it over a high heat. Add the sausage slices and sauté them at the same time.

Put the hot rice in a shallow serving dish and stir in all the prepared ingredients with a fork. Stir gently so as not to crush the rice. Decorate with *langoustines* (shrimps), mussels, and strips of red pepper.

Cantonese crab rice * Le riz cantonnais au crabe

FOR SIX PEOPLE

1 cup rice

½ cup oil

6 tomatoes

¾ cup diced mushrooms

1 cup small cleaned shrimp

1 can (8 ounces) crabmeat

2 slices cooked ham, diced

4 eggs

salt and pepper

Cook the rice in rapidly boiling salted water for 12 to 15 minutes or just until tender. Rinse in cold water. Drain well. Put in a baking dish. Sprinkle with oil and dry and reheat in a moderate (350° F.) oven, stirring occasionally with a fork.

*Substitute large shrimp or crawdabs for *langoustines*.—Ed.

Dip the tomatoes in hot water and slip off the skins. Halve them and press out the seeds. Cut in small dice.

Wash and trim the mushrooms and cut in small dice.

Sauté the tomatoes and mushrooms in 4 tablespoons of oil, and after a few minutes, add the shrimp, the crabmeat—broken into small pieces—the diced ham, and any leftover meat or poultry you might have on hand. When very hot, stir into the hot rice. Serve on a heated platter.

Garnish with 1 or 2 very thin omelets, cooked in a little oil until well browned and quite dry, and cut into thin strips like thin noodles.

Curried rice * Riz pilaf au cari

FOR FOUR PEOPLE

¾ cup rice	1 tablespoon curry powder
1½ cups boiling bouillon or water	salt
2½ tablespoons oil	

Measure out the rice and bring to a boil double that amount of bouillon or water. Stir the curry into the liquid; add the salt.

Heat the oil in a saucepan. Sauté the rice in the oil over moderately high heat for 2 to 3 minutes, stirring constantly with a wooden spoon. Add the hot liquid, and as soon as the liquid boils again, reduce the heat as much as possible, cover, and cook gently for 20 minutes. Do not stir during the cooking.

Provençale minced meat and rice
Hachis provençal

FOR EIGHT PEOPLE

2 cups diced leftover meat	pinch of saffron *or*
3 onions	1 tablespoon turmeric
oil	8 tomatoes
2 teaspoons flour	16 link sausages
½ cup bouillon or water	8 eggs
1 cup rice	cayenne
	salt and pepper

Dice the meat very fine; peel and slice the onions.

Heat 4 tablespoons of the oil in a skillet. Sauté the onions until pale gold. Add the meat. Stir until well mixed with the onions. Sprinkle with flour and moisten with bouillon or water. Season with salt, pepper, and a dash of cayenne. Cook slowly until the moisture completely disappears.

At the same time, boil the rice in a large pan of salted water to which the saffron or turmeric has been added. After 12 minutes, test the rice. It should be cooked just long enough to be tender, not soft. Rinse in cold water, drain and reheat in a baking dish in a moderate (350° F.) oven.

Heat oil in a large skillet. Wipe and halve the tomatoes. Sauté on both sides. Season with salt.

Finally, brown the sausages in butter. Deep fry the eggs in oil, as if you were poaching them, dropping them in one by one.

Put the meat mixture in the center of a heated platter. Surround with rice and surround the rice with tomatoes, eggs, and sausages.

Mushroom-stuffed ham on rice
Cornets de jambon aux champignons sur riz

FOR FOUR PEOPLE

1 small onion	½ pound mushrooms
½ carrot	1 cup heavy cream
1 stalk celery	4 thin slices cooked ham
¼ pound butter	salt and pepper
1¼ cups rice	

Mince the onion, carrot, and celery (white part only). Heat 3 tablespoons of butter in a saucepan and simmer the vegetables just until soft. Add the rice and stir, still over a very low heat, so that the rice will not brown. When the rice has absorbed the butter, add 2½ cups boiling water. Season well with salt and pepper. Cover and cook very slowly for 15 to 20 minutes or until the rice has completely absorbed the liquid. Uncover and continue cooking over very low heat until the rice has dried out. Stir gently with a fork.

Meanwhile, wash and trim the mushrooms. Slice them very thin and sauté in 2½ tablespoons of butter. Add the cream. Keep warm but do not boil.

Sauté the ham slices in the rest of the butter for just a moment. Roll the slices into cornucopias and fill with the mushroom mixture.

Place the rice on a heated platter and smooth it flat with a spatula. Place the cornucopias on the rice. Serve hot.

Mussel pilaff * Pilaf aux moules

FOR FOUR PEOPLE

2 quarts mussels	¾ cup milk
9 tablespoons butter	pinch of saffron or
1 onion, chopped fine	1 tablespoon turmeric
1¼ cups rice	1 cup heavy cream
2 tablespoons flour	salt and pepper

Put the mussels, which have been thoroughly scraped and washed, in a pan. Cook over a high heat just until the shells open. Remove the mussels from their shells and drain the broth through a cheesecloth to remove any sand. Save the broth.

Heat 3 tablespoons of butter in a heavy pan. Sauté the chopped onion gently until tender and add the rice. Stir until the rice has absorbed the butter.

Meanwhile, measure out a cup of the cooking broth and mix with ¾ cup of water, salt, and pepper. Bring to a boil.

Add the boiling liquid to the rice. When the liquid boils again, reduce the heat as much as possible, cover, and cook 20 minutes without stirring. Pile lightly into a ring mold and keep hot.

Heat 3 tablespoons of butter in a saucepan and stir in the flour. When blended, add the rest of the cooking broth and milk. Together they should measure about 2 cups. Season with salt, pepper, and saffron or turmeric. Simmer the sauce for a few minutes; if it is not smooth, strain it. Add the cream to the sauce and heat but do not boil. Stir ¼ cup of the sauce into the mussels. Unmold the rice ring on a hot serving platter. Fill the center with the mussels and serve the rest of the sauce in a separate bowl.

Rice with almonds and hazel nuts
Riz aux amandes et aux noisettes

FOR FOUR PEOPLE

6 tablespoons rice
3 tablespoons butter
½ cup chopped hazel nuts

½ cup slivered almonds
salt and pepper

Pour the rice into a large pan of boiling salted water and boil 12 to 15 minutes or just until tender, according to the rice. When just tender, rinse with cold water and drain.

Put the rice on a baking dish or heatproof vegetable dish. Dot liberally with butter and reheat the rice in a moderate (350° F.) oven, stirring occasionally with a fork.

When the rice is very hot, remove from the oven. Season with salt and pepper and stir in the nuts with a fork. Serve with fish.

Rice with bananas * Riz aux bananes

FOR SIX PEOPLE

¼ teaspoon saffron leaves or
3 tablespoons turmeric

18 link sausages
3 tomatoes

1 cup rice
½ cup oil

3 bananas
salt and pepper

Bring a large pan of salted water to a boil and add the saffron or turmeric. Pour in the rice gradually and boil 12 to 15 minutes or just until tender. Rinse in cold water and drain. Put in a baking dish and sprinkle with 4 teaspoons of oil. Dry and heat the rice in a moderate oven, stirring occasionally with a fork.

Brown the sausages in a skillet.

At the same time, heat the rest of the oil in a large skillet.

Cut the tomatoes in half, press out the seeds, and sauté them.

Cut the peeled bananas in half lengthwise and sauté them.

Serve the rice on a heated platter. Surround with tomatoes and bananas and place the sausages on top of the rice. Serve very hot.

Rice bowls (cold) * Coupes au riz

FOR EIGHT PEOPLE

1 cup rice
⅛ teaspoon saffron leaves *or*
2 tablespoons turmeric
1 cup small pitted prunes
2 cups strong tea
1 can (6½ ounces) oil-packed tuna
6 tablespoons chopped black olives

4 tablespoons chopped walnuts
1 small can peas
Mayonnaise (page 14)
juice of 1 lemon
1 small can red peppers
salt and pepper

Pour the rice into a large pan of fast boiling salted water to which the saffron or turmeric has been added. Cook 12 to 15 minutes or just until tender. Rinse in cold water. Drain well. Chill.

Soak the prunes in tea for 2 hours.

Break the tuna into small pieces and combine with the chopped olives, nuts, peas and the prunes cut into small pieces. Mix this combination into the cold rice and bind with mayonnaise, made with lemon juice. Season with salt and pepper. Add more lemon juice, if needed. Place the rice in individual bowls, garnished with strips of canned red peppers.

Rice ring with peas
Couronne de riz aux petits pois

FOR FOUR PEOPLE

6 very small onions
2 cups freshly shelled peas

1 cup rice
½ pound mushrooms

6 tablespoons butter   salt and pepper

Peel the onions and shell the peas. Place them in a small saucepan with a tablespoon of butter and a tablespoon of water. Cover tightly and steam until cooked.

Boil the rice in a large pan of salted water for 12 to 15 minutes or just until tender. Rinse in cold water and drain well.

Wash and trim the mushrooms and boil them in salted water for 3 minutes. Drain and chop fine. Sauté in butter for a few moments. Stir in the rice. Season with salt and pepper and the rest of the butter.

Butter a ring mold. Fill with the rice-mushroom mixture. Place in a moderate (350° F.) oven to reheat the rice. About 5 to 10 minutes should be enough.

Unmold the rice on a heated platter and fill the center with the peas and onions.

Risotto avon ∗ *Risotto avon*

FOR FOUR PEOPLE

½ cup rice
3 tablespoons butter
1 cup boiling bouillon (veal or
    chicken)
pinch of saffron *or*
2 tablespoons turmeric
¾ cup diced ham

1½ cups diced cooked chicken or veal
¼ pound mushrooms
juice of ½ lemon
1½ cups Béchamel Sauce (page 6)
butter
salt and pepper

Cook the rice in butter over a moderate heat, stirring frequently until it becomes transparent. At the same time, heat the bouillon with either a pinch of real saffron or with turmeric, which is used as a substitute. Season the hot bouillon and add it to the rice. When the liquid boils, cover and cook without stirring over a low heat for 12 to 15 minutes or just until tender. Remove the cover and continue cooking for 5 minutes.

Meanwhile, prepare the filling by dicing the ham and leftover meat. Wash and trim the mushrooms. Slice them and cook them in a little water with the juice of ½ lemon for 5 minutes.

Make the béchamel sauce. Mix a third of it with the rice and the rest with the meat and mushrooms. Season well with salt and pepper.

Butter a charlotte mold or other deep straight-sided baking dish. Line the bottom and sides with the rice mixture. Fill the center with the meat mixture. Press it down so that it will be tightly packed. Cover with rice. Put the mold or dish into a pan of hot water and bake in a moderate (350° F.) oven for 30 minutes. Unmold just before serving.

This may be served without sauce or with either a tomato or a béchamel sauce flavored with saffron or turmeric.

Sausages with rice and bananas
Saucisses au riz et aux bananes

FOR FOUR PEOPLE

1½ cups rice
4 tablespoons seeded raisins
1 pound Toulouse or Polish sausage

3 bananas
salt and pepper

Boil the rice in a large amount of salted water for 17 minutes. Run cool water into the rice. Drain well.

Soak the raisins in water at the same time.

Cut the sausage in ½-inch pieces and cook slowly in a skillet without butter or other fat. Brown on one side and turn. Add the bananas, cut in slices, and also the raisins. Brown the bananas slightly. Add the cooked rice, mix well. Season with salt and pepper. Cover and cook until the rice is very hot.

Pasta

Ham and tomato sauce
Coulis aux tomates
To serve with spaghetti, macaroni, and noodles

FOR FOUR PEOPLE

1 cup cooked ham
4 onions, chopped
2 pounds (6-8) tomatoes
5 tablespoons butter

bouquet garni (thyme, bay leaf, parsley)
2 lumps sugar
salt and pepper

Chop the ham. Peel and chop the onions. Dip the tomatoes in boiling water. Peel and cut in pieces.

Heat the butter in a heavy saucepan. Sauté the ham and the onions just until the onions are transparent. Do not brown. Add the tomatoes, *bouquet garni,* sugar, salt, and pepper. Cook gently for 2 hours. Remove the *bouquet garni* and taste for seasoning before pouring on cooked noodles or spaghetti.

Stuffed cannelloni * Canelonis farcis à l'italienne

FOR SIX PEOPLE

6 cannelloni*
2 cups Tomato Sauce (page 22)
3 tablespoons butter
1 tablespoon flour
1½ cups leftover boiled meat, chopped

1 cup bouillon
2 tablespoons chopped *fines herbes*
  (parsley, chervil)
¾ cup grated Gruyère cheese
salt and pepper

Cook the cannelloni (or pasta tubes) 15 to 20 minutes in a large kettle of boiling salted water, stirring occassionally so that they will not stick together. Drain them and rinse with cold water. Spread them on towels to dry.

Make the tomato sauce or heat a good canned tomato sauce.

Melt 2 tablespoons of the butter in a small saucepan. Add the flour and stir it into the butter. Still stirring, add the bouillon and simmer until the mixture thickens. Add the meat, herbs, salt, and pepper. The combination must not be liquid.

*Cannelloni are large, 5-inch pasta squares, which can be bought in Italian stores. If they are not available, force the stuffing into cooked pasta tubes (rigatoni), which are available everywhere.—*Ed.*

Put a good tablespoon of the filling in each cannelloni and roll them up. Place the cannelloni in a buttered shallow baking dish. Cover with the sauce into which you have mixed half the cheese. Sprinkle with the rest of the cheese and dot with butter. Brown in a hot (400° F.) oven for 10 minutes.

Macaroni caponi ∗ *Macaroni caponi*

FOR FOUR PEOPLE

½ pound finely ground beef
1 large onion
1 clove garlic
2 tablespoons oil
½ cup heavy cream
4 teaspoons tomato paste
2 tablespoons Madeira wine

2 tablespoons cognac
1¼ cups bouillon
½ pound macaroni
5 tablespoons butter
¾ cup grated Parmesan cheese
salt and pepper

Order the meat ground twice. Chop the onion and garlic very fine. Sauté the onion and garlic in oil just until tender. Add the chopped meat, and when lightly browned, add the cream, tomato paste, wine, cognac, and bouillon. Season with salt and pepper. Simmer very slowly for 2 hours.

Cook the macaroni in a large kettle of boiling salted water just until tender. Drain well. Mix well with the butter and the Parmesan cheese and add the sauce. Serve immediately.

Creole macaroni ∗ *Macaroni à la créole*

FOR SIX PEOPLE

1 clove garlic
4 tablespoons oil
3 small eggplants
2 green peppers
2 zucchini

½ can tomato paste
½ pound macaroni
1 cup grated Parmesan cheese
salt and pepper

Mince the garlic and sauté a moment in oil. Add the eggplants, the peppers, and zucchini not peeled but cut into pieces. Stir until well mixed. Add the tomato paste, salt, and pepper and simmer 2 hours.

Cook the macaroni in a large kettle of boiling salted water just until tender. Drain well. Mix with grated cheese and serve on a hot platter surrounded with the vegetable sauce.

Macaroni à la demidoff * Macaroni à la demidoff

½ pound macaroni
4 medium-sized carrots
½ celeriac
1 onion
½ pound mushrooms
3 tablespoons butter

1 small can truffle peelings
2 cups heavy cream
¼ cup Madeira wine
paprika
salt and pepper

Cook the macaroni in a large kettle of salted boiling water until it is about three quarters cooked. It will finish cooking later.

Chop the carrots, celeriac, and onion very fine. Simmer 30 minutes in lightly salted water. (Substitute ¾ cup of chopped celery hearts if celeriac is not available and cook it for the last 10 minutes with the other vegetables.—*Ed.*)

Wash, trim, and chop the mushrooms.

Heat the butter. Drain the vegetables well and simmer them in the butter for an hour. 5 minutes before serving, add the mushrooms and the contents of the can of truffles.

Mix the macaroni in a saucepan with the cream. Sprinkle liberally with paprika and season with salt and pepper. Put the pan over a low heat and bring the macaroni slowly just to the simmering point.

Put a layer of macaroni in a shallow buttered baking dish. Spread with a layer of the vegetables. Repeat the process and finish with a layer of macaroni. Sprinkle with the Madeira and bake 20 minutes in a moderate (350° F.) oven.

Ham and macaroni loaf * Pain de macaroni

¼ pound (1 cup) macaroni
½ pound cooked ham
2 eggs, slightly beaten
½ cup heavy cream

1 cup grated Gruyère cheese
2 tablespoons butter
salt and pepper

Cook the macaroni in boiling salted water just until tender. Drain and chop coarsely. Dice the ham in pieces of the same size. Place the macaroni and ham in a bowl and stir in the beaten eggs, the cream, and the cheese. Season well and stir until thoroughly mixed.

Line a charlotte mold or other straight-sided baking dish with buttered heavy wax paper. Pour in the macaroni mixture and bake 25 to 30 minutes at 350° F.

Unmold on a hot platter and serve with the sauce of your choice. I suggest béchamel sauce or tomato sauce.

*Macaroni in port * Macaroni au porto*

FOR FOUR PEOPLE

½ pound macaroni
1½ cups grated Gruyère cheese
1 truffle
½ pound mushrooms

5 tablespoons butter
2 cups port
salt and pepper

Cook the macaroni in a large amount of boiling salted water. You can test the macaroni by holding a piece between your thumb and finger. It should be tender but not soft. Drain in a collander.

Grate the cheese; cut the truffle in thin slices.

Wash, trim, and chop the mushrooms. Sauté them in 2 tablespoons of butter for 5 minutes.

Butter a shallow baking dish and spread half the macaroni in the bottom. Cover with mushrooms and the truffle slices. Sprinkle with pepper and half the grated cheese. Cover with the rest of the macaroni. Sprinkle with the rest of the cheese, with salt and pepper and dot with the butter. Sprinkle all over with the port and bake 20 minutes at 400° F.

Macaroni salad with shrimps and rémoulade sauce
Salade de macaroni rémoulade aux crevettes

FOR FOUR PEOPLE

1 cup macaroni pieces
Rémoulade Sauce (page 20)
½ pound small shelled cooked shrimp

2 tablespoons capers
juice of ½ lemon (optional)
8 small gherkin pickles

Cook the macaroni in boiling salted water just until tender. Drain.

Make the sauce. Combine the sauce, the shrimp, and the macaroni. Taste. If necessary, add a little lemon juice as well as salt and pepper.

Heap on a small platter. Smooth the macaroni into a dome shape. Put some of the capers on the top and make 2 circles with the rest of the capers around the dome: one around the center and one an inch from the base. Surround the platter with small gherkins, finely sliced, but not cut through at one end, so that they can be spread to look like fans.

*Macaroni timbale * Timbale de macaroni*

FOR SIX PEOPLE

3 ounces pork fat*
2 onions

½ pound ground beef
2 cups grated Parmesan cheese

*If only salt pork is available, parboil it 5 minutes, rinse, and use like fresh pork fat.—*Ed.*

2 tablespoons chopped parsley
½ cup olive oil
1 can (7½ ounces) tomato purée
⅓ cup soft breadcrumbs
milk

5 eggs
1 Italian or Polish dry sausage
5 ounces Gruyère cheese
2 pounds large macaroni
salt and pepper

Chop the fat, onions, and parsley very fine or force them through a meat grinder. Heat the olive oil in a saucepan and add the mixture. Cook gently until golden.

Mix the tomato purée with 2½ cups of hot water. Pour into the saucepan. Season with salt and pepper. Cover three quarters of the way and simmer very slowly for 2 hours. Watch to see that it does not become too dry.

Make meat balls by soaking the breadcrumbs in milk and squeezing out the milk. Put in a bowl with the ground beef, a little grated Parmesan cheese, a raw egg, salt, and pepper. Mix thoroughly and divide into little balls. Fry in 3 inches of fat or in a deep frying pan. Keep warm.

Hard-cook the 4 remaining eggs. Cut them, the sausage, and the Gruyère cheese into thin slices.

When the sauce has cooked 1½ hours, cook the macaroni in a kettle full of boiling salted water, using about 2 tablespoons of salt. Cook until tender, and when they are cooked, add a quart of cold water. This will keep the macaroni from sticking together. Drain immediately.

In a large baking dish, put a layer of macaroni. Dot the surface with meat balls, sausage slices, egg slices, and cheese. Spoon a little of the tomato sauce over it all. Sprinkle with Parmesan. Repeat this until everything has been used, finishing with tomato sauce. Sprinkle the top liberally with Parmesan.

Bake 20 minutes at 400° F.

Noodles, chicken and mushrooms au gratin
Nouilles crème volaille au gratin

FOR FOUR PEOPLE

¾ pound leftover chicken or turkey
½ pound mushrooms
2 cups Béchamel Sauce (page 6)
½ cup heavy cream

½ pound noodles
½ cup grated Gruyère cheese
2 tablespoons butter
salt and pepper

Chop the chicken; trim, wash, and chop the mushrooms.
Make a rather thin béchamel sauce.
Combine the chicken, mushrooms, béchamel, and cream. Mix well and season with salt and pepper.
At the same time, boil the noodles in a large kettle of salted water just until tender. Drain well.
Put a layer of noodles in a buttered baking dish. Cover with a layer of sauce.

Repeat the process until everything is used. End with a layer of noodles. Cover with grated cheese and dot with bits of butter. Brown in a hot (400° F.) oven.

Noodles with onions * Nouilles soubise

FOR SIX PEOPLE

2 pounds (8 to 10) onions	½ pound noodles
4 tablespoons butter	fine breadcrumbs
nutmeg	paprika
2 cups Béchamel Sauce (page 6)	salt and pepper

Peel and slice the onions very thin. Boil 15 minutes in salted water. Drain well. Heat 3 tablespoons of the butter in a saucepan and simmer the onions slowly until tender. They should not brown. Season with salt, pepper, and a little nutmeg.

Make a thick béchamel sauce and stir in the onions.

Cook the noodles in a large pan of boiling salted water. Drain well. Put the noodles in a buttered baking dish and cover with the sauce. Sprinkle with breadcrumbs and paprika; dot with butter. Brown in a hot (400° F.) oven for 10 minutes.

Noodle salad * Salade de nouilles

FOR FOUR PEOPLE

¼ pound noodles	4 gherkin pickles
Vinaigrette Sauce (page 29)	Mayonnaise (page 14)
1 can (7½ ounces) oil-packed tuna	

Cook the noodles in boiling salted water just until tender. Drain and rinse with cold water. Drain thoroughly. When cool, season with a vinaigrette sauce. Add the tuna fish broken into small pieces and the pickles sliced very thin.

Cover with a rather thin mayonnaise made with lemon juice.

Noodles with tarragon * Nouilles à l'estragon

FOR FOUR PEOPLE

½ pound noodles	¾ cup heavy cream
5-6 tarragon leaves	salt and pepper
3 tablespoons butter	

Cook the noodles in boiling salted water just until tender. Drain well. If the noodles are not well flavored, season with salt and pepper.

Put the noodles in a pan and add the chopped tarragon leaves. Stir in well, over heat, adding the butter by bits. When the noodles are very hot, add the cream. Taste and add more seasoning. Dishes with cream should always be well seasoned with pepper. Serve as soon as the cream is hot.

Ravioli ✳ *Ravioli*

FOR FOUR PEOPLE

Dough:
2 cups all-purpose flour
4 teaspoons oil
1 teaspoon salt
3 eggs
6-8 tablespoons lukewarm water

Filling:
1 hard-cooked egg
1 veal cutlet (¼ pound), cooked
3 ounces pork fat
4 teaspoons chopped parsley
1 raw egg
salt and pepper
Tomato Sauce (page 22)
grated Parmesan cheese

Heap the flour on a working surface and fashion a well in the center. In the well, put the oil, salt, and eggs. Working with the fingers of one hand, work the eggs and oil into the flour, adding the water with your other hand. Mix just until the dough forms a ball. Set it aside to rest for at least 2 hours.

Make the sauce.

Chop the hard-cooked egg, the ham, and the veal very fine. Chop the pork fat very fine or force through a meat grinder. Combine all the ingredients with parsley, salt, and pepper and stir in the raw egg to bind the mixture.

Roll out the pastry very thin. Divide in 2 equal squares. On one square put little mounds of the filling 1 inch apart in straight lines. Moisten the dough between each mound with a wet pastry brush. Lay the other pastry square over the first one and run a pastry wheel between the mounds, pressing down so that the dough will stick together and the ravioli will be divided into squares at the same time. Place the ravioli on a floured baking sheet or wooden board.

Bring a large pan of salted water to a boil. Throw the ravioli into the boiling water. Cook until the ravioli are tender. Test as soon as they float to the surface. They may, depending on the flour used, require a little longer cooking. Like spaghetti, the dough should be just tender.

Serve with tomato sauce and Parmesan cheese.

Spaghetti bolognese ✳ *Spaghetti bolonaise*

FOR SIX PEOPLE

⅓ cup oil
½ pound ground beef

1 can tomato paste
1 pound thin spaghetti

6 ounces lean pork belly*

6 onions

grated Parmesan cheese

salt and pepper

Heat the oil in a saucepan. Brown the meat lightly. Chop the pork very fine. Chop the onions and add them and the pork to the meat. Add 1½ cups of water and simmer 15 minutes. Add the tomato paste, salt, and pepper. Cover and simmer 30 minutes.

Cook the spaghetti in a large kettle of boiling salted water for 6 to 10 minutes, depending on the size of the spaghetti. It should be just tender. Drain well. Place in a hot serving dish and cover with the sauce. Serve with grated Parmesan cheese.

Spaghetti à la carbonara * Spaghetti à la carbonara

FOR FOUR PEOPLE

½ pound spaghetti

⅓ cup olive oil

1 clove garlic, minced

3 ounces pork fat, chopped**

2 eggs, slightly beaten

½ cup grated Parmesan cheese

salt and pepper

Cook the spaghetti in boiling salted water just until tender. Do not overcook. Drain well.

Heat the oil in a large skillet. Sauté the garlic and pork fat. When the fat is golden, add the spaghetti and the eggs. Season with salt, pepper, and Parmesan. Stir quickly until hot. Serve immediately.

Neapolitan spaghetti * Spaghetti à la napolitaine

FOR FOUR PEOPLE

4 tablespoons olive oil

2 cloves garlic

1 pound (3-4) tomatoes

1 large green pepper

½ pound spaghetti

1 cup grated cheese

salt and pepper

Heat the oil in a saucepan and brown the garlic well. Remove the garlic. Add the tomatoes, which have been peeled and cut into pieces. Season with salt and pepper. Cook over moderately high heat, stirring constantly. When the water from the tomatoes has evaporated, and the oil separates from the tomatoes, the sauce is done. Add the green pepper, seeded and cut into thin rounds.

Cook the spaghetti in a large pan of boiling salted water just until tender. Drain well. Mix with the sauce and the cheese. Serve immediately.

*If fresh pork is not available, parboil lean salt pork or pork jowl 5 minutes, rinse and use like fresh pork fat.—*Ed.*

**If fresh pork fat is not available, parboil pork jowl or salt pork 5 minutes, rinse and chop.—*Ed.*

Sautéed tagliatelli with cheese
Tagliatelles sautées au fromage

FOR SIX PEOPLE

½ pound wide thin noodles (tagliatelli)
3 tablespoons butter
½ cup fine breadcrumbs

½ pound small mushrooms
juice of ½ lemon
Parmesan cheese
salt and pepper

Cook the noodles in a large pan of boiling salted water for 3 to 4 minutes or just until tender. Drain well.

Heat the butter in a saucepan. Stir in the breadcrumbs and the drained noodles. Add the mushrooms, which have been trimmed, washed, and chopped. (This should be made with *cèpes,* but because these are not readily available, use small cultivated mushrooms, dried mushrooms, or field mushrooms, if you are sure of them.—*Ed.*) Sauté the combination for 5 minutes, stirring frequently.

Put in a warm vegetable dish. Sprinkle with lemon juice. Serve with a side dish of grated Parmesan cheese.

Tagliatelli chips * Tagliatelles chips

FOR FOUR PEOPLE

½ pound wide thin noodles (tagliatelli)

salt

Cook the tagliatelli in a large kettle of boiling salted water for 1 minute.

Drain and spread them out on a towel so that they will not stick.

Fry a few at a time in deep fat at 385° F., stirring with a long fork to keep them separate. Drain well and sprinkle with salt.

Tagliatelli in cream * Tagliatelles à la crème

FOR SIX PEOPLE

½ pound wide thin noodles (tagliatelli)
tarragon, chopped

3 tablespoons butter
¾ cup cream
salt and pepper

Cook the tagliatelli in a large pan of salted boiling water for 3 to 4 minutes or just until tender. Drain them and put them in a pan with 2 teaspoons of chopped fresh or ½ teaspoon dried tarragon, salt, and pepper. Heat and add the butter bit by bit, stirring until the butter melts. Add the cream, stir well, and serve immediately.

Tagliatelli with nuts * Tagliatelles aux noix

FOR SIX PEOPLE

2 thick slices cooked ham
12 walnuts
2 tablespoons chopped parsley
1 clove garlic

4 tablespoons oil
1 pound wide thin noodles (tagliatelli)
salt and pepper

Chop the ham; peel and chop the walnuts; chop the parsley and garlic.

Heat the oil in a small saucepan and add these ingredients, cooking just long enough to heat them thoroughly.

Cook the tagliatelli in a large pan of boiling salted water for 3 to 4 minutes or until just tender. Drain well and put in a hot dish. Season with salt and pepper and pour over the hot ham mixture. Stir well. Serve with a side dish of grated cheese.

Neapolitan tagliatelli omelet
Omelette napolitaine (à base de tagliatelles)

FOR SIX PEOPLE

½ pound wide thin noodles
  (tagliatelli)
8 eggs
¾ cup Gruyère cheese

2 tablespoons butter
tomato sauce (homemade or canned)
¼ cup grated Parmesan cheese
salt and pepper

Cook the noodles in a large pan of boiling salted water for 3 to 4 minutes or just until tender. Drain well.

Beat the eggs and stir in the noodles and the grated cheese. Season with pepper and some salt. The Gruyère has a salty flavor, so take care.

Heat the butter in an omelet pan. Add the mixture and stir very gently. When the omelet is lightly browned on the bottom, fold it in two with a wide spatula and slip it onto a warm (not hot) platter. Cover with tomato sauce, which, if canned, can be reheated in a double boiler. Sprinkle with Parmesan cheese.

(Remember that French omelets are not cooked as long as the American variety. The interior of a folded omelet has a creamy texture.—*Ed.*)

Brown vermicelli * Vermicelle grillé

FOR FOUR PEOPLE

½ pound vermicelli
⅓ cup oil

bouillon or water
salt and pepper

Put the vermicelli and oil in a pan and stir constantly over moderate heat until the vermicelli is light brown.

At the same time, bring water or bouillon to a boil. Pour enough of the liquid to cover the vermicelli by about ⅓ inch. Season with salt and pepper. Cover the pan, reduce the heat, and cook until the liquid is absorbed, which should take from 5 to 6 minutes.

This is a delicious accompaniment to braised meats.

Vegetables

Vegetables

If I like vegetables very much, and if we eat a great many in France, I must admit it is because we have so many ways of preparing them. We don't like them raw or simply boiled in water. I take as much care in preparing a vegetable dish as I do a meat dish or a dessert. And I have proved with my own children that it is very easy to get children used to eating vegetables, provided they are well prepared and well served.

The secret of success is to have the vegetables very fresh. This is easy in France where distances are short and where there are variations in climate that permit vegetables a slow ripening process. We eat vegetables as accompaniments of meat, poultry, or fish (we serve them in separate dishes, usually), but often they constitute a complete course in themselves—Spinach Soufflé, Leek Tart, Endive au Gratin, and so on.

Apples

Although strictly speaking, apples are fruit, they—better than all other fruits—can serve also as a vegetable and make a delicious companion to such meats as pork or veal chops, roast pork, or baked ham; to such poultry as goose, duck, and guinea hen; and to such fish as salmon, grilled tuna, and mackerel. In other words, apples go well with the rich meats and fish.

Apples vary greatly. For best results, choose those that are not too large and neither too tart nor too cottony in texture. Remember never to season apples like vegetables.

Sautéed apples * Pommes sautées

FOR FOUR PEOPLE

6-8 apples   6 tablespoons butter

Peel apples and core with an apple corer. Cut in quarters and cut each quarter in 3 or 4 slices.

Heat the butter in a large skillet. Put in the apple slices and sauté over a very gentle heat. When the apples are golden on one side, turn them with a wide spatula, such as are available in most hardware stores. (If you cannot find one in the kitchen department, look in the section where they sell painters' tools.—*Ed.*)

Turn the apples carefully so that they do not break. Do not season with salt or pepper.

If you are serving apples with Duck in Cider, add a little Calvados or apple brandy to the apples and touch with a lighted match. It is the only liqueur that will not detract from the flavor of the apples.

Apples in butter * Pommes au beurre

FOR FOUR PEOPLE

8 apples (not too tart)   6 tablespoons butter
1 lemon

Peel the apples without cutting them. Rub each one lightly with the cut side of a lemon to prevent their darkening. Cut a slice off the stem end of each apple to make a kind of cover. Core with an apple corer. Fill the center with butter and put back the cover on each apple.

Place the apples in a buttered baking dish. Pour in ¾ cup of water and bake in moderate oven (350° F.) until tender, the time depending on the apple. Test by inserting a sharp, pointed knife. The apples should be tender but not soft enough to crush.

Artichokes en cocotte * Artichauts en cocotte

FOR FOUR PEOPLE

8 small artichokes   3 tablespoons oil
3 tablespoons butter   1 carrot, sliced thin
3 shallots, finely chopped   1 onion, sliced thin
¼ pound mushrooms, chopped   1 clove garlic, sliced thin
5 ounces chopped lean pork belly   1 cup dry white wine, heated
  or bacon   4 teaspoons tomato paste
2 tablespoons chopped *fines herbes*   1 bay leaf
⅓ cup soft breadcrumbs   juice of 1 lemon
¼ cup milk   salt and pepper
1 large thin slice pork fat

Remove the choke and center leaves of tender artichokes. Cut off the top third of each artichoke.

Heat the butter in a small pan and sauté the chopped shallots, mushrooms, fat, and *fines herbes* (parsley, tarragon). (If you cannot get pork belly, parboil the bacon 5 minutes, rinse well and then chop.—*Ed.*) When the shallots are transparent, add the breadcrumbs, which have been soaked in the milk and squeezed dry. Mix well and stuff each artichoke with the mixture. Tie the artichokes with kitchen string.

Line the bottom of a porcelain-lined iron casserole with the pork fat. Pour in the oil and add the carrot, onion, and garlic. Place over direct heat until the vegetables are golden. Place the stuffed artichokes on the vegetables. Sprinkle with the heated wine mixed with the tomato paste. Add the bay leaf, salt, and pepper and cook uncovered 1 hour in a 350° F. oven. Season with lemon juice.

Braised artichokes * Artichauts braisés

FOR FOUR PEOPLE

8 young, tender artichokes
4 onions, peeled and chopped
4 tablespoons oil
3 teaspoons flour
2 tablespoons tomato paste

1 clove garlic, chopped
bouquet garni (½ bay leaf, thyme,
    parsley)
1 cup bouillon
salt and pepper

Remove the artichoke chokes. Cut off the top third of the artichokes.

Sauté the onions in oil for a few moments. Add the artichokes and continue cooking until the vegetables are lightly browned all over. Sprinkle with flour and stir with a wooden spoon until the flour disappears. Add the tomato paste mixed in ½ cup water. Add also the garlic, *bouquet garni,* salt, and pepper. Cover and simmer 15 minutes. Add the bouillon and simmer 2 hours. Serve very hot. The sauce should be thick.

Artichoke bottoms with eggs and cream (cold) Fonds d'artichauts froids à la crème

FOR FOUR PEOPLE

4 large artichokes
4 tablespoons chopped *fines herbes*
1 cup heavy cream

juice of ½ lemon
4 soft-cooked eggs
salt and pepper

Cook the artichokes 1 hour in boiling salted water. Drain, cool, and remove the leaves and the choke, leaving only the bottoms. (Canned artichoke bottoms may be used also.—*Ed.*) Place on a small serving platter.

Combine half the chopped *fines herbes* (parsley, chervil, tarragon) with 2½ tablespoons of very heavy cream and the juice of ½ lemon. Spoon the mixture into the artichoke bottoms.

Place an egg on each artichoke bottom. Whip the rest of the cream. Season with salt, pepper, and the rest of the herbs. Heap this on top of the eggs. Chill in the refrigerator. This dish should be served very cold.

Artichoke bottoms with spinach
Fonds d'artichauts aux épinards

FOR TWO PEOPLE

4 artichokes	3 tablespoons heavy cream
2 tablespoons butter	½ cup grated Gruyère cheese
½ pound spinach	salt and pepper

Cook the artichokes in boiling salted water for about 35 minutes. Drain and remove the inner leaves and chokes. (Or use canned artichoke bottoms.—*Ed.*) In either case, sauté the bottoms lightly in butter.

Cook the spinach until tender. Then force through a strainer or food mill or purée in a blender. Add the cream, salt, and pepper. Fill each artichoke bottom with the spinach. Sprinkle with grated cheese. Dot each one with butter and brown in a moderate oven.

Artichoke bottoms stuffed with mushrooms
Fonds d'artichauts farcis aux champignons

FOR FOUR PEOPLE

8 artichoke bottoms	¼ cup grated Gruyère cheese
3 tablespoons butter	salt and pepper
½ pound mushrooms	
¾ cup thick Béchamel Sauce (page 6)	

Prepare the artichoke bottoms as in the preceding recipe. Sauté in butter. Remove to a fireproof serving platter.

Wash and trim the mushrooms. Slice them thin and sauté them a few minutes in butter.

Make the béchamel sauce and mix it into the mushrooms. Season with salt and pepper. Fill the bottoms with the mixture. Sprinkle with the grated cheese, dot with butter, and brown in a 400° F. oven for 5 to 10 minutes.

Artichoke bottoms à la grimod de la reynière
Artichauts à la grimod de la reynière

FOR FOUR PEOPLE

4 large artichokes	rosemary
4-5 (1 pound) onions	½ cup grated Gruyère cheese

3 tablespoons butter
tarragon

dry breadcrumbs
salt and pepper

Prepare the artichoke bottoms as in the preceding recipes.

Meanwhile, peel and slice the onions very fine and sauté them in butter until golden. Season with tarragon, rosemary, salt, and pepper and let cool.

Fill the artichoke bottoms with the cold onions. Sprinkle with grated cheese and breadcrumbs. Brown in the oven.

Artichokes maraîchère * Artichauts maraîchère

FOR FOUR PEOPLE

8 tender young artichokes
3 tablespoons oil
1 leek
1 onion
2 tomatoes

several spinach leaves
several sorrel leaves
¾ cup white wine
salt and pepper

Remove the chokes and the inner leaves of the artichokes. Trim off the top third and remove the hard outer leaves.

Heat the oil in a porcelain-lined iron casserole and sauté the leek, onion, and tomatoes, all peeled and chopped. When they are very soft, add the artichokes. Add the spinach and sorrel leaves, also chopped, sprinkle with the white wine, season with salt and pepper, and cook covered for 2 hours in a 300° F. oven.

Artichokes à la provençale
Artichauts à la provençale

FOR FOUR PEOPLE

8 young tender artichokes
8 cloves garlic
vinegar

¾ cup olive oil
bouquet garni (bay leaf, thyme, parsley)
salt and pepper

Remove the chokes and cut the top third from the artichokes. Place them in a shallow, flat-bottomed pan just large enough to hold the artichokes. They should be pressed one against the other. Insert the garlic between the artichokes.

Pour a little vinegar into each artichoke, allowing about ¼ teaspoon to each one. Pour the oil in the pan and then fill with water. Sprinkle with salt and pepper and add the bouquet garni. Cover and simmer 3 hours. Then, 15 minutes befor the end of cooking, remove the cover and let the liquid boil away so that the artichokes brown slightly on the bottom.

Artichokes à la barigoule * Artichauts à la barigoule

FOR FOUR PEOPLE

4 artichokes	¼ pound lean pork belly
1 clove garlic	6 tablespoons oil
1 shallot	6 tablespoons white wine
3-4 sprigs parsley	salt and pepper

Choose very fresh medium-sized artichokes. Cut off the top third of the artichokes and remove the hard outer leaves. Cook in boiling salted water for 30 minutes. Turn upside down in a collander to drain.

Chop the garlic, shallot, and parsley very fine. Chop the pork belly fine. (If this is not available, parboil a piece of bacon for 5 minutes. Rinse and chop.—*Ed.*) Mix well and season.

Spread the leaves of the artichokes slightly and twist out the choke. Put some stuffing in each artichoke and tie the artichokes with kitchen string.

Put the oil in a heavy pan, and when it is hot, add the artichokes. Sprinkle with the white wine and cook covered over a low heat for 1½ hours. This is eaten with fork and knife, removing discreetly the leaves that are too hard.

Chinese artichokes with curry sauce
Crosnes sauce au cari

FOR FOUR PEOPLE

2 pounds Chinese artichokes	2 cups milk
4 tablespoons butter	3 tablespoons curry powder
4 teaspoons flour	salt and pepper

Peel the artichokes and boil them in salted water for about 20 minutes or until tender.

Make a sauce by heating the butter and stirring in the flour. Simmer a few moments and stir in the milk. When well blended, add the curry powder and season with salt and pepper.

Drain the vegetables and put them in the sauce. Simmer until the sauce is slightly thickened. Taste for seasoning and serve in a heated dish.

Chinese artichokes with tomato sauce
Crosnes à la sauce tomate

FOR FOUR PEOPLE

3 ounces pork fat*	1 can tomato paste

*If pork fat is not available, wash and parboil fat salt pork for 5 minutes and rinse. This will remove the salt.—*Ed.*

3 onions

2 tablespoons parsley, chopped

2 tablespoons chervil, chopped

2½ tablespoons oil

2 pounds Chinese artichokes

1 cup grated Parmesan cheese

salt and pepper

Chop fine the pork fat, the onions, and the herbs or grind them through a *moulinette*. Simmer 15 minutes in a heavy saucepon with the oil. Add the tomato paste and an equal amount of water. Season with salt and pepper. Cover and simmer 1 hour.

Peel the artichokes and cook 20 minutes in boiling salted water or until tender. Drain. Place in a hot serving dish. Cover with the sauce and serve the vegetable with grated Parmesan cheese.

Don't forget that cooked Chinese artichokes can be sliced and sautéed in butter like potatoes.

Chinese artichoke fritters * Beignets de crosnes

See Oyster Plant Fritters

Asparagus

Although both white and green asparagus are grown in France and in the United States, the white is eaten most commonly in France and the green in America. The two varieties differ in texture and in flavor, but the recipes for one apply equally well to the other, and the general method of preparing and cooking them differs only slightly. Both varieties should be eaten as fresh as possible. If it is not practicable to eat them as soon as they are picked, wrap the asparagus in a damp cloth and store in the refrigerator until just before cooking. Both varieties must be thoroughly washed before cooking.

Tie asparagus into bunches according to size so that they will cook evenly. Cut them to an even length.

Never overcook asparagus. It should be tender but not soft. Always drain thoroughly, and put on several layers of dish toweling for further draining. Never let asparagus cool in the cooking water.

Once the asparagus is arranged on a platter, cut and remove the string. Like artichokes, asparagus can be eaten with the fingers without fear of being thought impolite. Asparagus need not be served piping hot, and in fact should not be when served with emulsified sauces (hollandaise, mousseline, and so on).

White asparagus is all white except for a rosy violet tip. Yellow spears should be avoided, because they are comparatively dry and tasteless. They should be peeled before cooking. If they are just slightly scraped, they will hold their shape better and make a better-looking presentation, but they will not be as tender to eat. If they are peeled with a sharp knife from the tip to the end, they will be almost entirely edible. Cook 20 to 30 minutes in a large amount of boiling salted water.

The green variety does not have to be peeled, but the white end is cut off, and with very large spears, it is best to remove the pointed leaves. Cook the asparagus in 2 inches of boiling salted water, using a deep, covered pan, or asparagus steamer, for 12 to 15 minutes.

Hot asparagus can be eaten with hot or cold sauces, such as hollandaise or béchamel sauce mixed with cream or chopped, hard-cooked eggs, mayonnaise, tarragon French dressing, or a vinaigrette with chopped, hard-cooked eggs.

Cold asparagus is delicious with a variety of vinaigrettes and mayonnaises or tarragon-flavored heavy cream.

Asparagus louis XV * Asperges louis XV

FOR FOUR PEOPLE

4 pounds asparagus
Hollandaise Sauce (page 10)

1 egg white
salt and pepper

Prepare and boil the asparagus according to directions on page 483.

At the same time, make the sauce. Remove the sauce from the heat and fold in the stiffly beaten egg white.

Cut the well-drained asparagus on the bias in 3-inch pieces, or if you use the young green variety, leave whole. Arrange the asparagus on a warm platter and cover with the sauce.

Asparagus with crab * Asperges au crabe

FOR SIX PEOPLE

4 pounds asparagus
3 hard-cooked eggs

¾ cup Vinaigrette Sauce (page 29)
2 cans best crabmeat

Prepare white or green asparagus for cooking according to directions on page 483 and boil or steam until tender.

Chop the hard-cooked eggs and mix with some of the vinaigrette sauce.

Remove any filaments from the crab and flake it.

Arrange the asparagus on a salad platter. Cover with the vinaigrette sauce mixed with the eggs. Decorate the edge of the platter with crab and serve the rest of the sauce in a sauce bowl.

Asparagus with two cheeses
Asperges aux deux fromages

FOR FOUR PEOPLE

4 pounds young asparagus

½ cup grated Gruyère cheese

12 tablespoons butter   salt and pepper
½ cup grated Parmesan cheese

Wash and prepare the asparagus so that it is tender and edible right down to the end. Cook according to directions on page 483 and drain them well.

Melt half the butter and pour it into a shallow dish. Mix the cheeses and put them in another shallow dish. Dip the asparagus spears first in the butter and then in the cheese and arrange them in layers on a heated serving platter.

At the same time heat the remaining butter until brown. Pour very hot over the asparagus. Season with salt and pepper and serve.

Asparagus and ham (cold) * Asperges au jambon

FOR FOUR PEOPLE

2 pounds asparagus   1 hard-cooked egg
4 large thin slices boiled ham   2 teaspoons chopped parsley
1½ cups Vinaigrette Sauce (page 29)   salt and pepper

Prepare and boil the asparagus according to directions on page 483. Drain and cool.

Roll one or two spears, according to their size, in a quarter piece of ham. Arrange the rolls on a serving platter and serve with a vinaigrette sauce to which a chopped hard-cooked egg and parsley have been added. Season to taste.

Asparagus under a blanket
Asperges sous couverture

FOR FOUR PEOPLE

2 pounds asparagus   dry breadcrumbs
2 cups Béchamel Sauce (page 6)   salt and pepper
1 cup grated Gruyère cheese

Prepare white or green asparagus for cooking according to directions on page 483. Cook in salted water until tender. Drain and cool. Arrange on a heatproof serving platter.

Make the sauce and stir in the grated cheese. Season well with salt and pepper. Spoon some of the sauce over the tips and cover that part with heavy waxed paper. Pour the rest of the sauce over the stems. Brown in a 400° F. oven for 15 minutes. Remove from the oven. Take off the papers and sprinkle the stems with breadcrumbs.

Asparagus loaf * Pain de pointes d'asperges

FOR FOUR PEOPLE

2 small bunches green asparagus
2 cups Béchamel Sauce (page 6)
4 eggs slightly beaten

2 tablespoons butter
salt and pepper

Wash the asparagus and cut into small pieces. Boil 5 minutes in salted water. Drain thoroughly.

Make the béchamel sauce, and when cooled to lukewarm, add the eggs. Season with salt and pepper and mix in the asparagus. Butter liberally a charlotte mold or other straight-sided heatproof dish. Pour in the asparagus mixture and place the mold in a pan of hot water. Bake at 350° F. for 45 to 60 minutes. The way you can tell when the loaf is cooked is this: when you insert a knife, the blade will come out clean.

Unmold on a serving platter after loosening the edges with a knife blade. Serve with the sauce of your choice or with hot heavy cream seasoned with salt and pepper.

Asparagus à la polonaise * Asperges à la polonaise

FOR FOUR PEOPLE

3 pounds asparagus
2 hard-cooked eggs
2 teaspoons chopped parsley

¼ pound butter
½ cup dry breadcrumbs
salt and pepper

Prepare and cook the asparagus according to directions on page 483.

At the same time, divide the yolks and whites of the hard-cooked eggs. Chop the yolks and mix them with the parsley. Heat the butter until lightly browned. Stir in the breadcrumbs.

Arrange the very well-drained asparagus on a warm platter. Cover the tips first with the egg-yolk-parsley combination and then with the buttered breadcrumbs. Serve immediately.

Asparagus quiche * Quiche aux asperges

FOR FOUR PEOPLE

Pastry:
2½ cups flour
1 egg
6 tablespoons oil
½ teaspoon salt

Filling:
2 pounds asparagus
1½ cups heavy cream
4 eggs
salt and pepper

Pastry: Heap the flour on a marble or other working surface. Make a depression in the center and in it put the egg, oil, and salt and work the mixture with your fingertips, adding a little cold water when necessary, until you have a smooth ball. Let the pastry rest several hours before rolling out.

Prepare and cook the asparagus according to directions on page 483.

Roll out the pastry on a floured surface, using a floured rolling pin. It should be about ⅛ inch thick. Line a pie tin with the pastry and prick it well with a sharp-tined fork on the bottom and the sides. Bake in a 425° F. oven for 10 minutes.

Filling: Beat the cream and eggs together until thoroughly blended. Season with salt and pepper. Pour the mixture into the partially cooked pastry shell. Bake 10 minutes longer.

Cut off the top 2 inches of the asparagus. Remove the *quiche* from the oven and stick the asparagus tips into the filling, tip sides up. Put the *quiche* back into the oven for 5 minutes or until the custard has set. Serve hot.

Asparagus salad ✳ *Salade d'asperges*

FOR FOUR PEOPLE

16 large asparagus spears
1 head garden lettuce
1 bunch radishes

1 small cucumber
3 hard-cooked eggs
Mayonnaise (page 14)

Prepare and cook the asparagus according to directions on page 483. Wash the lettuce and radishes.

Place 2 leaves of lettuce on each plate. Trim the asparagus so that it is entirely edible and place 4 spears on the lettuce leaves on each plate. Garnish with egg and cucumber slices and decorate as you like with the radishes and mayonnaise.

Asparagus en soufflé ✳ *Soufflé aux asperges*

FOR FOUR PEOPLE

4 pounds medium-sized asparagus
3 egg yolks
1½ cups freshly grated Gruyère
   cheese

3 egg whites, beaten stiff
salt and pepper

Prepare and boil the asparagus according to directions on page 483.
(Cut off all but the tender part. All the asparagus in a soufflé must be edible.)
Divide and tie them into small bunches. Boil 15 to 20 minutes in salted water. When cooked, drain them very thoroughly before placing them on a fireproof serving platter. Remove the strings.

Beat the egg yolks with a fork and gradually add the freshly grated cheese. Season with salt and pepper and fold in carefully the beaten egg whites. Spread the mixture over the asparagus and bake 15 minutes in a 425° F. oven. The top should be well browned. Serve immediately.

Fresh fava beans à l'ancienne
Fèves nouvelles à l'ancienne

FOR FOUR PEOPLE

2 cups fresh shelled young fava beans*   ¼ cup heavy cream
¼ pound butter   1 egg yolk
1 teaspoon sugar   salt and pepper
1 sprig savory

Parboil the beans 10 minutes in salted water. Drain them well.

Heat the butter in a saucepan. Add the sugar, the savory, the beans, salt, and pepper. Cook covered for 25 minutes.

Remove the pan from the heat. Stir in the cream previously mixed with the egg yolk. Taste for seasoning and serve.

Fava beans in cream * Fèves à la crème

FOR TWO TO THREE PEOPLE

2 cups young shelled fava beans   ½ cup shredded almonds
2 tablespoons butter   salt and pepper
½ cup heavy cream

Be sure to use only the very young beans for this delicious recipe. Start the beans in cold salted water. Bring to a boil and maintain at boiling point for 15 minutes. Drain well and dry the beans by putting them back in the pan with butter and cooking them over high heat for 2 minutes.

Meanwhile, heat the cream with the almonds. Season with salt and pepper. Put the beans in a heated vegetable dish and pour over the almond cream. Serve immediately.

Fava beans à la blanquette * Fèves à la blanquette

FOR FOUR PEOPLE

4 cups fresh fava beans   juice of ½ lemon
5 tablespoons butter   2 teaspoons chopped fresh tarragon

*Fava beans, called broad beans in England, are available in some Italian markets and can easily be grown in home gardens. They resemble shell beans in appearance, but are very different in flavor. Unless very young, the beans have an outer skin that has to be removed before eating.—Ed.

2 egg yolks
⅓ cup heavy cream

salt and pepper

Wash the shelled beans and dry them carefully. Remove the outer skin.

Melt the butter, and before it gets hot, add the beans. Sprinkle with salt and pepper. Cover and cook over a low heat, shaking the pan from time to time. The time of cooking depends on the age of the beans.

When the beans are tender, add the yolks, beaten with the cream and lemon juice. Stir the sauce and let it heat but not boil. Taste for seasoning, adding the chopped tarragon, if you like the flavor, and serve. This dish ·is an excellent accompaniment for a roast shoulder of lamb, for example.

Green beans in cream * Haricots verts à la crème

FOR FOUR PEOPLE

2 pounds green beans*
3 tablespoons butter

2 tablespoons heavy cream
salt and pepper

Trim the beans, removing any strings if necessary. Boil uncovered in salted water for 20 minutes or until tender. Drain thoroughly.

Heat the butter slightly in a skillet. Add the beans and cook gently over a very low heat until the butter has penetrated the beans. Add pepper, and just before serving, add the cream.

Green beans à la bourguignonne
Haricots verts à la bourguignonne

FOR FOUR PEOPLE

2 pounds very young green beans
10 tablespoons butter
4 teaspoons flour
1 cup hot bouillon
½ cup hot red Bordeaux wine

2 tablespoons chopped *fines herbes*
  (parsley, chervil)
juice of ½ lemon
salt and pepper

Wash and trim the beans and boil them uncovered in salted water for 20 minutes or until tender. Drain thoroughly.

Heat 3 tablespoons of butter in a deep heavy pan. Add the flour and stir in with a wooden spoon. Stirring constantly, gradually add the hot bouillon and

---

Haricots verts differ from any of the American varieties of beans. The nearest approach in texture is found in very young, freshly picked green beans. The flat Italian green beans are perhaps the nearest in flavor.—*Ed.*

wine. Season with salt and pepper and cook slowly until the mixture begins to thicken.

Heat the rest of the butter in a saucepan and put in the beans and the herbs, which have been chopped very fine. Sauté 5 minutes, shaking the pan occasionally. Add wine sauce to the beans, stirring constantly.

Serve the beans in a heated vegetable dish and sprinkle with the lemon juice.

Green beans à la française
Haricots verts à la française

FOR FOUR PEOPLE

2 pounds green beans
1 pound tiny onions
2 heads garden lettuce
¼ pound butter

1 tablespoon sugar
bouquet garni (parsley, chervil)
salt

Trim the beans and, unless they are very small, cut them into pieces.

Peel the onions but leave them whole. Remove the large outer leaves from the lettuce heads, leaving the hearts. Wash well.

In a deep heavy pan, put 6 tablespoons of butter, all the vegetables, the sugar, some salt, and ¾ cup of cold water. Stir well and bring to a boil. Add the *bouquet garni,* cover, and cook very gently for 1 hour. Test. If the vegetables are tender, remove the *bouquet garni,* add the rest of the butter. Salt, if necessary, before serving.

Green beans au gratin * Gratin de haricots verts

FOR FOUR PEOPLE

3 pounds fresh young green beans
¼ teaspoon baking soda
5 tablespoons butter

¼ pound mushrooms
1 cup heavy cream

Trim the young beans, removing any strings if necessary. If only large beans are available, French-cut them, that is to say, cut thin lengthwise.

Boil the beans uncovered in a large quantity of salted water to which the baking soda has been added. Cook until about three quarters done—approximately 15 minutes. Drain well.

Meanwhile, trim, wash, dry, and chop the mushrooms. Heat 2 tablespoons of butter in a skillet and sauté the mushrooms for 2 minutes.

Drain the beans and finish cooking them in a saucepan with the cream over a low heat. Season to taste with salt and pepper and put the beans in a shallow buttered baking dish. Cover the beans with the chopped mushrooms. Melt the rest of the butter and pour it over the mushrooms. Brown in a hot oven 10 minutes. Serve very hot as a separate course or as an accompaniment to a roast.

Canned green beans with almonds and gruyère cheese (cold)
Haricots verts aux amandes

FOR FOUR TO SIX PEOPLE

1 large (2-pound) can French
   green beans
4 sections processed Gruyère cheese

½ cup blanched almonds
Vinaigrette Sauce (page 29)

Drain the beans thoroughly.

Dice the cheese very fine. Mix in a salad bowl with the beans and almonds.

Just before serving, mix carefully with the vinaigrette sauce. Serve this salad well chilled.

Horticultural beans with tomatoes
Haricots frais à la tomate

FOR FOUR PEOPLE

3 pounds horticultural beans
2 small onions
small *bouquet garni* (thyme,
   bay leaf, parsley)
3-4 tomatoes

4 tablespoons oil
paprika
½ cup heavy cream (optional)
salt and pepper

Shell the beans. Put them in cold, salted water with the onions and the *bouquet garni.* Bring to a boil and simmer 1 hour. Test to be sure they are cooked. Drain well.

Dip the tomatoes in boiling water and slip off the skins. Halve the tomatoes and press out the seeds and as much juice as possible from the halves. Cut them in large dice and sauté the dice in oil over a moderate heat for 10 minutes. Add the beans. Taste for seasoning and continue cooking for 10 minutes. Sprinkle with paprika and serve. If you like, add the heavy cream before serving.

Wax beans with fresh tomatoes
Haricots beurre à la tomate fraîche

FOR FOUR PEOPLE

3 pounds wax beans
1½ pounds (5-6) tomatoes
3 tablespoons butter

½ cup heavy cream
paprika
salt and pepper

Trim the beans and cook them about 20 minutes or until three quarters cooked.

Dip the tomatoes in boiling water for a few seconds. Slip off the skins. Halve them and press out the seeds and as much juice as possible. Simmer uncovered in a heavy saucepan until they become a rather thick purée. Season with salt and pepper.

Melt the butter in another saucepan. Add the beans and the tomatoes. Simmer until the beans are tender.

Just before serving, stir in the heavy cream. Season again with salt, pepper, and a dash of paprika. Heat the cream but do not let it boil.

Sautéed flageolet beans
Haricots flageolets sautés (frais)

FOR FOUR PEOPLE

2 cups fresh flageolets*
7 tablespoons butter
1¼ cups bouillon

chopped *fines herbes* (parsley, chervil)
salt and pepper

Wash the shelled beans well and put them in very hot but not boiling water for 2 to 3 minutes. Drain them and put them in a saucepan with 5 tablespoons of butter. Add the bouillon, salt, and pepper; cover and simmer slowly for 1 hour. Taste. If the beans are not tender, continue the cooking. They should remain whole.

Heat the remaining butter in a skillet. Sauté the beans in the butter without letting them brown. Just before serving, sprinkle with chopped herbs.

Chinese snow peas with mushrooms
Haricots mange-tout aux champignons

FOR FOUR PEOPLE

½ pound mushrooms
3 medium-sized onions

½ cup heavy cream
paprika

*Flageolets are rarely found in the United States, but very small lima beans make a satisfactory substitute.—*Ed*.

3 pounds snow peas*   salt and pepper
3 tablespoons butter

Trim the beans and cut them in small pieces. Boil in salted water for 25 minutes.

Meanwhile, trim and wash the mushrooms. Dry them and chop them.

Chop the onions fine and sauté a few minutes in the butter; add the mushrooms and cook two minutes.

Drain the beans and stir them into the mushroom mixture along with the heavy cream. Season with salt and pepper and a dash of paprika. Serve hot or very cold.

Beets

Choose beets with fresh leaves. Wash the beets thoroughly, cutting off all but an inch of the tops. Boil whole for 30 to 50 minutes or until tender. Or, better still, bake in a 325° F. oven for 60 to 90 minutes or until tender. Peel and prepare according to the following recipes:

Beets in cream * Betteraves à la crème
FOR FOUR PEOPLE

4 cooked beets   paprika
3 tablespoons butter   salt and pepper
½ cup heavy cream

Cut the cooked beets in slices. Heat the butter until frothy and reheat the beets in it over a low heat for 10 minutes, shaking the saucepan from time to time. Put in a vegetable dish. Heat the cream in the same pan and stir with the juices in the pan. Season with salt and pepper and pour over the beets. Sprinkle with paprika and serve very hot.

Deep-fried beets * Betteraves en fritot
FOR FOUR PEOPLE

2 medium-sized beets   nutmeg
2 teaspoons baking powder chervil or parsley
2 cups all-purpose flour   1 lemon
3 tablespoons oil   salt and pepper
2 onions

*Chinese snow peas are the *mange-tout* beans of France.—*Ed.*

Prepare the beets according to directions at beginning of section.

Dissolve the baking powder in ½ cup warm water. Sift the flour into a mound in a bowl. Make a depression in the center and into it pour the water, the oil, and a good pinch of salt. Stir with a wooden spatula, adding enough water to give a smooth light batter.

Cover and keep in a warm place for 3 hours.

Slice the beets very thin. Slice the onions thin. Place onion slices on beet slices. Season with salt, pepper, a dash of nutmeg, and a little chopped chervil or, lacking that, parsley. Cover with slices of beet. Dip these into the frying batter and fry in deep fat (385° F.) until golden brown. Drain, sprinkle with salt, and serve on a platter surrounded by slices of lemon.

Beets with onions * Betteraves aux oignons

FOR FOUR PEOPLE

2 large beets
2 onions
6 tablespoons butter

½ cup heavy cream
salt and pepper

Prepare and cook the beets according to directions given above. Heat the butter in a small fireproof serving dish. Add the onions, chopped very fine, and cook over low heat until soft. Add the beets and cook covered, still over low heat, for 10 minutes. Season with salt and pepper, and shortly before serving, add the cream.

Brussels sprouts in cream
Choux de bruxelles à la crème

FOR FOUR PEOPLE

4 pounds Brussels sprouts
1 cup heavy cream

3 teaspoons curry powder
salt and pepper

Carefully trim the sprouts, removing all the withered or yellowed leaves.

Put them in a pan of cold water and bring slowly to a boil. When the water boils, transfer the sprouts to a pan of boiling salted water and boil hard without a cover for 20 minutes. This operation makes the sprouts much more digestible.

Drain thoroughly and chop fine. Put them in a saucepan with the cream and curry powder. Season with salt and pepper. Heat until the sprouts have absorbed most of the cream. Stir constantly. Serve in a heated vegetable dish.

Cabbage casserole d'auvergne
Chou farci d'auvergne

FOR SIX PEOPLE

1 large cabbage
5 ounces pork fat
2 onions
1 cup ground cooked beef
7 ounces lean pork belly or bacon

2 tablespoons *fines herbes,* chopped
   (parsley, basil, tarragon, chervil)
4 teaspoons lard or butter
paper-thin slices salt pork or fat bacon
salt and pepper

Wash the cabbage and boil it 10 minutes in salted water with the pork fat. (If the only pork fat you can get is salt pork, add no salt to the water.—*Ed.*) Drain the cabbage well.

At the same time, peel and boil the onions in salted water for 15 minutes. Drain them.

Chop the beef and the lean pork belly. (If you can't get pork belly, parboil bacon 5 minutes and rinse to remove the smoked flavor.—*Ed.*) Set aside ¼ of the chopped pork or bacon. Chop the onions and mix everything together with the *fines herbes* and the lard or butter. Season with salt and pepper.

Line a casserole with the slices of salt pork or bacon and cover with a layer of cabbage leaves. Over this place a layer of stuffing. Continue this alternation, finishing with a layer of leaves. Sprinkle with the remaining chopped bacon. Cook 1½ hours in a 400° F. oven. Turn the contents out on a deep, heated serving dish. This may be served with brown sauce or tomato sauce.

Stuffed cabbage with chestnuts
Chou farci aux marrons

FOR FOUR PEOPLE

1 medium-sized cabbage
1 pound chestnuts
6 tablespoons butter
4 onions
1 cup finely ground cooked meat
6 tablespoons chopped pork fat or
   freshened salt pork
½ cup soft breadcrumbs

¼ cup milk
pork skin or bacon rind
2 cups bouillon
2 carrots
bouquet garni (thyme, parsley,
   bay leaf)
salt and pepper

Choose a good firm cabbage. Take off the outer curly leaves and wash the cabbage, leaving it whole. Cook 15 minutes in boiling salted water and drain well, pressing out all the water. Place on a board and spread open the leaves. Take out the core.

Make an X on the rounded side of each chestnut, piercing the shell with a a sharp-pointed knife. Boil in water for 10 minutes. Remove the chestnuts from the water and peel off the shell and skin. Put the chestnuts in a saucepan with very little water and cook covered until they crush easily with a fork. Take out 5 chestnuts and crush them. Set the others aside.

Heat the butter in a skillet. Add 2 onions that have been chopped and sauté them until they begin to brown lightly. Add the ground meat, the chopped pork fat, the crushed chestnuts, and the breadcrumbs, the last having been soaked in milk and squeezed dry. Mix very well and season with salt and pepper.

Put a little stuffing between each leaf and the rest in the center. Re-form the cabbage, tying it in place with kitchen string.

Melt a little butter in the bottom of a deep pan. Add a wide piece of pork skin or bacon rind that has been boiled 5 minutes. Place the cabbage on this and pour over the bouillon. Add the carrots, cut in thin rounds, and the remaining onions, peeled and quartered. Add the *bouquet garni,* salt, and pepper and simmer uncovered for 3 hours, basting the cabbage frequently with the bouillon.

15 minutes before the end of cooking the cabbage, add the rest of the chestnuts. Remove the *bouquet garni* and serve hot.

Cabbage stuffed with olives and rice
Chou farci aux olives et riz

FOR FOUR PEOPLE

1 medium-sized cabbage	2 small cans liver paste
¼ cup rice	½ teaspoon anise seeds
2 eggs	salt and pepper
2 tablespoons chopped black olives	

Parboil and prepare the cabbage for stuffing as above.

At the same time, boil the rice in salted water until just tender. Test it after 8 minutes. As soon as the rice is cooked, drain it and freshen with cold water. Drain thoroughly.

Hard-cook one of the eggs, shell it, and crush it with a fork.

Chop the olives very fine or force them through a food mill.

Mix the rice, olives, crushed egg, the liver paste, and the anise seeds very thoroughly. Taste for seasoning and bind with the raw egg.

Stuff and cook the cabbage as in the recipe for Stuffed Cabbage with Chestnuts.

Cabbage stuffed with ham * Chou farci au jambon

FOR FOUR PEOPLE

	1½ cups milk
1 medium-sized cabbage	1 shallot, chopped
8 slices white bread or	2 tablespoons *fines herbes,* chopped
½ loaf French bread	(parsley, chives, tarragon)

1 cup ground ham   3 egg yolks
1 cup finely diced bacon   salt and pepper

Parboil the cabbage and prepare it for stuffing as in the preceding recipe.

Put the milk in a bowl and break the bread into it. When it is soft, pour off the excess milk and squeeze out as much as possible from the bread. Mix the bread with the ground ham, diced bacon, shallot, and *fines herbes*. Season strongly with pepper but take care with the salt because of the ham and bacon. Mix thoroughly with a wooden spoon, adding the three egg yolks.

Stuff the cabbage and cook as above.

Cabbage stuffed with corn * Chou farci au maïs

FOR FOUR PEOPLE

1 medium-sized cabbage   1 egg
2 tablespoons butter   ¾ cup cooked corn kernels
1 cup ground uncooked meat   12 small onions
½ cup lightly seasoned sausage meat ¾ cup dry white wine
1 rusk   salt and pepper

Trim the hard exterior leaves from the cabbage and trim the stem. Boil in salted water for 15 minutes. Drain and spread open the leaves. Take out the hard core.

Heat half the butter in a skillet and sauté the meat and sausage meat until well browned.

Grate the rusk into the egg, slightly beaten. Add the meats and the corn. Mix well and season. Stuff the cabbage as in the recipe for Stuffed Cabbage with Chestnuts.

Melt the rest of the butter in a deep kettle. Add the onions and then the cabbage. Pour in the wine and cook covered for 2½ hours, basting frequently with the wine. Season with salt and pepper.

Individual stuffed cabbages * Choux individuels

FOR FOUR PEOPLE

1 cabbage   1 egg
1½ cups cooked ground meat   6 tablespoons butter
8 chestnuts   ¾ cup heavy cream
1 tablespoon chopped parsley   paprika
3 tablespoons soft breadcrumbs   salt
milk

Cut the cabbage in quarters and parboil in salted water for 10 minutes. Drain and separate the leaves, cutting out the thick ribs and the small center leaves.

Make a stuffing with the ground meat, the center cabbage leaves, the chestnuts (boiled 20 minutes, peeled, and chopped), the parsley, and the breadcrumbs, the last having been soaked in a little milk and squeezed dry. Bind it all with the raw egg and season with salt. Spread the leaves of the quarters with the mixture and tie them up to look like 4 small cabbages.

Heat the butter in a heavy pan. Put in the cabbages and sauté until golden. Add half the cream. Season with salt and simmer very gently for 1 hour.

Add the rest of the cream, sprinkle with paprika, and serve very hot with rice.

Cabbage purée * Purée de chou

FOR SIX PEOPLE

1 medium-sized cabbage	¾ cup milk, scalded
4 potatoes	salt and pepper
3 tablespoons butter	

Trim off the hard leaves of the cabbage, slice, and cook in salted water until tender. Drain and press out the water with your hands. Force through a food mill (or purée in a blender.—*Ed.*).

At the same time, peel the potatoes and boil them in salted water. Purée them also.

Combine the purées in a saucepan with the butter, adding enough milk to give the proper consistency. Season to taste.

This is delicious served with Burgundy beef.

Cardoons

Cardoons are a member of the thistle family and are closely related to the globe artichoke. They are grown for their stalks. (Although this vegetable is not widely marketed in the United States, it is grown in a large part of the country. White stalks of chard can be treated the same way.—*Ed.*)

Cardoons my way * Cardons à ma façon

FOR FOUR PEOPLE

2 pounds cardoons	10 tablespoons butter
8 anchovies	salt and pepper
¾ cup olive oil	

Wipe the stalks clean without washing them. Cut them lengthwise into little sticks. Place on a dish towel and set aside.

Put the anchovies and the oil in a large skillet and heat until the anchovies blend with the oil. Add the butter, cut in small pieces, and stir until the mixture is very hot. Add the little sticks and cook for 20 minutes without letting it burn, shaking the pan about every 3 minutes to turn the sticks. Taste for seasoning and serve very hot.

Cardoons with marrow I * Cardons à la moëlle I

1 large bunch cardoons	1 cup bouillon
4 teaspoons all-purpose flour	2-3 ounces beef marrow
12 tablespoons butter	salt and pepper
4 teaspoons pastry flour	

Remove the green leaves of the cardoons and cut the white stalks into 4-to-5-inch pieces and put them in a bowl of cold water.

Fill an enamel saucepan with water. Salt heavily and bring to a boil. Stir the all-purpose flour into a little cold water and add to the boiling water. Transfer the cardoons to the boiling water and cook until tender. Strain through an enameled collander, or lacking that, line a metal strainer with a towel. All these precautions are necessary because cardoons turn black if they touch or are associated with metal. Freshen them in cold water and remove the coarse exterior strings. Wipe the cardoons dry.

Sauté the cardoons in butter—again in an enamel pan—for 10 minutes. Sprinkle with fine flour and cook just until they are golden. Add the bouillon gradually, stirring with a wooden spoon. Continue to cook very slowly until the cardoons have absorbed most of the sauce. Transfer to a hot serving platter.

At the same time, melt the marrow in a double boiler. Pour this over the cooked cardoons and serve very hot.

Cardoons with marrow II * Cardons à la moëlle II

1 large bunch cardoons	marrow
3 tablespoons butter	8 toast rounds
juice of 1 lemon	salt and pepper

Prepare and boil the cardoons as in the previous recipe. After they have been freshened and trimmed, place them in a shallow, heatproof serving dish. Sprinkle with melted butter and lemon juice. Season with salt and pepper and brown in a hot oven.

Meanwhile, in simmering salted water, poach the marrow of a marrow bone, cut in eight slices. Toast 8 small rounds of bread. Surround the cardoons with toast topped with a piece of marrow.

New carrots à l'orientale
Carottes nouvelles à l'orientale

FOR FIVE PEOPLE

2 pounds new carrots
10 tablespoons butter
1 cup seedless raisins

3 teaspoons sugar
salt

Wash and peel the carrots and cut them into very thin rounds as you would for potato chips. Heat the butter in a heavy pan, and when it is hot, cover the dish tightly and cook over as low a heat as possible for 2 hours.

Meanwhile, soak the raisins in warm water for 1 hour. Drain them well and add them to the carrots 30 minutes before the end of cooking. Season with the sugar and salt.

New carrots with cream * Carottes à la crème

FOR FOUR PEOPLE

1 large bunch small new carrots
5 tablespoons butter
¾ cup heavy cream

juice of ½ lemon
salt and pepper

Scrape the carrots, if necessary, and boil them 30 to 45 minutes in salted water or until tender. Drain them well.

Heat the butter in a pan and sauté the carrots until golden brown. Add the cream just before serving. Heat but do not boil. Season with salt and pepper and serve very hot, sprinkled with the juice of half a lemon.

Fried carrots * Carottes frites

FOR AN INDEFINITE NUMBER OF PEOPLE

This is a recipe for carrots to accompany roasted and broiled meats. They are a pleasant change from potatoes.

carrots
oil

salt

Scrape the carrots and cut them in thin slices. Boil 10 minutes in salted water. Drain and dry.

Fry in deep fat (385° F.) for 3 minutes. Drain on paper toweling. Sprinkle with salt and serve very hot.

Carrots à la vichy * Carottes à la vichy

FOR FOUR PEOPLE

2 pounds carrots
4 tablespoons butter
2 tablespoons sugar

1 tablespoon chopped parsley
salt

Peel the carrots and cut in rounds as thin as possible. Put in a heavy saucepan with just enough water to cover. Add the butter, sugar, and salt. Simmer over very low heat until the water completely evaporates. There should be nothing but a little syrup in the pan, in which the carrots should be cooked until glazed. Shake the pan frequently so that the carrots will be evenly glazed and lightly browned in the syrup.

Season with chopped parsley.

Carrots à l'andalouse * Carottes andalouses

FOR FOUR PEOPLE

1 pound carrots
3 tablespoons butter
1 teaspoon flour
1 teaspoon cognac

nutmeg
1 egg white, beaten stiff
salt

Wash and peel the carrots and cook them whole in boiling salted water for 45 minutes. Drain and force through a food mill (or purée in a blender—*Ed.*). Add a tablespoon of butter, the flour, cognac, a small pinch of nutmeg (freshly grated, if possible), and salt.

Finally, fold in the beaten egg white. Heat the rest of the butter in a skillet and lightly brown the mixture.

Autumn carrots * Carottes d'automne

FOR FOUR PEOPLE

1½ pounds carrots
½ pound mushrooms

1 tablespoon chopped *fines herbes*
   (parsley, tarragon)

3 tablespoons butter   salt and pepper
1 teaspoon sugar

   Scrape the carrots and slice thin lengthwise. Cut each slice into thin strips. Boil 15 minutes in salted water. Drain well.
   Wash, wipe, and dice the mushrooms coarsely.
   Heat the butter in a skillet and sauté the mushrooms and the carrots. Season with salt, pepper, and sugar. When the vegetables are lightly browned, put them in a hot vegetable dish and sprinkle with the *fines herbes*.

Carrots à la catalane * Carottes catalanes

FOR FOUR PEOPLE

2 pounds carrots   2½ tablespoons concentrated bouillon
4 tablespoons olive oil   4 teaspoons Malaga or port
1 teaspoon sugar   salt and pepper

   Peel the carrots and cut into thin rounds. Put in a pan with the oil, sugar, salt, and pepper and cook over a high heat until the carrots are golden brown. Shake the pan frequently. Add the bouillon and the wine. Serve very hot.

Carrots and peas à la polonaise
Carottes à la polonaise

FOR FOUR PEOPLE

1 pound carrots   ½ cup extra heavy cream
5 tablespoons butter   paprika
2 pounds fresh peas, cooked, *or*   salt and pepper
1 small can peas

   Choose fresh tender carrots. Peel them and cut them into little match sticks. Place them in a heavy pan with the butter and ¾ cup of water. Season with salt, cover, and cook over a low heat for 45 minutes. Be sure that the water does not evaporate too quickly. If it seems to, lower the heat.
   Add the cooked or canned peas well drained. Continue cooking until the peas are hot. The vegetables should be almost dry. Add the cream and heat, stirring constantly. Do not boil. Season well with salt and pepper, and add a dash of paprika.

Cauliflower loaf * Pain de chou-fleur

FOR SIX PEOPLE

1 large cauliflower	2 pounds (6-8) tomatoes
1½ cups Béchamel Sauce (page 6)	2 tablespoons chopped parsley
3 eggs	paprika
2 tablespoons tomato paste	salt and pepper
3 tablespoons butter	

Wash and trim the cauliflower. Cook in boiling salted water for 25 minutes or until tender. Drain thoroughly and force through a strainer.

Meanwhile, make a thick béchamel sauce and mix it with the puréed cauliflower. Season highly with salt and pepper.

Beat 2 eggs and 1 egg yolk until well blended. Add the eggs and the tomato paste to the cauliflower. Mix well.

Beat the remaining egg white until stiff and fold it into the cauliflower.

Pour into a buttered charlotte mold or other straight-sided mold and place in a pan of hot water. Bake 45 minutes at 350° F.

At the same time, heat the butter in a shallow pan over moderate heat. Add the tomatoes, cut in pieces but not peeled or seeded. Season with salt, pepper, and chopped parsley. Cook uncovered for 45 minutes.

Unmold the cauliflower onto a heated platter. Strain the sauce over the loaf. Serve very hot.

Sprinkle with paprika.

Cauliflower in cream * Chou-fleur à la crème

FOR SIX PEOPLE

1 large cauliflower	¾ cup heavy cream
1½ cups Béchamel Sauce (page 6)	salt and pepper
1 cup grated Gruyère cheese	

Remove the green leaves from the cauliflower, wash, and cook whole in salted water for 20 minutes. Don't let the water boil too hard or the cauliflower will crumble.

Make the béchamel sauce and add the cheese. When the cheese has melted, add the cream, salt, and pepper.

Drain the cauliflower thoroughly and place in a hot serving dish. Cover with the sauce.

Cauliflower fritters * Fritots de chou-fleur

FOR FOUR PEOPLE

Frying Batter I (page 110)
1 cauliflower
6 tablespoons oil
juice of ½ lemon

Tomato Sauce (page 22)
several sprigs parsley
salt and pepper

Make the frying batter, which should be quite thin. Let stand for 2 hours.

Trim the cauliflower and divide the head into little bouquets. Boil them gently in salted water for about 15 minutes. Do not overcook, because they should remain firm though tender. Drain well and put them in a dish with the oil and lemon juice. Let them stand for 1 hour.

Meanwhile make the tomato sauce.

Dip each bouquet into the batter and fry in deep fat (385° F.) until golden brown. Fry the parsley.

Serve with the tomato sauce.

Cauliflower à la polonaise
Chou-fleur à la polonaise

FOR TWO PEOPLE

1 small cauliflower
2 hard-cooked eggs, finely chopped
2 teaspoons parsley, finely chopped

6 tablespoons butter
juice of 1 lemon
salt and pepper

Wash and trim the cauliflower and cook in boiling salted water just until tender. When you drain it, cover the strainer so that the cauliflower will not cool.

Put on a hot serving platter. Sprinkle with the chopped eggs and parsley, which can be ground through a *moulinette* or chopped fine.

Sprinkle with melted butter, heated until light brown, and season with the lemon juice, salt, and pepper.

Cauliflower à l'italienne * Chou-fleur à l'italienne

FOR FOUR PEOPLE

1 cauliflower
1 lemon
6 tablespoons butter

1 cup grated Gruyère cheese
pinch *orégano*
salt and pepper

Wash and trim the cauliflower and cook in a large amount of boiling salted water to which the lemon, cut in slices, has been added. This will keep the cauliflower white. After 20 minutes, test the cauliflower by pressing the stem gently with your finger. It should be pliable but not overcooked. Drain.

When cooled to lukewarm, divide the cauliflower into little bouquets. Place in a buttered baking dish, sprinkled with half the grated cheese. Sprinkle the rest of the cheese over the cauliflower, sprinkle with salt, pepper, and *orégano*. Dot with butter and brown the cauliflower for 10 minutes in a 400° F. oven. Heat the rest of the butter until light brown. Just before serving, pour the butter over the cauliflower.

Cauliflower with apples * Chou-fleur aux pommes

1 small cauliflower	lemon juice
1 pound (3-4) cooking apples	salt
6 tablespoons butter	

Wash and trim the cauliflower. Cook 20 minutes in boiling salted water or until tender but not soft. Drain well.

Peel and core the apples, cutting them in quarters. Cut into ¼-inch slices and cook them gently in 3 tablespoons of butter. Do not shake the skillet or the apples will be crushed.

Divide the cauliflower into little bouquets. Cook these in another skillet, using the rest of the butter, until golden.

Mix the apples and cauliflower just at the moment of serving. Season to taste and sprinkle with a little lemon juice. This is a delicious accompaniment to roast pork or veal.

Celeriac fritters I & II
Beignets de céleris raves I & II

Celeriac is a variety of celery having a large delicious root. Although not common in the United States, it is possible to find it. Here are two methods of serving celeriac like fritters.

I

Frying Batter I (page 110)	2 lemons
2 celeriac	

Prepare the batter. Let stand 2 hours.

Peel the celeriac and boil 20 minutes in salted water. Drain and cool. Cut them in sections like thin French fried potatoes.

Dip the sections into the batter and fry in deep fat (385° F.). Drain well and serve very hot with lemon wedges.

II

Frying Batter I (page 110)   parsley
1 celeriac   salt

Prepare the batter. Let stand 2 hours.

Peel the celeriac and cut into rounds ¼ inch thick, like potato chips. Boil 20 minutes in salted water. Drain and dry. Dip each piece in batter and fry until golden brown in deep fat (385° F.). Drain them and pile them in a pyramid on a hot platter. Sprinkle with salt and garnish with sprigs of fried parsley. Serve very hot.

Sautéed celeriac * Céleris raves sautés

FOR EIGHT PEOPLE

4 celeriac   juice of 1 lemon
3 tablespoons butter   4-5 tarragon leaves
3 tablespoons oil   salt and pepper

Peel the celeriac and cut into thin rounds. Boil 10 minutes in salted water. Drain.

Heat the butter and oil in a skillet and sauté the celeriac until golden. Season with salt and pepper.

Sprinkle with lemon juice and chopped tarragon leaves.

Celeriac à la grecque * Céleris raves à la grecque

FOR FOUR PEOPLE

This is a basic recipe that can be made with onions, leek, mushrooms, cauli-flower, and many other vegetables.

1 celeriac   2 small bay leaves
6 small onions   4 tablespoons oil
6 tablespoons dry white wine   paprika
¾ cup bouillon   salt
1 teaspoon peppercorns

Peel the celeriac and cut it in slices or in small sections like French fried po-tatoes. Boil in salted water for 15 minutes. Drain.

Combine the celeriac, onions, peeled but left whole, white wine, bouillon, peppercorns, bay leaves, oil, and some salt in a saucepan. Simmer over low heat for 45 minutes.

Cool and put in a serving dish. Sprinkle with paprika and serve very cold.

Celery aux fines herbes
Céleris en branches sauce fines herbes

FOR FIVE PEOPLE

2 bunches celery	¾ cup bouillon
2 teaspoons chopped tarragon	soft breadcrumbs
2 tablespoons chopped parsley	6 tablespoons butter
¾ cup dry white wine	salt and pepper

Wash, trim, and cut the celery stalks in 3-inch pieces. Boil in salted water for 20 minutes.

At the same time, simmer the herbs in white wine in an uncovered saucepan. Add salt and pepper and the bouillon.

Drain the celery and put in a buttered, shallow, ovenproof serving dish. Pour over the herb sauce, sprinkle with breadcrumbs, and dot with butter. Bake ½ hour at 350° F.

Chestnuts in bouillon * Marrons au bouillon

FOR FOUR PEOPLE

2 pounds large chestnuts	2 tablespoons butter
2 cups bouillon	salt
2 sugar lumps	

Peel off the outer skin of the chestnuts with a sharp knife. Put the chestnuts in a pan in a moderate oven for a few minutes. This will dry the inner skin, which will then come off quite easily.

Put the peeled chestnuts in a saucepan just large enough to hold them. Cover them with bouillon and add the sugar and a little salt. Bring to a boil and add the butter. Cover and reduce the heat. Simmer without stirring for 1 hour. The chestnuts will remain whole and will have absorbed all the liquid.

Chestnut purée * Purée de marrons

FOR EIGHT PEOPLE

4 pounds chestnuts	2 cups scalded milk
2 tablespoons sugar	6 tablespoons butter

1 stalk celery   salt and pepper

The hardest thing about making the purée is peeling the chestnuts. Slit the rounded side of the chestnut in several places, using a sharp pointed knife. Put them in a roasting pan with a little water and cook them in a 400° F. oven for 10 minutes. Take them out and peel off both skins while the chestnuts are warm.

Put them in a pan of cold water with the sugar and celery. Bring to a boil and cook until they are tender when you test them with a fork. Drain the chestnuts and force them through a food mill or, with a potato masher, through a strainer.

Put the purée in a saucepan and add milk gradually, beating constantly until you have a smooth though not too liquid purée. Add the butter, season with salt and pepper to taste, and serve hot.

Chicory loaf * Pain de chicorée

FOR FIVE PEOPLE

1 large head chicory (curly endive)   ½ cup grated Gruyère cheese or
4 cups Béchamel Sauce (page 6)   2 tablespoons tomato paste
5 eggs, beaten   salt and pepper
½ cup cream

Trim the root and hard leaves from the chicory. Wash it and boil in a large kettle of boiling salted water for 15 minutes. Drain and when cooled to luke-warm, press the water out of the chicory with the palms of your hands. Force it through a food mill (or purée it in a blender—*Ed.*).

Make a thick béchamel sauce and add half of it and the 5 beaten eggs to the chicory. Season well with salt and pepper. Pour into a well-buttered charlotte mold or other straight-sided baking dish. Place in a pan of hot water and bake 45 minutes at 350° F.

Thin the remaining béchamel sauce with cream and add the cheese or the tomato paste. Heat but do not boil.

Unmold the loaf on a hot serving platter and pour the sauce over it.

Corn soufflé * Soufflé de maïs

FOR FOUR PEOPLE

2 cups corn kernels   3 eggs
1½ cups milk   2 tablespoons heavy cream
2½ tablespoons sifted flour   salt and pepper
3 tablespoons butter

Scrape corn kernels off corn that has been boiled or steamed 20 minutes. Mix 3 tablespoons of cold milk with the flour and heat the rest of the milk to the boiling point. Pour the hot milk into the flour mixture and add the butter, the corn, and the egg yolks. Stir vigorously over moderate heat without letting the mixture boil. Season with salt and pepper. Remove from the heat.

Beat the egg whites stiff and fold them in along with the heavy cream.

Butter a soufflé dish and pour in the mixture. Bake at 400° F. for 25 minutes.

Corn fritters * Beignets de maïs

FOR SIX PEOPLE

2¼ cups all-purpose flour
2 egg yolks
1½ cups beer
1 teaspoon salt

6 ears fresh green corn
2 lemons
several sprigs parsley

Put the flour in a bowl and fashion a well in the center. In the well, place the two egg yolks, the beer, and the salt. Mix with a wooden spoon until you have a smooth thick batter. Let the batter rest at room temperature for an hour.

Husk the corn and boil 20 minutes in salted water. Cool and scrape off the kernels with a sharp knife.

Combine the batter and corn kernels. Drop this mixture by spoonfuls into hot deep fat (385° F.) and fry until golden brown. Serve very hot in a mound on a serving platter lined with a folded napkin. Accompany with lemon wedges and parsley fried in the deep fat.

Corn croquettes * Croquettes de maïs

FOR FOUR PEOPLE

2 cups corn kernels (boiled or
  steamed)
2 cups Béchamel Sauce (page 6)
3 egg yolks
2 whole eggs

flour
1 cup fine breadcrumbs
10 tablespoons butter
salt and pepper

Use corn kernels that have been boiled or steamed 20 minutes.

Combine the corn with a thick béchamel sauce, and when cooked and seasoned, beat in the egg yolks. Remove from the heat and pour it on a baking sheet. Let the mixture become cold before forming it into croquettes or ovals.

Beat the eggs until well blended.

Dip the croquettes first into beaten egg, then into flour, and finally into the breadcrumbs.

Heat the butter in a deep skillet and fry the croquettes until golden brown or deep fat fry them at 385° F.

Cucumbers with pepper cream
Concombres au poivre à la crème

FOR FOUR PEOPLE

3 pounds cucumbers.
1 cup Béchamel Sauce (page 6)
¾ cup heavy cream

1 sprig tarragon
freshly ground pepper
salt

Peel the cucumbers but leave them whole. Cut out small balls with a potato ball cutter. Cook the balls in salted water for 15 minutes. Drain thoroughly.

Make the béchamel sauce. Remove from the heat and stir in the cream. Season with salt and a generous amount of freshly ground black pepper. Pour this over the cucumber balls and sprinkle with chopped tarragon. This vegetable is good served hot, but it is especially delicious served cold with meats in aspic.

Fried cucumbers * Concombres frits

FOR FOUR PEOPLE

2 medium-sized cucumbers
Frying Batter I (page 110)

Tomato Sauce (page 22)
salt

Peel the cucumbers. Cut lengthwise in thin strips. Cover with salt and let stand for 2 hours.

Make the batter, which must also stand for 2 hours.

Make the tomato sauce.

Drain and pat dry the cucumber slices. Dip them in batter and fry in deep fat (385° F.) until golden brown. Drain and serve with the tomato sauce.

Cucumbers with mustard
Concombres à la moutarde

FOR FOUR PEOPLE

3 pounds (4-5) cucumbers
6 tablespoons oil
4 teaspoons spiced French mustard

juice of 1 lemon
fines herbes (tarragon, parsley)
salt and pepper

Peel the cucumbers and cut out small balls with a potato ball cutter. Do not include any of the seeds. Throw the balls into boiling salted water and cook 5 minutes. Rinse in cold water. Drain.

Put in a saucepan with the oil, mustard, lemon juice, salt, and pepper. Simmer very gently for 15 minutes. Put in a dish and cool. Serve very cold, sprinkled with chopped herbs.

Stuffed cucumber * Concombre farci

FOR SIX PEOPLE

1 large 4-pound cucumber
1 pound lightly seasoned sausage
  meat*
2 egg yolks
2 tablespoons chopped herbs
  (tarragon, parsley, chives)
2 tablespoons tomato paste

¼ cup fine breadcrumbs
8 tablespoons butter
¾ cup dry white wine
4 tomatoes
Tomato Sauce (page 22)
salt and pepper

Split the cucumber lengthwise. Remove all the seeds carefully and cook the cucumber in boiling salted water for 10 minutes. Drain thoroughly.

Mix the sausage meat with egg yolks, chopped herbs, and tomato paste. Season well with salt and pepper. Fill the cucumber with the mixture and sprinkle with breadcrumbs.

Melt the butter in an oven dish. Place the cucumbers in the dish and sprinkle with the wine. Bake in a 400° F. oven for 30 minutes, basting occasionally.

Cut the tomatoes into quarters and simmer them in 2 tablespoons of butter.

Transfer the cucumbers to a serving platter. Cut into serving pieces but re-form to make the cucumbers look uncut. Sprinkle with the juices in the cooking dish. Surround with the sautéed tomatoes and serve the previously prepared tomato sauce in a separate bowl.

Dandelion leaves in bacon * Pissenlits au lard

FOR FOUR PEOPLE

½ pound (2 quarts) dandelion leaves
½ pound (2-3) potatoes
1 tablespoon *fines herbes*
  (chives, parsley)

7 ounces (5-6 slices) bacon
2 tablespoons vinegar
pepper

Trim and carefully wash the dandelion leaves. Peel the potatoes and cut in thin slices. Chop the herbs quite fine.

Dice the bacon and sauté until slightly browned in a deep skillet.

Place the potatoes and the dandelion leaves in the skillet. Sprinkle with the chopped herbs, the vinegar, and the pepper. Cook over low heat until the potatoes are tender.

*You may substitute 1½ cups ground cooked meat mixed with ½ cup ground pork fat for the sausage meat.—*Ed.*

Eggplant with cream * Aubergines à la crème

FOR FOUR PEOPLE

4 small eggplants
flour
3 tablespoons oil
1½ cups Béchamel Sauce (page 6)
1 cup grated Gruyère cheese

2 teaspoons chopped parsley
soft breadcrumbs
½ cup heavy cream
juice of 1 lemon
salt and pepper

Cut the eggplants in two. Cut around the inside edge of the skin to loosen the flesh but do not pierce the skin. Sprinkle with salt and turn upside down on a plate for 1 hour to let the water drain out.

Sprinkle the eggplants with flour and sauté them in 2 tablespoons of very hot oil until they are cooked. Turn with a spatula so as not to break the skin. Drain and carefully remove the flesh.

Meanwhile, make the béchamel sauce.

Force the eggplant through a food mill (or purée it in a blender—*Ed.*). Mix with the sauce and add half the grated cheese. Season with pepper.

Put the skins in a shallow, heatproof serving dish. Fill with the mixture. Sprinkle with parsley, breadcrumbs, the rest of the cheese, and a little oil.

Brown the eggplants in a hot oven, and at the same time, heat the cream. Season with salt, pepper, and a little lemon juice and pour the mixture into the serving dish just before serving.

Stuffed eggplant saint sauveur
Aubergines farcies saint sauveur

FOR SIX PEOPLE

6 small eggplants
2 large, firm tomatoes
3 green peppers
1 large onion
1 clove garlic

1 cup olive oil
1½ cups boiled rice
½ cup grated Parmesan cheese
salt and pepper

Choose eggplants of equal size and shape, allowing 1 eggplant to a serving. Cut them in two. Cut the flesh a little without piercing the skin. Sprinkle with salt and turn upside down on a platter for 1 hour to drain.

Dip the tomatoes in boiling water for a few seconds and remove the skin. Cut them in half and press out the seeds. Dice the tomato flesh coarsely. Split and seed the peppers and slice them very thin. Chop the onion and crush the garlic.

Put ½ cup of oil in a skillet. Add the vegetables and cook gently for 30 minutes. Season with salt and pepper and add the boiled rice. Stir well.

Sprinkle the eggplants with a little oil and broil them slowly until tender. Carefully remove the flesh without cutting the skin. Chop the flesh and add to the mixture in the skillet. Stir in half the grated Parmesan cheese. Add pepper, if necessary. Place the eggplant shells in a shallow heatproof serving dish. Fill the shells with the mixture.

Sprinkle with more grated Parmesan and sprinkle with 5 or 6 teaspoons of olive oil. Brown in a hot oven (425° F.).

Stuffed eggplant toulonnaise
Aubergines farcies toulonnaises

FOR FOUR PEOPLE

4 medium-sized eggplants	1 tablespoon *fines herbes,* chopped
3 tablespoons oil	(parsley, tarragon)
6 ounces (¾ cup) sausage meat	1 raw egg
¼ pound mushrooms, chopped fine	¼ cup soft breadcrumbs
3 tablespoons butter	salt and pepper

Wash the eggplants and cut them in two lengthwise. Fry them in oil until they are soft, turning them with a spatula so as not to break the skins.

When the eggplants are soft, remove two thirds of the pulp from the center and mix it with sausage meat, raw chopped mushrooms, 1½ tablespoons of butter, and the chopped *fines herbes.* Bind with the raw egg. Season with salt and pepper.

Place the eggplant shells in a shallow heatproof serving dish. Fill with the mixture, sprinkle with breadcrumbs, dot with butter, and bake 45 minutes at 350° F.

Eggplant au gratin * Gratin d'aubergines

FOR FOUR PEOPLE

3 small eggplants	1 cup freshly grated Gruyère cheese
1 cup cottage cheese	salt and pepper
3 eggs	

Wash the eggplants and turn them on a spit or under a broiler until the skins turn black. Strip the skin from them and crush the pulp, mixing it with "white cheese." (This is like cottage cheese whipped smooth with a little skim milk, in a blender or with a wire whisk.—*Ed.*) Add the eggs, one by one, stirring constantly. Add the grated cheese, salt, and pepper. Put in a buttered shallow oven dish and bake 30 minutes at 400° F.

Eggplant with ham ∗ Aubergines au jambon

FOR FOUR PEOPLE

4 medium-sized eggplants	¾ cup milk
½ cup oil	½ lemon
3 tablespoons butter	dry breadcrumbs
6 ounces ham in ¼-inch slices, diced	salt and pepper
1 tablespoon flour	

Wipe the eggplants well. Cut in half lengthwise and dig out as much of the pulp as possible without breaking the skin. Dice the pulp.

Heat the oil moderately in a skillet and sauté the eggplant shells for 10 minutes, turning them with a spatula. Remove and drain.

In the same oil, sauté the diced eggplant.

In another skillet, heat 2 tablespoons of butter and sauté the diced ham until lightly browned. Add to the diced eggplant and sprinkle with the flour. Stir with a wooden spoon. Add the milk and the juice of the half lemon. Stir until the mixture starts to thicken. Season with salt and pepper.

Fill the eggplant shells with the mixture. Place them in a buttered baking dish. Sprinkle with breadcrumbs and dot with butter. Bake at 400° F. until browned.

Eggplant à la parmesane
Aubergines à la parmesane

FOR EIGHT PEOPLE

3 pounds (6-8) small eggplants	4 hard-cooked eggs, sliced
flour	5 ounces Gruyère cheese, sliced thin
oil	5 ounces grated Parmesan cheese
Tomato Sauce (page 22)	

Wash the small eggplants but do not peel them. Slice them thin lengthwise and place them on a shallow platter. Sprinkle with salt and put plates holding several heavy objects on the eggplant to weigh them. This will force out the water and, with that, the bitter flavor. Let them stand 45 minutes. Finish by pressing each slice beween the palms of your hands.

During this time, prepare a tomato sauce.

Dip each slice of eggplant in flour and fry in oil until browned on both sides. Drain on toweling.

Put a little tomato sauce in the bottom of a shallow baking dish. Cover with a layer of eggplant slices, then with hard-cooked egg slices, then with cheese slices, and finally with a sprinkling of grated Parmesan cheese. Continue this alternation, finishing with a layer of sauce and grated Parmesan. Bake 15 minutes at 375° F. Serve hot.

*Eggplant caponata (cold) * Caponata*

FOR SIX PEOPLE

1 pound small eggplants
olive oil
1 pound green peppers
1 onion
3 tomatoes
12 small pitted olives

1 tablespoon capers
1 celery heart
6 tablespoons wine vinegar
1 tablespoon sugar
salt and pepper

Wash the eggplants but do not peel them. Cut them in small dice and sauté them 15 minutes in 3 tablespoons of olive oil. Salt them and remove with a slotted spoon to a dish.

Wash the peppers. Split them, remove the seeds, and cut them in little pieces. Sauté them in the same skillet for 15 minutes, adding more oil, if necessary. Remove them to a dish.

Peel and slice the onion very thin and sauté the slices in oil, and when pale yellow, add the tomatoes, peeled and cut in pieces. Cook until the tomatoes are soft, and then add the olives, the capers, the celery heart cut in small dice. Cook it all together for several minutes. Add the eggplant and pepper and cook 1 minute longer.

Combine the vinegar with an equal amount of water and the sugar. Mix this well into the eggplant mixture and pour everything into a non-metal serving dish. Cool and place in the refrigerator. This dish is much tastier if it is prepared a day in advance.

*Fried eggplant * Aubergines frites*

FOR FOUR PEOPLE

4 thin eggplants   salt

Wipe the eggplant but do not peel them. Cut off the ends and slice in as thin rounds as possible.

Fry in deep oil at 385° F. for 2 minutes. Drain on paper toweling and sprinkle with salt. Eggplant cooked this way makes an excellent accompaniment to roasts.

Belgian endives

1 Never soak endives in water after washing them.
2 Always put a few slices of lemon and a crust of bread in the cooking water to keep the endives white.

3 Endives always absorb a lot of water in cooking. Take care to press out all the water before the final preparation.

4 Endives braised in butter in a covered dish are much better if they are not previously boiled, as is so often the custom.

Braised belgian endives * Endives braisées

FOR FOUR PEOPLE

3 pounds endives
6 tablespoons butter

salt and pepper

Wash and wipe the endives dry. Put them in a covered heavy saucepan with the butter. Season with salt and pepper and simmer very gently for 3 hours. Watch to see that they are evenly browned.

Belgian endives with mushrooms
Endives aux champignons

FOR FOUR PEOPLE

2 pounds endives
¼ pound mushrooms
3 tablespoons butter

1½ cups Béchamel Sauce (page 6)
1 cup grated Gruyère cheese
salt and pepper

Trim the endives, wash them, and cook 30 minutes in boiling salted water, according to directions on page 515.

Trim and wash the mushrooms; cut them in thin slices. Sauté 2 minutes in 2 tablespoons of the butter.

Make the béchamel sauce and add the mushrooms to the sauce. Season with salt and pepper.

Put the endives in an oven serving dish. Cover with the sauce and sprinkle with the grated cheese. Dot with little pieces of butter and brown 10 to 20 minutes in a hot (400°) oven.

Deep-fried belgian endives * Fritots d'endives

FOR FOUR PEOPLE

Frying Batter:
1 cup all-purpose flour
4 teaspoons oil

Endives:
1 pound endives
2½ tablespoons oil

1 teaspoon (scant) baking powder	juice of 1 lemon
2 eggs	parsley sprigs (optional)
1 teaspoon salt	salt and pepper

Frying Batter: Make the frying batter first, because it should rest at least 2 hours before being used. Sift the flour into a bowl and make a hole in the center. Pour in the oil, the baking powder dissolved in a little lukewarm water, the egg yolks, and the salt. Stir just until smooth. Cover and let stand in a warm place for 2 hours. Just before using, fold in 2 stiffly beaten egg whites.

Endives: Trim the endives and cook 30 minutes in salted boiling water, according to directions on page 515. Drain thoroughly and cool. When cold, press out all the water from the endives between the palms of your hands. Divide each endive in quarters lengthwise and marinate them in a shallow dish with the oil, lemon juice, salt, and pepper for 30 minutes.

Dip each piece in the frying batter and deep fry at 385° F. until golden brown. Drain them and pile them in a pyramid on a platter lined with a folded napkin. Serve with lemon wedges and fried parsley, if desired.

Belgian endives au gratin ✳ *Endives au gratin*

FOR FOUR PEOPLE

3 pounds endives	1 small can tomato purée
2 cups Béchamel Sauce (page 6)	½ cup heavy cream
1¾ cups grated Gruyère cheese	salt and pepper

Trim the endives and wash them well. Boil 45 minutes in salted water, according to directions on page 515. Drain and dry in a towel.

Make the béchamel sauce and stir in 1½ cups of grated cheese.

Arrange the endives in a large shallow baking dish. Cover with the sauce. Sprinkle with the rest of the cheese.

Mix the tomato purée with the cream. Spread it over the top. Sprinkle with salt and pepper and brown in a hot oven. Serve very hot.

Belgian endives in ham ✳ *Endives au jambon*

FOR FOUR PEOPLE

8 endives	¾ cup grated Gruyère cheese
4 large slices cooked ham, cut very thin	3 tablespoons butter
	pepper

Trim and wash the endives. Boil 30 minutes, according to directions on page 515. Remove from the water and drain thoroughly. Press out water between the palms of your hands.

Divide the ham slices in two and roll each endive in a piece of ham. Place the rolls seam side down in a buttered shallow baking dish. Sprinkle with pepper and, very generously, with grated Gruyère cheese. Put a large piece of butter on each roll and brown 12 minutes in a hot (400° F.) oven.

Fennel à la niçoise * Fenouil à la niçoise

FOR FOUR PEOPLE

3 bunches fennel	1 pound (3-4) ripe tomatoes
2 medium-sized onions	½ cup white Bordeaux wine, heated
2 cloves garlic	pinch powdered thyme
4 tablespoons oil	salt and pepper

Wash the fennel and trim off the leafy tops. Cut them in quarters and wash again. Boil in salted water for 10 minutes. Drain well.

Peel and chop the onions and garlic rather coarsely. Heat the oil in a heavy pan and sauté them gently until soft. Add the fennel. Dip the tomatoes in boiling water. Peel off the skin and cut the tomatoes in large pieces. Then add the white wine and sprinkle with thyme, salt, and pepper. Cover and cook slowly for 1 hour.

Stuffed grape leaves * Feuilles de vigne farcies

FOR FOUR PEOPLE

12 large grape leaves*	1 egg, slightly beaten
juice of 1 lemon	4 tablespoons oil
1¼ cups ground lean lamb	1 sugar lump
¾ cup cooked rice	bouillon
1 tablespoon chopped parsley	salt and pepper
1 onion, chopped fine	

Boil the grape leaves in water to which the juice of ½ lemon has been added. In a few moments, they will be tender. Spread the leaves out on a working surface and fill with the following stuffing:

Combine the ground meat with the rice, parsley, chopped onion, and beaten egg. Mix thoroughly and season with salt and pepper.

Put a good tablespoon of the stuffing on each leaf and fold over the sides and

*If grape leaves are not available, look in Greek food shops or food specialty stores for the canned variety.—*Ed.*

ends to make little packages. Place the stuffed grape leaves in a heavy saucepan or dish. Add the oil, the juice of ½ lemon, the sugar lump, and just enough hot liquid—half bouillon, half water—to barely cover the leaves. Sprinkle with salt and pepper and simmer uncovered for 2 hours. Watch to see that the liquid does not entirely boil away, adding more if necessary.

Stuffed kohlrabi * Choux-raves farcis

FOR FOUR PEOPLE

4 medium-sized kohlrabi	½ cup soft breadcrumbs
5 tablespoons oil	¼ cup milk
2½ ounces (3-4 slices) bacon, diced	1 hard-cooked egg, chopped
1 large onion	4 tablespoons fine breadcrumbs
2 tablespoons chopped parsley	salt and pepper

Peel the kohlrabi, cut each one in two, and cook in boiling salted water until tender. Drain and scoop out a little of the center of each half.

Heat 2½ tablespoons of the oil and sauté the diced bacon and the onion, peeled and chopped, until golden. Add the chopped parsley, the breadcrumbs soaked in the milk and squeezed dry, the chopped egg, salt, and pepper. Mix well.

Stuff the kohlrabi with the mixture. Sprinkle with fine breadcrumbs and with the remaining oil. Brown in a hot oven.

Braised leeks * Poireaux braisés

FOR FOUR PEOPLE

2 pounds leeks	¾ cup bouillon
5 tablespoons butter	salt and pepper

Buy leeks of the same average size so that the cooking will be even.

Remove the green tops and wash the white part of the leeks very carefully. Cut them in ¾-inch pieces.

Heat 4 tablespoons of butter in a heavy frying pan without letting it brown. Put in the leeks. Season with salt and pepper and add the bouillon. Cover and simmer gently for 45 minutes. Test to see if the leeks are tender.

Transfer the leeks to a heated serving dish. Add the remaining butter to the cooking broth. Taste for seasoning and pour over the leeks.

Leeks à la grecque * Poireaux à la grecque

FOR FOUR PEOPLE

2 pounds thin young leeks
¾ cup bouillon
6 tablespoons dry white wine
3 tablespoons oil
1 tablespoon tomato paste

8 tiny onions
4 bay leaves
1 teaspoon peppercorns
pinch paprika

Remove all the green from the leeks, trimming them to 4-inch pieces. Wash the white parts very carefully. Boil in salted water for 5 minutes. Drain.

Put the leeks in a pan with the remaining ingredients, except for paprika. Simmer uncovered 45 minutes. The liquid must be very concentrated at the end of the cooking time. Chill and serve as an hors d'oeuvre. Sprinkle with paprika.

Leeks à l'indienne * Poireaux à l'indienne

FOR FOUR PEOPLE

1½ pounds fresh young leeks
1 large onion, finely chopped
2½ tablespoons oil
bouquet garni (celery leaves, thyme,
    bay leaf, parsley)

3 teaspoons curry powder
¾ cup dry white wine
juice of ½ lemon
cayenne
salt and pepper

Remove the green from the leeks. (The green part of leeks can be used in soups.) Wash the whites carefully and cut them in 2-inch pieces. If only large leeks are available, cut them lengthwise also.

Put all the other ingredients in a pan and simmer 5 minutes. Add the leeks and cook, uncovered, until tender. This vegetable can be eaten hot or cold.

Leeks and potatoes * Poireaux aux pommes

FOR FOUR PEOPLE

3-4 leeks
1 onion
2 pounds (5-6) potatoes
4 tablespoons oil

5 teaspoons flour
1 cup scalded milk
2 teaspoons chopped parsley
salt and pepper

Trim off all the green parts of the leeks and wash the white parts carefully. Chop them and the onion quite fine.

Peel the potatoes and slice them thin.

Heat the oil in a heavy pan and sauté the onion and leeks just until transparent.

Sprinkle with flour and stir until the flour disappears. Add the hot milk gradually, stirring constantly. Season to taste.

Add the potatoes to the leeks. Bring to a boil. Reduce the heat and simmer until the potatoes are tender. Season and sprinkle with the chopped parsley.

Leeks balls * Boulettes de poireaux

FOR SIX PEOPLE

2 pounds leeks	½ cup fine breadcrumbs
1¼ cups raw or cooked meat	½ cup oil
2 eggs	salt and pepper

Remove most of the green ends from the leeks and wash the white parts carefully. Boil in salted water until tender. Force them through a food mill or chop very fine.

Combine the leeks with the meat. Bind with the raw eggs and season well with salt and pepper. Make little balls of the mixture. Roll them in breadcrumbs.

Heat the oil in a skillet, and when very hot, sauté the breaded leek balls until browned on all sides. Serve very hot.

Braised lettuce * Laitues braisées

FOR FOUR PEOPLE

8 small heads leafy lettuce*	½ pound butter
(Boston, Romaine, Escarole,	8 slices white bread
Oak Leaf)	salt and pepper

Remove any hard or wilted outer leaves. Wash the lettuce in several waters to remove the sand. Boil in salted water for 10 minutes. Remove carefully from the water, and when cool enough to handle, press out all the water between the palms of your hands.

Melt 6 tablespoons of butter in a shallow heatproof dish. Place the lettuce side by side in the dish or, if more convenient, fold them in two, end to end. Season with salt and pepper. Cover and simmer 40 minutes, turning the lettuce so that they will be well buttered on both sides.

Trim the crusts from the bread and fry the bread slices in butter.

Serve the lettuce on the croutons.

*Small heads of lettuce, picked fresh from the garden, are perfect. The larger heads of lettuce obtainable in the market can be quartered, using a portion of the root stem to hold them together, and prepared in the same way. Do not use iceberg lettuce.—*Ed*.

Stuffed lettuce * Laitues farcies

FOR FOUR PEOPLE

8 small heads of lettuce (see recipe for Braised Lettuce)
¾ cup Béchamel Sauce (page 6)
1½ cups leftover meat, ground fine

6 ounces lean pork belly*
¾ cup bouillon
salt and pepper

Trim, prepare, and drain the lettuce as in the preceding recipe.

Make a stuffing with the béchamel sauce, the ground meat, salt, and pepper. The stuffing should be rather firm.

Once the water is pressed from the lettuce, lay them out on a working surface and spread with the stuffing. Roll them up and tie with kitchen twine.

In a deep pan or heavy casserole, heat thin larding strips of pork belly. When some of the fat has been drawn out, place the lettuce rolls on the strips. Brown the lettuce rolls lightly, salting if necessary. Add the bouillon and simmer 30 minutes.

Lettuce with roquefort * Laitues au roquefort

FOR FOUR PEOPLE

8 small lettuce heads
6 tablespoons butter

1½ tablespoons Roquefort cheese
salt and pepper

Prepare and cook the lettuce as in the two preceding recipes. Drain them, covering the strainer so as not to let the lettuce get cold. Remove from the water carefully. Press each lettuce head between the palms of your hands to extract the water. Fold over, end to end, and place in a shallow serving dish. Keep warm.

Heat the butter and pour it slowly into another pan, leaving the white deposit in the first pan (this is called clarification). Crumble the Roquefort cheese into the butter. Season with salt and pepper and pour it over the lettuce. (Imported Roquefort is heavily salted; do not oversalt.—Ed.)

Lettuce with vermicelli (cold)
Laitues au vermicelle

FOR FOUR PEOPLE

8 small heads of lettuce
¾ cup dry white wine

¼ pound vermicelli
Vinaigrette Sauce (page 29)

*If pork belly is not available, parboil a piece of bacon or salt pork for 5 minutes and use in the same way.—Ed.

juice of 1 lemon
3 tablespoons oil

salt and pepper

Choose and prepare the lettuce as you would for braised lettuce. Boil the lettuce 5 minutes in salted water. Drain well and cook in a non-metal pan over low heat with the wine, the juice of ½ lemon, salt, and pepper for 20 minutes.

Combine the oil and vermicelli in a saucepan and stir it over moderate heat until the vermicelli become light brown. Add enough boiling water to fill to 1½ inches above the vermicelli. Season with salt and pepper.

Cook covered until water has been absorbed. They will be cooked. Cool and season with a vinaigrette sauce made with lemon juice.

Put the seasoned vermicelli in a dish and surround with the lettuce.

Okra à l'indienne * Gombos à l'indienne

FOR FOUR PEOPLE

1½ pounds okra
3 tablespoons butter
2 red peppers (fresh or canned)

1 tablespoon curry powder
¼ cup heavy cream
salt

Stem the okra and cook them 25 minutes in boiling salted water. Drain well.

Heat the butter in a skillet and sauté the okra and the red peppers cut in slices. Sprinkle with salt and curry powder. Add the cream and heat (not boil) 5 minutes. Serve.

Okra fritters * Beignets de gombos

FOR FOUR PEOPLE

Frying Batter IV (page 111)
1 pound okra
juice of 2 lemons
½ cup oil

1 tablespoon chopped parsley
several sprigs parsley
1 lemon
salt and pepper

Make the batter in advance so that it can stand for 2 hours.

Stem the okra and boil in salted water for 5 minutes. Drain and put them in a dish with the lemon juice, oil, chopped parsley, salt, and pepper. Let stand for an hour or so.

Dip the okra in the batter and fry in deep fat (385° F.). At the same time, fry the parsley sprigs.

Serve the okra on preheated individual plates garnished with parsley and lemon quarters.

Glazed onions * Oignons glacés

FOR FOUR PEOPLE

2 pounds small onions   3 teaspoons sugar
6 tablespoons butter   salt and pepper

Peel the onions carefully so that they will be round and smooth. Boil 10 minutes in salted water. Drain well.

Heat the butter in a heavy frying pan. Sprinkle with sugar and add the onions. Simmer very gently, stirring so that the onions will be glazed on all sides. Season at the end of cooking.

Fried onions * Oignons frits

FOR FOUR PEOPLE

8 Bermuda onions   salt and pepper
flour

Peel the onions very carefully and cut them in thick slices. Separate the onions into rings, breaking them as little as possible. Season with salt and pepper and dip them in flour.

Plunge the onions immediately in deep fat (385° F.). Fry until golden brown and drain. Do not fry too many at a time or the temperature of the fat will be reduced. Serve with roasts of all sorts or with broiled fish.

Onion purée * Purée d'oignons soubise

FOR FOUR PEOPLE

2 pounds onions   paprika, nutmeg
2 cups Béchamel Sauce (page 6)   heavy cream (optional)
6 tablespoons butter   salt and pepper

Peel and slice the onions very thin. Boil in salted water for 15 minutes.

Make the béchamel sauce. It should be fairly thick.

Drain the onions and put in a pan with half the butter. Cover and simmer until they are tender. Do not let them brown.

When they are cooked, add the sauce. Season with salt and pepper, a dash of paprika, and a dash of nutmeg. Cook over moderate heat for 10 minutes, stirring frequently.

Force the mixture through a strainer or food mill. Reheat with the rest of the butter, adding 4 or 5 tablespoons of heavy cream, if desired.

Stuffed onions * Oignons farcis

FOR FOUR PEOPLE

8 large onions
½ pound mushrooms
3 tablespoons butter

2 tablespoons chopped chervil or parsley
¾ cup bouillon
salt and pepper

Peel rather large and uniform-sized onions and cut off the top quarter of each one. Boil the onions (without the top quarters) in salted water for 7 minutes. Drain well.

Chop the raw onion "caps."

Trim and wash the mushrooms and chop them coarsely.

Heat the butter in a skillet and sauté the chopped onions and mushrooms together, just until the onions are tender. Season with salt, pepper, and the chervil.

Hollow out the parboiled onions, leaving a ½ inch shell. Fill with the stuffing and put in a buttered baking dish. Sprinkle with the bouillon and bake 25 minutes at 425° F.

Oyster plant in mayonnaise
Salsifis à la mayonnaise

FOR FOUR PEOPLE

2 pounds oyster plant
Mayonnaise (page 14)
juice of 1 lemon

1 can anchovy fillets
pitted black olives

Scrape the oyster plant carefully and wash well. Boil 20 minutes in salted water. Drain and chill.

Mix with mayonnaise, flavored with lemon juice. Put on a serving dish and decorate with anchovy fillets and black olives.

Oyster plant in cream * Salsifis à la crème

FOR FOUR PEOPLE

2 pounds oyster plant
5 tablespoons butter
1 teaspoon flour

¾ cup heavy cream
nutmeg
salt and pepper

Scrape the skin from the oyster plant and wash well. Boil in salted water for 20 minutes. Drain.

Heat the butter in a skillet. Sauté the oyster plant, turning so that the butter will color lightly all sides. Sprinkle with flour and add the cream. Add a dash of nutmeg and season highly with salt and pepper. Simmer 5 minutes.

Oyster plant fritters * Beignets de salsifis

FOR FIVE PEOPLE

Frying Batter IV (page 111)
1 bunch (6-7 roots) oyster plant
juice of 1 lemon *or*

2 tablespoons vinegar
2½ tablespoons flour
salt

Prepare the frying batter and let it stand at least 2 hours.

Peel the oyster plant and cut into long thin pieces of equal thickness. To a kettle of boiling salted water add the vinegar or lemon juice and the flour. Boil the oyster plant for 30 minutes. Drain and pat dry with toweling.

Dip the pieces in frying batter and fry in deep fat (385° F.) until golden brown. Drain and pile on a serving platter lined with a folded napkin.

Chinese artichokes are prepared in the same way.

Fresh peas à la française
Petits pois à la française

FOR FOUR PEOPLE

This recipe should be reserved for the sweetest, tenderest peas.

5 cups sweet small fresh peas
12 tablespoons butter
1 onion
1 lettuce heart

1 sprig parsley
6 tablespoons water
2 egg yolks
pinch of salt

Allow 1 pound of peas for 1 cup of shelled peas.

Put the peas in a saucepan (made of neither iron nor tin) with the butter, a whole onion, the lettuce heart tied with kitchen string, the parsley, and the water. Salt very lightly and bring to a boil over a high heat. Then, after a few minutes, reduce the heat, cover with a soup plate into which you pour a little water. This will keep the steam in the saucepan. Simmer 25 minutes.

Just before the peas have finished cooking, beat the egg yolks slightly.

Take out the lettuce and the parsley and remove the peas from the heat. Pour in the egg yolks, stirring constantly with a fork. This is called binding. Pour the peas immediately into a heated vegetable dish and serve.

Peas à l'alsacienne * Petits pois à l'alsacienne

FOR FOUR PEOPLE

5 cups small fresh green peas
6 tablespoons butter
several sprigs parsley
5 new onions
1 head lettuce

2 tablespoons sugar
1 cup very heavy cream
2 egg yolks
salt and pepper

Allow 1 pound of fresh peas for each cup of shelled peas. Heat the butter in an enamel-lined or stainless steel pan. As soon as it melts, pour in the peas gently. Sprinkle with salt and cover. Simmer for 15 minutes.

Add a ladle of boiling water, the parsley, tied in a bouquet, the onions, and the head of lettuce. Cover and continue cooking for 45 minutes. Season to taste with salt and pepper and add the sugar. Stir until well mixed.

Meanwhile, combine the cream and egg yolks in a small saucepan. Season with salt and pepper. Mix well with a whisk and heat but do not let the mixture boil. Pour the mixture over the peas just before serving.

Fresh peas with lettuce * Petits pois aux laitues

FOR FOUR PEOPLE

4 pounds of fresh peas
2 lettuce hearts
3 rather small onions
4 tablespoons butter

3 teaspoons sugar
1 sprig savory
2 teaspoons flour (optional)
salt and pepper

Shell the peas. Wash the lettuce hearts and peel the onions.

Heat 3 tablespoons of butter in an enamel or stainless steel saucepan. Add the vegetables, the sugar, savory, and a little salt. Cover with a soup plate that has a little water in it. Simmer for about 1 hour, stirring occasionally. Add a very little water from time to time as necessary. The peas must not be allowed to dry out but may not be too liquid.

Just before serving, add a little fresh butter, which may—if you like a thicker consistency—be mixed with 2 teaspoons of flour. Season to taste.

Fresh peas with pork fat * Petits pois au lard

FOR FOUR PEOPLE

3 pounds fresh peas
5 ounces pork belly*
3 tablespoons butter

10 tiny onions
3 teaspoons sugar
salt and pepper

* If pork belly is not available, parboil salt pork or pork jowl for 5 minutes in boiling water. Rinse and use.—Ed.

Shell the peas. Dice the pork fat rather coarsely.

Heat the butter in a saucepan and sauté the pork fat until golden, stirring occasionally to color the fat on all sides. Meanwhile, peel the onions.

Add the peas, onions, salt, and pepper. Cover and simmer 45 minutes. Halfway through cooking, add the sugar. Serve very hot.

Fresh pea purée * Purée de petits pois frais

FOR FOUR PEOPLE

2 quarts shelled fresh peas	10 tablespoons butter
1 lettuce heart	¼ cup heavy cream
½ teaspoon sugar	salt and pepper

Allow 8 pounds of peas for the 2 quarts of shelled peas.

Cover the peas with cold water. Add the lettuce heart, the sugar, and a little salt. Boil uncovered for 30 minutes or until very tender. Strain, retaining the water. Force the peas and lettuce through a food mill (or purée in a blender— *Ed.*). Meanwhile, boil down the liquid until it measures approximately ¾ cup.

Put the purée into a saucepan with the butter and stir hard over moderate heat until the butter melts. Add the cream and the concentrated pea broth. Season with salt and pepper and serve very hot.

Fresh peas printaniers * Petits pois printaniers

FOR FOUR PEOPLE

10 tablespoons butter	1 teaspoon baking soda
10 fresh mint leaves	salt
4 pounds fresh peas	

Cream the butter with a small spatula. Chop 2 mint leaves very fine or grind them through a *moulinette.* Work the mint leaves into the butter and let the mixture harden in the refrigerator. Make little balls or shells of this mixture and serve on a little plate when you serve the peas.

Shell the peas and cook them in a large pan of boiling salted water. Add the baking soda and 8 fresh mint leaves. Boil until tender. Drain and serve in a heated vegetable dish.

Stuffed peppers * Poivrons farcis

FOR FOUR PEOPLE

4 large green peppers	1 egg
1½ cups ground cooked meat	1 teaspoon chopped tarragon

2 onions, finely chopped
4 tablespoons boiled rice

4 tablespoons oil
salt and pepper

Parboil the green peppers in salted water for 2 minutes. Drain them. Remove the stems, and through the hole made by the stem removal, take out all the seeds.

Make a stuffing by combining the meat, chopped onions, and rice with the raw egg. Mix well, adding the tarragon, salt, and pepper.

Stuff the peppers with the mixture. Place in a baking dish with the oil. Bake 15 minutes at 400° F.

Peppers stuffed with tuna and rice
Poivrons farcis au riz

FOR FOUR PEOPLE

5 tablespoons butter
2½ tablespoons oil
1 cup rice
1 onion, finely chopped

4 green peppers
1 can flaked tuna
salt and pepper

Heat 2 tablespoons of butter and the oil in a heavy saucepan.

Add the rice and the onion and cook just until transparent, stirring constantly. Add 1½ cups boiling water and a little salt. Reduce the heat, cover, and cook very slowly without stirring until all the water has been absorbed. It will take 15 to 20 minutes.

Meanwhile, broil the green peppers, turning them so that the skin will be loosened on all sides. Peel the peppers, split them and remove the seeds.

Mix the rice with the flaked tuna. Season to taste with salt and pepper. Fill the pepper halves.

Heat the rest of the butter in a heavy frying pan. Place the peppers in the pan. Cover and simmer 30 minutes.

Ratatouille * Ratatouille

FOR EIGHT PEOPLE

2 pounds small eggplant
4 pounds tomatoes
2 pounds zucchini
1 pound green peppers

1 or 2 cloves garlic
1½ cups olive oil
salt and pepper

Wash all the vegetables but do not peel them. Slice them all quite fine. Peel the garlic and crush slightly. Heat the oil in a deep heavy pan. Add all the vegetables and cook over a high flame for about 20 minutes. Reduce the heat and continue cooking until it all looks like a thick brown marmalade. Season halfway through the cooking.

Ratatouille can be eaten hot or cold.

Sorrel with poached eggs * Oseille aux oeufs pochés

FOR FOUR PEOPLE

3 pounds sorrel	4 tablespoons heavy cream
¾ cup bouillon	3 egg yolks, slightly beaten
1 teaspoon sugar	4 poached eggs
5 tablespoons butter	salt and pepper

Trim and wash the sorrel very carefully. Put it in a heavy saucepan with 4 tablespoons of water and wilt it over a low fire. When it is soft, drain it thoroughly. Put it back into the pan with the bouillon, sugar, salt, and pepper. Simmer very gently for 2 hours.

Force through a food mill or strainer (or purée in a blender—*Ed.*). Add the butter and cream and stir over moderate heat. Remove from the heat and stir in the beaten egg yolks. Spread in a warm serving dish.

Serve with poached eggs or, if you prefer, put soft-cooked eggs, peeled but not broken, on the bed of sorrel.

Buttered spinach * Epinards au beurre

FOR FOUR PEOPLE

3 pounds spinach	salt and pepper
6 tablespoons butter	

Wash the spinach thoroughly, using only the leaves and smaller stems. Boil 15 minutes in a large kettle of boiling salted water. Remove from the water with long forks or spoons and drain immediately in a collander. Spinach that stays in hot water once it is cooked becomes brown and ugly.

Drain well and chop finely. Reheat in a saucepan with butter, salt, and pepper. (Add heavy cream, if you wish. Do not let the cream boil.)

Spinach in cream * Epinards à la crème

FOR FIVE PEOPLE

5 pounds fresh spinach	¾ cup heavy cream
1 cup bread squares	salt and pepper
8 tablespoons butter	

Trim the large stems from the spinach and wash carefully. Cook uncovered in boiling water for 10 minutes. Lift the spinach from the water and place in a collander. Run cold water through the spinach. Drain, press out the water between the palms of your hands, and force through a food mill (or purée in a blender—*Ed.*).

Meanwhile, cut thick slices of firm white crustless bread into croutons. Fry in 2 tablespoons of butter, shaking the pan frequently so that the cubes will brown on all sides.

Reheat the spinach in 6 tablespoons of butter in a saucepan. Season with salt and pepper. Just before serving, add the cream. Heat but do not let the mixture boil.

Serve in a preheated vegetable dish. Garnish with the croutons.

Spinach with mushrooms
Epinards aux champignons

FOR FOUR PEOPLE

3 pounds spinach
½ pound mushrooms
6 tablespoons butter

½ cup grated Parmesan cheese
salt and pepper

Wash the spinach, removing the large stems. Boil 10 minutes in salted water. Remove from the kettle and place in a collander. Run cold water through the spinach and press out the water between the palms of your hands. Force through a food mill (or purée in a blender—*Ed.*).

Trim and wash the mushrooms; wipe them well. Take off a few mushroom caps to be used for decoration. Chop the stems and remaining caps rather coarsely. Heat half the butter in a skillet and sauté the mushroom pieces over high heat for 2 to 3 minutes. Season with salt.

Put the spinach in a saucepan with the rest of the butter and season with pepper. Mix well. Transfer the mushroom pieces with a slotted spoon to the spinach and sauté the mushroom caps in the remaining butter. Stir the mushroom-spinach mixture, adding the Parmesan cheese. Continue stirring until the cheese is melted.

Put the spinach in a heated serving dish and decorate with the mushroom caps, which have been lightly salted.

Leaf spinach * *Epinards en branches*

FOR FOUR PEOPLE

4 pounds spinach
3 tablespoons butter

¼ cup heavy cream
salt and pepper

Trim the spinach of all thick stems and withered leaves. Wash very carefully and cook in a large kettle of boiling salted water over high heat for 10 minutes.

Remove the spinach from the kettle with long forks or spoons and rinse it in cold water. Press out all the water with your hands. Reheat the spinach in a saucepan with the butter and cream. Season with salt and pepper and serve.

Leaf spinach miroir
Epinards en branches miroir

FOR FOUR PEOPLE

3 pounds fresh spinach	juice of 1 lemon
3 tablespoons butter	salt and pepper
4 eggs	

Wash the spinach well and remove the thick stems. Boil uncovered in salted water for 10 minutes. Lift the spinach out of the water and place it in a collander. Run cold water through it. Drain well and press out the water between the palms of your hands.

Heat the butter in a skillet or in a heatproof serving dish. Reheat the spinach in the butter. When the spinach is very hot, break the eggs on top of it. Sprinkle with salt and pepper. Cover and simmer until the whites have completely set. Sprinkle with lemon juice, if you like.

Spinach croquettes * Croquettes d'épinards

FOR FOUR PEOPLE

3 tablespoons butter	6 tablespoons grated Parmesan cheese
3 tablespoons flour	nutmeg
1 cup milk	1 egg
2 pounds spinach	½ cup fine breadcrumbs
2 egg yolks	salt and pepper

Heat the butter in a small saucepan. When it is frothy, add the flour. Stir quickly for a few seconds and remove from the heat. Add all the milk and stir vigorously to avoid lumps. Put back on the heat and stir constantly until the sauce is thick. Remove and cool.

Trim the spinach, removing the large stems, and wash carefully. Boil 10 minutes in salted water. Freshen the spinach in a large pan of cold water. Drain for 5 minutes and then press out the remaining water between the palms of your hands. Force the spinach through a strainer with a potato masher or through a food mill (or spin in the blender—*Ed.*).

In a bowl, combine the spinach, the sauce, the egg yolks, and the cheese. Mix thoroughly and season to taste with a dash of nutmeg, salt, and pepper. Chill and then spread onto a marble or other working surface. Cut in large pieces and roll into croquettes. Dip them first into beaten egg and then in breadcrumbs. Fry in deep fat at 385° F. until golden brown.

Spinach fritters * Beignets d'épinards

FOR FIVE PEOPLE

2 pounds spinach	2 eggs
4 medium-sized potatoes	salt and pepper
3 tablespoons butter	

Trim the withered leaves and thick stems from the spinach and boil hard in salted water for 10 minutes. Drain thoroughly and force through a food mill or chop very fine.

At the same time, peel and boil the potatoes in salted water until tender. Force them through a strainer.

Mix the vegetables and beat in the butter, the beaten eggs, salt, and pepper. When well blended, drop by spoonfuls into hot (385° F.) deep fat and fry until golden brown. Drain and pile into a mound on a platter lined with a folded napkin.

Stuffed spinach * Epinards farcis

FOR FOUR PEOPLE

1 pound fresh smooth-leaved spinach	cayenne
½ pound raw ground meat	3 tablespoons butter
½ cup rice, boiled	juice of 1 lemon
1 onion, finely chopped	salt and pepper
1 shallot, finely chopped	

Remove the leaves from the stems. Wash them well and dip them in boiling salted water for a few seconds. Use 1 or 2 leaves, according to size, to envelop balls of the following stuffing:

Combine the meat, boiled rice, onion, and shallot. Mix well, seasoning with a dash of cayenne, salt, and pepper. Make small balls of this mixture. Wrap them in spinach leaves.

Melt the butter in a heavy dish or pan. Place the stuffed spinach in the pan. Sprinkle with lemon juice. Cover and simmer very gently for 2 hours.

Spinach soufflé ✳ *Soufflé aux épinards*

FOR FIVE PEOPLE

2 cups Béchamel Sauce (page 6)	5 egg whites
2 pounds spinach	½ cup grated Gruyère cheese
2 tablespoons butter	salt and pepper
5 egg yolks	

Make the sauce and let it cool.

Wash the spinach, trimming off all the large stems. Boil it hard in salted water for 10 minutes. Transfer the spinach to a collander, and when it has cooled somewhat, press the water out between the palms of your hands. Grind it through a *moulinette* or chop very fine. Put the spinach in a saucepan with the butter and stir over a high heat to dry out the spinach.

Remove the spinach from the heat and stir in the sauce and the egg yolks. Mix very vigorously and season with salt and pepper. Beat the egg whites stiff and gently fold them in with a wooden spoon, lifting the mixture as you fold. Pour the mixture into a buttered soufflé dish. Sprinkle with Gruyère cheese. Bake 15 minutes at 375° F. Serve immediately. Soufflés cannot wait.

Tomatoes

The tomato is no longer a seasonable vegetable but is available all year long. Nevertheless, the summer tomato that has been allowed to ripen on the vine is still the best.

In winter and spring the tomatoes coming from the far south are picked before ripening and lack both juice and flavor.

A freshly picked tomato, eaten raw, makes a delicious hors d'oeuvre. Cook tomatoes with natural summer companions, such as zucchini and eggplant, sprinkle all with olive oil, and touch it with garlic, and you will have all of Provence in your dish even if you are not able to be there.

Tomatoes in fresh cream ✳ *Tomates à la crème*

FOR FOUR PEOPLE

1½ pounds tomatoes	chopped tarragon leaves
5 tablespoons butter	salt and pepper
1 cup heavy cream	

Choose small, firm but ripe tomatoes. Cut them across in 2 parts. Heat the butter in a skillet and place the tomatoes, cut side down, in the butter. Prick in several places with a sharp knife and cook gently 5 to 10 minutes, turning them once. Add the heavy cream and stir gently just until the cream is hot, but not boiling. Sprinkle with salt and pepper and with chopped tarragon.

Grilled tomatoes * Tomates grillées

FOR FOUR PEOPLE

Grilled tomatoes are at their best when cooked over charcoal or, if one is on a picnic, over a wood fire. In any case, the heat must be gentle.

8 tomatoes   salt and pepper
oil

Cut the tomatoes in 2 parts and gently press out the seeds. Put them in a grill or on a broiling pan. Paint them with oil on all sides and cook over or under low heat for 10 minutes on each side. Season and serve.

Fried tomatoes * Tomates frites

FOR FOUR PEOPLE

Frying Batter: *Tomatoes:*
1 cup flour   1 pound firm young tomatoes
½ teaspoon salt   several sprigs parsley
1 teaspoon oil
¼ cup beer
2 egg whites

Frying Batter: Put the flour in a bowl and fashion a well in the center. Put the salt and oil in the well. Stirring constantly with a wooden spoon, gradually add the beer and ⅓ cup lukewarm water. Mix just until smooth. Cover and keep at room temperature for at least 1 hour.

Just before using, fold in the egg whites, beaten stiff.

Tomatoes: Meanwhile, dip the tomatoes in boiling water for a few seconds and slip off the skins. Cut the tomatoes in quarters, removing as many seeds as possible. Let the tomatoes drain for a few moments on a rack.

Wipe the tomatoes as dry as possible. Dip each piece in the frying batter and deep-fat fry them at 385° F. When golden brown, drain them on paper toweling, sprinkle with salt, and serve immediately with parsley fried in the same manner.

Tomatoes stuffed with cucumber cream
Tomates farcies au concombre à la crème

FOR FOUR PEOPLE

1 large cucumber
4 large tomatoes
1 cup very heavy cream

2 teaspoons chopped *fines herbes*
　(tarragon, chervil or parsley)
salt and pepper

Peel and halve the cucumber lengthwise. Scoop out the seeds with a spoon and dice the cucumber rather coarsely. Boil the dice 20 minutes in salted water. Drain and cool. This can be done in advance.

Cut off the top third of the tomatoes and scoop out the seeds. Turn the tomatoes upside down on a rack to drain.

Mix the cucumber with the heavy cream and chopped herbs.

Season with salt and pepper. Fill the tomatoes with the mixture. Chill. Serve very cold as an hors d'oeuvre or as an accompaniment to cold meats.

Tomatoes stuffed with crab
Tomates farcies au crabe

FOR FOUR PEOPLE

4 large tomatoes
1 green pepper
1 large cucumber

2 stalks celery
½ pound crabmeat
Mayonnaise (page 14)

Choose large round tomatoes of equal size. Dip them in boiling water a few moments and slip off the skins. Cut off the top third of each tomato and scoop out the flesh. Dice the flesh. Save the tops.

Cut 4 quarter-inch slices from the pepper and chop the rest.

Peel and split the cucumber. Scoop out the seeds and dice the flesh. Cut the celery in dice of the same size.

Whether you pick your own crabmeat from freshly boiled crab or buy it, chop it very fine and mix all the diced vegetables and the crab with mayonnaise.

Fill the tomatoes with the stuffing. Put on the hats and decorate with the pepper circles. Serve on a platter lined with fresh, crisp lettuce leaves.

Onion stuffed tomatoes
Tomates farcies aux oignons

FOR FOUR PEOPLE

8 tomatoes
4 slices bread

2 eggs, slightly beaten
1 clove garlic, minced

½ cup milk
2 cups chopped onions
oil

1 tablespoon chopped parsley
dry breadcrumbs
salt and pepper

Take off the top third of each tomato. Scoop out the centers and turn them upside down on a rack to drain.

Soak the bread in milk and squeeze out all the liquid. Sauté the chopped onions in 4 tablespoons of oil until they are transparent. Combine them in a bowl with the bread, the eggs, the garlic, and the parsley. Mix well and season highly with salt and pepper.

Fill the tomatoes with the stuffing. Place the tomatoes in an oiled baking dish. Sprinkle with the breadcrumbs and a little oil. Bake 1 hour in a moderate (350° F.) oven.

Tomatoes stuffed with mussels (cold)
Tomates farcies aux moules

FOR FOUR PEOPLE

8 medium-sized tomatoes
1 cup cooked or canned mussels
Mayonnaise (page 14)

2 hard-cooked eggs
1 tablespoon chopped parsley

Wash the tomatoes. Wipe them and cut off the top third of each one. Scoop out the insides with a little spoon, taking care not to pierce the skin.

Mix the mussels with mayonnaise, the hard-cooked eggs shelled and chopped, and the chopped parsley.

Fill the tomatoes with the mixture and chill well before serving.

Monaco tomatoes * Tomates monegasques

FOR FOUR PEOPLE

4 tomatoes
1 shallot
1 medium-sized onion
1 can oil-packed tuna fish

4 anchovy fillets
2 teaspoons chopped parsley
3 hard-cooked egg yolks
Mayonnaise (page 14)

Wipe the tomatoes and remove the top third of each one. Scoop out the interior, leaving a ½-inch shell. Do not pierce the skin.

Chop the shallot and onion very fine in a wooden bowl and add the tuna fish, the anchovy fillets, the parsley, and the egg yolks. Continue chopping until you have a blended mixture.

Mix well with mayonnaise. Fill the tomatoes with the mixture. Serve cold, garnished with watercress.

Veal stuffed tomatoes * Tomates farcies au veau

FOR SIX PEOPLE

6 large tomatoes
1½ cups ground cooked veal
Mayonnaise (page 14)
juice of 1 lemon
1½ cups boiled rice

6-8 black, pitted olives
1 tablespoon chopped *fines herbes*
   (parsley, tarragon, chives)
watercress
salt and pepper

Wash the tomatoes and cut off the top third of each one. Scoop out as much of the center as possible without piercing the skin. Combine the ground veal with mayonnaise, strongly flavored with lemon juice, the rice, the olives cut in little pieces, and the chopped herbs. Season with salt and pepper.

Stuff the tomatoes with the mixture. Chill and serve on a bed of watercress.

Baked stuffed tomatoes * Tomates fumées

FOR FOUR PEOPLE

4 large tomatoes
¾ cup chopped onions
¼ pound mushrooms
3 ounces Canadian bacon
1 tablespoon chopped *fines herbes*
   (chives, parsley)

6 tablespoons olive oil
1 egg, beaten
fine breadcrumbs
salt and pepper

Wash the tomatoes and cut them across in two. Take out about three fourths of the interior without piercing the skin.

Chop the onions; wash, trim, and chop the mushrooms; chop the bacon; chop the *fines herbes*.

Heat 4 tablespoons of oil in a skillet and sauté the chopped ingredients for 10 minutes, stirring frequently.

Remove the pan from the heat and stir in the beaten egg. Season with salt and pepper.

Fill the tomato halves with the stuffing. Put them in an oiled baking dish. Sprinkle with breadcrumbs and the remaining oil. Bake 40 minutes in a hot (400° F.) oven.

Tomatoes mordicus * Tomates mordicus

FOR FOUR PEOPLE

½ cup olive oil
1 clove garlic

4 thin slices Gruyère cheese
4 eggs

4 slices firm white bread salt and pepper
2 large ripe tomatoes

Heat 4 tablespoons of oil in a skillet and add the garlic finely minced. Brown the bread lightly on both sides in the oil.

In another skillet, heat the remaining oil. Wipe the tomatoes and cut them in half. Sauté the tomatoes over a gentle heat, beginning with the cut side down. Cook 10 minutes, turn, put a slice of cheese on each tomato, and cook the other side 10 minutes.

Put a slice of fried bread on each tomato and break an egg on each slice of bread. Season with salt and pepper. Cover and cook until the egg whites have set. Serve immediately.

Provençale tomatoes * Tomates provençales

FOR FOUR PEOPLE

8 medium-sized tomatoes 4 teaspoons *fines herbes*
6 tablespoons olive oil   (basil, parsley, chervil)
2 cloves garlic salt and pepper
4 teaspoons fine breadcrumbs

Wipe the tomatoes and cut them across in half. Press out the seeds gently.

Heat the oil in a skillet and cook them cut side down over low heat for 10 minutes. Prick them in several places with a sharp-pointed knife. Turn and cook 10 minutes longer or until cooked.

Transfer them carefully to a heatproof serving dish. Cover with a mixture of the garlic chopped very fine, the breadcrumbs, and the chopped *fines herbes*. Season with salt and pepper. Pour over all the liquid that is left in the skillet. Brown 5 minutes in a hot (400° F.) oven.

Tomatoes stuffed with tuna and rice
Tomates au thon et riz

FOR FOUR PEOPLE

4 large tomatoes 1½ cups boiled rice
4 onions soft breadcrumbs
1 can (7½ ounces) oil-packed tuna salt and pepper
3 tablespoons butter

Wipe the tomatoes and cut off the top third. Scoop out the interior, leaving a half-inch shell. Turn upside down to drain.

Chop the onions fine. Pour the oil from the tuna-fish can into a skillet. Add the butter and sauté the onions in the combination until transparent. Chop the tuna fish. Season with salt and pepper and lower the heat. Add the rice with the tuna and stir just until the mixture is well heated. Do not cook.

Fill the tomatoes with the mixture. Cover with breadcrumbs. Bake in a 400° F. oven for 20 minutes or until the tomatoes are tender.

Tomato soufflé * Soufflé de tomates

FOR FOUR PEOPLE

2 pounds tomatoes	1½ cups thick Béchamel Sauce
2 tablespoons olive oil	(page 6)
1 bay leaf	4 eggs
1 sprig thyme	salt and pepper

Dip the tomatoes in boiling water for a few seconds and slip off their skins. Cut them in half and gently press out the seeds. Cut the tomatoes into pieces. Heat the oil in a saucepan and add the tomatoes, bay leaf, thyme, salt, and pepper. Cook until you have a thick purée.

Make the sauce and separate the eggs. Beat the egg whites stiff.

Add the béchamel sauce to the tomato purée and add the egg yolks one by one, beating hard after each addition. Remove from the heat and fold in the beaten egg whites.

Pour the mixture into a buttered soufflé dish or deep, straight-sided baking dish. Bake 15 minutes at 350° F. and increase the heat to 450° for 10 minutes. Serve immediately.

Stuffed tomatoes with capers * Tomates aux câpres

FOR FOUR PEOPLE

1 cup cooked, boned fish	½ cup Vinaigrette Sauce (page 29)
3 anchovy fillets	4 large ripe tomatoes
½ cup green beans	1 head lettuce
2 hard-cooked egg yolks	Mayonnaise (page 14)
⅓ cup chopped pickles	16 tiny shrimps
2 tablespoons capers	

Cut the fish, the anchovy fillets, the green beans, the egg yolks, and the pickles in small pieces. Add the capers and the vinaigrette sauce. Marinate for 1 hour.

Wash the tomatoes and cut off the tops. Scoop out the seeds and fill the centers with the fish mixture. Arrange the tomatoes on a platter lined with crisp lettuce leaves. Garnish with mayonnaise and small unshelled shrimp.

Turnips in cream * Navets à la crème

FOR FOUR PEOPLE

2 pounds young white turnips
5 tablespoons butter

1 cup heavy cream
salt and pepper

Peel or scrape the young turnips. Never use the older, tough turnips. Cut them in rounds and put them in a saucepan with just enough cold salted water to cover. Cover and simmer 15 minutes after the water has been brought to a boil. Add the butter and continue cooking uncovered. The water will evaporate, and when the turnips begin to fry in the butter that remains, add the cream, salt, and pepper.

Serve as an accompaniment to veal chops or cutlets.

Glazed turnips * Navets glacés

FOR FOUR PEOPLE

3 pounds young white turnips
3 tablespoons butter
1 tablespoon sugar

¾ cup bouillon
salt and pepper

Peel the turnips and slice them evenly. Put them in a saucepan and just cover them with cold, salted water. Bring to a boil and simmer 15 minutes.

Drain the turnips and put them in a well-buttered heavy frying pan. Sprinkle with sugar, salt, and pepper and add the bouillon. Cover with a piece of buttered heavy paper. Bring the liquid to a boil. Lower the heat and simmer until most of the liquid has disappeared.

Turnips à la piémontaise
Navets à la piémontaise

FOR FOUR PEOPLE

3 pounds young white turnips
6 tablespoons butter
¾ cup scalded milk

1 teaspoon meat extract
¼ cup fine breadcrumbs
salt and pepper

Peel the turnips. Place them in a pan of cold, salted water. Bring to a boil and simmer 30 minutes.

Slice the turnips thin and put them in a baking dish with the butter and the milk, mixed with the meat extract. Season with salt and pepper and sprinkle with the breadcrumbs. Brown in a hot (400° F.) oven for 30 minutes.

Turnip potato purée * Purée de navets

FOR FOUR PEOPLE

2 pounds young white turnips
2½ cups bouillon
3 medium-sized potatoes

6 tablespoons butter
¾ cup scalded milk
salt and pepper

Peel the turnips and slice them thin. Place them in a pan of *pot-au-feu* bouillon. Boil the turnips 30 minutes. Drain them and force them through a food mill or a strainer (or purée them in a blender—*Ed.*).

At the same time, peel the potatoes and boil them until tender. Drain and purée them.

Mix the two purées in a saucepan with half the butter. Gradually add the scalded milk until you have a smooth, soft consistency. Season with salt and pepper and add the rest of the butter as you serve the purée.

Watercress in cream * Cresson à la crème

FOR TWO PEOPLE

Watercress cooked and prepared like spinach is an excellent vegetable to be served with roast of pork.

2 pounds watercress
3 tablespoons butter

¼ cup heavy cream
salt and pepper

Pick over the watercress, using only the leaves and the thinnest stems. Cook 5 minutes in a large amount of boiling salted water. Drain in a colander and rinse with cold water. Press out the water with your hands.

Heat the butter over low heat in a shallow saucepan. Add the watercress. Season with salt and pepper and simmer 10 minutes. Add the cream and heat without boiling. Serve as soon as the mixture is hot.

Stuffed zucchini * Grosse courgette farcie

FOR TEN PEOPLE

1 large zucchini
1½ cups ground beef
1½ cups boiled rice
½ cup soft breadcrumbs
milk

2 eggs
6 tablespoons oil
3 sprigs tarragon
salt and pepper

Wash and parboil the zucchini for 5 minutes in boiling salted water. Remove from the water and cut off one end. Using a knife, scoop out the seeds.

Make a stuffing by mixing thoroughly the ground meat, rice, soft breadcrumbs (soaked in milk and squeezed dry), raw eggs, salt, and pepper. The stuffing should be highly seasoned. Fill the zucchini with the mixture.

Pour the oil into a long baking dish. Put in the zucchini and place a sprig of tarragon on each side and another on top. Bake 1¼ hours at 350° F., basting often.

Small stuffed zucchini * Petites courgettes farcies

FOR FOUR PEOPLE

8 small zucchini	2 tablespoons soft breadcrumbs
½ cup finely chopped mushrooms	½ cup milk
1 onion	½ cup grated Parmesan cheese
6 tablespoons butter	2 eggs, beaten slightly
2 tablespoons chopped parsley	salt and pepper

Wash the zucchini and simmer them in salted water for 10 minutes. Drain them and split them lengthwise. Scoop out about three quarters of the pulp. Reserve the pulp and place the zucchini in a buttered baking dish.

Trim, wash, and chop a generous ¼ pound of mushrooms to obtain the ½ cup. Chop the onion equally fine. Heat 5 tablespoons of butter in a skillet and sauté the onion lightly before adding the mushrooms, parsley, and breadcrumbs (soaked in milk and squeezed dry). Add also the zucchini pulp and the Parmesan cheese and season with salt and pepper. Stir over heat for just a moment. Remove and mix in the beaten eggs.

Fill the zucchini shells with the mixture. Put a small piece of butter on each one and brown in a hot oven.

Cold stuffed zucchini * Courgettes farcies froides

FOR SIX PEOPLE

6 uniformly straight small zucchini	3 slices cooked ham, diced
½ pound mushrooms	3 tablespoons tomato paste
⅔ cup oil	juice of 1 large lemon
1½ cups boiled rice	salt and pepper

Wash the zucchini well and boil 15 minutes in salted water. Drain and cool. When they are cold, cut off little hats from the stem end—about ¾ inch. Save these pieces. Using a long iced-tea spoon, scoop out the pulp, leaving a shell approximately ½ inch thick.

Trim and wash the mushrooms and chop them rather coarsely. Heat the oil in a large skillet. Sauté the mushrooms 2 minutes and then add the cooked rice, the diced ham, and the tomato paste. Season with salt and pepper. Mix well and remove from the stove. Chill and mix in the juice of a whole lemon. Stuff the zucchini with the mixture. Place them on a serving platter and put back the little hats. Serve very cold.

Zucchini soufflé philippe
Soufflé philippe (à la courgette)

FOR SIX PEOPLE

1 large zucchini	4 eggs
3 tablespoons butter	salt and pepper
2 cups Béchamel Sauce (page 6)	

Wash the zucchini and split it in two lengthwise. Scoop out the flesh, being careful not to pierce the skin. Cut the flesh in little pieces. Heat the butter in a skillet and cook the zucchini over low heat until it becomes a thick purée, which is cooked until lightly browned.

At the same time, make the béchamel sauce. Remove the sauce from the heat and beat in the egg yolks. Add the zucchini pulp. Beat the egg whites stiff and fold them into the mixture.

Place the zucchini shells in a buttered baking dish. Fill with the soufflé mixture and bake 25 minutes at 350° F. Serve immediately.

Zucchini omelet * Courgettes en omelette

FOR FOUR PEOPLE

6 small zucchini	2 tomatoes
4 tablespoons oil	3 large eggs
1 onion	salt and pepper

Wash the zucchini well and cut off the ends, leaving the zucchini whole. Heat the oil over a low heat in a skillet large enough to hold the zucchini in a single layer. Sauté the onion, sliced very thin, until golden. Add the zucchini and sauté them gently, turning them so that they will be sautéed evenly all over.

Dip the tomatoes in boiling water and slip off the skins. Cut in half and press out the seeds. Cut the tomatoes in pieces and add to the zucchini. Season with salt and pepper and cook gently for 10 minutes. Preheat the oven to 400° F.

Beat the eggs as you would for an omelet. Season with a little salt and pepper. Pour the eggs into the skillet and transfer to the oven. Serve as soon as the eggs have set.

Salads

Salads

In France, we eat a lot of salad greens dressed simply with a vinaigrette sauce, seasoned with chopped herbs and mustard. This salad is served as an accompaniment to roast or broiled meat.

But we also classify as salads, vegetables of all kinds, cooked or raw, cut in slices or chopped and seasoned in the same way that we season salad greens, and we eat them as an hors d'oeuvre at the beginning of the mid-day meal.

Also, we eat another kind of salad which are various foods, vegetables, eggs, meat or fish mixed with boiled rice. This can constitute a main dish for a simple meal. The dressing can be a vinaigrette sauce, lemon juice and cream or mayonnaise.

Oil and vinegar, like seasonings, are a matter of taste and preference. For most salads a very fine olive oil is the best, but many olive oils are too heavy and too strong in flavor. In France, peanut oil or a mixture of peanut oil and olive oil is often used. Red or white wine vinegar is usually used in making dressings, but frequently lemon juice or a fruit juice is substituted for the vinegar. Recipes for the vinaigrette sauces are found in the chapter on Sauces.—Ed.

Eight green salads and their dressings
Huit salades et leurs assaisonnements

FOR FOUR PEOPLE

All salad greens must be well washed, well dried, and in many cases lightly crisped in the refrigerator before being dressed and served.

I. Garden Lettuce (Boston lettuce, Bibb lettuce, Oak Leaf, etc.)

Dressings:

Vinaigrette Sauce (page 29) made with 1 tablespoon chopped *fines herbes* (parsley, tarragon, chervil), hard-cooked egg quarters, paprika.

Mustard French Dressing (page 29) with chopped mint.

Cream French Dressing (page 30) made with lemon juice instead of vinegar and ½ teaspoon grated lemon rind.

Hard-cooked Egg French Dressing (page 30) with 3 teaspoons of orange juice and ½ teaspoon chopped basil.

Herb French Dressing (page 30).

II. Romaine

Dressings:

Vinaigrette Sauce (page 29) with chopped chives.
Roquefort French Dressing (page 30) with 1 tablespoon anise seed.
Cream French Dressing (page 30) with 1 teaspoon of capers.
Mustard French Dressing (page 29) with 1 teaspoon chopped parsley, ½ teaspoon chopped basil, ⅛ teaspoon celery salt.
Herb French Dressing (page 30)

III. Curly Endive or Chicory * Chicorée Frisée

Dressings:

Vinaigrette Sauce (page 29) with large garlic croutons (1 per serving). Rub 1½-inch-square pieces of French bread vigorously with garlic. Mix the salad well before serving.

Vinaigrette Sauce (page 29) with hard-cooked egg slices and 1 teaspoon of capers.

Vinaigrette Sauce (page 29) with raw chopped onion.

IV. Dandelion * Pissenlits

Dressings:

Vinaigrette Sauce (page 29) made with peanut oil, with hard-cooked egg quarters.

Pork Fat Dressing. Heat 3 ounces pork belly* in a skillet. When it has rendered its fat, add 4 teaspoons of wine vinegar. Season with salt and pepper. Serve warm with the fresh dandelion greens.

V. Watercress * Cresson

Dressings:

Always dress watercress just before serving.

4 tablespoons peanut oil, 4 teaspoons lemon juice, salt and pepper.

Mustard French Dressing (page 29) with diced Gruyère cheese.
Vinaigrette Sauce (page 29) with hazel nuts, fresh spinach leaves.
Mix a salad of half watercress, half lettuce with Cream French Dressing (page 30). Sprinkle with paprika.

---

*If pork belly is not available, substitute salt pork, parboiled 5 minutes and rinsed.—*Ed.*

VI. Corn Salad ✳ Mâche

Dressings:

Vinaigrette Sauce (page 29) with sliced beets.

Vinaigrette Sauce (page 29) substituting lemon juice for the vinegar, with beets and celery, finely diced.

Bacon Dressing. Sauté 4 slices of bacon, cut into small pieces, in a skillet. Place the corn salad in a warm salad bowl. Pour the bacon and bacon fat on the corn salad. Put 4 teaspoons of lemon juice in the hot skillet to warm. Pour that quickly on the corn salad. Sprinkle with pepper, but not with salt.

VII. Escarole ✳ Scarole

Dressings:

Mayonnaise (page 14) with chopped walnuts and chopped fresh tarragon.

Crush a clove of garlic in a salad bowl. Add Egg French Dressing (page 29). Mix thoroughly before serving.

Herb French Dressing (page 30) with hard-cooked egg quarters.

Cream French Dressing (page 30) with green pepper rounds, paprika.

VII. Belgian Endive ✳ Endives

Dressings:

Mayonnaise (page 14) with sliced, cooked beets and chopped tarragon.

Vinaigrette Sauce (page 29) made with peanut oil, with chopped walnuts.

Vinaigrette Sauce (page 29) made with grapefruit juice instead of vinegar, with 6 well-peeled orange segments, each cut in 3 pieces.

Anchovy salad ✳ Salade verte aux anchois

FOR TEN PEOPLE

1 tablespoon chopped parsley
2 teaspoons chopped tarragon
1½ cups Mayonnaise (page 14)
10 anchovy fillets

1 romaine
1 head chicory
1 head escarole

In the bottom of a large salad bowl, put the chopped herbs, the mayonnaise, made with tarragon vinegar, and the anchovies, cut in small pieces. Stir well.

Trim the salad greens, cut them, and wash them. Dry very thoroughly.

Mix the greens with the dressing and serve very cold.

✳ Corn salad, unfamiliar to some people, is a salad green or pot herb grown in late fall and early spring. It is sometimes called lamb's-lettuce.—*Ed.*

Artichoke salad * Salade de fonds d'artichauts

FOR SIX PEOPLE

6 large artichoke bottoms
1 small can red peppers

1½ cups Mayonnaise (page 14)
salt and pepper

Cook 6 large artichokes for 35 minutes in boiling salted water. Drain and remove the leaves and chokes, or use well-drained canned artichoke bottoms.

Reserve 1 red pepper for decoration and chop the rest. Mix the chopped peppers with mayonnaise highly flavored with lemon juice. Cut the reserved pepper in narrow strips.

Fill the cold artichoke bottoms with the mayonnaise mixture and place on a small salad platter. Surround the edge of the platter with crossed strips of red pepper.

Asparagus crab salad * Salade d'asperges au crabe

FOR SIX PEOPLE

4 pounds asparagus (white or green)
3 cans crabmeat
3 hard-cooked eggs

½ cup Vinaigrette Sauce (page 29)
salt

Trim the asparagus and cut off all the hard part of the stems. Boil in salted water for 12 to 30 minutes, depending on the variety of asparagus. Drain and cool.

Remove the crabmeat from the cans and divide into pieces, removing any hard filaments.

Peel and crush the hard-cooked eggs and mix them into the vinaigrette.

Put the asparagus on a salad platter. Cover with the vinaigrette. Decorate with the crab.

Assumption day salad * Salade du 15 août

FOR TEN PEOPLE

¾ cup rice
½ cup yellow raisins
1 large red pepper
2 cups shelled green peas
4 firm tomatoes

4 tablespoons chopped black olives
1 cup heavy cream
juice of 3 lemons
salt and pepper

Boil the rice in a large pan of salted water 12 to 15 minutes or until just tender. Drain quickly in a collander; rinse in cold water; drain again and chill.

Soak the raisins in warm water for 1 hour.

Split the pepper, remove the seeds and filaments, and slice into thin strips.

Cook the peas in boiling salted water just until tender. Drain and cool.

Wash the tomatoes and cut them in thin slices.

If possible, buy the imported black olives. Remove the pits and chop enough to give you the required amount.

Mix all these ingredients well in a large salad bowl.

Just before serving, combine the cream with the juice of 3 lemons, season with salt and pepper, and pour over the salad.

Avocado chicken salad
Salade aux avocats et poulet

FOR TEN PEOPLE

5 avocados	¾ cup heavy cream
juice of 1 lemon	2 tablespoons toasted slivered almonds
1½ cups diced cooked chicken	paprika
2 tablespoons chopped celery	salt and pepper
2 tablespoons chopped cucumber	

Split and seed the avocados. Remove some of the avocado flesh, making sure that you do not pierce the skin. Leave a ¼ inch of the flesh in the shell, and sprinkle with lemon juice to keep the flesh from darkening. Combine the diced avocado flesh, the diced chicken, chopped celery, and cucumber with the cream, seasoned with lemon juice, salt, and pepper. Stir in the almonds, and when everything is well mixed, fill the avocado halves. Sprinkle with paprika.

Serve very cold.

Avocado crab salad * Salade d'avocats au crabe

FOR SIX PEOPLE

3 avocados	chopped parsley
1 can crabmeat	paprika
Vinaigrette Sauce (page 29)	lettuce

Buy very ripe avocados. Cut them in two, lengthwise, and remove the seed. Carefully scoop out the flesh without cutting the avocado skin. Cut in small dice.

Remove all filaments from the crab. Mix with the avocado.

Make a vinaigrette and stir in some chopped parsley. Pour the vinaigrette over the mixture and fill the empty shells with the mixture.

Cover a serving platter with pretty lettuce leaves and arrange the filled avocados on the lettuce leaves. Serve as an entrée or in place of a green salad.

Bachelor's salad * La salade du célibataire

FOR FOUR PEOPLE

1 small head lettuce
1 large Idaho potato
4 tablespoons olive oil
1 large apple

1 avocado
juice of 2 lemons
salt and pepper

Trim, wash, and dry the lettuce. Tear or cut it into pieces.

Boil the potato in its jacket in salted water just until tender. Do not overcook. Cool, peel, and cut in as thin slices as possible. Put the lettuce and potato in a salad bowl. Season with oil, salt, and pepper.

Peel, core, and cut the apple and avocado into small pieces. Add to the salad. Sprinkle immediately with the juice of 1 lemon. Taste and add as much more lemon juice as desired.

Dried bean salad * Salade de haricots blancs

FOR FOUR PEOPLE

1 ½ cups cooked dried beans
3 tomatoes
2 tablespoons sliced black olives

3 hard-cooked eggs
1 clove garlic
Vinaigrette Sauce (page 29)

This is usually made when leftover beans are on hand.

Mix the beans, the tomatoes, cut in small pieces, the sliced olives (using the imported variety, if possible), and the eggs, cut in slices.

Crush the garlic and mince it or pound it and blend with the vinaigrette. Season the salad with this mixture.

Beef and cucumber salad
Salade de boeuf aux concombres

FOR FOUR PEOPLE

2 cups diced cucumbers
2 cups diced cooked beef
½ cup Mayonnaise (page 14) or
½ cup Vinaigrette Sauce (page 29)

or ½ cup heavy cream
lemon juice
paprika
salt and pepper

Put the peeled and diced cucumbers in a dish and sprinkle with salt, using the coarse variety, if possible. Let it stand 1 to 2 hours, drain well, and wipe in a clean towel.

Combine the cucumbers with the diced beef and mix with mayonnaise or a vinaigrette, or with my favorite, which is heavy cream beaten with a little lemon juice, a lot of pepper, very little salt, and ½ teaspoon of paprika.

This is served cold. If it is used as an hors d'oeuvre, put lettuce leaves on 4 individual plates and divide the salad among the 4 servings.

Berthault salad * Salade berthault

FOR SIX PEOPLE

2 pounds potatoes	½ bottle very dry champagne
1 pound (3½ cups) small green beans	2 tablespoons cognac
4 eggs	6 tablespoons olive oil
1 can anchovy fillets	1 teaspoon French mustard
12 green pitted olives	juice of ½ lemon
12 black pitted olives	salt and pepper

Boil the potatoes in their jackets in salted water for 20 minutes or just until tender. Let them cool. Peel the potatoes and slice them into thin rounds.

Trim the beans. Cook them uncovered in boiling salted water for 20 minutes. Drain and cool.

Cook the eggs in boiling salted water for 15 minutes. Plunge them in cold water. Shell them and slice into rounds.

Put a layer of potatoes in a china or glass salad bowl. Cover with a layer of beans, another layer of potatoes, a layer of egg slices, a layer of potatoes, a layer of olives, a layer of potatoes, a layer of anchovies, and finally, a layer of potatoes. Pour over it all ½ bottle of very dry champagne and let it stand several hours.

Just before serving, sprinkle with cognac and cover with a sauce made of oil, mustard, salt, pepper, and lemon juice. Serve very cold.

Cabbage bowl salad * Salade de chou

FOR SIX PEOPLE

1 cabbage	1½ cups Mayonnaise (page 14)
4 hard-cooked eggs	1 pound (3-4) medium tomatoes
¾ pound mushrooms	

Cut the cabbage in two crosswise. Hollow out one of the halves to make a bowl. Chop up the cabbage removed from the half with 2 of the hard-cooked eggs.

Trim, wash, and remove the caps from the mushrooms and reserve all the caps that are well formed and approximately of the same size. Chop the rest, rather coarsely, and mix with the chopped cabbage. Bind with mayonnaise.

Put the mixture into the hollowed cabbage half and fashion it into a dome, smoothing it with a knife or small spatula. Surround the bottom of the dome with tomato half slices and thin egg wedges, standing them up in the cabbage rim against the filling. Place the cabbage on a salad platter.

Put the mushroom caps on toothpicks and make a ring of them around the top of the dome.

Cabbage and carrot salad
Salade de chou et de carottes

FOR FOUR PEOPLE

1 small head green cabbage	1 green or red pepper
3 carrots	Vinaigrette Sauce (page 29) *or*
2 gherkin pickles	Mayonnaise (page 14)

Chop the cabbage very fine. Chop the carrots, the pickles, and the pepper. Mix everything in a salad bowl and season either with a vinaigrette or with a mayonnaise made with lemon juice.

If this salad is an opening course, serve on individual plates lined with lettuce leaves. Some people like a little sugar with carrot salads, so put the sugar bowl on the table.

Cooked cabbage salad * Salade de chou cuit

FOR FOUR PEOPLE

1 tender new cabbage	2 or 3 mint leaves, chopped
Vinaigrette Sauce (page 29)	

Remove the exterior hard leaves of the cabbage and trim the stem. Cut the cabbage in quarters, trimming out the hard center core. Cook 5 minutes in boiling salted water. Drain in a collander and rinse with cold water. Drain again. Pat dry in a towel.

Season with a vinaigrette to which the mint leaves have been added.

Red and green cabbage salad
Salade de riz, chou vert, chou rouge, raisins secs

FOR FOUR PEOPLE

½ cup seedless raisins	½ cup rice
¾ cup chopped green cabbage	Vinaigrette Sauce (page 29)
¾ cup chopped red cabbage	

Soak the raisins in cold water for 1 hour.

Chop the cabbage very fine.

Boil the rice in a large pan of salted water for 12 to 15 minutes or just until tender. Drain, rinse in cold water, drain again.

Combine the rice and raisins in a salad dish. Surround with the chopped cabbage and season with the vinaigrette.

Cauliflower and mushrooms (raw)
Chou-fleur et champignons (salade)

FOR FOUR PEOPLE

1 small cauliflower	juice of 1 lemon
½ pound mushrooms	Mayonnaise (page 14)

Remove the leaves from the cauliflower and divide the head into small flowerets.

Trim and wash the mushrooms. Cut them in slices. Sprinkle with lemon juice.

Alternate small bunches of mushrooms and cauliflower around a serving platter.

Make a mayonnaise using tarragon vinegar. Serve in a separate bowl.

Chicken almond salad
Salade de poulet aux amandes

FOR SIX PEOPLE

4-pound chicken, roasted or poached	2 tablespoons slivered almonds, toasted
4 tablespoons seedless raisins	½ orange
1 bunch watercress	1½ cups Mayonnaise (page 14)
3 stalks celery	salt and pepper

Roast or poach a chicken according to directions on page 230. Cool.

Soak the raisins in warm water for a few hours.

Remove the skin and bones from the cold chicken and cut the meat in thin slices.

Wash the watercress, discarding the thick stems. Wash the celery and cut it in small pieces.

Put the watercress, celery, chicken, toasted almond slivers, and the raisins in a large salad bowl. Season with salt and pepper.

Mix the juice of ½ orange with the mayonnaise and combine with the salad ingredients. Mix well. Serve very cold.

Cauliflower salad with roquefort and anchovies
Salade de chou-fleurs au roquefort et anchois

FOR FOUR PEOPLE

1 very white cauliflower	2 hard-cooked eggs
Roquefort French Dressing (page 30)	4 anchovy fillets

Trim the cauliflower, removing all the leaves and the hard base. Steam it whole until the stems are tender when pressed with your finger. Drain very thoroughly. Place in a bowl.

Make the dressing and pour it over the cauliflower. Let it stand for at least 30 minutes, basting frequently.

Just before serving, place the cauliflower on a serving platter. Pour the sauce over the cauliflower and decorate with hard-cooked egg slices and anchovy fillets.

Celeriac rémoulade with lemon
Salade de céleri rave rémoulade au citron

FOR FOUR PEOPLE

1 celeriac	French mustard
1½ lemons	2 teaspoons chopped parsley
½ cup Mayonnaise (page 14)	

Peel the celeriac. Cut it into thin strips and place them in a bowl. Sprinkle immediately with the juice of ½ lemon to keep the celeriac white. Let it stand at least 1 hour.

Make a mayonnaise with very little mustard and lemon juice. Mix the dressing with the celeriac and put on a small salad platter. Decorate with half a lemon sliced and chopped parsley.

Classic celery salad * Salade de céleri à l'ancienne

FOR SIX PEOPLE

3 celery hearts	3 small tomatoes
3 eggs	green and black pitted olives
½ cup Mayonnaise (page 14)	2 tablespoons walnut meats
French mustard	

Cut the celery in thin small strips about 1 inch long.

Hard-cook the eggs in boiling water for 15 minutes. Plunge into cold water.

Shell them and halve them. Remove the yolks and crush them with a fork, adding the mayonnaise, strongly flavored with mustard.

Cut the egg whites into strips like the celery. Mix the celery and egg-white strips into the mayonnaise mixture and spread in a salad platter. Let stand several hours in the refrigerator.

Decorate the top with half tomato slices, olives, and walnut meats.

Celery and salmon salad
Salade de céleri et saumon

FOR FOUR PEOPLE

1 can salmon
4 stalks celery
2 tablespoons slivered almonds

½ cup heavy cream
3 tablespoons grapefruit juice
salt and pepper

Drain the salmon and cut it into small pieces.

Wash the celery and chop it fine.

Mix the salmon and the celery with the slivered almonds and season highly with salt and pepper. Place in a small salad dish and cover with a mixture of heavy cream and grapefruit juice.

Christiane salad * Salade christiane

FOR EIGHT PEOPLE

4 artichoke bottoms
  (cooked or canned)
4 medium-sized potatoes
2 bananas
2 apples
1 celery heart

4 hard-cooked eggs
½ cup Vinaigrette Sauce (page 29)
1 teaspoon chopped tarragon
2 teaspoons chopped parsley
8 walnuts
salt and pepper

If using fresh artichokes, boil them 25 minutes in salted water. Discard all but the bottoms. Cool.

Boil the potatoes in their jackets until tender. Cool.

Cut the artichoke bottoms, potatoes, bananas, apples, and celery heart into thin slices of approximately the same size.

Chop the hard-cooked eggs.

Put everything into a salad bowl and season with the vinaigrette, to which you add the chopped herbs.

Decorate the top with walnut halves.

Coconut salad * Salade de noix de coco

FOR SIX PEOPLE

1 coconut	12 black olives
2 red peppers	3 teaspoons tomato purée
2 green peppers	1 cup Mayonnaise (page 14)

Cut the coconut in two crosswise. Scoop out the coconut meat and cut it into medium-sized dice.

Wash the peppers. Split them to remove the seeds and filaments and cut them into pieces.

Pit the olives, using the imported variety, if possible, and cut them in quarters.

Combine the tomato purée with the mayonnaise and mix with the peppers, olives, and coconut. Serve in a salad bowl.

Countryside salad * Salade campagnarde

FOR SIX PEOPLE

1 small cooked beef tongue	4 tomatoes
3 Idaho potatoes	4 hard-cooked eggs
1 celery heart	5 gherkin pickles
1 head lettuce	Mayonnaise (page 14)

Trim the tongue and cut into small dice.

Boil the potatoes in their jackets, starting in cold salted water. When tender, drain, cool, peel, and cut the potatoes in pieces.

Wash the celery and cut into small dice.

Trim the lettuce and wash it well. Dry thoroughly.

Dip the tomatoes in boiling salted water for a moment. Slip off the skins and cut in thin slices.

Peel and quarter the hard-cooked eggs.

Chop the pickles rather coarsely and combine with the mayonnaise.

Mix all the ingredients in a large salad bowl and bind with the mayonnaise. Serve very cold.

Cooked cucumber and crab salad
Salade de concombre cuit et de crabe

FOR FOUR PEOPLE

1 very large cucumber	⅔ cup Mayonnaise (page 14)
1 can crabmeat	2½ tablespoons catsup

Peel the cucumber and split it. Remove the seeds and cut the flesh into small dice. Cook in boiling water for 10 minutes. Drain for 2 hours.

Flake the crabmeat, removing all filaments.

Combine the mayonnaise and catsup.

Mix the cucumber, crabmeat, and mayonnaise, stirring until well blended. Chill in the refrigerator. Serve in stemmed sherbet glasses.

December salad * Salade de décembre

FOR TEN PEOPLE

2 pounds canned French string beans
2 pounds Chinese artichokes
2 small cans truffle peelings

juice of 2 lemons
⅔ cup oil
salt and pepper

Buy the finest and smallest canned green beans available. Drain them well and let them stand.

Rub the artichokes with 2 tablespoons of coarse salt in a rough towel, and cook them 20 minutes in boiling water. Drain.

Mix the beans and the artichokes in a salad bowl with the truffle peelings. Season with a dressing made of the lemon juice, oil, salt, and pepper. Serve very cold.

Belgian endive, orange, and grapefruit salad
Salade d'endives aux pamplemousses et oranges

FOR FOUR PEOPLE

3 endives
½ grapefruit
1 orange

2 tablespoons diced Gruyère cheese
Vinaigrette Sauce (page 29)

Trim the endives and wash them well. Dry thoroughly.

Peel the grapefruit and orange, removing all the white skin and fibers.

Cut each orange segment in two and each grapefruit section in thirds. Cut the Gruyère in very small dice and mix everything together in a salad bowl with a vinaigrette sauce.

Orange endive salad * Salade d'endives à l'orange

FOR FOUR PEOPLE

3 pounds Belgian endives
2 oranges

4 tablespoons oil
salt and pepper

Trim and wash the endives and cook them whole in boiling salted water for 45 minutes. Drain them carefully and cool completely.

Make a sauce by combining the juice of the oranges with the oil, salt, and pepper. If the oranges are very sweet, add a little lemon juice.

This is a salad fit for a king.

Fennel and anchovy salad
Salade de fenouil aux anchois

FOR FOUR PEOPLE

2 Belgian endives	Vinaigrette Sauce (page 29)
1 fennel heart	juice of 1 lemon
10 radishes	3 teaspoons anchovy paste

Chop the endives, the fennel heart, and the radishes. Place them in a shallow dish, putting the radishes in the center.

Make the vinaigrette, using lemon juice instead of vinegar, and blend thoroughly with the anchovy paste.

Pour the sauce over the vegetables. Serve as an hors d'oeuvre.

Garden salad * Salade de jardin

FOR SIX PEOPLE

1 small cauliflower	2 teaspoons sugar
2 medium-sized onions	1 teaspoon powdered thyme
1 cucumber	1 teaspoon marjoram
1 green pepper	1 teaspoon paprika
4 red peppers	½ cup Vinaigrette Sauce (page 29)
1 pound spinach	

Soak the cauliflower trimmed of all leaves, in cool, salted water for 30 minutes. Drain and cut off the stems, leaving just the flowerets.

Peel and chop the onions and cucumber. Split the green and red peppers. Remove the seeds and filaments. Cut 2 of the red peppers into strips and set aside. Chop the rest of the peppers.

Wash the spinach. Remove all the stems and cut the leaves into pieces with a scissors.

Mix the cauliflower, raw onion, cucumber, and chopped peppers with the sugar, herbs, and the vinaigrette in a salad bowl. Mix well and chill. Just before serving, add the spinach leaves and decorate with the red-pepper strips.

Ham and cheese sal
Salade de jambon et au gruyère

FOR SIX PEOPLE

1 head escarole	1 cucumber
1 pound lean cooked ham	1½ cups Mayonnaise (page 14)
6 ounces Gruyère cheese	1 tablespoon tomato purée
3 hard-cooked eggs	

Trim and wash the escarole. Dry well.

Cut the ham and cheese into little strips.

Peel and slice the eggs.

Slice the cucumber without peeling it.

Combine the mayonnaise and tomato purée. Put the mixture in a small bowl.

Place the bowl in the center of a large salad platter. Surround with lettuce leaves and arrange the eggs, cucumber, ham, and cheese on the leaves. Each person will help himself to sauce as he is served.

Cooked lettuce salad à la constance
Salade de laitues constance

FOR FOUR PEOPLE

8 small heads lettuce	¾ cup rice
¾ cup dry white wine	4 tablespoons oil
juice of 1 lemon	salt and pepper

Trim and wash the lettuce thoroughly, but do not cut off the stem end. Cook in boiling salted water for 5 minutes. Drain them well, pressing out the excess water with your hands. Put them in an enamel saucepan with the wine, the juice of ½ lemon, salt, and pepper. Cook covered over a very low flame for 15 minutes.

Boil the rice in salted water for 12 to 15 minutes or until tender. Drain quickly in a collander; rinse in cold water, and drain again. Season with lemon juice and oil.

Put the rice on a salad platter and surround with the cold lettuce.

Lettuce with cheese * Laitues au fromage

FOR SIX PEOPLE

1 large head of lettuce (Boston, escarole, romaine)	¼ cup chopped walnuts
	1 onion

1 8-ounce package cottage cheese   Vinaigrette Sauce (page 29)
2-3 tablespoons milk   celery salt
4 carrots   pepper
2 green peppers

Wash the lettuce well and remove any hard or wilted leaves. Remove also the center leaves to make room for the stuffing.

Beat the cottage cheese with a little milk until smooth. (This is quickly done with an electric beater or blender.—*Ed.*)

Grate the carrots; dice the green peppers very fine, chop the nuts and the onion, and mix all the vegetables into the cheese. Season with celery salt and pepper.

Place the lettuce in a serving dish. Fill the center with the stuffing and serve very cold with the vinaigrette sauce in a separate bowl.

Lettuce hearts with roquefort cheese
Coeurs de laitues au roquefort

FOR FOUR PEOPLE

2 lettuce hearts   2 tablespoons Roquefort cheese
1 pound (4) tomatoes   Mayonnaise (page 14)

Buy the lettuce hearts or remove them from 2 heads of lettuce. Divide each heart in half and wash well.

Wash the tomatoes. Cut them in quarters. Arrange the lettuce hearts in a row on a serving platter. Surround with tomato quarters.

Crumble the Roquefort cheese into the mayonnaise and serve in a separate bowl.

Macaroni and ham salad
Salade de macaroni au jambon

FOR FOUR PEOPLE

¼ pound macaroni pieces   1½ cups Mayonnaise (page 14)
6 ounces cooked ham   ⅓ cup heavy cream
2 hard-cooked eggs   juice of 1 lemon
2 gherkin pickles   salt and pepper

Cook the macaroni in boiling salted water just until tender. Drain well.

Cut the ham into small dice. Slice the eggs and pickles into rounds. Make the mayonnaise, add the heavy cream, and season well with lemon juice, some salt, and quite a lot of pepper.

Mix the sauce with the rest of the ingredients and serve very cold.

Cooked mushroom salad
Salade de champignons cuits

FOR FOUR PEOPLE

½ pound mushrooms
3 tablespoons butter
6 tablespoons Mayonnaise (page 14)

juice of 1 lemon
salt and pepper

Trim the mushrooms and separate the caps from the stems. Cut them all in thin strips.

Heat the butter in a saucepan, and when very hot, add the mushrooms. Cook until the moisture disappears, but do not brown the mushrooms. Season with salt and pepper and cool completely.

Mix with the mayonnaise or, if you prefer, with oil. In either case, sprinkle with the juice of a lemon. Add the lemon juice little by little, because a whole lemon might be too much. Serve in a small salad dish.

Hazel nut salad ✳ *Salade de noisettes*

FOR FOUR PEOPLE

1½ cups cooked dried white beans
1½ cups cooked green beans
1 stalk celery, chopped

½ cup small roasted hazel nuts
Vinaigrette Sauce (page 29)

Combine the cold cooked beans with the celery in a small salad bowl.

Add the nuts to the bowl, stirring carefully so as not to break the beans. Mix with the vinaigrette, which can be mildly or highly seasoned, according to your taste.

Oyster plant with mayonnaise
Salsifis à la mayonnaise

FOR FOUR PEOPLE

2 pounds oyster plant
⅔ cup Mayonnaise (page 14)
juice of 1 lemon

1 can anchovy fillets
black olives

Trim and scrape the oyster plant. Cook in boiling salted water until tender. Drain and chill.

Make the mayonnaise and season it with lemon juice. Mix well with the oyster plant.

Place in a salad platter and decorate with anchovy fillets and black olives, using the imported variety, if possible.

Niçoise salad * Salade niçoise

FOR FOUR PEOPLE

½ pound small green beans
2 green peppers
¼ pound salt-packed anchovies
1 large onion
1 pound tomatoes

3 hard-cooked eggs
12 pitted black olives
1 can (6½ ounces) oil-packed tuna
Vinaigrette Sauce (page 29)
salt and pepper

Trim the beans, wash them, and boil uncovered in salted water for 20 minutes. Drain and cool.

Wash the peppers and cut them in half. Remove the seeds and filaments. Split the anchovies and remove the spinal bones, the head, and the tail and let a thin stream of cold water run over them for an hour. (If whole anchovies are unavailable, use 2 cans of anchovy fillets and cut them into 1-inch pieces.—*Ed.*)

Peel the onion and slice very thin.

Dip the tomatoes in boiling water for a moment. Slip off the skins and cut them in thin slices.

Having boiled the eggs 15 minutes in salted water, plunge them in cold water, shell, and quarter them.

In a large salad bowl, mix the tomatoes, anchovies, green beans, onions, peppers, and olives, using the imported variety, if possible. Add the tuna, flaked into rather small pieces, and mix with a vinaigrette made with olive oil. Stir gently so as not to break the various vegetables. Decorate with the eggs. Chill before serving.

Paprika salad * Salade de paprika

FOR FIVE PEOPLE

1 large celeriac
4 Belgian endives
4 mushrooms
1 apple

3 tablespoons chopped almonds
1½ cups Mayonnaise (page 14)
paprika
salt and pepper

Peel the celeriac. Cut it into slices and then into matchlike strips. Parboil 5 minutes in boiling water.

Wash the endives and chop the leaves. Trim, wash, and mince the mushrooms. Cut the apple into small dice.

Combine everything in a small salad bowl with the almonds. Season with salt and pepper. Cover with mayonnaise and sprinkle with paprika. Serve very cold.

Sweet pepper salad * *Salade de piments doux*

4 sweet red peppers
4 ripe tomatoes
½ cup olive oil
1 tablespoon vinegar

4 scallions
2 teaspoons chopped parsley
salt and pepper

Broil the peppers, turning them so that they are evenly browned.

Cut them open to remove the seeds and cut into strips. Place in a shallow salad dish.

Broil the tomatoes and force them through a strainer over the peppers.

Season with a dressing made of the olive oil, vinegar, salt, and pepper and sprinkle with a mixture of the scallions, sliced very thin, and the chopped parsley.

Pineapple and shrimp salad *Salade d'ananas avec crevettes*

1 pineapple
3 stalks celery
½ cucumber

½ pound small, cooked, shelled shrimp
1½ cups Mayonnaise (page 14)

Cut the pineapple in half. Scoop out the flesh and cut in small cubes.

Wash the celery and cut into small pieces.

Cut the cucumber into small dice without peeling.

Reserve some of the shrimp, but mix most of them with the chopped ingredients, binding it with the mayonnaise. Fill the pineapple halves with the mixture. Decorate with the remaining shrimp and serve very cold.

Pork and apple salad * *Salade de porc et pommes*

1½ cups cold diced roast pork
1½ cups diced eating apples
juice of 1 lemon

1½ cups Mayonnaise (page 14)
salt and pepper

Dice the pork.

Cut the apples without peeling them. Remove the seeds and cut them in small dice.

Combine the pork and apples and sprinkle immediately with lemon juice so that the apples will not turn brown.

Because lemon has been added to the apples, mix the apples and pork with a mayonnaise that is mild. Taste to be sure that there is enough salt, and if you wish, add more lemon juice.

Alsatian potato salad
Salade de pommes de terre alsacienne

FOR FIVE PEOPLE

2 pounds (6-8) medium-sized potatoes
¾ cup bouillon
2 cooked beets
½ cup Vinaigrette Sauce (page 29)
2 hard-cooked eggs

gherkin pickles
1 tablespoon chopped parsley
Mayonnaise (page 14)
salt and pepper

Start the potatoes in cold salted water. Bring to a boil and cook in their jackets just until tender, the time depending on the size of the potatoes. Peel the potatoes and slice them very fine into a salad bowl. Sprinkle with salt and pepper and pour boiling hot bouillon over the potato slices so that they will absorb the bouillon. Crush one of the beets and add its juice to the potatoes. Add the vinaigrette and mix well.

Decorate the top of the salad with the other beet, chopped, and the hard-cooked eggs, the yolks forced through a sieve or a *moulinette,* the whites, chopped fine— the whites and yolks being kept separate—pickle slices, and parsley. Serve the mayonnaise in a separate bowl.

Potato, egg, and anchovy salad
Salade de pommes de terre, anchois et oeufs

FOR FIVE PEOPLE

1½ pounds (5-6) potatoes
6 eggs
½ cup Mustard French Dressing
    (page 29)

2 cans (2½ oz.) anchovy fillets
cayenne
salt and pepper

Put the unpeeled potatoes in a pan of cold salted water and bring to a boil. Cook just until tender. Drain and cool. Peel and cut into thin slices. Put the potato slices in a salad bowl.

At the same time, boil the eggs for 15 minutes. Plunge them into cold water and peel. Cut 2 of the eggs into thin strips. Slice the rest into rounds.

Mix the mustard dressing into the potatoes along with the egg strips. Taste for seasoning.

Decorate the top of the salad with radiating strips of anchovies and egg slices.

New potato salad
Salade de pommes de terre nouvelles

FOR FOUR PEOPLE

1½ pounds tiny new potatoes
Mustard French Dressing (page 29)
1 slice cooked ham

2 hard-cooked eggs
1 tablespoon chopped *fines herbes*
   (parsley, tarragon)

Wash the potatoes and steam just until tender. Cool slightly and remove the skins. Place in a salad bowl and mix with the mustard dressing. Sprinkle with shredded ham, hard-cooked eggs, which have been finely chopped or forced through a *moulinette,* and herbs.

Potato and mussel salad
Salade de pommes de terre et moules au safran

FOR TWO PEOPLE

1 pound tiny potatoes
1 quart mussels
Mayonnaise (page 14)

1 teaspoon turmeric *or*
small pinch of powdered saffron
juice of ½ lemon

Start cooking the small new potatoes in their jackets in cold, salted water. Bring to a boil and cook just until tender. Cool, peel, and slice very fine.

Open thoroughly cleaned mussels by putting them in a pan over a moderate heat. When they are open, remove from the shells.

Make a mayonnaise and flavor it with turmeric or saffron and the juice of ½ lemon. Mix the salad and let stand 1 or 2 hours before serving.

Radish salad * Salade de radis

FOR FOUR PEOPLE

¾ cup sliced radishes
¾ cup cooked green beans

¾ cup boiled rice
Vinaigrette Sauce (page 29)

Mix the radishes, beans, and rice and season with the vinaigrette made with lemon juice.

Almond rice salad * Salade de riz colorée

FOR TEN PEOPLE

½ pound prunes
strong tea
1 pound rice
1 small can red peppers

½ cup slivered almonds
2 tablespoons chopped chervil or
   parsley
¾ cup Vinaigrette Sauce (page 29)

Put the prunes in a bowl and cover with strong tea. Soak at least 1 hour.

Cook the rice in a kettle of boiling salted water for 12 to 15 minutes or just until tender. Drain quickly in a collander, rinse in cold water, and drain again.

Cut the peppers in small dice.

Remove the pits from the prunes and cut into small dice.

In a large salad bowl, mix the rice, peppers, prunes, almonds, and chervil, using the parsley if chervil is not available. Add the vinaigrette and mix well. Serve cold.

Curry rice salad * Salade jaune

FOR TWELVE PEOPLE

½ cup seedless raisins
2 cups rice
3 tablespoons curry powder
1 cup hazel nuts

1 large can tiny peas
3 cups Mayonnaise (page 14)
lemon juice
salt

Soak the raisins for 1 hour in warm water.

Cook the rice in a kettle of boiling salted water, to which the curry powder has been added, for 12 to 15 minutes or just until tender. Drain quickly in a collander, rinse in cold water, and drain again.

Combine the rice, raisins, whole hazel nuts, and the drained canned peas. Bind with the mayonnaise, strongly flavored with lemon juice. Salt to taste. Serve very cold.

Rice and pepper salad * Salade de riz aux poivrons

FOR SIX PEOPLE

1 cup rice
½ pound Belgian endives
½ cup walnut halves

1 green pepper
1 red pepper
¾ cup Vinaigrette Sauce (page 29)

Boil the rice in a large pan of salted water for 12 to 15 minutes or until just tender. Drain quickly in a collander, rinse well in cold water, and drain again.

Wash the endives and chop them rather coarsely.

Split the peppers and remove the seeds and filaments. Chop them coarsely also. Mix all the ingredients in a salad bowl and mix with well-seasoned vinaigrette.

Shrimp and potato salad
Salade de crevettes et de pommes de terre

FOR EIGHT PEOPLE

¾ pound small cooked and cleaned shrimp
3 gherkin pickles
2 tablespoons chopped parsley
1 teaspoon chopped tarragon leaves
1 tablespoon white wine vinegar

2 cups cooked diced potatoes
1 cup cooked peas
2 apples
1½ cups Mayonnaise (page 14)
2 teaspoons French mustard
romaine lettuce

Mix the shrimp with finely chopped pickles, parsley, tarragon, and vinegar. Let stand 10 minutes so that the shrimp will absorb the flavors.

Mix the shrimp with the cold cooked vegetables and the apples, peeled and diced. Bind with the mayonnaise mixed with the mustard. Serve very cold on leaves of romaine.

Spinach and bacon salad
Salade d'épinards au bacon

FOR SIX PEOPLE

1½ pounds spinach
6 slices bacon
juice of 1 large lemon

6 tablespoons oil
pepper

Wash and trim the spinach, discarding the stems. Chop coarsely. Place the leaves in a salad bowl.

Cook the bacon until quite crisp. Break into pieces and add to the spinach. Make a dressing of the juice of a lemon, the oil, and pepper. Do not add salt because the bacon will be salty. Serve immediately while the bacon is warm.

Romance salad * Salade romantique

FOR FOUR PEOPLE

1 small cauliflower
4 hard-cooked eggs

1 bunch watercress
4 or 5 black olives, pitted

2 small carrots   Vinaigrette Sauce (page 29)
1 bunch of radishes

Remove the leaves from the cauliflower. Cook it whole in salted water for 20 minutes or until the small stems are just tender. Drain and cool.

Shell and slice the hard-cooked eggs.

Slice the carrots very thin and cut the red peel away from the white part of the radishes to make them look like flowers.

Chop the watercress leaves.

Place the cauliflower in the center of a round salad plate. Surround first with the carrots, then the radishes, then the watercress, and finally the egg slices.

Cut the olives in slices and make a star on top of the cauliflower. Serve the vinaigrette in a separate dish.

Raw spinach and carrot salad
Salade d'épinards crus aux carottes

FOR FOUR PEOPLE

1 pound spinach   ⅔ cup Mayonnaise (page 14)
1 pound carrots   juice of 1 lemon
1 head garden lettuce   paprika
2 eggs

Wash the spinach and remove the leaves. Discard all the stems. Tear the spinach leaves into pieces.

Grate carrots; trim, wash, and break the lettuce head into leaves.

Hard-cook the eggs in salted water for 15 minutes. Plunge into cold water. Peel and slice.

Mix the spinach and carrots with the mayonnaise and add a little lemon juice.

Line a salad platter with 4 large lettuce leaves. Divide the mixture among the four leaves. Decorate with egg slices and sprinkle with paprika.

Cooked spinach and mussel salad
Salade d'épinards aux moules

FOR SIX PEOPLE

4 pounds spinach   4-5 tarragon leaves
2 quarts mussels   2 hard-cooked eggs
½ cup Vinaigrette Sauce (page 29)

Wash and trim the spinach, taking off the thick stems. (These stems, cooked in boiling water to which lemon juice has been added, and seasoned with a vinaigrette sauce, make an excellent hors d'oeuvre.)

Cook the spinach in a large amount of boiling water. Do not cover. After 8 to 10 minutes, when the spinach is cooked, drain in a collander and run cold water over the leaves, stirring them so that all the spinach will cool. Let drain a few minutes and then press out the rest of the water between the palms of your hands.

Place thoroughly cleaned mussels in a large kettle. Put over high heat uncovered until the mussels open. As soon as they are opened, they are cooked. Shell the mussels and put them in a salad bowl. (Canned mussels may be substituted for the fresh variety.—*Ed.*)

Make a vinaigrette, adding chopped tarragon and the hard-cooked eggs crushed very fine. If possible beat with an electric mixer to make the dressing creamy in texture. Mix with the spinach and mussels and serve very cold.

Cooked spinach salad * Epinards cuits en salade

FOR FOUR PEOPLE

4 pounds spinach	4 hard-cooked egg yolks
¾ cup heavy cream	salt and pepper
juice of 2 lemons	

Boil the spinach uncovered in a large kettle of salted water, allowing 10 minutes after boiling has started. As soon as it is cooked, drain in a collander and immediately rinse in cold water. Drain and press out the water between the palms of your hands. This must be done quickly if the spinach is to retain its bright green color. Discard any yellow leaves.

Combine the cream and the juice of 1 lemon, salt, and pepper. Add the rest of the lemon juice, little by little, according to taste.

Force the egg yolks through a strainer or *moulinette*.

Mix the spinach with the sauce and heap into a dome on a salad platter. Sprinkle with the egg yolks.

Spinach and tomato salad
Salade d'épinards aux tomates

FOR FOUR PEOPLE

1 pound new spinach	juice of 1 lemon
1 pound (3-4) tomatoes	*orégano*
2 hard-cooked eggs	salt and pepper

Trim the spinach, discarding all the stems and using only the leaves. Tear into small pieces.

Dip the tomatoes in boiling water for a moment and slip off the skins. Cut into small pieces.

Peel and quarter the hard-cooked eggs.

Put the vegetables and eggs in a shallow salad bowl.

Make a sauce by combining the cream with the juice of ½ lemon and season with salt, pepper, and a pinch of *orégano.* Taste. Add more lemon juice, if desired. Spoon this over the salad.

*Spring salad * Salade de printemps*

FOR FOUR PEOPLE

1 large bunch corn salad*	Vinaigrette Sauce (page 29)
¼ pound mushrooms	2 teaspoons chopped tarragon
3 large artichoke bottoms (fresh or canned)	

Trim and wash the corn salad.

Trim and wash the mushrooms. Slice them very thin.

Cook the fresh artichokes in salted boiling water for 25 minutes. Remove the leaves and chokes and use only the bottoms. Canned or fresh, the bottoms should be diced.

Mix the corn salad, mushrooms, and artichokes carefully so as not to break them and place in a salad bowl. Pour over the vinaigrette and sprinkle with chopped tarragon.

*Summer salad * Salade d'été*

FOR FOUR PEOPLE

2 tomatoes	8 pitted olives
1 cucumber	6 walnuts
6 radishes	Vinaigrette Sauce (page 29)
2 celery hearts	

Peel or trim the vegetables and cut them into large dice. The olives should be cut in half and the walnuts shelled and quartered. Put everything into a shallow salad bowl and mix with a vinaigrette. Serve as an hors d'oeuvre or as an accompaniment to cold poultry.

---

*Corn salad, unfamiliar to some people, is a salad green or pot herb grown in late fall and early spring. It is sometimes called lamb's-lettuce.—*Ed.*

Tomato salad * Salade de tomates

To make a really good tomato salad, choose firm red tomatoes and peel them after having dipped them in boiling water for a moment. Cut them in slices and remove the seeds. Place the tomatoes in a dish wih several slices of onion. Sprinkle with salt and pepper. Let stand for 1 hour. Remove the onion slices and pour off the juice. Pour on a vinaigrette and sprinkle with chopped *fines herbes* (chives, tarragon, parsley).

Accordion tomatoes * Tomates en accordéon

FOR SIX PEOPLE

6 large tomatoes
1 small can salmon
3 hard-cooked eggs
2 teaspoons chopped parsley
½ teaspoon chopped tarragon

1½ cups Mayonnaise (page 14)
1 head Boston lettuce
2 carrots
1 small cauliflower

Choose tomatoes that are oval rather than round. Dip them in boiling water and slip off their skins. Place them on a table, stem side down, and cut them from the top in thin slices without cutting through at the base.

Crush the salmon with a fork. Chop the eggs fine and combine the salmon, the eggs, the herbs, and enough mayonnaise to bind the mixture.

Line a square or rectangular salad platter with lettuce leaves. Put the tomatoes on the lettuce, and with the help of a small spoon, put some of the salmon mayonnaise between the slices.

Grate the carrots and cut the cauliflower into little flowerets. On opposite corners of the platter, put a pile of carrots and a pile of cauliflower. Divide the rest of the mayonnaise between the other 2 corners.

Cooked tomato salad * Salade de tomates cuites

FOR FOUR PEOPLE

2 pounds tomatoes
1 cucumber
1 large stalk celery
½ cup oil

juice of 1 lemon
pinch of ginger or sage
salt and pepper

Dip the tomatoes in boiling water for a moment and slip off the skins. Cut the tomatoes in quarters and remove the seeds.

Peel and cut the cucumber in large dice.

Cut the celery in thick slices.

Heat the oil in a deep skillet and put in all the vegetables. Sprinkle with salt and pepper and the ginger or sage. Cook until the water from the vegetables has evaporated. Cool completely.

Just before serving, sprinkle with lemon juice. This is excellent with cold meat.

Tomato crab salad * Salade de tomates au crabe

FOR SIX PEOPLE

1 can crabmeat	2 tablespoons curry powder
2 stalks celery	6 large tomatoes
2 red peppers	6 black olives
¾ cup Mayonnaise (page 14)	1 head Boston lettuce
juice of 1 lemon	salt and pepper

Flake the crabmeat so as to remove all the filaments. Chop the white part of the celery very fine and do the same thing with the red peppers. Mix the crabmeat and vegetables with mayonnaise seasoned highly with lemon juice and with curry. Season with salt and pepper.

Dip the tomatoes in boiling water and slip off the skins. Cut them crosswise in 3 parts. Spread the two lower thirds with the crab mixture. Put on the top third and fasten the parts together with a toothpick. Put a black olive on each pick.

Serve on a salad platter lined with lettuce leaves that have been washed and well dried.

Picnic tomatoes * Tomates de pique-nique

FOR SIX PEOPLE

12 medium-sized tomatoes	½ cup Vinaigrette Sauce (page 29)
1½ cups cooked green beans	2 teaspoons chopped *fines herbes*
1½ cups cooked or canned flageolets*	(tarragon, parsley)
1 hard-cooked egg	salt and pepper

Wash the tomatoes well and cut off the top quarter of each one.

Scoop out most of the flesh, taking care not to pierce the skin. Turn them upside down to drain.

Chop the green beans and mix them with the flageolots. Crush the hard-boiled egg with a fork and add it to the vinaigrette, well seasoned with salt, pepper, and chopped herbs. Mix well with the vegetables.

Fill the tomatoes with the vegetables and put back the tops.

*If flageolets are not available, use tiny lima beans.—*Ed.*

Tomato salad with green beans
Salade de tomates aux haricots verts

FOR FOUR PEOPLE

1 pound small green beans
6 medium-sized tomatoes
6 hard-cooked eggs

1 tablespoon chopped chervil or parsley
Vinaigrette Sauce (page 29)
salt

Trim and wash the beans and cook them uncovered 20 minutes in boiling salted water. Drain and cool.

Choose firm red tomatoes. Dip them in boiling water for a moment and slip off their skins. Cut in rather thick slices.

Shell and slice the eggs, using an egg slicer, if possible.

Spread the beans on a salad platter. Make little piles, alternating tomato and egg slices, and place them on the bed of beans. Sprinkle with chopped chervil or parsley and serve the vinaigrette in a separate bowl.

Turnip salad * Salade de navets

FOR FOUR PEOPLE

1 pound (3-4) turnips
4 teaspoons sugar

2½ tablespoons wine vinegar
salt

Peel the turnips and cut them as thin as possible. Put them in a dish and sprinkle with salt. Let stand 1 hour. Wash them and dry them carefully with a towel. Place in a small salad dish and sprinkle with sugar and vinegar.

Watercress, egg, and bacon salad
Salade de cresson aux oeufs et bacon

FOR EIGHT PEOPLE

1 very large bunch of watercress
8 slices bacon
6 hard-cooked eggs

¾ cup Vinaigrette Sauce (page 29)
Worcestershire sauce

Trim the watercress, discarding all the thick stems. Wash well, dry, and crisp in the refrigerator. Don't mix until just before serving or the watercress will wilt.

Cook the bacon until crisp and cut or break it into small pieces.

Shell the eggs. Reserve 2 eggs and cut the rest into thin rounds.

Make the vinaigrette, using tarragon vinegar.

Put the vinaigrette, the watercress, the eggs, and the bacon in a salad bowl. Mix well and carefully. Decorate the salad with the rounds cut from the other eggs and put a drop or two of Worcestershire sauce on each one.

Watercress salad with grapefruit and hazel nuts
Salade de cressons aux noisettes

FOR FOUR PEOPLE

1 large bunch watercress
½ cup coarsely chopped hazel nuts
juice of 1 grapefruit

4 tablespoons oil
salt and pepper

Trim and wash the watercress. Put in a salad bowl with nuts and season with a dressing made of equal parts of fresh grapefruit juice, oil, salt, and pepper. Mix well before serving.

Hot weather salad * Salade pour temps chaud

FOR SIX PEOPLE

1 escarole lettuce
1 pound lean cooked ham
½ pound Gruyère cheese
3 hard-cooked eggs

1 cucumber
1½ cups Mayonnaise (page 14)
1 tablespoon tomato purée

Trim and wash the lettuce and divide into leaves. Cut the ham and cheese into little strips. Slice the hard-cooked eggs and slice the cucumber without peeling it.

Cover a large platter with lettuce leaves and arrange the ham, cheese, egg slices, and cucumber on the leaves around a bowl containing a mixture of the mayonnaise and the tomato purée.

Zucchini mayonnaise * Courgettes mayonnaise

FOR FOUR PEOPLE

3 medium-sized zucchini
½ cup Mayonnaise (page 14)

juice of 1 lemon
salt and pepper

Wash the zucchini, trimming off the stem and base. Do not peel. Boil 25 minutes in salted water. Drain and cool.

Cut the zucchini in thin rounds and season with mayonnaise strongly flavored with lemon juice and pepper.

Desserts

Desserts

Under the title, Desserts, fall many kinds of sweets including cooked desserts, pastries, cooked fresh and dried fruits and raw fruits which we use a great deal as an end to our meals.

The modern tendency in French restaurants is to limit the choice of desserts to a few specialties of the house, but this is not the case at the family table where there is a large variety of desserts such as I give you in the following pages.

Vanilla Sugar

(available in specialty shops)

The vanilla sugar called for in many recipes is made by putting a long vanilla bean in a quart jar of sugar. The sugar absorbs the flavor of the vanilla. When some of the sugar is used, it can be replaced with more so that you can have it always on hand.

Caramel

Caramel is used for coloring sauces and for lining dessert molds.

To color a gravy: Make the caramel in a special pan reserved for that alone. Put 2 lumps or two teaspoons of sugar in a small saucepan with a teaspoon of water. Cook over high heat without stirring until the sugar turns dark brown. Then add 4 tablespoons of water and pour into the sauce.

To line a mold: Heat 4 tablespoons of sugar in a metal mold with 2 tablespoons of water. When the sugar turns light brown, tilt the pan so that the caramel covers the bottom and sides.

Custard creams

In the rich and abundant cuisine of France, custard cream holds a very important position. It is the basis or the accompaniment of a large percentage of our desserts. But it is also served by itself, in which case it is always served along with —but quite separately from—little cookies or cakes.

When custard cream is thickened with a little flour, it becomes pastry cream, which is used in tarts under fruits or in cream puffs or éclairs or in the middle of a large dessert, like a Saint-Honoré.

Custard cream is flavored in a great many ways, which keeps one from becoming tired of it.

Advice on Custard Creams:

1 Never let custard creams made with egg yolks and no flour reach the boiling point or they will separate. If this does happen, pour it through a funnel into a bottle. Cork the bottle and shake hard. If you do this immediately, you will save the custard cream.
2 Custard creams made with flour may, on the contrary, be allowed to boil. Flavor them before cooking, if you are using a flavoring without alcohol, such as coffee, chocolate, praline, and so on. Do it after cooking, if you are using Cointreau, kirsch, armagnac, cognac, or, as in America, flavoring extract.
3 Never serve a lukewarm custard cream. It ought to be hot or very cold. The only exception to this rule is the White Wine Custard Cream.
4 Custard creams can be decorated with candied cherries, sweetened coffee grains, or drops of caramel. Be sure to add something, because it makes the dessert more attractive.

Cream brûlée * Crème brûlée

FOR FOUR PEOPLE

10 tablespoons sugar	4 egg yolks
3 cups milk, scalded	

Cook the sugar and ¼ cup of water, preferably in an unlined copper saucepan, until dark brown. Stirring constantly, add the hot milk and mix well. Boil 1 minute and remove from the heat. Add the egg yolks, one by one, stirring vigorously. Strain the mixture and cool. Chill in the refrigerator.

White butter cream (frosting for certain cakes) Crème au beurre

TO FILL A CAKE FOR SIX TO EIGHT PEOPLE

4 egg whites	flavoring
1¼ cups sugar	½ pound unsalted butter

Beat the egg whites stiff and fold in the sugar. Put in a large saucepan and work with the whip over heat until well blended. Remove from the heat and continue whipping until cool. Add ½ teaspoon vanilla powder or 1 teaspoon of vanilla extract, or 2 tablespoons liqueur, or 3 tablespoons strong coffee, or 2 squares melted chocolate. Cream the butter until soft and whip it into the first mixture. Use this filling for mocha cakes.

Egg white cream * Crème aux blancs d'oeufs

FOR FOUR PEOPLE

This is an excellent way of using up extra egg whites.

10 egg whites
2 cups milk
¾ cup sugar

3 tablespoons strong coffee *or*
2 squares bittersweet chocolate
  (melted) *or*
3 tablespoons liqueur

Beat the egg whites stiff.

Scald the milk and add the sugar and whatever flavor you wish. Combine the liquid with the egg whites and cook over heat, stirring constantly until thick.

Almond custard cream * Crème aux amandes

FOR FOUR PEOPLE

1⅓ cups blanched almonds
2 cups milk
¾ cup sugar

2 egg whites
orange blossom water

Pound and rub the almonds in a mortar with a pestle, or lacking that, use a wooden pounder and bowl. Add a little water as you do it, to make a smooth almond paste.

In a bowl, combine the milk, sugar, and the unbeaten egg whites. Whisk well until thoroughly blended. Pour into a saucepan and boil down over a low heat to half its original quantity. Add the almond paste and boil 2 minutes. Flavor with a little orange blossom water. Strain through a sieve and chill in the refrigerator. Serve very cold.

Custard cream aurore * Crème aurore

FOR FOUR PEOPLE

2 cups milk
7 tablespoons sugar
4 eggs

1 jar raspberry or currant jelly
3 ounces candied cherries

Scald the milk with 3 tablespoons of sugar.

Separate the eggs. Beat the egg yolks slightly and gradually add the hot milk, stirring constantly. Put the mixture into the saucepan and stir over a low heat until the mixture thickens, but do not let the mixture boil. When the custard coats the spoon, it is ready. Remove from the heat and stir in 6 to 7 tablespoons of melted jelly. Pour into a serving dish. Cool thoroughly.

Beat the egg whites stiff, and still beating, add the sugar so that you will have a stiff meringue. Drop tablespoonfuls of the mixture into barely simmering water and poach 1 minute on each side. Drain on a towel.

Place the cooked meringue on the custard cream and decorate with candied cherries.

Chocolate butter custard * Crème prise au chocolat

FOR SIX PEOPLE

4 squares bittersweet baking chocolate   3 eggs
½ pound very soft butter   1 cup sugar

Make this dessert a day in advance.

Melt the chocolate in the top of a double boiler. Cool. Add the soft butter, little by little, beating constantly. Add the eggs, one by one, beating hard after each addition. Finally, add the sugar, which will also require long beating.

Put the mixture in a dessert bowl and chill in the refrigerator.

Chocolate custard mold
Crème renversée au chocolat

FOR SIX PEOPLE

1¼ cups sugar   4 egg yolks
1 quart milk   2 whole eggs
7 squares bittersweet chocolate

Boil the sugar and milk together.

Cut the chocolate in small pieces and melt in the top of a double boiler. Combine with the hot milk.

Beat the eggs together well, and stirring constantly, add the milk-chocolate combination gradually to the eggs.

Butter a charlotte mold or other straight-sided baking dish and strain the custard cream into it. Put in a pan of hot water deep enough so that the water comes halfway up the side of the dish but no more. Bake at 350° F. for about 45 minutes or until firm. Let the custard set in the refrigerator for several hours.

To unmold: Dip the mold in lukewarm water and turn it upside down on a serving dish.

Chocolate custard cream * Crème au chocolat

FOR TEN PEOPLE

1 quart milk
½ pound bittersweet chocolate,
  grated

6 egg yolks
1 whole egg
7 tablespoons sugar

Bring the milk to a boil. When it has reached a full, rolling boil, add the grated chocolate and bring the milk to a boil again. Beat the eggs and sugar until thick and creamy. Still beating, add the chocolate milk gradually. Pour the mixture into a saucepan and heat without boiling. There is a special way of stirring: Using a wooden spoon, criss-cross the pan from left to right instead of going round and round. As soon as you feel the sauce thicken, remove from the heat. Strain into a dessert bowl. Chill before serving.

Classic chocolate custard cream
Crème au chocolat à l'ancienne

FOR SIX PEOPLE

½ pound bittersweet baking chocolate
2 cups milk
10 tablespoons sugar

¾ cup heavy cream
8 egg yolks

Cut the chocolate in small pieces and melt in the top of a double boiler. Add the milk and bring to a boil over direct heat.

Stir the sugar, cream, and egg yolks together until thoroughly mixed. Add the boiling chocolate milk gradually, stirring constantly with a wooden spoon. Pour the mixture into individual custard cups and place them in a pan of hot water. Bake 25 minutes at 300° F. Chill before serving.

Chocolate mousse (uncooked)
Crème mousse au chocolat (sans cuisson)

FOR EIGHT PEOPLE

7 squares bittersweet baking chocolate
8 eggs

½ cup sugar

To make this *mousse,* you use neither milk nor water. Cut the chocolate into pieces and melt in an enamel double boiler.

Separate the egg yolks from the whites. Beat the egg yolks until light and add the sugar, adding more if you like. Add the chocolate as soon as it is melted.

Beat the egg whites very stiff and add them to the chocolate mixture.

Put in a serving bowl and chill in the refrigerator. This dessert will last 2 to 3 days in the refrigerator. If you like the *mousse* to be lighter, add 1 or 2 extra beaten egg whites.

Cocoa custard * Crème prise au cacao

FOR SIX PEOPLE

5 egg yolks	4 tablespoons cocoa
2 whole eggs	2 cups milk
¾ cup sugar	

Beat the eggs, sugar, and cocoa together hard and long with a whip or with an electric beater.

Scald the milk, and when it boils, add it to the egg mixture gradually, still beating. Strain the mixture into a shallow heatproof serving dish or into individual custard cups. Place them in a pan of hot water and cook either in the oven or on top of the stove. Take care that the water never really boils. Cook until the custards set or until they are no longer liquid when you touch them with your finger.

Frothy cocoa custard cream
Crème mousseuse au cacao

FOR FOUR TO FIVE PEOPLE

2 egg yolks	2 teaspoons cocoa
2½ tablespoons sugar	1½ cups scalded milk

Mix the egg yolks and sugar together and add the cocoa.

Stirring constantly, add the hot milk. Pour into the top of a double boiler and cook, stirring with a whip until the custard is thickened and frothy.

Coffee custard cream * Crème au café

FOR SIX PEOPLE

2 cups milk	5 egg yolks
1¼ cups sugar	1½ cups heavy cream
1 cup very strong coffee	

Boil the milk and sugar. Add the coffee.

Beat the egg yolks well, and still beating, add the milk and coffee combination gradually. Pour the mixture into a saucepan and stir over moderate heat until the sauce thickens. Do not let it boil.

Remove from the heat when quite thick and pour through a strainer. When it is cold, add the heavy cream. Chill in the refrigerator. This should be served icy cold but not frozen.

Instant pudding * Crème instantanée

FOR FOUR PEOPLE

This dessert is a great help when unexpected guests arrive for dinner.

3 egg whites
3 teaspoons sugar

4 tablespoons apricot jam
1 tablespoon cognac

Beat the egg whites stiff. Add the sugar, the apricot jam, and the cognac. Mix everything together well, beating a little to be sure the mixture is blended. Serve immediately. Serve small cakes or cookies with this dessert.

Kirsch custard cream * Crème au kirsch

FOR ONE PERSON

1 egg yolk
1 teaspoon kirsch

1 tablespoon sugar

For each guest to be served, allow the above proportions. Mix everything together in a bowl and beat with a whip or electric beater until frothy. Pour into individual dessert glasses and serve very cold.

Lemon caramel custard * Crème renversée au citron

FOR SIX PEOPLE

1 quart milk
grated rind of 2 lemons
6 eggs

¾ cup sugar
5 sugar lumps

Boil the milk with the rind of the lemons. Strain the milk in order to remove the lemon rind.

Beat the eggs in a bowl with the sugar until lemon-colored and creamy in texture. Add the milk gradually, stirring constantly with a wooden spoon. Skim off the froth that forms on the top. Do not let the mixture boil.

Cook the sugar lumps with 2 teaspoons of water in a charlotte mold or other straight-sided baking dish. Tilt the mold so that the caramel will reach all sides. Pour the egg mixture into the mold and place in a dish of hot water deep enough so that the water comes halfway up the sides of the mold. Bake at 300° F. about 45 minutes or until firm when you press it with your finger. Chill thoroughly before unmolding.

Lemon and white wine custard cream
Crème au citron au vin blanc

FOR SIX PEOPLE

4 lemons	1½ cups white wine
10 tablespoons sugar	12 egg yolks

Squeeze the lemons and put the juice in the top of a large enamel- or porcelain-lined double boiler. Add the sugar, white wine, and egg yolks, beaten until lemon-colored. Beat constantly over simmering water until thick. The custard is apt to thicken quickly, and because it must never boil, remove the top part from time to time, if there seems to be any danger of curdling. This dessert may be eaten lukewarm or cold. Serve in individual dessert glasses.

Marbled custard cream * Crème marbrée

FOR FOUR PEOPLE

4 egg yolks	2 cups milk
10 tablespoons sugar	½ teaspoon grated lemon rind
2½ tablespoons flour	8 sugar lumps

Beat the egg yolks, sugar, and flour together, adding the milk gradually. When well blended, cook over a moderate heat, stirring until the mixture thickens. Remove from the heat and add the lemon rind. Cool and strain into a shallow serving dish. Chill thoroughly.

Make a caramel with the sugar lumps (see page 579) and drop it here and there over the surface of the custard cream. Trace it gently with the point of a knife to give the surface a marbled appearance. Serve very cold with cookies.

Classic pineapple custard cream
Crème ancienne à l'ananas

FOR EIGHT PEOPLE

3-pound pineapple
3 pounds (6 cups) sugar

4 egg yolks

Weigh the pineapple, because traditionally one uses the same weight of pineapple as sugar. Peel the pineapple and grate it. Put the grated pineapple, sugar, and ¾ cup of water in a saucepan and boil 15 minutes.

Beat the egg yolks well and add them, stirring constantly, to the pineapple. Stir until the mixture thickens, but do not allow it to boil. Remove from the heat and cool. Serve cold.

Raspberry custard cream * Crème aux framboises

FOR FOUR PEOPLE

1½ cups raspberry juice
¾ cup milk
5 egg yolks

½ cup sugar
3 egg whites

Force enough raspberries through a fine sieve to give the 1½ cups of juice. Heat the juice and the milk in separate saucepans. Beat the egg yolks and sugar until light and creamy. Add the hot raspberry juice and then the milk, beating constantly. Cook in a double boiler until thickened. Do not let it boil. Remove from the heat and cool to lukewarm.

Beat the egg whites stiff and fold them into the custard cream. Chill in the refrigerator and serve very cold.

Strawberry custard cream * Crème aux fraises

FOR SIX PEOPLE

1 quart milk
1¼ cups sugar
1 vanilla bean
8 egg yolks

1½ pints wild strawberries or
　　small cultivated berries
1 pint large strawberries

Bring the milk and 1 cup of sugar and the vanilla bean to a boil. Cut the bean lengthwise to release as much flavor as possible. (If a vanilla bean is not available, add 1 teaspoon vanilla extract at the end of the cooking.—*Ed.*)

Beat the egg yolks well and add the hot milk gradually, beating constantly. Cook the mixture over a low heat, stirring until it thickens. Do not let the mixture boil. Remove from the heat. Cool.

Crush the small berries until they are a liquid purée. Add the rest of the sugar and mix with the cool custard cream. Pour the mixture into a dessert bowl and chill in the refrigerator. Before serving, garnish with the large berries.

Tea custard cream * Crème au thé

FOR FOUR PEOPLE

1 pint heavy cream	½ cup sugar
½ cup very strong tea	3 egg yolks

Scald the cream over low heat until it has reduced a bit in quantity. Remove from the heat and stir in the tea, the sugar, and finally the egg yolks, beating constantly. Continue beating a few moments and then strain the mixture through a cheesecloth-lined strainer. Pour into individual custard cups and put them in a pan of hot water. Cook on top of the stove until the custard is set. Do not cook in the oven.

Vanilla custard cream * Crème à la vanille

FOR FOUR PEOPLE (TWO CUPS)

1 pint milk	1 vanilla bean
½ cup sugar	4 egg yolks

Scald the milk and sugar with the vanilla bean cut in half so that all the flavor will be released. (If no vanilla bean is available, add 1 teaspoon of vanilla extract at the end of the cooking.—Ed.)

Beat the egg with a wooden spoon. Remove the vanilla bean and slowly add the hot milk to the eggs, stirring constantly. Pour the mixture into a saucepan and stir over very low heat until the mixture thickens. Do not let the mixture boil. Serve cold.

White wine custard cream * Crème au vin blanc

FOR TWO PEOPLE

3 egg yolks	6 tablespoons sugar
1 whole egg	1 tablespoon potato flour
1 cup white wine	1 vanilla bean

Put the egg yolks and whole egg into a bowl and gradually add the white wine, the sugar, and the potato flour blended with a little cold water, stirring constantly and vigorously. When well blended, put the mixture in a saucepan with a small vanilla bean and cook over a very low heat, stirring constantly until the mixture thickens. Do not let it boil. Remove the vanilla bean (or lacking a vanilla bean, add a teaspoon of vanilla extract at this point—*Ed.*). Pour into a dessert dish and serve lukewarm with cookies.

Pastry cream ✳ *Crème pâtissière*

FOR FOUR PEOPLE

4 egg yolks	2 cups milk
2½ tablespoons flour	flavoring (see below)
10 tablespoons sugar	

Combine the egg yolks, flour, and sugar in a bowl. Mix in the cold milk and whisk until smooth. Strain into a saucepan. Add the flavoring: ½ teaspoon grated lemon rind, or 1 teaspoon vanilla powder (if not available, add 1 tablespoon vanilla extract at the end of cooking—*Ed.*), or 3 ounces cooled, melted bitter-sweet chocolate, or 3 tablespoons liqueur, or 2 tablespoons instant coffee. Stir over moderate heat until the mixture thickens. This mixture can boil because it contains flour. Let it thicken according to what use you intend to put it to. Eaten by itself, as a custard cream, it should not be as thick as when you use it to fill éclairs or cream puffs.

Alsatian apples ✳ *Pommes à l'alsacienne*

FOR SIX PEOPLE

2 pounds apples	2½ tablespoons flour
14 tablespoons butter	2 cups milk
1½ cups sugar	2 egg yolks

Peel the apples, core them, and cut in thin slices.

Melt 10 tablespoons of butter in a heavy skillet and cook the apples in the butter until almost tender. They should be pale pink and transparent. Sprinkle with 1 cup of sugar and cook until the sugar caramelizes lightly. Remove from the heat and transfer the apples to a heatproof serving dish.

Heat the rest of the butter and stir in the flour. Add the milk and stir until you have a fairly thin sauce. Add the rest of the sugar. Remove from the heat and cool to lukewarm. Stir in the egg yolks and spread the sauce over the apples. Bake 30 minutes at 400° F. Serve hot.

Sabayon cream * Crème sabayon

FOR TWELVE PEOPLE

2½ cups sugar
12 egg yolks

4 cups dry white wine
½ cup cognac, armagnac, or kirsch

Beat the sugar and egg yolks together. Beat the mixture hard and long or until lemon-colored and creamy. Add the white wine and continue beating. Cook over simmering water in a large enamel- or porcelain-lined double boiler, beating constantly until thick. It will triple in quantity. Never let the mixture boil. Add the liqueur.

Serve warm or ice cold in individual dessert glasses. You can substitute port, marsala, or sherry for the white wine.

Velvet cream * Crème velours

FOR SIX PEOPLE

1 quart milk
20 sugar lumps
6 egg yolks
1 teaspoon potato flour

5 tablespoons ground hazel nuts
5 tablespoons cocoa
5 tablespoons instant coffee

Scald the milk with half the sugar. Make a caramel with the other half. See page 579. Combine the caramel and milk.

Mix the egg yolks and potato flour and add the warm milk gradually. Cook the mixture over very low heat until it thickens. Do not let it boil. Remove from the heat. Combine the nuts, cocoa, and coffee and add to the custard cream. Mix well and chill in the refrigerator.

Apple delight * Pommes délice

FOR FIVE PEOPLE

5 very large apples
1¾ cups sugar
5 tablespoons flour
3 egg yolks
2 cups milk

2 tablespoons macaroon crumbs
grated rind of ½ lemon
raspberry jelly
1 egg white, beaten stiff

Peel and core the apples but leave them whole.

Make a syrup in a saucepan with 1 cup of sugar and 1 cup of water. Put in the apples and poach over a low heat for about 10 minutes.

In a small bowl mix the flour, the egg yolks, the rest of the sugar, and the milk. Stir over moderate heat until the mixture boils a few moments. Remove the custard cream from the heat and cool thoroughly. Add the macaroon crumbs and the grated rind of ½ lemon.

In the bottom of an ovenproof serving dish, put a layer of the custard cream. Arrange the apples on the custard cream and fill the center of each apple with raspberry jelly. Fold the beaten egg white into the rest of the custard cream and cover the apples with the mixture. Bake at 350° F. for about ½ hour.

Flambéed apples * Pommes flambées

FOR FOUR PEOPLE

8 apples
1¼ cups sugar

½ jar currant jelly
½ cup cognac

Peel and core the apples, leaving them whole. Put them in a saucepan with 1 cup of water and ¼ cup of sugar. Cover and simmer for about 25 minutes, the time depending on the variety and quality of the apples. They should be just tender but not soft.

Transfer the apples to a heatproof platter and fill the centers with currant jelly.

Boil the rest of the sugar with ¾ cup of water until you have a thick syrup. Add the cognac and pour it over the apples. Touch with a lighted match and serve immediately.

Apple fritters * Beignets de pommes

FOR FOUR PEOPLE

1¼ cups sifted all-purpose flour
2 egg yolks
pinch of salt
¾ cup beer

1 teaspoon Calvados
4 large apples
sugar

Make the batter several hours in advance. Put the flour in a bowl and make a well in the center. In the well, put the egg yolks and a pinch of salt, the beer, and the Calvados. Stir with a wooden spoon until you have a smooth, fairly thick batter. Cover and let rest.

Peel 4 large apples, preferably pippins, and core them with an apple corer. Cut them across in thin slices. Dip them in batter separately and fry in deep fat (370° F. to 380° F.). When they are golden brown, drain them on paper toweling and serve on a napkin-lined serving platter. Sprinkle with sugar.

N. B. If you want to vary this recipe, use Frying Batter I—given to me by Dr. de Pomiane.

Apple dessert with apricot sauce
Entremets aux pommes, sauce abricots

FOR TWELVE PEOPLE

7 pounds apples
1 pound butter
1 cup sugar

1 quart Vanilla Custard Cream
    (page 588)
3 tablespoons apricot brandy

Peel and core the apples and cut them in thin slices.

Put the apple slices in a large skillet with all but 2 tablespoons of the butter and the sugar. Cook uncovered over moderate heat until the apple slices become transparent. Remove from the heat and cool to lukewarm. Pack the apples into a a well-buttered ring or charlotte mold and press them down well. Chill in the refrigerator overnight.

Make a double recipe of the vanilla custard cream and flavor with the apricot brandy. Cool.

Unmold the apples onto a platter and cover with the custard cream.

Apples bonne femme * Pommes bonne femme

FOR FOUR PEOPLE

8 medium-sized apples
⅔ cup sugar

3 tablespoons butter
currant jelly

Peel the apples, leaving them whole. Core them with an apple corer.

Cream the sugar and butter together with a knife blade, and when well mixed, fill the center of each apple with the mixture. Put a little water in the bottom of a baking dish. Make a slight incision around each apple so that they won't burst and place them in the pan. Cook at 400° F. for about 1 hour or until tender. Serve with currant jelly.

Apples with lemon cream
Pommes du rouergue a la crème de citron

FOR FOUR PEOPLE

½ pound (48) sugar lumps
8 medium-sized apples
1 cup milk
2 egg yolks
¾ cup sugar

8 teaspoons flour
grated rind of 1 lemon
1½ tablespoons butter
2 egg whites, beaten stiff

Prepare a syrup by boiling the sugar lumps and ½ cup water for 10 minutes in a saucepan just large enough to hold the apples. Do not cover the pan.

Peel the apples, leaving them whole. Poach in the syrup for 5 minutes or just until they are tender. Some varieties of apples require more time than others, but make sure that they are *just* cooked and no more, or they will crush.

Remove from the syrup and drain. When cool enough to handle, cut a thick slice off the top and save carefully on a plate.

Gently scoop out the core and seeds from each apple, but do not pierce the outside.

Make a pastry cream by scalding the milk. At the same time, in a small saucepan beat the egg yolks and half the sugar thoroughly with a whip and add the flour and lemon rind. Put the pan over moderate heat and add the hot milk, stirring constantly. As soon as the boiling point is reached, remove from the fire and cool thoroughly. Fill the apples with the pastry cream and cover with the reserved slices. Place the apples in a well-buttered baking dish. Cover with a meringue made of the beaten egg whites mixed gently with the rest of the sugar. Bake 30 minutes at 275° F. Serve warm.

Apples with raisins
Pommes aux raisins de corinthe

FOR SIX PEOPLE

½ cup seedless raisins
6 large apples
¼ cup sugar

butter
½ cup white wine

Soak the raisins 1 hour in lukewarm water.

Do not peel the apples. Wash and core them with an apple corer. Place the apples in a buttered baking dish. Fill the centers with well-drained raisins. Sprinkle lightly with sugar, dot with butter, and pour the wine into the bottom of the dish. Bake about 25 minutes at 400° F. Serve warm or cold in the dish in which the apples are cooked.

Saint christopher apples
Pommes saint-christophe

FOR SIX PEOPLE

3 pounds apples
8-10 sugar lumps

⅔ cup sugar
1 jar apricot jam

Peel the apples and cut them in thin slices.

Heat the sugar lumps and 1 tablespoon of water in a charlotte mold or other straight-sided metal baking dish until dark brown. Tilt the mold so that the caramel covers all of the interior. Put in a layer of apples and sprinkle with sugar. Continue doing this until the mold is full. Pack them down well.

Place the mold in a pan of hot water and bake 3 hours at 400° F. Cool to lukewarm and unmold onto a serving dish. Cover with apricot jam.

Apricot bananas * Bananes aux abricots

FOR SIX PEOPLE

12 small bananas	1½ cups heavy cream, whipped
⅓ cup apricot jam	½ cup sugar
4½ tablespoons kirsch	

Choose bananas of equal size. Peel off a third of the skin lengthwise and remove the banana flesh. Crush it and mix with the apricot jam and the kirsch. Fill the banana shells with the mixture and cover them with the sweetened whipped cream. Chill in the refrigerator.

Banana cream * Crème de bananes

FOR FOUR PEOPLE

This is quickly and simply made and is particularly delicious.

4 bananas	5 tablespoons sugar
1 package (3 ounces) cream cheese	5 tablespoons currant jam
2 tablespoons cream	chopped almonds

Crush ripe bananas with a fork until smooth. Add the cream cheese blended with the cream. Mix well and add the sugar. Mix again and spread on a small serving dish. Cover with the jam and sprinkle with almonds. Serve very cold.

Chocolate bananas * Bananes au chocolat

FOR FOUR PEOPLE

4 bananas	1 cup extra heavy cream
¾ cup sugar	2 ounces bittersweet baking chocolate
4 teaspoons liqueur (kirsch, cointreau, and so on)	

Cut the bananas in thin rounds into a shallow dessert platter.

Make a syrup by heating the sugar with 2 tablespoons of water in a heavy saucepan and adding whatever liqueur you choose.

Pour the syrup over the banana slices. Spread the heavy cream over the top and sprinkle liberally with the finely grated chocolate. Chill in the refrigerator and serve very cold.

Banana diplomat * Diplomate aux bananes

FOR SIX PEOPLE

4 tablespoons yellow raisins
10 ounces lady fingers
3 cups milk
½ cup rum

6 bananas
6 tablespoons sugar
3 egg yolks

Soak the raisins 2 hours in lukewarm water. Drain well.

Dip the lady fingers for a moment in a mixture of 1 cup of milk and ½ cup of rum. Line the bottom and the sides of a charlotte mold or other straight-sided baking dish with the lady fingers.

Peel and cut the bananas into rounds and place a layer of them on the bottom layer of lady fingers. Sprinkle with some of the raisins and cover with a layer of moistened lady fingers. Continue this alternation, finishing with a layer of lady fingers.

Boil the rest of the milk with the sugar. Beat the egg yolks in a bowl with a fork. Gradually add the hot milk, stirring constantly with a wooden spoon. Pour the mixture into the mold and let stand 30 minutes. Place the mold in a pan of hot water.

Bake 45 minutes at 350° F. Cool to lukewarm before unmolding.

Flambéed bananas * Bananes flambées

FOR EIGHT PEOPLE

12 bananas
10 tablespoons butter

½ cup sugar
6 tablespoons rum

Peel the bananas. Cut them in half lengthwise.

Melt the butter in a skillet and add the bananas. Sauté 2 minutes. Turn the bananas and sprinkle with the sugar. When the sugar has melted, add the rum and touch with a lighted match. Serve immediately.

N.B. This can be effectively cooked in a chafing dish in the dining room.

Banana fritters * Beignets de bananes

FOR FOUR PEOPLE

1 cup sifted all-purpose flour	4 teaspoons rum
¾ cup beer	1 egg white, beaten stiff
pinch of salt	4 bananas
4 teaspoons sugar	confectioner's sugar
1 tablespoon oil	

Make a batter by combining the flour, beer, salt, and sugar. This should have the consistency of cream. Add the oil and rum and let the mixture stand several hours. Just before using, stir in the beaten egg white.

Peel the bananas and cut them across in half. Dip them lightly in the batter and fry them in deep fat at 380° F. When they are golden brown, remove them from the fat and drain on paper toweling. Serve quickly, covered with confectioner's sugar.

Small banana soufflés * Petits soufflés aux bananes

FOR FIVE PEOPLE

Pastry Cream:

1 egg yolk	5 bananas
1 teaspoon flour	1 egg
3 tablespoons milk	2 tablespoons Vanilla Sugar (page 579)
2 tablespoons sugar	

Make the pastry cream by combining the egg yolk, flour, milk, and sugar in a small bowl and stir (without beating) the combination until blended. Put the mixture into a saucepan and stir constantly over moderate heat until it has boiled a few seconds and coats the spoon. Do not let the mixture scorch. Remove from the heat and cool.

Choose bananas that are rather large and not overripe. Cut them in half lengthwise. Remove the flesh, but save the skins and place them on a baking sheet. Force the flesh through a strainer.

Separate the yolk from the white of the egg. Stir the egg yolk into the bananas along with the cold pastry cream and the vanilla sugar. Finally, fold in the egg white, beaten stiff.

Fill the skins with the mixture and bake 10 minutes at 350° F. Serve immediately.

Cherry charlotte * Charlotte aux cerises

FOR SIX PEOPLE

18 lady fingers	10 tablespoons sugar

kirsch
2 pounds cherries

Vanilla Custard Cream (page 588)

Dip the lady fingers in kirsch; they must be thoroughly moistened. Drain them.

Cook the pitted cherries with the sugar and just a little water to make a thick compote. If there is too much syrup, pour off some of it.

Butter a long baking dish or loaf tin. Put in a layer of lady fingers and cover with the cherry compote. Cover that with another layer of lady fingers and bake 30 minutes at 350° F. Remove from the oven and cool.

Meanwhile, make the vanilla custard cream and cool.

Unmold the charlotte onto a serving platter and cover with the custard cream. Serve very cold.

Auvergne cherry flan
Clafoutis comme en auvergne

FOR FOUR PEOPLE

2½ cups sifted pastry flour
3 eggs, separated
pinch of salt
milk or water

1 tablespoon armagnac
6 tablespoons sugar
1 pound black cherries
butter

Put the flour into a bowl. Make a hole in the center and in it put the egg yolks and a pinch of salt. Stir well, adding enough milk or water to give a consistency of light cream. Add the armagnac. Beat the egg whites, adding the sugar gradually. Fold them into the first mixture and add the unpitted cherries.

Butter a deep pie tin and pour in the mixture. Sprinkle the surface with bits of butter and bake at 300° F. for 30 to 45 minutes.

Cherry meringue * Cerises meringuées

FOR FOUR PEOPLE

2 pounds cherries
1½ cups sugar

2 egg whites

Remove the stems and stones from the cherries and cook with 1 cup sugar and 1½ cups water. Cook until the syrup is thick but not so long that the cherries will lose their shape.

Place the compote in a heatproof serving dish.

Beat the egg whites stiff and add ¼ cup of the sugar gradually, beating until you have a glossy meringue. Spread the meringue over the cherries. Sprinkle with the rest of the sugar and bake at 375° F. just until lightly browned. Serve immediately.

Currants mont blanc * Groseilles en mont-blanc

FOR SIX PEOPLE

2 pints red and white currants   1 cup milk
1 pound pot or cottage cheese   1 cup sugar

Wash and stem the currants and put them in a serving dish.

Beat the cheese with the milk and add the sugar. (A blender is excellent for this operation.—*Ed.*) Mix them with the currants and serve very cold.

Pearly currants * Groseilles perlées

FOR FIVE PEOPLE

1 pint white currants   1 cup extra fine sugar
2 cups sugar

Stem currants. Dip them in a syrup made of 1 cup of sugar and 1 cup of water boiled 5 minutes and cooled to lukewarm.

With a slotted spoon transfer the currants to a surface spread with very fine granulated sugar. Roll the currants in sugar and place them on a sheet of white paper. Spread them around so that the currants do not touch each other. Place them in the sun or in a very slow oven to dry. The sugar will crystallize and the currants will become pretty little pearls with a delicious flavor. These should be eaten soon.

Grape flan * Clafoutis aux raisins

FOR FIVE PEOPLE

1 large bunch grapes   3 eggs
¾ cup sugar   6 tablespoons soft butter
2½ cups sifted pastry flour   1 cup milk

Stem the grapes and put them in a saucepan with 4 tablespoons of sugar and 1½ tablespoons of water. Cover and simmer 10 minutes.

In a bowl mix the flour, eggs, soft butter, and the rest of the sugar. Add the milk and stir until you have a smooth batter. Add the poached grapes. Put into a buttered shallow baking dish and bake 40 minutes at 400° F. If the top browns too quickly, cover with heavy waxed or brown paper. Serve warm or cold.

Cold lemon mousse * Mousse froide au citron

FOR FOUR PEOPLE

5 egg yolks
¾ cup sugar
juice of 2 lemons

5 egg whites, beaten stiff
currant jelly

Beat the egg yolks with the sugar until light and lemon-colored. Add the juice of 2 lemons and mix well. Stir over hot water in the top of a double boiler until thick. Remove from the heat and fold in the egg whites. Pour into a serving dish and chill in the refrigerator. Decorate with currant jelly.

Lemon soufflé * Soufflé au citron

FOR FOUR PEOPLE

8 sugar lumps
1 large juicy lemon
6 tablespoons hot milk
1 heaping tablespoon flour
2 scant tablespoons butter

pinch of salt
2 egg yolks
4 teaspoons finely chopped orange peel
4 teaspoons finely chopped lemon peel
2 egg whites, beaten stiff

Rub the sugar lumps hard against the outside of a lemon so that they will be well flavored with the essence of the lemon rind. Stir the sugar in the milk until it dissolves. Peel the lemon and chop the lemon rind very fine.

Put the flour in a small saucepan and stir in the milk with a wooden spoon until the lumps disappear. Put the pan over low heat and add the butter, stirring constantly. When you have a thick smooth sauce, add a pinch of salt and remove from the heat.

Beat in the egg yolks, one at a time. Add the orange and lemon rind and finally fold in the stiffly beaten egg whites.

Pour into a well-buttered charlotte or soufflé dish. Bake at 350° F. for about 30 minutes. Serve as soon as it comes from the oven. A soufflé cannot wait.

Melon

Is melon a fruit or is it a vegetable? It is good eaten salted or sugared, enjoyable in a salad or in a dessert. It is, in all cases, delectable, soothing, and refreshing.

Melon had its origin in Africa and Asia. It was first cultivated in Italy. We in France owe its culture to King Charles VIII, who brought it back from one of his transalpine adventures and had it grown in Languedoc in the lands of the Counts of Toulouse. From then on it was celebrated as part of noble and imperial menus.

Nowadays, it is available to everyone. Melons are grown in large quantities and have a long season, from late spring to late autumn.

Advice about melon:

1 When you buy it, weigh it; it should be heavy.
2 The end opposite to the stem should be slightly tender.
3 The stem should be easily removed and the skin around it crackled.
4 The melon should smell good, even through the skin.
5 The melon should be served cold, but never put ice on the flesh of the fruit or it will lose its flavor.
6 If you plan to serve the melon just in slices, put sugar, salt, and pepper on the table. Some like melon salted, and some prefer it sugared.
7 Some people like lemon on melon, so be prepared for this also.
8 The custom is to drink red wine after eating melon.

(The melon referred to above are the nettled variety, such as cantaloupe and black jack.—*Ed.*)

Ginger melon * *Melon au gingembre*

FOR FOUR PEOPLE

1 melon	1 tablespoon ginger
4 tablespoons sugar	4 fresh mint leaves

Cut a melon in 4 slices.

In a bowl mix the sugar and ginger and sprinkle each melon slice with the mixture. Decorate each one with a mint leaf and chill in the refrigerator before serving.

You can increase or decrease the amount of sugar ginger you use, but always keep the same proportions.

Meringued melon * *Melon meringué*

FOR FOUR PEOPLE

2 medium-sized melons	6 tablespoons maraschino or cointreau
½ pint raspberries	2 egg whites
4 large peaches	2 tablespoons sugar

Cut the melons in half and remove the seeds and filaments.

Put the raspberries and the peaches, which have been peeled and sliced, into the melon halves. Sprinkle with the liqueur of your choice. Put in the refrigerator for 1 hour.

Preheat the oven to 450°F.

Beat the egg whites stiff, adding the sugar gradually. Put a 2-inch topping of meringue on each melon half. Lightly brown the meringue, but don't keep it in the oven longer than necessary, and never over 5 minutes. Serve the melon warm or cold.

Melons with port * Melons au porto

FOR FOUR PEOPLE

2 medium-small melons
4 tablespoons sugar

1½ cups port

Cut the melons in half and remove the seeds and filaments. Sprinkle each one with a tablespoon of sugar and 6 tablespoons of port. Chill in the refrigerator for an hour and serve at the beginning of a meal.

Melon with wild strawberries
Melon aux fraises des bois

FOR FOUR PEOPLE

1 melon
½ cup powdered sugar

½ pint wild or small strawberries
3 tablespoons kirsch

From the stem end of the melon cut off a ¾-inch top. Through this opening scoop out the seeds and the filaments. Then, with a spoon, carefully scoop out the flesh without piercing the skin. Cut the flesh in large dice.

Sprinkle the interior with the powdered sugar. Alternate layers of strawberries and melon inside the melon. When filled, sprinkle with the kirsch and put back the cover. In order to seal the melon tight, twist it in a cheesecloth. Let stand in the refrigerator at least 2 hours before serving.

Baked oranges * Oranges au four

FOR TWO PEOPLE

2 oranges
4 teaspoons sugar

1 tablespoon butter
4 teaspoons Cointreau

Cut the oranges in half. Remove as much of the seeds and white center filaments as possible. Sprinkle each half with a teaspoon of sugar.

Melt the butter and brush each orange half with it. Bake at 400° F. just until the oranges are lightly browned. Serve hot; spoon a teaspoon of Cointreau over each one.

Chantilly oranges * Oranges chantilly

FOR FOUR PEOPLE

4 oranges	1½ tablespoons maraschino
¾ cup heavy cream	4 tablespoons chopped walnuts
4 tablespoons sugar	2½ tablespoons orange juice

Cut off carefully the top third of 4 large oranges. Scoop out the flesh from the fruit without piercing the skin. Save the juice and the pulp. Cut the pulp, free of seeds or filaments, into small pieces.

Whip the cream and mix in the sugar, the maraschino, the orange pieces, the walnut meats, and 2½ tablespoons of orange juice. Mix well and fill the orange shells with the mixture. If possible, decorate the top with orange leaves. Chill thoroughly in the refrigerator.

Orange on pineapple * Oranges à l'ananas

FOR SIX PEOPLE

1 can pineapple	6 seedless oranges

Arrange 6 slices of pineapple on a serving platter. Boil down the syrup until it is quite thick.

Meanwhile, peel the outer skin of the rind of 1 orange and cut it into very thin strips. Boil 5 minutes and drain.

Peel all the oranges, very carefully removing all the white filaments. Place an orange on each slice of pineapple. Spoon the syrup over each orange and sprinkle with the orange peel. Chill thoroughly in the refrigerator.

Orange surprise * Oranges surprise

FOR FOUR PEOPLE

1 apple	1 bunch black grapes
2 bananas	2 tablespoons hazel nuts
juice of 1 lemon	2 tablespoons sugar
4 large oranges	4 teaspoons cognac

Peel the apple and bananas and cut them in small dice. Sprinkle with lemon juice to keep them from darkening.

Cut off the top third of each orange. Scoop out the flesh of the oranges into a strainer in order to get the juice.

Remove the grapes from the stem. Combine them with the apple and bananas. Mix with the nuts, the sugar, a little of the orange juice, and the cognac. Fill the oranges with the mixture. Put on the covers and chill in the refrigerator.

Provençale peaches * Pêches à la provençale

FOR SIX PEOPLE

6 large peaches	12 fresh ripe figs
4 cups sugar	1½ cups heavy cream, whipped
½ cup Vanilla Sugar (page 579)	1 cup wild or small strawberries
4 cups water	2 tablespoons slivered almonds
4½ tablespoons kirsch	

Dip the peaches in boiling water and slip off the skins.

Bring 3½ cups sugar, ½ cup vanilla sugar, and 4 cups of water to a boil. Reduce the heat and simmer the peaches in the syrup for 20 minutes. Remove the peaches to a shallow serving dish and sprinkle with 3 tablespoons of the kirsch.

Peel the figs and force the pulp through a strainer or *moulinette*. Cook in a saucepan with ½ cup of sugar for 5 to 8 minutes over a high heat, stirring with a wooden spoon until quite thick. Cool and add the rest of the kirsch and the whipped cream.

Cover the peaches with the fig cream and sprinkle the surface with wild strawberries and slivered almonds. Chill in the refrigerator before serving.

(Because fresh figs are often hard to find in the market, you can substitute fig jam for the cooked fresh figs.—*Ed.*)

Pears

Pears were known by the Greeks in the Golden Age. Brought by Pyrrhus to Italy, Cato the Elder knew six varieties of the fruit, and Pliny accounted for 41.

In France (as in America), fresh pears are to be had almost the entire year, from July to May. Naturally, there are different varieties at different seasons of the year, and in some seasons there are several varieties available. They differ in texture of the flesh as well as in the color of the skin, and they certainly differ in flavor.

When you test a pear to see if it is ripe, take care to press the skin at the stalk end. If you touch the pear elsewhere, it will spot and spoil the fruit.

You can easily use overripe pears for pear sauce.

A pear is very thirst-quenching, which accounts for the old expression, "Keep a pear for thirst." Another proverb, "Peel a pear for your friend, and a peach for your enemy," means that it is better not to eat the skin of this excellent fruit.

Pears barbotton * Barbotton de poires

FOR FIVE PEOPLE

2 pounds pears
1 quart sweet white wine

¾ cup sugar
currant jelly

Peel the pears and cut them in slices. Put them in a deep serving bowl and cover with white wine. Sprinkle with sugar and chill in the refrigerator for several hours. Before serving, cover the top with currant jelly.

Pears bourdaloue * Poires bourdaloue

FOR FOUR PEOPLE

4 large firm pears
1½ cups sugar
1¼ cups milk
1 vanilla bean

4 egg yolks
2 tablespoons flour
2 tablespoons toasted almonds, ground

Peel and quarter the pears and remove the seeds. Bring ¾ cup of water and half the sugar to a boil and poach the pears in the syrup over low heat for 15 minutes.

Meanwhile, bring the milk to a boil with the rest of the sugar and the vanilla bean. Mix the egg yolks and the flour. Remove the milk from the heat and pour into the egg mixture slowly, beating constantly. Put back over a moderate heat and cook, stirring constantly, for 5 to 7 minutes or until the mixture thickens. Remove the vanilla bean (or add 1 teaspoon of vanilla extract—Ed.).

Pour into a shallow serving dish and cool. Place the cooked pears on the sauce and sprinkle with ground almonds. Serve very cold.

Burgundy pears * Poires bourguignonne

FOR FIVE PEOPLE

2 pounds small pears
1½ cups sugar

1 teaspoon cinnamon
1 cup red Burgundy

Peel the pears but keep them whole. Put them in a saucepan with the sugar, ¾ cup of water, and cinnamon and simmer, covered, for 15 minutes. Add the wine and simmer 15 minutes longer, but this time without a cover.

Put the pears in a shallow serving dish. Boil down the juice until it has the consistency of a light syrup. Pour the syrup over the pears and chill in the refrigerator. This dessert must be served very cool.

*Pears au gratin * Gratin de poires*

FOR FIVE PEOPLE

6 tablespoons yellow raisins
3 pounds pears
¾ cup sugar

1 tablespoon grated lemon rind
½ cup fine breadcrumbs

Soak the raisins 1 hour in lukewarm water.

Peel the pears and cut them in quarters, removing the cores and seeds. Put them in a saucepan with ½ cup sugar, the grated lemon peel, and 4 tablespoons of water. Cover and simmer 30 minutes.

Force the pears through a strainer and combine them with the well-drained raisins.

Put the mixture in a shallow buttered baking dish. Sprinkle the top with the breadcrumbs and the rest of the sugar and bake 10 minutes at 450° F. so that the sugar will caramelize. Serve hot or cold.

*Pears à l'impératrice * Poires à l'impératrice*

FOR FOUR PEOPLE

1 cup rice
2 cups milk
1 vanilla bean
1⅔ cups sugar
2 egg yolks

¾ cup heavy cream
4 large pears
juice of 1 lemon
pinch of salt

Boil the rice for 2 minutes in water.

Boil the milk with a pinch of salt and a vanilla bean cut lengthwise. (If the bean is not available, add 1 tablespoon of vanilla extract at the end of the cooking.—*Ed.*)

Drain the rice and pour it into the milk. Reduce the heat and cook uncovered over a very slow heat for 15 minutes or until the rice is cooked. Remove from the heat and stir in ⅔ cup of sugar and the egg yolks. Mix carefully. Cool thoroughly.

Whip the cream and stir into the rice. Use a fork while stirring so as not to crush the grains of rice.

Make a syrup by boiling 1 cup of sugar with 1 cup of water. Reduce the heat and simmer the pears whole or in halves just until tender.

Put the rice mixture in a serving dish and arrange the pears on the rice. Pour over the syrup, to which you will have added a little lemon juice.

Meringued pears * Poires meringuées

FOR SIX PEOPLE

This can be made equally well with apples and pears. It is good for using fruit too bruised to be eaten at table and the whites of eggs left over from making a custard or a sauce.

4 pounds pears	4 egg whites
½ cup sugar	

Peel carefully and core the pears. Cut them in pieces and cook in a saucepan with ¾ cup of water and 4 tablespoons sugar. (You would use more sugar for apples.) As the pears cook, crush them with a fork to make a thick sauce like applesauce.

Put the pear sauce in an ovenproof serving dish. Cover with a meringue made of the beaten egg whites, into which 4 tablespoons of sugar have been gently folded. Bake at 300° F. for 1 hour. Serve hot or lukewarm.

Pear and prune compote
Compote de poires et pruneaux

FOR FOUR PEOPLE

1 pound prunes	½ cup sugar
2 cups strong tea	1 vanilla bean
4 large pears	½ teaspoon cinnamon
1 lemon	

Soak the prunes overnight in strong tea.

Peel the pears and rub the outside immediately with lemon so that they will not darken. Make a syrup by boiling the sugar with 2 cups of water and a vanilla bean, if available, cut lengthwise, to permit as much of the flavor to get into the syrup as possible. (If not available, add 1½ teaspoons of vanilla extract at the end of the cooking.—*Ed.*) Add the cinnamon. Poach the pears just until they are tender when tested with a fork.

Cook the prunes 5 minutes in boiling water.

Put the pears in the middle of a serving dish with the syrup. Surround with the prunes and chill in the refrigerator. Serve very cool, accompanied by macaroons.

Pineapple with rum * *Ananas au rhum*

FOR SIX PEOPLE

1 very ripe pineapple
rum
3 egg yolks

12 tablespoons butter
4 tablespoons sugar
4 tablespoons toasted almonds, ground

Peel the pineapple and cut into thin slices. Soak 1 hour in ½ cup of rum.
Meanwhile, make the sauce:

In the top of a double boiler, stir the egg yolks with the butter over simmering water until blended. Add the sugar and 4 tablespoons of rum and continue to stir until the sauce begins to thicken and to coat the spatula. Remove from the heat.

Drain the pineapple slices and arrange them on a long serving platter. Pour the sauce over the pineapple. Sprinkle with the almonds. Chill in the refrigerator.

Pineapple surprise * *Ananas surprise*

FOR SIX PEOPLE

1 grapefruit
2 oranges
2 apples
1 pineapple

6 ounces candied cherries
½ cup maraschino liqueur
½ cup sugar

Peel the grapefruit and oranges carefully, removing all the white inner skin and filaments. Divide the fruits in sections and cut each section in half.

Peel the apples and cut them in average size dice.

Cut off the top fifth of a ripe pineapple and set the top aside, with its leaves, for future use. Scoop out the interior, leaving a ⅛-inch-thick shell. Cut the pineapple flesh into ¾-inch cubes.

Put all the prepared fruit and the candied cherries into a bowl and sprinkle with the maraschino and the sugar. Stir and let stand 10 minutes. Fill the pineapple shell. Cover with the top part of the pineapple and chill in the refrigerator.

The pineapple is placed in the center of the table for dessert. Each person helps himself by spearing the fruit with a toothpick.

Plums

The plum has a Caucasian origin. It came to France via Syria and Italy. The queen of plums is unquestionably the Reine-Claude or greengage. It owes its

French name to Queen Claude, daughter of King Louis XII and wife of François I.

The greengage, like all other plums, are only good when fully ripe, and these are difficult to find in the market. If plums are eaten half ripe, they are bitter and tart.

If you want to make compotes with unripe plums, you will waste your sugar because the result will be mediocre. The *quetches,* from which the famous liqueur is made, are best eaten cooked and are especially good when served well sweetened and with heavy cream. The American damson plum is perhaps the nearest approach to the *quetch.*

Plum flan * Flan aux prunes

FOR FOUR PEOPLE

2 pounds plums	3 eggs
¾ cup sugar	2 cups milk
2 cups sifted pastry flour	

Choose pale purple plums that are ripe but not overripe. Wash them, halve them, and remove the stones. Put them in a saucepan with ¼ cup of sugar and 1½ tablespoons of water and cook very gently for 10 minutes.

Put the flour in a bowl. Add the rest of the sugar and the whole eggs. Mix well and add the milk gradually, stirring constantly until thickened.

Put the plums in a shallow buttered baking dish. Pour the batter over the plums and bake about 40 minutes at 400° F. Serve warm or cold.

Almond stuffed plum fritters
Beignets de reines-claude

FOR FOUR PEOPLE

Frying Batter:

1¼ cups sifted all-purpose flour	2 pounds greengage plums
1 egg yolk	½ cup sugar
¾ cup beer	blanched almonds
1 teaspoon cognac	¼ cup Vanilla Sugar (page 579)
pinch of salt	

Place the flour in a bowl and make a well in the center. Put the egg yolk, salt, beer, and cognac in the well and stir with a wooden spoon until smooth. The mixture should not be too thin. Let the batter rest for several hours.

Wash the plums and keep them whole. Put them in a saucepan with a tablespoon of water and ½ cup of sugar. Simmer 10 minutes. Remove from the pan and drain well. When they have cooled, remove the stones delicately and fill the centers with almonds. Dip each plum in the frying batter and fry in deep fat at 380° F. When golden brown, drain well and pile them on a serving platter lined with a folded napkin. Sprinkle with vanilla sugar and serve very hot.

Raspberry charlotte, vanilla sauce
Charlotte aux framboises

FOR EIGHT TO TEN PEOPLE

8 tablespoons kirsch	½ vanilla bean
½ pound lady fingers	½ cup (scant) sugar
1 pint raspberries	3 egg yolks
2¼ cups milk	3 level teaspoons rice flour

Combine the kirsch and 4 tablespoons of water in a soup plate and dip each lady finger briefly in the mixture. Line the bottom and sides of a charlotte mold or straight-sided baking dish with the lady fingers, pressing them very close together. Moistened this way, they will adapt themselves to any shape you wish.

Put half the raspberries in the lined mold and cover with a layer of moistened lady fingers. Add the rest of the raspberries and cover with another layer of lady fingers. Cover with a plate the exact dimensions of the mold and put on enough weight to press the cake down gently. Let stand in the refrigerator at least 7 to 8 hours.

Boil the milk with the vanilla and dissolve the sugar in the milk. (If necessary, substitute 2 teaspoons of vanilla extract after the sauce is cooked.—*Ed.*) Beat the egg yolks, adding the hot milk gradually while beating continuously. Add the rice flour beaten in a little cold milk and cook over a low heat, stirring constantly until the sauce thickens. The sauce must not reach the boiling point. Strain through a fine sieve. Cool.

Then 10 minutes before serving, unmold the cake onto a serving platter. Pour the sauce over it so that it covers and surrounds the cake.

Strawberry chantilly * *Crème fouettée aux fraises*

FOR FOUR PEOPLE

1 pint small strawberries	10 tablespoons sugar
1 pint heavy cream, whipped	

Hull the strawberries, washing them only if necessary and then very briefly in cold water, or the strawberries will lose some of their flavor.

Put aside several of the smallest strawberries for decoration. Force the rest through a strainer lined with a dish towel or cheesecloth in order to extract the juice.

Beat the cream stiff and sweeten with the sugar. Add ½ cup of strawberry juice. Divide the mixture among 4 sherbet glasses and decorate with the strawberries. Chill in the refrigerator and serve very cold.

Strawberry charlotte * Charlotte aux fraises

FOR SIX PEOPLE

3 pints strawberries
¾ cup Vanilla Sugar (page 579)
2½ tablespoons kirsch

10 ounces lady fingers
½ cup maraschino liqueur
1½ cups heavy cream, whipped

Hull the strawberries and cut them in half. Put them in a bowl with 6 tablespoons of the sugar and the kirsch.

Moisten the lady fingers with a mixture of ½ cup of maraschino and ½ cup of water. Line the bottom and sides of a charlotte mold or other straight-sided dish with some of the lady fingers.

Put a layer of strawberries over the bottom layer of lady fingers. Cover with a layer of the whipped cream, sweetened with sugar. Cover with moistened lady fingers. Continue this operation, finishing with a layer of lady fingers.

Chill in the refrigerator. Unmold and serve with sweetened whipped cream.

Charlotte rose * Charlotte rose

FOR EIGHT PEOPLE

2 pints small strawberries
¾ cup Vanilla Sugar (page 579)
10 ounces lady fingers
½ cup maraschino liqueur
1½ cups heavy cream, whipped

Frosting:
4 egg yolks
1¼ cups sugar
½ pound soft butter
red coloring
3 ounces candied fruits

Hull the strawberries, washing them briefly in cold water if they are dirty.

Put the strawberries in a bowl with 6 tablespoons of the sugar. Cover and let stand 1 hour.

Dip the lady fingers very briefly in a mixture of ½ cup maraschino and ½ cup water. Line the bottom of a mold or straight-sided baking dish with some of the lady fingers. Put a layer of strawberries on the bottom layer of lady fingers. Cover with a layer of whipped cream sweetened with the rest of the sugar. Cover with a layer of moist lady fingers. Continue this until you fill the mold, finishing with

a layer of lady fingers. Press down well. Chill in the refrigerator for several hour
Unmold and frost with the following butter cream. Decorate with candied fruit
preferably strawberries.

To make the frosting: Beat the egg yolks with the sugar for a long time. Yo
want a very light and frothy mixture. At this point, begin adding the soft butte,
little by little. Beat with a wooden spoon for 20 minutes (or somewhat less, if
you want to use an electric beater—*Ed.*). Add just a few drops of coloring matter
to give a pale pink color.

Strawberry compote ✳ *Compote de fraises*

FOR FIVE PEOPLE

2 pints strawberries   ¾ cup sugar
2 tablespoons Vanilla Sugar (page 579)

To make a good strawberry compote, you must not cook the berries. Hull the
strawberries and put them in a bowl.

Boil the two kinds of sugar with 1½ cups of water rapidly until the syrup
forms a good thread when dropped from the edge of the spoon. If you have a
candy thermometer, it should register 230° F. Remove from the heat and cool
5 minutes. Pour this over the strawberries. Cover and cool completely.

Strawberries curaçao ✳ *Fraises à l'orange*

FOR FOUR PEOPLE

1½ pints strawberries   1½ tablespoons curaçao
4 large oranges   1¼ cups powdered sugar

Hull the strawberries, washing them quickly in cold water, if necessary.
Pile them in a pyramid on a serving platter.
Squeeze the juice from 2 oranges and heat it with the curaçao. Pour the hot
mixture over the strawberries and garnish the edge of the platter with peeled
orange slices.

Strawberry mousse ✳ *Mousse aux fraises*

FOR EIGHT PEOPLE

¾ pint strawberries   ½ cup sugar
1 teaspoon lemon juice   2 egg whites, beaten stiff
1¼ cups heavy cream, whipped   pinch of salt

Hull the strawberries, washing them quickly under cold water if necessary. Drain well.

Force the strawberries through a strainer and mix the purée with the lemon juice and a small pinch of salt.

Beat the whipped cream gently into the strawberries with a whisk or whip and add the sugar.

Fold the egg whites in tablespoon by tablespoon, lifting the mixture high so that the egg whites will not fall. Pour into a serving bowl and chill in the refrigerator for several hours.

Strawberry omelet * Omelette aux fraises

FOR FOUR PEOPLE

¾ cup strawberries	8 eggs
2½ tablespoons kirsch	3 tablespoons butter
4 tablespoons sugar	pinch of salt

Hull the strawberries, leaving them whole unless large. Let them soak in a soup plate with the kirsch and 2½ tablespoons sugar for 1 hour.

Beat the eggs until blended and add a pinch of salt and 1½ tablespoons of sugar. Heat the butter in a skillet and make the omelet as usual. Just before folding, put the strawberries in the omelet and turn onto a hot serving platter. Serve immediately.

Fruit cup * Coupes aux fruits

FOR FOUR PEOPLE

¾ cup seedless raisins	1 cup hazel nuts
2 grapefruits	4 tablespoons orange marmalade
3 oranges	4 tablespoons kirsch
3 bananas	

Soak the raisins in lukewarm water for at least 2 hours.

Peel the grapefruits and oranges carefully, removing all the white filament. Cut into thin rounds and put in a bowl with the bananas peeled and cut into rounds. Add the nuts and the well-drained raisins.

Heat the orange marmalade with the kirsch and a tablespoon of water in a small saucepan. When the marmalade has melted, pour it over the fruit. Mix well and put into individual dessert glasses. Chill in the refrigerator.

Winter compote ✳ *Compote d'hiver*

FOR FIVE PEOPLE

2 tablespoons yellow raisins
5 large apples
¾ cup sugar
rind of ½ lemon

1½ tablespoons rum
½ cup walnut meats
¾ cup heavy cream

Soak the raisins in lukewarm water for at least 1 hour.

Peel the apples and cut them in eighths. Place in a saucepan with 10 table-spoons of the sugar and the rind of ½ lemon and ¼ cup water. Simmer over a slow fire until the apples become translucent. Cool before adding the rum.

Put the apple compote in a serving bowl. Remove the lemon peel. Add the well-drained raisins. Around the edge, make a ring of nut meats and fill the center with the cream whipped and sweetened with the rest of the sugar. Serve very cold.

Winter fruit salad ✳ *Salade de fruits d'hiver*

FOR SIX PEOPLE

½ pound dried apricots
½ pound prunes
½ jar plum jam
3 oranges
2 bananas

⅔ cup blanched almonds
1½ tablespoons kirsch
½ cup sugar
½ cup heavy cream

Soak the apricots and prunes overnight. Drain and cut into small pieces. Put the jam into a fruit dish. Add the oranges and bananas peeled and cut into small pieces, the cut-up apricots and prunes and the almonds. Add the kirsch and stir well. Add the sugar and stir again. Chill in the refrigerator. Just before serving, stir in the cream.

Desserts with dried and canned fruits

Here are a few desserts based on dried or canned fruits, which are the standbys of winter. Obviously, you could use these recipes with fresh fruits when they are in season, or you could use recipes from the preceding section, substituting canned or dried fruits for the fresh variety.

For example, if you want to make a cherry flan in the winter, you would follow the recipe already given on page 597, substituting the canned cherries for the fresh, or you could use canned pineapple in making a rum pineapple dessert (page 607). We will not repeat these recipes but will leave it to you to make the substitutions.

Date dessert * Entremets aux dattes

FOR SIX PEOPLE

Vanilla Custard Cream (page 588)   4 ounces slivered almonds
4 ounces dates   4 egg whites
½ cup sugar

Make the custard cream and let it cool.

Stone and cut the dates into thin slices. Mix them with the sugar and the almonds.

Beat the egg whites stiff and fold them into the date mixture. Line a shallow heatproof serving dish with buttered wax paper and pour the mixture into it. Bake at 300° F. for about 30 minutes or until the blade of an inserted knife comes out dry. Serve with the custard cream.

Sweet chestnut dessert * Entremets aux marrons

FOR TWELVE PEOPLE

4 pounds chestnuts   8 eggs
4½ cups sugar   vanilla powder

Make a light incision around each chestnut and cook them in boiling water for 10 minutes. Remove and cool slightly and peel off the outer skin. Cook them in another pan of boiling water until tender. Remove, cool, and remove the inner skin. Crush the chestnuts coarsely with a fork. (If you prefer, use canned chestnuts.)

Make a syrup by boiling 4 cups of sugar with 6 tablespoons of water for a few moments. Stir in the chestnuts and cook 3 to 4 minutes. Remove them from the heat. Cool to lukewarm and then stir in the eggs, beaten until blended, and 4 teaspoons of vanilla powder (or 1½ tablespoons vanilla extract—*Ed.*).

Cook the rest of the sugar and 2 tablespoons of water in a charlotte mold or other straight-sided metal baking dish until it becomes a very thick syrup that will form a hard ball when dropped into cold water. Tilt the pan to coat the mold evenly. Fill the mold with the chestnut mixture. Place in a deep pan of hot water and bake 1 hour at 350° F.

Unmold while lukewarm and serve with sweetened whipped cream or cold vanilla custard cream.

Chestnuts in caramel * Marrons au caramel

FOR SIX PEOPLE

2 pounds chestnuts
1 quart milk
1½ cups sugar

3 cups Vanilla Custard Cream
   (page 588)

Make a light incision around each chestnut and cook them in boiling water for 10 minutes. Remove them from the water and cool slightly. Peel off the outer skin.

Cook the chestnuts in boiling milk until tender. Remove them from the pan, cool, and peel off the inner skin.

In an unlined copper sugar pan, or in a heavy saucepan, cook the sugar with 3 tablespoons of water until it turns light brown. Add the chestnuts and roll them around in the pan until each is well coated with caramel. Dry and cool on a grill.

Make the custard cream and cool.

Put the chestnuts in a serving dish containing the custard cream. Serve quite cool.

Chestnut charlotte
Charlotte aux marrons et crème fouettée

FOR EIGHT PEOPLE

¾ pound lady fingers
½ cup rum
2½ cups heavy cream

½ cup sugar
¾ pound *marrons glacés*

Dip the lady fingers lightly in a mixture of equal parts rum and water. Line the bottom and sides of a charlotte mold or other straight-sided baking dish with the moist lady fingers.

Whip the cream stiff and stir in the sugar. Refrigerate a third of the cream for decoration and mix the rest with the *marrons glacés* chopped fine.

Make alternate layers of the chestnut cream and lady fingers until the mold is full. Finish with a layer of lady fingers. Refrigerate 24 hours. Unmold and cover with the rest of the whipped cream.

Chocolate ardechois * Ardechois au chocolat

FOR TEN PEOPLE

2-pound can unsweetened
   chestnut purée
10 eggs
2 cups sugar

4 ounces bittersweet chocolate
7 tablespoons sweet butter, softened
walnuts

The commercial chestnut purée, although not sweetened, should be well flavored with vanilla. Add powdered vanilla or vanilla extract, if necessary. Put the purée in a bowl with 6 egg yolks and mix well with a wooden spoon. Stir in the sugar.

Beat 6 egg whites stiff and fold them gently into the chestnut mixture.

Butter a deep baking dish generously and put in the chestnut mixture. Bake in a preheated 300° F. oven for 1 hour. Cool and unmold onto a dessert platter.

Meanwhile, cut the chocolate into small pieces and melt with 2 tablespoons of water in a small saucepan over low heat, stirring constantly with a wooden spoon.

Remove from the heat and add the butter. Mix well and add 4 egg yolks, slightly beaten. Stir well and allow to cool thoroughly. Pour over the dessert in order to cover it completely. Decorate with walnut halves.

Chestnut mont blanc * Mont-blanc

FOR EIGHT PEOPLE

1 pound sugar lumps	5 tablespoons butter
2 vanilla beans	2½ cups heavy cream
2-pound can unsweetened chestnut purée	10 tablespoons Vanilla Sugar (page 579)

In an unlined copper sugar pan or in a deep heavy saucepan cook the sugar lumps with ¾ cup of water and vanilla beans until you have a syrup that registers 230° F. on a candy thermometer, or until it forms small balls when dropped into cold water. Remove from the heat. (If you do not have vanilla beans, add 2 tablespoons of vanilla extract to the chestnut purée.—Ed.)

Blend the chestnut purée and butter together. Remove the vanilla beans and stir the syrup gradually into the purée. Beat well. Force the mixture through a collander onto a serving platter, letting it rise in a mound. The chestnut purée should look like spaghetti.

Whip the cream and sweeten with vanilla sugar. (Lacking that, mix in regular sugar and flavor with 1½ teaspoons vanilla extract.—Ed.) Using a pastry tube fitted with a large fluted tip, force the cream around the edge of the platter and make a ring around the top of the mound. Serve very cold.

Fruit condé * Condé aux fruits

FOR SIX PEOPLE

6 egg whites	*Custard Cream:*
¾ cup assorted candied fruits	6 egg yolks
1 teaspoon vanilla	3 cups milk
12 tablespoons sugar	½ cup sugar

Beat the egg whites stiff and fold in 8 tablespoons of sugar, the candied fruits finely chopped, and the vanilla.

Heat 4 tablespoons of sugar with a tablespoon of water in a charlotte mold or other straight-sided baking dish. Tilt the pan so that all the interior will be coated with the caramel.

Fill with the fruit mixture and place in a pan of hot water. Bake 30 minutes at 350° F. Cool.

Make a vanilla custard cream, using the above remaining ingredients. Cool.

Unmold the dessert just before serving and cover with the custard cream. If you have saved out a few candied fruits, you can use them for decoration.

Flambéed peaches * Pêches flambées

FOR EIGHT PEOPLE

2 cans peaches   ¾ cup kirsch

Put the peaches and their syrup in a small saucepan with 6 tablespoons of kirsch. Heat slowly. Pour into a heated serving dish.

Heat the rest of the kirsch and pour it over the peaches. Touch with a lighted match and serve immediately.

This can be done with other fruits, such as pears and pineapple.

Prune stuffed crepes
Entremets de crêpes aux pruneaux

FOR EIGHT PEOPLE

16 Crepes   1¼ cups confectioner's sugar
2 pounds pitted prunes   2 cups heavy cream, heated

Make the crepe batter and let it rest.

Soak the prunes several hours. Put them in a pan of cold water. Bring to a boil and boil 10 minutes. Drain the prunes in a strainer, and when all the water has drained off, force them through a strainer to get a purée. Mix the purée with the confectioner's sugar.

Make the crepes according to directions on page 92 . Put a few tablespoons of prune stuffing in each crepe and roll them up loosely. Place them in a rather deep rectangular heatproof serving dish. Cover with the heated cream and bake for 5 minutes in an oven preheated to 400° F. Serve lukewarm and not burning hot. Some people will want more sugar, so have sugar on the table.

Peach charlotte * Charlotte aux pêches

FOR SIX PEOPLE

1 can peaches	¾ pound lady fingers
2½ tablespoons cognac	1½ cups heavy cream
½ cup maraschino	½ cup Vanilla Sugar (page 579)

Cut the peaches into small pieces and put them in a bowl with the cognac.

Mix the maraschino and ½ cup of water and dip the lady fingers lightly into the mixture. Line the bottom and sides of a charlotte mold or a straight-sided baking dish with the lady fingers.

Whip the cream and sweeten with the vanilla sugar (or, lacking that, add ordinary sugar and 1 teaspoon vanilla extract—*Ed.*).

Alternate layers of peaches, whipped cream, and moistened lady fingers until the mold is filled. End with a layer of lady fingers. Chill several hours before unmolding on a dessert platter and serving.

Prune delight * Délice aux pruneaux

FOR EIGHT PEOPLE

1 pound pitted prunes	4 eggs
strong tea	1 cup milk
10 tablespoons butter	⅞ cup sugar
white bread	Vanilla Custard Cream (page 588)

Soak the prunes several hours in tea. Drain and boil in water for 5 minutes. Drain.

Sauté in butter 6 to 8 pieces of decrusted white bread cut slightly less than ½ inch thick. When browned on both sides, cut them into ¾-inch strips. Line the bottom and sides of a buttered charlotte mold or a straight-sided baking dish with the strips, pressing them closely together.

Put the prunes in the mold and fill with a mixture of the eggs, milk, and sugar beaten until well blended. Put in a pan of hot water deep enough so that the water will come halfway up the sides of the mold and bake in a preheated 400° F. oven for 45 minutes. If the top browns too quickly, cover with a piece of wax paper.

Make the custard cream.

Cool the dessert to lukewarm and unmold onto a serving platter. Cover with the cold custard cream.

Prune mousse * Mousse aux pruneaux

FOR SIX PEOPLE

¾ pound pitted prunes	1 lemon
10 tablespoons sugar	5 egg whites

Soak the prunes several hours in water.

Cook the prunes with the sugar and enough water just to cover for 30 minutes. Drain and force the prunes through a sieve to make a purée. Season with ½ teaspoon of lemon rind and the juice of the lemon.

Beat the egg whites very stiff and fold them into the prune mixture, lifting the mixture high as you fold. Bake about 30 minutes at 350° F.

Quince jelly charlotte
Charlotte à la gelée de coings
FOR SIX PEOPLE

½ cup kirsch
¾ pound lady fingers
1 jar quince jelly

2 cups Vanilla Custard Cream
   (page 588)

Mix the kirsch and ½ cup of water and dip the lady fingers lightly into the mixture. Line the bottom and sides of a charlotte mold or other straight-sided baking dish.

Spread the bottom layer with jelly and continue alternating layers of jelly and moistened lady fingers until the mold is full. Finish with a layer of lady fingers. Cover with a small plate weighted with something heavy so that the cake will be pressed together firmly. Chill several hours in the refrigerator.

Make the custard cream.

Unmold the cake onto a dessert platter and cover with the custard cream.

Raspberry jelly coupe * Coupe à la framboise
FOR EIGHT PEOPLE

8 egg yolks
1 cup sugar
12 ounces raspberry jelly

4 tablespoons kirsch
8 egg whites, beaten stiff
3 dozen candied cherries

Combine the egg yolks and the sugar in the top of a double boiler. Beat well with a whisk or electric beater, and when frothy, add the jelly and kirsch. Cook over boiling water until thick.

Fold the beaten egg whites into the hot custard and pour into individual dessert glasses. Chill in the refrigerator.

Decorate with candied cherries.

Chocolate desserts

Chocolate flavors many desserts, and although we have given recipes using chocolate in other sections—custards, crepes, soufflés, and ice creams—here is a short chapter on nothing but chocolate desserts.

The chocolate most used in France is a bittersweet baking chocolate. One ounce equals a square of chocolate.

Christmas coupe * Coupe de noël

FOR EIGHT PEOPLE

½ pound bittersweet chocolate
10 tablespoons sweet butter, softened
8 egg yolks
8 egg whites, beaten stiff

1 cup heavy cream
½ cup Vanilla Sugar (page 579)
8 *marrons glacés*
toasted slivered almonds

Cut the chocolate into small pieces. Place in a saucepan with a tablespoon of water and melt over a very low heat, stirring with a wooden spoon until the chocolate is smooth and thick. Remove from the heat and beat in the butter and the egg yolks. Cool completely.

Fold in the beaten egg whites, lifting the mixture high as you do it so as not to break the egg whites.

Put the mixture into individual dessert glasses. Cover with the cream whipped and sweetened with the vanilla sugar. (If you do not have this on hand, sweeten with ordinary sugar and add 1 teaspoon vanilla extract.—*Ed.*) Garnish each glass with a *marron glacé* on top of the cream and sprinkle with the almonds.

Chocolate almond dessert
Entremets au chocolat aux amandes

FOR SIX PEOPLE

1 cup milk
1 cup sugar
3½ ounces bittersweet chocolate
4 egg yolks, slightly beaten

10 tablespoons sweet butter
4 ounces ground almonds
½ pound dry lady fingers

This dessert is best made the day before serving.
Scald the milk with the sugar.

Melt the chocolate, cut in small pieces, in the top of a double boiler and stir it with a wooden spoon to a smooth paste. Remove from the heat and stir in the egg yolks and then gradually add the hot milk, stirring constantly. Cook the mixture over very low heat, stirring until it thickens, but do not let it boil. Remove from the heat and cool.

Cream the butter until soft and work into it the ground almonds. Blend in the cool chocolate mixture.

Pound the lady fingers to fine crumbs and stir them into the mixture. Put everything in a buttered mold and chill several hours in the refrigerator. Unmold onto a dessert platter and serve plain or covered with a coffee custard cream.

Black and white dessert * Nègre en chemise

FOR SIX PEOPLE

4 squares bittersweet chocolate
1 cup sugar
¼ pound sweet butter, softened
2 egg yolks

1 cup kirsch
¾ pound lady fingers
½ pint heavy cream

Melt the chocolate, cut in small pieces, in the top of a double boiler. Stir to a smooth paste with a wooden spoon. Remove from the heat and stir in ½ cup of sugar, the butter, egg yolks, and ½ cup of kirsch. Mix thoroughly.

Butter a charlotte mold or other small straight-sided baking dish.

Mix the remaining kirsch with an equal amount of water. Dip each lady finger in the mixture and put a layer of lady fingers in the bottom of the mold. On the lady fingers put a layer of chocolate cream. Alternate these layers until the mold is filled, ending with a layer of lady fingers. Chill in the refrigerator for several hours.

To unmold, dip in a pan of very hot water for 2 minutes. Unmold onto a dessert platter and serve covered with the cream whipped and sweetened with the remaining sugar.

Chocolate marguerite * Entremets marguerite

FOR EIGHT PEOPLE

1 pound bittersweet baking chocolate
4 teaspoons sugar
4 teaspoons flour

¼ pound sweet butter, softened
4 egg yolks
4 egg whites, beaten stiff

Melt the chocolate, cut in small pieces, in the top of a double boiler. Stir to a smooth paste with a wooden spoon.

Remove from the heat and stir in the sugar, flour, and soft butter. When thoroughly blended, mix in the egg yolks and finally fold in the beaten egg whites.

Line a charlotte mold or other straight-sided baking dish with a buttered sheet of aluminum foil. Pour in the chocolate mixture and bake 15 minutes at 400° F. Cool thoroughly before unmolding. You can serve this with a coffee or vanilla custard cream.

Chocolate marquise * Marquise au chocolat

FOR EIGHT PEOPLE

1 pound bittersweet baking chocolate
12 tablespoons sweet butter, softened
4 tablespoons sugar

8 egg yolks
5 egg whites, beaten stiff
1 teaspoon cognac

Melt the chocolate, cut in small pieces, in the top of a double boiler. Stir to a smooth paste with a wooden spoon.

Remove from the heat and stir in the butter and sugar. When well blended, add the egg yolks one by one, beating hard after each addition. Finally, fold in the beaten whites carefully and add the cognac.

Chill in the refrigerator for several hours.

Chocolate moscovite * Moscovite au chocolat

FOR FIVE PEOPLE

3½ ounces bittersweet baking
  chocolate
4 tablespoons sugar
¼ pound sweet butter, softened

4 egg yolks
grated rind of 1 orange
4 egg whites, beaten stiff

Make this a day in advance.

Melt the chocolate cut in small pieces in the top of a double boiler. Remove from the heat and stir in the sugar and the butter. When well blended, add the egg yolks one by one, beating hard after each addition; add the grated rind of the orange.

Finally fold in the egg whites carefully and put in a dessert bowl. Chill in the refrigerator for 24 hours.

The queen of sheba * Reine de saba

FOR SIX PEOPLE

2 ounces slivered almonds

¼ pound sweet butter

4 squares bittersweet baking
   chocolate

2 teaspoons instant coffee

10 tablespoons sugar

3 tablespoons flour

3 eggs

Pound the almonds to a smooth paste, adding just a little water as you do it.

Melt the chocolate, cut in small pieces, in a saucepan with the coffee dissolved in 2½ tablespoons of boiling water.

Remove from the heat. Beat in the butter, the almond paste, the sugar, the flour, and finally the eggs one by one. The important thing is to beat hard after each ingredient is added.

Pour the mixture into a buttered charlotte mold or other straight-sided baking dish. Place in a pan of hot water and bake 35 to 40 minutes at 350° F. Cool thoroughly before unmolding.

This may be served with sweetened whipped cream or with a coffee custard cream.

Chocolate velvet mousse
Mousse de velours au chocolat

FOR FOUR PEOPLE

4 squares bittersweet chocolate

4 tablespoons sugar

4 tablespoons heavy cream

4 egg yolks, slightly beaten

4 egg whites, beaten stiff

Melt the chocolate, cut in small pieces, in the top of a double boiler, stirring it to a smooth paste with a wooden spoon. Remove from the heat and add the sugar, cream, and the egg yolks. Stir thoroughly.

Fold in the stiffly beaten egg whites, lifting the mixture high during the folding process. Pour into a dessert bowl or into individual dessert glasses. Chill several hours in the refrigerator.

Sweet omelets and soufflés

Cherry omelet * Omelette aux cerises

FOR FOUR PEOPLE

1 pint cherries

8 tablespoons butter

8 eggs

½ cup sugar

4 teaspoons rum

salt

Remove the stems and stones from the cherries and sauté them for 5 minutes in half the butter.

Beat the eggs hard with the sugar, rum, and a pinch of salt. Add the cherries.

Heat the rest of the butter in an omelet pan and make the omelet in the usual manner. See page 130.

Bride's omelet * Omelette à la jeune mariée

FOR FOUR PEOPLE

8 eggs
½ cup sugar
4 teaspoons orange blossom water
4 teaspoons slivered pistachios

1 large dry macaroon
10 candied cherries
3 tablespoons butter
salt

Beat the eggs very hard with ¼ cup of the sugar, orange blossom water, and a pinch of salt. Add the pistachios and the macaroon pounded into crumbs and the cherries cut into small pieces. Mix well.

Heat the butter in an omelet pan and make the omelet in the usual manner. See page 130. As soon as it is cooked, place it on a heated serving platter and sprinkle with the rest of the sugar. Serve immediately.

White grape omelet * Omelette aux raisins blancs

FOR FOUR PEOPLE

8 eggs
4 ounces candied angelica
1 cup sugar

3 tablespoons butter
1 large bunch white grapes
4 tablespoons rum

Beat the eggs until blended. Add the angelica, chopped into small pieces, and ¼ cup of sugar. Mix well. Heat the butter in a omelet pan. Make the omelet in the usual manner. See page 130. Turn it onto a warm platter. Sprinkle with ¼ cup of sugar.

Heat the rest of the sugar with 1½ tablespoons of water. When it becomes a thick syrup, drop in the white grapes free of any stems. Bring to a boil and after a second or two, remove from the heat. Meanwhile, bring the rum to a boil in a small saucepan.

With a slotted spoon, remove the grapes from the syrup and place them around the omelet. Pour the syrup over the omelet and immediately spoon the hot rum over the omelet. Touch with a lighted match and serve immediately.

Rum omelet * Omelette au rhum

FOR FIVE PEOPLE

10 eggs
6 tablespoons sugar

3 tablespoons butter
4 tablespoons rum, heated

Beat the eggs together with 2 tablespoons of the sugar. Heat the butter in an omelet pan and pour in the eggs. Let it brown on the bottom for a few seconds. Lift up the edges gently so that the uncooked eggs will seep to the bottom. When the omelet is cooked, fold it onto a hot platter and sprinkle with the rest of the sugar. Pour over the hot rum and touch with a lighted match. Serve immediately.

Sweet omelet * Omelette sucrée

FOR FOUR PEOPLE

8 eggs
¼ cup sugar
1 tablespoon cognac

3 tablespoons butter
1 jar apricot jam
salt

Beat the eggs very hard with the sugar, cognac, and a pinch of salt. Heat the butter in an omelet pan and make the omelet in the usual manner. See page 130. Just before folding, fill with half the apricot jam. Heat the rest of the jam in a small saucepan.

Put the omelet on a heated platter and cover with the warm jam. Serve immediately.

Strawberry omelet * Omelette aux fraîses fraîches

See page 612.

Apple omelet * Omelette aux pommes

FOR FOUR PEOPLE

8 eggs
5 tablespoons sugar
3 apples
7 tablespoons butter

5 tablespoons heavy cream
2 tablespoons Calvados
salt

Beat the eggs until blended with a pinch of salt and 4 teaspoons of sugar.

Peel and core the apples. Cut them into thin sections and sauté them lightly in half the butter for 15 minutes, turning them occasionally. Add the cream, the rest of the sugar, and the Calvados.

Heat the rest of the butter in an omelet pan and make the omelet in the usual manner. See page 130. Just before folding the omelet, fill it with the apple mixture. Serve very hot.

Almond soufflé * Soufflé aux amandes

FOR FIVE PEOPLE

4 tablespoons butter	4 egg yolks
4 tablespoons flour	½ cup ground blanched almonds
1 cup milk, scalded	6 egg whites, beaten stiff
6 tablespoons sugar	4 teaspoons toasted slivered almonds

Melt the butter in a small saucepan over low heat and stir in the flour with a wooden spoon. Mix well. Add the hot milk gradually, stirring constantly. When the sauce thickens, remove from the heat and add the sugar, the egg yolks, and the ground almonds. Beat well.

Preheat the oven to 350° F.

Fold in the egg whites gently, lifting the mixture high during the folding process so that the egg whites will not fall.

Pour the mixture into a buttered soufflé dish or other straight-sided baking dish. Sprinkle with the toasted, slivered almonds. Bake at 350° F. for 10 minutes. Increase the heat to 450° F. and cook 10 minutes longer. Just before serving, you can sprinkle the top with confectioner's sugar.

Chocolate soufflé * Soufflé au chocolat

FOR FOUR PEOPLE

4 ounces bittersweet chocolate	4 tablespoons sugar
3 egg yolks	4 egg whites, beaten stiff

Cut the chocolate in little pieces and melt in the top of a double boiler. Remove from the heat.

Beat the egg yolks until lemon-colored and add the sugar. Add this slowly to the chocolate, stirring constantly.

Fold in the stiffly beaten egg whites, lifting the mixture high during the folding process. Put the mixture in a buttered soufflé dish and bake 15 minutes in a 400° F. oven. Serve immediately.

Cointreau soufflé * Soufflé au cointreau

FOR SIX PEOPLE

6 egg yolks
1¼ cups sugar

6 egg whites
4 tablespoons Cointreau

Preheat the oven to 400° F.

Beat the egg yolks and sugar until lemon-colored and smooth.

Beat the egg whites very stiff and fold them in carefully, raising the mixture high during the folding process. Fold in the Cointreau equally carefully.

Put the mixture in a buttered soufflé dish or other straight-sided baking dish and bake in an oven that has been preheated 10 minutes before putting in the soufflé.

Grand marnier soufflé * Soufflé au grand marnier

FOR FOUR PEOPLE

1 cup Pastry Cream (page 589)
½ cup Grand Marnier

6 egg whites
6 tablespoons sugar

Make the pastry cream without flavoring and cool to lukewarm. Stir in the Grand Marnier.

Beat the egg whites stiff and gradually add 4 tablespoons of sugar while still beating. Fold the mixture gently and carefully into the pastry cream.

Butter a soufflé dish or other straight-sided baking dish and sprinkle it with the rest of the sugar. Pour the soufflé mixture into the dish and put it over heat. The dish can go on an electric stove, but if you are using gas, protect the dish with a Pyrex plate or asbestos mat. Leave the soufflé there for 5 minutes and then transfer it to a 450° F. oven for 10 minutes.

Rothschild soufflé * Soufflé rothschild

FOR SIX PEOPLE

3½ ounces assorted candied fruits
4 tablespoons kirsch

4 egg yolks
1 cup sugar

Chop the candied fruits as fine as possible. Stir in the kirsch and let stand for 15 minutes.

Beat the egg yolks and sugar until light-colored and frothy. Add the fruits and kirsch.

Fold in the stiffly beaten egg whites, lifting the mixture high during the folding process in order not to let the egg whites fall.

Preheat the oven to 300° F.

Pour the mixture in a generously buttered baking dish or soufflé dish. It should be three fourths full so that the soufflé can rise.

Bake for 15 minutes. Increase the heat to 450° F. and bake 10 minutes longer. Serve immediately.

Twin soufflé * Soufflé l'un l'autre

FOR EIGHT PEOPLE

10 eggs
1 cup sugar
2 cups milk, scalded
5 tablespoons triple-strength coffee

3 squares bittersweet baking chocolate
3 tablespoons confectioner's sugar
salt

First soufflé: Separate 5 eggs. Beat the egg yolks vigorously with half the sugar and a pinch of salt. Add half the hot milk gradually, stirring constantly. Cook over low heat, stirring until the mixture thickens, but do not let the mixture boil. Remove from the fire, add the coffee, and cool to lukewarm. Beat the egg whites stiff and carefully fold them in.

Second soufflé: Melt the chocolate, cut in small pieces, in the rest of the milk. Separate 5 eggs and beat the egg yolks, remaining sugar, and a pinch of salt. Slowly add the chocolate milk and cook over low heat, stirring until the mixture thickens. Do not let it boil. Cool to lukewarm. Beat the egg whites stiff and fold them in.

Butter a large soufflé dish or other straight-sided baking dish. Cut a clean piece of cardboard the right size to divide the dish in 2 parts. Pour one mixture on one side and the second mixture on the other. Bake at 400° F. for 15 minutes. Withdraw the cardboard and continue cooking for 5 to 6 minutes. Serve immediately, sprinkled with confectioner's sugar.

Sweet crepes

I have already given you two recipes for crepes and directions for making them. I will not repeat them here, because what I said applies to desserts as well as to entrées, but I will add a third recipe, for a batter that is especially good for light and sweet crepes.

Dessert crepe batter * Pâte à crêpes pour entremets

FOR TWENTY CREPES

2 cups milk
3 cups sifted pastry flour
4 egg yolks

¼ cup sugar
½ pound butter
4 egg whites, beaten stiff

Blend the milk and flour in a bowl with a whisk. Add the egg yolks, stirring well until blended. Add the sugar and stir again. Melt the butter in a double boiler and pour it into the mixture. Fold in the beaten egg whites and mix well. Use like other crepe batter.

Crepes au cointreau * Crêpes au cointreau

FOR FOUR PEOPLE

Dessert Crepe Batter
2 cups Pastry Cream (page 589)

½ cup Cointreau
4 tablespoons sugar

Follow the preceding recipe for crepe batter and cook twelve crepes, keeping them in a dish over hot water. See page 92.

Make the pastry cream and add 4 tablespoons of Cointreau.

Spread the cream on the crepes and roll them up. Place them on a heated serving platter. Sprinkle with sugar. Just before serving, sprinkle with the rest of the Cointreau, which has been heated, and touch with a lighted match. The Cointreau will not burn unless it is very hot.

Crepes morateur * Crêpes morateur

FOR FOUR PEOPLE

12 crepes
canned chestnut purée

apricot jam
½ cup slivered almonds

Make the crepes using the Dessert Crepe Batter (see recipe above).

Spread each one with the chestnut purée and roll them up like cigars. Melt the jam and spoon it over the rolled crepes. Sprinkle with the slivered almonds, which have been browned lightly in a dry skillet.

Crepes suzette * Crêpes suzette

FOR EIGHT TO TEN PEOPLE

Crepes:
Dessert Crepe Batter

½ cup sugar
4 tablespoons cognac

2 tablespoons cognac
Filling:
8 tablespoons butter

To flame:
5 tablespoons cognac

Make the crepe batter and add the cognac. Cook 20 crepes (see page 92).

Cream the butter and the sugar until smooth and mix in 4 tablespoons of cognac.

Butter a metal serving platter and heat it lightly.

Spread the crepes with the butter mixture and fold them in quarters. Arrange them on the heated platter.

Heat 5 tablespoons of cognac in a small pan and pour it over the crepes. Touch with a lighted match and serve immediately.

Frozen desserts

I am not going to waste time enumerating all the ice creams and all the sherbets that you can buy so easily or that you know how to make yourself. I will make an exception of Tea Ice Cream, which I find delightful and which I have never seen in America. Other than that I will limit myself to frozen desserts, which may be a bit more complicated but which are typical of what we in France serve at dinner.

Dairy maid's heart ∗ *Coeur fermière*

FOR EIGHT PEOPLE

1 cup sugar
8 egg yolks
2 cups heavy cream
6 tablespoons sugar

½ teaspoon vanilla powder
1 quart Vanilla Custard Cream
 (page 588)
Cat's Tongues (page 695)

Make a syrup with the sugar and 4 tablespoons of water by boiling until it forms a long thread when it falls from the spoon or measures 220° F. on a candy thermometer.

In the top of a double boiler, beat the egg yolks with a fork until blended. Gradually add the hot syrup, stirring constantly with a wooden spoon. Place over simmering water and cook for 45 minutes, stirring frequently. The mixture should have the consistency of a thin mayonnaise.

Remove from the heat and beat with a whisk or electric beater until cold.

Whip the cream until stiff and add the sugar. Fold this into the custard sauce and flavor with vanilla. (If vanilla powder is not available, use 2 teaspoons of vanilla extract.—*Ed.*) Pour into heart-shaped molds and place in the coldest part of your refrigerator.

Make the custard cream.

Unmold the desserts on individual plates. Cover with custard cream and serve with cat's tongue cookies.

Cointreau frozen dessert
Entremets glacé au cointreau

FOR EIGHT PEOPLE

Follow the preceding recipe, but when you add the whipped cream, add also 6 tablespoons of Cointreau. Line with a cheesecloth or handkerchief a mold that is not too deep. This will make the unmolding easier. Fill with the mixture and place in the coldest part of the refrigerator for several hours.

Unmold and decorate with candied orange peel.

Tea ice cream * Glace au thé

FOR SIX PEOPLE

3 cups milk
1 cup very strong tea

8 egg yolks
2 cups sugar

Heat the milk and tea together.

Beat the egg yolks and sugar together until they fall from the beater in a ribbon. Add the hot milk and tea mixture gradually, stirring constantly. Stir over very low heat until the mixture thickens. Do not let it boil. Cool and then freeze in an ice cream freezer.

Strawberry (peach or pear) melba
Fraises melba (ou peche melba ou poire melba)

FOR SIX PEOPLE

2 cups milk
¾ cup sugar
1 vanilla bean
4 egg yolks

1 pint strawberries *or* 3 pears *or*
3 peaches
currant jelly
4 tablespoons slivered toasted almonds

Scald the milk with the sugar and the vanilla bean split in two. (If no vanilla bean is available, add 2 teaspoons of vanilla extract when the cooking is completed.—*Ed.*)

Beat the egg yolks in a small pan with a fork. Add the hot milk after removing the bean, stirring constantly with a small whisk. Put the mixture over very low heat and stir until it thickens. Do not let the mixture boil.

Cool the mixture and put it in a freezer tray. At the end of one hour, remove the mixture and beat it hard with a whisk or electric beater. Place it back in the freezer tray and repeat the process at the end of the second hour. It takes 3 hours to freeze the dessert totally.

Put a portion of this ice cream into 6 individual dessert glasses. Cover with hulled strawberries. Pour over each dessert 4 to 5 teaspoons of melted, but cooled currant jelly. Sprinkle with toasted almonds.

This dessert is equally good made with peaches or pears.

Frozen coffee meringues * Meringues glacées au café

FOR SIX PEOPLE

Meringues:
5 egg whites
10 tablespoons sugar
4 ounces ground almonds
1 tablespoon flour

Filling:
3 cups milk
6 tablespoons triple-strength coffee
¾ cup sugar
5 egg yolks

Beat the egg whites stiff. Fold in the sugar, almonds, and flour. Put the mixture in a pastry bag fitted with a smooth medium-sized tip and force little mounds, the size of pullet eggs, onto a baking sheet lined with heavy paper sprinkled with sugar. Leave space between the mounds. Bake 7 to 8 minutes at 350° F. Remove from the oven and cool.

For the filling, scald the milk, coffee, and sugar together. Beat the egg yolks slightly and add the hot milk gradually, stirring constantly. Cook the mixture over very low heat, stirring constantly until it thickens. Never let the mixture boil. Cool and put in one or two freezer trays. At the end of 1 hour, remove from the trays and beat hard. Put it back in the trays and repeat the operation at the end of another hour. Allow 3 hours for the freezing of the filling.

Just before serving, put 2 large tablespoonfuls of the filling between 2 meringues.

Norwegian omelet * Omelette norvégienne

FOR EIGHT PEOPLE

Let us say right off that this dessert is an omelet in name only. It really is a Genoise cake, covered with ice cream and topped with a hot meringue. Why is it

Norwegian? Doubtless because of the surprise of cold ice cream found in the center of a hot dessert.

Anyway, it is a much appreciated dessert with us and one that is easy to make and as delicious as it is intriguing for the uninitiated. I am sure that when you make it, you will make a great impression on your guests.

Cake:
8 eggs
1½ cups sugar
4 teaspoons cognac
2½ cups pastry flour
7 tablespoons butter, melted
3-pint brick vanilla ice cream

Meringue:
6 egg whites
6 tablespoons sugar

Using a large, stainless steel bowl, whip the eggs and sugar over a very low heat until the mixture falls like a ribbon from the whip. The mixture must be less than lukewarm, even if it is whisked over heat. If necessary, remove from the heat occasionally. When it has reached the proper point, remove from the heat and keep beating until the mixture is cool. Fold the cognac, the flour, and the butter, which has been melted over a very low heat, into the egg mixture, lifting it high to introduce as much air as possible.

Butter or flour a baking sheet and spread the mixture into a rectangle ¾ inch thick, spreading it smooth with a spatula. Bake 15 minutes at 400° F. Remove the cake and cool on a rack. When the cake is cool, cut it into a piece just slightly larger than the dimensions of the ice cream brick. Place on a heatproof serving platter.

Beat the egg whites stiff, adding gradually the sugar. When the meringue is glossy, it is ready.

Place the ice cream on the cake and cover with the meringue as quickly as possible. Place in a 450° F. oven just until the meringue is lightly browned. Serve immediately.

Frosty oranges * *Oranges givrées*

FOR SIX PEOPLE

6 oranges   1 cup sugar

Cut off the top third of the oranges. Scoop out the interior and press out the juice from the pulp.

Add 2 tablespoons of water to the sugar and cook until it forms a long thread or measures 220° F. on the candy thermometer. Remove the pan from the heat and add the orange juice. Put back over the fire until it starts to form a thread. Freeze the mixture in an ice cream freezer.

Fill the orange shells with the mixture and chill in the refrigerator until just before serving.

Frozen raspberry soufflé
Soufflé glacé aux framboises

FOR EIGHT PEOPLE

1 cup sugar
8 egg yolks
1 pint heavy cream

6 tablespoons sugar
½ pint raspberries

Boil the sugar and 4 tablespoons of water until it falls in a long thread from the spoon or registers 220° F. on the candy thermometer.

Beat the egg yolks lightly with a fork in the top of a double boiler. Add the hot syrup slowly, stirring constantly with a wooden spoon.

Cook in the top of a double boiler for 45 minutes. Stir frequently until the sauce has the consistency of a thin mayonnaise.

Whip the cream and add the sugar.

Crush the stemmed raspberries with a fork and mix with the whipped cream.

Combine the mixtures and mix well.

Choose a soufflé dish or other round baking dish that is a little too small for the amount of dessert. Line the sides of the mold with a piece of wax paper that comes ¾ inch above the rim. Fill the dish with the mixture and place in the cold part of the refrigerator.

Before serving, trim off the paper rim and the dessert will look like a soufflé. Serve immediately.

Other desserts

Sweet french toast (classic recipe)
Pain perdu (recette classique)

FOR FOUR PEOPLE

2 cups milk
10 tablespoons sugar
1 vanilla bean
2 eggs

¼ pound butter
8 slices dry bread
confectioner's sugar

Boil the milk with 8 tablespoons of sugar and the vanilla bean split in half lengthwise. (If the vanilla bean is not available, add 2 teaspoons of vanilla extract when the milk is removed from the heat.—*Ed.*)

Cool the milk. Beat the eggs with the rest of the sugar.

Melt the butter in a skillet over a moderate heat.

Dip the bread first into the milk. Drain and then dip into the beaten eggs. Brown the bread lightly on both sides. Serve on a heated platter sprinkled with confectioner's sugar.

Sweet french toast herminie * Pain perdu herminie

FOR FIVE PEOPLE

2 cups Dessert Crepe Batter
  (page 629)
1½ cups milk
2 tablespoons sugar

6 tablespoons butter
10 slices dry bread (⅓ inch thick)
confectioner's sugar
cinnamon

Make the crepe batter.

Mix the milk and sugar.

Melt the butter in a skillet.

Dip the bread first in the sweet milk, then in the crepe batter, and brown the bread in the butter on both sides. Serve on a heated platter sprinkled with confectioner's sugar and cinnamon. Accompany with jam, if you like.

Angel's hair pudding * Gâteau de cheveux d'ange

FOR SIX PEOPLE

¼ cup seedless raisins
½ pound thin vermicelli
3 eggs
¾ cup sugar

½ cup walnut meats
1½ tablespoons cognac or rum
jam

Soak the raisins in lukewarm water for several hours.

Boil the vermicelli in slightly salted water for 4 to 5 minutes. Put the vermicelli in a collander and rinse it under cold water. Drain well.

Beat the eggs and sugar together.

Grind the nuts very fine.

Combine the vermicelli, egg mixture, nuts, and raisins and flavor with either cognac or rum.

Butter a charlotte mold or other straight-sided baking dish very generously and put in the mixture. Bake 1 hour at 350° F.

Cool before unmolding and serve covered with jam melted over a low heat.

Rice pudding with candied fruits
Gâteau de riz aux fruits confits

FOR SIX PEOPLE

1 cup rice	4 eggs
3 cups milk	7 ounces assorted candied fruits
1 vanilla bean	2½ tablespoons rum
1 cup sugar	salt
2 tablespoons butter	

Cook the rice in a large kettle of boiling salted water just until tender. Drain well.

In another saucepan, scald the milk with the vanilla bean split in half length-wise. (If not available, add 2 teaspoons of vanilla extract when the rice is cooked. —Ed.)

Remove the vanilla bean and stir the milk in the rice. Cook covered for 15 minutes. Remove from the heat and add ¾ cup of sugar, the butter, and 3 whole eggs plus 1 egg yolk beaten until blended. Stir well.

Beat the remaining egg white until stiff and fold into the mixture. Then add the candied fruits, diced small and mixed with the rum.

Melt the remaining sugar with 2 teaspoons of water in a charlotte mold or other straight-sided baking dish. When the sugar is light brown, tilt the mold so that the syrup will cover the bottom and sides. Fill with the rice mixture and place in a pan of hot water. Bake 30 minutes at 350° F. Cool to lukewarm.

Unmold onto a serving platter. Serve garnished with whipped cream, or melted jam, or vanilla custard cream.

Rice pudding * Gâteau de riz

FOR EIGHT PEOPLE

¼ cup seedless raisins	4 egg yolks
1 cup rice	4 egg whites, beaten stiff
3 cups milk	8 sugar lumps
⅞ cup sugar	1 can mixed fruits
1 tablespoon grated lemon rind	

Soak the raisins in lukewarm water for several hours.

Wash the rice in a large amount of water. Drain and cook in boiling milk for 15 minutes over a low heat. Add the sugar and the lemon rind. Stir and remove from the heat. Add the raisins. Stir in the egg yolks, and finally, fold in the beaten egg whites.

Caramelize a charlotte mold or other straight-sided baking dish with the sugar lumps and 1 tablespoon of water as in the preceding recipe. Place in a pan of hot water and bake at 350° F. for about 35 minutes. Cool to lukewarm. Unmold onto a dessert platter and surround with the mixed fruit in the syrup.

Lemon rice pudding * Riz au lait au citron

FOR FOUR PEOPLE

1 cup rice	¾ cup sugar
3 cups milk	2 lemons
1 vanilla bean	salt

Wash the rice quickly in cold water and boil 2 minutes in salted water to remove the starch. Drain and pour the rice into boiling milk. Add a pinch of salt and a vanilla bean. (If this is not available, add 2 teaspoons of vanilla extract when the rice is cooked.—*Ed.*) Cover and cook over low heat for 15 minutes.

Dissolve ½ cup of sugar in a little milk over low heat, and when the rice is cooked, remove it from the fire and add the sweetened milk to the rice, mixing it gently with a fork.

Cut the lemons in thin slices and parboil them for 3 minutes. Drain.

Make a thick syrup with the rest of the sugar and a tablespoon of water. Poach the lemon slices 15 minutes in the syrup.

Arrange the lemon slices on the rice and serve hot or cold.

Semolina pudding * Gâteau de semoule

FOR SIX PEOPLE

1 quart milk	3 eggs, separated
6 tablespoons sugar	1 jar of jam
1 vanilla bean	3½ ounces angelica
⅔ cup semolina	

Boil the milk with 4 tablespoons of the sugar and the vanilla bean split in half lengthwise. (If the vanilla bean is not available, add 1 tablespoon of vanilla extract when the semolina is cooked.—*Ed.*)

Reduce the heat under the milk, and while the milk simmers, add the semolina. Cook gently for 5 to 10 minutes. Remove from the heat and cool to lukewarm. Add the egg yolks one by one, beating hard after each addition. Fold in the beaten egg whites.

Melt the rest of the sugar with 2 teaspoons of water in a charlotte mold or other straight-sided baking dish. When it caramelizes, tilt the dish so that the bottom and sides will be coated. Fill with the semolina mixture.

Bake at 350° F. for 30 minutes. Cool to lukewarm and unmold onto a serving dish. Heat the jam and pour it over the pudding and decorate with pieces of angelica.

Vermicelli pudding * Gâteau au vermicelle

FOR EIGHT PEOPLE

¼ cup seedless raisins
2½ tablespoons rum
1 quart Vanilla Custard Cream
  (page 588)
4 cups milk
⅞ cup sugar

⅓ pound vermicelli
4 egg yolks
4 egg whites, beaten stiff
candied cherries
walnut halves

Soak the raisins in the rum for 1 hour.

Make the custard cream.

Boil the milk with the sugar. When it reaches the boiling point, add the vermicelli broken into pieces and cook gently for 8 to 10 minutes, stirring with a wooden spoon.

Remove the pan from the heat and add the raisins, then the egg yolks, one by one, beating after each addition.

Fold in the beaten egg whites, lifting the mixture high as you fold.

Put 4 tablespoons of sugar and 1 tablespoon of water in a charlotte mold or other straight-sided baking dish. When it caramelizes, tilt the dish so that the bottom and sides will be coated. Fill with the vermicelli mixture and bake at 400° F. for 15 to 20 minutes.

Cool before unmolding.

Unmold onto a dessert platter and decorate with cherries and nuts.

Pastry

Pastry

In speaking of pastries, we refer to all dishes that are based on pastry dough. Some of these doughs are used for savory preparations—usually in entrées—as well as for desserts and are, moreover, made in the same way, but because pastry dough is generally more connected with desserts than with other courses, we have placed the recipes and directions for making them within the dessert chapter.

Let us begin by making one important observation: If the rest of cooking can be classified as art, this particular branch must be likened to science. In making a sauce, a stew, or a soup, a free hand guided by your taste buds is permissible, but when you are making pastry, it is important to follow the directions precisely and to measure the ingredients with care.

Once this is said, we can examine the many kinds of pastry dough—Flaky Pastry (*Pâte Feuilletée*), Tart Pastry (*Pâte Brisée*), and Sweet Pastry (*Pâte Sablée*).

The sweetened varieties are generally used for dessert tarts and pies. Unsweetened, they are used for quiches, *vols-au-vent,* and other entrées. Then there are many other pastry bases, such as Cream Puff Pastry (*Pâte à Chou*), Brioche Dough (*Pâte à Brioche*), and a cake dough (*Pâte à Génoise*), which are used mostly for desserts.

When you make this kind of pastry, it is important and easier to make enough at a time. In general, I like to say that one should never make less than a pound of Flaky Pastry, Cream Puff Pastry, or Brioche Dough. For Tart or Sugar Pastry, a half pound is the minimum. If you are serving just a few people, and you would like to serve a *vol-au-vent* or another entrée that requires less than a pound of Flaky Pastry, use the rest, for example, for an apple tart (obviously to be served at another meal).

We will examine each one carefully, and finally, we will talk of the icings, which are an indispensable part of many cakes and desserts.

Flaky Pastry

Of the three great and famous French pastries—Flaky Pastry, Tart Pastry, and Sugar Pastry—the most admired is the Flaky Pastry, which serves as a basis for both entrées and desserts. It is perhaps the most difficult one to make successfully.

As a dessert, Flaky Pastry is used for the famous *milles-feuilles,* filled with pastry cream or jam for certain tarts and tartlets, for cream-filled cornucopias, or for little cakes and cookies that go with desserts, such as *palmiers,* bird's tongues, and so on, and finally for large cakes—Pithiviers made with *frangipane* and others.

As entrées, you will use Flaky Pastry to make *vols-au-vent* and fill them with (1) seafoods à l'armoricaine, or (2) a mixture of brains, quenelles, green olives, and cockscombs in a cream sauce, or (3) leftover chicken mixed with mushrooms in a strong curry sauce, or (4) macaroni combined in a tomato sauce with truffles and diced ham.

You can make pastry shells and fill them with (1) scrambled eggs, or (2) fillet of sole cooked in vermouth, garnished with mussels, and covered with a béarnaise or choron sauce. Another wonderful filling is (3) a combination of diced ham, foie gras, mushrooms, and truffles in a brown port sauce. Then there is (4) a mushroom purée topped with a poached egg and sauced with hollandaise, which makes a delightful entrée.

You can make Flaky Pastry *dartois* filled with sardines, minced meat, or chicken or spinach, or you may have them as a sweet and fill them with jam or with apple or pear sauce. With these *dartois,* serve heavy cream, seasoned with lemon juice, and if the bars are served as an entrée, add plenty of pepper to the cream.

Flaky Pastry serves well as a covering for deep-dish pies, which are very economical dishes made with (1) beef and kidneys, or (2) chicken, or (3) rabbit mixed with hard-cooked eggs, sausage, and olives, or (4) fish fillets made with mushrooms and quenelles. As a sweet, these pies are made with cooked fruits. Always serve the pies hot and accompany them with cream as you would a *dartois.*

Rissoles are made with Flaky Pastry filled with all kinds of minced substances. The Flaky Pastry fried in deep fat rises and flakes beautifully, but the rissoles must be served immediately. You can cover poached eggs with Flaky Pastry and fry them in the same manner.

Small garnishes, made in the shapes of little rosettes or crescents are made with Flaky Pastry to decorate meat, fish, and vegetable dishes.

Tiny sausages, wrapped in Flaky Pastry and fried in deep fat, make a perfect accompaniment to a preprandial drink, as do cheese sticks, which are made with the same pastry.

Finally, don't forget all the entrée tarts, which are filled with chopped vegetables (leeks, spinach, and so on), or dessert tarts filled with pastry cream and cooked or raw fruit. These become part of *très grande cuisine* when made with Flaky Pastry.

Practical advice for making flaky pastry

1 *La détrempe* (the preliminary mixture of flour and water) should be made quickly and with one hand. Don't knead it, or it will become elastic.

2 If possible, make the pastry on marble. (A porcelain-covered kitchen table makes a satisfactory substitute.—*Ed.*)

3 It is most important that the butter and flour mixture should have the same consistency. They should feel the same to the touch and should be firm without being hard.

4 It is impossible to make the pastry successfully if either the *détrempe* or the

butter are soft. When the weather is hot, this is difficult, and it is important that during the resting intervals the pastry be kept in the refrigerator.

5 Use the best flour available. In France, I use the best wheat flour. (American flours differ slightly and a well-mixed and sifted combination of approximately ⅔ pastry [cake] flour and ⅓ all-purpose flour gives a very satisfactory result. —*Ed.*) Some flours require more water than others. Measure after sifting. Use best quality unsalted butter.

6 When you roll out the pastry, take care that the sides are straight and that the pastry is of a uniform thickness.

7 Unlike some pastries, it is necessary to bake Flaky Pastry immediately. Once the pastry has been finally prepared and is cut into its proper form, it must be put in the preheated oven.

8 When you cut Flaky Pastry with a pastry or cookie cutter, do it quickly and evenly, otherwise the pastry will rise irregularly.

9 When you are making tarts or covering a deep-dish pie, give the pastry only four turns. You will have a pastry that will rise less and will be better for these particular dishes.

*Flaky pastry * Pâte feuilletée*

YIELD: APPROXIMATELY 2 POUNDS

3 cups sifted pastry flour
2 cups sifted all-purpose flour
½ teaspoon salt

¾ cup cold water (approximately)
1 pound plus 3 tablespoons butter

Heap the well-mixed flour on a marble or other working surface. Fashion a well in the center and into it put the salt. Working with the fingers of one hand and pouring with the other hand, pour the water, very gradually, into the center, working the flour and water together just until the dough no longer sticks to your finger. Roll into a ball and let it rest 20 minutes.

Meanwhile, knead the butter with your hands so that it will be of the same firmness as the flour and fashion it into a flattened round, slightly smaller than the dough.

If the butter is too soft, it will break through the flour mixture. This is not a catastrophe, but it does mean that you will have to use more flour on the working surface and rolling pin and that in turn will mean that the pastry will not rise as much as you would like it to.

Dust the working surface lightly with flour and roll out the dough with a lightly floured rolling pin to a circle large enough to envelop the butter. Place the butter in the center and fold over the edges of the dough on all sides to completely seal in the butter. With gentle, deft strokes, roll out the pastry to a long rectangle. Dividing the strip (mentally) in thirds, fold the third nearest you toward the center. Cover with the other third so that you will have 3 layers. Turn the square by 90 degrees and roll out again. Fold in the same manner. Sprinkle the pastry lightly with flour and let it rest in a cool place for 20 minutes.

These are considered the first two turns. Repeat the process, giving the third and fourth turns. Rest again for 20 minutes. After the fifth and sixth turns, the pastry is ready for use.

N.B. If you wish, let the pastry rest as long as necessary before the final two turns, which should be made immediately before cutting and baking.

This pastry can be used after 4 turns for some tarts and deep-dish pies. At this stage, it is like semiflaky pastry.

Semiflaky pastry * Pâte demi-feuilletée

YIELD: APPROXIMATELY 1 ½ POUNDS

3¾ cups sifted pastry flour
2 cups sifted all-purpose flour
½ teaspoon salt

¾ cup cold water (approximately)
½ pound plus 2 tablespoons butter

This recipe is made like the regular flaky pastry. Its advantage is that although it demands as much work as flaky pastry, it is more economical and serves the same purpose as the flaky pastry with 4 turns which is recommended for pies and some tarts.

Vol-au-vent * Vol-au-vent

FOR EIGHT PEOPLE

3 cups pastry flour
1⅓ cups all-purpose flour
1 teaspoon salt
¾ cup water

¾ pound plus 2½ tablespoons
  unsalted butter
1 egg, slightly beaten

Make a flaky pastry, using the above ingredients and following the directions on page 643. After the sixth turn, roll out the pastry to a rectangle having the thickness of a little over ½ inch and measuring 18 x 9 inches. The strip should be of an even thickness and with straight parallel sides.

Preheat the oven to 450° F.

Divide the rectangle into 2 equal parts. Place one part on a moistened heavy baking sheet. Place a 7-inch pastry circle or saucepan cover on the pastry and cut it sharply and evenly. Trim away the excess pastry.

Cut the other part, resting on the pastry board, in the same way and cut out a center circle about 4½ inches in diameter, leaving a 2½-inch ring.

Moisten the edge of the lower circle and place the ring on top, making sure that they stick together well.

Paint the top of the circle with a pastry brush dipped in egg and paint the bottom. Take care that the egg does not touch the interior or exterior sides because this would keep the *vol-au-vent* from rising.

With the sharp point of a knife, make a slight incision, without cutting through, around the exposed part of the bottom. This is the part that, once the pastry has risen, will form a cover. Still with the knife point, trace a lattice design on the bottom and make little lines on the top circle, leaving a narrow border on both sides of the ring. Bake 30 minutes. Use the trimmings to make a tart or small cookies.

Tart pastry and sugar pastry

These pastries, because they are easier to make and the butter is more easily incorporated, are made in the home more often than some of the others. They are also used for large dinner parties and other important occasions, when the recipe calls for pastry that should not rise very much, as, for example, in tarts.

Tart pastry is often unsweetened, but even so, it is used for desserts as well as for entrées.

Sugar pastry is, of course, always made with sugar and is used exclusively for desserts.

For both kinds of pastry it is important that, once made, the pastry is allowed to rest for at least 2 hours. If it is allowed to rest overnight, so much the better. The resting should take place in a cool place but *never* in the cold parts of the refrigerator.

The following rules are important for success in making tarts, tartlets, and deep-dish pies.

Advice on tarts, tartlets, and pies

1 In the first place, remember to make your pastry in advance so that it will have time to rest. Flaky Pastry has to be baked as soon as it is made, whereas Tart and Sugar Pastries require long waiting periods. Time your pastry so that it will be ready when you want it.

2 Read the recipe of your choice to see if the butter needs softening and allow time for it. Use only the best unsalted (sweet) butter available. Butter can be softened by letting it stand at room temperature or by melting it gently in the top of a double boiler.

3 Flours vary. Some require more liquid than others. The following recipes are made with a combination of two thirds sifted pastry (cake) flour and one third sifted all-purpose flour, which has proved very satisfactory in making pastry. —Ed.

4 Tartlets are baked in individual buttered shallow tins of various sizes and shapes. Tarts are baked either in a plain or fluted straight-sided tart tin (*tour-*

tière) or in a flan ring placed on a baking sheet. (A false-bottomed cake pan is an excellent substitute.) If the crusts are to be baked unfilled, they must either be well pricked with the tines of a fork or filled with dried beans. Either method will keep the crust from rising during the baking. Tart shells must be allowed to cool before turning them out of the tins. Pies have only a top crust and are served in the dishes in which they are baked.

5 Making pastry. Roll the pastry out on a floured surface, using a floured rolling pin. The best pastry surface is marble, but a pastry board or a porcelain-topped table are very satisfactory. The pastry should be rolled deftly and gently, usually to a thickness of ⅛ inch. It should be cut the proper shape for the tart tin or flan ring or individual tins that are to be used. Roll the pastry up on the pin, and unroll it over the baking utensil. Using your fingers, press the pastry on the bottom and sides, pushing the sides ⅛ inch above the edge to form an even rim. This can be left plain or pressed with the dull side of a knife to give a fluted appearance. Take care not to pierce the pastry with your fingernails if the tart is to be filled with anything liquid.

6 Preheat the oven 10 minutes before baking. If the baking sheet is an integral part of the oven, remove it before heating the oven. Pastry must not be put on hot baking sheets.

7 In most cases, the amount of pastry in the recipe referred to will be about the right amount for the tart. If there is pastry left over, roll it into a ball and cover with wax paper. Keep it in the refrigerator for use the following day or two. (Or, if you prefer, make and bake unfilled tart or tartlet crusts. They can be stored in the freezer.—*Ed.*)

Tart pastry I * Pâte brisée I

YIELD: APPROXIMATELY 1 POUND

2 cups sifted pastry flour	¼ teaspoon salt
1 cup minus 2 tablespoons sifted all-purpose flour	1 egg
2½ tablespoons sugar	9 tablespoons butter

Heap the well-mixed flours on a working surface and fashion a well in the center. Into the well put the sugar, salt, egg, and slightly softened butter cut in small pieces. With your fingers gradually work the flour toward the center and add just enough water, teaspoon by teaspoon, until you have a very smooth and shiny ball of pastry. The pastry has to be kneaded slightly, but do it no longer than necessary. Let this pastry rest for several hours.

Tart pastry II * Pâte brisée II

YIELD: APPROXIMATELY ¾ POUND

2 cups sifted pastry flour	¼ teaspoon salt

1 cup minus 2 tablespoons sifted   9 tablespoons butter
   all-purpose flour

Mix the flours well and heap them on a working surface. Fashion a well in the center and into it place the salt and the softened butter cut into pieces. Work the mixture together very quickly with your fingertips, adding just enough water to give a smooth pastry. If it is too soft, add a little flour. Rest several hours if possible before using.

Tart pastry III * Pâte brisée III

YIELD: APPROXIMATELY ¾ POUND

1½ cups sifted pastry flour   2 tablespoons sugar
1 cup minus 2 tablespoons sifted   ¼ teaspoon salt
   all-purpose flour   1 egg
1 teaspoon baking powder   7 tablespoons soft butter

Mix the flour and baking powder well and heap them on a working surface. Fashion a well in the center and into it put the sugar, salt, egg, and soft butter. Mix them all together, working the flour toward the center with your fingertips and adding just enough water to give a dough that no longer sticks to your fingers. Roll it into a ball and cover with a clean towel. Let it rest for 24 hours.

Rouville tart pastry * Pâte brisée rouville

YIELD: APPROXIMATELY 1 POUND

2 cups sifted pastry flour   11 tablespoons soft butter
1 cup minus 2 tablespoons sifted   ¼ teaspoon salt
   all-purpose flour

Make the pastry in the usual manner, but let it stand overnight.

Sugar pastry * Pâte sablée

YIELD: APPROXIMATELY 1 POUND

9 tablespoons butter   1 cup sifted all-purpose flour
¼ cup sugar   1 egg
2½ cups sifted pastry flour   ⅛ teaspoon salt

Soften the butter over extremely low heat and stir in the sugar with a wooden spoon. It should have a creamy consistency.

Mix the flours well and heap them on a working surface.

Fashion a well in the center and into it put the whole egg, the sweetened butter, and the salt. Work with your fingertips only long enough to blend the ingredients.

Roll out the mixture very carefully, because it is crumbly. Both the working surface and rolling pin must be well floured.

Seven-minute sweet pastry
Pâte sablée sept minutes

YIELD: ABOUT 1 POUND

9 tablespoons butter
½ cup sugar
1½ cups sifted pastry flour

1 cup minus 2 tablespoons sifted
    all-purpose flour
1 egg

Soften the butter over very low heat and gradually stir in the sugar with a wooden spoon.

Mix the flours and heap them on a working surface. Fashion a well in the center and into it put the egg and the butter mixture. Work quickly with your fingertips to form a ball. Let it rest several hours, if possible. Roll out on a floured surface with a floured rolling pin.

It is practically impossible to roll out sugar pastry without its breaking. Don't worry. Fit the pieces together, and it will all go together during the baking. This pastry will cook in 7 minutes, which is a little faster than the preceding pastry.

Other pastries

Besides the three great pastries with their many uses, there are several other pastries or cake batters that are more often used for desserts than for entrées. For the most part, we will give the recipe for the dough or batter for each dessert, but there are two in particular that I would like to write about. They can be considered basic, because they have so many uses. I refer to Cream Puff Pastry (*Pâte à Chou*) and Brioche (*Pâte à Brioche*).

Brioche dough * Pâte à brioche

YIELD: ABOUT 1 POUND

1 package (¼ ounce) dry yeast
3 cups sifted pastry flour
2 eggs

2½ teaspoons sugar
¼ teaspoon salt
9 tablespoons soft butter

Dissolve the yeast in ½ cup of lukewarm water and mix to a soft dough with 1 cup of flour.

Put the rest of the flour in a large bowl and make a well in the center. Into it put the eggs, sugar, salt, and the yeast-flour mixture. Then, add the soft butter and mix it all well, working the dough until smooth and soft. (A hand makes a good beating tool.)

Cover and rest for at least 1 hour.

Cream puff pastry * Pâte à chou

YIELD: ABOUT ¾ POUND

We owe this pastry to Popelin, pastry chef to Queen Catherine, who invented it in 1540. The queen called it oven-dried pastry. In 1790, the great chef Tirolay, in service in the House of Orléans, thought up the idea of frying this pastry dough and invented souffléed fritters.

It was in 1800 that it took the name of *pâte à choux,* and it was then for the first time that pastry bags appeared on the scene.

1⅛ cups water	2½ tablespoons sugar
5½ tablespoons butter	1¼ cups sifted all-purpose flour
¼ teaspoon salt	3 eggs

In a saucepan, bring to a boil the water with the butter, salt, and sugar.

Remove from the heat and add the flour, all at once. Stir well and put back on the heat. Stir until the mixture no longer sticks to the sides but leaves dry parts on the bottom on the pan. Remove from the heat and cool a little. Add the eggs one by one, beating hard and long after each addition.

If you were making an entrée, you would, of course, leave out the sugar.

Tarts, tartlets, and pies

Almond tart * Tarte aux amandes

FOR SIX PEOPLE

Tart Pastry (page 646)
1⅛ cups toasted slivered almonds
1 cup sugar

1 cup heavy cream
4 teaspoons Cointreau *or* Grand Marnier

Make the pastry in advance and let it rest.

Roll out on a floured surface, using a floured rolling pin, and line a tart tin with the pastry. See introductory remarks.

Preheat the oven to 400° F.

Mix the nuts, the sugar, the cream, and the liqueur in a bowl and pour the mixture into the tart. Bake 25 minutes. Serve warm, preferably.

Almond strawberry tart
Tarte aux fraises aux amandes

FOR SIX PEOPLE

2 cups sifted pastry flour	1 egg yolk
1 scant cup sifted all-purpose flour	currant jelly
½ teaspoon salt	1 pound strawberries
10 tablespoons soft sweet butter	½ cup slivered almonds
2 eggs	

Make the pastry in advance.

Mix and resift the flours onto a working surface. Fashion a well in the center and in it put the salt, butter, and eggs. Work the flour into the other ingredients with your fingertips. Knead well until the pastry is perfectly blended. Cover and let rest several hours.

Preheat the oven to 400° F.

Roll out the pastry ⅛ inch thick.

Cut out a circle, which will serve as the base of the tart. Place on a buttered baking sheet. With a small cookie cutter cut little crescents out of the rest of the pastry, and moistening one end of each crescent, stick them around the edge of the tart with the other point sticking up in the air. Paint the crescents with an egg yolk mixed with a teaspoon of water. Bake 20 minutes. Cool on the baking sheet before moving; otherwise the crust will break.

Put a layer of jelly on the bottom of the tart. Put the stemmed and washed strawberries in the tart and stick one on the end of each crescent. Sprinkle the strawberries with almonds.

Apple tart * Tarte aux pommes

FOR SIX PEOPLE

Pastry:	*Filling:*
1¼ cups sifted pastry flour	3 pounds apples
⅘ cup sifted all-purpose flour	3 tablespoons butter
1 egg	½ cup sugar
8 tablespoons soft sweet butter	¾ cup white wine
salt	cinnamon
	1 teaspoon grated lemon rind

Make the pastry in advance.

Mix the flours and resift onto a working surface. Fashion a well in the center and into it put a pinch of salt, the egg, the soft butter, and 3 tablespoons of cold water. Work the flour into the center gradually, blending all the ingredients. Make a ball of the pastry and set it aside to rest for several hours.

Peel half the apples and cut them in quarters, removing the core and seeds, which should be kept in reserve.

Melt the butter in a large saucepan and put in the peeled apples. Add ¼ cup of sugar, the wine, the cinnamon, and lemon rind. Cook uncovered until soft, stirring often. Watch that they do not scorch. When the apples are cooked, force them through a sieve or food mill. Cool.

Roll out the pastry and line a buttered tart tin. See introductory notes. Prick the bottom with a fork.

Preheat the oven to 400° F.

Peel, core, and slice the rest of the apples quite thin.

Fill the tart two thirds full with the applesauce and arrange the apple slices in concentric circles, alternating direction with each ring and making the apple slices overlap a little. Bake 30 to 35 minutes. If the top browns too quickly, cover with a piece of paper.

Meanwhile, boil down the apple skins, cores, and seeds with the rest of the sugar to a thick syrup that will form a jelly. When the tart is cooked and cooled, strain and spoon this over the apples.

Apple tart mapie * Tarte aux pommes mapie

FOR SIX PEOPLE

Tart Pastry (page 646)
¼ pound butter
1¼ cups sugar
4 eggs

3 tablespoons flour
2 apples
confectioner's sugar

Make the pastry in advance and let it rest.

Heat the butter over a low heat just until it turns a light brown color. Place the sugar in a bowl and pour the butter over it, stirring well. Add the eggs one by one, beating after each addition. Add the flour and mix well. This is part of the filling.

Roll out the pastry and line a buttered tart tin. See introductory notes.

Preheat the oven to 400° F.

Peel the apples and cut them in small dice. Put them in the bottom of the tart and cover with the egg mixture. Bake 30 minutes. Serve warm or cold, sprinkled with confectioner's sugar.

Apple meringue tart
Tarte aux pommes meringuées

FOR SIX PEOPLE

Tart Pastry (page 646)   currant jam
2 pounds apples   apricot jam
7 tablespoons sugar   plum jam
3 egg whites

Make the pastry in advance and let it rest.

Preheat the oven to 400° F.

Roll out the pastry and line a buttered tart tin. See introductory notes. Prick the pastry well and bake about 15 minutes. Remove from the oven and cool.

Peel the apples. Quarter them and remove the core and seeds. Cook these apples with 4 tablespoons of sugar and 2 tablespoons of water just until soft. Force them through a sieve or food mill. Cool.

Beat the egg whites stiff and fold in 3 tablespoons of the sugar.

Reduce the heat of the oven to 300° F.

Put the applesauce into the tart. Using a pastry bag fitted with a small tip, force the meringue to make a lattice over the top of the tart. Space the strips well so that the squares will be rather large. Bake 10 minutes or until the meringue is lightly browned. Remove from the oven and fill the squares alternately with the various jams. Serve warm or cold.

Banana tart * Tarte aux bananes

FOR SIX PEOPLE

Sugar Pastry (page 647)   6 tablespoons sugar
1½ tablespoons butter   rum
7 bananas   ½ jar apricot jam

Make the pastry in advance and let it rest.

Slice 3 bananas and place them in a bowl with 2 tablespoons of sugar and 3 tablespoons of rum. Let stand 10 minutes.

Preheat the oven to 400° F.

Roll out the pastry and line a buttered tart tin. See introductory remarks. Prick the pastry well with a fork. In another bowl, crush 4 bananas with a fork and stir in 1½ tablespoons of rum and 4 tablespoons of sugar. Mix well and spread the mixture in the tart. Over this arrange the sliced bananas in concentric circles. Cover with wax paper and bake 20 minutes.

When the tart is baked, paint it with melted apricot jam or any other jam that you prefer.

Cherry tart * Tarte aux cerises

FOR SIX PEOPLE

Tart Pastry (page 646)
2 pounds large ripe cherries

1½ tablespoons butter
1 jar currant jelly

Make the pastry in advance and let it rest.

Remove the stones from the cherries. There are special gadgets on the market for this procedure.

Preheat the oven to 350° F.

Roll out the pastry and line a buttered tart tin. See introductory remarks. Arrange the cherries in the tart, pressing them closely together.

Bake 25 minutes.

Melt 4 tablespoons of jelly and spoon it over the warm tart. Serve warm or cold.

Alsatian black cherry tart
Tarte aux cerises noires à l'alsacienne

FOR EIGHT PEOPLE

Tart Pastry (page 646)
3 bread rolls
4 tablespoons butter
1 cup milk
butter
8 tablespoons sugar

⅓ cup ground almonds
4 egg yolks
1 teaspoon cinnamon
1 pound black cherries
4 egg whites, beaten stiff

Make the pastry in advance and let it rest.

Soak the rolls in milk.

Heat the butter in a double boiler. Remove from the heat and add 6 tablespoons of the sugar, the almonds, the egg yolks, and the cinnamon. Mix well.

Squeeze the milk from the rolls and force the bread through a grinder or a *moulinette* and stir into the butter mixture.

Remove the stems and stones from the cherries.

Beat the egg whites and add 2 tablespoons of sugar to keep them from falling. Fold into the first mixture, gradually and gently. Fold in the cherries without stirring.

Preheat the oven to 300° F.

Roll out the pastry and line a buttered tart tin. See introductory remarks. Pour in the filling and bake 45 minutes.

Chocolate tart * Tarte au chocolat

FOR SIX PEOPLE

Pastry:
1¾ cups sifted pastry flour
¾ cup sifted all-purpose flour
8 tablespoons soft sweet butter
2½ tablespoons sugar
1 teaspoon oil
salt

Filling:
1 cup milk
4 teaspoons flour
2 eggs
2½ tablespoons sugar
½ pound bittersweet baking chocolate
2½ tablespoons confectioner's sugar

Preheat the oven to 350° F.

Mix all the ingredients for the pastry with your hand until well blended. Knead lightly. Roll the pastry out on a floured surface, using a floured rolling pin and line a well-buttered tart tin with the pastry. See introductory remarks. Prick well with a fork. Bake 15 minutes.

While the crust is baking, make a pastry cream by combining the milk, flour, whole eggs, and sugar in a saucepan. Whisk until blended and stir over moderate heat just until the mixture starts to boil. Pour this into the partially cooked crust and continue cooking for 5 minutes.

Melt the chocolate over low heat with a teaspoon of water and the confectioner's sugar. Stir to a smooth paste and spread over the pastry cream. Bake 5 minutes longer.

Jam dartois * Dartois à la confiture

FOR EIGHT PEOPLE

Flaky Pastry (page 643)
jam (strawberry, raspberry or apricot)
1 egg yolk

1 cup heavy cream
juice of ½ lemon

Make the pastry. When it has been given the final turn, roll out 2 rectangles of equal size and shape.

Spread one of the rectangles with jam, leaving a 1-inch border. Moisten the border with water. Place the other rectangle on top and press the edges together.

Paint the surface with egg yolk mixed with a teaspoon of water. Bake 20 minutes.

Serve warm with a bowl of heavy cream flavored with lemon juice.

Lemon tart I * Tarte au citron I

FOR SIX PEOPLE

Pastry:
2½ cups sifted pastry flour

Filling:
1 cup sugar

1 scant cup sifted all-purpose flour
1 egg
½ cup sugar
14 tablespoons (7 ounces) soft sweet
    butter
1 teaspoon baking powder
salt

3 egg yolks
3 tablespoons flour
2 cups milk, scalded
1 lemon
lemon marmalade
3 egg whites
2½ tablespoons confectioner's sugar

Make the pastry in advance and let it rest several hours.

Pastry: Mix and resift the flour onto a marble or other working surface. Fashion a well in the center and into it put the egg, sugar, butter, baking powder, and a pinch of salt. With your fingertips work the flour toward the center until all the ingredients are well mixed. Roll into a ball and let stand.

Filling: Mix together in a bowl the sugar, egg yolks, and flour. Add the hot milk gradually, stirring constantly. Pour into a saucepan and stir over moderate heat, letting the mixture boil 2 to 3 minutes. Remove from the heat and add the juice and grated peel of 1 lemon.

Preheat the oven to 350° F.

Roll the pastry out on a floured surface and line a well-buttered tart tin with the pastry. See introductory notes. Put in the bottom of the tart a good layer of lemon marmalade. Cover with the lemon pastry cream. Beat 3 egg whites stiff and add the confectioner's sugar. Spread it over the lemon pastry cream. Bake 25 minutes. Chill thoroughly before serving.

Lemon tart II * Tarte au citron II

FOR SIX PEOPLE

Semiflaky Pastry (page 644)
2½ tablespoons sugar
3 tablespoons butter

2 lemons
3 egg yolks
2 egg whites

Make the pastry in advance. Preheat the oven to 350° F. Roll it out and line a buttered tart pan with the pastry. Prick well with a fork and bake 15 minutes.

Beat the sugar and butter in a saucepan until well blended. Add the grated rind and juice of the lemons, the egg yolks, and the egg whites. Stir over a low heat until the mixture thickens. Pour the mixture into the partially cooked crust and continue baking for 5 minutes. Serve warm.

Linz tart * Tarte linz

FOR EIGHT PEOPLE

3¾ cups sifted pastry flour
2 cups sifted all-purpose flour

1 teaspoon ground cloves
1 large lemon

1¾ cups sugar
¾ pound soft sweet butter
6 egg yolks
1 tablespoon cinnamon

1 teaspoon baking powder
1½ teaspoons salt
raspberry jam *or*
plum jam

This tart should be made 2 or 3 days in advance.

Combine all the ingredients in a bowl except for the jam and knead them together until well blended. Cover and let stand for several hours.

Cook down the jam until very thick. Cool.

Roll out and cut in a round. Line a buttered tart tin. See introductory notes. Fill the tart tin with the jam.

Preheat the oven to 400° F.

Roll out thin the remaining dough and cut into ⅜-inch strips. Cover the tart with these strips in a lattice, pressing the ends down on the rim. Brush the strips with an egg yolk mixed with a teaspoon of water. Bake for about 25 minutes.

Orange cream tart
Tarte à l'orange et à la crème

FOR SIX PEOPLE

Flaky Pastry (page 643)
4 egg yolks
¾ cup sugar

2½ tablespoons flour
2 cups milk
3 oranges

Make the pastry, and when it has had its final turn, roll out and line a buttered tart tin. See introductory notes.

Preheat the oven to 400° F.

Fill the pastry with dried beans for weight and bake 15 minutes. Remove the beans and cool.

Stir the egg yolks and sugar in a saucepan with a wooden spoon. Add the flour and gradually add the strained milk, which has been boiled with the skin of an orange cut in pieces. Place the mixture over heat, and still stirring, let the mixture boil until thick. Remove and cool.

Fill the tart with the pastry cream and decorate with well-peeled orange sections.

Pear dartois * Dartois de poires

FOR SIX PEOPLE

Flaky Pastry (page 643)
2 pounds pears

1 egg yolk
1 cup heavy cream

½ cup sugar   lemon juice

Time the making of the pastry so that it will be ready when you want it.

Peel the pears. Cut them in slices, removing the core and seeds. Make a syrup with the sugar and 2 tablespoons of water. Cook the pear slices just until tender. Cool to lukewarm.

Preheat the oven to 400° F.

Roll the pastry out in one long strip and divide in half so that you will have two equal rectangles. Spread the pear compote on one of the rectangles, leaving a ¾-inch border. Moisten the border and put the other rectangle over the pear compote, pressing the edges together. Trace designs on the surface with a knife and paint with the egg yolk mixed with a teaspoon of water. Bake 20 minutes.

Serve warm with a side dish of heavy cream seasoned with a little lemon juice.

Pear tart * Tarte aux poires

FOR EIGHT PEOPLE

Sugar Pastry (page 647)
2 cups Pastry Cream (page 589)
3 pounds pears
1 cup sugar

1 vanilla bean *or*
1 teaspoon vanilla extract
2 tablespoons toasted slivered almonds

Make the pastry in advance and let it rest.

Preheat the oven to 400° F.

Roll the pastry out on a floured surface, using a floured rolling pin. Line a buttered tart tin. See introductory notes. Prick the bottom with a fork and bake 12 minutes. Cool.

Make the pastry cream and let it cool.

Peel the pears. Cut them in half and remove the core and seeds. Poach them in a syrup made of the sugar, 2 tablespoons of water, and the vanilla bean. Boil 5 minutes. (If the vanilla bean is not available, use vanilla extract.—*Ed.*) As soon as the pears are tender but not soft, remove from the syrup with a slotted spoon.

Line the bottom of the tart with the pastry cream. Arrange the pear halves on the cream and spoon over the pear syrup, cooked down until it has a pale caramel color. Sprinkle with the slivered almonds.

Pineapple tart * Tarte à l'ananas

FOR SIX PEOPLE

Sugar Pastry (page 647)
4 egg yolks

2 cups milk, scalded
1 can sliced pineapple

¾ cup sugar   candied fruits
2½ tablespoons flour

Make the pastry and let it rest.

Preheat the oven to 400° F.

Roll out the pastry and line a buttered tart tin. See introductory remarks. Prick the pastry well with a fork and bake 15 minutes.

Mix the egg yolks, sugar, and flour in a bowl. Stirring constantly, add the hot milk gradually. Pour the mixture into a saucepan and stir over moderate heat, letting the mixture boil for 5 minutes or until very thick. Let the mixture cool completely.

Drain the syrup from the pineapple and boil it down until very thick.

Put the pastry cream in the baked shell. Cover with slices of pineapple arranged in a circle, with each slice overlapping the next. Cover with the concentrated syrup and decorate with candied fruit.

Raspberry jam tart * Tarte à la framboise

FOR SIX PEOPLE

Tart Pastry (page 646)   1 egg yolk
1 jar raspberry jam

Make the pastry in advance.

Roll it out and line a buttered tart tin. See introductory notes. Prick the bottom well with a fork.

Preheat the oven to 400° F.

Gather up the trimmings of the pastry and roll out again. Cut in ⅜-inch strips.

Fill the tart with raspberry jam. Make a lattice over the top, pressing the edges on the moistened rim of the tart. Paint the lattice with an egg yolk mixed with a little water. Bake 25 minutes.

Raspberry pear tart
Tarte aux poires à la framboise

FOR SIX PEOPLE

Tart Pastry (page 646)   1 vanilla bean or
2 pounds pears   1 teaspoon vanilla extract
½ cup sugar   raspberry jelly

Make the pastry in advance and let it rest.

Roll the pastry out as thin as possible and line a buttered tart tin. See introductory notes.

Peel the pears, quarter them, and remove the core and seeds. Make a mixture of the sugar, 2 tablespoons of water, and the vanilla bean slit in half (or the vanilla extract—*Ed.*). Poach the pears in the mixture for 10 minutes or until just tender but not soft. Remove with a slotted spoon and drain. Reserve the syrup.

Preheat the oven to 350° F.

Spread a thin layer of jelly in the tart and place the pear halves close together on top of the jelly. Bake 20 minutes.

While the tart is baking, boil down the pear syrup with 4 tablespoons of jelly. Pour the thickened syrup over the tart as soon as it comes from the oven.

Strawberry meringue tart
Tarte aux fraises meringuées

FOR SIX PEOPLE

Tart Pastry (page 646) *or*
Sugar Pastry (page 647)
1½ pints strawberries

2 egg whites
4 tablespoons sugar

Make the pastry in advance and let it rest.

Preheat the oven to 400° F.

Roll out the pastry and line a buttered tart tin with it. See introductory notes. Prick well with a fork and bake 10 minutes.

Arrange the strawberries, pointed side up, in the tart. Beat the egg whites stiff and fold in the sugar. Spread the meringue over the berries and bake at 300° F. for 15 to 20 minutes or until the meringue is lightly browned.

Strawberry orange tart
Tarte aux fraises à l'orange

FOR FOUR PEOPLE

9 tablespoons sweet butter
¼ cup sugar
2½ cups sifted pastry flour
1 scant cup sifted all-purpose flour
1 egg

1½ pints large strawberries
1 orange
3 tablespoons confectioner's sugar
salt

Soften the butter over a very low heat, stirring in the sugar with a wooden spoon.

Resift the flour onto a marble or other working surface. Make a well in the center and in it break a whole egg and the sweetened butter and a pinch of salt. Work the ingredients together just long enough to blend them; the less you work the pastry, the better.

Preheat the oven to 400° F.

Roll out carefully on a well-floured surface, using a floured rolling pin. Line a buttered tart tin and if the pastry breaks, don't worry. Press the pieces together in the tin, and it will all smooth out in the baking. Bake 20 minutes.

Fill the tart with hulled strawberries. Sprinkle with the juice of ½ orange and with confectioner's sugar. Decorate with well-peeled orange sections.

Tatin tart * Tarte tatin

FOR SIX PEOPLE

Tart Pastry (page 646)   1 cup sugar
¼ pound soft butter   4 pounds apples

Make the tart pastry of your choice in advance in order to give it time to rest. You will need enough for 1 crust.

Spread the butter in the bottom of a deep iron skillet or *sauteuse.* Lacking either of these use a shallow metal baking dish. Sprinkle the butter with ¾ cup of sugar.

Peel and core the apples and cut them in thick, round slices. Place these flat and closely packed in the pan and sprinkle with the rest of the sugar. Cook over moderate heat until the apples just begin to be tender. Remove from the heat and cool to lukewarm.

Preheat the oven to 400° F.

Roll out the pastry into a round the same diameter as the skillet or *sauteuse.* Place the pastry over the apples inside the pan so that the pastry meets the sides. Bake just long enough to cook the pastry.

Remove from the oven and immediately place the pan over high heat for 5 minutes. Turn the tart upside down on a platter and serve.

Cherry barquettes * Petites barquettes aux cerises

FOR TEN PEOPLE

Barquettes *are individual 3-inch-long oval tartlet tins. These can be bought in stores dealing in foreign cookware. If not available, use small round tartlet tins.—* Ed.

Tart Pastry (page 646)   1 jar currant jelly
1 can pitted cherries

Make the tart pastry of your choice in advance and let it rest.
Preheat oven to 400° F.

Roll and cut the pastry and line the individual buttered tartlet tins. See introductory remarks. Prick the pastry well with a fork.

Bake 10 minutes. Remove from the oven and cool. Remove the tarts from the tins. Fill each of them with cherries and cover with a teaspoon of currant jelly, melted but not hot.

Chestnut barquettes * Barquettes de marrons

FOR FIVE PEOPLE

Flaky Pastry (page 643)   ½ cup heavy cream
1 can chestnut purée   2 tablespoons sugar

Make the flaky pastry in advance. Preheat the oven to 400° F. After the final turn, roll it out to a thickness of ⅛ inch. Cut the pastry into appropriate shapes and line the well-buttered tins. See introductory remarks. Fill with dried beans to keep them from rising and bake 15 minutes.

Remove the dried beans and let the tartlets cool in the tins. Take them out and fill with the chestnut purée. Cover with sweetened whipped cream.

N.B. Another way to make Chestnut *Barquettes* is to put a layer of pastry cream in each tartlet and cover with *marrons glacés,* sprinkled with ground almonds.

Fig tartlets * Tartelettes aux figues

FOR FOUR PEOPLE

½ pound dried figs   ½ cup sugar
Tart Pastry (page 646)   6 tablespoons heavy cream

Soak the figs overnight in water.

Make the pastry in advance so that it can rest.

Preheat the oven to 400° F.

Roll out the pastry ⅛ inch thick on a floured working surface, using a floured rolling pin. Cut it out in rounds and line individual tartlet tins. See introductory remarks. Fill with dried beans so that the pastry will not rise. Bake 10 minutes. Remove the beans and let the tartlets cool in the tins before taking them out.

Cook the figs 30 minutes in very little water. Force them through a sieve and mix the purée with the sugar and cream. Fill the tartlets with the mixture.

Grape tartlets * Tartelettes aux raisins

FOR SIX PEOPLE

Tart Pastry (page 646) *or*   3 egg yolks
Sugar Pastry (page 647)   2 cups milk, scalded

10 tablespoons sugar
3 tablespoons flour

1 pound grapes
apricot jam

Make the pastry in advance.

In a small bowl, mix the sugar, flour, and egg yolks. Stirring constantly, add the hot milk gradually. Pour the mixture into a saucepan and stir over moderate heat, letting the mixture boil about 5 minutes or until thick. Cool completely.

Preheat the oven to 400° F.

Roll out the pastry, cut in the proper shapes, and line buttered oval or round tartlet tins. See introductory remarks. Prick the pastry well with a fork and bake 10 to 12 minutes. Cool before removing the tartlets from the tins. Line each tartlet with the cold pastry cream. Cover with the grapes, pressed closely together.

Melt apricot jam over low heat and spoon over the grapes.

Lemon tartlets * Tartelettes au citron

FOR EIGHT PEOPLE

Pastry:
2½ cups sifted pastry flour
1 cup sifted all-purpose flour
14 tablespoons (7 ounces) soft
  sweet butter
½ cup sugar
1 egg
¾ teaspoon baking powder

Filling:
3 egg yolks
1 cup sugar
3 tablespoons flour
2 cups milk, scalded
juice and rind of 2 lemons
½ jar raspberry jam
3 egg whites, beaten stiff
2½ tablespoons confectioner's sugar

Make the pastry by combining all the ingredients and working them together just until blended. Roll the pastry out thin on a floured surface and cut into rounds. Line small buttered tartlet tins. See introductory remarks.

Stir the egg yolks and sugar together without beating. Add the flour and, stirring, add the scalded milk gradually. Put the mixture into a saucepan and stir over heat, letting the mixture boil for 2 to 3 minutes or until thickened. Stir constantly or the sauce will scorch. Remove from the heat and add the grated rind and juice of the lemons.

Preheat the oven to 350° F.

Put a thick raspberry jam in each tartlet. Cover with the lemon cream.

Cover with a meringue made of the egg whites and sugar, sealing in the lemon cream. Bake about 25 minutes.

Pineapple tartlets * Tartelettes à l'ananas

YIELD: ABOUT THIRTY SMALL TARTLETS

Sugar Pastry (page 647)
2 cups Pastry Cream (page 589)

1 can pineapple

Make the pastry in advance.

Preheat the oven to 400° F.

Roll out the pastry and cut in small rounds. Line small round buttered tartlet tins. See introductory remarks.

Prick the pastry well with a fork and bake 8 to 10 minutes. Cool to lukewarm before taking the tartlets out of the tins.

Meanwhile, make the pastry cream and let it cool. Flavor it with kirsch or vanilla.

Cut the pineapple in uniform pieces. Put a layer of pastry cream in each tartlet and cover with a piece of pineapple.

Raspberry pasties * Tartelettes aux framboises

YIELD: THIRTY PASTIES

1 jar raspberry jam
4 cups sifted pastry flour
1⅘ cups sifted all-purpose flour
1½ cups minus 2 tablespoons soft
   sweet butter

1 teaspoon baking powder
¾ cup sugar
2 eggs
3 tablespoons light cream

Boil down the jam until quite thick. Cool.

Mix the flours and butter together until you have a pebbly texture. Stirring constantly, add the baking powder, then the sugar, the eggs, and finally the cream.

When well blended, roll out thin on a floured surface and cut in small rounds. Preheat oven to 400° F.

Line small buttered tartlet tins with the rounds. Cover each round with raspberry jam and cover with rounds of pastry, sealing the edges together. Decorate the top of each one with a little bit of pastry in the shape of a crescent or triangle or anything that suits your fancy. Bake 12 to 15 minutes.

Apple pie * Pie aux pommes

FOR SIX PEOPLE

Flaky Pastry (page 643)
4 pounds apples
½ cup sugar

1 egg yolk
heavy cream

Make the pastry in advance, timing it so that it will be ready when the apples are prepared.

Peel and core the apples. Cut them into large wedges and put them in a saucepan with the sugar and 2 tablespoons of water. When tender but not mushy, pour everything into a deep ovenproof serving dish.

Preheat the oven to 400° F.

Give the pastry its final turn and cover the dish, pressing the pastry firmly to the rim. Paint with egg yolk mixed with a teaspoon of water. Draw little decorative lines on the pastry. Make a hole in the pastry and insert a little roll of paper to act as a chimney. Bake 20 minutes.

Serve hot with heavy cream in a separate bowl or pitcher.

Apricot pie * Pie aux abricots

FOR SIX PEOPLE

Flaky Pastry (page 643)	1½ tablespoons Grand Marnier
4 pounds apricots	1 egg yolk
¾ cup sugar	heavy cream

Make the pastry, timing it so that the apricots will be cooked when the pastry is ready for its final 2 turns.

Wash the apricots well and cut them in half. Remove the stones. Put them in a saucepan and add the sugar and enough water to come to the top of the apricots. Cook over a moderate heat until they are very tender, but not soft and mushy. Remove from the heat and add the liqueur. Place in a Pyrex or earthenware dish.

Preheat the oven to 350° F.

Give the pastry the final 2 turns and cover the dish with a layer of pastry. Fashion a little chimney on the top by making a hole in the pastry and inserting a small tube of paper. Paint the surface with an egg yolk, mixed with a teaspoon of water. Sprinkle lightly with sugar. Bake 20 minutes.

Serve hot with heavy cream, served in a separate bowl. If you cannot find fresh apricots, make this pie with soaked dried apricots.

Pear and prune pie * Pie aux poires et pruneaux

FOR SIX PEOPLE

1 pound prunes	6 tablespoons sugar
Flaky Pastry (page 643)	1 vanilla bean or
2 pounds small pears	1 teaspoon vanilla extract
1 lemon	heavy cream

Soak the prunes in water for 24 hours.

Make the flaky pastry, timing it so that after its final turn, it will be ready to be baked.

Peel the pears and leave them whole. (The Seckel pear is very good for this recipe.—Ed.) Rub each one with the cut side of a lemon.

Make a mixture with the sugar, 2 tablespoons of water, and a small split vanilla bean (or the vanilla extract—*Ed.*). Poach the pears in the mixture for 10 minutes or until almost cooked. Test with a sharp knife.

Put the pears, prunes, and the syrup in a deep heatproof serving dish.

Preheat the oven to 400° F.

Give the pastry its final turns, roll out, cut, and cover the dish with a round of pastry, pressing the sides down. Make a hole in the pastry and insert a small tube of paper as a chimney.

Bake 15 to 20 minutes or until the pastry is golden brown. Serve hot with heavy cream.

Raspberry and currant pie
Pie aux groseilles et framboises

FOR FIVE PEOPLE

Tart Pastry (page 646)
2 pounds currants
1 pint raspberries
1½ cups sugar

powdered sugar *or*
whipped cream *or*
Vanilla Custard Cream (page 588)

Make the pastry in advance and let it rest.

Choose very ripe currants and remove the stems. Mix them with the raspberries. Put a layer of the fruit in a deep dish and cover with sugar. Alternate sugar and fruit. Because currants are quite acid, you may want to increase the amount of sugar.

Preheat the oven to 350° F.

Roll out the pastry and cover the dish, pressing the edge on the rim of the dish to seal in the berries. Make a small hole in the pastry and insert a small paper tube. Bake until the crust is a golden brown.

Serve hot or cold, accompanied with powdered sugar or sweetened whipped cream or vanilla custard cream.

Large dessert cakes

Almond cake ✳ *Gâteau d'amandes*

FOR EIGHT PEOPLE

3 cups sifted cake flour
6 eggs
1¼ cups sugar

7 tablespoons sweet butter, melted
1¼ cups slivered almonds
1 teaspoon baking powder

Mix the flour, eggs, sugar, and melted butter and beat well.

Add the almonds and baking powder and beat until blended. Cover and let stand for at least 1 hour.

Preheat the oven to 400° F.

Put the batter into a buttered cake pan and bake 30 minutes. If you want to, you can sprinkle the surface of the cake as it comes from the oven with finely grated bittersweet chocolate.

Baba au rhum * Baba au rhum

FOR EIGHT PEOPLE

2½ cups sifted cake flour
5 tablespoons lukewarm milk
1 package dry yeast
2 eggs
1 teaspoon sugar

5 tablespoons soft sweet butter
2 cups sugar syrup
½ cup rum
⅛ teaspoon salt

Sift the flour into a bowl. Fashion a well in the center and into it put the milk in which the yeast is dissolved and the eggs. Using your hand as a tool, beat this dough vigorously for 10 minutes. Cover and let rise in a warm place for 1 hour. The dough will rise to double its original size. At this point, add the sugar, a pinch of salt, and the soft butter and knead the mixture delicately for 5 minutes, lifting the dough up high with your fingers.

Preheat the oven to 300° F.

Fill a buttered mold half full with the dough.

Place in the oven, and when the dough has risen to the top of the pan, increase the heat to 450° F. When the cake is well browned, reduce the heat to 350° F. and continue cooking. The total baking time is 45 minutes. Cool in the pan before unmolding onto a serving platter.

Make the syrup by boiling 2 cups of sugar with 2 cups of water for 5 minutes. Add the rum. Spoon this hot over the cake.

Basque cake * Gâteau basque

FOR EIGHT PEOPLE

Pastry:
3 cups sifted pastry flour
1¾ cups sifted all-purpose flour
1 teaspoon baking powder
1 cup sugar
14 tablespoons soft sweet butter

3 egg yolks
1½ tablespoons cognac
juice of ½ lemon

Pastry Cream:
1 cup sugar
4 egg yolks
½ cup sifted all-purpose flour
2 cups milk, scalded

Make the pastry a day in advance. Sift the mixed flours and the baking powder onto a working surface. Fashion a well in the center and in it put the sugar, the soft butter, the egg yolks, the cognac, and the juice of ½ lemon. Work the flour into the other ingredients and knead well until the pastry is perfectly blended and no longer sticks to your fingers. Let rest overnight.

Make the pastry cream the day before also. Stir the sugar and egg yolks together without beating in a saucepan. Add the flour, and when well mixed, add the hot milk gradually. Stir over heat until thick. Remove from the heat and pour into a dish to cool.

Preheat the oven to 400° F.

Roll out half the pastry on a floured working surface, using a floured rolling pin. Line a layer cake pan or tart tin with a piece of buttered wax paper. Cover this with a round of pastry. If the pastry breaks, press the pieces together firmly with your fingers. Pour the pastry cream in the center and cover with another pastry round, rolled out to the same size. Press the edges together to seal in the pastry cream. Bake 30 minutes.

Breton cake * Gâteau breton

FOR EIGHT PEOPLE

6 egg yolks
1 egg
6¼ cups sifted cake flour
½ pound plus 2 tablespoons soft
    sweet butter

1¼ cups sugar
4 teaspoons rum
salt

Beat 5 egg yolks and a whole egg with a fork until well blended. Add the flour, butter, sugar, rum, and a pinch of salt. Stir with a spoon, and then knead with your fingers without adding any liquid, until the dough detaches itself from the sides of the bowl.

Preheat the oven to 350° F.

Butter a deep cake pan. Fill it evenly with the dough and paint the surface with an egg yolk mixed with a teaspoon of water. With the point of a knife, trace a zigzag on the surface. Bake 30 minutes. Insert a knife in the center of the cake to be sure it is baked. If it comes out dry, the cake is cooked. If not, continue baking a few minutes longer, but cover the top if it is browning. Cool before unmolding. Eat the cake cold.

Brioche * La brioche

FOR SIX PEOPLE

3 ⅛ cups sifted cake flour	½ teaspoon salt
1 package dry yeast	2 teaspoons sugar
2 eggs	9 tablespoons soft sweet butter

A brioche is traditionally baked in a special mold with a small base and large fluted sides. These can be found in stores selling foreign cookware.

Take about 1 cup of flour and place it in a small bowl. Fashion a well in the center and in it put the yeast dissolved in 2 tablespoons lukewarm water. Mix together with the flour. This is called *levain.*

Put the rest of the flour in a larger bowl and make a well in the center. In it put the eggs, salt, sugar, *levain,* and the butter. Mix and beat this mixture vigorously. Hands are the best tools. Draw up the dough and let it fall back into the bowl. Continue this until the dough no longer sticks to the side of the bowl. Cover and let it stand at least 8 hours in a lukewarm place so that it will rise.

Butter a large fluted brioche mold. The mold should be large enough so that the dough only half fills it. Put the dough in the mold and let it stand 15 minutes before baking so that it will settle well.

Preheat the oven to 400° F.

Cover the dough with a piece of wax paper and bake about 1 hour. Test the cake by inserting a thin knife. If it comes out dry, the brioche is baked.

N.B. Some desserts call for brioches "with hats" in various sizes. The fluted, bowl-shaped molds in which these are cooked are sold in stores selling foreign cookware. A quart-size Pyrex bowl and individual Pyrex custard cups make good substitutes.—*Ed.*

Large Brioches: When the dough is ready for baking, take three fourths of it and place it in a buttered brioche mold or Pyrex bowl. Roll the remaining dough on a lightly floured surface with the palm of your hand to make it pear-shaped. Insert the pointed end in the center of the dough in the mold. Let stand 15 minutes before baking. Brush the surface with egg yolk mixed with a teaspoon of water, but do not paint the place where the "hat" joins the base. Bake 45 to 60 minutes.

Small Brioches: Take three fourths of the dough and divide it into 20 very small portions or 12 large portions. Place them in individual buttered molds or cups. Divide the remaining dough into the same number of pieces and roll them into pear-shaped "hats." Insert them in the center of the portions in the molds. Let stand 15 minutes. Paint each one with egg yolk, mixed with a teaspoon of water, avoiding the place where the 2 parts meet. Bake 20 minutes.

When brioches are filled, the "hats" are removed and the inside part scooped out. Usually, the "hats" are then replaced.

Cherry brioche * Brioche aux cerises

4 slices dry Brioche (page 668)   raspberry jelly
2 pounds cherries   1½ tablespoons kirsch
1¼ cups sugar

This is a good way to use up leftover brioche a day or two after it has been baked.

Cut the slices and place them in a 400° F. oven so that they will toast a little.

Remove the stones from the cherries and place them in a saucepan with the sugar and ¾ cup of water. Poach the cherries in the syrup until they are tender and remove them with a slotted spoon. Keep the cherries warm. Add the jelly to the syrup and boil down until quite thick. Remove from the heat and add the kirsch.

Arrange the brioche on a serving platter. Cover with the cherries and pour over the hot sauce.

Filled brioche * Brioche fourrée

1 large Brioche (page 668)   6 tablespoons sugar
1 can mixed fruits   1 jar apricot jam
1 jar currant jelly

Reheat a baked brioche. Remove the "hat" and scoop out three fourths of the interior. Place on a dessert platter.

Heat the canned fruits in a fourth of their syrup and add the currant jelly and the sugar. Put the fruits in the brioche and replace the hat. Serve warm accompanied by well-heated apricot jam.

Brioche with candied fruits
Brioche aux fruits confits

Brioche Dough (page 648)   4 tablespoons apricot jam
4 ounces assorted diced candied fruits   4 teaspoons rum

Follow the recipe for making the dough, allowing 8 hours for letting it rise.
Mix the candied fruits well with the apricot jam and rum.

Put half the prepared dough in a well-buttered brioche mold. Cover with the fruit mixture and cover the fruit with the rest of the dough. The mold should be three fourths full. Let stand 15 minutes.

Preheat the oven to 400° F.

Cover the mold with a piece of heavy wax paper and cook for about 1 hour. Test by inserting a sharp knife in the center. If it comes out dry, the brioche is cooked.

Brioche mousseline * Brioche mousseline

FOR TWELVE PEOPLE

6¼ cups sifted cake flour
2 packages dry yeast
4 eggs
4 teaspoons sugar

1 teaspoon salt
½ pound plus 2 tablespoons soft
    sweet butter
6 tablespoons milk

Measure out 1¼ cups of flour and put it in a bowl. Fashion a well in the center and in it put the yeast dissolved in ¼ cup lukewarm water. Mix well. Cover and let rise for 2 hours in a lukewarm place.

Put the rest of the flour in a large bowl and make a well in the center. In it put the eggs, sugar, salt, yeast mixture, and the soft butter. Mix and beat vigorously with your hand until the mixture no longer sticks to the side of the bowl.

Finish by adding just enough milk to give you a dough that is neither hard nor soft. Cover and let the dough rise for 8 hours.

Butter a large fluted brioche mold. Put in the dough and let it stand 15 minutes to settle.

Preheat the oven to 400° F.

Cover the pan with a piece of wax paper and bake approximately 1 hour. Test the cake by inserting a knife. If it comes out dry, the cake is baked. Serve with sabayon sauce.

Cherry cake * Gâteau aux cerises

FOR FOUR PEOPLE

3 eggs
¾ cup sugar
2½ cups sifted cake flour
1 teaspoon baking powder

1 teaspoon vanilla powder *or*
1½ teaspoons vanilla extract
½ pound black cherries
½ cup heavy cream, whipped

Preheat the oven to 350° F.

Beat the eggs and sugar well. Stir in the flour, 2½ tablespoons water, baking powder, and vanilla.

Remove the stones from the cherries and dredge them lightly with flour before adding them to the batter. Fold them in gently and pour the mixture into a floured cake pan.

Bake 40 minutes and unmold when warm. Serve covered with whipped cream.

Coconut cake * Gâteau de noix de coco

FOR EIGHT PEOPLE

Cake:
6 egg yolks
1¼ cups sugar
1 cup sifted cake flour
½ cup potato starch
6 egg whites, beaten stiff

Icing:
5 egg whites
6 tablespoons confectioner's sugar
2-3 cups freshly shredded coconut

Preheat the oven to 400° F.

Beat the egg yolks and sugar until pale yellow. Add the flour and potato starch and stir until blended. Fold in the beaten egg whites and put in a deep cake pan lined with buttered paper. Bake about 45 minutes or until an inserted knife comes out perfectly dry. Cool and unmold the cake. Divide the cake into 2 equal parts horizontally.

Beat the egg whites stiff for the meringue icing and fold in the confectioner's sugar and part of the shredded coconut. Place one of the cake layers on a baking sheet. Cover with a thin layer of the meringue. Put the other layer on top of this and cover the top and sides with the meringue. Sprinkle with grated coconut and place in a 200° F. oven to let the meringue brown very lightly.

Coffee mille-feuilles * Mille-feuilles au café

FOR EIGHT PEOPLE

Flaky Pastry (page 643)
2 cups Pastry Cream (page 589)

¼ cup triple-strength coffee
⅔ cup confectioner's sugar

Make the pastry and divide it into 4 parts. Roll out each one into squares of equal size and shape. Place them on baking sheets and prick them very thoroughly with a fork.

Preheat the oven to 400° F.

Bake the pastry sheets for 10 minutes and let them cool.

Make the pastry cream and flavor it with coffee. Cool completely. Spread 3 layers with the cream and pile them up one on top of the other, trimming them with a very sharp knife so that they are perfectly even. Cover with the fourth layer and sprinkle liberally with confectioner's sugar.

Hazel nut cake * Gâteau de noisettes

FOR SIX PEOPLE

¾ pound shelled hazel nuts	6 egg whites, beaten stiff
6 egg yolks	3 cups Vanilla Custard Cream
1¼ cups sugar	(page 588)

This dessert must be made several hours in advance.

Force the nuts through a food grinder or pulverize them in the blender so that you will have a rather coarse flour. Measure the nut flour in a cup and mix three fourths of it with the egg yolks and beat until well blended. Add the sugar and beat again.

Preheat the oven to 425° F.

Fold in the stiffly beaten egg whites, delicately lifting the mixture high as you fold.

Divide the batter between 2 buttered layer cake pans. Bake 30 minutes. Cool. Remove from the pans.

Make the custard cream and thicken with the rest of the ground nuts. Spread the cream between 2 layers. Chill in the refrigerator. Decorate, if you wish, with candied fruits.

Chocolate four-part cake
Quatre-quarts au chocolat

FOR SIX PEOPLE

This classic recipe is made by weighing the eggs and measuring out equal weights of sugar, flour, butter, and chocolate. Because most American kitchens do not have scales, choose large eggs and follow this recipe.—Ed.

1¼ cups sugar	½ pound bittersweet chocolate
4 large eggs	3 cups sifted cake flour
½ pound soft sweet butter	

Preheat the oven to 350° F.

Beat the sugar and eggs long and hard until they have tripled in volume. Add the soft butter and the chocolate melted in a double boiler. Finally, add the flour. Mix well and put in a buttered cake pan or in a special *quatre-quarts* mold.

Bake about 45 minutes or until an inserted straw or needle comes out dry. If the top browns too quickly, cover with wax paper. Remove from the pan when cold.

Lemon four-part cake * Quatre-quarts au citron

FOR FOUR PEOPLE

2 large eggs
¼ pound soft sweet butter
10 tablespoons sugar
5 teaspoons lemon juice

1¾ cups sifted cake flour
1 teaspoon baking powder
1 cup confectioner's sugar

Preheat the oven to 400° F.

The eggs should weigh 4 ounces. Therefore, beat ¼ pound of butter with the sugar until smooth. Add the eggs one by one, beating long and hard after each addition. Stir in 4 teaspoons of lemon juice and the flour mixed with the baking powder.

Pour this mixture into a buttered cake pan or *quatre-quarts* mold and bake about 30 minutes. Remove from the pan when cold.

Ice with a mixture of confectioner's sugar, a teaspoon of lemon juice, and enough water to give a spreading consistency. Spread with a knife dipped in boiling water.

Honey and hazel nut cake
Gâteau de miel et noisettes

FOR SIX PEOPLE

4 ounces (5½ tablespoons) honey
5 egg yolks
⅔ cup sifted cake flour
⅔ cup powdered ground hazel nuts

5 teaspoons sugar
4 tablespoons heavy cream
5 egg whites, beaten stiff

Preheat the oven to 300° F.

Stir the liquid honey and the egg yolks with a wooden spoon until well blended. Add the flour gradually, stirring constantly, and then add the nuts pounded with the sugar in a mortar or wooden bowl (or pulverized in a blender—*Ed.*).

Stir in the cream, and finally, fold in the beaten egg whites, lifting the mixture during the folding process.

Put the mixture in a buttered cake pan and bake 30 minutes.

King's cake * Galette des rois

FOR EIGHT PEOPLÉ

This is the traditional cake baked for Epiphany, or the Three Kings' Day.

*The person who gets the piece in which the bean or little statuette is hidden be-
comes the "king" or "queen."*

4 cups sifted pastry flour	1 teaspoon salt
1⅘ cups sifted all-purpose flour	¾ cup water (approximately)
1 pound plus 3 tablespoons sweet butter	1 egg yolk

Follow directions for making and rolling flaky pastry, using all the above
ingredients except the egg yolk. The only difference is that after the *détrempe* is
made, it should be allowed to rest at the very least 20 minutes in the refrigerator.
(American flours seem to profit by long resting periods.—*Ed.*) After the butter
is enfolded, the pastry should be replaced in the refrigerator for another 20 minutes. After the first and second sets of turns, the pastry is allowed to rest 10
minutes in the refrigerator.

Preheat the oven to 400° F. Roll out the pastry. It should be rather thick. Cut
quickly and neatly with a large cutter or sharp-edged pan. The thicker the pastry,
the higher it will rise. Place on a baking sheet and trace a lattice on the surface
with the sharp point of a knife. Paint with egg yolk mixed with a teaspoon of
water. Make a little incision somewhere in the cake and insert a dry bean or tiny
statuette. Bake 30 to 40 minutes. If the cake browns too quickly, cover with wax
paper or aluminum foil.

Alsatian kugelhopf * Kugelhopf d'alsace

FOR TEN PEOPLE

*The famous Kugelhopf can be baked in a charlotte mold or other deep, straight-
sided baking dish or in a special Kugelhopf mold, a decorative mold with a center
part that gives the cake a deep center well.*—Ed.

½ cup seedless raisins	10 tablespoons sugar
4 teaspoons kirsch	¼ pound sweet butter
1 cake moist yeast	2 eggs
6¼ cups sifted cake flour	confectioner's sugar
1 cup scalded milk	salt

Soak the raisins in the kirsch.

Dissolve the yeast in 2 tablespoons lukewarm water.

Resift the flour into a large bowl.

Scald the milk and remove it from the heat. Stir in the sugar, salt, and butter
cut in small pieces. Add gradually to the flour, stirring with a whisk. Then beat
the dough 5 minutes. Add the eggs one by one, beating hard after each addition.
The dough should become elastic and should no longer stick to your hands. Add
the yeast and mix well. Cover and let stand for 2 hours in a lukewarm place. Beat
down and mix in the soaked raisins.

Butter the mold and fill it three fourths full with the dough. Cover and let rise in a lukewarm place until it fills the mold.

Preheat the oven to 350° F.

Bake about 40 minutes. Cool and unmold. Sprinkle with confectioner's sugar before serving.

Marie's cake * Gâteau marie

FOR SIX PEOPLE

8 egg whites
1½ cups sugar
2 cups minus 1 tablespoon sifted
   cake flour

11 tablespoons sweet butter, melted
1 jar apricot jam or currant jelly

Preheat the oven to 400° F.

Beat 6 egg whites very stiff, and still beating, add the sugar gradually. Stir in the flour and melted butter.

Line the bottom and sides of a deep cake pan with buttered wax paper. Pour in the batter and bake 45 minutes.

Unmold when lukewarm and cool completely.

The next day, cut the cake horizontally in thin slices. Spread each slice with apricot jam or currant jelly and re-form the cake.

Beat the remaining 2 egg whites stiff, and while still beating, add 2 tablespoons of sugar. Cover the cake with the mixture and bake at 225° F. until the meringue is cooked, or approximately 60 minutes. Keep your eye on it so that it will not brown too much.

Mocha cake * Gâteau moka

FOR TEN PEOPLE

Cake:
1¼ cups sugar
8 egg whites, beaten stiff
1 cup plus 1 tablespoon sifted
   potato starch
juice of ½ lemon

Mocha Butter Cream:
1¼ cups sugar
4 egg yolks
½ pound soft sweet butter
4 tablespoons triple-strength coffee
walnut halves

Preheat the oven to 275° F.

Cake: Beat the egg yolks and sugar until pale and frothy. Fold in the stiffly beaten egg whites along with the potato starch. Add a little lemon juice. Pour the mixture into a buttered cake pan and bake about 1 hour. Cool and remove from the pan.

Cut the cake in 3 or 4 horizontal slices. Cover the bottom layers with the mocha cream. Re-form the cake and completely cover the top and sides, smoothing it with a small spatula. Decorate with walnut halves.

Mocha Butter Cream: Beat the sugar with the egg yolks. When the mixture is light and frothy, add the soft butter (softened, if necessary, in a double boiler). Beat hard at least 30 minutes. An electric beater is a great help in this recipe. Still beating, rapidly add the coffee.

Bertha's nut cake * Gâteau de noix berthe

FOR EIGHT PEOPLE

Cake:
2 cups walnut meats
½ pound plus 2 tablespoons soft
   sweet butter
6 eggs
5 tablespoons sifted cake flour
1¼ cups sugar
1½ tablespoons kirsch

Nut Custard Cream:
7 ounces (14 tablespoons) sweet butter
1¾ cups ground walnuts
1¼ cups sugar
4 egg yolks
Kirsch Icing (page 703)

Preheat the oven to 350° F.

Cake: Force the walnut meats through a meat grinder, using the finest blade, or through a *moulinette.* Add the soft butter and stir until blended. Still stirring, add the eggs one by one. Add the flour, mix well, and finally stir in the sugar and kirsch.

Butter a charlotte mold or other deep straight-sided baking dish and bake 45 minutes.

Nut Custard Cream: Melt the butter in a saucepan over a low heat. Add the ground walnuts, sugar, and egg yolks. Stir the mixture vigorously over heat until very thick. Never let the mixture boil. Remove from the heat and cool.

Cool the cake in the pan. Turn it out of the pan and cut it horizontally in 3 layers. Between each layer, put a layer of nut custard cream. Re-form the cake and cover it with kirsch icing. Serve very cold.

Grandmother's orange cake
Gâteau à l'orange mère-grand

FOR SIX PEOPLE

Cake:
4 egg yolks
10 tablespoons sugar

Icing:
1 jar orange marmalade
1 orange

¾ cup sifted cake flour
9 tablespoons potato starch
grated rind of 2 oranges
4 egg whites, beaten stiff

2½ tablespoons curaçao
1 cup confectioner's sugar

Preheat the oven to 300° F.

Beat the egg yolks and sugar until pale and light. Add the sifted flour and potato starch and the finely grated orange peel. Fold in the beaten egg whites gently. Butter a charlotte mold or other small straight-sided baking dish and sprinkle it with sugar. Pour in the batter and bake 1 hour. Test by inserting a sharp knife. If the blade comes out dry, the cake is baked. Cool in the mold.

Remove the cake from the pan and cut it horizontally in 3 slices. Spread the 2 bottom layers with orange marmalade and re-form the cake. Spread a thin even layer of marmalade over the entire surface of the cake, using a small spatula.

Beat the juice of 1 orange, the confectioner's sugar, and the curaçao until smooth. Spread this frosting over the cake, using a small spatula.

Pain de gênes * Pain de gênes

FOR SIX PEOPLE

7 tablespoons butter
½ pound Almond Paste (page 697)
3 eggs

4 teaspoons rum
3 tablespoons potato starch

Preheat the oven to 300° F.

Melt the butter over a low heat. Remove from the heat and cool.

Put the almond paste into a bowl and add 1 whole egg, 2 egg yolks, and the rum. Save the egg whites. Beat hard and long until the mixture becomes light in texture. Add the potato starch, and when blended, fold in the 2 egg whites, beaten stiff.

Finally fold in the cooled melted butter.

Line a layer cake pan with buttered wax paper and pour in the cake batter. Bake 20 minutes. Cool and unmold. This cake will keep fresh for a long time in an air-tight container.

Perpignan cake * Pain de perpignan

FOR SIX PEOPLE

5 egg yolks
¾ cup sugar
5 egg whites, beaten stiff
1¾ cups sifted cake flour

1 teaspoon grated orange or
    lemon rind *or*
1 teaspoon vanilla extract

Preheat the oven to 350° F.

Beat the egg yolks and sugar long and hard until they triple in volume.

Beat the egg whites very stiff. Fold into the egg yolk and gradually add the cake flour, folding continuously, mixed with the lemon or orange rind or the vanilla extract.

Butter a 10-inch cake pan and pour in the cake batter. Bake about 40 minutes. Cool and unmold.

Pithiviers cake * Gâteau pithiviers

FOR EIGHT PEOPLE

Flaky Pastry (page 643)	½ cup sugar
⅔ cup blanched almonds	6½ tablespoons butter
7 bitter almonds	4 teaspoons kirsch *or*
3 egg yolks	orange blossom water

Make the flaky pastry. You will need ½ of the recipe. Roll out in 2 rounds of equal size and shape.

Using a mortar and pestle or a wooden bowl and pounder, pound the almonds to a paste adding very gradually 2 of the egg yolks. (If bitter almonds are not available, use ¾ cup of blanched almonds and add ¼ teaspoon almond extract which is made from bitter almonds.—*Ed.*) Let the mixture rest for a few minutes and then work in the sugar and then the butter in small bits. Finally work in the kirsch or orange blossom water. You should have a very smooth paste.

Preheat the oven to 375° F.

Spread the paste on one of the pastry rounds leaving a small border. Paint the border with a pastry brush dipped in lukewarm water. Cover with the other round and press the edges together firmly with your thumb. Paint with the remaining egg yolk mixed with a teaspoon of water and design a lattice on the top with the sharp point of a knife.

Bake 25 to 30 minutes.

Raisin cake estienne
Gâteau aux raisins secs d'estienne

FOR EIGHT PEOPLE

1¼ cups seedless raisins	1 cup milk
6 cups sifted cake flour	6 eggs
1¼ cups sugar	9 tablespoons soft sweet butter
4 ounces diced candied fruits	1 teaspoon baking soda
½ teaspoon nutmeg	salt

Decoration:
apricot jam
slivered almonds
candied cherries
angelica

Soak the raisins in lukewarm water for at least 1 hour.

Preheat the oven to 400° F.

Drain the raisins thoroughly and put them in a bowl with the flour, sugar, candied fruits, nutmeg, a pinch of salt, and the milk. Mix well and add the eggs. Beat well.

Stir the butter until creamy and add to the rest of the ingredients. Finally, add the baking soda.

Line a cake pan with well-buttered heavy wax paper and pour in the batter. Bake 1 hour. If the top browns too much, cover with wax paper.

Remove the cake from the pan when cold and spread with a layer of melted apricot jam. Decorate with little daisies made of cherries surrounded by the slivered almonds for petals and with little leaves of angelica.

Classic raisin cake
Gâteau aux raisins secs à l'ancienne

FOR EIGHT PEOPLE

⅔ cup seedless raisins
⅔ cup yellow seeded raisins
½ pound plus 2 tablespoons soft
   sweet butter
1¼ cups sugar
2 eggs

3 egg yolks
3 cups sifted cake flour
¼ teaspoon cinnamon
3 cloves
1½ tablespoons rum
3 egg whites, beaten stiff

Soak the raisins for at least an hour in lukewarm water.

Preheat the oven to 350° F.

Beat the butter with a spoon until creamy. Add the sugar, the whole eggs, and the egg yolks. Mix well.

Drain the raisins thoroughly and mix them into the flour with the cinnamon and cloves. Mix with the egg mixture.

Fold in the rum and stiffly beaten egg whites.

Pour into a large cake pan lined with well-buttered heavy wax paper. The cake pan should not be too full.

Bake 1½ to 2 hours. Test by inserting a straw to see if it comes out dry.

Saint-honoré * Saint-honoré

FOR SIX PEOPLE

½ recipe Tart Pastry I (page 646) 2½ cups heavy cream
Cream Puff Pastry (page 649) 4 tablespoons Vanilla Sugar (page 579)
10-12 sugar lumps

Make the tart pastry, allowing time for it to rest.

Make the cream puff pastry and put it in a pastry bag fitted with a small plain tip.

Roll out the tart pastry and cut out a round 10 inches in diameter. Put on a buttered baking sheet. Prick the pastry with the tines of a fork.

Preheat the oven to 400° F.

While the oven is heating, force a line of cream puff pastry all around the edge of the pastry circle. Bake 15 to 20 minutes.

Force the rest of the cream puff pastry in little mounds the size of a hazel nut onto another buttered baking sheet and bake 15 minutes.

Heat the sugar lumps with 2 tablespoons of water in a small saucepan, and when it turns a light caramel color, dip each tiny cream puff in the caramel and attach them all around the cream puff ring.

Fill the center with sweetened whipped cream.

Saint valentine's cake
Gâteau de la saint-valentin

FOR EIGHT PEOPLE

7 tablespoons butter 2 egg whites, beaten stiff
½ pound almond paste 1 jar raspberry jam
2 egg yolks 1¼ cups confectioner's sugar
1 whole egg 1½ tablespoons kirsch
4 teaspoons rum red coloring
3 tablespoons potato starch

Preheat the oven to 300° F.

Melt the butter in a double boiler and let it cool.

Using commercial almond paste, place the paste in a bowl with the egg yolks, whole egg, and rum. Beat vigorously until soft and light. Add the potato starch. Fold in the beaten egg whites, and finally add the cold melted butter.

Line a square cake pan with buttered wax paper and pour in the cake batter. Bake about 20 minutes. Remove from the oven and cool.

Take the cake from the pan. Cut in the shape of a heart, and then cut it in half horizontally. Spread with a good layer of raspberry jam. Re-form the cake. Place on a cake rack.

Mix the confectioner's sugar with the kirsch in the top of a double boiler, adding a few drops of water. Don't add much, because the icing must not be too liquid. Stir over hot water until slightly lukewarm. Add a few drops of red coloring to give the icing a pretty pink color. Spread over the cake, using a spatula to smooth it evenly. Let the icing dry.

Savarin * Savarin

FOR EIGHT PEOPLE

3 cups sifted cake flour
2 packages moist yeast
7 tablespoons sweet butter
3 eggs
5 teaspoons sugar
1 teaspoon salt

1 cup sugar
6 tablespoons rum
½ jar apricot jam
2 cups Pastry Cream (page 589) *or*
2 cups heavy cream, whipped and
    sweetened

Start by making the yeast mixture *(le levain)*. Put ⅔ cup of flour onto a working surface. Fashion a well in the center and in it put the yeast cakes crumbled into ¼ cup lukewarm water. Stir just until mixed. Sprinkle with flour and flatten the soft dough.

Melt the butter in a double boiler and cool.

Put the rest of the flour in a heap and fashion a well in the center also. In it put the eggs, 5 teaspoons of sugar, and salt and work the center ingredients into the flour with your fingertips. Knead the dough for a good 10 minutes, beating it against the marble or other working surface. Put the yeast mixture in the dough and continue kneading for a few moments.

Put the dough in a bowl and gradually add the melted cool butter. When you are through, you should have a soft but firm batter that will fall from your fingers in a large ribbon.

Fill a buttered ring mold three-fourths full with batter. Let rise in a warm place until the ring mold is full.

Preheat the oven to 400° F. Bake the savarin 45 minutes. Unmold.

Heat the sugar, 1 tablespoon of rum, and 1 quart of water together and boil 5 minutes. Remove from the heat and soak the cake in the syrup, turning it so that the whole cake is impregnated. Drain on a cake rack over a pan to catch the drippings.

Spoon the remaining rum over the cake, respooning any that falls in the pan.

Spread the cake with apricot jam boiled down until thick. Place on a serving platter and fill the center with pastry cream or sweetened whipped cream.

Pineapple savarin * Savarin à l'ananas

FOR EIGHT PEOPLE

1 cup sugar

1 can diced pineapple

6 tablespoons rum
½ jar apricot jam

2 cups heavy cream, whipped and
sweetened

Follow the preceding recipe for making, baking, and soaking the cake.

Boil down the apricot jam until very thick and paint the surface of the savarin with the jam. Place on a serving platter.

Fill the center with pineapple dice and cover with whipped cream.

Layered spice cake * Pain d'épices fourré

FOR SIX PEOPLE

3 cups sifted cake flour
1 teaspoon anise seeds
5½ tablespoons honey
10 tablespoons sugar

1 teaspoon baking soda
orange marmalade
2 tablespoons kirsch
1½ cups confectioner's sugar

This cake is made a day in advance.

Preheat the oven to 400° F.

Sift the flour into a bowl and mix it with the anise seeds.

In another bowl, put the honey and the sugar. Dissolve the baking soda in ½ cup boiling water and add it to the honey and sugar, stirring until the sugar dissolves. Add this mixture to the flour and mix well.

Put in a buttered cake tin. Bake about 45 minutes.

Cool to lukewarm and remove from the pan to a cake rack. Let it cool completely.

Cut the cake in half horizontally and spread with a thick layer of bittersweet orange marmalade. Replace the top part of the cake. Brush it free of any loose crumbs.

Mix the kirsch and sugar with a wooden spoon in the top of a double boiler and heat it slightly over hot water, adding just enough water to give a spreading consistency. Pour it over the cake and spread it smooth with a moistened knife. Let the frosting dry.

Sponge cake chantilly
Gâteau de savoie à la chantilly

FOR EIGHT PEOPLE

4 egg yolks
1 cup sugar
⅞ cup potato starch, sifted
juice of ½ lemon
4 egg whites, beaten stiff
9 tablespoons kirsch

2½ cups heavy cream
3 tablespoons Vanilla Sugar (page 579)
½ cup slivered almonds
candied violets, silver candy balls,
    blanched almonds, and so on.
salt

Preheat the oven to 425° F.

Beat the egg yolks with the sugar and a pinch of salt until pale and frothy. Mix in the potato starch and the juice of ½ lemon. Fold in the beaten egg whites, gently lifting the mixture high in the process.

Butter a deep cake pan and fill the pan two thirds full so that the cake may rise. Bake 40 to 45 minutes. Watch to see that it does not overcook. The cake is baked when an inserted knife comes out dry. Cool in the pan and remove the cake.

Cut the cake with a sharp, long knife in 3 or 4 horizontal slices. Mix the kirsch with the same amount of water and spoon the mixture over each slice. Whip the cream stiff and sweeten it with the vanilla sugar.

Put a part of the whipped cream in a bowl with the slivered almonds and mix well to make a stiff filling. Spread all but the top slice with the mixture. Re-form the cake and spread with the rest of the whipped cream. Decorate with candied violets, almonds, and silver candy balls.

Orange sponge cake * Eponge à l'orange

FOR SIX PEOPLE

3 eggs
1¾ cups sifted cake flour
2¼ cups sugar

1 teaspoon baking powder
8 juice oranges
6 tablespoons rum

Preheat the oven to 400° F.

Beat the eggs until light. Add the flour and ¾ cup of sugar. Mix well and add the baking powder and the grated rind of 2 oranges. Pour the batter into a small buttered cake pan and bake 30 minutes.

Meanwhile, squeeze the juice from the oranges. Place in a saucepan with 1½ cups of sugar and the rum. Heat without boiling.

Unmold the baked cake onto a dessert platter and spoon the orange syrup over the hot cake. The cake should absorb all the syrup.

Savoy sponge cake * Gâteau de savoie

FOR TEN PEOPLE

8 egg yolks
1¼ cups sugar
1 cup plus 3 tablespoons sifted
  cake flour
5½ tablespoons potato starch

grated rind of 1 lemon
8 egg whites, beaten stiff
Mocha Butter Cream (page 675)
  (optional) or
orange marmalade (optional)

Separate the egg yolks from the whites very carefully.

Beat the egg yolks and sugar together hard and long or until they fall in a thick ribbon from the spoon or the beater.

Add the flour and potato starch and finely grated rind of a small lemon. Mix well.

Preheat the oven to 300° F.

Beat the egg whites stiff and fold them into the other mixture. Do not stir but fold, lifting the mixture high as you do so and just long enough to blend the mixtures.

Fill a buttered mold three fourths full. The cake will rise, so it must not be any fuller. Bake 1 hour.

If you want to fill and ice the cake with Mocha Butter Cream or with orange marmalade, it is absolutely necessary that the cake be completely cold before you cut it.

Strawberry cake
Gâteau de fraises ou hérisson de fraises

FOR EIGHT PEOPLE

8 egg yolks
2 cups sugar
1¾ cups potato starch
juice of ½ lemon
8 egg whites, beaten stiff
flour

1 quart wild strawberries or small
   cultivated strawberries
1 pint heavy cream
½ cup Vanilla Sugar (page 579)
kirsch
⅛ teaspoon salt

Preheat the oven to 400° F.

Beat the egg yolks and sugar with a pinch of salt until they are pale and creamy. Add the potato starch and the juice of ½ lemon. Fold in the beaten egg whites very carefully, lifting the mixture high as you fold.

Butter a deep cake pan and sprinkle it with flour. Pour in the batter, filling it not more than two thirds full, because the cake will rise. Bake 45 minutes. Test by inserting a knife. If the knife comes out dry, the cake is baked.

Cool the cake completely. Hull the strawberries and wash them quickly.

Whip the cream and sweeten it with the vanilla sugar, or lacking that, add the plain sugar and a teaspoon of vanilla extract.

Cut the cold cake into 3 horizontal layers. On the first layer sprinkle 4 teaspoons of kirsch. Cover with strawberries and a layer of whipped cream. Cover with a layer of cake and repeat the process. Cover the top with whipped cream and dot the entire surface with strawberries. Chill in the refrigerator for several hours.

Chocolate thoiriat * Gâteau de thoiriat

FOR SIX PEOPLE

9 tablespoons sweet butter

1½ cups sifted cake flour

4½ ounces bittersweet chocolate   3 very fresh eggs
10 tablespoons sugar

Melt the butter in a double boiler. Add the chocolate cut in small pieces. When the chocolate melts, remove from the heat and add the sugar. Mix well and add the flour. Stir again, and finally, add the 3 egg yolks. Stir some more.

Preheat the oven to 400° F.

Beat the egg whites stiff and stir them into the chocolate mixture.

Butter a charlotte mold or other straight-sided baking dish. Pour in the cake batter and bake 30 minutes. The cake is cooked when the top is hard and cracking; the interior should remain soft.

Cool before serving.

Large apple turnover ✳ *Chausson aux pommes*

FOR THREE PEOPLE

½ recipe Tart Pastry I (page 646)   ¼ cup sugar
2 pounds apples   ½ teaspoon cinnamon
3 tablespoons butter   1 egg yolk
grated rind of 1 lemon

Make the pastry in advance and let it rest.

Peel the apples. Cut them in quarters and remove the core and seeds.

Heat the butter in a saucepan and add the apples, 6 tablespoons of water, the grated rind of 1 lemon, sugar, and cinnamon. Cook uncovered until the apples are very soft. Remove from the heat.

Preheat the oven to 400° F.

Roll the pastry into a large round. Trim it evenly and moisten the edge with water. Put the apple mixture on one half and fold over the other half. Press the edges together and paint the surface with the egg yolk mixed with a teaspoon of water.

Bake 15 to 20 minutes.

Large banana turnover ✳ *Chausson aux bananes*

FOR EIGHT PEOPLE

Flaky Pastry (page 643)   ½ cup sugar
10 bananas   1 egg yolk
1 tablespoon rum

Make the flaky pastry.

Before the final turn, peel the bananas and boil them 5 minutes. Drain well and force them through a sieve. Add the rum and sugar and beat well.

Preheat the oven to 400° F.

Roll out the pastry as thin as possible. Trace a large circle on the surface with a large pan cover or flan ring. Cut it out with a pastry wheel. Moisten the edge.

On half the round, put the banana purée, leaving a ¾-inch border. Fold over the other half and seal the edges well. Paint the surface with egg yolk mixed with a teaspoon of water. Bake 15 minutes.

Walnut cake ✻ Gâteau de noix

FOR EIGHT PEOPLE

1¾ cups ground walnuts	5 egg whites, beaten stiff
1¼ cups sugar	apricot jam

Preheat the oven to 350° F.

Grind the walnuts through a meat chopper, using a fine blade, or through a *moulinette*. Add the sugar and fold in the beaten egg whites.

Butter a baking sheet and sprinkle it with flour. Trace out 2 circles with the top of a sauce pan or with a flan ring. Fill each circle with half of the batter.

Bake 10 minutes. Cool.

Spread a layer of jam between the cake layers, and just before serving, cover with jam. You can substitute vanilla, chocolate, or coffee custard cream for jam.

Mesnards walnut cake
Gâteau de noix des mesnards

FOR TEN PEOPLE

Cake:

2 cups walnut meats	1 tablespoon sifted potato starch
½ pound plus 2 tablespoons soft sweet butter	3 tablespoons kirsch
¾ cup sugar	1½ cups milk, scalded

Pastry Cream:

Chocolate Sauce:

4 tablespoons sugar	½ pound bittersweet chocolate
4 egg yolks	⅓ cup triple-strength coffee
1 tablespoon sifted flour	3 tablespoons sugar
	2½ tablespoons heavy cream
	5 tablespoons butter

Pastry Cream: Start this dessert by making the pastry cream. Put the sugar in a bowl and add the egg yolks one by one, beating hard after each addition. Add the flour, potato starch, and kirsch. Mix well. Still beating, add the scalded milk gradually. When all the milk has been incorporated, pour the mixture into a saucepan and cook over low heat, stirring constantly. Don't let the sauce get too thick. Remove from the heat after it has boiled a few seconds. Cool thoroughly.

Cake: Chop the nuts for the cake quite fine but do not grind them. Beat the butter and sugar together until light and very smooth. Still beating, add the ground nuts and the cold pastry cream. Line the bottom and sides of a charlotte mold or other deep straight-sided pan with wax paper. Pour in the mixture and chill overnight in the refrigerator. Unmold onto a dessert platter and decorate with walnut halves. Serve accompanied with warm chocolate sauce.

Chocolate Sauce: Cut the chocolate in small pieces and heat in the top part of a double boiler over boiling water. When it has melted, stir in the coffee, and when well blended, lower the heat and stir in the sugar. Stir until the sugar has dissolved and add the cream. Let the sauce thicken. Just before serving, add the butter. Stir well and cool to lukewarm.

Walnut delight * Délice aux noix

FOR FOUR PEOPLE

10 tablespoons sugar
4 egg yolks
1 cup sifted potato starch

1 cup finely chopped walnuts
4 egg whites, beaten stiff

Preheat the oven to 350° F.
Beat the sugar and egg yolks until light and creamy. Add the potato starch very gradually, stirring constantly. Then stir in the nuts, and finally, fold in the egg whites, carefully lifting the mixture high during the folding process. Pour into a buttered cake pan.
Bake 35 minutes. Cool the cake completely in the pan before removing it.

Yule log * Bûche de noël

FOR EIGHT PEOPLE

Cake:
6 egg yolks
2 whole eggs
½ cup sugar
3 cups sifted cake flour
6 egg whites, beaten stiff

Butter Cream:
1¼ cups sugar
¾ cup water
6 egg yolks
½ pound plus 2 tablespoons soft
   sweet butter
1½ tablespoons Grand Marnier

Cake: Beat the egg yolks, whole eggs, and sugar long and hard or until the mixture is pale and frothy. Mix in the flour well and fold in carefully the beaten egg whites, lifting the mixture high in the process.

Preheat the oven to 400° F.

Line a baking sheet with a well-oiled piece of heavy wax paper. Spread the cake batter over the paper to an even thickness of ¼ inch. Bake 8 minutes.

Turn the cake out on a clean dish towel. Remove the paper and roll the cake up like a jelly roll. Keep it tightly rolled and covered while it cools.

Butter Cream: Boil the sugar and water for 5 minutes. Put 6 egg yolks in a bowl, and beating constantly, add the sugar syrup very gradually. Add the soft butter in bits, still beating, and finally add the Grand Marnier. This process may be done with a whisk or with an electric beater.

Unroll the cooled cake and spread with some of the butter cream. Re-roll the cake and place it on a long serving platter. Cover with the rest of the butter cream. Run lines along the surface with the tines of a fork and cut off the ends of the roll on the bias to make it look like a log. Garnish with little mushrooms and candy holly available in French candy shops. (If this is not possible, decorate with holly made of green-colored icing and red candy berries.—*Ed.*)

Small cakes

Small filled brioches * Petites brioches fourrées

FOR TEN PEOPLE

20 small brioches	2 tablespoons rum
1 cup heavy cream	4 tablespoons macaroon crumbs
¾ cup sugar	

Buy or bake small brioches. See page 668. Remove the "hats" and scoop out a good part of the interior. Whip the cream and add the sugar and rum. Fold in the macaroon crumbs. Fill the brioches with the mixture. Replace the hats and serve very cold.

Strawberry-filled brioches
Brioches farcies aux fraises

FOR SIX PEOPLE

6 large individual brioches	1 pint small strawberries

½ cup sugar   ½ jar raspberry jelly
1½ tablespoons kirsch

Buy or bake the brioches; see page 668. Remove the "hats" and scoop out as much of the center as possible without piercing the sides.

Make a syrup by boiling the sugar, kirsch, and 2 tablespoons of water for a moment. Remove from the heat and soak the brioche crumbs in it.

Hull and wash the strawberries.

Reheat the brioche shells.

Heat the raspberry jelly.

Fill the brioches with a mixture of the soaked brioche crumbs and strawberries. Cover with the heated jelly and serve hot.

Coffee éclairs * Eclairs au café

FOR EIGHT PEOPLE

Cream Puff Pastry (page 649)   *Icing:*
Filling: ⅓ cup coffee extract
1 cup sugar   1¼ cups confectioner's sugar
4 egg yolks
¾ cup sifted all-purpose flour
2 cups milk, scalded
½ cup triple-strength coffee

Preheat the oven to 400° F.

Make the pastry. Put the pastry in a pastry bag fitted with a large plain tube. Force the pastry in 3-inch lengths onto a baking sheet. Bake 15 minutes, without opening the oven door. Cool and slit them on the sides.

Meanwhile, make the filling: Beat the egg yolks and sugar in a saucepan until light and frothy. Add the sifted flour, and when well mixed, gradually add the scalded milk mixed with the coffee, stirring constantly. Stir over heat until thick. Remove from the heat and cool completely.

Make the icing by heating the coffee and 6 tablespoons of water without boiling it. Add the sugar gradually, stirring constantly. Cool to lukewarm.

Fill the éclairs with the coffee custard cream from the side and place on a cake rack. Spread each one with a thin layer of icing.

Chocolate éclairs * Eclairs au chocolat

FOR EIGHT PEOPLE

Follow the preceding recipe, substituting 3½ ounces of bittersweet chocolate, melted in a double boiler, for the coffee in the filling. Substitute 3½ ounces of chocolate for the coffee in the icing, melting the chocolate with the water.

Coconut rocks * Rochers

YIELD: TWELVE ROCKS

4 ounces grated coconut　　　　　2 egg whites, beaten stiff
10 tablespoons sugar

Preheat the oven to 275° F.

Mix the coconut and sugar thoroughly before folding in the egg whites. Drop the mixture from the end of a spoon onto a buttered baking sheet in little mounds. Bake about 30 minutes.

Remove each mound while warm, but cool thoroughly before storing in an airtight container.

Eyeglass cakes * Gâteaux lunette

FOR FIVE PEOPLE

2 cups sifted cake flour　　　　　2 tablespoons sugar
1 cup minus 2 tablespoons sifted　　1 jar currant jelly
　all-purpose flour　　　　　　　confectioner's sugar
1 egg　　　　　　　　　　　　⅛ teaspoon salt
10 tablespoons soft sweet butter

Mix the sifted flours in a bowl. Fashion a well in the center, and in it put the egg, the butter, the sugar, and a pinch of salt. Mix well and knead until well blended. Cover and let the pastry rest for several hours.

Preheat the oven to 375° F.

With a floured rolling pin roll out the pastry on a floured working surface.

With a long oval cookie cutter, cut out pastries 3 inches long. In half the pastries cut out 2 little circles the size of a nickel, to make them look like eyeglasses. Place them on a buttered baking sheet and bake 10 minutes.

Spread the plain pastries with currant jelly and cover with the other pastries already sprinkled with confectioner's sugar. Put a little more jelly in the holes.

Golden flatcakes * Galettes dorées

YIELD: TWELVE CAKES

14 tablespoons (7 ounces) soft　　1 cup milk
　sweet butter　　　　　　　　1 teaspoon baking soda
1¼ cups sugar　　　　　　　　2 eggs, slightly beaten
6¼ cups sifted pastry flour

Preheat the oven to 425° F.

Cream the butter and sugar together until well blended. Stir in the flour, milk, baking soda, and eggs until you have a firm, well-blended dough.

Roll out onto a floured working surface to a thickness of ⅜ inch. Cut out rounds with a 4-inch cookie cutter. Place them on a buttered baking sheet. With the sharp point of a knife trace geometric designs on the tops. Paint the surfaces with a little cold milk and bake 8 to 10 minutes.

Pastry flatcake * Galette en pâte brisée

FOR SIX PEOPLE

4 cups sifted pastry flour
1⅘ cups sifted all-purpose flour
¾ pound soft sweet butter
salt

3 tablespoons sugar
1 cup water (approximately)
1 egg yolk
confectioner's sugar

Mix and resift the flours into a bowl. Make a well in the center and into it put the butter, a pinch of salt, the sugar, and enough water to give a firm dough. Do not knead any more than necessary. Let rest, if possible.

Preheat oven to 350° F.

Roll out the pastry on a floured surface to a thickness of about 1½ inches. Cut all around the edges with a knife to give the cake a fluted rim. Place on a baking sheet and cut a lattice design over the top with a sharp-pointed knife. Paint the surface and sides with an egg yolk mixed with a teaspoon of water. Bake about 45 minutes. When an inserted knife comes out dry, the pastry is cooked. As soon as it comes from the oven, sprinkle with confectioner's sugar. Serve on a napkin-lined plate. This is eaten warm at tea time, warm or cold as an accompaniment to compotes and custard creams, and cold with ice cream or sherbet.

Little génoises * Petites génoises

FOR SIX PEOPLE

3 eggs
10 tablespoons sugar
½ teaspoon grated lemon rind
⅛ teaspoon salt
1½ cups sifted pastry flour

7 tablespoons potato starch
4½ ounces (1 cup) ground almonds
9 tablespoons butter, melted and cooled
2½ tablespoons rum

Preheat the oven to 300° F.

Beat the eggs and sugar together until light and creamy. Add the lemon rind, salt, flour, potato starch, and ground almonds together with the melted butter and rum. Mix well.

Line small square or round cake or muffin pans with buttered paper and fill ¾ full with the mixture. Bake 25 to 30 minutes. Cool thoroughly before removing from the pans.

You can frost these with jam or sprinkle with confectioner's sugar.

Madeleines * Madeleines

FOR FIVE PEOPLE

Madeleines *are little cakes baked in small, shell-shaped tins. These are available in stores carrying foreign cookware.*—Ed.

3 eggs	9 tablespoons sweet butter
10 tablespoons sugar	4 teaspoons rum
1½ cups sifted pastry flour	

Preheat the oven to 350° F.

Beat the eggs and sugar until pale yellow and frothy. Stir in the pastry flour with a wooden spoon.

Melt the butter over very low heat so that it will not brown. Add to the flour mixture and add the rum. Mix well.

Butter the tins and fill with the mixture. Bake about 25 minutes and let them cool to lukewarm before taking them out of the tins. Place them on a cake rack to dry and cool. These will keep for several days in an airtight container.

Madeleines de commercy
Madeleines de commercy

FOR SIX TO EIGHT PEOPLE

1¼ cups sugar	3 cups sifted pastry flour
4 eggs	9 tablespoons sweet butter

Put the sugar in a bowl and add the eggs one by one, beating constantly. Beat the mixture until it becomes pebbly in texture. Add the flour gradually, putting in no more than 2 tabléspoons at a time, until the dough is smooth.

Melt the butter in the top of a double boiler and add it to the dough. If there are milk solids in the bottom of the pan, do not let them get into the dough. Stir until the butter is completely blended in. Let the dough rest for 2 hours.

Preheat the oven to 350° F.

Butter *madeleine* pans and fill the tins three quarters full with a spoon. Bake 25 to 30 minutes.

Meringues * Meringues

YIELD: TWENTY TO THIRTY MERINGUES

Making meringues is very easy if you follow each direction carefully.

4 egg whites   1 cup sugar

Separate the yolks from the whites very carefully; the least bit of yolk will keep the egg whites from rising.

Beat the egg whites very stiff and add ¼ cup of sugar. Continue beating for a few moments before adding the rest of the sugar. If you add all the sugar at once, the egg whites will fall.

Clean the baking sheet carefully and paint with a little oil. A clean baking sheet is necessary; otherwise the meringues will stick.

Preheat the oven to 170° F. Too hot an oven will brown the meringues and leave them soft.

With the aid of a tablespoon drop little mounds of the meringue on the baking sheet. Bake for 1 hour, watching carefully to see that the meringues do not brown.

Remove from the oven and cool completely before taking them from the baking sheet. Otherwise they will break.

These meringues are eaten plain as an accompaniment to every kind of custard cream. They are served as a dessert when a filling is spread between 2 of them. The filling used most often is simply sweetened whipped cream.

Almond meringues * Meringues aux amandes

YIELD: ABOUT TWENTY MERINGUES

4 egg whites   10 tablespoons Vanilla Sugar
¾ cup powdered almonds   (page 579)
2½ tablespoons flour

Preheat the oven to 350° F.

Beat the egg whites stiff and fold in the powdered almonds, the flour, and the sugar.

Put the mixture in a pastry bag fitted with a plain tip. Drop little mounds the size of a pullet's egg onto a buttered baking sheet. Bake 7 to 8 minutes.

This recipe differs greatly from the preceding one because of the almonds. You can, if you wish, fill the meringues with sweetened whipped cream or with jam.

Coffee meringues * Meringues au café

YIELD: ABOUT TWENTY MERINGUES

4 egg whites   salt

several drops of coffee essence   vanilla
1 cup extra fine sugar   powdered sugar
butter and flour

Beat the egg whites very stiff and add the coffee. Stirring with a wooden spoon, add the sugar and a pinch of salt. Add also a pinch of vanilla powder or 1 teaspoon of vanilla extract. Beat until the mixture falls in a ribbon from the spoon.

Butter lightly a baking sheet and dust it with flour.

Put the mixture in a pastry bag fitted with a small plain tip and force the meringue in small mounds onto the baking sheet. Sprinkle with powdered sugar and let stand for 10 minutes.

Preheat the oven to 200° F.

With the help of a pastry brush, brush off any sugar that has fallen on the baking sheet.

Bake the meringue 1 hour with the oven door slightly ajar.

Jam turnovers * Chaussons à la confiture

FOR FOUR PEOPLE

Semiflaky Pastry (page 644)   1 egg yolk
1 jar apricot jam

Make the pastry, and after it is prepared, roll out ⅛ inch thick and cut into 8 3½-inch rounds.

Preheat the oven to 400° F.

Put jam on half of each round, leaving a narrow border. Moisten the border with water. Turn the other halves over the jam, pressing the edges together.

Place on a baking sheet, and paint each turnover with egg yolk, mixed with a teaspoon of water. Bake about 15 minutes. Like all turnovers, they are better eaten warm.

Little prune turnovers
Petits chaussons aux pruneaux

FOR FOUR PEOPLE

12 prunes   1 egg yolk
Semiflaky Pastry (page 644)   ½ cup heavy cream
12 toasted almonds   4 tablespoons sugar

Soak the prunes several hours in strong sweet tea.

Make the pastry so that it will be ready when you want it.

Drain the prunes and remove the pits and replace them with the almonds.

Preheat the oven to 400° F.

Roll out the pastry and cut 8 2½-inch rounds. Moisten the edges with water. Place a prune in each round and press the edges together. Place on a baking sheet and paint each little turnover with egg yolk mixed with a teaspoon of water. Bake 10 to 15 minutes.

Serve accompanied by a bowl of heavy cream, heated and sweetened.

Small cookies

Cat's tongues * Langues de chat

YIELD: FIFTY TO SIXTY PIECES

9 tablespoons soft sweet butter
10 tablespoons sugar
3 egg whites

1½ cups sifted pastry flour
1 teaspoon powdered vanilla or
1½ teaspoons vanilla extract

Preheat the oven to 400° F.

Work the butter and sugar together until smooth and creamy.

Add the unbeaten egg whites one by one, stirring well after each addition. Resift the flour into the mixture and add the vanilla.

Using a pastry tube fitted with a small plain tip, force 3-inch strips onto a buttered baking dish, leaving space between each strip. Bake 6 to 8 minutes or until lightly browned around the edge.

Cigarettes * Cigarettes

FOR SIX PEOPLE

9 tablespoons soft sweet butter
1¼ cups confectioner's sugar

1½ cups sifted all-purpose flour
5 egg whites, beaten stiff

Preheat the oven to 350° F.

Work the butter with your hand until soft and creamy. Add the sugar and mix well. Add the flour, and when well blended, stir in the beaten egg whites. Stir until the mixture is very smooth.

Drop from the end of a teaspoon onto a buttered baking sheet little mounds well spaced apart to allow for spreading. Bake 8 to 10 minutes. When the edges of the cookies begin to brown, remove them from the oven and roll them around a thick pencil while still hot. Let them dry. They will be very crisp.

Little sugar cookies * Petits sablés sucrés

YIELD: ABOUT THIRTY COOKIES

3 cups sifted pastry flour
15 tablespoons soft sweet butter

½ cup sugar
¼ teaspoon salt

Preheat the oven to 400° F.

Mix and knead the ingredients together until thoroughly blended. Roll out thin on a floured working surface and cut with a fluted cookie cutter. Place on a lightly buttered baking sheet and bake 15 minutes.

Raisin devils * Diables aux raisins secs

FOR SIX PEOPLE

¼ cup seedless raisins
9 tablespoons soft sweet butter
1¼ cups confectioner's sugar

1⅞ cups sifted pastry flour
rind of ½ lemon
5 egg whites, beaten stiff

Soak the raisins 2 hours in lukewarm water. Drain thoroughly.

Preheat the oven to 350° F.

Work the butter with a wooden spoon until soft and creamy. Add the sugar, and when blended, stir in the flour, the grated rind of ½ lemon, and then the raisins. Finally fold in the beaten egg whites, lifting the mixture as you fold.

Drop onto a buttered baking sheet into little mounds well spaced to allow for spreading. Bake 8 to 10 minutes.

Financiers * Financiers

YIELD: FORTY PETITS FOURS

½ cup egg whites
1 cup plus 2 tablespoons confectioner's sugar
3 tablespoons powdered almonds

1 cup plus 2 tablespoons sifted pastry flour
9 tablespoons sweet butter

Preheat the oven to 400° F.

Put the egg whites in a bowl and add the sugar and powdered almonds. Mix well with a wooden spoon and gradually add the flour, stirring constantly.

Heat the butter in a small saucepan over a low heat until it turns a light brown. Pour it hot into the mixture. Mix well.

Fill small candy papers with this combination and bake for about 15 minutes. Watch them well. They should become firm to the touch but must not burn.

Macaroons * Macarons

YIELD: ABOUT EIGHTY MACAROONS

1 pound, 10 ounces Almond Paste
  (see below)

8 egg whites
1⅔ cups confectioner's sugar

Preheat the oven to 225° F.

Soften the almond paste by stirring with a wooden spoon in a bowl, adding 3 unbeaten egg whites.

Beat the remaining 5 egg whites until stiff. Fold in the sugar.

Gradually add the beaten egg whites to the almond mixture and stir gently, just long enough to blend the mixture.

With a pastry bag fitted with a large plain tip, force the mixture in small mounds onto a baking sheet lined with brown paper. In order to keep the macaroons soft, put another baking sheet under the one on which the macaroons are. Bake about 30 minutes.

To remove the macaroons from the paper, wait until they are cold. Moisten the back of the paper and they will lift off.

Almond paste * Pâte d'amandes

Almond paste can be bought in some stores but is not available everywhere. It can be made at home in the following way.—Ed.

YIELD: 1½ POUNDS

3 egg whites
2¼ cups powdered almonds

4 teaspoons apricot jam
2⅓ cups confectioner's sugar

Mix the egg whites, powdered almonds, apricot jam, and sugar very thoroughly. If not to be used immediately, store in airtight containers.

Marzipan * Massepains

FOR EIGHT PEOPLE

½ pound blanched almonds
2 egg whites
1¼ cups sugar

pinch of vanilla powder *or*
½ teaspoon vanilla extract
grated rind of ¼ lemon

With a pestle pound the almonds in a mortar, adding the egg whites gradually to prevent the almonds from becoming oily. (This can be done in small quantities with a blender.—*Ed.*) When the mixture is a smooth paste, add the sugar, the vanilla, and the lemon rind. Mix well.

Preheat the oven to 225° F.

Make little balls of the mixture and place them on a sheet of white paper, leaving space for the balls to spread. Bake 10 to 15 minutes. Do not open the oven during the baking for the first 10 minutes. If sufficiently cooked, remove the cakes from oven. Do not detach them from the paper until completely cold.

Palmiers * Palmiers

FOR TEN PEOPLE

Flaky Pastry (page 643)   ½ cup coarse sugar

Make the pastry and after the final turn, roll it out in 2 long rectangles. Sprinkle the pastry with sugar. Fold the ends toward each other in 3- to 4-inch folds until they meet in the middle. Roll them together and cut in as thin slices as possible. Repeat with the other rectangle.

Preheat the oven to 350° F.

Put the slices on a buttered baking sheet, leaving space between them. Bake 15 minutes.

Almond tiles I * Tuiles aux amandes I

FOR EIGHT PEOPLE

10 tablespoons sugar   10 tablespoons slivered almonds
5 tablespoons soft sweet butter   ½ orange *or*
½ cup sifted pastry flour   ½ lemon

Preheat the oven to 400° F.

Cream the sugar and butter together and add the flour, the slivered almonds, and the juice and grated rind of either the half orange or lemon. Mix well.

Butter a baking sheet and drop very small mounds of the mixture from the tip of a teaspoon. Space them very well apart. They will spread. Watch them, because they cook very quickly.

Remove from the oven and let stand for 2 to 3 minutes. With the aid of a spatula, lift them from the baking sheet and place them on a rolling pin to give them their traditional rounded shape. Work quickly and delicately, because the cookies are very fragile. Cold cookies will not bend on the rolling pin.

If you choose to make these with orange, you can add a few drops of red coloring matter.

Almond tiles II * Tuiles aux amandes II

FOR EIGHT PEOPLE

4 egg whites, beaten stiff   1 cup chopped almonds

¾ cup sugar   12 tablespoons sifted pastry flour

Preheat the oven to 350° F.

Combine the above ingredients and bake 5 to 10 minutes. Treat them in the same way as in the preceding recipe, to give them the traditional shape.

Toscas * Toscas

FOR SIX PEOPLE

Sugar Pastry (page 647)   ¾ cup sugar
¾ cup toasted almonds

Make the pastry in time to let it rest. Roll it out to a thickness of ⅛ inch and cut into rounds with a 2½-inch cookie cutter or with a Bordeaux wine glass. Place the rounds on a buttered baking sheet.

Sprinkle with the almonds.

Preheat the oven to 400° F.

Heat the sugar with a teaspoon of water, and when it has melted, spoon a little over each cookie. Bake about 8 minutes.

Cheese biscuits * Sablés au fromage

YIELD: TWENTY TARTS

9 tablespoons soft sweet butter   1¼ cups grated Gruyère cheese
1½ cups plus 1 tablespoon sifted   ¼ teaspoon salt
   pastry flour

Mix all the ingredients with your hand until you have a well-blended dough.

Preheat the oven to 400° F.

Roll out the dough on a lightly floured surface to a thickness of ¼ inch. With a glass or cookie cutter, cut out rounds and place them on a lightly buttered baking sheet. Bake 10 minutes or until browned lightly at the edges. Watch carefully, because these biscuits cook very quickly and depend upon the thickness of the pastry.

Cheese sticks * Bâtonnets au fromage

FOR TEN PEOPLE

1 cup boiled potatoes   3 egg yolks, slightly beaten
½ pound plus 2 tablespoons soft   milk
   butter   1 teaspoon salt

2 cups sifted all-purpose flour	dash cayenne
2 cups grated Gruyère cheese	

Preheat the oven to 425° F.

Boil and sieve potatoes to measure 1 cupful. Put in a bowl and mix in the butter with a wooden spoon. Stirring continuously, add the flour mixed with the salt and cayenne gradually. When well blended, add the cheese and finally the egg yolks. Mix thoroughly.

Rolling small portions of this mixture between the palms of your hands, make round thin sticks the size of small candles. Paint each one with a little milk, using a pastry brush, and place them on a baking sheet lined with buttered paper. Bake 15 minutes.

Cheese straws * Brins de paille

YIELD: TWENTY STRAWS

4 tablespoons butter	2½ tablespoons milk
⅓ cup grated Gruyère cheese	⅛ teaspoon salt
9 tablespoons sifted all-purpose flour	

Preheat the oven to 425° F.

Mix all the ingredients and knead them well, like dough. Place the ball of dough on a working surface, and with the heel of your hand, push off small bits of the dough from the further end of the dough onto the working surface. This method of blending the flour and butter together is called *fraisage.* Once you have worked all the dough in this manner, scrape it up with a spatula and form it once more into a ball.

Roll bits of the dough into small sticks the size of a pencil and cut them into uniform lengths. Place on a lightly buttered and floured baking sheet and bake for 5 minutes. Serve hot or cold with tea or cocktails.

Icings

Almond icing * Glaçage aux amandes

2 egg whites	½ ounce (1½ tablespoons) ground
10 tablespoons sugar	or slivered sweet almonds
	1 teaspoon ground bitter almonds

Beat the egg whites stiff and fold in the sugar. Add the 2 varieties of almonds. (Substitute ¼ teaspoon bitter almond extract, if the bitter almonds are not available.—*Ed.*)

Place the cake on a cake rack and cover the top and sides with the icing, smoothing it evenly with a small spatula. Place in a 400° F. oven for 3 to 4 minutes.

Almond cream icing * Crème d'amandes

7 tablespoons butter
¾ cup sugar
4 egg yolks

¼ pound powdered almonds
1½ teaspoons kirsch

Cream the butter and sugar together with the egg yolks until you have a very smooth, well-blended mixture. Add the powdered almonds, which have been flavored with the kirsch. Mix thoroughly before spreading on a cake.

Icings for babas * Glaçage pour babas

1 cup sugar
1 teaspoon very finely ground almonds
1 teaspoon very finely ground
   hazel nuts
3 tablespoons honey

1 teaspoon orange flower water
1 teaspoon rum
1 teaspoon curaçao
1 teaspoon maraschino
1 teaspoon anisette

Boil the sugar and 1 cup of water for 5 minutes and cool completely. Add the remaining ingredients. Mix thoroughly and strain the mixture over the baba placed on a cake rack, which should be placed in a shallow dish to catch whatever liquid falls from the cake.

Chocolate icing * Glaçage au chocolat

3½ ounces bittersweet chocolate   ⅔ cup confectioner's sugar

Cut the chocolate into very small pieces and put them in a saucepan with approximately 3 tablespoons of water and stir over low heat with a wooden spoon until smooth. Stir in the sugar and heat a few seconds before spreading it over the cake placed on a cake rack. Smooth the frosting on the top and around the sides.

Cold icing * Glaçage à froid

1 cup confectioner's sugar   flavoring

Beat the confectioner's sugar well with just enough water to give a shiny and runny frosting. Add a few drops of flavoring (vanilla, lemon, orange, and so on) and spread over the top and sides of a cake placed on a cake rack. Smooth with a small spatula.

Icing for éclairs and cream puffs
Glaçage pour choux et éclairs

1 cup confectioner's sugar   1 tablespoon triple-strength coffee
1 tablespoon coffee extract *or*

Heat the sugar with 2 tablespoons of water to make a syrup. Remove the syrup from the heat and add the coffee extract mixed with 2 tablespoons of water. Stir well and spoon over the éclairs or cream puffs to coat the tops. Spread smooth with a spatula.

Unbeaten egg white icing
Glaçage aux blancs d'oeufs non battus

3 egg whites   4 teaspoons rum
½ cup sugar

Whip the egg whites with a fork until frothy; they are not to be beaten stiff. Dissolve the sugar in the rum and add the mixture to the egg whites. Put the cake on a cake rack and cover with the icing.

Honey frosting * Glaçage au miel

1¼ cups sugar   1½ tablespoons kirsch
2 tablespoons honey

In a small saucepan, preferably one made of copper, put the sugar, ⅓ cup of water, and honey. Stir until smooth, and when the mixture boils, cover and simmer very gently for 5 minutes. Flavor with kirsch.

Pour this immediately over a cake placed on a cake rack and smooth with a small spatula.

Kirsch icing * Glaçage au kirsch

1⅔ cups confectioner's sugar   2 tablespoons kirsch

Mix the sugar with the kirsch in the top of a small double boiler. If the icing is too thick, add a few drops of water, but it should not be too thin. Heat it slightly over boiling water and pour it over a cake placed on a cake rack. Smooth with a small spatula and let the icing dry.

Red-hot iron icing * Glaçage au fer rouge

This method of making designs on cakes can be done with whatever icing you choose. There is a special tool, but a long skewer or trussing needle will do.

Once the cake is iced, heat the tool until it almost turns red, and with this make whatever designs you wish: lattice work, parallel lines, or crisscross.

Starch icing * Glaçage à la fécule

¾ cup sugar   2 tablespoons potato starch
3 egg whites

Beat the sugar and egg whites, and when they become frothy but not stiff, add the potato starch. Spread over a cake placed on a cake rack and place in a hot oven for a few moments.

Wine

Wines

In France, as everyone knows, we drink wine when we eat. For everyday living the wine we drink is called table wine—good, ordinary wine that corresponds to the beer of other countries. There is always both a carafe of water and a carafe of wine on the family table.

When we are entertaining guests we put aside the table wine and serve wines of good, or indeed exceptionally good, vintage, for if it is true, as Brillat-Savarin wrote, "A meal without cheese is like a beautiful woman with one eye," it is even more true that a meal composed of excellent dishes is incomplete without excellent wines.

There is poetry in wine; there is also a science of wine. Both are subjects dear to the heart of every gourmet, but lack of space forces us to limit ourselves to a few practical considerations.

True to the principle "a good wine for a good dish," each course at a large formal dinner is accompanied by a different wine, and the host makes every effort to choose the most harmonious combination of food and wine. Obviously the gourmet drinks very little of each wine, because he is only trying to enhance the flavor of the sauce, the essence of game, or the savor of cheese. Wine does not serve to quench thirst; there is always a row of glasses before each guest, and the largest one is filled with water. As the well-known author Colette, daughter of the noble land of Burgundy, used to say, "First the eye, then the nose, and finally the mouth." That is to say, you admire the attire of the wine first, then you breathe the aroma, and finally you taste the bouquet.

And then? Then you talk about it.

For smaller but still elegant occasions two wines are generally served, one to accompany the lighter dishes at the beginning of the meal and another for the heavier dishes and the cheese.

Here I would like to recall an essential rule that applies to a meal whether it offers two wines or several wines. A succession of wines must go from good to better, because a guest must never be allowed to think that the preceding wine is better than the one he is drinking at the moment.

With the simplifications that modern times impose on our lives, it is becoming more and more usual to dine "au champagne"—that is, to serve nothing but champagne not only throughout the meal but also as an *apéritif*. With cheese, however, you serve red wine and then come back to champagne for dessert.

Finally there are the small informal dinners, where just one wine is served. This is chosen with special care as a pleasant accompaniment to the entrée, the main dish, the cheese, and the dessert.

Whether you are serving one wine or several, each wine must be brought to the table at the temperature that best brings out all its qualities.

How do you choose these wines? There is no absolute rule. There are only the general rules of good sense and good taste.

White wine, if it is dry or mellow, is usually chosen to accompany shellfish, fish, and entrées. A sweet white wine is good with desserts and pastries. It is drunk chilled but not icy. You can put it in the refrigerator for one or two hours, never more. Better yet, cool the wine under running cold water. In any case once white wine has been put in the refrigerator—even if it is not used—it must never be returned to the wine cellar, because chilling in the refrigerator is a little brutal for wine, which cannot really stand rapid changes in temperature.

The principal regions from which these wines come are:

Bordeaux (Sauternes, Barsac, Graves, Entre-Deux-Mers, and so on). The white Bordeaux wines are the dry varieties, which one should drink in the first five years. There are the sweeter varieties, with a high flavor and almost velvety texture, that can wait up to fifteen years.

Burgundy (Chablis, Mersault, Pouilly-Fuissé, and so on). The white Burgundy wines are rather dry and should be drunk before they are ten years old.

Alsace (Reisling, Traminer, Pinot, and so on). Some Alsace wines have a gunpowder taste, others have a fruity flavor, mellow or highly perfumed. They are good for only a few years.

Jura, Loire Valley, Côtes du Rhône, Provence. Wines of these regions are difficult to buy in the United States.

Rosé Wine. Rosé, like white wine, generally accompanies entrées and light dishes. It is drunk cool but not cold. Cool rosé under running cold water, never in the refrigerator or in a cooler. The rosé wines come principally from the Loire Valley (Anjou, Saumur, Cabernet, and so on), from the Côtes du Rhône (Tavel, for example), or from the Côtes de Provence.

Red wine (except Beaujolais, which like rosé is drunk cool), must be "chambré," that is to say, it must be allowed to come slowly to room temperature, and in this regard one must differentiate between the Burgundies and the Bordeaux.

Red Burgundy. Red Burgundy is the classic accompaniment to meat, poultry, and particularly game. It must be brought slowly to room temperature if room temperature is not above 65° F. If the room is warmer than that, do not put the bottle in the dining room until two hours before the meal. Uncork the bottle a half hour before the meal to let the ethers escape and to enhance the quality of the wine; take care to place the cork on the bottle.

Red Bordeaux. Like red Burgundy, red Bordeaux can also accompany poultry, red meat, and especially cheese. Because it has more need for contact with the air than Burgundy and because it can stand a slightly higher temperature than Burgundy, it can be put into the dining room ten to twelve hours before the meal and uncorked two to six hours before the meal.

Champagne. As I have said before, champagne can accompany an entire meal —even after the champagne has been served as an *apéritif.* For this purpose it must be "brut," that is to say, very, very dry. It will momentarily yield its place when cheese is being served, preferably to a Bordeaux.

Champagne must be icy cold. It can stand a very low temperature. Chill it one to two hours in the refrigerator or one hour in a cooler, the latter making a particularly attractive receptacle for it when it is served as an apéritif. Champagne must not be chilled too long or it will "break" and lose its goodness.

All champagnes come from the province of Champagne, east of Paris, the vineyards being grouped around the cities of Reims and Epernay. There also exist in France some excellent sparkling wines, particularly the wines of Gaillac, which are less expensive and naturally cannot be called champagne. But if they are less expensive, they are also less good. No one would think of offering them at an elegant dinner; they are most often drunk at large public gatherings, such as city banquets, holiday celebrations, and functions of all kinds.

Index

(ENGLISH AND FRENCH)

Index

(ENGLISH)

Beef

Desserts

Eggs

Entrées

Ham

Lamb

Pastry

Salads

Variety Meats

Veal

Index

(FRENCH)

Boeuf

Entrées

Entremets

Légumes

Mouton et Agneau

Oeufs

Pâtisserie

Salades

Sauces

Soupes et Potages

Veau

Viandes

Volailles et gibiers